HISTORY OF PEASANT REVOLTS

HISTORY OF PEASANT REVOLTS

The Social Origins of Rebellion in Early Modern France

Yves-Marie Bercé

Translated by Amanda Whitmore

Cornell University Press
Ithaca, New York

English translation copyright © Polity Press 1990
First published in France as *Histoire des Croquants* © Editions
du Seuil, 1986

For information address Cornell University Press, 124 Roberts
Place, Ithaca, New York 14850.

ISBN 0-8014-2544-1 (cloth)
ISBN 0-8014-9775-2 (paperback)

Library of Congress Catalog Card Number 90-053182
Library of Congress Cataloging-in-Publication Data in process.

This translation first published 1990 by Cornell University
Press.

Typeset in 10 on 11 pt. Ehrhardt by Photo·graphics, Honiton, Devon
Printed in Great Britain by T J Press, Padstow

Contents

and poor women, 174. The town council and the policing of the
grain trade, 175. Tolerance and pity in society as a whole, 175.
Results of the bread riots, 177. Object and purpose of the bread
riots, 178.

Closing the gates or an ambush, 180. The justification of the
rioters, 183. The communal nature of the riots, 186. Resistance to
marauders in the eyes of society, 189. The formation of rebel areas,
192. The villager's ethic – and the soldier's, 193.

Tax-gathering practices that led to revolt, 198. The neighbourhood
to the rescue, 201. The dramatis personae of the revolt, 205.
Recriminatory lawsuits, 206. Typical bouts of rebellion, 208. The
advantages of a rising, 212.

Trouble provoked by the agents, 215. Besieging the inn, 217.
Haling the exciseman, 219. The riot of jubilation, 221. Rescuing the
smugglers, 223. Abusing the excisemen, 225. Dramatis personae:
the victims, 228. Dramatis personae: the rioters, 229. The mayor
versus the agents, 231. The local judges versus the agents, 232.
Retribution and patronage, 234. Rebellion in triumph and defeat,
236.

Taxes condemned in subversive manifestos, 245. Taxes condemned
in warnings, 246.

The king deceived, 248. The king robbed, 250.

The grand remission, 251. Remission on the king's death, 255.
Remission after a peace, 256.

The legend of the *gabelle* in south-west France, 259. Taxes on life,
261.

Preface

This is an abbreviated edition of a thesis published in 1974 by the Librairie Droz, Geneva, in the series *Mémoires et documents* issued by the Société de l'École des Chartes, number XXII. The thesis was accepted by the university of Paris-Sorbonne on 13 May 1972. The original version consisted of 974 pages with maps and illustrations. The constraints of an abbreviated version have obliged me to reduce the study by more than half. With much regret, therefore, I have had to omit almost all of the first part, which is entitled 'Background'.

In explaining the background to peasant revolts, I discussed the 'misfortunes of the age' – inclement weather, high prices, plagues and poverty. I examined institutions which were fundamental to seventeenth-century France, especially those connected with war; I analysed military taxation, the destruction of castles, army supplies, enlisting of soldiers, maintenance of prisoners and billeting. I surveyed the royal taxes, the state's most important source of revenue, which were a burden borne almost entirely by the peasantry, and observed how they were increased, allotted and sometimes waived. It is clear that from around 1640 there was a major change in the tax administration, as financial officials were dismissed, exemptions that had once been enjoyed were undermined and formidable new methods of recovering taxes were introduced. The repeated popular uprisings provoked reactions at all levels of society. I analysed the behaviour of the nobility in this respect by examining their own beliefs and the relations between landlords and tenants. The aristocracy practised their own traditional forms of violence, participated in their own political assemblies and often took up arms themselves against the state's fiscal activities. When disorder erupted, royal officials enjoyed a dual role: their public role and their role as private individuals able to intervene to protect their own interests. These were apt to be damaged by the overlapping of newly created jurisdictions or by an increase in the sale of offices. The peace of the country was undermined by the precarious nature of the policing powers of the *maréchaussée* (mounted constabulary) and by countless rebellions organized by officials themselves. All the chapters of my original work concerning these matters have had to be omitted, with the result that the present edition begins at what was originally the sixth chapter, which is about the communes.

I was obliged to delete the account of the great wave of rebellions that hit the towns of Guyenne in 1635, and likewise that of the minor revolts which occurred in Angoumois and Saintonge in 1636. These were in the section of the book entitled 'The Chronology of Revolts'. Also missing are the chapters on popular demonstrations during the Fronde and a concluding discussion of the rebellion staged by the *Tard Avisés* of Quercy at the end of the period, in 1707. All that remains are the critical examinations of the two great campaigns conducted by the Croquants in 1594 and 1637.

By contrast, the last part, 'Types of Riots', has been retained in its entirety. But most of the footnotes, lengthy explanations and critical apparatus are excluded. Serious and scholarly readers will need to refer to the original text of 1974 for all the necessary details. To compensate for this, a Postscript several pages long has been added after the Conclusion.

Yves-Marie Bercé

Introduction

Not so long ago, when the history of the seventeenth century was still widely taught, the most memorable and comprehensible impression of the period was undoubtedly left by the *Fables* of La Fontaine. There, in the well-known tale of the dove and the ant, we have our first encounter with that obsolete insult, 'croquant'. The archer who threatened the bird was a villager who was following the course of a stream as he hunted.

> A barefoot Croquant passed that way:
> This Croquant carried a crossbow.

Imprinted on our minds forever after was the idea that he was an uncouth fellow who was so poor that he had to catch his supper with a crossbow, a weapon that was a century and a half out of date. All the same, this 'croquant' was not any old rustic as the word implies nowadays; he was an armed peasant. The definitions and examples given in Furetière's dictionary emphasize his aggressive appearance. 'A croquant', says the entry, 'is an impoverished beggar with no possessions to his name who has only a hook to defend himself with in time of war. Peasants who revolt are just poor croquants.' He gives as an example, 'a poor croquant who has not so much as a *sou*'. Originally, and most frequently during the years 1590–1660, the term referred to a participant in a popular revolt, especially one from south-west France.

In fact, that long period which lasted from the Wars of Religion until Louis XIV consolidated the machinery of the state saw countless prolonged and widespread peasant revolts. They were the most serious in French history, second only to the tremendous western uprising against the Revolution and the ruthless policy of extermination by the republican state. These peasant wars of the first part of the seventeenth century were almost all concentrated in what may broadly be defined as the south-west of France. This is the area that runs from the marshes of Bas-Poitou to the valleys of the Pyrenees; from the borders of Saintonge to the uplands of Marche and Limousin; from the heathlands of Gascony to the plateaux of Quercy and Rouergue. But why, in some seasons, would these peasants see fit to leave their fields and flocks to go and harass neighbouring towns with their ill-assorted militias that bristled with old muskets and back-hafted sickles? And why were there so many of these demonstrations of peasant unrest during the decades between 1590 and 1660? What was it about south-west France that meant that most rustic uprisings happened there? If we are to attempt to answer any of these questions, we must reconstruct events totally ignored by conventional history and give an account of them before explaining them. After all, like all knowledge, and indeed more than any other kind of knowledge, history is essentially and necessarily no more than a narrative.

It remains for me to justify my choice of this subject. One reason why I was attracted to it was, I suppose, the irritation I felt on reading countless books where the past is not judged on its own merits or considered in its own right. The writers exhibit the age-old habit of viewing the past only in terms of the relation it bears to the present. Either they are looking for a model or pattern which reflects their own time, or they are judging past events according to what happened later. They attach special importance to aspects of a period which seem to have had a particular effect on posterity. Events are linked together into an inevitable sequence by these authors, who use them to read the present back into the past or to show that opinions existed which in fact were contrary to all modes of thought at the time in question. History takes on a linear quality. Every occurrence is critically examined; it is praised if it proves that an attitude or development already existed, and criticized if it reveals an earlier state of affairs. The notion of 'already' is all-important. In these pages, by contrast, I have tried to trace lines of evolution that died out; aspirations that were defeated, paths that were abandoned. If all these aspects are ignored, our knowledge of the past is diminished and our understanding of it impoverished.

In many respects, there has been no better history written than that of the Count of Cosnac who documented the Fronde in a detailed study which filled eight volumes. He liked to imagine himself a man of the seventeenth century and called his work *Souvenirs du règne de Louis XIV* (1866).

The virtues of this little-known historian do not stop here. When researching the background of some unimportant battle in Bas-Limousin for his book, the Count of Cosnac rode around the place where it happened, explored the clumps of brushwood and asked the nearby farmers about the peculiarities of the landscape.

This concern for visual reconstruction seems to me to be symbolic. Where the history of mentalities is concerned the smallest, most trivial detail can be valuable. A touch of ethnology is an improvement on scholarship pure and simple. In the present work, I felt it worthwhile to point out, for example, that the guards of the *prévôté de l'Hôtel* (grand provostship of the Royal Household) wore jackets decorated with fleurs-de-lis and that a bunch of straw over a door indicated an inn to passers-by. The fleur-de-lis stood for royal authority, while the bunch of straw signified that the people inside had uncorked their barrels of wine, and represented the freedom of everyone to sell the wines of their cellar. It is essential then to visualize behaviour and flesh out abstractions which would otherwise remain incomprehensible.

We must try to understand all that was implied by the phrase 'The peasants are in revolt'. We must find out how they gathered together, whether they did this often, how far they travelled to meet up with others, how they were informed of events, what they took with them and how they behaved when they arrived. To sum up, our task is to make a small contribution to the long history of behaviour.

1
The Communes

The communes in the seventeenth century

In the seventeenth century, the word commune no longer carried with it any overtones of the medieval institution of that name – of the ties of collective vassalage which the citizens of certain towns had formed with the local landowners in the distant past. It referred to local communities of every description from the gathering of residents in a rural parish to the magistrates of the big city. In a related sense, it denoted specifically 'the common people of a town or borough', even 'the populace' and, in the plural, 'the people of country parishes'. In edicts and ordinances, the phrase 'communal assembly' was used to refer either to a meeting of delegates who had come from the parishes of a *sénéchaussée* (seneschal's jurisdiction) or a province to confer with their governor, or to a band of armed peasants who had set out to hunt wolves, bandits or invaders. Used in this manner to suggest a crowd banded together, the word had connotations of violent unrest, and lexicographers who wished to illustrate its usage gave such examples as 'to gather the communes', 'he was killed by the commune in the province of . . .', 'the commune was aroused', 'to stir up the communes'. It was unrest, consequently, that seemed to express the character of the commune most exactly in contemporary eyes. And similarly throughout seventeenth-century France, unrest was the expression of a local consensus that entailed collective responsibility. Indeed, that basic social unit, the local community, was to breed a variety of collective loyalties designed to unite its members against the insecurity caused by war, against the tax collector and against the sovereign. The commune was the first rung on the ladder of corporations and colleges through which subjects were linked to their king.

Any attempt to study the social unrest of the seventeenth century must lead us to investigate the strength of the communal unit of that time. In particular, it is necessary to establish whether the institutions of the community lost their function and importance during the course of this period as a fairly well-known historiographical tradition maintains.

The election of urban authorities

It is well known that election to the office of consul, magistrate, alderman or any other post which had been established by custom usually amounted to a process whereby officials were co-opted from a circle of leading families. It was a system that gave free rein to a factional rivalry among townspeople that, at times, developed into violence. In Gascony, where a number of *pariage* agreements between noblemen had been made (under which the weaker of two nobles procured the protection of the stronger in exchange for part of his revenues) the influence exercised by the supporters of the two parties concerned was apt to give rise to disputes. In the largest towns, there was often hostility between Catholic and Protestant families, and sometimes there were conflicts between the burgesses of the long robe and the burgesses of the short robe – the office holders and the merchants. More often, however, it was different groups of office holders who were in competition with one another.

During the civil wars, the parties of the Reform and the League had been known to seize municipal magistracies and to exercise absolute power in the towns concerned, in defiance of the authority of the crown. Prompted by the experiences of the years of disorder, the Royal Council took care from then on to subject the nomination of local magistrates to close supervision and to make sure of the loyalty of those who won. Electoral procedure at Bordeaux in 1623 and at Poitiers in 1626 was regulated by Council decrees which forbade the 'soliciting or canvassing of votes in order that the electors may have complete freedom to nominate and elect such persons as seem good to them and in such manner as they may deem in their conscience to be for His Majesty's good and in his interests'. Under the terms of these decrees, only official candidates were allowed to stand – those men to whom authority was entrusted each time it seemed that a great city of the kingdom was likely to become the centre of unrest. When the secretary of state, Servien, learnt of the admission of Calvinist officials into the *présidial* (intermediate court) of Saintes, he instructed the lieutenant-general, the Count of Jonzac, 'to be mindful of the future and have the chief officials ensure that no office holder whatsoever is chosen or accepted among them who does not possess all the qualities required of a good citizen and a faithful subject and servant of the king, especially where those of the town corporation are concerned'. This was tantamount to saying that the governors and intendants of provinces should have no hesitation in intervening in the annual ballot at the town hall. Accordingly, in 1635, Servien wrote to an official of the *présidial* of Poitiers whose candidature was unacceptable: 'It is not at all sensible for an individual to place himself at the head of a faction in a town.'

In Bordeaux, the Dukes of Épernon were always careful to ensure that the magistrates were chosen exclusively from their associates. By the same token, the officials of the ducal faction were replaced by the allies of the archbishop, *parlement* (provincial court) or the Fronde when events turned against them in 1634, 1638 and 1648. To punish a town, the king could even deprive it for a time of the right to nominate its own dignitaries; thus, in Limoges, where the citizens refused to submit to the imposition of a tax known as a *subvention*, the intendant received a letter instructing him to appoint the consuls himself, 'without regard for the right to nominate the popular magistrates which privilege and custom have accorded them'.

The tightening of control over municipal institutions culminated in the edict of August 1692 which threw municipal offices open to purchase. Despite this much-emphasized institutional development, it is clear from any study of contemporary behaviour that people in fact retained a stubborn attachment to their local statutes. Above all, they retained their loyalty to the commune. This can be illustrated by the persistence of their own symbolic tradition.

Communal emblems

The identity and the powers of the commune were symbolized in a variety of ways. Two symbols in particular, the consular livery and the town bells, carried special ritual meaning and bore witness to the survival of the commune's prestige.

The dignity of a consul or alderman was sustained in a number of ways. He had a place of honour in church and a part to play in public ceremonies, such as processions, bonfires or the traditional banquets which were held in the town hall. Consuls displayed their office by parading with an escort of bowmen of the watch, town constables or heralds; and they made it yet clearer by wearing a costume, 'the king's livery', which marked them out in the eyes of the public as the representatives of the crown. At Limoges, for example, it was said that the consuls had donned 'their liveries and hoods for the first time in the year 1520 on the entry of the king of Navarre. In view of the fact that the citizens had come out in large numbers to pay their respects to him, the consuls had adopted red damask hoods to distinguish themselves from the masses. They wear these hoods to the present day.' When they were not attending ceremonies, the consuls, who were almost always lawyers or notaries, dressed in serge gowns and black felt hats. Over their gowns, they wore a red hood which was slung back across their shoulders. This hood was made of fine scarlet fabric, decorated with golden fringes or velvet facings: the extent of the decoration depended on the wealth of the city concerned. Even the humblest townships wanted their officials clad in scarlet and the cost of making their liveries sometimes represented a considerable burden on the community's funds. In the large cities, a livery cost about 100 *livres*. The liveries of each of the six or so consuls had to be replaced every so often – probably at least once every four years.

The hood embodied the collective authority of the commune. Even the most trivial street scene revealed its symbolic power. People made way for it, hailed it and bowed before it. Consuls always made a point of putting on their livery before setting out on official business, whether to issue an edict, to distrain the goods of a debtor or to break up a mob. On one occasion, a notary of Agen, Antoine Cabos, struck the consuls who had arrived in their hoods to conduct an official sequestration of his property. The *parlement* at Bordeaux sentenced Cabos to a fine of 100 *livres*, and ordered him to make a public apology, on his knees, in the great chamber of the town hall. 'Fresh from their shacks', a chronicler grumbled, 'the tribunes of the people swagger no less than kings once they have the mark of public authority on their shoulders. . . . There's nothing more arrogant than a louse in a velvet cloak.' If a dissenter wanted to show his contempt for the consular function, he aimed his abuse at the livery. Consider, for instance, the fate of the consuls of Bergerac during the unrest provoked by the billeting of troops in the town.

Carrying out their official duty of ensuring that this gathering gave rise to no upheaval, particularly in view of the extreme danger of the times, and wearing their livery on their shoulders to this end, they were grievously affronted in both word and deed, to the point where the said royal liveries were snatched from them and trampled underfoot, their gowns and cloaks were torn and the mob was incited to disregard their authority.

In the same way, a gentleman of the Agenais region who was engaged in a legal dispute with the consuls of the adjoining commune made a show of riding through the town with the local livery trailing from the tail of his horse. The records of various inquiries held after periods of unrest reveal the special place which the consular liveries occupied in civil sensibility, whether as objects of insult or as the focus of respect.

Unlike the liveries, which played a purely symbolic role, the town bells also served a number of practical purposes in communal life. Village meetings took place 'at the sound of the bell' and the pealing of bells was a sign of public celebration and mourning. Different functions were summed up in the inscription engraved in 1775 on the great city bell of Bordeaux: '*Convoco arma, signo dies, noto horas, compello nubila, concino loeta, ploro rogos*' (I call to arms, I tell the days, I mark the hours, I drive the clouds, I sing of joys, I mourn for woes). Insofar as they summoned the populace to meet, calling them to the rescue or bidding them to prayer, the bells of the church or belfry were thought of as guardians. People attributed an individual character to them which was instilled by a blessing solemnly bestowed on each bell when it was installed. This ceremony was referred to as the 'christening' of the bells. They were given names and high-ranking godparents, and miraculous powers were ascribed to them such as the ability to drive demons away and ward off any catastrophes that might threaten the town. The legends inscribed on the waists of bells bore witness to these beliefs: '*Malorum terror, bonorum amor*' (Feared by the evil, loved by the good) (bell at Drayaux, 1683); '*A fulgure grandine et tempestate libera nos domine*' (From lightning, hail and tempest, Lord, deliver us) (bell at Cubas, 1696); '*Ante sonitum meum fugiant ignita jacula inimici, fulminum, lapidum et tempestatum*' (Let there flee before my peal the burning spears of the enemy, of lightning, hail and storm) (bell at La Roque-Gajac, 1598). The powers most widely ascribed to them were those of dispelling storms and driving away lightning and hail. In wine-growing regions, all the bells were therefore set ringing the traditional 'thunder peal' the moment the black clouds loomed.

A similar tutelary function was embodied in the tocsin which was sounded to call people to the rescue when a common danger arose. The officials of the *maréchaussée* were authorized, for example, to seek succour from the communes in the case of emergency 'by gathering them at the sound of the tocsin'. Riding through the Quatre-Vallées, the vice-seneschal of Armagnac noticed how the bells maintained the unity of the local population.

The dwellers in the aforesaid valley go about their lives in a state of astonishing vigilance. They are led by two deputies whom they appoint on the first of January each year and they obey them as if they were kings. In the event of any crisis, they ring their bells to such effect that the thirty-six towns or villages are alerted and at arms in the space of less than two hours.

But not all gatherings were sanctioned by edicts and ordinances. Right up to the nineteenth century, the prompt and unanimous response which the clanging of the tocsin awakened made it the chosen signal for every revolt. To gather the communes by tocsin or to sound the alarm from the belfry was a crime officially acknowledged and condemned by the courts. When the authorities took action against a rebel community, the punitive measures they adopted often included bringing down the bells and destroying them or moving them to a parish which had stayed loyal. As part of the measures the Constable of Montmorency took to suppress the uprising which had broken out against the salt tax around Bordeaux and Saintonge, for example, he gave the order on 26 October 1548 that 'Each and every bell, large and small, which they keep in their churches and public places is to be broken, smashed and shattered, without exception.' In the rebel district around Angoulême, the bells seem to have been effectively destroyed. The intention was not merely to prevent any future summons being made with the tocsin, but also, more importantly, to use the fate meted out to the bells as a way of demonstrating the humiliation of the commune as a whole. This was the reason, for instance, why the town hall bell was melted down after the fall of La Rochelle, and why the laws devised by the intendants to curb the communes which had risen up against the imposition of taxes authorized the removal of bells from the rebel churches and proscribed their replacement as a crime.

Records of contemporary practice make plain the immense psychological importance which was attached to these communal emblems. Our next step must be to examine the same sources for evidence of the five ancient powers which the communes enjoyed in respect of their political, judicial, military, fiscal and security affairs.

Political powers

Consuls, aldermen or *jurats* (town magistrates) acted as masters of ceremonies at the rituals organized to express the community's loyalty to the throne. They presided, for instance, at singings of the *Te Deum*, and led the thanksgiving processions which were customarily held to celebrate events such as births and marriages in the royal family, or victories won by the king's armies in the field. At such festive times these processions would wind their way through the towns down streets ablaze with torchlight. The magistrates led them into the squares, and lit the bonfires there. Every so often a town would be visited by a dignitary: the president of a crown court, the local bishop, the intendant, the lieutenant-general or provincial governor, ambassadors sent by a foreign monarch, princes of the blood and, sometimes, the king himself. Great ceremonial attached to the arrival of such visitors, and on these occasions, too, the magistrates presided. They put on their finest liveries and came out of the town to greet the distinguished guest at a point several leagues from his destination. Greetings accomplished, they brought him all the way to the gates, with a large mounted escort provided by the gentlemen and burgesses of their retinue. They presented him with the keys of the town, and welcomed him with a flowery speech. The guest advanced through the streets with a canopy over his head, and his feet protected by greenery or by carpets spread over the cobblestones. The crowd cheered, the bells rang, the town cannon thundered on the ramparts and the militia, in battle order, discharged their muskets in a resounding salute. The guest was then ushered on to a grandstand hung with tapestries and adorned with panels bearing the noble devices of heraldry in brilliant paint. He was showered with gifts and required to listen to a series of addresses delivered by the spokesmen of each of the town guilds. The next event in the programme was a high mass, or sometimes a tournament. Finally the guest and his entourage were treated to a banquet, lodged in style in the most comfortable houses the town could provide, and entertained, for the duration of their stay there, at the community's expense.

It was a society where appearances counted, and where the powerful felt a need for outward show. In conducting public festivities, the magistrates consequently made a point of demonstrating to the public that they were, within their territory, the lawful representatives of the crown. At the time they assumed their duties they had bound themselves to uphold the privileges of the municipality and to preserve the common weal; but they had, at the same time, sworn loyalty to God, their king and their country. They were invested with their power by the votes of their fellow-citizens; but they were also, by the same token, liable to be held to account for it in time of trouble. It quite often happened that they took the side of the court at a time when the entire community was up in arms against it. At Figeac, for example, in June 1643, the consuls alone opposed the decision of their fellow-townsmen to take part in the uprising launched by the Croquants of the Rouergue. In April 1649, at Poitiers, the mayor made a solitary stand in favour of Mazarin, and was nearly assassinated on several occasions. The *jurats* of Bordeaux made an attempt, at the same period, to obstruct the union which had been initiated with the *parlement* of Paris (the supreme sovereign court). The attempt met with general derision, and the *jurats* found themselves substantially excluded from the communal policing councils set up by the Fronde.

A rebel town could expect to have its institutions abolished and its personality erased. This punishment was a reminder that the powers the commune exercised were tenuous at best. They were bestowed by the king and exercised in his name. And what the king gave the king could take away. The best-known example of royal retribution was the fate which befell the town of La Rochelle on 18 November 1628. The communal life of the town and its corporate organizations were brought to an end. The king abolished the institutions of mayor and aldermen and the ranks of peer and burgess. The seneschal assumed the responsibility for administering justice and policing the town. The town's traditional revenues were absorbed by the royal estate. The town hall was taken over, and the title deeds and records in the municipal treasury were carried off to Paris.

Judicial powers

Magistrates who were also seigneurs or co-seigneurs of their town and the surrounding countryside had the right to administer supreme justice; and they were determined to retain this impressive and fearsome function in spite of the steady growth in the jurisdiction of the crown. They enforced the law through the agency of a series of specialist officers, an assessor, a crown attorney, a clerk, a gaoler and an executioner. The Ordinance of Moulins had deprived these local courts of the right to hear civil cases, and their role consisted largely of investigating breaches of the community regulations. Their procedures were simple and inexpensive. They were entitled to judge all criminal offences committed within their domain, and to pass the death sentence where appropriate. If the condemned man appealed against the sentence the courts were obliged to refer his appeal to the *parlement*: if the sentence was upheld, consuls, *jurats* or aldermen would appear in person to escort the miscreant to the scaffold in the market-place.

Dossiers listing an almost unbroken series of sentences passed from 1600 onwards are preserved in the records of the court of *jurats* at Bordeaux. The dossiers give an impression of the extent to which the status of this local court was still acknowledged by the ordinary citizen, on the one hand, and the competing judicial authorities, on the other. In the thirty years between 1614 and 1644, ninety local murder cases were tried by the court, and some twenty of the criminals condemned as a result of these hearings were eventually brought to the gallows. In the single year June 1635 to May 1636 the court passed no more than fifty-one sentences of any kind. Twenty-eight of these were acquittals, or prescribed nothing more than an apology, and ten were procedural rulings. Only eight involved fines, and only five entailed some form of physical chastisement. A survey of the sentences passed over a period of fifty years reveals that 51.7 per cent of the condemned criminals were strangers to the town, immigrants or travellers, while 48.2 per cent of them derived from fluid social groups such as journeymen, boatmen and students.

It is clear, then, that the town courts concerned themselves essentially with a range of sordid offences committed by the poor. They enforced the law through proceedings of an *ad hoc* and informal nature, but remained none the less effective enough to inspire fear, to keep order on the streets and to reassure the burgesses and the rest of the citizen body.

Military powers

The community's right to self-defence was given tangible expression in the town wall. Even the humblest villages were surrounded by walls, and a stranger reaching a town was obliged to make his entry through a gateway fortified with drawbridge, portcullis and tower. The ramparts bristled with look-out

turrets and crenellated battlements, and were girded with a protective ring of
ravelins and moats. Seen from a distance the towns looked wholly enveloped
in their walls, with only the church steeples and in some cases the keep of
the citadel peering above the fortifications. When the vice-seneschal of
Gascony made a tour of his province between October 1626 and April 1627,
he observed that 228 of the 246 places he visited – 92.6 per cent – were
fortified with ramparts. Only seven were undefended, not counting eleven
Huguenot townships which had recently had their walls removed.

Towns were expected to hold out against the king's enemies. Cities which
rose in rebellion had their ramparts razed to the ground. Montauban, Nérac,
Bergerac, Saint-Jean-d'Angély, La Rochelle, famous towns of the south-west
which had risen against the king, were branded for posterity by the destruction
of their battlements. Their walls were 'laid low as the earth, and the foundations
were torn away. The moats were filled up in such fashion that the town may
be approached and entered from every side, and a plough can drive through
it like arable land.' To avert this eventuality, the 'political magistrates' of a
town were accordingly held responsible for ensuring its defence. They were
expected to oversee the upkeep of the walls with the help of *corvée* labour
(work usually undertaken for one's lord) – to clear the moats and repair any
breaches in the fortifications. In addition they had the task of maintaining a
number of cannon, together with a full arsenal of powder and matches, muskets
and halberds, which were stored either in the town hall or in one of the larger
defensive towers. One of the consuls took charge of the town keys when the
gates were locked at night. In times of war and pestilence, one gate only was
left open during the daytime, and the magistrates bound the citizens to
keep watch. The *jurats* of Bordeaux, for instance, had 'the time-honoured
responsibility of seeing that the drum was sounded at every point in the town
and of constraining all the citizens to do guard duty, inasmuch as they were
the governors of the said town and enjoyed the supreme political authority
there'. Some towns were still dominated by a castle, and there the consuls
found their authority challenged by that of the commander of the garrison.
They bridled at the challenge. Frequent disputes arose as to who gave the
orders, who directed the *corvée* contingents, who was responsible for giving
the password and who had charge of the keys.

Provided it had its gates locked and its citizens manning the ramparts, the
smallest township could resist a besieging army for quite some time. The
garrison of the citadel at Blaye, for example, was reinforced in emergencies
by a company of 300 to 400 arquebusiers formed from among the burgesses,
as well as by several hundred peasants who converged from the surrounding
county to take refuge within the walls. The citizens of the town of Dax and
the residents of the local *prévôté* (provost's jurisdiction) kept 'watch and ward
together continually at all times, by day and by night, both at the gates and
on the walls'. The thirty-odd parishes of the *prévôté* were ready to dispatch
1,000 armed men to the town at the earliest summons. Other towns exhibited
a similar vigilance. The residents of Tulle, for instance, fielded a force of
almost 500 armed men in response to a sudden crisis on 30 November 1607.
The men were mustered after dark, in the space of two hours. In 1633 a new

governor was dispatched to the province of Limoges. The residents of the town organized a guard of honour of 1,200 horsemen to meet him on the orders of their colonel-in-chief. On the night of 31 July 1635, a band of Navarrese set out to raid the livestock belonging to the villages of Itxassou and Espelette. Village after village rang the tocsin to warn of the danger, and by one in the morning the news had spread as far as the town of Bayonne. Thinking that the Spanish were coming

the entire population, burgesses and gentlemen alike, rose up at this alert in every part of the town. Everyone hastened to arms and took up his appointed station with a speed and wrath so amazing that 1,600 or 1,700 musketeers and more than 800 pikemen were mustered in less than half an hour. They assembled in silence and were astonishingly obedient to the commands of their magistrates.

In September 1650 Mazarin and the marshal of La Meilleraye besieged Bordeaux. Thirty-six companies of burgesses, comprising not less than 7,200 men, held out in the city on behalf of the Fronde. Their valour was equalled only by their lack of discipline.

Governors and lieutenants-general were well aware that they could, in an emergency, ask the local magistrates to gather 'the communes of the province'. These 'communes' were contingents of men supplied by each community. The men served as labourers, carters or sappers in haulage operations or siege works. Sometimes they were even used as auxiliary troops, though their quality was dubious. Levies of this sort were conscripted for the campaigns against the Protestants between 1621 and 1628, and again for the wars with the Spaniards in 1636, 1638 and 1639. From 1672 to 1674, 1690 to 1692 and 1704 to 1707 'militias' recruited in similar fashion were raised to guard the coasts. The communal levy would be commanded by a consul, or alternatively by a local notable whom the consuls had approached: this leader was known as the captain or colonel of the commune. Cut-price soldiers of the levy were not necessarily local citizens, but might well be any old mercenaries paid and equipped at the town's expense. Burdensome and resented, conscription of this kind was a very different matter from the upkeep of the town militias, in which the communities gloried and the citizens were proud to serve. 'Sons of the town' in arms, the members of these militias were organized according to the street or district they inhabited into a number of companies and sections, which were placed under the command of captains and corporals appointed by the citizen body. All the burgesses were automatically included in the militia, irrespective of their station in life, and the officers were selected from among the most prominent merchants and functionaries. The companies of militia were expected to take turns in keeping watch. Serving militiamen had to perform a number of duties each evening: they presented arms before the house of their commanding officer, received the password at the town hall, supervised the closing of the gates and stood guard on the ramparts. Any dereliction of duty would be visited with a fine. On festive occasions like the visits of dignitaries or Midsummer's Eve, the militia paraded proudly through the town, filling the squares with the din of their celebratory musket-fire. It was a way of bearing witness to the rights and freedoms of the commune.

Fiscal powers

Tax agents collected a variety of modest communal dues. They levied duty on the livestock passing in through the town gates, on the stalls of travelling merchants in the market-place and on the wine sold by innkeepers up and down the streets. Farmed out to a wealthy local trader, this municipal tax gathering could generally be relied on, year in year out, to augment the coffers of the town hall by some hundreds or thousands of *livres*. With the addition of customs duties and the seigneurial dues that were levied on the surrounding countryside, the total income was barely enough to cover the community's day-to-day expenses. In a crisis year the towns inevitably had to borrow, and the resulting indebtedness proved to be irreversible as the seventeenth century wore on, partly because of the stagnation both in prices and in the commerce which generated virtually the entire wealth of a town, but more especially because of the growing tendency to interference by the state, which was threatening to upset the precarious but long-sustained municipal balance of payments beyond hope of recovery. In the first place the central authorities had induced the towns to pay a number of new taxes by a kind of fiscal sleight of hand. The royal superintendents had installed tax clerks in each of the communities, and had assigned them a substantial commission deductible from the local tolls. By doing so they had forced the town halls to try to buy each separate appointment in order to keep the office of tax clerk within the municipal jurisdiction.

The towns were forced into making a number of other purchases of the same type. In 1635 they had to buy the office of commissioner for cash distraints, and in 1635–7 the office of broker in the market towns. Finally, in 1641, they found themselves having to buy up all the local property rights to which the king was able to stake a claim. Costs of this kind were thrust directly on the town halls. But the government also offered the magistrates a poisoned chalice by giving them the chance to make a profit out of raising the royal taxes.

In some towns the *jurats* or consuls were undoubtedly entitled by ancient custom to a useful choice. They could share out the task of tax-gathering among their fellow-townsmen, or relieve them of that duty while at the same time augmenting the profits they themselves made from the *tailles* (poll tax). In every part of the kingdom it was they who apportioned the financial burden which was imposed on the community when troops passed through. Royal edicts, however, invariably stipulated that tax inspectors and collectors should be chosen from outside the municipal governments. It was hoped that this would deter town councils from farming out tax-gathering contracts corruptly and misappropriating the revenues raised. Decrees of the Council, indeed, confined the levying of taxes to mayors, aldermen, consuls or receivers. The decree of 26 August 1639 made these functionaries responsible for raising military provisions. And the principle of collective punishment ensured that, in case of abuses, their property and that of the town hall would be forfeit before any goods belonging to the rest of the citizens.

Insofar as they succeeded in buying up the various new offices which the crown had instituted in their midst and in asserting their right to administer the taxes imposed on their fellow-townsmen, the municipal authorities preserved at least an outward independence. They even signified their acceptance, in principle, of the taxes demanded by the crown through the provincial assemblies which brought together the receivers from the communities and the *lieutenants–généraux* (presiding judges) of the regional jurisdictions under the name of *états* or *assemblées de la police* (administrative estates or meetings). Authorized by the government or the provincial intendant, these assemblies sought to avert from their province the threat of a new demand for taxes or military provisions, or at any rate to discuss ways in which the burden might best be borne. All they could do in practical terms was to send a delegation to haggle with the Council over the compromise assessment which was bound to be reached in the end. It was the price the communities paid for surrendering real power and opting to live by their wits.

Traditional sources of revenue were so meagre that in times of abnormal expenditure caused by a disaster such as a storm, plague or irruption of troops requiring billets, communities were obliged to resort to drastic expedients. As a first step they alienated their goods. Next they sought the Council's permission to impose an extra tax on themselves subsumed in the usual *tailles*.

These steps were normally taken in the following manner. Consuls were forced to sell off community lands or part of the monies raised by the town dues, usually to a hospital or a religious foundation. Even when that had been done they were still sometimes unable so much as to pay the interest on their debts, and were subjected consequently to the harassment of bailiffs dispatched by the community's creditors. Official reports drawn up by the Treasurers of France reveal how large these communal debts could sometimes be. In 1636, for example, 78,000 *livres* were owed by the community of Verdun-sur-Garonne. Other reports refer to debts of 120,000 *livres* at Moissac, 248,000 at Bordeaux, and so forth.

Liabilities on this scale could be liquidated only in one possible way. If the town authorities could not reverse the inflation, they might at least hope to check it by obtaining permission to levy an extraordinary tax on the citizen body.

With this aim in view the authorities convened a general assembly of the citizens. Once the citizens' consent to the levy had been recorded, as custom demanded, by the local judge, the authorities proceeded to submit a petition expounding the needs of the community to the *cour des aides* (court for tax appeals). Many months later the *cour des aides* would grant *lettres d'assiette* (tax warrants) authorizing the requested levy. The board of finance would then issue *lettres d'attache* (authorizations) commanding the town's representatives to add this sum to the expenses registered for the community in the appropriate *département* (administrative area). Rulings given by the Council in 1632 and 1633 limited the basic tax awarded by the *cours des aides* to 300 *livres*. For any award in excess of this amount a community had to make a special application to the Council. The Council would appoint a Treasurer of France to go and verify the community's debts, and would rule on the size of the tax to award on the basis of his report. Even after the Council had issued its ruling, the receivers still had to wait for the award to be recorded in the tax warrants. This confirmatory step could well be postponed for years. The Council had no desire to jeopardize the raising of the royal *tailles*, which was difficult enough already. One final hurdle consisted in extracting the monies gathered from the tax collector in the local *élection* (fiscal administrative court). The collector would agree to part with his takings only after he had been bombarded with writs by the municipal authorities and had received the formal instructions of the board of finance.

The *élections* most often burdened with local taxes were Agenais, Condomois and Saintonge. Agen, Bazas and Nérac were the most heavily taxed of the towns.

Taxation was heaviest in the years 1632–3, in the aftermath of the crisis of 1628–31, and again in 1638–9, during the phase of maximum exertion in the war with Spain. Three to six per cent of the sums levied at these periods were diverted to cover the administrative expenses incurred in obtaining the *lettres d'assiette*, and the town officials and tax collectors deducted commissions for their services amounting to approximately a further 10 per cent. The upshot was that the community treasurers received no more than 84 per cent of the total levy raised.

Most of these funds were unfortunately consumed in public expenditure of a non-productive kind. It is revealing to examine the reasons cited by the communities for their petitions to tax themselves. The purpose of the proposed levies was specified in 365 cases. Just forty-two of these levies (11.5 per cent) were directed to a useful end such as paying the salaries of a schoolmaster, shepherd, printer or similar community employee, or carrying out necessary maintenance work on bridges, roads and walls. In eighty-one cases, however, (22.1 per cent) the communities were merely seeking to raise funds which would enable them to comply with an ephemeral obligation imposed from outside: to quarter troops, dismantle fortifications, relieve poverty or plague. The remaining 242 taxes (66.3 per cent) were an unqualified waste of money. Ninety of them (24.6 per cent of the total) were to be spent on legal proceedings which the communities wished to initiate against other townships or against a citizen seeking to evade the communal dues, either before the *élection*, the *cour des aides*, or the *parlement*. The final 152 (41.6 per cent) were to be levied to no better purpose than to appease the more pressing of the communities' creditors by paying the accumulated interest on the debts which were owing to them.

The sums raised were modest. These taxes none the less provoked countless indignant lawsuits, which took up much of the time of the *cours des aides*. Plaintiffs often brought actions against the consuls for their conduct of affairs. Town officials found themselves accused of malpractices, called on to open their accounts and prosecuted for fraud. Catholics living in the Huguenot cities blamed their consuls for raising taxes unauthorized by any royal warrant, and using them to finance the Protestant sect and pay the salaries of clergymen of the 'supposedly reformed religion'. In other places legal proceedings were engendered by the rivalries of different city factions. Prominent families vied with each other to bribe their way into office, and funds raised in special taxes were consequently sometimes diverted to improper ends. The *cours des aides* were regularly obliged to instruct the *élus* (officials of the local fiscal administrative court) to report on any such malpractices they encountered in the course of their tours of duty.

The *cours des aides* were themselves under attack from the *parlement*, which disputed the jurisdiction the *cours* claimed to exercise over municipal affairs. The *parlement* at Toulouse accused the *cour* at Montpellier of exacting anything up to 300,000 *livres* a year from the syndics or chief magistrates of communities which appealed to it, payment taking the form of spices and contributions to the travelling expenses of the *cour's* representatives. The accusation was voiced in a decree of 20 April 1630. 'It so happens', declared the *parlement*, 'that there is a consulate which pays no more than twenty to thirty *livres* in taxes to the king, while yielding almost 150 *écus* (crowns) to the *cour des aides* in travelling expenses for the assessors, legal fees and spices.' The *parlement* at Bordeaux even sought to restrict the jurisdiction of the *cour des aides* to royal taxes alone. The *parlement's* decrees began to encroach on the *cour's* domain, and the *cour* was forced to appeal to the Privy Council to annul them.

Following the crisis of 1628–31 the superintendents of finance were confronted by a flood of petitions from communities seeking to tax themselves in order to liquidate the debts they had incurred during the outbreaks of famine and plague. They were perturbed by these local levies, which were hard to control and gave rise to so much wrangling, and dismayed to find them competing with the royal treasury for the taxpayer's money. In 1636 all the municipal levies due to be raised in the *généralités* (fiscal regions) of Bordeaux and Montauban were suspended: the superintendents cited 'the great difficulties which the inhabitants of Guyenne are encountering in the payment of their ordinary taxes, both because of the disorders which have for some time been afflicting this area and because of the levies which are being raised there in the interests of communities and private persons'. A similar step was taken in 1644.

Awards of special levies were in any case accompanied by the proviso 'that they shall not delay the collection of His Majesty's revenues'. Communities could be paid, in other words, only out of the portion of the taxes which remained after all the revenues due to the treasury had actually been raised. On 2 March 1636 the Council issued a decree commanding the Treasurers of France at Montauban to provide details of any unauthorized levies collected by the townships. Nearly all the cities in the province had suffered from riots the previous year, and the decree went so far as to blame the disturbances on this illicit tax gathering.

Warrants of this kind for general or special taxes were issued once again in the aftermath of the Fronde. The awards were made with such frequency that the right to bestow them was granted, on a permanent basis, to the provincial intendants. The intendants regularly condemned the malpractices perpetrated by the city councils. The councils, in their view, had passed into the hands of cliques of families and officials, all of whom were trying to cover up the fraudulent profits they were making by ensuring that their own group remained the sole source of recruitment to any municipal office. This suspicion of the local oligarchies was formally recorded, and the authorities in due course used it as a pretext for stepping in to discharge the debts of the communities and take control of their budget for good and all. The takeover proceeded in two stages. In the first stage the state assumed control of municipal tax collection: in the second stage it simply confiscated the funds. Ever since the sixteenth century the authorities had been trying to implement the first stage of the takeover through a series of financial edicts which made the post of town tax collector a royally appointed and purchasable office. These attempts were frustrated, on each occasion, as the towns bought back the post and continued to assign it to salaried employees who were answerable exclusively to the elected consuls or aldermen. From 1663, however, tax collectors were obliged to go through their accounts at the Audit Office once every six years; and from 1683 this inspection took place annually in the presence of one of the members of the provincial intendant's staff. This first stage of state intervention culminated in the edict of August 1692, when the tax collector finally became an officer of the crown.

The second stage had its origins in the fiscal edicts which the crown had, over the years, felt justified in issuing in view of the difficulties encountered by the townships in raising the local tolls. The crown would threaten to abolish the tolls altogether, or alternatively to deduct a portion of the proceeds. The town councils then sent delegates hurrying to court to appeal against the ruling, and following some negotiation the crown would agree to revoke its edict in exchange for acceptance of a minor tax which it proposed to levy upon all the towns in the kingdom. In 1647, however, finding itself in desperate financial straits, the crown went further. On 21 December it issued a statement proclaiming the formal confiscation of all the revenues collected in civic tolls. Th proclamation adjudged that the sovereign had the right to reclaim the financial concessions he had granted in the past and use them to his own advantage. All the *deniers d'octroi* (towns' customs dues) were accordingly to be conveyed to the Treasury. If the towns needed any sums over and above the modest amounts they raised from their *revenus patrimoniaux* (traditional tolls), they had permission to levy two sets of dues, one for the king and the other for the municipal treasury. Circumstances prevented the crown from implementing this decree. After the Fronde, however, the Financial Council revived the scheme. A fresh order of confiscation was issued on 28 June 1653. The order affected only half of the local revenues: the towns were allowed to retain control of the rest. This decree evidently had as little effect as its predecessor, since the crown felt obliged to reassert it in further proclamations issued in August 1657 and November 1661. In 1662 the local tolls were amalgamated and leased to Jean Rouvelin as part of the general farming out of *aides* (sales taxes). A large force of armed bailiffs was required to carry out the ensuing plunder of the towns, and in some cities these officers had to contend with violent resistance. Riots broke out at Limoges in October 1653, April 1654 and February–March 1661, at Fontenay-le-Comte on 28 June 1659, at Le Dorat in September 1660, and at Châtellerault on 11 November 1660.

In the meantime the provincial intendants were embarking on a new survey of community debts. They drew up timetables for paying off the communities' creditors, and proposals for balanced budgets which were designed to regulate community spending thereafter. Their decisions were formally endorsed by decrees of the Council, and from that time on the day-to-day expenditure of the townships was unchanging and predetermined. Communities could no longer use their resources to provide against future contingencies. The amount they could spend was confined to a fixed proportion of their revenues officially authorized by the state.

This move extinguished local resistance to the fiscal offensive of the crown. The commune, as an institution, was left with no further room to manoeuvre, and its magistrates were reduced to playing an empty ceremonial role.

Policing powers

One function of the community magistrates was seldom challenged. Few people, naturally, questioned their right to police their town. Policing involved a number of different duties: repairing the roads, supervising trade and maintaining public order. These duties were spelt out in the set of civic rules known as 'police regulations' which were posted up at the crossroads on market day. Sometimes the regulations appeared individually, as separate printed notices, and sometimes they were amalgamated into a code of community by-laws. These rules were invariably headed by a number of provisions enforcing respect for religious observances. Some prescribed punishments for blasphemy; others forbade the opening of taverns during hours of service as an affront to public decency, or restricted the sale of meat during Lent and other fast days to sick persons alone. Most of the rules, however, were intended to control the business activities of publicans and innkeepers, butchers and bakers. It was in the taverns, after all, that brawls took place and riots began. Inns were the haunt of foreigners, of spies in the service of dissident magnates, of quacks and swindlers and unruly journeymen and travellers retreating from a district infested by plague. And butchers' and bakers' shops attracted crowds of hungry beggars in the months of dearth.

Consuls divided among themselves at the time they came into office the various policing duties and the different streets and squares where those duties were to be taken up. The allotment of duties was determined partly by their rank, and partly by the location of their homes. Matters relating to food supply and public sanitation were supervised in the big cities by *ad hoc* committees known as 'police assemblies' or 'police councils'. Membership of these committees was not confined to the consuls, and an assortment of leading citizens, royal assessors and representatives of the principal schools and corporations also took part in them. Bodies of this kind were invested with emergency powers in times of famine and plague. Towns often had, in addition, special boards which went under the name of 'paupers' syndicates'. These boards were set up to administer the charitable legacies which had been entrusted, over the years, to the town hall or the hospital for the benefit of the poor. Finally there were the teams of town sergeants, bowmen or constables who had the task of enforcing the police regulations. These police forces were small. Two officers were employed at Cognac in 1630. Bergerac had a force of two at the beginning of 1645, rising to four in the course of that same year. In Agen, similarly, in 1649, a force of six was increased to twelve. Bordeaux had twelve constables, supported by a company of bowmen of the watch. These policemen were generally described as inferior people. Easily inclined to arrogance, they were good for evicting vagrants, but helpless in the face of a mob run riot – if they were not actually abetting it.

One other policing duty was the enforcement of customary rights. In some areas this function loomed large in community life. Certain regions, for example, contained a quantity of waste land so intractable that boundaries could not be properly demarcated and common use was the rule. In regions of this kind one of the principal roles of the community magistrates was to ensure that these customary arrangements were respected, and to safeguard the land traditionally held in common against the encroachments of newly arrived landowners and the attempts to assert a variety of spurious state rights which were apt to be made by the intendants and lessees of the royal demesne. The problem the magistrates faced was particularly acute in districts consisting of marshland, moorland, mountain and forest, where outsiders challenged the traditional rights connected with livestock rearing (e.g. the right to *parcours*, or untaxed residence in either of two adjoining seigniories, the right to graze cattle and the right to gather the acorn harvest) or forestry (*affouage*, or the right to cut wood on communal land). The benefits derived by the peasantry from these activities were trivial from the point of view of a townsman; but they represented, none the less, a bonus which was sometimes essential for the well-being of the poorest in the community – grass for their goat, acorns for their pig, and wood for their fire. Now the peasants saw their common land being alienated as the communities struggled to keep pace with their mounting debts. In addition they were confronted by the efforts to curtail the ordinary citizen's access to crown lands which were initiated for fiscal purposes in the reign of Louis XIV, and by the territorial claims put forward by the new seigneurs in the first feudal reaction at the end of the seventeenth century. The effect of these developments was to inhibit age-old practices, to nudge rural households below the subsistence level, and to incense communities which found themselves menaced by an attack on rights they regarded as sacred.

The best-known of these onslaughts against the freedoms enjoyed by the rural communities was the celebrated ordinance on waters and forests of August 1669. Article 19 of this document imposed a harsh prohibition on the grazing of sheep – not merely in the forests, as might have been expected, but even on the surrounding moorland. Article 20 revoked, in similar fashion, the rights known as *chauffage* and *affouage* (heating) which had previously entitled the peasants to collect wood. Article 18 restricted the right to gather acorns and to engage in pig-grazing or pasturage to a season of four months, October to January. These measures ran clean contrary to time-honoured custom. Indeed, they challenged the very basis of such custom, founded as they were on the assumption that practices derived solely from an unquestioned customary right could be made subject to the production of title deeds. The attempts made by the government from 1661 onwards to introduce forest reform met with considerable resistance, especially in south-west France. The consuls of the various communities and the local gentry all endeavoured to shield the traditional users of the land who had suddenly become poachers in the eyes of the law. The authorities struck back by imposing collective sentences on whole groups of parishes. Government agents were sent to administer fines, and constables were dispatched to impound the livestock roaming the forests. These officers found rebellions on their hands.

The king's agents did not dare to enforce their new law too rigorously in the mountains, and the mountain folk of the Pyrenees went on exploiting their forests without serious state interference right up to the nineteenth century. The most serious outbreaks of mass violence took place in other kinds of terrain, as the local peasants fought to defend the lands they were accustomed to graze in common in the marshlands, moorlands, open meadows, water-meadows and poplar plantations. Riots broke out, for example, in defence of community rights at Chaillé-les-Marais in the marshlands of Poitou in August 1644, at Geay in the marshlands of Charente in July 1667, and at Bègles in the marshlands of the Bordeaux region in January 1706. The largest uprising provoked by this particular discontent took place in Agenais in June and July 1681. On 29 April that year the *parlement* had issued a decree providing that peasants who allowed their livestock to graze freely on the commons should be subject to a fine. The publication of this decree was accompanied by the seizure of a quantity of livestock on the orders of the magnate who farmed the crown estates in the Agenais region. Rumours of trouble began to circulate at the end of June, and in early July the peasants took up arms. The uprising started on 5 July, in the villages of Sainte-Radegonde and Monbalen in the hills around Agen. Fresh trouble followed on 9 July, at Savignac and Saint-Aubin, villages lying between Villeneuve and Montflanquin on the right bank of the Lot. Armed bands made up of the residents of five or six rural parishes set guards in the country churches and sallied forth to burn the smallholdings of the townspeople, only to be dispersed by a company of mounted bowmen and burgesses sent over from Villeneuve. Similar disturbances took place in a number of parishes to the north of Périgueux, Chancelade, Agonac and Sorges. Partly because the *parlement* was anxious to make up for the leniency it had shown in 1675, and partly because the authorities feared a Protestant conspiracy, the uprising was suppressed with exceptional harshness. Three of the rebels were broken on the wheel, and one was sent to the galleys. These incidents were not merely examples of the efforts made by the peasantry to defend community rights: they were, in addition, episodes in the long history of conflict between the people of the countryside and the dwellers in the towns. It was an age-old conflict, and traces of it are discernible in most of the Croquant risings.

These upheavals can also be seen as the protest of a peasant culture based on oral tradition and custom – of people who looked for their values to the unchanging habits of earlier generations, who clung to practices rooted in the hoariest antiquity and regarded the very obscurity of such practices as an adequate reason for venerating them. Their law was a communal law, unwritten, deeply embedded and long established. Into their world abruptly came the officers of the crown, products of a new law that was written and prescriptive, men who demanded evidence and title deeds and grants of land drawn up in good and due form,and who validated their own identity with printed documents bearing an official stamp. Their attempt to replace the old law entailed a painful collision of cultures, and the royal commissioners sometimes learnt to their cost that to establish a new order is no easy matter.

To make too much of this concept of a collision of cultures would, however, be pompous and simplistic. Forest reform was not intended to deprive the mountain-dwellers altogether of the minor communal benefits they enjoyed: the object was merely to supply the naval dockyards with timber. In the same way the process by which the state took control of the towns' finances would seem to have been not so much the result of a deliberate policy as of the growing elaboration of the tax system. As the impulse to state control gathered head the authorities destroyed the traditional powers of the commune without being fully aware of what they were doing. The communes continued to issue edicts asserting their own strength and durability. But by encumbering their budgets with new taxes and then, for good measure, confiscating their revenues, the Council was steadily ruining them.

The final blow was the edict of August 1692 which converted the positions of mayor, clerk, tax collector, bowman and other local functionaries into offices open to purchase and hereditary succession. But it did not mark the end of civic freedoms. Those had already vanished thirty years earlier, when the young Louis XIV had plundered his own towns as a useful expedient in time of civil war and had, in so doing, extinguished the ancient community liberties for good and all.

The excitements of the people

The community structure was firmly implanted in the minds of the people and embedded in their customs. If we study any manifestation of popular excitement described in contemporary accounts of days of rejoicing or disorder, we find that this sense of community asserts itself time and again. This is only to be expected in an age of intense social activity characterized by shared feeling and a collective consciousness.

Fairs

Peasant society affirmed its collective identity by coming together at fairs which were held in a nearby town beneath the vaults of the covered market or in a large meadow on the town's edge. These gatherings of people were too incessant to be explained simply by economic need. Crowds flocked to every possible event, from the grand fairs endowed by charters to the little markets in the *châtellenies* (minor administrative districts). An eighteenth-century agronomist counted no less than 450 fairs in Angoumois alone. 'Fairs', he observed, 'have proliferated so greatly in this region that to suppress the bulk of them might well be beneficial to farming, and no great loss to trade. Cowherds and labourers often frequent them for no good reason, out of sheer force of habit.' Gatherings of this kind did, in fact, serve a genuine social purpose. People went there in search of news and novelties, and to take part in the collective merry-making which offered a diversion from the monotonous and isolated life of the country parish. They left for the fair before daybreak and returned at dead of night, after a satisfying dawdle through the wayside taverns. Fairs buzzed unceasingly with the astounding tales of pedlars: whole towns in Spain, from the steeples down, were being submerged by floods; the queen of England had arrived in Limoges;[1] the king was remitting the country's tax arrears. Fairs were the places where plagues could spread or subversive ideas take root. All it took was a foreign merchant to die in an inn near the fairground, or a village malcontent to hand out seditious pamphlets. These risks forced local consuls into urgent preventive action at times when disease was rife or disorder threatened. They ordered their trumpeters to denounce the evils of the fairground, forbade the citizens to go there and closed the town gates.

The west of France was a region of good pasture and well-fed oxen. Cattle fairs were consequently frequent, and these fairs served as a meeting-place for Croquant groups. Crowds are said to embolden people to vent their emotions, to strengthen the social ties which bind them together and to encourage them to voice demands they might otherwise repress. At all events, it was at these fairs that rebel communes passed their subversive resolutions. It was there that they rounded on tax collectors sent to inspect the trading in barrels of wine or salt and drove them out ignominiously. And every now and then some unfortunate 'scapegoat' would find himself torn to pieces by a lynch mob 'after a trip to the fair'.

Festivals

The social intercourse characteristic of fairs in cattle-raising country was also a common feature of an assortment of festivals: political ceremonies, high days and holy days and traditional revelries.

A great host of religious holidays had accumulated over the centuries, part of the ever-growing body of Christian tradition. These ranged from great Church festivals to days set aside for simple processions and services organized at the level of the diocese or parish to extol a particular apostle, martyr or local patron saint. A hundred such holidays were recognized, for example, by the statutes of the synod of Bordeaux. Consuls of the various communities prescribed, in addition, a number of secular celebrations intended to commemorate every important event in the life of their town. The consequence was that almost one day in four was a holiday.[2] A hundred years later this passion

1 In May 1628 the magistrate's court at Limoges sentenced a woman for passing herself off as Henrietta Maria, queen of England. Incident recorded in the unpublished manuscript annals known as the *Annales de Limoges*, which were edited at this period by François Roussaud, priest of the Limoges parish of St. Michel des Lions.

2 See Yves-Marie Bercé, *Fête et Révolte*, Hachette, Paris, 1976.

for pomp and leisure would be derided and condemned by the acolytes of the
new religion of industry and profit. But the festivals made up for many other
days in the calendar when the seventeenth-century labourer had to toil from
dawn to dusk.

Political ceremonies

Communes in every part of the kingdom were expected, as we have seen, to
mark victories of the king's armies and joyous events in the lives of the royal
family with a lavish celebration. The arrival of eminent visitors was attended
by solemn ceremonies, and so were the anniversaries of red-letter days in the
history of the town – of the passing of a destructive plague, or the date of the
town's liberation from the English or Huguenots. On days like this the consuls
would parade in their finest robes, holding aloft the canopy above the Holy
Sacrament as the clergy bore it through the streets. They were accompanied
by bands of fiddlers and an escort of paupers carrying great candles of white
wax. After the procession was over bonfires were lit and the citizens danced
in the squares. An even more dazzling exhibition of royalist sentiment took
place each August during the Feast of the Assumption, an occasion especially
commemorated at the express wish of Louis XIII. And at the end of the
century the intendants presided over a series of unparalleled festivities in
honour of Louis XIV, the glorious monarch who had triumphed over heresy
and over the alliances of hostile powers.

Criminals were punished in public to edify the masses. Punitive spectacles
also helped to strengthen social solidarity, insofar as they attracted as many
people as the more festive events. Heralds went round proclaiming the news
of an imminent execution, and these grim proceedings invariably unfolded in
the presence of dense crowds. Two thousand people gathered, for example,
on 24 April 1630 in the amphitheatre at Limoges to witness the execution of
three witches from the surrounding countryside. On 18 August 1633 a crowd
of 6,000 packed, similarly, into the small town square of Loudun to see Urbain
Grandier burnt at the stake.

Scaffolds were erected in the evening in every part of the square of the Holy Cross
in the aforesaid town of Loudun. More than 6,000 persons were assembled there, on
foot and on horseback, on the rooftops, in the windows and on the scaffolds themselves.
The crowd had arrived to view this strange sight from every point of the compass, for
I believe there were more than 8,000 visitors in the town of Loudun. They hailed from
every region, and particularly from Poitiers, Tours, Orléans and Anjou.

Church festivals

Every secular celebration bore the stamp of the Church. Conversely, each
procession which wound round the town to commemorate one of the regular
festivals in the Church's year was headed by the full body of community
officials. The consuls, for instance, marched at the head of some twelve
processions yearly, irrespective of whether the occasion was sacred or secular.

The churchgoing public naturally took part in all the major festivals of the

Christian calendar. In addition, however, they also sought out other religious ceremonies of a more special nature, colourful devotions which drew in the layman by virtue of their aesthetic and imaginative appeal. They flocked, for example, to see their local bishop celebrating a mass prescribed by the Pope to give thanks for the delivery of a gang of slaves who had been ransomed from the pirates of the Barbary coast. They hurried to catch a glimpse of a passing religious notable, an itinerant holy man or a Father Provincial, sometimes even the head of a major religious order, and scuffled over the shreds they had torn from his robe. Every so often the town would host a provincial synod organized by a local monastic community, or would offer hospitality to the arriving inmates of a new religious house, Carmelite nuns or sisters of the order of St Ursula or the order of Our Lady, pious Augustinians, Jesuits or Capuchin friars. The townsfolk would throng to listen to a celebrated preacher whom the consuls or the members of a local religious brotherhood had invited to the town at their own expense to deliver himself of an Advent or Lenten sermon, and would pack the squares to hear him challenging the Protestant ministers in public debate. Crowds of peasants gathered to play their part in religious observances ranging from the biggest pilgrimages to the tiniest local cult. Shops and taverns sprang up around the little rural chapels where the faithful came to adore a particular miracle-working image. For ten leagues around, the countryside was emptied as entire communities marched in procession behind their parish priest and their sacred banners to make their devotions at the shrines of Garaison in Gascony, of Rocamadour in Quercy, of Verdelais in the Entre-Deux-Mers, of La Chapelle-Saint-Laurent in Gâtine, and of Sainte-Aquitère-de-l'Houmeau and Grâce-Dieu-de-Benon in Aunis. The ceremonies took the form of a solemn mass, followed by a feast. Pedlars sold ribbons, candles and almanacs, and the worshippers danced and drank till late at night. Tens of thousands of pilgrims are said to have poured in for the *pardons*, the great festivals which took place periodically at Rocamadour, and even on ordinary days it was not uncommon to see up to thirty processions piously ascending the long flight of steps which led to the rock-hewn church.[3]

In about the period 1580–1610 a mystical movement began to win a following in a number of towns of central and southern France. The movement consisted of *confréries de pénitents* (brotherhoods of penitents), and its success had an impact on social life for at least a century. The brotherhoods were originally founded in various different places by an assortment of fervent priests and pious officials. They took their cue from Rome, dedicating themselves, in a reaction to Protestant teachings, to the worship of the Eucharist, the Virgin Mary and the Saints. Within a few decades a good many towns had two or three of these brotherhoods, one being based, as a rule, in each major parish. The extent of their proliferation depended on circumstances. In some places they benefited from their connection with the Catholic League; in others, however, they had to contend with the suspicion of a certain number of clergymen and officers of the crown. The various different brotherhoods took

---

3 More than 20,000 people are said to have attended the *pardon* held on 23 June 1546. Almost 15,000 appeared at the festival of 24 June 1666.

their names from the colours they wore, colours of repentance and mourning, white, blue, black and grey. Members of each order dressed, in their meetings and processions, in a single identical costume designed to conceal the differences in social station within their ranks. This costume consisted of a gown or cassock, a cowl to cover the face, a woollen girdle, a wooden staff which they held in their hands, and the emblem of their patron saint which was patched on to the shoulder of their garment. The statutes of the order were approved by the ordinary. They provided for the election, each year, of a number of officials whose duty it was to oversee the daily life of the brotherhood: a prior, rector or syndic with his attendant assessors or theological advisers. The brotherhood financed itself by means of entrance fees, annual subscriptions and such gifts and bequests as were made to it by the more affluent members. Penitents joining the order vowed to help each other, to come to the aid of poor or sick fellow-members, and to attend the funerals of those who died. They submitted themselves to a harsh regime of Christian living: daily prayers, regular communions, and personal attendance at a large number of religious services and processions. Each brotherhood had a chapel of its own, and the members did all in their power to make the most of this place of worship: to dignify it with holy relics and indulgences, adorn it with splendid, candlelit altars and furnish it with eloquent preachers. The magnificent processions they organized brought the brotherhoods hundreds of instant recruits. In theory, at least, the orders were not exclusive. No one was barred from an institution explicitly 'not intended for men of one particular trade' (*non pro hominibus specialis artis*): the only people refused admission were those who had offended against public decency, 'heretics, simoniacs, brawlers, blasphemers, usurers and persons living in sin' (statutes of the Blue Order of Villeneuve-sur-Lot, 1611) – a category which on one occasion specifically included police constables and butchers (statutes of the Grey Order of Tulle, 1601). For practical purposes, however, the expense involved in making up the obligatory gown, the entrance fee which generally came to about an *écu* and a yearly subscription amounting to several tens of *sous* all combined to restrict admission to property-holders. Holding an office in a brotherhood was a still more costly business, since the holder was generally expected to make a handsome donation to his order, and the various annually elected posts were consequently monopolized by the legal profession. As the years passed, however, the orders were joined by increasing numbers of merchants, master-craftsmen and even common artisans, and in the course of the eighteenth century these groups at last got access to offices of an honorific kind.

The Blue Order of Villeneuve-sur-Lot included, for example, a number of masters of riverboats and citizens of other small towns in the Lot valley.[4] Its

---

4 Filing in procession in their dark cowls and the glimmer of candlelight, with psalms of remorse on their lips, the penitent brothers readily stirred the public to devotion. One typical devotee was a young peasant from the province of Limousin, who had lodgings with a master-builder in Tournepiche, a suburb of Périgueux. This young man was said to have lost his voice as the result of witchcraft. In May 1634, however, he recovered it by following a procession of penitents of the Black Order.

members were Christians deriving from a relatively wide range of social backgrounds. They promoted each other's material and spiritual welfare, as the statutes of the order required them to do, and pursued, in addition, a number of other activities of a pious and charitable nature. They distributed alms to those less fortunate than themselves, provided poor girls with a dowry, visited prisons and hospitals and took part in processions on feast days. Good works of this kind were highly visible, and the brotherhoods of penitents became, by performing them, a sure and powerful force for social integration.

Professional guilds

In the age of the Counter-Reformation these privileged bodies were the most important forum for shopkeepers and artisans. More numerous and more conspicuous than the craft associations, they numbered among their members virtually all the inhabitants of any given town – all, at least, who had a craft and a roof under which to practise it. These guilds had varying histories. Some could point to a pedigree of several centuries, while others might have been registered with a local notary the day before. But all of them came into being for the same basic reason. In each case a handful of master-craftsmen were impelled by a desire to dignify their calling, to ensure that it enjoyed a recognized place in the social hierarchy and to impress the general public with the numbers and cohesion of those who engaged in it. Every year they elected an officer known as the *mage* or *baile*. They placed themselves under the protection of a patron saint and undertook to hold a service on that particular saint's day and to take the day off. This annual celebration entailed a range of expenses such as the fee for the priest, the lighting for the church and above all the cost of the banquet which the guild brothers shared when the service was over. They met the expenses out of their regular subscriptions together with the rather heavier charges which they levied on new members and on any members who happened to marry, open a shop or engage an apprentice. Guilds had to win approval for their statutes from the local church authorities. Local churches enjoyed a reasonable amount of independence, and the guild brothers could accordingly be confident that this procedure would not take years. Otherwise their principal function was to take part in festivals and parades. Guilds marched in line in the community's formal processions, their place in the procession depending variously on the length of their pedigree or the place which the consuls accorded them in the social hierarchy. At Bordeaux, for example, the sack-makers, dressmakers and masons led the parade, while at Agen pride of place was taken by the guild of lawyers, the guild of St Ivo, who marched in front of both the merchants and the goldsmiths. At Cahors the largest guild was that of the cobblers; at Tulle, however, the cobblers, weavers and paper-makers were equally well represented. The best-known and most active guilds in Bordeaux were those of the watermen and cask-makers; at Agen, on the other hand, the masons and weavers cut the greatest dash. These holiday parades often had a distinctly military air. In Agen, for instance, there advanced through the streets on Ascension Day 'a company of masons armed with swords and beating a drum.

They carried a standard and marched in battle formation. Two of them acted
as captains, leading the way, and flanked by three sergeants with halberds and
swords.'

There is, in fact, no evidence that guilds, corporations or leagues of journeymen were directly involved in any disturbance at any time. Equally, however,
there was no outbreak of mass violence which did *not* involve a large number
of individual journeymen and artisans. The townships consequently forbade
the guilds to hold festivals in troubled periods, since they feared that these
gatherings might take on a seditious character. When the *mages* came, for
example, 'to the town hall to ask permission to march their guild in rank and
file to the sound of the drum as it had been their custom to do in previous
years', the authorities refused permission

in order to avoid any kind of misadventure. And they very particularly forbade them
to march in formation through the town and to carry either arms or drum. All they
allowed them to do, indeed, was to gather to say their prayers, and to play their fiddles,
if they chose, in the church where they had been wont to conduct their annual
ceremonies.

Disciplined and vigorous as they were, the guilds were also anxious to safeguard
their privileges. They were not going to compromise their position by getting
entangled in riots and revolts. They were dependent on the favour of the
municipal governments, and inextricably connected with the celebrations and
ceremonies of city life. They too felt part of the commune.

Jollifications

Guild festivals were carefree revelries which started with masquerades and
ended with drinking bouts. They formed part of a whole series of jollifications
which stood out like milestones in the course of the passing year. It is easy to
ridicule the bland conventional picture of a rural Arcadia. But it must be said,
all the same, that the record books are not merely a chronicle of tragic
incidents, that they speak also of moments when 'life was good, for that while'.
These were the 'fat months' of the folk tales as opposed to the 'lean months'
– the seasons of Lent and Advent, the times when bread was dear and the
whole day was occupied in harvesting the corn or the grapes. It is clear from
the parish registers that marriages varied in frequency through the year in
accordance with this cycle of dearth and plenty. In Gascony, for example,
most marriages took place in January, February, June and November. These
months corresponded, respectively, with the Christmas weeks best suited to
weddings and banquets; with the season when pigs were slaughtered between
Christmas and carnival time; and with the feasts of Midsummer's Day and
Martinmas, 24 June and 11 November, when the country people danced. They
were times for eating and drinking. The annual series of days devoted to
merrymaking, drunkenness and periodic violence can be traced by another
method – through a study of the letters in which the authorities granted pardon
for various crimes. These letters reveal that brawls invariably took place on

the same occasions, saints' days, carnival week and Shrove Tuesday, May Day and Midsummer's Day.

Guild brothers celebrated their annual festival by bestowing mock titles on certain of their number. This custom was known as queening. It involved choosing kings and queens along with an entourage composed of dignitaries who took the names of chancellor, standard-bearer, sword-bearer, throne-bearer, favourite and goblet-filler or wine-taster. These worthies won their appointments either by election or through a kind of auction in which they bid for the posts by offering to buy candles and posies for the guild. They spent most of their brief reigns drinking and getting everyone else to do the same. They were enthroned in the churches and paraded through the streets. For many centuries the authorities were content to turn a blind eye to this activity; by our period, however, it was beginning to cause a certain amount of scandal.

The childish custom the guilds had of creating kings and queens was as widespread in Quercy as in every other province. They came into the churches with lighted tapers, beating their drums and banging their instruments. They crept right up to the altars, bristling with pikes and halberds, and making faces at everyone, especially the women and girls. Finally they pranced around with their candles in their hands and cavorted up to the offertory. The kings and queens of the festival were always the most conspicuous for their brazen and shameless behaviour.

In the week after Ascension Day the watermen of Bordeaux raced through the streets with a panoply of banners, fifes and drums to advertise the pilgrim-age they would be making the following Saturday to the church of Plassac near Blaye. They went there by boat and indulged in twenty-four hours of spectacular junketings. The people of Bas-Limousin set out in similar fashion, to 'abduct the kings of the guilds of the most mechanical craftsmen and escort them to church beneath a canopy or awning. At the same time they honoured the said guilds with banquets and public feasting. Most of the guilds provided their own pewter plate and kitchen utensils.'

On New Year's Day people in western France celebrated the festival of 'aquilaneuf'. It was a pretext for young parishioners to go from house to house soliciting drinks, chickens and money.

On the first Sunday of Lent the people of Gourdon held the Feast of Savages. To 'play the savage' you dressed up and put on a mask. For four days the maskers had the run of the streets: they booed the passers-by and drenched them with hoses of muddy water. The lieutenant-général left the town 'so as not to make an ass of the law'. Shrove Tuesdays at Agen were famous. The market was draped with tapestries, carts were lashed together as a makeshift stage and musicians perched on the top, and the main square was filled with dancers. In addition the Duke of Épernon had the streets cleared to make room for equestrian carousels performed by members of the nobility. Gentlemen masked and clad in the magnificent garb of knights-errant or the traditional costume of Agen formed into companies and tilted at the ring or the quintain. Everywhere the carnival season was a time of licence and revelry.

At the beginning of May boisterous citizens went round putting up maypoles.

The maypoles were swathed with garlands and ribbons, and the citizens raised them in front of the window of any eminent person they wished to honour, while young people and passers-by threw them a little largesse.

They wanted to march through the town in a band of about eighty to entertain the public. They wanted to ride with horse-pistols, in breastplates, to the sound of a trumpet. Another group of eighty or a hundred men were to follow them on foot, with muskets, flags flying and beating a drum. In this formation they meant to present arms at the town hall and raise a maypole.

In Poitou and Angoumois the May Day customs were bound up with the tradition of *bachelleries* (bachelor festivals) or dancing parties. Young people in each parish were permitted, by common consent, to choose an unmarried youth to act as their 'captain' during the weeks between Easter and Whitsun. The 'captain' repaid his promotion by celebrating masses and giving feasts. One of his duties was to set up a maypole in front of the local château – a practice reflecting the feudal origins of the tradition. The *bachelleries* were still very popular in the seventeenth century, and the young people revelled in every province of western France. For the duration of this special season they were usually entitled to ride about the neighbourhood, tilt at the quintain, drink to their hearts' content and take the girls dancing.

Midsummer's Day, the feast of St John the Baptist, was the excuse for an outbreak of still more general gaiety. Every village made merry in the glow of a towering bonfire lit by the consuls and the local parish priest. When the stack collapsed and the flames burnt low over the embers, the young people vaulted the fire, snatched the glowing brands and flailed them around the streets. Certain other Midsummer customs were beginning by now to arouse official disapproval. The cask-makers of Bordeaux, for example, went round the city performing a kind of pantomime in which they re-enacted the baptism of Christ. Some of them dressed up as Jesus, some as St John the Baptist and some as apostles, with shaggy hair, coats of many colours and wooden trenchers on their heads to represent haloes. At Périgueux the community appointed five Masters of Midsummer (*officiers de la Saint-Jean*), one for each district of the town. These dignitaries went under the titles of emperor, king, marquis, duke and abbot. The consuls entrusted a range of powers to them to exercise over the holiday period, 'authority within the town, and, in particular, authority over weddings. At one time this was an honour confined to the leading citizens. At present, however, these officers have brought themselves into disrepute to such a degree that the case is altered entirely.' At Saint-Sever and Bazas, access to the main square was blocked with carts, and bullfights were organized. The chief picador was known as the Prince of the Moon. At Tulle, finally, Midsummer was the time of the Moon Festival, a procession held in moonlight to commemorate the passing of the Black Death in 1348. The procession was also known as the Pilgrimage of St John, since popular tradition maintained that the plague had been dispelled through the personal intervention of St John the Baptist. The assembled company set out from the cathedral at six in the evening, and made their way round a series of little country chapels before returning to town, while arquebusiers, trumpeters and bell-ringers stationed in the church towers and belfries took it in turns to keep up a festive din. The procession was headed by the King of the Moon Festival, and fiddlers, flautists and drummers brought up the rear. The king was elected by an assembly made up of all the guilds in the town. He 'reigned' with an entourage of cronies for the duration of the festival, which lasted a whole nine days. His duties included lighting the bonfires which the citizens had made ready at the crossroads, giving the signal for the dancing to begin and receiving showers of mock honours.

In the course of their fleeting dominion as tribunes of the people, these lords of misrule were widely entitled to one particular privilege. They were allowed to preside over weddings, and to amuse themselves at the expense of the newly-weds. They inherited the rights connected with the feudal custom of *droit de seigneur*, rights which were sometimes bestowed by the citizens, with all due formality, on the countless Provençal youth leagues or on the *bachelleries* of Poitou. In other provinces where no such formal office had been created for them, young parishioners and couples engaged to be married were accorded, by common consent, a sort of light-hearted eminence as the watchdogs of public morality. They were entitled to penalize, for instance, anyone engaging in marriages generally judged to be scandalous or grotesque through the custom of the *charivari*, or mock serenade. The ragging this entailed was aimed especially at persons remarrying or entering into any kind of ill-assorted union. Every evening for several days gangs of exuberant youths conducted a cacophonous orchestra made up of cooking-pots, horns and cattle-bells beneath the windows of the unfortunate couple. The symphony was enlivened with gibes, obscene ditties and volleys of stones and mud. The only way for the victim to put an end to the racket was to abandon any resistance and stand drinks all round. Sometimes the *charivari* had official sanction, since the organizers had secured the blessing of the local magistrate; even so, it was not uncommon for the revelry to take an ugly turn, as the husband responded to the ragging by snatching up a musket and opening fire on his tormentors – or at any rate took them to court. Evidence suggests that this custom already existed at the beginning of the fourteenth century; and it survived until very recent times. Legal records, individual memories and investigations conducted by students of folklore all make it plain that the *charivari* lingered on in the countryside of south-west France almost to the present day. By comparing the minutes of inquiries presided over by seventeenth-century judges with the police reports of more recent times we can see how little the custom changed over the years. A seventeenth-century miller of Barsac who married a widow met with the following indignities: 'When they found his house, they fastened cuckold's horns round the walls and stuck them in his garden; in a word, they libelled him in every possible way they could, and rumour has it that the magistrates were the ringleaders.' This incident was cited in the chronicle of Gaufreteau. The chronicler believed that the custom originated in the Haut-Pays, near Toulouse. He goes on,

If the husband wants to protect himself he must pay a sizeable sum and must wine and dine the very people who are littering his house with cuckold's horns, breaking down his door, barging into his nuptial chamber and insulting him in a thousand other ways besides. The *parlement* may pass decrees for all it is worth: there is no one who will obey them, neither the honest journeymen of the country parishes nor those persons who have some influence on the journeymen by virtue of their social status or financial means.

In February 1643 a citizen of Lectoure married a widow. For four nights after his wedding his house was besieged by about a hundred neighbours armed with pots and pans. They blackened the walls with excrement, smashed the windows and drove off a soldier from the local garrison whom the governor had sent to keep the peace. When the victim still refused to stand them drinks they actually blocked up the doors of his house with cobblestones torn from the street. Six of the ringleaders were summoned before the magistrate's court. They complained that it had 'always been the custom in this kingdom to stage a *charivari* against boys who marry widows . . . and girls who marry widowers'. They had acted, they said, 'not to create a scandal, and not out of ill intent, but solely to uphold their right to stage the said *charivari* . . . to observe the fine and praiseworthy custom of the *charivari*'.

Another source of merriment for the 'guardians of morality' was the *azoade*, or donkey tour, a ceremony designed to make fun of henpecked or cuckolded husbands. The decision to launch this mock procession would be taken at an inn. Decision made, the company would set off to find a donkey, and the procession would form up. Sometimes one of the party would get astride the animal the wrong way round, brandishing its tail in his hands and proclaiming to all and sundry that he represented a certain person before whose house they were going to have some fun. Alternatively the donkey would be saddled with a grotesque dummy and lured down the road by means of a bag of millet which was dangled before it at the end of a long pole. On one typical occasion the consuls at Agen went to break up a crowd which had gathered beneath the windows of the house of a craftsman in the rue du Temple.

A donkey procession had been organized by the landlord of a neighbouring inn in conjunction with a draper, a grocer and a blacksmith. They stood around insolently, without doffing their hats. The donkey tour first made its appearance in the fourteenth century. In the course of the nineteenth century it began to die out; but the custom was still known in some country regions in the early 1900s.

These jollifications are something more than extinct curiosities. They should not be ignored or despised. Authorized, accepted, spontaneous, and constantly indulged in, they were, in their day, the token of an unquestioned solidarity which was felt by the inhabitants of every village and district. Through them the population showed that it thought as one.

This popular culture drew its strength from a simultaneous devotion to tradition and excess. It was ill-equipped to resist the advent of a rationalized religion and an orderly and meticulous policing system. Humanist magistrates infused with an urge to lay down the law, priestly reformers buoyed up by demanding standards of piety – all of these did their best to undermine the grip of popular custom through a barrage of orders and decrees. They denounced and prohibited the feasts of misrule, the masquerades and the boisterous processions. In a series of celebrated judgements the Sorbonne condemned the secret rites of the leagues of journeymen – primitive imitations of the Catholic liturgy which the journeymen staged to sanctify their exploits. The *parlement* at Bordeaux suppressed on grounds of blasphemy the performances which the city's cask-makers and saddlers put on at festival time. One sternly reformist clergyman was Alain de Solminihac, a distinguished bishop who occupied the see of Cahors from 1636 to 1657. His biographers recall the assiduous zeal with which

he deployed against popular gatherings every spiritual weapon up to and including excommunication, and gave the chief clergy and curates a mandate to do all within their power to prevent excesses ... There were even some officials who supported these orgies on the pretext that they had been the custom from time immemorial ... But these *tempora* and *mores* were extinguished thanks to constant exhortations and ordinances resolutely enforced.

In a chronicle compiled at the end of his life to edify his children, a wealthy notary of Tulle commented with satisfaction on the end of the noisy processions which had previously been a feature of the guild festivals and the carnival season: 'Many old customs which were grotesque and unseemly have been rightly abolished.' In 1680 the consuls of Gourdon broke up the Shrove Tuesday Feast of Savages by force of arms. Guards of burgesses were posted at the town gates and on the thoroughfares. They had orders to arrest every troublemaker, 'because masquerades of this kind have been forbidden alike by royal decree and through the excommunications which the bishops of Cahors have pronounced these thirty years on those who have played the savage in this town'.

This ancient custom was relegated to the fringes of society. Banned in the towns, it survived only in outlying country districts. Other festivities were diluted out of all recognition. 'Queenings' increasingly had to be conducted by auction rather than election. Elections had fostered disorder insofar as the journeymen tended to choose the most boisterous of their number; but auctions were won by well-heeled notables anxious to make their mark with a conspicuous show of largesse. Old peasant revelries gave way to the customs instituted by 'guilds of the rosary'. On the feast of Our Lady's Nativity or the local saint's day the parish priest gave a sermon in which he invited the congregation to bid for the titles of king or *dauphin*. Parents believed that by holding these offices they could place their children under the protection of the Virgin Mary or the local patron saint, and the competition was keen. In spite of all these changes one or two of the older customs did, none the less, linger on tenaciously, like the *charivaris* and bullfights.

The history of the bullfights is an instructive case in point. These bloodthirsty spectacles became popular in France at the end of the Hundred Years War, and encountered little serious criticism till the seventeenth century. Bullfights were held at Bordeaux in carnival time, at Bazas and Saint-Sever during the Midsummer festival, and at Mont-de-Marsan on the feast day of the local patron saint, Mary Magdalene. They attracted large crowds and were often, consequently, the scene of violent incidents. The first known mention of a bullfight occurs in a pardon accorded in 1457 to an archer who kept a tavern at Saint-Sever. The archer had been implicated in a brawl which broke out in his tavern after a day of bullfighting. In 1604 a bullfight was staged in the ditches of the Hâ at Bordeaux. The show ended violently when a group of carters in the audience came to blows. The episode caused some scandal. In 1628 Jean Jaubert of Barrault, bishop of Bazas from 1611 to 1631, made an attempt to ban these riotous spectacles. The response to his pastoral letter was immediate and hostile: 'The people are in a state of mutiny and revolt. He is consequently in peril of his life, and so is his brother the Count of Barrault, seneschal of Bazadois.'

Various other attempts were made to abolish bullfighting. The *parlement* passed decrees, and the bishops of Aire sent out pastoral letters. The public paid no attention. In January 1648 letters patent were issued by the crown, but even these were ignored.[5]

The clergymen of south-west France justified their campaign by citing a papal bull promulgated by Pope Pius V in 1567 under the title *De salute gregis*. The decree condemned any shows which involved the baiting of animals, and its strictures were taken up in the pastoral letters of the bishops, in the decrees passed by the *parlement* at Bordeaux and even in the letters patent issued by Louis XIII in December 1620 and by Louis XIV in January 1648. The authorities condemned bullfighting as a bloody and dangerous pastime. They described how the victims ran through the narrow streets of the towns, maddened by the shouting, by the blows of the *banderillas*, the barking of the dogs and the volleys of musket-fire; how they broke into the market-place only to find that the exits had already been blocked with carts. Crowds stampeded to the spectacle, and citizens were injured and even killed. Wine flowed in torrents, and the very picadors and matadors were drunk. Gangs of youths challenged and fought each other, and old scores were settled in blood. At service-time the churches were empty, and the voices of the priests were drowned by the din of shots and yells from the streets. The community bankrupted itself in organizing the festival to the point where it could no longer pay the authorities the normal festival dues. Instead the money went to the *'tenanciers'* or bullfight contractors, local butchers or merchants who were elected annually to stage the event, and who financed the preparations by raising a toll from their fellow-citizens. In short, the authorities concluded, this custom had to be suppressed in the interests of public order, and to ensure due payment of taxes and respect for the rites of the Church.

In the dioceses of Bordeaux and Bazas successive condemnations had the desired effect. Bullfighting was stamped out and had totally disappeared by about the end of the 1630s. In the diocese of Aire, however, the resistance was harder to break. Gilles Boutault, bishop from 1626 to 1649, issued repeated ordinances without any apparent success. Bullfights were still in

---

5 See Yves-Marie Bercé, 'Les courses de taureaux dans le sud-ouest aquitain' ('Bullfights in Aquitaine, South-West France'), in *Les Jeux à la Renaissance* (Colloque de Tours), Paris, VRIN, 1982, pp. 19–31.

vogue, for example, in 1665 in the town of Saint-Sever, which contemplated giving them up in token of submission to the crown after the failure of the uprising against the salt tax in which it had taken part. The aldermen acknowledged that they had failed to comply with the bans pronounced on bullfighting in the previous thirty years. One pious tradition ascribes the credit for finally extinguishing the custom in this diocese to Jean-Louis de Fromentières, who occupied the see of Aire from 1673 to 1684.

By way of compensation, clergy and intendants allowed the communities to organize bullfights 'in the Spanish style'. The distinction was significant. Crueller than the traditional French contests, Spanish-style bullfights none the less seemed to the authorities more orderly and less liable to cause a breach of the peace. In the first place they took the form of a performance rather than a festival in which all took part. Secondly the bull was not chased through the city, and the performance took place in a confined arena. Finally the Spanish-style fights were staged by professionals, rather than improvised by gangs of local youths. This shift to the Spanish style was hastened by a political event of the early eighteenth century – the succession of Philip, Duke of Anjou, to the Spanish throne. Bullfighting came back into favour. A great Spanish-style bullfight was staged at Bayonne on 17 January 1701 before the kings of both France and Spain. From that time onwards the traditional French bullfight survived chiefly in saint's day festivals and the carnivals which were held in some of the parishes of Lannes and Béarn.

Both customs, in other words, had their social status inverted. In the early seventeenth century the traditional bullfight was a festival held in the towns with the official sanction of judges and aldermen. As the years passed, however, it sank down the social scale and became no more than a despised recreation of the rural masses. The Spanish bullfight, by contrast, began its career as an orderly and aristocratic spectacle and was transplanted into the French towns by the chances of politics. The process began in 1701 with the coronation of Philip V of Spain and the historic bullfight of Bayonne, and culminated in 1853 with the Spanish marriage of Napoleon III and the rule which was made at that time permitting bullfighting to take place south of an imaginary line between Bordeaux and Avignon – a rule that is still in force to the present day.

Seventeenth-century clergymen and nineteenth-century prefects both campaigned against traditional bullfighting with varying degrees of success. Both, however, were at one in connecting the bullfights with a shameful past – a past which they wished to present to their public as a contrast offsetting the new order of things. For the clergy, this popular custom was an abominable legacy of the days of paganism; for the prefects, it bore the stamp of the 'savage manners of feudal society'. For both groups this cultural legacy was nothing more than a piece of folklore consigned to a dark age with which they wanted to mark a break. They believed that their new social order should have a new culture worthy of it.

Lastly we may turn for a moment to a custom practised in a completely different region. The Swiss wrestling matches are a good final example of the political and cultural transition which took place in the seventeenth century.

During the seventeenth century these tournaments were cast out by urban society. Denounced by the preachers and banned by the magistrates, they disappeared from the life of the towns, valleys and plateaux of Switzerland. From that time on they became a simple country pastime confined to the slopes of the Alps and their foothills, where the shepherds continued for many years to vie with each other in wrestling bouts during the festivals which were held at the end of every summer.

This long survey of festivities reveals, consequently, that two historical processes were unfolding side by side. As the state pursued its gradual takeover of the ancient functions of the townships it was launching, at the same time, a continual onslaught against the free and easy ways in which the townspeople traditionally gave vent to their excitement. The communes were losing not only their institutional identity but their emotional underpinnings. Violent displays of local fellowship and long-established customs were vanishing steadily – and vanishing, in particular, in the reign of Louis XIV.

Taverns

Every merrymaking called for wine. Each festival was a booze-up, and taverns played an essential role in the social life of the time.

Our descendants will say for sure that it was the innkeepers who invented this phenomenal number of feast days. Religion for peasants and craftsmen means getting drunk to celebrate the festival of a saint they have never heard of in any other connection. These days of idleness and debauchery are precisely the time when all the crimes get committed. It is the feast days that fill prisons and provide the watchmen, court clerks, gaolers and hangmen with their sordid livelihood.[6]

Incidents provoked by drunkenness give scope to righteous indignation in every age. In the seventeenth century, however, there is some evidence to suggest that the problem of drinking grew more acute. More vines were planted in this period, and the cellars filled with brandy as inferior vintages were fortified in the countryside of Gascony and Angoumois. Taverns sprang up in the suburbs which stretched out around the highways on the outskirts of every town, and the edicts issued by the town hall could do little to prevent them. All a would-be innkeeper needed to do was to hang up a bush in his doorway. So long as he took care to dodge the insidious attentions of the taxman, he could sell his own brew at a profit and keep open house.

Wherever there was a rural chapel frequented by pilgrims or a Protestant church consigned to the suburbs of a town by municipal regulations, local peasants put up tables and established inns. The larger towns of south-west France were endowed with medieval privileges which stipulated that only local wine could be sold within their walls. This meant in practice that the import of wines from outside was strictly prohibited from the time of the grape

6 See 'Festivals' entry in Voltaire's *Dictionnnaire philosophique* (1764). Voltaire ascribes this sententious judgement to a 'sound magistrate'.

harvest (variously dated from Michaelmas, 29 September, or Martinmas, 11 November) right up to Palm Sunday or Easter. Craftsmen who subjected the local vintage to unfair competition by smuggling in wines from outside and selling them on the cheap were punished with the full rigour of the law.

Town councils reported with dismay that the local wines were selling at a loss or going off in their casks as a result of the competition from the 'countless taverns which are being set up the whole time by craftsmen who have no wine of the local vintages'. Good or bad, wine flowed freely in every citizen's house, and this domestic consumption was one of the principal causes of urban drunkenness. Each house gave board and lodging to a contingent of servants and footmen. They were never short of barrels to help themselves from.

The social role of the tavern needs little explanation. People went there to gamble, gossip, drink and amuse themselves. In addition they also sometimes went to do business as creditor and debtor, or merchant and customer, to arrange leases, draw up a tax assessment or pay over their apportioned tax to the collectors. At the risk of sounding blasphemous, we may fairly say that tavern and church were the twin poles of village society.

Every so often, in towns like Saint-Émilion, Dax or Cognac, the authorities denounced the evils of the bottle: the riotous conduct of men returned from a drinking session, the indecency of inns which stayed open late at night or at service-time, the shouts, the oaths and the general booziness which seeped out from behind the tavern door.

Most of the craftsmen in the town . . . are so dissipated that they never leave the inns and taverns either by night or by day. They sit there squandering their assets and all the income they are able to win by their labours and industry. The result is that most of their families are on the verge of starvation. And that is not the end of their profligacy. Once in their cups these wine-bibbers perpetrate all manner of affronts and blasphemies against the holy name of God. And at night, when they leave the taverns, they head straight for the neighbouring houses, to burgle them.

A priest in Limousin attributed a temporary rise in the price of wine to divine displeasure. 'In previous years those rascals insisted on having the best bottles in town. Their constant drinking and blasphemy vexed our good Lord so greatly that the wine which was once so abundant has become extremely dear when they least expected it.' On Sundays and feast days the ploughmen went straight from mass to a neighbouring hostelry, where they spent the sacred hours in a protracted binge that ended only at nightfall. The legal records give vivid accounts of the orgies which accompanied the annual dinners of the grape pickers and vine dressers, the saint's day festivals and the local celebrations of Poitou. The revellers gambled away their earnings at dice, playing cards, tarot cards, bowls and ninepins, and their debts burnt a hole in the pockets of their friends and relatives. Layabouts beat up any innkeepers who refused to serve them, broke down the doors of their cellars and broached their casks. On Saturday nights the drunks slept heavily, flat out on the ground at the edge of the tavern fire. Sometimes a few of the company amused themselves by peeling off the clogs and hose of one of the slumberers and throwing them in the grate, or even singeing the beard of the unfortunate victim. One regular drinker was the parish priest of Genac. His parishioners accused him of sitting around all day 'in a tavern which he never left till he had taken more wine than was good for him. Usually we had to help him to his chamber by lifting him under the arms.' Another record speaks of the befuddled footmen and peasants who spent their evenings brawling in front of the chapel dedicated to the patron saint of Saint-Roch. Still another describes the excesses of a journeyman cobbler known as 'Boozer' (*Boischopine*). He laid about him with his stool and started a free-for-all. Dutch courage played its part in every outburst of civic rioting. The seventeenth century was a period in which drunkenness strengthened its hold on the lower orders in the townships, and any sketch of the popular excitements of the time must take account of it.

Dangerous social groups

Certain social groups played a particularly prominent role in outbreaks of public disorder. To analyse their activities we must turn, once again, to the contemporary legal records. The bulk of the punishments meted out by the court of aldermen at Bordeaux were imposed on three unruly groups, journeymen, watermen and students. These three groups represented 48.2 per cent of the city's total manpower. Their membership was inherently fluid, their status low and their reputation shocking.

Students took lodgings in the streets near the colleges. Far from their homes, and emboldened by youthful insolence, fire and extremism, they were, for a time at least, free from the constraints of their social background. They formed themselves into cells, electing priors to lead them and exacting dues from the freshmen. They wore swords, duelled with each other and lorded it in the streets. Sometimes they hung around taverns swindling simple-minded customers and jostling passers-by. At night they made the town re-echo with their songs, brawls and general uproariousness as they larked about with their pistols, knives and guns, threw stones at the citizens' windows and coshed the constables. The magistrates fined them heavily or drove them out of town. Sometimes their brawls led to bloodshed, and the magistrates responded with sentences of a more drastic kind. In April 1636 the old Duke of Épernon used student trouble as his pretext for picking a quarrel with the aldermen of Bordeaux. 'I should like to know', he demanded, 'on whose authority you invited students to the town hall to witness the execution of Lureau? This has never been done before, either during the Toulouse riots or at any other time. Your answer, please, aldermen! What kind of people do you think these students are?' 'Your Grace,' ventured an alderman, 'the students are mostly young men of good family. Some of them are gentlemen, sons of presiding magistrates, councillors and other qualified persons. They are subjects of the king and residents of the city.' 'Do you not realize that they are vagabonds, loafers, wool-gatherers?' The alderman persisted. 'We punish anyone of that sort we find here. We give them short shrift.' 'Be silent, insolent blockhead!' thundered the Duke.

Journeymen loom large in the crime figures of every town. They were in the thick of every tavern brawl. Every so often they banded together to agitate against guild-masters with whom they had fallen at odds in a quarrel over employment. The courts handed down stiff sentences, but the lifestyle of the journeymen continued unchanged.

Watermen and ferrymen were another particularly unruly and dangerous group. Coarse, brutal and quarrelsome, these 'rascally waterfowl' had a hand in all the disturbances which broke out on the banks of the Vienne, the Charente, the Corrèze, the Isle, the Dordogne, the Garonne or the Lot.They included not only ferrymen but bargees and fishermen, raftsmen coming down on their timbers from the Haut-Pays, sailors who dealt in cargoes of salt, prunes, wine, corn or sand, convicts, picklocks and deck hands, dockside porters and stevedores. Their women were laundresses or fishwives and they lived in the ports. They were blamed for all kinds of misconduct, for general insolence, for foisting their own fares on passengers, turning them away at a whim, putting them ashore in mid-journey if the tide turned suddenly or a contrary wind sprang up, and sometimes even making off with travellers' clothes. They were also in the thick of civil disorders. It was the watermen at Agen who gave the signal for the revolt which broke out in that town on 17 May 1635. The watermen at Bordeaux were equally turbulent. On 14 May 1635 they helped to storm the city hall, and on 16 August 1675 they burnt the official dispatch-boat before the documents it carried could be unloaded on the banks of the Garonne. Finally they were responsible for massacring the servants of the Baron de Fumel. Summoned to Bordeaux in the rising of 1649 by the Duke of Épernon, this gentleman had proceeded there by boat with a retinue of well-armed servants and friends. He arrived at the Chapeau-Rouge wharf on 24 July, at the precise moment when the duke was leaving town with the rebels hot on his heels. Even as the usual picklocks were collecting to carry the luggage, some of the local children denounced the new arrivals as supporters of Épernon. The port was soon crowded. The Baron's vessel was surrounded by other craft, and in a matter of minutes the watermen had plundered his baggage and had cut the throats of virtually all his entourage or drowned them in the river.

With the possible exception of the carters, the river people were the most unsavoury characters in the entire population – the most foul-mouthed, the most violent and the most feared.

One other group often given to disorderly behaviour were the footmen and servants employed in the more prosperous households. They too were apt to fall foul of the local magistrates, when the townsfolk complained of their pilfering and of their arrogant and dissolute conduct. They used their employers' status as an excuse to put on airs, loafing around the streets with swords, pistols and daggers. Footmen trafficked in stolen goods, and chambermaids sold their bodies. One observer protested how 'several whores posing as nurses and wet-nurses of new-born children have taken shelter in this town ... A number of servants and other young men are slipping into our houses by night under the pretext of having a tête-à-tête and are indulging in lewdness and adultery.' In every town the police regulations prescribed that the bowmen of the watch should make their rounds with the object of ensuring that no one walked the streets with arms and without lanterns 'after the sounding of the tattoo' and of preventing attendants and footmen from 'loitering' or roaming about at night after the town gates were closed, unless they had been 'dispatched by their masters on the said masters' business'.

But no amount of edicts and ordinances could stop the footmen acquiring some of the superficial trappings of upper-class life. It was a kind of social nemesis. The footmen were usually protected by the tacit support of their masters, who were concerned for the honour of their livery and could be expected to view the arrest of a servant as a personal insult. The bowmen held back, and the lackeys continued to wield their arms in spite of the regulations, in an assortment of vicious blood-feuds, honourable vendettas and squalid brawls.

Finally we should bear in mind the challenge posed by the poor. Their sheer numbers made them a scandal and challenge to the community. They were a scandal in the sense that no Christian townsman could conscientiously stand by while his less fortunate fellow-citizens starved to death in a nearby street; a scandal which weighed on him daily when the bolder paupers ventured into churches and even private houses in search of alms. They were a menace, a terrible menace, when the community found itself in the path of an epidemic, since its hundreds of beggars had had their resistance weakened by hunger to the point where they might easily let in the virus like a sort of fifth column in a city besieged by plague. Townspeople drew a distinction between the poor of their own community and paupers arrived from outside, whether professional beggars or peasants compelled by famine to beg their bread on the roads. Outsiders were not wanted. The citizens gave them enough alms to last them a day, threatened them with a flogging if they turned up a second time and drove them out of town. Poor fellow-citizens – old people, invalids, widows and waifs – were treated with more solicitude. They could turn to the town hospital, where the authorities provided relief with the help of the quite considerable sums which generations of pious burgesses had bequeathed for that purpose in their wills. Those sums were administered, as we have seen, by an official known as the syndic of the poor. The office of syndic existed in all the larger towns. It was occupied by a citizen conspicuous for his wealth and piety, and involved him in an unending round of financial litigation. In times of economic crisis the body of registered paupers is known to have been swelled, to a frightening extent, by large numbers of petty craftsmen, day labourers and their families who were unable to make ends meet during months of continuous dearth.

In the years 1657 to 1662 the government launched a great reform of the hospital network. This entailed the founding of general hospitals throughout the kingdom on the model of the one in Paris. Such hospitals could cater for hundreds of paupers – a significant improvement on most of the older establishments, which had been able to accommodate only a few dozen people.

This step has been viewed, with justification, as a major turning-point in the social history of the seventeenth century. It was the beginning of a whole process by which the poor were segregated and shut away. By creating the general hospitals the government began, in effect, to stamp out begging.

Previously beggars had asked for alms in an open and brazen manner, and society had generally accepted their right to do so. From now on, however, their activities were increasingly viewed as contemptible and shameful, and society persecuted them for all it was worth. The medieval hospitals in which they had once taken refuge had been, admittedly, cramped and limited places – but they had lain at the heart of the town and been an integral part of it. The huge new buildings which now arose were sited deliberately at arm's length, outside the town walls on the edge of the fields. They were a closed world, sealed off, self-sufficient and isolated from normal community life.

Group violence

Sometimes the records allude to events of an unpredictable kind. A crowd would gather without warning, or the commune would be disturbed by a piece of news or a development its members felt to be scandalous and offensive, and would take up arms. A rumour would spread, for example, that an exciseman had come to town, a riotous crowd would sally forth to attack him and the magistrates would signal their acquiescence by standing aside. The chronicles merely mention that 'the commune was aroused; it rose up.' On one occasion a crown commissioner arrived in La Rochelle with a brief to negotiate the disbanding of the local Protestant convocation. The envoy was bombarded all the way to his lodgings with warnings to the effect 'that the town was a dangerous place for him, since he had brought bad news. Rumours were spreading and the commune was about to rise up.' Another time a master-distiller was sent to his town by the *cour des monnaies* (a high court concerned with currency) with the assignment of posting up a sheaf of the latest fiscal regulations. The man was denounced in the street. 'Gentlemen,' a citizen shouted, 'it's a monopolist, come and help me throw him in the river! He ought to be lynched, that's the way to treat monopolists!' The wrath of the commune was an ever-present spectre, conjured up regularly by taxpayers to threaten their persecutors and by tax collectors as a way of blaming others, or excusing themselves, for the paucity of the moneys they had raised. And with good reason. Communes often were involved, in a corporate sense, in every stage of a riot, from its first beginnings right through to its final results.

The usual cause of a disturbance was an assault launched from outside upon the community as a whole. Sometimes all that was needed to provoke an outbreak of rioting was an event which people made out to be an assault, or perceived as one. Under certain circumstances incitement to violence might come from the highest local authority – the consuls themselves. At Auch, for example, the representatives of the surrounding *élection* claimed the right on one occasion to take first place in the procession which the town held annually on the Feast of Corpus Christi. The senior consul barred their way, overturned the candle carried by the assistant magistrate of the *élection*, and called on the bystanders to come to his aid. The crowd ran riot. Faced by a mob of nearly 400 angry citizens, the officials of the *élection* took to their heels. In August 1636 the consuls of Périgueux summoned their citizens to arms in a similar fashion, and in November 1662 the consuls of Auch did so for a second time: the object in each case was to drive off passing soldiery. In 1639 a more protracted disturbance took place in Le Dorat. Pierre Robert, the *lieutenant-général*, had brought a lawsuit that summer against the community, with a view to getting himself exempted from the charges he had incurred by billeting troops in the town. He appealed to the Council, and his appeal was upheld. On 8 September he went back to Le Dorat. The following day the citizens called a meeting in the garden of a nearby monastery, and throughout the evening armed bands marched and countermarched beneath the windows of Robert's house discharging menacing volleys of musket-fire. Next morning Robert retreated to his country house. On 14 September, however, he was obliged to return once more to perform his official function of presiding over the military roll-call. That night drums beat in the streets. The citizens armed themselves, and gathered at the town hall, where they divided into two companies of a hundred strong. One company stationed itself in front of the *lieutenant-général's* lodgings, and the other waited in ambush behind the house, among the walnut trees which lined the paths running through the Hosanne cemetery. Drums sounded the charge, and the mob proceeded to shatter the *lieutenant-général's* windows with a hail of stones and bullets, shouting as they did so, 'Blood-sucker, come out and let us finish you off!' The siege went on until one o'clock in the morning. At daybreak Robert evacuated the town for a second time, and for more than a month the citizens refused to let him back. Each time he tried to enter, the great bell of Saint-Louis sounded the tocsin, and companies of burgesses formed up in the squares.

Rioters made good use of the symbolic emblems of the commune. They rang the bells and the tocsin in the belfry, beat the drum and the tabor to rally support to their cause. To sound the alarm with bells or beat drums were 'political acts' which normally required the authorization of the local judges or the city magistrates. Recruiting sergeants, for instance, or circus managers usually had to solicit permission at the town hall to sound the tabor through the streets. When an enemy approached a town, the tocsin sounded, and the whole town re-echoed with its insistent, sinister peals. The guards rushed to close the gates, and the citizens ran to the town hall where the consuls distributed arms to them from the civic arsenal. In time of crisis the consuls made a point of locking the bell-towers, removing the ladders inside them and hanging the bell-ropes high and out of reach. The drum was not merely a soldier's device for ordering the daily routine in camp, or signalling a roll-call. Consuls also used drums to draw attention to the ordinances they wished to impose. In garrison towns drums were beaten through the streets with their pattern of beats inverted to sound the alarm. It was the army's version of the tocsin, a signal designed to warn of a sudden attack, or an outbreak of mutiny or fire. In wartime drums were carried into action alongside every attacking column. The drum was associated with qualities of freedom and fearlessness, and as if to underline this connection the drummers who marched at the head of the processions organized in the towns by guilds and corporations and the riotous demonstrations of rebels were usually boys. When the people of Villefranche-de-Rouergue rose up against the excisemen on 13 August 1627 their drummer was a craftsman's wife. Wandering tumblers enlisted the services of children who marched at the head of their troupe with drums and flags.

At Montpellier the populace were summoned to insurrection by 'a little boy who went through the town beating a drum and calling out at the top of his voice that he wanted all the wives and serving-women to go to the law courts, where they meant to hang two men without just cause'. Riots were no more than another manifestation of community spirit, and as such they tended, not surprisingly, to develop on much the same lines as the commotions which took place in a town on festival days. Excisemen, for example, were ridiculed in the same way as cuckolded husbands. Rioters were not disposed to break with community customs: on the contrary, they liked to re-enact the fantastic traditional rituals. They loaded themselves up with the props used at festivals, put on masks and staged their protests to the sound of music. One August night, for example, some citizens of Cognac went and made a racket beneath the windows of the agents of the crown estates, yelling abuse and letting off firearms in the tradition of the *charivari*. A larger demonstration which took place at Bourges was led, correspondingly, by a dozen maskers. The demonstration was aimed at some bailiffs from Paris who had come bearing injunctions against the local *élus*, and the object was to drive them from their inn. The maskers were armed with sticks and skewers. They announced themselves light-heartedly by sending two fiddlers through the streets to herald their arrival. Festivals of this kind, however, could end in a killing. At Barbezieux in 1636 the offending excisemen were thrown in the river. At Marennes in 1644 they were torn to pieces by the crowd.

The essentially communal nature of a riot was demonstrated by the spontaneous way in which the rioters took to the streets and by their readiness to snatch at the slightest pretext for doing so. The potential for rioting was always there, long established, tacitly accepted, and liable to manifest itself at any time in the most fantastic guises. Anyone who knew how to speak to the populace and play on their grievances could easily stir up a riot at any time he chose. At Cahors, for instance, a disturbance was provoked by 'a rumour which had spread far and wide among the people that the *cour des aides* had passed a decree authorizing a fraudulent tax assessment. Actually it was the merchants and innkeepers who were defrauding the masses. They went round announcing that the *gabelle* (salt tax) was being levied, and the masses were so stupid as to believe them.' A similar sort of incitement was practised by an agent of the Treasury who had been sent from Paris to bring claims against the chief tax collector of Limoges. The agent had no hesitation in arresting the man in public, in the streets of Orléans, and pointing him out to the crowd. The crowd duly screamed abuse 'at the excisemen and blood-suckers, and said they ought to be killed'. Throngs of this kind knew nothing of the people and facts involved; but they rioted notwithstanding, noisily, blindly and without a moment's thought. 'Late one evening', a chronicle tells us,

some persons of rank from the Haut-Pays above La Réole arrived by boat at Tourne. They had meant to reach Bordeaux, but the tide had come on faster than expected and prevented them from proceeding farther downstream. They sought out an inn there and went to bed. Now the host, who was a wicked and treacherous man, conspired with a number of other citizens of the town – birds of the same feather as himelf – to plunder and despoil those poor travellers who had no other thought than to rest, and took it upon himself to carry out that infamous deed. Since this was a time when the Huguenots were in arms, he spread the word that the travellers were Huguenots and had the tocsin rung. The populace gathered, and the upshot was that the travellers were piteously done to death and thrown into the river ... The criminal trial which followed had a deep and lasting effect on this parish of Tourne, insofar as all or nearly all of the parishioners had the blood of the victims on their hands.

On another occasion bands of citizens in Bordeaux sprang to arms in response to a spurious report that the Protestants of Médoc were attacking their town.

On repairing to Saint-Projet, [the aldermen] found a large number of people standing at their doors with arms in their hands, but could not tell the reason for this demonstration ... [They found likewise] that the butchers had barricaded the street at three different places in the market and underneath the Mû ... [and they found] a large crowd assembled in the Saint-Michel district.

These accounts bring out the full sense of the expression 'popular emotion'. On the one hand they reveal it to be a matter of intense and fleeting responses to some external event – a random manifestation of collective feeling in a form that is usually both violent and banal. At the same time we should note that the actual root of the word 'emotion', the mechanical concept of a moving body, conveys very aptly the group spirit and the communal solidarity from which these outbreaks drew their strength. It is this basic meaning which enables us to appreciate most clearly the quintessential structures of community life.

The community rioted collectively, and was punished collectively. The collective guilt of the commune was assumed at the very outset, in the preventive measures the state took to forestall an anticipated outbreak of sedition. It sometimes happened, for example, that tax agents whom the crown had sent to a community to carry out an unpopular order were threatened and put to flight. They appealed to the Council, and the Council accordingly agreed 'to place them under the safekeeping of the citizen body'. This meant that the blame for any misfortunes which might befall them in the process of executing the decisions of the crown was laid, in advance, at the door of the community as a whole. When rebellion, therefore, broke out in the town, as almost always happened, the community found itself saddled with joint liability in the eyes of the law. The crown resorted to this harsh device with particular frequency to suppress any resistance to the contentious business of raising taxes. In the great tax code promulgated in 1600 the government specified a number of cases in which persons found to be in arrears in a given locality might draw down on their commune the fiscal equivalent of joint liability – collective distraint. Any citizen, for example, who resisted the bailiffs sent to enforce the claims of the tax collectors would invite such retribution almost for sure. These provisions were upheld through a strict adherence to legal precedent throughout the seventeenth century. But the crown was not content to rely on the routine procedure of debt collection as its sole means of punishing unrest. Sometimes it also initiated criminal proceedings against the offending community. Legal theorists cast the blame around the whole community by hypothesizing either that the riots had received official blessing in the form of some kind of publicly adopted resolution, or else that the violence had simply spread round the town like a plague, '*communicato consilio aut tumultu*' ('as intrigue or disorder made their way through the streets'). The government decreed that the ringleaders should be arrested. But the ringleaders had to be identified, and to facilitate this the government also decreed, as a first step, that *all* the residents of the commune should be subpoenaed on an individual basis. For the purposes of the trial the community was represented by a syndic or an official trustee, on the grounds that it was, after all, 'no more than a fictitious and imaginary entity, dragged this way and that by troublemakers without being able to control them and without any notion of where they are leading it. That is why Homer compares a people to the sea. Left to itself it is tranquil, and is never ruffled except when it is whipped up into fury by the winds.'

A community which was sentenced would typically find itself subject to a collective indemnity in the form of a fine. In addition, however, communities might be stripped of their privileges or branded in a number of other conspicuous ways. Towns 'were punished, when they deserved it' by having their walls, fortifications and public buildings pulled down, and through the crown 'changing their administration and depriving them of their prerogatives, privileges and superior rights, treating them in the same way that the Romans treated the Campanians, and Septimius Severus treated the citizens of Byzantium and Laodicea'. Article XXI of the criminal code of 1671 ordained that rebel towns should be punished collectively by sentencing their magistrates and tearing down their public statues. This law was no innovation: it merely enshrined in the statute books a form of brutality which had been practised routinely for many years. Some of the more striking examples of this brutality may be found in the measures taken by the crown to chastise the Huguenot cities. But the legal records refer also to other acts of vengeance which the authorities perpetrated as a means of punishing disaffection among the administrative or commercial leadership of other French towns. One example was Limoges. From 17 July to 4 August 1642 the city seethed with rumours and seditious demonstrations directed against the collectors of a government levy who were forced to take to their heels. Frémin, the provincial intendant, sent a report to the Council in Paris, and the Council accordingly issued a decree directing that troops should be sent to the region and granting the tax-farmers in charge of raising the levy the right to subject the citizens to collective distraint. During the following weeks the agents of the tax farmer got to work in the neighbourhood of Limoges. They confiscated the goods of any citizens who came their way, from their livestock to their crops and laden mule trains. And in December the king sent a letter suspending the consular elections in the city. The intendant was told to appoint three consuls to take the place of the six who were usually elected each year, 'notwithstanding the traditional privileges and customs of the town, which His Majesty does not propose to take into account on this occasion'.

Bordeaux suffered a similar fate at the hands of Marshal d'Albret, who became master of the city after the troubles of 1675. D'Albret aimed to subject the city to an even harsher punishment than the Constable of Montmorency had visited on it when it rebelled against the salt tax in 1548. In an edict issued on 17 January 1676 the marshal insisted that the citizens should pull down the Saint-Michel bell-tower which soared over a hundred metres above the Port de la Lune 'because Bordeaux should not be slow to comply with the king's laws, and because the dismantling of every bell in its steeples would not suffice to atone for all its crimes'.

Details of yet another case of government retribution are preserved in the account of the legal proceedings which were initiated as the result of the rebellion of the village of Abjat in Périgord. A subpoena was served individually on each of the inhabitants of the village and the surrounding parish. Foullé, the provincial intendant, imposed a stringent sentence without right of appeal.

The officials and part of the resident population were to be condemned to death on the wheel and the gallows, and all the population were to be subject to a collective payment of fines, costs, indemnities and interest on their arrears. The bells of Abjat were to be dismantled, and to stamp their rebellion even more indelibly upon the minds of posterity, the market of Abjat was to be demolished and a pyramid raised in its place.

Such methods were copied from the wars of antiquity, and the Council's representatives warmly commended them. But they smacked none the less of a kind of judicial fanaticism, and magistrates in the appeal courts recoiled with sheer horror from endorsing their use. In any event, group violence was not always the result of communal solidarity. Some cities were torn apart by internal struggles between contending factions or social classes. A riot, as we have seen, could reflect a local consensus; but the citizenry tended to split into two unequal segments when the government stepped in to quell the unrest. On the one side were the dignitaries, officials and leading burgesses. They are referred to in the chronicles as 'the decent citizens' or 'better class of residents', 'men of property' who 'had something to lose'. Relatively few in number, they were effective and well armed. Opposed to them were the irresponsible masses. The chronicles call them 'the rabble', 'the dregs of the people', 'men of little substance or none at all'. Several disturbances ended in a social confrontation of this kind. At Villefranche-de-Rouergue, for instance, a 'multitude of lowly people' who had risen against the excisemen tried to shut the local magistrates up in the church during mass 'to strengthen their grip on the town'. The rebels were 'all from the dregs of the people', and their cry was 'Kill, kill, plunder!' Even though their number rose to a strength of 2,000, 'some fifty decent citizens' were enough to scatter them. Each night the following month, to prevent any further disorders, the consuls mounted 'a guard of burgesses' on the gate-towers and in the main square. The series of major disturbances which flared up in the towns of Guyenne in the summer of 1635 revealed internal fissures of much the same sort. People in every community took part in these outbreaks, but their involvement varied in form, degree and timing according to their social class. The 'decent citizens' only took part in the initial bout of protest against excessive taxation with which the troubles began. The craftsmen were responsible for the first violent incidents. The last group to make their appearance were the people of the suburbs and the outlying villages, who flocked to take part in the looting which ensued on the following days. In Bordeaux, the crowded and turbulent capital of the province, social groups were virtually segregated according to district, and the accounts of the riots which took place there indicate just how deep the flaws in the community ran. The turmoil centred on the parishes of Saint-Michel and Sainte-Croix. When night fell the rebels encamped in the two parish cemeteries, and it was there, the following morning, that Marshal d'Albret was obliged to appear in person to take delivery of their subversive manifestos. The authorities in the larger towns prescribed a range of precautionary measures to be adopted in case of riot. A study of the consular records shows that such measures varied little from one town to another. A small force of burgesses – the numbers would total no more than a few dozen, or a few hundred – were called upon to bear arms and oversee the maintenance of order in the town. They were expected to form guards regiments and carry out patrols. At the first sign of trouble they were to occupy a number of strategic positions, namely the approaches to the town, its gates, bridges and main streets. In addition the consuls were to make a daily tour of the markets, taverns and butchers' shops 'in order to speak to the people and recall them to their duty'. Every step taken, in other words, reflected the prejudice which the magistrates entertained towards the majority of their fellow-citizens, and the gulf of mistrust which isolated this small group of worthies the chronicles labelled 'men of property, well affected and devoted to the service of the King and the interests of public order' from the greater part of the people in their town.

This gulf between the men of property and the mass of the population was a feature of every urban community. The gulf was not merely a social but also a cultural one. All the activities we have looked at – the ceremonies of the craft guilds, the jollifications of the young, the frequenting of taverns and the rites with which rioters dignified their marauding – were different parts of what was, in effect, a popular culture. This culture was the sum of an assortment of perceptions, traditions and ways of life. It did not always conform to the standards set by society as a whole, but it exerted its own authority. It laid down its own norms of behaviour, and enforced them by means of a body of sanctions which amounted to nothing less than a popular or traditional code of law.

This was not a unique phenomenon. All societies, in all ages, are known to have been governed informally by at least one body of traditional, customary and oral law. This law survived on the fringes of the written and prescriptive legislation drawn up by the state, and was recognized, or at least tolerated, by the state authorities.[7] It was particularly favoured by the spirit of an age like

---

7 See René Maunier, *Introduction au folklore juridique*, Publications du département et du Musée national des arts et traditions populaires, Paris, 1938, 38 pp. Maunier stated that he was preparing a substantial volume on popular justice or the punitive aspects of traditional law. This book however was never published, and Maunier's work seems nowadays to suffer from a neglect it does not entirely deserve.

the seventeenth century, when people looked back nostalgically to an idealized past, and ancient customs still carried decisive weight the greater part of the time. Under these circumstances traditional law continued to regulate significant areas of social life which had not yet been annexed by the official legal system. Aldermen, consuls, judges and the other community magistrates were close to the ordinary people, shared in their culture and consequently tended to turn a blind eye when they chose to settle their affairs by popular law. It was even possible to cite popular customs, the need to maintain them and respect their air of legality, as a line of defence in court. We saw earlier how the defendants at the magistrate's court in Lectoure justified their involvement in a charivari as the observance of a 'fine and praiseworthy custom'. A lawyer in Bordeaux made a similar plea on behalf of a group of peasants who had been summoned before the parlement for staging a donkey tour to make fun of a henpecked husband. The laywer declared that the donkey tour

seems a frivolous idea, but the ceremony actually serves a serious and useful purpose ... This ceremony is nowhere explicitly forbidden by any law or ordinance; and where there is no civil law there can be no civil penalty. Even today people still get invited, as a matter of custom, to take part in forbidden gambling games and to join in the practical jokes and horseplay of the household lackeys. We tolerate such customs as the bullfight at Bazas and a thousand other activities little deserving of praise.[8]

The story of the Croquant revolts will give a further indication of the strength of this unobtrusive but tenacious popular law.

Urban ecology

By studying the customs of a community we can detect in a number of ways how the social and institutional structure of the community was built into the townscape. We shall examine here how the changes which took place in the townscape over time affected the collective outlook and the community life of the townsfolk. By so doing we can catch a glimpse of the ecology, as it were, which prevailed in the towns of south-west France in the period of Croquant revolts.

Up till the end of the seventeenth century the girdles of ramparts which hemmed in every town were preserved as a matter of military necessity. The result was that the medieval habitat of a town survived unaltered within its defensive outer shell. Pictures painted of towns in the seventeenth century do not differ greatly from the town scenes which the medieval illuminators emblazoned on their manuscripts two hundred years before. Old towns like this consisted of narrow, often winding streets in which the jutting roofs of the overhanging houses blocked out all view of the sky. Even the church was

---

8 Plea made by the lawyer Matisson in 1610 on behalf of some peasants from the Aiguillon region. See *Revue de l'Agenais*, 1880, p. 171.

embedded in the mass of the houses, and there was barely room for a small parvis in front of the porch. The maze of streets was broken up by a handful of public squares which were walled in on every side and could be reached only by the alleys, also walled, which ran into them at each of their four corners. It was in those squares that the populace assembled to take part in the major social activities of the town, in its festivals, processions, markets and executions. Here and there a road was widened to make room for a well or fountain, or a cross was raised at a crossroads, and landmarks like these sometimes served as alternative meeting-places. At the approach to bridges, and before the town gates, the houses stood back creating small areas of cobbled space. People crossed these areas constantly, and they were also used for trade. Sometimes the townsfolk arranged to meet in the pathways of a cemetery, or gathered in a square in the shade of a tall and solitary tree. In Bordeaux, for example, a gathering took place in 1635 in the cemetery of the parish of Sainte-Eulalie, and in 1675 in the cemetery of the parish of Saint-Michel. In Le Dorat, as we saw earlier, in 1639, the citizens assembled in a monastery garden. Such meetings were sometimes official, called by heralds at the sound of the trumpet; but sometimes the populace gathered with seditious ends in mind.

The heart of the town consisted of a 'golden mile', an area within whose confines all the local institutions were concentrated together. The town hall had pride of place. A clock, a bell and sometimes a belfry were erected on top of the mansion in which it was housed. The adjoining streets were occupied by the church and the ecclesiastical buildings – the bishop's palace together with his chancellery, tribunal and prison, a chapter house and its cloister, a deanery and a presbytery, in other words the bishop's and canons' establishments and the houses surrounding them. This compound constituted a legally privileged enclave within the town. It was a *sauveté*, a self-contained township exempt from the authority of the local magistrates. Typical *sauvetés* were those of Saint-André and Saint-Seurin in Bordeaux: others were established in the towns of Limoges, Aurillac and Tulle, each of them the seat of a bishop. This same central district also contained the headquarters of the secular tribunals along with the office of the clerks of the court and the town gaol. Often there was just one courtroom, where a number of different tribunals took turns to preside. All the chief magistrates lived within easy reach of this main judicial building. In each town this central preserve of the leading citizens occupied a clearly demarcated area. In Niort it was the rue du Pont; in Angoulême the two tiny districts at the foot of the cathedral, the quartier de la Pain and the quartier du Petit-Saint-Cybard; in Bordeaux, the large parish of Saint-Pierre; in Tulle, the walled core of the city and the adjoining suburb of Le Trech; at Cahors, the Pont-Neuf district; at Villeneuve-sur-Lot, the area surrounding the rue de Montflanquin; and at Moissac, the rue de la Place and the grand-rue Malaveille. These central areas were easily recognizable on any town plan as a result of the sheer numbers of mansions and public monuments which the citizens built in them. They were also the areas which got assessed at the highest rates when the tax rolls were drawn up.

Medieval towns contained a number of other special quarters which came into being to serve a professional need. There were quarters for merchants and craftsmen. Butchers, goldsmiths or blacksmiths, for instance, often plied their trade in streets reserved exclusively for their calling, where their shops stood side by side. Sometimes the shopkeepers congregated for reasons of simple convenience. They could get their raw materials from a common source of supply, could draw on each other's complementary skills and call on each other's assistance in case of need. At other times the instinct to congregate was reinforced by the pressure of the municipal regulations. The authorities were anxious to monitor trades they regarded as essential and equally trades they considered unhygienic and dangerous. They wished to keep the tradesmen in one place, and under their control. Each of the various markets, the *halles* or *cohues* which served as exchanges for herbs and livestock, the *minage*, or corn market and the butchers' and fishmongers' stalls, was, correspondingly, sited in a single specific place. A market was often covered with a wooden shelter and fenced off with a ring of posts. These posts were used as notice-boards. They carried edicts and ordinances issued by the town authorities, writs made out by the bailiffs and pamphlets circulated by seditious malcontents. Citizens looked to them for the latest official announcements, for news that the tax collectors had come to town or a new toll was being raised; and they looked to them also for warning that a riot had broken out. These bustling markets were more than simply places to buy and sell. They served as arenas for every kind of wordly activity, and as early news agencies. And they were, not surprisingly, hotbeds and seedbeds of public unrest. Countless disturbances began in the market-place. Rioters sallied forth from the markets to protest about the dearness or scarcity of corn, or to voice their anger at the latest dues which the city governments had slapped on to foodstuffs imported from the surrounding countryside. Often they made for the homes of prosperous local merchants who had hoarded a scarce commodity, or set out in search of some excisemen or moneylenders' agents who had come to town and taken lodgings in a neighbouring inn. Rich merchants' houses were a particularly obvious target. Rows of them lined the busy central streets of every town. The Place Royale at Montauban, with its fine colonnaded mansions, is a typical example. This square was assailed by arsonists on two occasions, on 12 November 1614 and 15 June 1649. The flames were fed by the goods of the local silk merchants' and apothecaries' stores which had also been set ablaze. The damage to the square was so serious that the Council in Paris on both occasions granted the town authorities permission to raise a surtax to pay for the repairs. The money was to be levied over and above the regular *tailles* of the jurisdiction. The catalogue of victims is revealing. Twenty of the twenty-six people rescued in 1614, and twelve out of eighteen rescued in 1649, were shopkeepers or wholesale merchants. The onslaught had been directed at a specific social group. This in turn had political consequences, since it enabled the Council in Paris to maintain in the decree it issued on 30 July 1649 that the thirty-odd families which had suffered in the catastrophe had all been 'among the families which had shown themselves most zealous and most devoted to the service of the king in the recent civil disorders'. Inns were an equally tempting destination for rioters. Among the large buildings at the heart of a town were a number of handsome hostelries, renowned throughout the provinces, which provided accommodation for distinguished strangers and wealthy travellers. One typical concentration could be found in the south-west corner of the old walled part of Limoges, at the junction of the roads from Angoumois and Périgord. The most famous inn in Limoges was the Cheval Blanc. It was used as a headquarters by the Catholic League during the Wars of Religion, and its landlord died on the scaffold in 1589. In 1602 a government agent sent to set the rate for a local tax took lodgings in the Cheval Blanc – only to be evicted by a crowd of angry women from the market of Saint-Pierre. At Niort the top hotel was (from 1616 onwards) the Salle Dorée in the Place de la Halle; at Angoulême it was the Grand Cerf near the Palet and Beaulieu markets. In Tulle the outsanding inn was the Lion d'Or. It gave its name to an entire district of the city – the area which fronted the left bank of the Corrèze at the point where the Pont de la Cité met the road to the south of France. One last example of a celebrated hostelry is the Chapeau Rouge, most famous of all the inns of Bordeaux. It stood not far from the wharf named after it, where travellers from Blaye and the north disembarked from their barges. Royal commissioners, moneylenders and speculators from Paris, dignitaries like Montauron, the chief collector of taxes, stayed there as a matter of course.

Beyond the bustling central streets where the leading citizens lived were a number of districts inhabited mainly by craftsmen. They were squalid and densely populated. Accommodation consisted of either overcrowded tenements or shacks thrown together haphazardly with wood and daub. Land registers indicate that such buildings occupied only a limited stretch of ground, and their rateable value was low. Streets in these districts were named after the trades of the various workmen who had lived there already for many generations. Such clusters of streets grew up typically on the edge of the old medieval towns, on patches of land which had been left undeveloped when the enclosing walls were built. In fortified towns and other towns built on the newer grid system, working people lived in the side streets beyond the axes formed by the central thoroughfares which ran across the settlements from gate to gate. These humble districts were the centre of much of the communal activity we examined earlier. It was their parish churches the craft guilds used to stage their annual ceremonies, and it was their streets which served as the breeding-ground for rioters in times of civil unrest. In Poitiers, for example, a riot was confined, from start to finish, to two craftsmen's districts – the districts of La Chaussée and Saint-Sulpicien. In La Rochelle, similarly, the hard core of Protestant resistance drew its support from the people who lived in the districts of Le Perrot and Saint-Nicolas. 'Almost all craftsmen', the chronicle calls them, 'men of no substance, all of them well armed'. Sometimes the craftsmen's part of a town can be guessed from obvious clues. The most crowded district of Niort was situated, suggestively, at the northern end of the town, where the streets ran up against the ramparts in the area surrounding the Place du Vieux-Marché. In Angoulême, a community divided into eight parishes, the two with the lowest rateable values were Beaulieu and Saint-Jean. They were located at the western end of the old walled town. The social topography of Cahors may be deduced from the land register of 1650, which rated the houses one to nine in descending order of value. The further the houses lay from the cathedral and city centre, the lower the ratings were. Most of the houses in the Pont-Vieux district at the eastern end of town got, at best, a grade-seven rating, and the district was notable for its lack of any official buildings. It was a craftsmen's quarter. Four prominent guilds, the vine growers, cobblers, joiners and innkeepers, worshipped there in the churches of Saint-Urcisse and Saint-Laurent. Some of the city's craftsmen owned real estate in one or other of the districts and were consequently listed in the register, and a high proportion of these lived in Pont-Vieux: eight of the nineteen weavers, nine of the twenty-five masons, fifteen of the fifty-three tailors and sixty-two of the 186 vine growers. In Villeneuve-sur-Lot, which was built on a grid, the craftsmen lived in the side streets. You reached them by following the line of the ramparts, then turning into the city at an angle of ninety degrees. Contrasts in social standing among the townsfolk were reflected in the size of their properties. Villeneuve-sur-Lot contained about ten noble families scattered throughout the town. Their houses covered an area of anything up to 200 to 300 square metres, not counting the gardens and outbuildings. The houses of the burgesses in the rue de Montflanquin covered 50 to 100 square metres. The homes of the craftsmen, however – typical examples were the houses in the rue du Puits-Couleau – had a surface area of 15 to 40 square metres at most. The town was also divided socially into two very different sections by the river which flowed through it. The left bank of the Lot was inhabited only by craftsmen, brewers and vine growers. They had the right to elect no more than one of the town's four consuls. Their local brotherhood of penitents, the Whites of the church of Saint-Étienne, deferred socially to the Blues of the parish of Sainte-Catherine on the right bank, in recognition of the fact that the Blues were an older and wealthier order which attracted members of the town's most eminent families. Moissac, also a grid town, was equally revealing from a social point of view. The most expensive houses were the ones that lined the principal thoroughfares. The nearer you got to the central square, the more of them you found. Conversely, the further you followed a main street towards the edge of the town, the lower the rateable value of the houses sank. The rates varied from 120 *livres* on the grand-rue Malaveille to 10 to 15 *livres* in the side streets and the districts which adjoined the walls or the river, and as little as 2 *livres*, 10 *sous* if you happened to live in one of the suburbs or on one of the filled-in moats which had once encircled the walls. Everywhere tradespeople were consigned to claustrophobic districts in the outlying parts of a town. Such districts, however, could easily turn into hotbeds of rebellion. Rioters could very quickly block the alleys with chains and barricades, creating a fortified stronghold which any force of dragoons dispatched to quell the insurrection could venture into only at the utmost peril to themselves. In June 1635, for example, when riots broke out in Bordeaux, it was only after repeated charges that the mounted carabineers of the Duke of Épernon broke their way through the bulwarks the rebels had thrown up in the streets. Similar difficulties confronted the guards whom the Marshal de Schomberg sent into action in Montpellier in July 1645. The guards found themselves advancing at full gallop upon rebels 'entrenched in streets so narrow that two men on horseback could barely ride there abreast and they could only force an entry with much bloodshed'. Each of the craftsmen's districts was a pocket of seething humanity: each could be made, within minutes, an impregnable redoubt.

In most towns, however, it seems to have been unusual for a district to be occupied exclusively by a particular social group. Certain classes did predominant in certain areas; but there was seldom a stark contrast between one district and another. Bordeaux was the spectacular exception which proved the rule. This city was fragmented, throughout its history, into sharply defined social enclaves – one town for the nobles and dignitaries and another town for the artisans. The nobles and dignitaries made their homes for century after century within the confines of the old city wall of 1227. The craftsmen's town grew up to the south of the old nucleus, in the new districts which had been settled farther up the Garonne in the course of the thirteenth century and brought within the bounds of the city by the second wall of 1302. The moat which surrounded the first wall was filled in, but no attempt was made to build on the new land so created. It was an expanse left open to the public for walking, games and fairs, a great esplanade which ran almost all the way from the château of Le Hâ at the eastern end of the city to the Porte des Salinières (the Salters' Gate) on the banks of the Garonne. It was also a visible border. To the south of it lay a huge area inhabited almost entirely by craftsmen: the parish of Saint-Michel, which was wholly enclosed by the new wall, and the parishes of Sainte-Croix and Sainte-Eulalie, which stretched out beyond the wall and into the open fields. It is true there were plenty of craftsmen in other parts of the city. Many, for instance, lived in the *sauveté* of the cathedral or the parishes of Saint-Christoly and Saint-Rémi. But because this southern belt was settled so uniformly by craftsmen, it developed a strong local character. Its inhabitants were known for their independence, not to say aggressiveness. Detailed records survive of the pious observances of the craft guilds, and some of these also testify, in passing, to the concentration of craftsmen in the southern part of the town. One chronicle, for example, lists a total of twenty-eight craft guilds which assembled in the cathedral for the Whit Sunday service of 1676. The record indicates that about a quarter of these guilds worshipped on ordinary days at a church in one or another of the southern parishes. The chronicler actually specifies the church in twenty-three cases; and in sixteen of these cases the church turns out to lie in the southern zone. Nine guilds, for instance, attended the parish church of Saint-Michel: the sailors, the packers who unloaded the crates of salted fish, the cask-makers and the timber-workers, the cabinet-makers, the thatchers, the wool carders, the journeymen tailors and the pedlars. The journeymen bakers, corn-sifters and nailsmiths worshipped at the church of the Augustinians, and the joiners, pastrycooks and vinegar-makers at the church of the Carmelites. The sixteenth and last guild, the glovers, made their devotions at the parish church of Sainte-Eulalie. These lists of guilds, incidentally, reveal the importance of the local wood-working trades. Carpenters of various kinds exploited the stocks of timber that were floated down to Bordeaux on the river and assembled the vessels that were used to sail on it. The town boatyards were also located in the southern parishes, on the stretch of the Garonne which flowed from the Porte de Grave to the Porte de Sainte-Croix; and the nearby streets were appropriately called Carpenteyre and Fusterie (Carpenters' Lane and Timberyard). The whole southern district was grossly overcrowded. A census conducted in 1631 testifies amply to the congestion. The census was held in each of the town's twelve parishes, and came up with a total of 25,400 registered communicants. Almost half of that total, 11,000 people, lived in the southern parishes: 1,000 in Sainte-Croix, 2,000 in Sainte-Eulalie and 8,000 in Saint-Michel. The parish priest of Saint-Michel was obliged to rely on the assistance of twenty-two curates. Gaufreteau noted that 'there are so many people in these parishes that it is almost impossible for the priest to know them all'. He added that 'Sainte-Eulalie and Saint-Michel are the parishes which breed the city's bravest and hardiest soldiers. As the local saying has it 'Saint-Eulalie and Saint-Micheau / Make up one half of all Bordeaux.' The social chasm which ran through Bordeaux is illustrated, finally, by the history of the riots which took place there. The craftsmen's districts were in a state of constant revolt. The residents resorted to violence with a singular unanimity which distinguished them sharply from their cautious fellow-citizens. In the troubles of 1635, for instance, the heart of the disorder was the parish of Saint-Michel. It was there that the barricades went up, in the rue des Faures and the rue de la Grave which led to the parish church. The craftsmen of the southern parishes showed a similar pugnacity in 1652, during the second phase of the Fronde. The Fronde held Bordeaux, but its leaders were divided in the face of the besieging royalist troops. The parishioners of Saint-Rémi wished to negotiate with the enemy, but the craftsmen of Saint–Michel were all partisans of the Ormée ('Elm') movement which had embraced the cause of the Fronde. On 26 June they clashed with the Saint-Rémi faction in a bloody skirmish on the rue du Pas-Saint-Georges. The sequel to this conflict took place in July the following year. Opinion by then had clearly swung in favour of the crown, and the people in the northern parishes were determined to surrender. They set guards on the rue Neuve and the rue de la Rousselle to prevent any possible attempt by the craftsmen of Saint-Michel to break out and carry on the fighting. In 1675 the pattern repeated itself. The riots were once again confined to the south of the old city moat. The rebels held the southern districts, and the *parlement* and the *jurats* kept order everywhere else. When the government troops arrived to put down the disturbances in the city, it was the southern zone they penalized. Their commanders talked of stationing a garrison in the bell-tower of the church of Saint-Michel, and even of tearing down the steeple. In the end, however, they contented themselves with building the Fort Saint-Louis alongside the city wall, and training its guns on the crowded streets of the most unruly parishes, Sainte-Croix and Saint-Michel.

Each city had several districts serving an economic function. The most easily recognizable was the port district. Rivers played a vital role in transporting foodstuffs or travellers, and the wharves were consequently among the liveliest parts of a town. The rateable value of the houses there was generally low, since the air was made foul by the smell from the water-mills, laundries and tanneries which were set up on the river-banks to exploit the flow of the stream. In addition the wharves were inhabited by an assortment of cohesive and turbulent social groups, fishermen and carpenters, laundresses, boatmen and bargees. Large numbers of journeymen, stevedores and general labourers were attracted to the docks, where they found work unloading vessels and dismantling timber rafts. Most of them, as we have seen, lived from hand to mouth and were easily stirred to riot. But the wharves were not wholly given over to the homes of such people. The rivers were also lined by a number of other buildings of a more distinguished character: merchants' houses, for instance, and the taverns or inns which sprang up wherever a bridge or ferry attracted travellers wishing to cross to the other bank. Limoges, on the Vienne, had a good example of a strategically situated river-port. The port was located at the south-east end of the town in a place known as Le Naveix. Le Naveix was the place where the timber rafts stopped when they came down the river from Eymoutiers; and it was, at the same time, the point where the bustling streets of the Basse-Cité came out on the waterfront near the bridge of Saint-Étienne. Niort had a port which extended, from the fourteenth century onwards, all the way down the Sèvre from the islands to the suburb of Bessac on the right bank. L'Houmeau, in Angoulême, was a typical case of a flourishing port district. Richest and most vigorous of all the town's five suburbs, it prospered by serving the busy traffic which plied on the River Charente. Districts in several other cities thrived on the river trade. In Tulle, for example, the boats were served by the suburb of La Barussie; in Périgueux, by the suburb of Taillefer; and in Cahors, by the low-lying district around the Pont-Neuf. Bordeaux illustrates the violent nature of life on the wharves. The carpenters who worked in the boatyards were the most unruly grouping in the whole unruly parish of Saint-Michel. Yet there too, as in the other towns, the port generated prosperity. Right down along the Garonne as far as the marshes beyond Les Chartrons, stalls jostled each other at the foot of the city ramparts and taverns, wine shops and warehouses did a steady trade.

Often the ramparts which ringed the town were reinforced by a castle. Gloomy and vast, it reared up in the background of the townscape, battlements bristling with artillery calculated as much to menace the citizens as to protect them from outside foes. The castle stood well back from the nearest streets, secluded by its moat and by an esplanade which ran in front of the drawbridge. In times of civil unrest the crown officials and tax collectors scurried behind the shelter of its portcullis.

Typical castles were the donjon which overlooked Niort; the château of Le Hâ and the château Trompette, twin fortresses of Bordeaux; and the citadels which dominated the towns of Blaye and Dax. Each of these buildings occupied something like a quarter of the entire walled area of the town concerned.

If you strolled at the foot of the ramparts your eye would fall, to begin with, on orchards and convent gardens. Beyond that lay stretches of waste ground which had a bad reputation after dark. Sometimes there were also alleys which climbed up the outside of the town wall and screened the wall from view. Outlying alleys of this kind were a favourite haunt of prostitutes. At Niort, for instance, they plied their trade in a cul-de-sac to the west of the Vieux-Marché. At Agen they frequented the approaches to the ramparts, and the tower which overlooked that part of the town perimeter was consequently known as the Tour du Bordel (Brothel Tower). In Bordeaux they usually liked to lurk in the ruelle de Londres, a lane which ran between the town wall and the garden of the Augustinian house. The outer edge of a town was also vile with accumulated refuse. Citizens insisted on throwing their rubbish over the ramparts, and no amount of ordinances could deter them from doing so. Great piles of filth filled the moats and overtopped the walls. Sometimes they even cluttered up the gates and the avenues. The Dijeau gate at Bordeaux was especially noted for its squalor.

The Fronde was the last time the old town walls were used for defensive purposes. In the decades which folowed the Fronde wars the threat of armed conflict receded everywhere except in the frontier provinces. The stones in the walls caved in, and the gaps grew ever wider, and the town councils, deeply in debt, no longer had the resources to carry out repairs. Towns began to expand beyond their old defensive limits. Teams armed with pickaxes set about demolishing the old and useless postern gates. The old outer moats were replaced by tree-lined avenues, and the line of the moat which had once marked the boundary of the commune was no more now than a barrier where the *octroi* duty was levied on foodstuffs coming in.

There was a shift of population. The *nouveaux riches* of the period, burgesses who had made their pile and crowned their careers by buying prestigious posts in the civil administration, were abandoning the gloomy streets of the old medieval cities and moving out to the new suburbs beyond the city walls. These suburbs were being laid out by a new breed of town planners. The objective now was to build on as vast a scale as possible, with plenty of room for gardens and open space. It was one more way of enhancing the state's prestige. By installing themselves in fine mansions, provincial intendants and magistrates appointed by the government could awe the mass of the townsfolk with the splendour of their office. This was the reason why the intendants of Haute-Guyenne, for example, built lavishly on the outskirts of Montauban. And wealthy local citizens followed suit. The shipowners of Bordeaux began building homes for themselves in Les Chartrons, a low-lying district to the north of the old walled city, where the banks of the Garonne were already lined with the houses of English and Flemish merchants. Traders who had made their fortune in Cahors or Tulle were on the move already by the end of the sixteenth century, leaving the warren of streets in the medieval city centre and putting up mansions and outbuildings in the new suburban districts. In Cahors the favoured district was the suburb of La Barre, in Tulle the suburb of Le Trech. One result of this flight to the suburbs was the growth of the magnificent residential areas in which towns of the eighteenth century took such pride. But the new town planning also entailed a rigid social segregation. It marked the end of the old neighbourliness, the cluttered intimacy in which people of the medieval towns had lived from day to day. In the past the community had been thrown together by the need to defend the same small settlement. A few thousand people had been packed, over many centuries, into the same few acres of streets and houses – and within that cramped environment the social distinctions between them had tended to grow blurred. There were, certainly, rich districts and poor ones; but the distances between them were very small. You could get from district to district by walking a few steps, or at most by turning a corner. Some idea of this medieval intimacy may be gathered by considering the dimensions of Bordeaux, the capital of south-western France. Bordeaux was a city of barely 30,000 souls. It contained, according to the census of 1631, 4,700 houses, 6,000 men of arms-bearing age and 25,400 communicants. The population lived within a walled area whose circumference measured just over 5,500 metres. At Limoges and Niort the circumference of the walled town was less than 2,500 metres; at Périgueux it was only 1,500. This meant, in practice, that everyone knew everyone. No matter how short a time a person had lived in a town or taken part in its social life, he could still recognize every citizen who passed him in the street, and could without trouble recall that citizen's name, his family, his trade and the house where he lived. Each evening after the church bells had sounded the angelus, the town gates were barred and the residents shut up for the night in their little walled enclosure. Citizens rubbed shoulders daily. If war came, they bore its hardships side by side. Communal solidarity was rooted in tradition, inevitable and essential: there was no way any of them could avoid being bound by its ties. The character of the commune was built into the townscape. When the towns began to expand beyond their medieval walls, the change that took place was not merely a demographic shift but the death of a social order.

The jurisdiction of the magistrates sometimes extended for several leagues outside the town walls. The ultimate frontiers of the town were marked by a ring of boundary stones which the town officials inspected at regular intervals. These stones represented the limits of the urban seigniory, or in other words, of the suburbs and the whole belt of territory which enjoyed the freedom granted to the town by the terms of its charter and in which, consequently, the writ of the town hall ran. As the towns grew beyond their walls their expansion naturally followed the line of the main roads. The various suburbs which grew up outside the city gates offered services to travellers. People could get their horses shod in the roadside smithies, or take refreshment in the local taverns and inns. These cheap suburban hostelries were patronized exclusively by lowly strangers making their way to town, journeymen, pedlars, drovers, peasants and so forth. They were, consequently, channels for plague. The epidemic which ravaged Bordeaux in 1603 was introduced by a student who arrived in the city infected, and stopped for a drink in a tavern in the suburb of Saint-Seurin. Similarly, the pestilence which spread through Limoges at the end of September 1630 was brought to the town by a traveller who had taken lodgings at the sign of the Three Angels in the suburb of Arènes. Often suburban innkeepers were prepared to take in poor people who had been turned back at the town gates, or had failed to find any shelter inside the walls. In return for a small consideration, the innkeepers let them huddle together in a barn, or under the stairs. Large numbers of taverns in the suburbs of Agen and the Sainte-Croix parish in Bordeaux were known to indulge in this practice, and every so often the watch were obliged to raid offending establishments to drive out the beggars and vagrants who had taken refuge there. In times of dearth the vagrant population of the suburbs increased. Bowmen were posted at the town gates, and patrols of 'hunters' were organised within the walls to roam the streets and 'cull' the unhappy paupers for a premium of two *sous* per vagrant caught. Anyone caught was turned out of town or led to the hospital. The authorities issued constant ordinances directing boatmen and gatekeepers to bar the way to ragamuffins who tried to take shelter in the garden sheds near the ramparts. Innkeepers who put up beggars usually got a few *sous* out of the arrangement, and their servants also profited by buying whatever the beggars had managed to filch. When the bowmen raided the inn the servants blamed them for the pilfering and forced them to let the beggars go, to the mirth of the bystanders.

A large patch of land was left deliberately untended in the suburbs of most towns. It was here that the great fairs were held. The amphitheatre in the north-west of Limoges was also used for public executions.

Lectoure had areas designated for both of these functions. The most important fair of the year, the Martinmas fair, was held on a stretch of waste ground which ran parallel to the ramparts. Executions took place on a hillock which rose up, surmounted by windmills, at the point where the road from Agen met the road from Saint-Clar.

In Angoulême sentences were carried out on a hill that rose alongside the road from Limousin. The great meeting-point at Périgueux was the place known as Les Terrières, a large field on the banks of the river Isle. A chapel stood in the field, and a spring welled up from the depths of the ground. It was there that the communes of the province first assembled when they rose up in rebellion in May 1637. The people of Laplume behaved in a similar fashion when they ran riot against the local excisemen. They sallied forth from their township and gathered together on a patch of ground they judged the appropriate place to adopt their seditious resolutions. Shadier folk in Bordeaux slipped off to the Palais Gallien in the north-west of the city. Some people said the ruins were the site of a witches' coven. Duellists went there from time to time, and prostitutes abounded. To ask the way to the Palais was a standing joke.

The growth of the suburbs which began, in spite of the civil wars, in the course of the sixteenth and seventeenth centuries was evidence not only of the flight from the city centre but also of the power of attraction the towns exerted on the surrounding countryside. The links between the walled town and the lands which lay around it were always close. In the first place the town owned the countryside. Burgesses gazing from the ramparts looked out on their property – fields, barns, smallholdings and country houses, all belonging to them. In addition even the largest towns had a rustic air about them. Poitiers, for example, contained at the end of the seventeenth century 326 gardens and 1,827 houses: almost one property-holder in six had a garden attached to his house. There were also thirty-six barns and twenty-two monastic compounds within the city walls. A number of towns had 'green belts' in the form of districts covered with gardens, orchards and even vines. In

Niort the greenest area was the southern part of the walled town, in Cahors the La Barre district and in Angoulême the district of Beaulieu. Every town contained a host of religious houses, and each of these houses was set in a large and leafy enclosure full of kitchen gardens and tree-lined alleyways. Monasteries and their outbuildings covered, in the seventeenth century, as much as a third of the whole walled area of Angoulême, and a fifth of the walled area of Bordeaux. The links between town and country were reinforced by the presence of labourers who lived in the towns but went out at dawn every morning to work in the fields. Their numbers were often substantial. Of the 400 working people registered, for example, on the citizens' roll in Cahors, 186 were vine growers. Most of them lived in outlying districts close to the city gates. Sixty-two hailed from Pont-Vieux at the eastern end of the town, fifty-three from La Barre right out in the west. *Bourgades* (ordinary townships) were almost entirely countryfied. A visitor would find barns and byres dotted among the houses, and streets full of rotting straw and thatch the townspeople were saving up to use as stable litter.

But if towns were bound to the countryside, so, too, was the countryside dependent on the towns. Villages near the towns were wholly occupied in meeting the citizens' needs. They supplied them both with foodstuffs and a domestic labour force. Market gardeners moved into the outskirts of every town, regardless of how poorly watered or unsuited to cultivation the land might be. No less than two groups of cultivators settled, for example, on the edges of Angoulême. One group chose an area at the foot of the plateau on which the city stood, close by the point where the road from Bordeaux crossed the streams flowing into the Charente. This area became known as the suburb of Saint-Ausone. The other group founded a cluster of villages on the right bank of the river, beyond the Saint-Cybard bridge. Bordeaux had a comparable district in the parish of Saint-Rémi. As early as the fourteenth century this parish had expanded beyond the city wall into the marshes of Les Chartrons. The expansion was caused by an influx of country people, who built cottages in the marshes and made ends meet by going to town each morning to work in the burgesses' houses as gardeners, domestics and day labourers. To the west of the city, on the road from Médoc, another township sprang up in the form of the *sauveté* which surrounded the ancient basilica of Saint-Seurin. This township was gradually merging into the city proper. Tradesmen's stalls and the shacks of labourers, brewers and craftsmen proliferated relentlessly by the side of the road, in spite of the devastation inflicted on the area each time Bordeaux was besieged. Half townspeople, half peasants, these folk of the suburbs looked to the cities for their living. When an enemy drew near they took refuge inside the ramparts, as villagers from the depths of the country had done in earlier times; and they raised contingents of soldiers for the town militia. When they got embroiled in legal disputes or tax battles they went to the city courts. They went into town to hire out their services as labourers, or to sell their crops and livestock in the nearest market-place. In time of dearth they went there to beg their bread.

We may conclude, then, that the girdle of fortifications which ringed a town was a permeable barrier. Townsfolk and villagers were dependent on each other and constantly in touch. When disorders broke out in a town the common people of the suburbs ran riot in sympathy. Often they tried to break through the gates to take part in the disturbances and help themselves to loot if the chance arose. Riots in which they joined took on an extra savagery. When houses were laid waste by arson, murder and looting, as happened in Bordeaux and Agen in 1635, the perpetrators were seldom city craftsmen with homes of their own. Nor, for that matter, were they peasants from distant communities in the heart of the countryside. The trouble came almost always from the same little circle of brewers and market gardeners who hung about in the villages on the outskirts of the town. Craftsmen rose up to achieve a concrete objective – to remedy a specific injustice or abuse. The men of the suburbs, however, were simply thugs, unskilled and unattached to a stable community; and the violence they committed was of a random and primitive kind. People like these were immune from the ties of civic solidarity. They lived outside the basic nucleus of the commune, and were spurned by the citizens as an unwelcome appendage to it, a growth on the skin of society, disturbing and despised.

We have now completed our survey of the relationship between the townscape and the mentality of the people who lived in the town. This survey proves that in the early seventeenth century the age of walled cities was still far from over, and that the institution of the commune, deep-rooted in the soil, still exerted its age-old grip on the whole society.

The people of the high roads

Various other types of people spent their lives outside the matrix of the commune. Some of them did so because their trade was nomadic by tradition; others simply lacked the wherewithal to belong to a settled group. Pedlars and journeymen and seasonal labourers went round from village to village, staying in a barn one night and a country inn the next. Migrant workers set off for Spain in hopes of getting a job there, and with it a few gold coins. The countryside was also roamed by bands of refugee peasants. Vulnerable to calamity, peasants were quickly driven on to the roads, and their numbers swelled particularly in the darkest years of the seventeenth century. Finally there were vagrants of a more pernicious kind, such as beggars, bandits and gipsies. They occupied the lowest rung of the social ladder. We shall look at each group in turn, at its functions in society, and the part it played in outbreaks of collective violence.

We may safely assume that large numbers of people at this period spent their entire lives, so to speak, in the shadow of the local steeple. Certain individuals were, none the less, impelled by sheer Christian faith and hope to go on pilgrimages, journeys they had vowed to perform and proceeded to discharge patiently, no matter how long or short the road might be. Some of them had vowed to visit a shrine in thanks for what they believed to have been a divine intervention – unexpected release from an illness or a birth which had passed off without mishap to mother or child. Others were sorely afflicted by a terminal disease, and hoped that by visiting a shrine they might be healed. The poorest pilgrims asked for alms in the towns they passed through, at the gates of the hospitals or monasteries. The king was also the object of a sort of pilgrimage. Crowds of tuberculosis victims flocked when he passed through a town, in the hope that the royal touch would cure the 'king's evil'. In Bordeaux, for example, a scrofulous crowd of 1,500 people gathered to be touched by Louis XIII on All Saints' Day, 1615. A mob of 2,670 sufferers approached him when he visited Surgères at Whitsun 1628.

Other classes of wanderers made their living by loitering about the roads and haunting the wayside taverns. Chief among these were the pedlars. These itinerant salesmen dealt in a variety of pots and pans, in ribbons and lace and cloth. When they got to a town they spread out their goods on a cloak in a suitable public meeting-place like a market or a churchyard. A relatively prosperous salesman would strut about with a pistol and wear a felt hat. He would have assistants to help him and ponies laden with bundles. A humbler pedlar, on the other hand, would make his tour on foot with his earnings wrapped in a cloth around his waist. His clothes would be so full of vermin that as soon as he reached an inn he would have to remove them and roast them at the oven for a few seconds to kill the vermin off. The taverns were also frequented by numerous journeymen who were known by nicknames reflecting their drinking and fighting abilities – 'Boozer', for instance (*Bois-chopine*), or 'First Strike' (*Frappe-d'abord*). You could hire them for a few *sous* to help a bailiff by acting as his escorts, his witnesses or his heavies.[9]

Neighbouring regions were linked by a flow of regular, seasonal exchanges which enabled one locality to draw on another's skills. The valleys of the Charente and Garonne were filled each year by a long procession of migrant craftsmen and labourers – masons from Limousin, coppersmiths and watch-makers, smelters and knife grinders from the Auvergne, and above all team upon team of harvesters and grape pickers from the moors of Saintonge, the forests of Périgord and the limestone plateau of Quercy. Hired labourers of this kind went home at the end of the summer with a few *sous* and a sack of corn to support their families. They were widely distrusted, on the grounds that they might not fulfil their contract. If dissatisfied with their wages they would leave for home before their work was done. In addition they were held to be brutish, stupid and somewhat ridiculous. Numerous Gascon tales revolved around the obtuseness of the Auvergnats and the idiotic blunders they made.

The people of the high roads were the spreaders of epidemics, and of the choicest pieces of news. They brought word of new taxes and the approach of soldiery. Sometimes they spread a rumour that an uprising had started, to panic the neighbourhood. They were universally suspected, and blindly believed. Peasant society could never have done without them. They were its envoys and its informants, seldom reliable and always listened to.

---

9 All the customs cited here may be found in the record of the investigations conducted by the bailiff's court at Angoulême in 1643. See *Archives Départmentales*, Charente, B 1–975.

Migrants in Spain

Working in Spain was traditional. The route there was long established and the journey had been made for many generations. The people of the Massif Central had trekked to the south of France since the dawn of history, and once there an Auvergnat worker could take an ancient and well-trodden route which led to the south-western frontier and the roads to Spain. As early as the twelfth century the scallop-shell worn by the pilgrims who travelled to the shrine of St James of Compostela was engraved on the seal of the consuls of Aurillac.

The migration from France to Spain reached its peak in the sixteenth century. Evidence for this may be found in the registers which were kept by the hospitals of Catalonia. The registers for this period consistently show that more than a third of the patients were French. Most of the migrants, then as earlier, were Auvergnat craftsmen of various kinds: coppersmiths, tinsmiths, glaziers, sawyers, masons, cobblers and gelders of livestock. But there was also a large new contingent of Pyrenean mountain people. By this date the last waves of settlers had occupied the highest mountain valleys and had brought under cultivation the last patches of fertile ground it was possible to reach. Many of the mountain villages were overpopulated. Grain was scarce, and there was no soil left for the young people to till. They were forced to go south through the passes to Spain and hire themselves out as farm-hands at seed-time and harvest-time. Pyrenean herdsmen roamed through Aragon in the winter in search of pasture land. They came home the following summer with supplies of grain, olive oil and duty-free salt.

The Gascons were the next to head for the frontiers. Peasants driven from their homes by climatic disasters or political vicissitudes were readily attracted by the prospect of earning Spanish wages, which by the sixteenth and seventeenth centuries were worth twice as much as they could hope to earn in Gascony – and were paid in Spanish gold. People from Agen and Quercy, too, struck out on the roads to Spain. We can follow the ebb and flow of this migration and can form an impression of its importance at any given time by looking at some of the surviving documents. In 1613 the hospital of Saint-Louis-des-Français was founded for the benefit of Frenchmen in Madrid. Like the Catalan hospitals this establishment kept a register of admissions,and its register has been subjected, like theirs, to a detailed scrutiny. Between 1617 and 1673, the period covered by the register, 2,647 patients were admitted to Saint-Louis-des-Français. A majority of these – 1,369 or 52 per cent – were Auvergnats. Next after that came the Gascons. There were 388 of them, or 14.5 per cent of the total. There were 146 patients from Béarn, and 116 from Limousin, 5 and 4 per cent of the total respectively. Finally there were 103 people from Quercy and 48 from Agen. Some nearby provinces, however, were scarcely represented at all. Almost none of the patients hailed, for example, from Périgord, Angoumois, Saintonge or Poitou. If we plot these places of origin on a map we can trace the route the migrants followed through south-west France to Castile. Some of them started in Auvergne and made for the Pyrenees: some came from Bas-Limousin and reached the frontier at Béarn. The route was traditional and consequently confined to certain specific areas. People who lived in the territories the Auvergnat travellers passed through would sometimes rise up from their fields and take part in this ancient migration; but only if their villages happened to lie on the travellers' line of march.

The numbers of Frenchmen who made the migration varied over the years. The exodus was most dramatic, as one might expect, at times when grain was dear – in years like 1619 and 1626, the disastrous year of 1630, 1643 and 1647, 1655 and 1657. People crossed to Spain when they found they could no longer afford the price of bread on the wages they earned at home. This general trend, however, could easily be reversed by changes in the political situation. In the course of these years the Spanish authorities frequently pursued an anti-French policy. In 1625 they confiscated the goods of Frenchmen living in the country. In 1635 they declared war. At another time they annoyed the French expatriate population by introducing a range of minor discriminatory measures and by obstructing the free conversion of the Spanish currency. The influx of labourers from France dwindled appreciably in response to all of these developments. It did not, however, dry up. The numbers of French in Madrid fell sharply from 1631 to 1635, but the fall was not permanent. Labourers went on slipping through the Pyrenean passes; the Spanish authorities threatened them with a battery of edicts, but the immigrants seldom got caught. It is clear, none the less, that the migration gradually lost its momentum in the course of the seventeenth century. Estimates made at this period of the total French community in Spain are apt to be vague; but they point unmistakably, even so, to an overall downward trend. To judge from the figures given by successive French ambassadors who were stationed in Madrid, the community seems to have numbered some 200,000 in 1626. By about 1680 it was less than half that size.

Some of the migrants, as we have seen, were far from being unskilled. Of the patients listed in the hospital records at Madrid, 850 had a trade of some description. Certain trades were mentioned in the lists with particular frequency. Twenty-two per cent of the 850 were bakers, for example, 11 per cent domestic servants, 11 per cent shoemakers, 10.5 per cent pedlars, 8 per cent tailors and 7 per cent water-carriers. Most of the migrants were young people. Two-thirds of them were aged between fifteen and twenty-five. Those who were married already had left their wives and children at home. They had gone to spend a few years making their fortune beyond the mountains, and would come back in due course bringing with them a store of gold doubloons, wrapped up for safety and tucked at their waists with a belt of coarse Spanish cloth. We may note in this connection an official report which survives on the subject of the Auvergne. The report is usually attributed to the provincial intendant, Lefèvre d'Ormesson. It contains a financial assessment which is commonly cited as evidence for the practice of importing Spanish gold. Lefèvre d'Ormesson observes that some 5,000 to 6,000 migrants went to Spain each year. Most of them originated in the region of Basse-Auvergne. When they came home to their provinces they brought with them a total of 700,000 or 800,000 *livres*. Further evidence for the circulation of Spanish currency may be found in the accounts of the mints and the tax receipts in every part of south-west France. It was the result of the journeys made by travellers of this type and the modest but steady flow of funds they brought home with them.

Journeymen and craftsmen drifted across the Pyrenees in hundreds and thousands. This constant drain of skilled labour reflects the stagnation which reigned in the French provincial economy – the shortage of liquid money and the heaviness of the taxes. We may reasonably suppose that some of the migrants were recruited to serve the Spanish as informants, spies or *agents provocateurs*. Some indication of this is given by Cardinal de Retz, the one-time leader of the Fronde who arrived in Saragossa after his escape from France in 1654. De Retz was astonished at the number of Frenchmen he noticed in the streets. 'Vast numbers of them', he observed, 'are more Spanish than the Spanish, the craftsmen in particular'. We shall see later on that this phenomenon played an appreciable part in the revolts which took place in Guyenne in 1635 and the Fronde-related conflicts in Bordeaux.

Refugee peasants

The flight to Spain was continual. For century after century migrants took the same roads across the Pyrenees to escape an impoverished land. But it is also clear from the sources that peasant society in the seventeenth century was in a state of upheaval unique to that period. Homeless peasants were drifting about the countryside. This was no migrants' trek along a specific, traditional route: the upheaval affected whole provinces. Villages were largely abandoned, as the bulk of their inhabitants left their lands and took to the roads for a period under the sudden pressure of circumstances beyond their control. They set off with their wives and children and a few domestic animals to seek their living elsewhere. Rain poured through the collapsing roofs of their deserted cottages, and weeds crept up through the floors. Their fields lay fallow and overgrown with scrub. The *élus* rode around the villages drawing up reports on the number of cold hearths and untended acres. But the villages were never abandoned permanently. Either the refugees would come back to resume their old occupations with the help of the savings they had earned by hiring out their labour, or new bands of settlers would arrive to till the neglected soil. Everyone hoped to return home, and no settlement was ever allowed to die. No village vanished from the map in the course of this upheaval, as some had been known to do in earlier periods in regions like La Gâtine. The countryside of La Gâtine was totally reshaped as a result of the depopulation which took place in the fifteenth century. As lands lost their value because of the shortage of agricultural labour, the old forms of feudal land tenure gave way to sharecropping. Estates were reorganized, and smallholdings farmed by sharecroppers sprang up on the sites of the medieval villages. The old cottages were left derelict or converted into byres and barns.

Changes of this kind took centuries, and only a survey covering the economic history of many generations can properly chronicle them. The short-term desertion of villages in the seventeenth century was another matter altogether. We rely for our knowledge of this phenomenon on the more tangible evidence of day-to-day events.

Upheaval on the land was caused by a number of factors. Inevitably from time to time the countryside succumbed to a natural disaster which shattered the peaceful rhythm of agricultural work. Sometimes the crops failed, causing a famine that lasted for several months. Starving peasants left their farms and set out, in hundreds or even thousands, to beg their bread at the gates of the nearest town. Some provinces were also exposed to the ravages of war. Numerous towns in Gascony and the Pyrenees, for instance, were taken by storm in the course of the Wars of Religion, and parts of them were burnt in the process or even razed to the ground. Reports drawn up by the local *élus* in 1623 reveal that twenty-five to thirty of the parishes in Bas-Armagnac were deserted, and the population had fled. One telling report was submitted by the consuls in the town of Saint-Bertrand-de-Comminges. The consuls contrasted the state of their town before and after the wars. 'This town', they noted,

was formerly one of the largest in the province, as well as being the capital of the bishopric of Comminges. It was densely populated, and large numbers of merchants came there from all parts. Ever since the civil wars, however, the town has been wholly abandoned. The only people left are the priests or clergy and a dozen or so of the citizens. The result has been not only that the town has remained deserted, but all the surrounding lands have been left lying fallow and unfruitful, and the trade which used to come there has been taken away by other towns in the neighbourhood.

But the upheaval was not caused solely by the classic calamities of famine and war. The documents also refer quite frequently to two other factors specific to this particular period which drove peasants to flee their land: the havoc wrought by hailstorms and the crushing burden of taxes.

Modern meteorological statistics demonstrate that hailstorms strike with varying frequency, and that some decades are more afflicted than others. During the seventeenth century outbreaks of bad weather were noted systematically both in the record books maintained by English families and in the reports submitted by the *élus* of Gascony; and it is apparent from both sources that the incidence of hail at this period was particularly severe. This phenomenon can be accounted for in two different ways. It is possible that the spring temperature of the Gulf Stream was warmer than usual in these years, or alternatively that the upper layers of the atmosphere were abnormally cold. Whichever the case, it seems certain that hail in the seventeenth century fell exceptionally often and exceptionally hard. Stricken communities submitted constant requests for tax relief supported by the same monotonous tales of woe. They explained how the hail had dashed their hopes for that year's crops and the next year's too, how the whole population had been forced to leave their homes and go begging for work and bread in neighbouring settlements which the storm had passed by. 'Your poor petitioners', they lamented, 'have nothing left to them but their own tearful voices with which to bewail their misfortune and beg their living in the fields.' Thanks to the havoc wrought by a series of ruined harvests, Gascony by the middle of the seventeenth century had become a desolate region where the yield from taxes was poor and whole communities of peasants had been driven to vagrancy or revolt. In one or two places tax exemptions were indeed accorded by the authorities. But they backfired for the simple reason that the taxes remained in force in the other parishes round about. The tax assessment had been inequitable in the first place: the remedy now adopted tended to exacerbate the inequities and was, consequently, worse than the disease. On one occasion an intendant of Haute-Guyenne looked into the cause of the *croquandages* (Croquant risings) which ravaged the province in the years 1634 to 1641. He ended by blaming the *élus*. 'Under the pretext of hailstorms', he noted, 'they have changed the old basis of taxation in favour of the wealthiest taxpayers to such an extent that the old basis has been abandoned in most of the *élections* of Gascony.' Disorder was seen to be spreading through the institutions of government as well as the fields.

On other occasions the peasants were goaded to leave their soil by taxation alone. Sometimes, too, the twin scourges of hail and taxes struck a place simultaneously.

Various reasons for flight were cited by peasant communities in the complaints they lodged with the government, and echoed by the Board of Finance in the rulings it delivered in response. Peasants complained of the unfairness of the tax rates, the bias of the *élus* who imposed the taxes and the excessive zeal of the bailiffs who were sent to enforce their demands. Everywhere local officials drew the attention of the government to the depth of social distress. The aldermen of Fontenay-le-Comte described how their city had been 'reduced to such a condition of poverty and wretchedness that half the people have left it and it is now a ghost town'. The consuls of Castillon reported that their citizens had been 'forced for the most part to abandon their ancestral homes and withdraw to other places in the surrounding district where the crops were better and the tax less burdensome'. The consuls of Tartas maintained there were no more than a few dozen families still living in their town. This overall picture was confirmed by the findings of the intendant of Haute-Guyenne. The intendant related how the citizens of towns throughout the province had taken to flight in the face of oppressive taxes and the exactions of garrison troops. 'Some towns are overtaxed to an extraordinary extent, even more than the countryside. The reason for this is that business has slackened instead of increasing, while the taxes have gone up. The rents to be had from the houses are only modest, while the rates have risen sixfold. Consequently a good number of people have abandoned their homes.' The parishes belonging to the *châtellenies* of Mortagne, Cosnac and Montbron claimed that they had been the objects of discrimination on the part of the *élus* of Saintes. The *élus* had denied them justice, and their people had consequently been forced 'to abandon everything, to forsake their houses, leave their lands uncultivated and seek safety in flight. This was because their dues had increased by more than two-thirds.' One final example of a distressed community was the parish of Genac in Cognaçais. This parish was striken simultaneously by an outbreak of plague, a series of distraints imposed by the tax collectors and the obligation to billet rapacious troops. By 1657 it was virtually deserted and the fields had reverted to waste land. The better-off people had taken smallholdings in other parishes, and the poorest had either died or left to beg their bread on the roads.

Migrant peasants sought refuge in places either exempt from taxation or favoured by the *élus*. The viscountcy of Turenne was one of these privileged regions, and it 'attracted people from all parts'. This phenomenon was reflected in the population figures. It has been calculated that the populations recorded in the low-tax districts were higher than would have been expected from their natural rate of growth; in neighbouring *élections*, however, the opposite was the case. Peasants in the west of France could also take refuge in the parishes of Marennes and those of the offshore islands of Saintonge which enjoyed an almost total exemption from taxes by virtue of their strategic location and role as salt-producing centres and were required to pay the crown no more than a fixed collective 'contribution'.

The extent of the migration and the degree to which a community was affected by the constant upheavals varied from place to place. All depended on the heaviness of the taxes and the intensity of the hailstorms. Agenais was one of the worst affected regions. We still possess the memorials which sixteen of its parishes addressed to the throne in 1649. No less than eight of these documents talk of deserted villages. There is, then, ample evidence to suggest that in many provinces large numbers of craftsmen and peasants were drifting across the land.

Cast out of their communities, these people soon became used to a wandering life. They were easily inclined to rebellion. The moment the signal was given to rise up in revolt they armed themselves and flocked from every highway and by-way to swell the crowds of insurgent Croquants. In the intervals between these exceptional times of turmoil they roved across the landscape beneath the open sky, living from day to day and free from the ordinary rules of village morality. They had passed into the wide world of vagrants. Vagrancy was a scourge of the age. It was at the same time pitiful and disturbing: a burden on the conscience of every dutiful Christian and a constant threat to the welfare of the humblest property-owner. Hospitals of the period kept account-books in which they recorded the passage of vagrants. Some of these account-books have survived and enable us, consequently, to trace the history of contemporary vagrancy. Large-scale vagrancy set in at the time of the Wars of Religion, and persisted right up to the period when Louis XIV began to rule in his own right. It was the age of pervasive beggary, when authors produced romances written in popular slang and artists painted coarse scenes of rustic merrymaking. 'Poor wayfarers', as they were called, who took shelter in the hospitals were given a bowl of soup and a roof for the night, and sent on their journey with a charitable offering of one or two *sous*. Alms of this kind were known as the '*passade*'. In two average years, 1640 and 1641, the hospital bursar at Treignac, a large market town in Limousin, dispensed as many as thirty '*passades*' each month. Paupers told a range of hard-luck stories to arouse the pity of almsgivers. Some of them declared that they were soldiers maimed in the wars. Others explained they were pilgrims worn out on distant journeys, merchants robbed on the roads, slaves newly ransomed from Turkish captivity or peasants whose livelihood had been ruined by wars or storms. They supported their claims by producing certificates signed by a judge or a parish priest, and drew attention to their wretchedness by trudging along the highways with their wives and children in tow.

Vagrants were helped, or at least tolerated. They were hunted down only when the authorities wanted extra manpower for military purposes. We may notice once again in this connection the change in social outlook which was reflected in the establishment of large general hospitals from 1657 on. Up to that time the authorities had been content to deal with the problem of vagrancy through a series of ordinances which prescribed that vagabonds should be press-ganged or sent to the galleys. These ordinances were essentially an expedient intended to fill out the regiments and galley crews, and the preambles which introduced them made little attempt to conceal the fact. Equally it was accepted as a natural mark of high rank for an eminent person to be followed by a procession of beggars. By the mid-1650s, however, the scourge of vagrancy had abated; and possibly for this reason, begging in the churches, at the gates of towns or in front of bakers' ovens seemed more of a scandal than it would have done a few decades before. In the edict by which it established the Paris general hospital in April 1656, the government declared its intention of 'putting an end of the idle begging of the poor, in the interests of religion, charity and public order'. A contemporary notice which was put up to draw attention to the rise of the new, secluded type of hospitals in the provinces proclaimed with good reason that this was 'a general trend which is spreading throughout the kingdom'. Most of the people forced to take up residence in these hospitals were women and children: children, in particular, were rounded up in droves.[10]

Hardened vagrants were handled not by the officials of charitable bodies but by the judges of the *prévôtés*. It was only a short step, after all, from vagrancy to delinquency, as an army provost-marshal observed. 'Idleness', he grumbled

soon works mischief among vagrants and gipsies and people like that. It leads them to drunkenness, debauchery, gambling and card games, blasphemy, quarrelling and sedition . . . Brutes like these refuse to obey the divine injunction to earn their bread by the sweat of their brow. They sink into shameful poverty, which drives them to theft and sacrilege and abominable murders. There are so many of them that the wheels and gallows often groan beneath their weight.

A similar moral is drawn by another commentator from the career of three bandits who haunted the countryside of Poitou.

They started as soldiers of fortune, and sponged for a long time on men of property. After that they went into hiding in a wood near Nantes. At first they had no intention of committing any wrongdoing, but merely sought to get something out of the travellers

10 Evidence for this may be found in the record of the search for vagrants conducted by the Paris police in March 1657. The police expected to pick up about 5,000 paupers. These included 1,000 women, about 500 destitute men and no more than 360 disabled soldiers. All the rest were children.

who came that way. They asked alms from passing merchants, and helped themselves to a handful of fruit or a few chickens from the baskets of the poor ... Little by little, in other words, they settled into this wicked way of life, and ended by becoming dangerous robbers.

Provosts and their 'game'

Sometimes delinquents got cross-examined by the authorities. The cross-examinations were recorded, and the records enable us to catch a glimpse of a number of tragic individual lives. We can trace the decline and fall of one common type of delinquent by examining the career of François Blancheteau. François Blancheteau, commonly known as 'Grease' (*Graillon*), was a thirty-year-old manual labourer from the village of Brie. He inherited some chattels from his mother, but was shortly afterwards accused of stealing a 14-*livre* pewter bottle from a tavern: the chattels were seized by the magistrates and the landlord compensated from the proceeds. Following this disaster Blancheteau left his village and wandered around the countryside, hiring himself out as a vine-dresser and harvest hand. He slept where the evening found him, sometimes in barns or taverns, sometimes under the open sky in a meadow or ruined mill. Later he bought a mare and earned his living by transporting salt, timber and various other goods. Finally he became a horse-thief, and that was the end of him. A similar fate was experienced by his comrade Philippe Godeau, commonly known as Lamarche. Godeau, like Blancheteau, was a native of Brie. In 1640, at the age of eighteen, he enlisted in the Aubeterre regiment, but was demobilized after only two campaigns. He returned to the village and there, by his own account, eked out a precarious existence, chopping wood, cutting corn and 'doing the *baillarge*', or in other words roaming the district and helping with the barley harvest which was in progress in one place or another throughout the summer months. As often as not Godeau took the opportunity to practise a little subterfuge. He went, his accusers inform us, into parts of the countryside where he was unknown, and there 'asked for corn on the pretext that his own crops had been ruined by the hail or that he had been the victim of some other calamity of fire or flood. Most of the people of Brie go in for this kind of trickery.' Before long Godeau had to come back home to get married and settle down. His accusers report that he extorted cash from his neighbours and was widely feared by them. He went around armed with a sword and a brace of pistols, and spent his time in the taverns 'living it up, even though he hadn't got a penny to his name'. Similar vignettes, incidentally, may be found in many accounts of the village braggarts of the period. They wore feathers in their hats, and swords at their waists, and cultivated the image of gentlemen of leisure – idle, but armed to the teeth, and always ready for a quarrel. Actually Godeau was a horse-thief. He went about at night raiding the stables of carters, postmasters and local justices, and making off with their horses, donkeys and mules. Finally he tried burgling a wealthy butcher of Angoulême, but this time he was caught. On 6 August 1644 he was hanged in an Angoulême square.

To judge from contemporary memoirs, some of the chief haunts of bandits and robbers were, rather surprisingly, in western rather than south-west France. One famous bandit of the west coast was Péchon de Ruby, whose *Vie généreuse des mercelots* was published in 1596. He described himself as a Breton, and set the scene of his adventures in Bas-Poitou. Another bandit, Guilleri, claimed to have plundered the same area. These assertions were supported by Aubigné in a work published in 1617, *Les Aventures du baron de Faeneste*, and by Nicolas Gye in *Le Jargon ou langage de l'argot réformé*, which appeared in 1634.

The towns of Niort and Fontenay were particularly notorious, and their fairs had the reputation of being meeting-places for beggars.

Among the various troublesome vagrants who frequented the fairs and high roads, gipsies occupied a special place. For one thing they were organized. They roamed the countryside in bands or companies with a 'captain' at their head. They travelled on fine horses, and carried guns and swords. When they arrived in a new locality, they sought permission to stay there from the seigneur or local justice before setting up their encampment in an isolated barn. Now and again they were wanted for pilfering by the magistrates of the place where they had settled. When that happened, however, they simply moved on a little, and got themselves taken in at the local château. They could entertain the seigneur with conjuring tricks, or could offer to act as his hit-men in a private vendetta. The government would have liked to see them all packed off to the galleys. 'It is the king's desire', said the ordinances, 'that they be driven from the kingdom'. In the first half of the seventeenth century, however, the gipsies were consistently protected by the gentry, and rulings of this nature were never strictly enforced.

In the course of the sixteenth century the government found it necessary to create a specific office for controlling the assorted people of the high roads. This office was known as the *prévôté*. The duties it entailed were set out in a variety of edicts dating from the reigns of François I and Henri II, as well as the Edict of Roussillon issued in August 1564 – documents which have been preserved through being quoted in the eighteenth-century ordinances governing the *maréchaussée*. According to these edicts, officers of the *prévôté* such as the provosts, vice-bailiffs and vice-seneschals were expected to have charge of the countryside at all times, 'to keep it free of vagrants and soldiery . . . and to make the high roads safe for trade and travellers'. They were supposed to ensure 'the defence of public freedom', and to combat a variety of social evils including nomadism (i.e. gipsies), vagrancy and begging (i.e. refugee peasants), looting and banditry (i.e. out-of-work soldiers and deserters), unlawful assemblies, and duels and private vendettas (i.e. upper-class crime). In times of crisis the ministers of the crown would require the provosts to keep the security forces attached to them at full strength and well equipped. Full mobilization of this kind would be called for at periods when large troop movements were taking place in the countryside, when a war had just broken out or drawn to an end, and when particularly large groups of men were concentrated at one place – as happened, for example, during the sieges of Montauban and La Rochelle. In an average year, by contrast, only a quarter of the theoretical security force would actually be serving.

Provosts were expected to be constantly riding about the countryside and doing their best to enforce the ambitious government ordinances with the very limited means at their disposal. They drove gipsies and other vagrants out of their area, and did what they could to ensure that people respected the law which forbade private citizens to bear arms. In addition they kept track of pilgrims, and maintained a supervisory presence at festivals and fairs. They were expected to stop duels, to break up illicit public meetings, to stamp out corruption and blood-feuds and to station peace-keeping forces in territory disputed between rival seigneurs. Their chief task, however, was to police any bands of soldiery that passed through their jurisdiction or were billeted there. They were expected to follow such troops from the moment they entered the area to the moment they left it, and to make sure the soldiers kept to their intended route. When the soldiers were quartered in their area it was the provosts' duty to guard the approaches to the camps or garrison towns and to head off any deserters or bands of looters who tried to stray from their base. The provosts were also supposed to gather evidence for legal inquiries and to deploy guards to keep the crowds in order when executions were held. Finally they were expected to organize escorts. The task of these escorts was to carry prisoners safely from one centre to another, and to convey the year's taxes through the province on their way to the royal treasury.

Numerous though their duties were, the provosts were never the only competent authorities in any single sphere. They did not, for example, have exclusive jurisdiction over any particular type of crime: their involvement depended on the circumstances. Provosts took cognizance of crimes committed outside the cities, and in general concerned themselves with any offenders they caught red-handed in the course of their tours. Their proceedings were typically swift and informal. The authorities were keenly conscious of the breakdown in social order that had resulted from the rise in population and the unhappy conditions of the time. They had seen that if public tranquillity were to be safeguarded there would have to be room for some sort of instant judicial action which 'could not be held up in order to receive the imprimatur of several layers of authority'. This new form of justice was consequently given the trappings of a military operation or a hunt. Provosts were referred to as 'judges in boots', and the men they prosecuted were their 'game'. They were entitled 'to break down the doors of the lairs where their game took shelter ... to condemn any criminals they caught on their tours without any manner of trial and to hang them on the nearest tree'.

In fact the provosts' resources were as scarce as their powers were great. According to a set of returns which were dispatched to the controller-general in about 1680, the combined strength of the various security forces employed by the forty-one provosts in charge of policing the provinces of south-west France totalled no more than 590 men. The *généralité* of Poitiers had a force of 127 bowmen; Bordeaux had 109; Pau and Limoges had 103 each; Montauban had seventy-nine, and La Rochelle, sixty-nine. These figures, furthermore, were only theoretical, representing the total number of men the provosts would have been able to muster if their forces were at full strength. And the theoretical combined figure of 590 was 18 per cent of the total security force of the entire kingdom, which was officially said to consist of 3,271 men. It was true that the bowmen were splendid. They wore red or blue surcoats embroidered in gold and silver with the provost's monogram, and yellow bandoliers. The ones who served in the *prévôtés générales* (jurisdictions of the provincial provosts-general) and the *prévôté de l'Hôtel* actually had the king's arms embroidered on their surcoats or jackets. But both provosts and bowmen had to appeal for help from the public if they were to have any hope of performing the tasks which the government had entrusted to them. They had royal permission, consequently to 'gather the communes at the sound of the bell to reinforce their companies . . . and to call together our vassals, both noble and plebeian, ploughmen and commoners and other community members, at the sound of the tocsin and the cry of the public herald'. There was no difficulty in getting the communes to rally together against bandits, gipsies and plundering soldiers, and the peasantry flocked willingly to the provosts' aid. The world of the high roads really was a world of outcasts, of people who had cut themselves off from the group loyalties imposed by the settled life. It was diametrically opposed to the world of the communes.

During the reign of Louis XIV the powers of the *prévôté* were strengthened, confirmed and clarified by a whole series of measures. The effect of these measures was to intensify the suppression of vagrants by the state. On 18 December 1660 the government issued a proclamation that called for closer supervision of citizens carrying arms. In March and May 1668 it delivered two successive decrees requiring the *prévôtés* to bring their forces up to strength. In August 1670 it passed a great ordinance regulating the proceedings to be followed in criminal cases, and on 23 September 1678 it issued a further proclamation designed to 'purge the realm of vagrants'. The first step to this end had already been taken in July 1667, when the Saint-Sauveur cul-de-sac in Paris, site of the *cour des miracles* (the meeting-place of beggars and thieves) was raided and cleared by the police. Gipsies were the next victims. The attack on them was initiated in Colbert's ministry, and formed part of his programme for strengthening the authority of the crown. From April 1679 the provincial intendants began to file reports, on Colbert's instructions, detailing the numbers of gipsies they had captured and sent in chains to Marseilles. In the meantime, on 11 July 1682, a new proclamation on vagrants was issued that complemented the earlier one of September 1678. The letters addressed to Paris by the provincial intendants bear witness to just how effectively the government's orders were carried out. Freedoms preserved by the custom and tradition of many centuries had been shattered beyond repairing. The sun was setting on the exuberant age of the Baroque. The liberties once enjoyed by the communes in arms on their ramparts, the young men who staged *charivaris* in the city streets at night and the gipsies who wandered the high roads were all disappearing together, pounded into fragments by the remorseless hammer of state control.

2

The First Croquants: The Assemblies of the *Tard Avisés* in Limousin and Périgord in 1593–1595

By the time Henri III died in 1589, the provinces of south-west France had been racked by civil war for thirty years. In every canton in the region one or several contending armies had marched and countermarched, pillaging as they did so, living off the land and sometimes even burning villages and slaughtering any villagers who had not had the wit to flee. The various rival factions had entrenched themselves in their most impregnable strongholds. Their armies had worn each other out in a profitless stalemate, and their most committed adherents were sick of the struggle. By 1590 local truces were being arranged. Gentry and magistrates belonging to the rival parties agreed to suspend hostilities for the duration of the ploughing season or the harvest or grape-picking time. Sometimes these truces even extended to whole provinces, and lasted for periods ranging from several months to a year. Then came the great sensation. At the end of July 1593 word spread throughout the country that the king of Navarre had abjured Calvinism and had concluded a general truce with the Duke of Mayenne at La Villette. From then on peace was visibly breaking out. The Catholic towns which had already taken the side of Henri IV received with delight the sealed dispatches of 25 July 1593 in which he announced his abandonment of heresy, and the subsequent royal proclamation of March 1594 in which he made public his conversion to the Catholic faith. These loyalist towns lit bonfires in every part of the kingdom. As for the towns which had sided with the Holy Catholic League, they too began little by little to rally to the crown. Some of them were heartened by the news of the king's conversion; others were simply exhausted or had lost all hope of success. The Royal Council spent the whole spring of 1593 in drawing up edicts of pacification and sending them out to every part of the country. These edicts guaranteed that the king would refrain from chastising any rebel towns or châteaux which submitted of their own accord.

In Guyenne the local truces were renewed in the usual fashion at the beginning of 1594. The estates of Périgord held a general meeting in February. The meeting made it plain how eager the people were for peace, and two months later they took action to bring it about. Périgueux rallied to the king on 7 April, and Sarlat followed two days later. On 20 April Marshal de Monluc came out in favour of submission. The marshal was seneschal of Agenais, and he brought the whole of the Agenais district with him. A few days later he also secured the surrender of Quercy. After that the only disaffected towns in Guyenne were Marmande and Blaye, and within the space of a few months, in August and September, they too had opened their gates to the royal forces. By that time the only lingering resistance in Guyenne was offered by a small handful of isolated gentry such as the Marquis de Villars, who served as lieutenant-general of the Catholic League for the entire Guyenne region. The Baron de Gimel similarly held out in Bas-Limousin, where he acted as head of the League. Diehards like these continued to garrison a small number of impregnable fortresses in the hope that reinforcements would sooner or later reach them from the Auvergne, the Languedoc or Spain.

Each day saw whirlwind developments, and the atmosphere was one of mounting hope for a general peace. The euphoria was somewhat marred, however, by reports that the communities of Limousin and Périgord were holding seditious assemblies. These mobs of peasants were obviously behind with the news. They were given the appropriate nickname of the *Tard Avisés* – the 'Out-of-dates'.

History of the assemblies and exploits of the *Tard Avisés*

All contemporary sources agree that the movement of the *Tard Avisés* began with the risings of the people who lived in the viscountcy of Turenne. The communities whose homes lay within the borders of this great fief had grown accustomed to arming themselves and holding assemblies with a view to confronting the soldiers who sallied forth from the strongholds of the various factions to raid the countryside. The communities were given permission to organise by the Duke of Bouillon, and some of the local gentry even served as their officers. Before long the nearby parishes of Bas-Limousin were joining in the assemblies of Turenne. Bas-Limousin consisted mostly of villages scattered in forest clearings some distance from any large town. The garrisons stationed in the district by the Catholic League were forever raiding these villages, and the villagers had realized they were defenceless on their own. Eventually the whole peasantry of Périgord and Limousin were issuing from their barren fields, deep valleys and wooded plateaux to take part in the assemblies and make their voices heard. In the autumn of 1593 the pace began to quicken. Great crowds of peasants gathered for two successive meetings which were held in Lubersac and Magnac. A third assembly took place in the town of Dognon, and as many as 12,000 well-armed Limousin peasants are said to have been there. The gathering decided to send two delegates to the king, to draw his attention to the woes of the countryside.

Then Périgord started stirring. On Palm Sunday the following year, 3 April 1594, a group of parish syndics met together in a place called Château-missier, in the forest of Vergt, and drew up a list of their grievances. A larger meeting took place at Abzac on 23 April. The Périgourdins in their turn decided to send delegates to the king, and from 23 to 27 May all the various envoys from Limousin and Périgord were granted a hearing by the Council in Paris. They were chiefly concerned that the Council should grant their region a tax exemption and rid them from the menace of marauding soldiery. The Council responded in favourable terms to most of their requests.

The arrival of delegates in Paris did not mean the end of the assemblies: they went on regardless. By this time veritable armies were taking part. The parish captains had learnt by now how to organize their peasants into relatively disciplined companies, armed and ready for war. Colonels, and even a general, had been elected, and whole regiments had been formed. From now on the *Tard Avisés* or Croquants, as they were also called, could count on deploying a degree of military force; and they went forth to challenge the garrisons of plundering soldiers that were installed in the local châteaux. In Limousin, for example, they succeeded in driving out the garrisons which had been troubling the people of Chalus and of Isle, a town near Limoges. In Périgord they managed to secure the withdrawal of soldiers from Excideuil, Grignols and Lisle near Périgueux; and they threatened the châteaux of Tayac and Saint-Martial-de-Nabirat.

The movement grew steadily bolder. By June it had spread beyond its early regional bounds. The peasants crossed into Haut-Limousin, Angoumois and Agenais, and advanced as far as the left bank of the Garonne.

The Croquants of Bas-Limousin set out to rally the towns of the uplands. Armed band of peasants massed beneath the walls of Saint-Yrieix, Aixe, Saint-Léonard and Limoges. At this point the authorities began to retaliate. Chambaret, the provincial governor, took the field on 9 June at the head of a force of 200 soldiers and gentry. He marched on a crowd of *Tard Avisés* that had gathered in the town of Bujaleuf, hanged the captain of the local parish and burnt a number of barns. Fresh groups of *Tard Avisés* approached, however, and Chambaret had to retreat. He left his command in the hands of the consuls of Saint-Léonard, and asked them to conclude a truce with the rebels on his behalf.

Chambaret made good use of the interlude. He gathered up all the funds which had been raised in local taxes, and summoned the governors of the Auvergne and Marche to his aid. Several days later he took the field again – with 600 horsemen this time. He succeeded in catching a mass of peasants in open country. The Croquant musketeers failed to stand firm before the charge of Chambaret's troopers. They broke ranks, and the fugitives were cut down right and left. No less than 1,500 peasants were killed in the massacre. This battle took place on Midsummer's Day, 24 June, at Les Pousses close to Saint-Priest-Ligoure. News of the slaughter quickly spread, and the Croquants of Limousin retreated in panic to their homes.

During this same month of June the movement spread into Angoumois, where several of the gentry joined it. Massès, the king's lieutenant in the province, stamped out the rising by the same brutal methods as his colleague Chambaret. At the beginning of July he broke up an assembly of some 2,000 peasants. More than 100 of them were killed in the clash.

The movement for peasant assemblies spread into Agenais from the direction of Bas-Périgord. On 10 July the peasants of Agenais held an assembly at the town of Ledat, in the Lot valley. They decided to launch an attack on the château of Penne, which was held by a predatory garrison, and sent delegates to Agen with instructions to call on the citizens to come to their support. The consuls of Agen joined forces with Monluc, the provincial governor; they fended off the envoys with delaying tactics, and eventually induced the peasant crowd to leave.

The fashion for assemblies was gaining ground even beyond the Garonne. On 12 June a number of local communities met at Mézin. They called on the citizens of Condom to rally to their cause, and arranged for a further assembly which was due to be held at Nérac but apparently never took place.

The movement now flagged for some months. The peasants throughout the region were busy with the harvest and grape-picking. Further assemblies were held in Périgord in October, but only a small contingent of syndics and parish captains took part in them.

At the end of 1594 the various royal governors set about capturing the last surviving bases of the Catholic League. Matignon took the offensive in Guyenne, Thémines in Quercy and Chambaret in Limousin. Each of them called on the communes in their province to help in the different sieges by providing reinforcements and supplying and maintaining the royalist troops. The communes responded. Between August and December 1594 bands of Limousin peasants arrived to help besiege the château of the Baron de Gimel near Tulle; and from December 1594 to March 1595 a regiment formed of the members of the Third Estate of Périgord ravaged and plundered the lands of the Marquis de Cauzac, who had served as the League's seneschal for the province of Agenais.

In February 1595 the estates of Périgord held a general meeting. Further delegations were sent to the king, and the people of the province continued to hope that tax rebates might be granted. Peasant assemblies gathered once more in July in the neighbourhood of Périgueux, and the town was badly frightened. On 8 August the consuls of Périgueux held a parley with the heads of the peasant communes. Bourdeille, the provincial seneschal, had other ideas, however. He collected a force consisting of 100 mounted gentry and 800 footsoldiers, and scattered the Croquants for good and all in a series of engagements which took place at Negrondes on 19 August, at Saint-Crépin-d'Auberoche on 24 and 25 August, and at Condat-sur-Vézère on 4 September.

Further assemblies were also held at about the same period in Saintonge and Angoumois. In September the garrison at Barbezieux was slaughtered by peasant bands. Order was restored only at the end of October, when the Marquis de Pisani staged a military demonstration in the area.

In spite of the universal repression of Croquant unrest, the king kept his promises. Action was taken to redress the grievances of the countryside as soon as the crown's authority had been established, the civil wars were over and religious harmony prevailed once more. In two proclamations issued in 1596 and 1600, the king confirmed the tax rebates which the Council had granted to the delegates from the provinces in 1594. There were no further peasant disturbances in the reign of Henri IV.

The eight Wars of Religion had ended with a curious turn of events. In the space of a mere two or three years the peasants had suddenly slipped free of their humdrum daily existence and had burst into the political arena. It is clear from the interest of the court historians and the fright of the local chroniclers that this assertion of peasant power took contemporaries wholly by surprise. We shall now take a systematic look at these peasant assemblies – both at their composition and the way they operated, at the individuals who led them and the documents they produced.

Composition of the assemblies of the Third Estate

It was not, in itself, unusual for the people of the countryside to meet for discussions or even to take up arms. Peasants had done so instinctively from a very early period to resist an approaching enemy. They had gathered together in the woods and lain in ambush for intruders behind the hedges overlooking a sunken road. They had rung the tocsin in the bell-tower, steeple bringing word to steeple of imminent danger or reinforcements to come. When the enemy entered their village they had barricaded themselves in the church and prepared to withstand a siege. During the Wars of Religion they were often obliged to arm in response to the perils of the time. The Bordeaux chronicler Jean Darnal described, for example, in the spring of 1590 how 'the people of the Entre-Deux-Mers have risen and armed themselves, ready to charge at any marauding soldiery'. Village communities adopted the same defensive tactics in every part of the country, in Burgundy as well as Saintonge.

Landed gentry regarded it as their duty to set an example when danger threatened their estates. They placed themselves at the head of their assorted tenant farmers who had gathered to defend their homes. The Viscounts of Turenne, in particular, drilled and disciplined their tenants from an early date with a view to preventing any invasion of their fief, and their military exercises were famous throughout the region. As a result of these exercises the towns and villages of Turenne became so strong militarily that marauding bands of soldiers usually preferred to leave them alone. There were several other examples. When Aubeterre rallied to the cause of the king of Navarre he bought with him several contingents of trained Périgourdin peasants. Galiot de La Tour, the seigneur of Limeuil, a former comrade-in-arms of Marshal de Monluc, organized his tenant farmers into a number of companies. The city clerk of Bordeaux reports that Galiot did more to train the peasantry for war than any other noble in the province. 'He forced all his tenants to arm, reviewed them personally and formed them into squadrons . .. his arquebusiers were 2,000 strong.' Similar hosts of armed tenants could be seen here and there throughout the country. 'The example set by the lord of Limeuil was promptly followed by several other seigneurs. They too obliged their tenants to take up arms, in order that they could parade their forces as he had done.'

Sometimes, then, peasants took up arms at the behest of the local gentry. Another form of mobilization was inspired by the seneschals. They frequently summoned large numbers of parish syndics to meet them, with a view to getting the parishes to levy men and money and to make a badly needed contribution to the costs of the current war. Popular assemblies of this kind took place quite commonly. All of them, however, were short in duration, and confined to a limited area. They were also respectable in the eyes of the authorities, either because they took place as a matter of ancient custom or because they were held in response to a royal edict or the command of a local official. The assemblies which began to be held in 1593 were another thing altogether. They took place incessantly. They attracted people from many parts of the countryside. And they had no official blessing of any kind.

The basic unit of these gatherings was the parish. Parishioners customarily came together for many purposes – to take part in votive processions, to hunt wolves, to submit to the tax assessments, and in general to engage in every aspect of community life. They elected a village notable to serve as their syndic and act as a spokesman for the parish. Sometimes they also chose the same notable as their captain; but the captain might equally be any other villager who had a good seat on horseback and could wield a sword. The Croquant movement typically took root in a parish through the arrival of a letter. This letter summoned all the parishes in a given jurisdiction to meet together in order to 'adopt resolutions for the common good'. The letter was a circular which had been copied out by a village scribe and signed by him in the name of the *Tard Avisés* of the province or the 'Third Estate of the countryside'. It was brought to the parish by a resident of a neighbouring jurisdiction, and would subsequently be forwarded to parishes further on. In this way the summons travelled from township to township, and the rebels were able to contact dozens of jurisdictions in the space of a few weeks. Villagers who did not see fit to respond to the first summons would shortly get a second, more pressing one. Alternatively the rebels would change their tune from promises to threats, and the villagers would find themselves pressurized into attending by the prospect of having their lands laid waste and their cottages burnt down.

The results were dramatic. At least twenty-one assemblies are known to have been held in the two years which elapsed between the autumn of 1593 and the autumn of 1595 – thirteen in Périgord, six in Limousin and two in Agen.

The summons was usually issued at least one week before the date which had been set for the assembly. Sometimes it came several weeks earlier. Dates were carefully chosen. Assemblies could be held only on a day which fell outside the periods of major agricultural work, and Sundays and holidays were particularly favoured. (Eight out of the sixteen assemblies whose dates we know were held on Sundays. Three were held on Tuesdays, but this is undoubtedly a coincidence.) The meeting-place was generally a large patch of open ground where communities could spread themselves out and the peasants could have room to stretch their legs. Open waste land was desirable for another reason: the rebels had to be able to guard the approaches to their rendezvous to avoid being surprised by hostile troops. They set watchmen at these approaches to challenge any newcomers. Typical meeting-points chosen were broad forest clearings, or open fields covered with heather or weeds. Places of this sort were easy to find in these heavily forested provinces. The assemblies at Châteaumissier, La Trappe, Abzac, Atur and La Bessède all took place in this kind of scenery. Other assemblies, however, at La Boule,

Trémolat and Limeuil, were held in the low-lying meadowlands on the banks of the Dordogne.

The numbers present varied. Only a few hundred men would appear for a meeting of syndics and consuls or a gathering organized by the residents of a single jurisdiction; but an assembly intended to bring together the Third Estate of several provinces could attract ten thousand or more. One typical modest gathering was held at Lalinde on 22 May 1594 by the syndics of the parishes on the left bank of the Dordogne. Only 120 people took part. On 8 August 1595 the syndics of Haut-Périgord arrived at Rognac, where they had been summoned to a conference by the consuls of Périgueux. These syndics had come escorted, and the meeting was consequently larger: almost 2,000 men were present in all. The peasant force which paraded before the walls of Saint-Yrieix and Saint-Léonard in May 1594 also totalled 2,000 men. But these were far from being the largest Croquant contingents. The mass of peasants who were routed by Chambaret on 24 June 1594 at the battle of Saint-Priest-Ligoure numbered 5,000 to 6,000, and the main assemblies of Limousin and Périgourdin rebels were vaster still. 12,000 peasants met at Dognon at the beginning of 1594, and 7,000 to 8,000 gathered in the forest of Abzac on 23 April. The largest recorded assembly was the one which was held at La Boule on 31 May 1594. Twenty thousand people were present according to Canon Tarde, 30,000 according to the city clerk of Périgueux, and 40,000 according to the chronicler Palma Cayet.

Most of the assemblies were attended by peasants from four or five leagues around. They went there and came back the same day, as though they were making a trip to a fair. The signal for the assembly was given before daybreak by drummers who made the rounds of the nearby fields; the meeting itself was usually set to begin at midday. Each commune marched to the meeting-place and took up its station there in a fairly orderly manner. The great crowd of visitors deliberately brought their own provisions with them so that they could eat their meals on the spot and would not be obliged to despoil the neighbouring hamlets. The journey home meant a night march, and the wayside taverns were consequently full of dawdlers enjoying their liquor. The largest assemblies like those held at La Boule and Chéronnac, where people from several provinces rubbed shoulders with each other, were more protracted affairs. Some of them lasted for up to five or six days.

The actual meeting resembled a council of war. The parish syndics all spoke in turn, freely setting out their grievances and debating the merits of possible courses of action. Leaders were not selected nor decisions adopted by vote; rather, the final word was left to a small core of notables who had sufficient prestige and authority to impose their will on the rest. The cheers of their supporters left no doubt who these notables were. Palma Cayet records the method used by the assembly at Abzac to choose the delegate whose task it would be to carry the peasants' petitions to the king. It is clear from his description that the village orators played the decisive role. They went to and fro among the various groups, heckling each other noisily, sticking their necks out when necessary and promoting the interests of their friends. Different parties were formed by different groups of parishes. Each party tended to place its trust in a local worthy whom everyone knew and whose counsel everyone followed. The proceedings were not wholly solemn. If the meeting took place anywhere in the neighbourhood of a town, casks were rolled out from the cellars and the wine flowed plentifully.

The function of these assemblies was not so much a deliberative as a military one. Their purpose was to organize a common defence against the incursions of passing soldiery, regardless of what faction the soldiers belonged to and regardless of whether they came to collect supplies, levy taxes or indulge in open looting. This military purpose was reflected in both the terminology used at the gatherings and the way they were organized. The leaders dignified themselves with military ranks. Each parish organized itself into a company with a 'captain' and 'lieutenant' at its head. Regiments were formed from contingents supplied by one or several jurisdictions, and were commanded by 'colonels'. For a time there seems actually to have been a 'general' in command of the Third Estate of Périgord. Before and after the assemblies the peasants went on parade. 'Colonels' inspected contingents of 500 and 1,000 men who shouldered their muskets in true military fashion and kept in line. Tarde relates in his chronicle how the peasants 'marched to their assemblies in battle order, flying their standards and beating their drums. They bought arms and elected captains in every parish and settlement. They beat their drums as they marched and rang the tocsin to summon their assemblies and to call their general parades. They maintained guards, stationed garrisons and kept every other form of military order.'

Arms were not difficult to find: there was a lively arms trade in the provinces. A peasant's natural weapon was his stick. Usually the bearer hardened the end of his stick in the fire, or shod it with iron and fitted it with a blade. Peasants also carried spades, forks and axes. Nearly all the Croquants had served in the wars, and had subsequently managed to hold on to their swords, pikes and halberds. Many peasants even had arquebuses and muskets, corselets and breastplates. In peacetime all this weaponry was hidden away in a cellar or beneath a pile of faggots, or was locked in a chest and buried in the ground near the owner's home. The Limousins, for example, went home and buried their arms after their defeat at Les Pousses. Their idea was to hide them safely for the duration of the summer months till the harvest was gathered in. After that they would bring them out and use them again.

Once the parish captains had agreed on a plan, and an adequate force of armed men had been raised through successive meetings, the Croquants went forth to threaten one of the fortified strongholds in the neighbourhood, and to put an end to the terror which its garrison was inflicting upon the country-side. They proclaimed to the nearby towns that their aim was 'to get this place to surrender and renew its allegiance to the king'. It was important to win the townspeople to their cause. That way they might get access to the weapons and artillery which were stored in the town halls, and might also hope to legitimize their activity by winning the blessing of the local officers of the crown. With these ends in view the Croquants issued their summonses to city after city – to Limoges in May 1594, Périgueux in June and Agen in July. Agen received a further summons in January the following year.

The Croquants were numerous enough to besiege a stronghold effectively, but unless they had cannon they could not take even the smallest fortress by storm. All they could do was to launch attacks on the outlying fields and buildings which belonged to the fortress. At Limoges, for example, and at Penne in Agenais, they threatened to wreak havoc in the surrounding territory, and at Saint-Martial, Tayac and Cauzac they carried out their threat and devastated the neighbouring cornfields, vineyards and barns.[1] No actual fighting took place, and attackers and defenders were parleying from the very first day of the siege. Judges or local gentry or other dignitaries offered their services as go-betweens, and the upshot was that the garrison came to terms. Bourdeille, the provincial seneschal, was instrumental, for instance, in getting the garrison at Excideuil to make itself scarce, and the lord of Laborie-Saunier got the garrison at Grignols to leave. At Saint-Martial 'some persons possessed of property and the wit to go with it mixed with this multitude and calmed them down.' The terms of the surrender were generally lenient. The garrison would be required to evacuate the stronghold; but their lives would be spared, they could keep their arms and baggage, and the rebels would not molest them on their journey out of the district. In Châlus and Aixe, however, the Croquants took the garrison commander prisoner and held him to ransom; and they usually indulged in some looting. In Châlus and Isle, near Limoges, and at Cauzac and Pechsec in Agenais, they forced their way into the stronghold, seized any goods they could find and even brought horses and carts to help them carry off the booty more easily. Once they had finished plundering, the Croquants handed the stronghold over to its rightful seigneur or the local seneschal. Mission accomplished, they returned to their homes.

The Croquants never attempted to set upon crown officials like provincial governors and seneschals. They did not fight at all unless actually forced to do so. If caught in the open country they formed up in battalions with the musketeers in front. Tarde comments how 'they had the impudence to array themselves in battle order, for all the world as though they meant to defend themselves . . . These regiments of the people made a show of standing firm.' At the first clash of arms, however, the peasant ranks broke. D'Aubigné scoffs that the Croquants 'had several commanders and disregarded them all. Some of them took shelter inside their battalions, and others ran for the woods.'

---

1 The practices followed by the regiments of the *Tard Avisés* were not exceptional. Similar measures were ordered in the course of the Wars of Religion by the royalist commander, Matignon. When besieging the town of Grenade, which was held by the Marquis de Villars, Matignon ravaged the countryside and burnt the mills right up to the town walls. See the letter by Matignon to the king on 22 October 1594, *Annales historiques de la Gironde*, vol. 14, p. 324. Similar measures were also decreed by the *parlement* of Bordeaux as a form of punishment to be inflicted on members of the Catholic League. One decree prescribed that the houses of the League supporters besieged in Montpezat should be 'razed, and their property confiscated; and the forest should even be felled which adjoins the said town' (Decree of 29 January 1595). *See Annales historiques de la Gironde*, p. 335.

Palma Cayet reports that they 'all fired at the same time, after which they immediately abandoned their barricades'. Once scattered in the woods the fugitives were helpless, and all they could do was return to their villages. They took their arms to the syndics, who handed them over in their turn to the clerk of the nearest town court as the provincial seneschals had ordered them to do. Croquant soldiers who had previously served in the Wars of Religion re-enlisted in the armies of the king.

The military campaigns which were launched by the peasant assemblies were, then, both short in duration and limited in their aims. They were undertaken for strictly defensive reasons. The Croquants of 1594–5 had no grand strategic design.

The leaders of the assemblies

Just twenty-six of the shadowy figures who played a leading role in the assemblies are mentioned in the records by name. Sixteen of these people were from Périgord, five from Limousin and five from Agenais. We know nothing more of most of them than their names and the places they came from, but the records do add some information about the background of ten of the twenty-six. Seven were legal practitioners of one sort or another. They included four local justices, a tax attorney, a notary and a lawyer. Two of the others were impoverished gentlemen, and the last one was a physician. The only reason these leaders are referred to by name in the chronicles is because they took part in the delegations which emerged from the depths of the countryside to summon the towns to support the Croquant cause and to remonstrate with the king. Village worthies of this kind were not the only leaders. The Croquants were also led, as we have seen, by the captains of their parishes. Parish captains owed their position solely to their (real or pretended) military prowess. The city clerk of Périgueux maintains with heavy sarcasm that two of the local parishes were led, in the early stages of the rising, by 'a *galafre* and a *pilat* from Sarlebous'. Translated from the Gascon, this meant a tavern regular and a village beanpole from the forest of Vergt.

The clerk of Périgueux drew a distinction between the ringleaders who incited the peasants to revolt and the syndics and parish captains. The latter were chosen to head the rising whether they liked it or not, and were forced to take up arms even though they might have no stomach for the struggle. 'At the beginning', the clerk reports, 'they had men volunteering to lead them; but they ended up by forcing people to serve as their captains. They singled out the wealthiest members of the community, and even the local judges.' One of the willing rebels was the judge of Excideuil. He personally led the revolt in his jurisdiction, and his leadership played a decisive part in spreading the insurrection. Four other leaders undoubtedly became involved of their own free will. Their involvement is quite well documented, and we know rather more about them than we do about the other Croquant chiefs.

The best known of them, La Saigne, first attracted attention as early as April 1594. He was prominent throughout the disturbances, and was still

ASSEMBLIES OF THE TARD AVISÉS, 1593–1595

leading the Croquants of Périgord in July 1595. He was a notary from the town of La Douze in the forest of Vergt. His name appears for the first time at the foot of a circular inviting the communities of Périgord to take part in an assembly which was shortly to be held at La Trappe in Sarladais. The original of this circular was written in the town of La Douze on 29 March 1594, a date which bears out an ironical assertion of Palma Cayet's. 'It is generally agreed', says the chronicler at the start of his account of the rising, 'that the rebellion was instigated by a small-town lawyer or notary called La Saigne, who, being at a loose end one day, amused himself by making out a large number of circular notices.' Later in the year La Saigne took part in the great Croquant assembly held at La Boule, and was there apparently accorded the title of 'general of the Third Estate'. In February 1595 he went to Périgueux for the general meeting of the estates of Périgord. He attended in the capacity of deputy for Mouleydier, a small river port on the banks of the Dordogne at the edge of the Liorac forest. In March, when the meeting was over, he set out for Paris to seek an audience with Henri IV in the hope of impressing on the monarch the demands of the countryside. On his return to Périgord he found that the tax exemptions promised the previous May were being held up by officials anxious to prosecute the war with Spain. He responded by issuing a new batch of circular letters. As the chronicler put it he 'began to rush round and circulate instructions from parish to parish, telling the people to hold themselves in readiness'. Finally, La Saigne led the colonels and captains who took part in the conference held at Rognac. We can see his hand clearly at work in two separate insurrections – the revolt which began in Périgord in April 1594, and the upheaval which shook the province in July the following year.

The Croquants of Périgord had a second prominent leader, who was condemned along with La Saigne in the proclamations issued by the *parlement* at Bordeaux. His name was Papus, and he was generally known as Pauillac. He was a tax attorney from the *châtellenie* of Ans, a group of eighteen parishes on the borders of Périgord and Bas-Limousin which belonged to Princess Catherine of Bourbon, the sister of the king. Palma Cayet describes him as 'a little man dressed just like a craftsman. His cloak was shabby and he rode without boots, on a mare.' The chronicler adds, however, that he 'put on the airs of a commander'; and he dominated the assembly of communes which took place in the forest of Abzac on 23 April 1594.

Another important leader was a man named Porquery. He was by profession a lawyer attached to the *parlement* at Bordeaux, and had also been elected syndic of the fortified town of Monpazier. He too distinguished himself at the Abzac assembly, where he made an immediate impact with his sound pro-fessional record and intellectual gifts; and the assembly consequently chose him as one of the delegates entrusted with the task of conveying their grievances to the king. On 5 May 1594 Porquery arrived in Paris in the company of a fellow-delegate. This other delegate's name has not been recorded, and we have no information about him except that he was the syndic of either Limeuil or Saint-Alvère. His mission completed, Porquery returned to his native region and appeared at an assembly held at Limeuil on 12 June. At the request of the gathering, he gave an account of his journey and of the answers the Council had given to each of the points contained in the Croquant remonstrance. Palma Cayet describes him as a skilful orator, capable of some subtlety and eager to act as a moderating force.

Lastly we know something about the leader of the Croquants of Agenais. This leader's principal exploit was to devastate the lands of the seigneur of Cauzac. His name was Boissonnade, and he was a physician from the town of Agen. He is referred to in the records as a 'colonel of the Third Estate', a rank he was probably granted some six months before his exploit by the assembly held at La Boule. From December 1594 to March 1595 he is said to have commanded 'three to four thousand footsoldiers of the Third Estate . . . who were authorized to bear arms by Marshal de Matignon'. Given that Boissonnade organized his campaign of pillage against Matignon's express orders, this authorization seems dubious, to say the least. Cauzac, however, failed to get the physician convicted by the *parlement* at Bordeaux. D'Aubigné reports how 'the whole multitude withdrew to their homes and were left in peace. Even Doctor Boissonnade, who had acted as their general, was left unmolested and allowed to practise his profession in Bordeaux.'

It is clear from the scattered notices about the Croquant leaders that none of them were fearsome bandit chiefs. They were village dignitaries. Their social status is further indicated in the chronicles at a number of different points. In the conference held at Rognac, for example, we are told that the Croquant delegates undertook to convey to Bourdeille, the seneschal, the resolution which their movement had adopted in favour of peace. This resolution had been signed by 'all the leading men of the market towns'. The captain elected by the jurisdiction of Châlus, a certain Pierre Deschamps, is described as having been a 'man of quality, intelligence and considerable resources'; and the captain of the parish of Château-Chervix is similarly reported to have been a 'man of imposing stature and ample wealth. He was also an eloquent speaker and had borne arms all his life.' All of these leaders, then, were well-to-do people. They had made money or had held public offices, and were generally respected by their neighbours on that account. They had something to lose from widespread civil unrest. At the same time they were also literate enough to act as a voice for the discontented peasants and to formulate their resentments in political terms. They made the theoretical demands of the peasants sharper and more precise, but consistently played a moderating role in any practical attempt to urge those demands on the authorities. Each time they were invited to parley by the seneschals and the town magistrates, they argued for compromise. They pleaded for the authorities to 'receive their remonstrances graciously', and promised to submit to the rule of law in exchange for an adequate hearing. And their attitude paid off. They got the marauding garrisons to move out of their region, and they got the king and his Council to remit their tax arrears. They also got the authorities to promise that they would be treated more fairly in the lawcourts. The promise was not an idle one, and royal commissioners were sent to travel among the communities and listen to their complaints.

Centres of dissidence

The rising of the *Tard Avisés* affected almost the whole of Limousin and
Périgord, and part of Saintonge and Agenais. Within these provinces, however,
we can also identify certain groups of parishes which caught the attention of
contemporary observers because the troubles there were particularly acute.
They were the epicentres of the social earthquake: it was in them that the
turbulence started, and out of them that it spread in successive waves of
rebellion across the countryside. We shall look at four of these major centres
of dissidence. In the first place there was Xaintrie, a group of parishes situated
in Bas-Limousin, on the borders of Haute-Auvergne. Xaintrie was a district
of bleak and barren tablelands cut through by narrow river valleys. It consisted
of two distinct parts, White Xaintrie and Black Xaintrie. White Xaintrie was
the area which surrounded the town of Mercoeur. The château there belonged
to the seigneurs of Merle. Black Xaintrie was a more thinly populated area
which centred on the town of Saint-Privat. This whole small district bordered
on the viscountcy of Turenne, and it benefited indirectly, in certain ways, from
the privileges enjoyed by the viscountcy. People who lived in Turenne, for
instance, were wholly exempt from taxes, and their tax-free status was confirmed in letters patent issued by a series of kings in Paris. This privilege also
favoured Xaintrie in the sense that any property owned by the people of the
viscountcy was treated as tax-free, regardless of whether it lay within Turenne
or across the border. In the same way the readiness of the people of the
viscountcy to take up arms against intruders helped to keep not only Turenne
but all the surrounding country free from the depredations of passing soldiery.
So Xaintrie quickly assimilated a spirit of resistance from Turenne. As early
as 1591 the people of the district were refusing to pay their taxes. When the
men of Turenne took up arms against the marauding troops from the garrisons
the men of Xaintrie followed suit. They lived under the constant threat of
garrisons stationed in Miremont and Saint-Chamant, two local châteaux which
were held by the Catholic League, and hoped that by imitating the tenant
militias of Turenne they could rid themselves of the menace. Xaintrie began
to be noticed. The Treasurers of France in Limoges denounced the district
for obstructing the tax collectors. 'In this *élection* of Tulle', they observed, 'are
a certain number of parishes which are known by the collective name of
Xaintrie. These parishes lie close to some lands owned by Monseigneur de
Bouillon, Viscount of Turenne; and under the present circumstances he could
give us valuable help be restoring order in Xaintrie and persuading the
inhabitants to pay His Majesty's dues.' But the district was not to be pacified.
Four years after the Croquant rising, in 1598, the people of Xaintrie were still
withholding their taxes and resisting the bowmen who came to collect them.
They had not paid a penny since 1591, and their arrears had mounted to a
total of 14,000 *livres*.

Another rebel heartland lay further to the north, in that part of Limousin
which stretched from Saint-Yrieix to Châlus. This district occupied the border

with Périgord, and was right at the centre of the rising. Peasants of both provinces flocked there from several leagues around. They moved about the district holding assembly after assembly and calling on the townspeople to rally to their movement and the garrisons to make themselves scarce. This group of cantons, like Xaintrie, aroused the ire of the Treasurers of France for persistently withholding their taxes; and it was their contingents who were routed by Governor Chambaret at the battle of Les Pousses. They marched on that occasion under no less than forty-two standards, each representing a different parish in one of the two insurgent provinces. An anonymous chronicler described them as 'a bunch of peasants'. The chronicler listed thirteen of the parishes they came from. Six of these parishes were in Limousin and seven in Périgord. All of them lay in the forest lands which straddled the provincial border and were carved up between the three noble families of Hautefort, Chalais and Des Cars.

Another district to play an important part in the early assemblies was the neighbouring *châtellenie* of Excideuil in Périgord. This *châtellenie* consisted of twenty-five parishes which belonged to the Chalais family. From Excideuil the waves of rebellion spread through the province as far as the outskirts of Périgueux. Assemblies or battles took place in every part of the surrounding countryside. In the north of the province the trouble centred on the parishes of Negrondes and Agonac and the parishes attached to the *châtellenie* of Ans-sur-l'Auvézère. Other disturbances broke out still nearer the provincial capital, in the parishes of Sarliac and Bassillac on the banks of the river Isle and in those of Saint-Laurent, Atur, La Douze and Saint-Crépin-d'Auberoche in the forest of Vergt. It was the villages of this part of Périgord that produced the movement's leaders, La Saigne and Papus, as well as the host of 'colonels and captains' from 'beyond the Isle' or from 'this side of the Dordogne' whom the citizens of Périgueux saw gathered at their gates in the summer of 1595. It was in this region, too, that Bourdeille, the provincial seneschal, scattered the peasant bands the following August, and it was there that the final battle took place on 4 September at Condat-sur-Vézère, a village at the eastern edge of the Ans district, on the border with Bas-Limousin.

One final group of parishes that attracted the notice of contemporaries were those of Black Périgord. Black Périgord was the belt of densely forested country to the south of the Dordogne which ran from the forest of La Bessède near Campagnac de Ruffenc to the forest of La Trappe near Villefranche. It was the home of most of the communities that signed a protest memorandum on behalf of the 'Third Estate of the countryside' and submitted it to the general meeting of estates which took place in Périgord in February 1595. Tarde calls them the 'united parishes'. According to him they were roughly forty in number. Twenty-seven of them lay to the south of the Dordogne, including some eleven situated on the borders of Quercy in the heart of the forest belt and twelve on the borders of Agenais. Eleven of the parishes occupied the actual banks of the Dordogne. Only three parishes lay on the far, northern side of the river.

It is evident from these details that the rebellion broke out in a wooded landscape – in a countryside covered with great tracts of untamed forest, barren to the plough and dotted only with scattered townships where small numbers of peasants reared livestock and ate chestnuts behind whatever frail defences had been raised to shelter them. Safe behind their ramparts, the large walled towns had little interest in the rising. Only a very few provided the Croquants with reinforcements, a tiny handful of places such as Châlus and Lubersac, Excideuil and Limeuil. The other towns certainly shared in the peasants' discontent and their anger with the tax collectors, and they lent their names to the decisions adopted by the Croquant assemblies. But they fought shy of the actual military campaigns, and were careful not to take up arms. The Croquant bands, in other words, were exactly what they proclaimed themselves to be. They represented the open countryside of western France, where the peasants lived in patchwork fields and isolated hamlets and were helpless in face of the plundering soldiers who roamed the roads.

We shall now look briefly at the content of the Croquant documents. In each of them the revolt is justified with the same arguments, and the arguments are couched in almost identical terms. The resemblances are so striking as to raise the possibility that most of the documents were actually written by a single author – La Saigne.

The letters of the *Tard Avisés* begin by invoking God and dedicating their cause to his service. They go on to describe the wretchedness of the times, to relate how the local truces are constantly being broken and the countryside is scoured by soldiery. They complain how the townspeople, snug behind their walls, are ignoring the rural misery, how the officers of the law are powerless to curb the marauding garrisons or are actively colluding with them. Finally they call on peasants and villagers to form a common front – to forget their religious quarrels and rise up with a view to ensuring that the truces are respected and the king's authority is once more recognized. In other words they propose that the peasant captains should lead their contingents forth to besiege the most destructive bands of soldiers in their strongholds and rid the land of them.

The sheer repetitiveness of the Croquant texts, their tendency to harp on certain arguments and reiterate certain words, is a useful aid to analysis. It enables us to set out the reasons the rebels advanced to justify their rebellion, and to weigh those reasons up. Anyone who reads the documents is inevitably struck by the recurrence of a number of words which appear incessantly and which point, in their turn, to a number of basic themes. The name most commonly mentioned, for example, is that of God: it appears in eighteen different places. In the preambles to their documents, the *Tard Avisés* view the disasters which are afflicting the realm as a mark of divine anger. Plague, war and famine, in their eyes, are scourges sent by God to punish men for the wickedness and ambition which fill their hearts. The continued absence of peace is seen as a further divine chastisement. Later in the discourse, however, God is also presented as a source of pity and justice. 'God will look down on our enterprise', the Croquants assure their readers: 'May it please God so.' God is called on to witness the vows of solidarity and mutual assistance which the peasant bands are taking, and the letters of the assemblies held in Limousin and Marche even enjoin obedience to God and his Church. Finally, the documents all conclude by expressing the wish that God may protect the recipient of the letter.

In the list of current miseries, the exactions of the soldiery get pride of place. In describing these exactions the *Tard Avisés* speak, no less than fourteen times, of robbers and robberies. The term 'robbers' is employed a good deal more often than its variants such as bandits, men-at-arms, soldiers and oppressors. This usage reflects the feeling of the people of the countryside that their cause is profoundly just. All they are doing is to defend their property; and they call themselves, appropriately, 'the robber-hunters' (*Messieurs les chasse-voleurs*). The robberies are also described in a number of other ways. They are called variously exactions, lootings, mobbings, oppressions, outrages and, above all, tyrannies. This latter word appears in as many as ten places. The Croquants proclaim that they must 'prevent' tyrannies, 'redress' them, and 'defend themselves' from them. A tyrant at this period meant the same as a torturer, and tyranny was what happened when a person used his authority to inflict violence in a wicked and horrifying manner, as the mad Roman emperors had done. The assemblies feel that in resisting the soldiery they are rising up against the intolerable demands of a power which they detest, whose legality they dispute and whose sway over them has been achieved by purely terrorist methods. Tyranny in practice means for the *Tard Avisés* the soldiers' ruthless demands for 'taxes' and 'levies': these words occur fourteen times. The Croquants explain how if the people supposed to owe these spurious dues are unable to pay them, they are promptly thrown into prison: the word 'prison' appears in twelve different places. They die wretchedly behind bars, leaving their families ruined: the word 'ruin' is used nine times. The documents talk at length about 'prisons full of peasants' and how the inmates pay their ransoms only to die of exhaustion or hunger when they get back home. These are the crimes which have directly caused the rebellion. By the same token, the release of prisoners from the gaols is the most pressing demand contained in the summonses which the *Tard Avisés* are issuing to the towns and fortified strongholds.

Croquant anger is also directed at those individuals who are making a profit out of the general misery. Such profiteers are described in contemptuous terms. They are parvenus 'who have got rich at the expense of the king and the people', fortunate individuals 'who were beggars not long ago'. They have made their pile, the Croquants say, by robbing the king and his subjects. 'They are richer than they have ever been, but it is we who have paid for their riches ... all the wealth they have amassed is money taken from us ... their greatness has been built on the ruins of His Majesty's fortunes and ours.' One document actually mentions the names of three financial officials, but usually the people of the countryside are content to direct their indignation at the walled towns as a whole. 'The towns care nothing if the people are ruined: our ruin is their wealth.' Wealthy profiteers get honours while the poor get misfortune and prison. The *Tard Avisés* rail at the scandal of justice denied: 'We cannot pin our hopes on receiving justice, for there is no justice for us ... It appears from what they tell us that the gentlemen who administer justice are either unable or unwilling to redress all these tyrannies.' The words 'just' or 'justice' occur ten times.

The men who are rising in revolt are 'the men of property'. The phrase appears in eight places. They are the poor folk, the poor people, the poor ploughmen: the word 'poor' is used eight times. They say they are 'victims partaking of the sufferings of this period', and call themselves the 'Third Estate of the countryside'. Their leaders are the 'best qualified representatives of the Third Estate', and their cause is 'just', 'good' and 'holy'. They claim that their uprising is a legitimate protest of honest men. Their conviction that this is the case is reflected in the names they use for themselves such as 'robber-hunters' and 'out-of-dates'. (Nicknames of this kind expressed the customary patience of the peasant and his slow-burning resolution – a stereotype which the signatories of the rebel letters were happy to adopt. In later documents, however, written when the assemblies had grown more numerous and more formal, the rebels started describing themselves as the 'Third Estate of the province' and the 'Third Estate in arms'.) The letters are typically addressed to Messieurs the officials and inhabitants of such-and-such a *châtellenie* or to Messieurs the consuls of such-and-such a town. The rebels identify themselves as the 'brothers' of the addressees, and 'warn' them instead of commanding: the word 'warn' is used in eight places. They sign themselves at the end in the style then current in letters, describing themselves as the 'humble and loving servants' of the recipients, as their 'good friends' (this phrase occurs three times), or as their 'comrades and servants'. The name people called them, Croquants, is never found in anything written by them. It was a nickname used by the chroniclers to make fun of these armies of country bumpkins. Fanciful etymologies were constructed to explain the term, and d'Aubigné and Cayet believed them; but we can safely leave these aside. A Croquant was simply a yokel armed with his stick. But when the peasants of Limousin and Périgord met together in assembly, they never regarded themselves as a band of Croquants insofar as that phrase implied a disorderly mob of yokels. They saw themselves as the Third Estate of the countryside, representatives of one of the principal social orders, namely the order of those people who lived in the villages and worked in the fields. They were the true Third Estate, and as such were filled with the sense of legitimacy and dignity that characterizes a social order assembled to discuss the affairs of the realm.

The *Tard Avisés*, then, devoted their letters to condemning the plundering of the people and insisting on the need to hunt the robbers down. They denounced unwarranted taxes and proclaimed their determination to pay them no more. They protested against the imprisoning of ploughmen and called for the ploughmen to be set free. They lamented the breaking of truces and the denial of basic rights. They railed at the profiteering towns and demanded justice for the countryside. All of these themes, however, amounted to no more than a programme for self-defence and non-cooperation with the taxman. The Croquants had only a limited number of constructive proposals to make. These included a tax rebate and the abolition of the posts of the local financial officials. In addition they wanted the authorities to accept that the peasantry had a right to take up arms against the foes of the king and his people, and to appoint a permanent syndic to represent the interests of the countryside. Apart from the times when they sent delegations to the king, or intervened in the meetings of the estates of Périgord, the *Tard Avisés* had very few opportunities to spell out their constructive demands in any kind of detail; and we are dependent on a handful of second-hand accounts for the little we know of these crude political manifestos.

The demand for a tax rebate was a sweeping one. The Croquants wanted a remission of all the arrears which had accumulated in previous years, an exemption from part of the taxes being levied in the current year and a reduction in the taxes to be raised in the years to come 'to the level they were at before the wars'. More generally, they called for the abolition of all those taxes which the government had instituted in recent times. 'They were quite unable', they declared, 'to pay as many special taxes and duties as they had done in the past. They would rather die. That was the reason why they had risen up.' The assemblies insisted on several occasions that they were no longer prepared to pay anything except 'the regular *taille* (poll tax) due to their king and the *taillon* (a special addition to the *taille* imposed for military purposes).

The Croquants maintained that the local financial officials should all be dismissed. They were dishonest, and not even necessary. The post of *élu*, for example, could easily be abolished, and the *élu*'s function of carrying out the local tax assessments could be taken over by the lieutenant of the *sénéchaussée*. The task of tax gathering, performed up till now by tax collectors in the service of each *élection*, could also be done away with. Instead the country parishes would pay their taxes direct to the king himself. The Croquants sketch out this classic utopian fantasy in the fourth of their collected documents. 'We wish', they declare, 'to take the king's tax to him personally without letting the money pass through the hands of all those individuals who have enriched themselves from it at the expense of the king and his people.'

The most urgent demand was formulated by Porquery in his interview with the king. He sought permission for the peasants to 'take the field in order to hurl themselves upon the enemies of the king and force them to submit and obey him'. The demand is made in several Croquant documents. 'If the robbers continue to prey upon the people any longer, we shall charge at them as we would at ravening wolves.' In a sense the action suggested was traditional. The authorities had long been accustomed to deal with outbreaks of lawlessness by getting the vice-seneschals to make their tours, to raze the houses of local gentlemen turned bandits and to arm the communes to fight them. The novelty consisted solely in the fact that on this occasion the people of the countryside were proposing to take the initiative themselves, and were not prepared to wait for the permission of local magistrates they regarded as being hand in glove with the bandits.

The final demand of the *Tard Avisés* was for the election of permanent deputies to represent the interests of the countryside in its dealings with the state. Such representation, in their view, was the only way of ensuring that a higher standard of justice would be meted out to them. The demand was the most specific in the whole Croquant programme. In the eyes of provincial officials, it was also the most subversive. It would undermine their inequitable and heavy-handed rule. The *Tard Avisés* of Périgord envisaged three 'special delegates of the Third Estate'. Each of them would represent one of the three *sénéchaussées* in the province; all, however, would be chosen outside the towns of Périgueux, Sarlat and Bergerac, where the jurisdictions were based. One of the three would be the 'special syndic of the Third Estate in the region of Périgord'. Tarde observes that insofar as this 'syndic of the country folk' was supposed to be 'chosen from towns and parishes outside the three local capitals', he would be 'like a tribune of the people, appointed with a view to maintaining them in their freedoms and privileges'. Both the consuls of the smaller towns and the syndics of the country parishes made a stand in favour of the idea in the general meetings held by the estates of Périgord. They formed themselves into a party of the countryside, and made a point of airing the same grievances each time a general meeting took place. As early as June 1583, for example, the syndics of eight towns in Sarladais and Bergeracois drew attention to the havoc being wrought by marauding soldiers in the countryside and complained that the townspeople were aiding and abetting the plundering bands. Twelve years later, in February 1595, an identical protest was submitted by almost the same group of towns. The difference was that this time the towns were supported by forty other communities. The attorney-general denounced this agitation before the assembled estates. 'There are', he declared, 'certain persons among the mass of the population who wish to meddle in the affairs of the realm. They call themselves the Third Estate, but are actually aiming to set up a Fourth. They aspire to appoint a syndic, breaking away in the process from our true Third Estate which consists of the three main towns.' The attorney-general advised the estates to reject the protest from the countryside, and the estates decided accordingly. The outcome was the same as it had been in 1583, when the complaint of the country syndics had been pronounced 'uncivil and impudent'.

Some thought was given to mustering the resources the Croquants would need to realize this last demand in their programme. The people of the countryside agreed to submit themselves to a special levy which would be raised each year from the different parishes. The funds collected would be used to support their proposed syndic and to pay the costs of any missions and legal proceedings his work might entail. Money actually was collected by the rebels who rose up in 1594, and Boissise, one of the commissioners sent out at the end of the rising, estimated that a total sum of 300,000 *livres* was spent on the various popular assemblies which were held in every part of Guyenne. Boissise was probably exaggerating, but it is clear that the expenditure was quite considerable.

The old social order in the countryside had been overturned by the wars, and the country people were anxious to see it restored. They wanted priests to attend to their ministry, and maintained that Church revenues should be paid only to clergy who took active charge of their parish. Many lands once owned by commoners had passed during the wars into the possession of the gentry, and the peasants wanted to see those lands contributing just as high a proportion of tax to the royal coffers as they had done in the past. They held that nobles should have their titles to nobility verified, that any parvenus found to have usurped such titles should be taken to court, and that the honours, legal privileges and tax exemptions enjoyed by the nobles should be made available only to families of genuine blue blood.

The *Tard Avisés* were driven by nostalgia. The whole thrust of their programme was to reverse the unpalatable changes which had taken place, during the war years, in the political structure of the kingdom, the social hierarchy and the rhythm of rural life. They longed to turn the clock back to the old days of religious harmony and general peace, when the king was content to get his regular *taille* from the people and everyone in the land knew his proper station; when the gentleman kept to his château and the merchants to the highways, and the peasant stayed in the meadow, watching his cattle graze.

In a moment we shall consider the repercussions of the demands put forward by the Croquants, and look at the final outcome of their campaign. First, however, we must try to assess the validity of the allegations they made. We must estimate the effect upon the mass of ordinary people of the minor local wars and the broken truces, the burden imposed on them by the raids of marauding garrisons and predatory gentry and the constant extortion of taxes both on legitimate and on wholly spurious grounds.

What the wars were really like

The *Tard Avisés* made it plain that they were not prepared to endure the havoc of war any longer. But how, in fact, did it affect them? What aspect of the fighting disturbed the life of villages deep in the forests of Périgord? Contemporary authors drew a distinction between two types of military engagement. On the one hand there were the great battles recorded in the history books, when generals hurled great armies against each other in bloody confrontations. On the other hand there were the mundane campaigning seasons, long months spent in chaotic manoeuvres, marches and countermarches, settling into winter quarters and garrisoning forts. During those months the troops of all three contending factions scattered through the provinces reorganizing their companies and enrolling new recruits. At the same time they also continued to harry the enemy. This day-to-day routine of the conflict was known as 'waging war' (*la guerre guerroyable*).

We can put together a fairly accurate picture of the way in which war was 'waged'. Whole areas were torn between the various contending factions. One faction, for instance, would occupy a canton while its opponents held the neighbouring château. In the Garonne valley or on the south bank of the Dordogne, the towns were Protestant outposts in a Catholic countryside. Montauban, capital of the Protestant faction in south-west France, was surrounded by dozens of Catholic châteaux and market towns; and the Huguenots sallied forth to besiege these local Catholic strongholds whenever they were strong enough to do so. Armies scattered through the land, and garrisons were installed in the smallest fortified places. Four soldiers were often enough to hold a small, poorly fortified hamlet so long as it occupied a strategic position. They could defend it effectively by the simple expedient of taking cover behind the stout walls of a church or barricading a little village lane. Sometimes, however, the attackers could turn the tables. A dozen horsemen could capture even a well-defended mansion by strapping scaling ladders to the backs of their sturdiest ponies and launching a surprise assault in the middle of the night. For months at a stretch the war would be a sporadic affair of isolated ambushes, a handful of horsemen skirmishing at a bend in the road. Here and there a township would be frightened into submitting to the enemy by the bombardment of a cannon drawn by a team of oxen a few leagues off. There were countless local truces, agreements and compromises. Now and again a garrison would surrender. The soldiers would fold their standards, douse their powder-matches and march out from their stronghold, carrying their arms. Then they would simply go and entrench themselves in a new stronghold a little further on.

It was a war that consisted of endless minor operations, a war 'waged' over great tracts of territory by trivial numbers of men. It cost the countryside very dear; but it also taught the communities how to defend themselves. A few peasants gathered in a market square could drive off a band of looters. Townspeople kept on continual alert, and if soldiers threatened the suburbs the burgesses would leap on their horses in an instant and put them to flight. Precautions of this kind were often formidably effective. In 1590, for instance, a company of citizens armed with arquebuses rode out from Périgueux and routed the garrison stationed at Grignols. In April 1576 the people of Fontenay-le-Comte kept their enemies at bay by adopting a policy of constant vigilance. They left only one of the town gates open at any time and held their market in a meadow inside the city walls. In defying the predatory garrisons the *Tard Avisés* were doing nothing new. Their campaign was only one in a long series of similar risings that began when communities grew sick of marauding soldiers and snatched up arms to resist them in a burst of spontaneous rage.

It is easy enough to imagine the damage which the wars inflicted on the countryside, harder to express that damage in concrete figures. We know that a garrison was a major liability for the host population, even when its expenses were properly paid. In Bas-Périgord, for example, the Viscount of Turenne owned two important strongholds. The cost of maintaining garrisons in those strongholds represented a significant slice of the revenues which Turenne raised in taxes each year. It cost 864 *livres* to provide for the annual upkeep of a corporal and seven soldiers in the château of Limeuil, 432 *livres* to support a captain and four soldiers in the château of Lanquais. But the burden was often appreciably greater than these figures suggest. Most of the time commanders simply did not have the money to pay their troops. In 1594, for instance, Périgord was full of royal garrisons, but Bourdeille, the provincial seneschal, did not have so much as a penny with which to pay them. To maintain their forces, consequently, garrison commanders were obliged to shift for themselves. They empowered their adjutants to scour the countryside, foraging and raising taxes, mobilizing labourers to widen the ditches around the castle and mend the gaps in the walls, and rounding up herds of livestock, loads of corn and casks of wine. All of the various factions tried to secure bases from which they could issue forth and harvest the crops of the surrounding lands. Marauders were continually pouring out of their strongholds, some acting under instructions and others out for themselves; and the country people were forced to remain on a constant war footing. But the marauding could not be avoided. Garrison commanders and captains could not afford to be deprived of munitions or food supplies. Faced with such a calamity they had no alternative but to dismiss their soldiers and go back home themselves.

Soldiers resorted to a total of three different tactics for getting the money they needed out of the peasantry. The first was to raid the villages. The second was to wait in ambush at the roadside, kidnap the first peasants or merchants who came by, and hold them in prison for ransom. The third was to hijack the taxes which had been gathered in a locality for the benefit of the king.

Raids and ransoms

A account still survives of the soldiers who occupied the port of Marans in Bas-Poitou in 1575–6. It gives us a fair idea of how a typical garrison behaved. 'They went out on raids incessantly. They seized oxen and cows and, moreover, held people to ransom, without having the slightest regard for religious principles. They spared no one, saying that a peasant who couldn't give them so much as a sheep or a donkey must be poor indeed.'

A range of complaints was made about the excesses perpetrated by the garrisons who occupied strongholds in the provinces of Limousin, Périgord and Agenais. One of the principal ones concerned the captain of the garrison installed in the château of Isle, near Limoges. He was, said the peasants, 'a man of evil life, who made off with both cows and oxen. He raised levies, and kidnapped anyone who was not prepared to pay.' The Croquants stormed his stronghold and sacked it. The peasants had equally harsh words for the Baron de Gimel in Bas-Limousin. They complained that the baron 'is rampaging through the whole of this region, plundering the people, devastating the land, and helping himself to as much as he can of His Majesty's revenues'. The provincial Bureau of Finance submitted a series of remonstrances relating to the the conduct of the garrison which occupied the château of Saint-Chamant on the borders of Haute-Auvergne. The château had been deserted by its owners, and the Bureau protested that it had now turned into a lair for marauding troops. Those troops set out periodically to 'levy taxes and take them by force. They kidnap the country people, and anyone going to and fro on business between the local cities and market towns, and hold them to ransom'.

In Périgord the fortresses of Lisle and Grignols had been notorious for a long time for the havoc their garrisons wrought. Bourdeille, the provincial governor, was particularly afraid of the garrison at Lisle, who were stationed only a league away from his own château of Brantôme. The citizens of Périgueux were driven to take up arms against the troops at Grignols on a number of different occasions. Their Black Book records that 'in these past wars the soldiers at Grignols put over a hundred men to death in the castle dungeons'; and the *Tard Avisés* claimed that several dozen unfortunates were still imprisoned there. Both Lisle and Grignols were seized by the Croquants in 1594. The seigneurs of Tayac and Saint-Martial had a similar reputation for maltreating or killing the peasantry, and the assemblies of Périgord threatened their château too.

The chief focus of resentment in Agenais was the château of Penne. Delegates sent by the Croquants to take part in the meeting of the Three Estates which was organized at Agen explained how the people of Penne had fled to the village of Hautefage, and the town had been left at the mercy of the soldiery. 'Not content with this', the garrison commander at the château had 'extorted funds from the local people on his own private authority, forcing them to contribute to the upkeep of his garrison to the tune of whatever sum the garrison might see fit. To get these poor peasants to pay, he raided them daily, making off with them and their livestock and anything else of value he found in their homes.' The château of Penne was duly attacked by the *Tard Avisés*. Further destruction was wrought in the province by the Count of Montpezat, who served as the local head of the Catholic League. He harried the royalist towns in the valley of the Garonne, 'raiding right up to the gates of Agen and [abducting] men and livestock alike'.

Military taxes

The levies which the contending groups inflicted on the people were wholly arbitrary. But the soldiers liked to conceal this fact by dressing up their exactions in some kind of official guise. To this end they also raised formal taxes which were entered in their account-books. These taxes were explained to the taxpayer in various ways. Sometimes the soldiers said they were special taxes, and sometimes they said they were part of the regular, royal *tailles* which had to be levied immediately and put to instant use. The soldiers never attempted to justify them on any grounds other than current military needs, or to support them with any warrant apart from the seal of the garrison commander.

Each faction levied taxes upon the territory it controlled. The funds were collected 'by force of arms', through a 'military operation'. Now and then the sources give us a glimpse of such an operation in progress. We find references to a squad of twelve horsemen touring the countryside, or a party of twenty footsoldiers going from village to village in search of lodgings. Faction leaders behaved like nothing short of viceroys in the region where they held sway. Turenne, for example, set up an entire administration to help him extract revenues from his domain of Languedoc. A treasurer-general and registrar handled the funds as they came in, and a council of Protestant notables issued ordinances, drew up tax rolls and made out receipts. In Guyenne the old Marshal de Monluc relied on a similar apparatus. He had an inner council composed of his captains, the local Catholic magistrates and a Treasurer of France attached to the Bureau of Finance at Bordeaux. Several of the chronicles give an idea of the size of the taxes raised. In 1593, for instance, the Duke of Ventadour imposed on the inhabitants of his duchy a special tax designed to raise a total of 9,000 *livres*. The proceeds were used to keep his garrisons in fighting trim. The following year the Count of Clermont instituted a series of levies intended to maintain the garrisons he had stationed in his châteaux of Montaigut and Aubusson. The levies were imposed not merely on the *bailliage* (local administrative unit) of Montaigut and the countryside round Aubusson, but throughout the province of Marche. In Agenais and Quercy the Count of Montpezat raised taxes on behalf of the Catholic League. The upshot was that the communities in those unfortunate provinces had to pay tax twice over. Jean Blaise de Monluc's tax collectors wanted their money for the royalist cause, and Montpezat's took anything they had left to support the League.

Encouraged by the example of such powerful nobles, the lesser warlords all proceeded to follow suit, from the garrison commanders to the lowliest captains. On 20 June 1594 the Bureau of Finance at Bordeaux reported to the king how

the great majority of the commanders and captains in this *généralité* have been taking outrageous liberties. They have been forcing the people, on their own authority, to pay them the money due to Your Majesty in *tailles, taillon* and other levies. The result has been that the tax collectors specially appointed to recover these funds cannot carry out their task, and not so much as a penny reaches the chief collector's office.

The Bureau of Finance at Limoges saw nothing new in this phenomenon. They observed that soldiers had been in the habit of gathering the king's *tailles* for their own use ever since the civil wars started thirty years before.

The nouveaux riches

The *Tard Avisés* were able to identify a number of individuals who had profited out of the suffering of the times – the unbridled levying of funds, the exactions of passing soldiery and the scandalous episodes in which communities got 'taxed twice over' by rival groups. As early as 1583 the syndics who spoke out on behalf of the countryside at the general meeting of the estates of Périgord pointed the finger at the burgesses of the main provincial towns. 'Most of the citizens of Périgueux', they complained,

are brothers or brothers-in-law of the tax collectors and agents, or are closely related to them. They are responsible for countless exactions ... All they can think of in Périgueux, Bergerac and towns like that ... is to get their share of the plunder ... The robbers can get into the towns at any time they please: they can come and go more easily than men of property.

La Saigne in one of his circulars mentions three profiteers by name, Crémoux, Gontrand and Gourgues. Pierre Crémoux and Barthélemy Gontrand were the two tax collectors for the *élection* of Périgord. Crémoux held the post of senior tax collector. He is referred to in a document as early as 1584, and was still in office in 1608. Barthélemy Gontrand occupied the junior post. His brother Pierre was a judge on the *présidial*. When Barthélemy died in February 1594, his office was reckoned to be worth no less than 4,500 *livres*. Crémoux and Gontrand were Périgueux men who never strayed far from the sound of the bells of the cathedral of Saint-Front, and their fortunes were large ones by local standards. Ogier de Gourgues, by contrast, was the president of the Bureau of Finance at Bordeaux, and his career was on an altogether different scale. He first appears in the records about 1550, as a merchant in Bordeaux. In 1558 he was appointed to the office of tax collector for Guyenne, and consequently became involved for the first time in handling the royal revenues. From then on he was a full-time agent of the fiscal authorities. Tax after tax was farmed out to him in every part of south-west France. In 1567 he obtained the post of Treasurer of France at Bordeaux, and he served as tax gatherer extraordinary throughout the civil wars. By 1582 he was one of the richest men in his province. He was actually able to lend the king a sum of more than 170,000 *livres* for use in commissioning ships. When he died in October 1593 he bequeathed to his children a wealth of estates scattered up and down south-west France. These lands included the viscountcy of Julhiac and the barony of Vayres, near Libourne, where Gourgues had acquired a château on the banks of the Dordogne, and every passer-by could stare at this massive pile which the one-time Bordeaux merchant had bought from the king himself. Gourgues's riches are an example of the outrageous fortunes which profiteers managed to make in the course of the civil wars. To the people of the countryside, the spread of this kind of wealth was a glaring scandal.

Reactions to the *Tard Avisés*

The *Tard Avisés* were by no means alone in their discontent. The evils they complained of were not new, but had aroused resentment ever since the civil wars broke out. And the letters of provincial governors, royal officials and city magistrates indicate that the grievances voiced by the Croquants were widely shared at the opposite end of the social hierarchy.

General hostility to taxes

Taxes had been increased out of all proportion under the pressure of wartime needs, and a cry of protest was going up from every part of the kingdom. Paris was bombarded by petitions from the meetings of estates in the provinces, and anguished letters came in from the consuls of the major towns. Everyone called for a tax rebate, just like the *Tard Avisés*, and couched his request in the same terms that the *Tard Avisés* used. Even the assemblies of noblemen used the same phraseology. The gentry of the Charente region rose up in 1590 against the 'plunder and ravaging ... the exactions and levies ... the constant demands for the people to provide huge sums of money, sums they could not raise even if they sold all the goods they possessed'. They implored the king to 'lighten the burden of his poor people'. In June 1594 the gentry of Guyenne who had gathered for the traditional feudal muster took the opportunity to call for 'the wholesale abolition of the levies and excises … Thanks to them the king is faced with the utter ruin of both the nobility and the commons.'

Many petitions insisted on the notion that the tax farmers were robbing both the king and his people. In doing so they implicitly condemned the very financial officials and businessmen who were lending money to the crown. At any other period such a charge would have been regarded as plain seditious; but many provincial authorities made it, none the less, in the letters they wrote to the king. The *jurats* of Bordeaux denounced the 'tax farmers who alone derive profit from serving Your Majesty in these unhappy times, and who batten on the ruin of all your decent subjects'. Such persons even threatened, they said, to cause 'some irreparable disaster. An offence so serious could not be overlooked under any circumstances short of a special pardon or amnesty.'

Merville, the seneschal of Guyenne, warned the king similarly against 'those persons whose sole ambition is to get their cut from the new levies and to make their fortune out of the ruin of your state'. He called for 'an end to overtaxing' and an 'adjustment of State finances'. The seneschal of Périgord, Bourdeille, demanded for his part that 'the tax arrears accumulated by these poor people should all be waived, right up to the present year'. Everyone was agreed that the country people had good reason for their discontent. Even the king was pleased to express his sympathy. 'Swearing by his holy drunken gluttony and jesting in his usual manner', Henri IV declared 'that if he were not what he was and had a little more spare time, he would gladly become a Croquant'. This anecdote is reported by both d'Aubigné and L'Estoile. It confirms that the unhappy *Tard Avisés* were not alone in their protest, and that their resolutions reflected a general dismay at the evils of the period which was shared by people far beyond their ranks.

But this broad consensus is misleading. The rising in the countryside was not popular with the rest of society. Townspeople generally viewed it with a mixture of fear and contempt. A number of chroniclers made out that the peasant bands had radical and even revolutionary aims. No trace of such aims can actually be detected either in the manifestos drawn up by the Croquant assemblies or in anything they did. But the chroniclers claimed that the Croquants were bent on overthrowing the monarchy, the nobility and even the Christian faith.

Alleged irenical tendencies

'The first of these decisions', reports the Black Book of Périgueux, 'was that from now on they would no longer fight or quarrel over religious differences; and everyone would live as the fancy took him'. Guyon de Maleville maintains that the *Tard Avisés* wanted to 'dictate to God in Heaven. They called upon him to give free rein to every form of religion, and to allow changes to be made in the raising of the tithes.' These writers make the Croquant aims sound extremely radical. But all these aspirations reflect was simple war-weariness, coupled with a wish to have priests in the villages once again and to make sure that they, and only they, got the money raised in the tithes. The peasants were no longer seeking to resist the raising of tithes *per se*, as some of them had done in the early days of the Reformation. Their demand was more limited than that, and in no way anti-religious. It recurs, indeed, in all the petitions submitted in 1614 and 1649 by the parishes of the Third Estate, and in many of the sermons delivered by clergymen under the impact of the Counter-Reformation. In any case there is clear evidence to indicate that country priests accompanied their flocks to the Croquant assemblies.

The peasantry had noticed in the course of the civil wars that people who sided with one or other of the rival factions sometimes did so for reasons that had very little to do with religion. Petitioners from Poitou complained in 1576 that the gentry were taking it easy: they joined whichever faction would bring them most glory and profit. And indeed the gentry often did change sides for reasons as trivial as a family quarrel, an insult or the chance to carry out a profitable raid. As for the marauding garrisons, they cared little if anything what religion their victims professed. By the time of the Croquant rising there were further grounds for disillusionment. The war had been both too long and too frightful for anyone to believe that his faction could win more than, at best, a Pyrrhic victory. Increasingly the religious distinction was blurred. Towns which had previously adhered to the Catholic League were resigning themselves to accepting a king who had once been a Huguenot. Followers of both the opposing creeds were serving the same commander. The tenant farmers who lived on the lands of the Viscount of Turenne and the Marquis de La Force marched in the Protestant armies in the service of their seigneurs without renouncing their personal devotion to the Catholic faith. It was only natural, then, that the people of Saintonge and Angoumois joined forces irrespective of their Huguenot or Catholic leanings to resist the introduction of new taxes. The Protestant towns of Saumur and Sainte-Foy formally authorized the delegates they were sending to the Croquant assemblies in Charente and Périgord to associate with Catholics there. Religious beliefs in the late sixteenth century were simple and uncritical. Decisions of the kind taken at Saumur and Sainte-Foy did not mean that anyone's convictions were faltering. They were not a manifestation of growing scepticism, let alone a foreshadowing of the modern ecumenical movement. All they meant was that utter intolerance had ceased to be realistic in the grimness and confusion of the times.

The nightmare of revolution

Contemporary observers showed signs of alarm from the moment the Croquant assemblies began to grow sizeable in April 1594. Bourdeille, the seneschal, claimed that some of the peasant bands which met at that time in Périgord had 'spoken openly of ruining the nobility and wiping them out'. Frightened by this warning, two dozen of the local gentry hurried to Bourdeille's side and urged him to break the assemblies up. By June a league of noblemen had begun to take shape in response to the threats which the *Tard Avisés* had made against the châteaux of Tayac, Saint-Martial and Penne. The gentry declared that in refusing to pay their taxes and tithes the peasants were rebelling against both their king and their God. In refusing to contribute towards the upkeep of the garrisons in the châteaux they were 'conspiring against our way of life, and trying to escape the subjection to which God had destined them'. The only solution was to form a league of like-minded nobles against the common threat. The moving spirit behind this association was the seigneur of Tayac, Jean-Guy de Beynac. Beynac was one of the gentlemen who had joined the Catholic League. His château had been attacked by the *Tard Avisés* in protest against the exorbitant amount of tax he had raised in the countryside. Beynac succeeded in rallying a total of thirty-three supporters, and they all took an oath to support each other against the schemes of the masses. This compact was similar to many other agreements concluded in the sixteenth century by factions of noblemen. Beynac and his fellows made a formal vow of friendship. They renounced any quarrels which had arisen between their families and agreed to refer to any personal disputes which had sprung up between them on matters of honour to the judgement of mediators chosen from among their number. Finally they promised to help each other when danger threatened them. This compact was signed in July 1594. All of the gentry who signed it were natives of Sarladais, a region straddling the river Dordogne where the Croquant assemblies had been particularly active. The confederate gentry hoped that they would be able, in an emergency, to raise a force of 400 cavalry under the leadership of the Marquis de La Force. Many of their names are unknown to us, but one or two stand out. One of Beynac's associates, for example, was Saint-Martial, a fellow-member of the Catholic League who had also, like him, been a victim of the *Tard Avisés*. Another was Vivans, a young Huguenot captain who commanded the garrison in the town of Domme. Two other prominent figures were Saint-Alvère and Auberoche. They owned lands in the forest of Vergt and were friends of Bourdeille. All of these men had either seen the Croquant assemblies at close quarters or been set upon by them. But no matter how vengeful they felt they were unable to take the field against the rebels. Marshal de Matignon had issued orders specifically forbidding them to take action of any kind.

Alarm at the Croquant turmoil was voiced again a year later, in May 1595. The cause of the turmoil at this point was a brief but spectacular rise in prices in the interval between two harvests. Hundreds and even thousands of impoverished peasants, most of them from Limousin, had surged to the gates of Périgueux, and carts bringing sacks of grain to the city had been plundered in the vicinity of Bassillac and Saint-Laurent. The citizens of Périgueux took fright in much the same way as the provincial gentry had the year before. The city clerk expressed the general consternation. 'Some of the rebels', he wrote in his chronicle, 'were brazenly advocating the destruction of the nobility and calling for total freedom. Even the sharecroppers were defying their rightful masters. The multitude were so inhuman that they tried on several occasions to stop grain and other commodities from being brought to this town'.

Many observers felt that the turmoil threatened the stability of the entire kingdom, and even the world. The consuls of Périgueux declared that the

Croquant rising represented an assault 'on the general tranquillity of France and the world as a whole'. An anonymous chronicler of Limousin made a similar comment. 'They are threatening and spurning the nobility', he noted, 'and are even uttering diatribes against the towns ... They had actually convinced themselves that they could dispense with the king's authority and make new laws of their own. In a word, they were terrifying large numbers of people, and it seemed as though this was truly the world turned upside-down.'

It looks very much from the testimony of these various sources as though the peasant population had begun to develop feelings of active hostility towards the nobles. At the very least it is clear that many observers thought this would happen, and feared it. The thirty years of religious wars had in fact been something of a heyday for the warrior aristocracy. Thanks to the wars they no longer needed to cross the Alps to Italy in quest of martial glory: on the contrary they scarcely even had to leave their provinces to take part in satisfying raids. Their mentality is accurately depicted by François de La Noue in the *Discours* he composed between 1580 and 1585 with the object of establishing a basic code of ethics among the nobility. De La Noue singled out for condemnation two particularly destructive attitudes which prevailed among his peers: an appetite for gallant adventure and a contempt for anyone who lived peacefully on their estates. In *Discours X* he denounced the mansions of the nobles as 'those vile trophies which are built out of the spoils they have wrung from the peasantry'. Few tenant farmers ever actually saw their seigneur in his mansion, since he was always away on campaign. But the seigniorial system had been based on the ideal of the benevolent gentleman protecting his peasants; and the new breed of absentee landlords no longer matched up to that. They no longer appeared at all except to demand special taxes intended to maintain their armies in the field. The petition submitted by the Poitevins in 1576 is evidence that even at this relatively early date the common people looked on the war games of the gentry with profound mistrust.

As time went on the kingdom was openly carved up among the various contending factions. The powers of the crown were increasingly usurped by the local warlords, and the royal armies were too weak to prevent this loss of control. Nobles who up till then had been busy fighting in Italy were free to prey as they fancied on the provinces at home. Confronted with the daily realities of war, with the whole range of tribulations we looked at earlier, the country people naturally tended to develop feelings of resentment towards the nobility. Contemporary observers were aware of this latent antagonism, and frightened of the upheaval it might lead to. Their fear gave rise to a whole mythology of subversion. We can identify among the various fantasies a Huguenot myth, a mercenary myth and a Swiss myth.

The Huguenot myth can probably be traced to the shocking tales which had spread about Protestants in other parts of Europe – about the 'peasants who rose up in Germany in 1525 to ransack the property of the nobles and wealthy people', or the 'league of crazy Anabaptists'. Protestantism was also tainted with scandal in France itself. The Reformation had barely taken root in the Agenais region when the Catholic Baron de Fumel was murdered by his Huguenot tenants. Marshal de Monluc claimed that at the time this murder took place members of the Protestant clergy were heard proclaiming in their sermons the end of both seigniorial rights and the payment of royal taxes. They assured the peasants that if they converted to the new religion they would no longer have to pay 'any homage to the gentry, or any tax to the king'. If tax agents came to ask for the rents on their property the peasants could answer simply 'that they would show them what the Bible said about whether they had to pay'. This myth was apparently current then, at the start of the wars of religion in 1562. By the time of the Croquant rising, however, it was an old chestnut. It was well known by now that there was nothing in Protestant doctrine which posed any challenge to the established social order.

The mercenary myth appears in two independent sources, both of them provincial chroniclers. These chroniclers trace the origins of the *Tard Avisés* and their gatherings right back to the darkest years of the reign of Jean the Good. They list a whole series of famous mercenaries of the past, recalling, for instance, the havoc wrought by Seguin de Badefol, a soldier who fought in Périgord in 1361 and was known as the 'king of the companies', and Rodrigue de Villandrando, who headed a band of the brigands known as *écorcheurs* in Armagnac in the years after 1430; by the rioters known as *maillotins* who rose up in Paris in 1382 and the peasants called *Jacques* who revolted in Beauvaisis in 1385; by the princes who organized the rebellion which went by the name of the *Praguerie* in 1440 and the peasants called *Gautiers* who ravaged Normandy as recently as 1589. Many provincial scholars of this kind would no doubt have remembered the devastation caused by mercenary bands in earlier centuries; and in this sense the Croquant assemblies may have aroused old spectres. At the same time the connection made between Croquants and mercenaries could well have owed something to a similarity of name. The *Tard Avisés* were reminiscent of the *Tard Venus*. The companies of mercenaries who roamed through France in the mid-fourteenth century were known as the *Tard Venus* (Latecomers) because they arrived on the scene after twenty years of fighting, when England and France had concluded the Treaty of Brétigny and people had begun to hope that peace might be returning at last.

The Swiss myth was the most widespread of the different fantasies. Observers claimed that the *Tard Avisés* had got their ideas of revolt from studying the example of the free cantons of Switzerland. Bourdeille noted that they 'beat their drums in the Swiss fashion'. The compact drawn up by the nobles of Sarladais accused the Croquants of aiming 'to establish a democracy on the model of the Swiss'. 'In the Swiss style' was positively a common phrase at this period. Each faction tried to besmirch the reputation of its rivals by accusing them of planning to launch a revolt 'in the Swiss style'. The *Tard Avisés* were not the only group accused of wanting to imitate the Swiss: the same accusation was hurled at both Protestants and members of the Catholic League. De La Noue wrote how 'some of the people complain of the arrogance of the nobles and would like to deal with them in the Swiss way – even though the Swiss have not in fact done all they things they suppose'. The system by which the cantons were organized in Switzerland was plainly thought of as anarchy. Power in that country was felt to have passed wholesale into the hands of an ignorant populace. The myth was reinforced by the presence of

Swiss troops in every army on the continent. Visitors to every camp in Europe could glimpse their mountain customs or hear their yodelling and their coarse Teutonic speech. Maskers at carnivals delighted in copying their long pikes, baggy breeches and great blond beards. Pamphleteers drew attention to the military renown they had won through their victories against the Austrians and Burgundians in the previous century, and the startling speed with which their largest cities had succumbed to the Reformation.

Gentry in the assemblies

The best informed chronicler of the rising, Palma Cayet, has very little to say about Croquant hostility to the nobles or the myths of revolution to which such hostility gave rise; and the original documents put out by the *Tard Avisés* themselves say nothing on these subjects at all. The circular letter composed on 2 June 1594 by the assemblies at Chéronnac and Saint-Julien – at the very time those assemblies were besieging towns and châteaux – gives, on the contrary, a most unrevolutionary impression. The Croquants spoke of 'living and dying for the service of the king' and of maintaining 'the orders of Church, nobility and judiciary' without which 'the state cannot survive'. In particular they noted the adherence to their cause, in Limousin and Angoumois, of 'a large number of seigneurs and gentry of blameless character ... who have vowed to give us every assistance against these robbers'. The seigneurs of Périgord and Limousin did undoubtedly play an important role in the rising. We have seen how a number of landowners such as Galiot de La Tour 'forced their subjects to arm' and in so doing helped to launch the assembly movement. The Bureau of Finance at Limoges knew very well that the resistance to taxation in their region would not have grown as it had done without the blessing of the landowners. The only way to get the people paying their taxes once again was, in their judgement, to advise the seigneurs to lend a hand. The Croquants for their part reckoned that the seigneurs had the power to make their tenants join the assemblies. None of this would make sense if the atmosphere in the provinces had been truly one of class war.

In August 1595 Marshal de Matignon censured the seneschal Bourdeille for taking the field against the Croquants. The Council sent letters extending an amnesty to the rebels, declaring that Bourdeille had misconstrued the nature of the assemblies and had encroached on the authority of the crown. Some remarks of Tarde's throw light on the government's attitude. 'The Croquant army', he observed, 'did not consist wholly of peasants or craftsmen. A third of their following were young people of good family or veterans who had borne arms in the late wars. In view of this the nobles trod warily.' Some of the gentry actually took part in the assemblies. Their involvement is clearly attested in the letters sent to the king by the governors of Marche and Guyenne and the delegates who served in the *parlement* at Bordeaux. These dignitaries reported how 'a number of seigneurs gave secret support to these popular insurrections ... and some of the nobility took part in them'.

Only two of these dissident gentry are known to us by name. One was an individual called Joseph de La Ville, who is listed in our sources as one of the captains of the *Tard Avisés* of Agenais. The documents describe him as a knight. The other, outstanding example was Marc de Cugnac, the lord of Giverzac. Giverzac's family mansion was in Sarladais, close by Domme, and he also had a second stately home at Sermet, in the woods of Villefranche-du-Périgord. Two of the assemblies organised by the *Tard Avisés*, the assemblies of La Trappe and La Bessède, were held near his residences. We know for certain that Giverzac was present at the first of these meetings, and that he promised 'his help to the Third Estate'. When La Saigne issued his summons to the citizens of Domme, Giverzac backed it up with a note recommending them to heed it. These two letters were addressed to the consuls of Domme and to Vivans, the Huguenot gentleman who commanded the garrison in the town. La Saigne and Giverzac ordered these worthies to rally to the *Tard Avisés* and to free the prisoners whom they had interned in their château for non-payment of taxes – prisoners who included a number of tenant farmers from Vivans's country estates. Vivans took the letters as a personal insult. As soon as the assembly had dispersed he got his soldiers to wheel out a *couleuvrine* (a long, slender cannon) and blast Giverzac's mansion to the ground. Vivans became a conspicious defender of the established order. Bourdeille mentions him in a list of the gentry who were most vehemently opposed to the Croquants, and he was also, as we saw earlier, one of the league of Sarladais nobles who signed a compact to help each other against the insurgency. Later he served as deputy for Basse-Guyenne in a number of political assemblies that were organized by the Huguenots, and was rewarded for his loyalty to the authorities by a series of appointments to prestigious garrison commands. Giverzac, however, was ruined by his part in the adventure. He went on fighting up to the end of the civil wars in the ranks of the Catholic League. In the summer of 1605 he snatched at a new chance of glory by joining in the Bouillon plot. He was given the assignment of raising a force of 500 cavalry and seizing control of the town of Cahors. The plot was a failure. Giverzac was sentenced to death *in absentia*, but granted a pardon in August the following year.

The assemblies which met in Saintonge in September 1595 were also headed by gentry. Some of these gentlemen bore names of considerable distinction. They were not connected exclusively with any single faction: some of them had fought on the Catholic and some on the Huguenot side in the course of the civil wars. These various examples present a picture very different from what one might have expected to find. At the very least they show that the cause of the *Tard Avisés* cannot be simply identified with any particular religious faction or social group.

The end of the assemblies

All the sources agree that the revolt of the *Tard Avisés* disintegrated abruptly. After the battles of Pousses in Limousin and Saint-Crépin in Périgord, the Croquants scattered, and in a matter of a few days all trace of them had vanished from the roads. The anonymous chronicler of Saint-Léonard records the transformation: 'From that time on there was no more talk of Croquants.'

Tarde sums up similarly: 'They lost heart, split up, ran out of money and went back to ploughing.' The swift defeats of the Croquants are easily explained. It is clear from the history of every revolt which took place at this period that bands of common people were unable to stand firm when confronted by a contingent of mounted noblemen or professional soldiers. They broke ranks no matter how numerous they were, and no matter how well armed. Harder to account for is the apparently total collapse of any urge to rebel.

The simplest explanation of this phenomenon is that the grounds for the uprising had been removed. The peasant demands had been satisfied. By the spring of 1595 the south-western provinces had been completely pacified; the Catholic League no longer maintained any garrisons outside a handful of isolated regions such as the central Pyrenees or the mountains of the Auvergne. Marshal de Matignon was exerting all the authority he possessed to forestall disorders and risings. As soon as he learnt the news of Bourdeille's operation at Saint-Crépin he sent off a gentleman with urgent commands for the seneschal. Bourdeille was to halt his campaign and disband the force he had mustered as soon as possible. The peasants were not hunted down. The Count of Ambleville resisted all moves to hang the Croquant captains taken at Condat-sur-Vézère, and no proceedings were initiated against the syndics of the rebel parishes or the colonels of the rebel regiments. In August 1595 the government rushed through its edict of amnesty, without even waiting till the last of the Croquant assemblies had drawn to an end. Certain judicial inquiries were set in motion at the *parlement* in Bordeaux as the result of complaints received from a number of Catholic gentry whose property had been pillaged by the troops of the Third Estate. In July 1596, however, all these inquiries were suspended on Matignon's orders. On 30 November 1596 the Council issued a decree forbidding any further legal investigation of the events which had taken place.

The end of the civil wars meant also the end of private taxation and the holding of peasants to ransom; and the Council abandoned all attempts to collect those tax arrears that could plainly not be recovered. The authorities were slower to countenance any reduction in tax for the current year. The campaign against the Catholic League had been brought to a successful conclusion in September 1595; for another three years, however, from 1595 to 1598, the armies on the frontiers were still engaged in the war with Spain. And their operations had to be financed. Peasants in Poitou and Limousin continued to offer sporadic resistance to the taxman right up to the end of the Spanish war.

After the war, however, this resistance abruptly ceased. From 1598 onwards the decrees put out by the Council make no further reference to peasant agitation in any province of France. Hostility to the taxman undoubtedly continued. In 1597 the Council judged that they could get away with imposing a tax on the circulation and consumption of goods in the towns at the rate of 'a *sou* for every pound', and in 1599 they made an attempt to introduce it. Opposition to the new tax was instant and nation-wide. Riots broke out in Poitiers in May 1601, and in Limoges in April 1602. These riots, however, were exclusively the work of the poorer people in the towns, and no disturbance whatever took place in the countryside. The plots of Biron and Bouillon were confined to the minor aristocracy of Périgord and Limousin, and in any case had hardly been woven before they unravelled. So far as the countryside was concerned, the reign of Henri IV really was what tradition depicts it: a peaceful time when taxes were collected without difficulty and the peasants had the leisure to dance. The assemblies of the *Tard Avisés* had stopped short, the rebels had calmed down, and the whole upheaval had ended without any after-effects. This lack of an aftermath is not, in fact, surprising. The peasant revolts of 1594–5 were not the result of any kind of endemic social conflict, but simply expressed discontent with the chaotic political situation which happened to prevail at that particular time.

Peasant risings caused by the civil wars

We noted earlier how peasant movements similar to that in Périgord sprang up to some degree in every part of France in response to the continuing civil strife. We can see from a brief survey of these other disturbances how nearly they coincided with the troubles in the south-west, and how closely they resembled them. In April 1589, for example, the Gautiers rose up in Perche and Lower Normandy. The Gautiers were peasants who adhered to the Catholic League, and they followed their seigneurs into action against the royalist army commanded by the Duke of Montpensier. In Cornouaille and Léon, in 1589–90, other Catholic peasants laid waste the châteaux of the Huguenot and Navarrese gentry. The mountain people of Le Comminges armed themselves to resist the incursions of bands of soldiery coming up from the plains. In the autumn of 1592 they took revenge on the Huguenot raiders, setting off under the leadership of captains employed by the Marquis de Villars to devastate the countryside of Bigorre. In August 1594 they took up arms yet again in a rising which continued into the early months of the following year. They formed themselves into a mutual defence league which went under the grandiose title of the 'Conference and Holy Congregation of the Catholic, Apostolic and Roman faith'. Their leaders on this occasion were the Baron de Larboust, the seneschal of Aure and a village merchant by the name of Jean Désirat who was well known to the valley-dwellers of the High Pyrenees.

In Burgundy the position was reversed. Huguenot peasants sounded the tocsin to warn of the advent of troops of the Catholic League. These peasants were active in the regions of Beaunois, Chalonnais and Mâconnais. They were known as the 'Redcaps' (*Bonnets Rouges*). They rose up in January 1594, and again in 1597. In the Velay mountains the disturbances were instigated by the lord of Chevrières, who served as governor of the region on behalf of Henri IV. He stirred up the peasants against the towns of Puy and Yssingeaux, which were holding out for the League. The peasants who massed in the Velay region were actually known as 'Croquants' like their fellows in Périgord. They took to the roads in the spring of 1595, and kept up their campaign till the summer.

These movements were all disorganized and lacking in cohesion. They reflected solely the natural instinct of peasant communities to guard their homes – the frustration of country people who had been goaded beyond endurance by the constant breaking of truces and the bandit raids of marauding soldiery. They did not in any way weaken the ties of loyalty which bound the peasants to their superiors, and specifically to the local seigneur: on the contrary, the seigneur often played a conspicuous part in leading his tenants against the enemy raiders. The factions in each region exploited the peasant assemblies with considerable skill, playing on local grievances and prodding the peasants to take the field for the Catholic League or the king of Navarre as the case might be. Each of these movements, finally, was limited in terms of both the time it lasted and the area it affected. The rising of the *Tard Avisés* in south-west France lasted longer and spread further than any of the other disturbances. It was an altogether larger affair.

The *Tard Avisés* began their agitation, as we have seen, at the end of 1593, and did not disperse completely till September to October of 1595. At the time when the assembly movement achieved its greatest geographical expansion, in June 1594, the waves of revolt had rolled across the country from the 'epicentre' in the Limousin-Périgord region and were spreading south into Agenais, Quercy and even Gascony, west into Angoumois and Saintonge, and north as far as Marche and the borders of Berry. There was no disturbance, however, in the countryside of either Gascony or Poitou; and the peasant movement never crossed the Loire. The area covered corresponded closely to that affected by the rebellion of 1548. Most of the later outbreaks of resistance to the taxman which took place in our period were also confined to this area. These later risings were often organised on much the same lines as the movement of the *Tard Avisés* had been. Many of the procedures were identical. Peasant assemblies were held in every part of the countryside; local communities were bombarded with invitations to attend, which grew steadily more pressing as the peasant bands drew closer; manifestos were drawn up by the more literate rebel villagers, written and copied and circulated to every *châtellenie*; peasant recruits were formed into regiments and the larger towns were summoned to rally to the cause. The rising which flared up in south-west France in 1594 served, accordingly, as a prototype for all the revolts which followed. The rebels of 1594 were, incidentally, the first to be known as the Croquants; and they also bequeathed their name.

The *Tard Avisés* rose up against the predatory nobles and their marauding garrisons, ever-present evils spawned by thirty years of war. These enemies had taken over the royal function of raising taxes, and were consequently, in the Croquant view, robbing both the king and his people. In protesting against this usurpation of the traditional kingly powers, the *Tard Avisés* may well have been mounting an unconscious rebellion against the advent of the modern state. By resisting the garrison soldiers, however, they were also, at a more basic level, defending their freedom and dignity. Ordinary people were anxious to defend themselves against the billeting of troops and the garnering of taxes, and this defensive urge remained a characteristic ingredient of the revolts that broke out in the course of the next hundred years.

One feature in particular may perhaps be said to distinguish the revolt of the *Tard Avisés* in 1594–5 from the other contemporary movements we have glanced at. They were uncompromisingly hostile to the towns. Their documents voice more clearly and more explicitly than any other source of the period the growing popular reaction to the rise of the urban bourgeoisie. La Saigne's manifestos, for instance, portray the city as being the bane of country people. It is the instrument by which the peasant population has been oppressed and reduced to slavery. It has snatched away their rustic liberties, encroached on their lands, and shattered the old cohesion of their small communities. From beginning to end of their rising the *Tard Avisés* were, first and foremost, the party of the countryside.

By 1598 the kingdom of France was at long last rid of both civil and foreign conflicts, and Henri IV was able to reign in peace. Unfortunately he had little more than a dozen years left to live. Contemporaries soon looked back on this time as a golden age. The minority of Louis XIII was equally untroubled by either political upheavals or natural disasters, and so were the first few years in which he ruled in his own right. The power struggles which took place at court in the course of the regency barely had any effect on daily life in the provinces. The local wars of religion were another matter. Fresh outbreaks of these racked the countryside in 1621–2, 1625–6 and again in the period between the summer of 1627 and June 1629 when the government troops laid siege to La Rochelle. South-western France was particularly affected by the fighting. Immediately after these wars, from 1628 to 1632, the kingdom was convulsed by a demographic catastrophe. A series of disastrous harvests coincided with the advent of a Europe-wide epidemic of plague. The effects of this double calamity were little short of apocalyptic. In towns such as Aurillac, Cahors and Bergerac, nearly half the population appears to have died.

It was in these dramatic circumstances that Cardinal Richelieu arrived at his decision to plunge France into the conflict that had raged through Germany and Austria ever since 1618 – the Thirty Years War. War necessarily meant an increase in taxation; and Richelieu's decision gave a fresh impetus to the French monarchy's protracted effort to create a centralized tax system. The pursuit of this effort was marked, however, by outbursts of popular resentment. In June 1624, for example, a band of Croquants in Quercy took up arms in a short-lived expression of anger at the government's attempt to extend the tax network by setting up élections. The administration of taxes was to be handled by the offices attached to the élections, rather than channelled through the local estates as had formerly been the case. In 1628 riots broke out in response to the establishment of bureaux de traites (customs offices). Wine and salt were shipped down the rivers Charente and Sèvre, and so, at this surprisingly early date, were spirits; and the authorities had set up these bureaux with a view to taxing the river trade. The general discontent reached its climax in 1635. In the very year in which the government finally entered into open war with Spain, widespread unrest boiled over in a series of the most dangerous popular risings the French monarchy had ever to face. The turmoil continued almost uninterrupted for a period of nearly two decades.

From May to July 1635 a terrible series of riots broke out in the towns. The cause of these riots was a tax which the authorities had ill-advisedly imposed on low-grade wine. The tax was levied on innkeepers, and its effect was to make them put up the price of the wine they sold. The first burst of rioting took place at Bordeaux on 14 May. On 17 June further bloody clashes shattered the calm of Périgueux and Agen, and before long dozens of small towns and villages in the middle Garonne, the lower Dordogne, Bourgès, Blayais and the southern part of Saintonge were experiencing disturbances of a more or less protracted and murderous nature, as the rioters vented their fury on the bailiffs who had been sent to collect the taxes and the officials in the employment of the élections. *I have studied this phenomenon in the greatest possible detail, and have reconstructed the spread of rumours, slogans and patterns of violence. The events of these months constituted a positive 'epidemic' of rebellion, unmatched till the Great Fear* (Grande Peur) *of July 1789. The Great Fear, of course, broke out on the eve of the French Revolution, and is consequently better known.*

These events of 1635 are described in detail on pp. 294–363 of the 1974 edition. To a great extent they were confined to the cities, and the rioters had little contact with the surrounding countryside. I have accordingly felt it reasonable to cut the 1635 riots from this narrative, to meet the demands of the present, drastically shortened, version of the book.

During 1636 the resistance to taxation centred on Angoumois and Saintonge. The protesters were peasants this time. The spring fairs which were held in the Charente region became the scene of a succession of peasant assemblies. The peasants drew up political manifestos addressed to the king and demanding that he should administer their taxes in a just and conciliatory manner as they imagined his forebears had done (see pp. 364–402 of the 1974 edition). I have also omitted this chapter to satisfy the requirements of the present, abridged text.

3

The Rising of the Communes of Périgord, 1637–1641

The beginnings of the rising

The rising of the communes of Périgord between 1637 and 1641 is the best known of all the events considered in this book. It was, in fact, the largest peasant revolt in the whole of French history. More peasants gathered to fight in it than in any other rising, not counting the wars of the Vendée in 1793–6; and no other rising got nearer to achieving its goals.

When contemporaries in the seventeenth century and historians of later times spoke of Croquant rebellions, it was this revolt, *par excellence*, which they meant. People's imagination was caught by the unfamiliar spectacle, as armed peasant hosts unfurled their flags in the meadows of the Dordogne, obscure country squires sallied forth to fight from the shelter of their mansions, and the local village cocks of the walk took on high-sounding titles and convinced themselves, for a season, that they were celebrated warriors and dispensers of the law.

The taxes at the root of the rising: 'rations' and 'borrowings'

Various taxes were due to be paid in the course of 1637. All the chroniclers agree, however, that the most pernicious of these levies, the one directly responsible for the great uprising that followed, was the special tax which went under the name of 'rations for the army at Bayonne'. On 16 December 1636 an ordinance had been issued under the signature of the Duke of Épernon, then governor of Guyenne, and the Duke of La Valette, who commanded the Army of the Basque region. This ordinance directed the judges of all the crown courts in the province to levy corn from the communities in their jurisdiction, the quantity depending on the relative size and importance of each place taxed. The grain was to be loaded in sacks and transported in carts and barges to the warehouses of Dax and Mont-de-Marsan which were used to store the provisions of the army at Bayonne. In February 1637 the requested shipment began to take place. In view of the market price which corn fetched at that period, the 'rations' represented a pretty substantial imposition upon the peasantry. Exactions costing 9,228 *livres* were made, for instance, from the *sénéchaussée* of Agenais, and 6,348 *livres* were raised from the small region of Rivière-Verdun. The communities had to borrow the corn from the granaries of merchants or charitable foundations, and pay them back by levying a tax upon themselves. The effect of the 'rations', then, was to add considerably to the overall tax burden.[1] Épernon and La Valette went ahead with the tax without either awaiting the authorization of a specific royal warrant or submitting it to the scrutiny of the local financial officials. These irregular proceedings caused considerable public comment. In May, after three months, the army warehouses had still not been restocked.

As the year 1637 wore on it became known that the *élection* officials were working on the apportionment of a special increase designed to raise a total of 150,000 *livres* from the *généralité* of Bordeaux. The authorities justified this increase, like the 'rations' before it, by the need to supply the army at Bayonne, and the tax was referred to formally in the official documents as 'an increase for equipping our forces in Guyenne'. This increase was calculated on the same base of assessment as the original taxes, but was levied separately from them and before the beginning of the fiscal year. The taxpayers were also required to make a special contribution towards the expenses of the taxmen, at a time when they had barely recovered from paying for the upkeep of the troops who had been billeted all over the province in winter quarters. The tax increase only served to strengthen the growing popular feeling that the province was being systematically milked.

The methods used to conduct the regular tax assessment changed quite appreciably in the course of 1637, and so did the amounts of money the government sought to raise. The crown announced these changes in a proclamation issued on 18 December 1636, and decrees implementing them were sent out to every part of the kingdom the following March. In each *généralité* the sum to be raised was divided into two equal parts. One half of the taxes were to be gathered from the peasant taxpayers in the countryside, and the other half were to be contributed by the people of the cities and market towns. On the pretext of combating the danger which threatened on the frontiers and defending the crown, the government extended the scope of this second half of the levy to cover not only the cities which were ordinarily subject to taxes, but also the privileged towns which had hitherto been accorded special rights or tax-free status. The authorities tried to distinguish this new tax from the traditional levies imposed elsewhere by calling it a 'lending and borrowing grant', or a 'borrowing' for short. The idea was to give the impression that the citizens affected were making a voluntary donation of emergency funds in response to the exceptional peril of the time. The device fooled no one. Provincial intendants took little trouble even to sustain the pretence, and talked bluntly in their letters of the 'taxes raised from the borrowing'. In the same way the government aimed to convince the peasants that the extra taxes imposed on the towns would lighten the burden on them. The preamble to the royal edict emphasized this point. 'We have cast our eyes', said the king, 'on our poor people in the countryside who have been reduced to poverty by the ravages of war, and have taken pains to relieve them, so far as has lain in our power, by according a considerable decrease in the taxes they have paid us in recent years.' The truth was rather different. When the taxes farmed out in 1636 and 1637 were compared systematically, on a parish-by-parish

---

1 The 'costs' given here can be only approximate, since the documents express the weights in *conques* (one *conque* corresponds to 60 pounds in weight).

basis, total taxation proved to have actually risen by a third. This point was conceded by no less a figure than Villemontée, the intendant of Poitou.

The urgency of the government's needs and its total ignorance of the real situation in the provinces drove it to tax its subjects to an extent they were no longer able to endure. On 10 March 1637 a decree was issued prescribing the immediate renewal of demands for the arrears that had accumulated in the two previous years, and revoking the rebates which had been accorded during that time. One of the taxes reinstated by this measure was the hated levy known as the *droits aliénés*, a surtax imposed in addition to the *tailles* in 1634 as a form of remuneration for the tax collectors. In previous years a portion of the *tailles* had been diverted or 'alienated' for their benefit. This levy was commonly believed to benefit no one but tax farmers and usurers. The government's decrees did not take effect immediately. The assessment of the 'borrowings' was difficult to make and delayed any effort to collect them, and the tax collectors' agents got to work only in the course of the summer. Already, however, word was spreading through the countryside that taxes were going up, that the government was imposing new levies without good reason and was going back on its rebates. People remarked on the fact that the rations were being raised without the authorization of a royal warrant; that the taxmen were assessing them for the new-fangled borrowings; and that levies they thought had been abolished were being imposed once more. They were growing increasingly certain that the king was being cheated, and his people robbed. The increase in taxes happened to coincide with the arrival in Bordeaux of the niece of Cardinal Richelieu, the youthful Duchess of La Valette. People claimed that the duchess was misappropriating the tax revenues, and the levies which had been raised to support the army at Bayonne were commonly referred to as 'the dowry of Madame de La Valette'. Serious trouble was brewing. As early as January the bailiffs were refusing to go to the villages with the warrants for gathering the funds intended to equip the forces in Guyenne – out of fear that the people might attack them. The chief tax collectors of Bordeaux and Montauban stayed prudently in Paris, and were content to operate through agents. 'I note', said the intendant Verthamont, 'that they have fully appreciated how difficult and dangerous it would be for them to carry out their business in this province at the present time.' By April sergeants had to be used to collect the rations in Périgord. The dispatch of these sergeants goaded the peasants to open revolt. 'The Duke of Épernon had directed that certain sums of money should be levied from this region, saying that he needed these funds to provision his army, which was currently engaged in the defence of Bayonne. The peasants however reacted so violently to this order that they lynched the sergeants who had been sent to distribute the tax warrants.' A leading citizen of Agen recorded his shock at these developments. 'People are going quite crazy and are openly denouncing these rations and taxes on corn. We are seriously frightened that everyone will follow the example of the men in Périgord.'[2]

---

2 This quotation is taken from the *Histoire du duc d'Épernon* ('Life of the Duke of Epernon') which was composed in about 1660 by his secretary, Guillaume Girard, and published successively in Paris (3 vols, 1663; 4 vols, 1730) and Amsterdam (1736). Épernon and his son La Valette both

The onset of the rising

The revolt flared up with a speed that astonished contemporaries.

Most of the risings of this kind unfold, as a general rule, in several stages, and we usually notice the trouble brewing before it breaks out. This insurrection, however, raged with unparalleled fury from the moment it was conceived. It was like one of those great fires which lie smouldering for a long while, then suddenly shoot out flames so high that they become virtually impossible to quench.

It was common enough for the subject population to voice their resentment at taxes they regarded as excessive. But resentment seldom bred violence. Such violent protests as did take place were isolated and failed to spread. Now, unexpectedly, the authorities found themselves confronted with the spectacle of organized rebel bands which poured out of the countryside and merged, within a week, into a fully-fledged peasant army. The time of petty skirmishes with scattered gangs of malcontents was suddenly over. Instead they were dealing with a multitude of tens of thousands of rebels, and a whole province was in arms.

The rising had in fact been brewing in the country parishes for a good two years. In June 1635 the citizens of Périgueux sounded the tocsin to summon the peasants from the neighbouring districts to help them drive out the excisemen who had forced up the price of their wine. In the final months of 1635 and throughout 1636, sergeants sent to gather the taxes had been lynched in the most distant villages, and it was only by providing their officers with an escort of bowmen that the authorities had been able to collect any taxes at all. Some of the peasants went to fairs in the neighbouring province of Angoumois, and brought back news of the assemblies which were being held there by people in the local *châtellenies*; and the manifestos drawn up by the rebels at those assemblies were read in the Périgord taverns. News also spread through the countryside of the amnesties and tax rebates that had been granted by the king, and these acts of royal clemency aroused considerable discussion. The time was ripe for a rising. The peasants of the communes were long since used to gathering in time of peril and running when the tocsin rang. They were hardened to warfare by years of living in constant insecurity, embittered by their hatred for the public enemy, the exciseman, and gravely disturbed to learn in the official proclamations that new kinds of taxes were being intro-duced. They were all prepared to rally together as soon as the summons reached them and organize a grand campaign of resistance to the ceaseless demands for tax.

The initial outbreak of violence took place, as we have seen, in the spring of 1637. On 22 April two sergeants sent to raise taxes for their *élection* in the

---

played a major role in suppressing the Croquant revolt of 1637, and this work is consequently one of the most important primary sources for the events of that year.

Périgord countryside were murdered by the peasants. Their bodies were found not far from Nanteuil de Bourzac, on the high road from Auriac, or in other words on the borders of the two most disaffected *châtellenies* in Angoumois, Montmoreau and Aubeterre. In the days that followed a similar fate befell a number of other agents who had set off with their escorts to distribute the warrants for the tax being levied on behalf of the army at Bayonne. The peasants killed them, injured them or put them to flight. This distribution of warrants seems to have triggered off the rising. Everywhere the peasants responded by arranging meetings and choosing leaders. Much of the organization of the rising seems to have taken place in the canton known as Le Paréage.

Paréage was a term of seigniorial law which referred to the joint exploitation by two seigneurs of a given seigniory. Le Paréage was a group of some twenty parishes which had been administered jointly since 1307 by the counts of Périgord and the cathedral chapter of Saint-Front in Périgueux. These parishes covered a forest region 15 by 20 kilometres in area. The forest was called the forest of Vergt, and it lay astride the immediate approaches to Périgueux, a league to the south of the River Isle. The forest also straddled the road from Périgueux to Bergerac, which served as the major highway between Limousin and Guyenne. Burgesses from Périgueux owned all the larger houses in the forest, and farmed smallholdings in the glades.

The warrants for raising taxes for the army at Bayonne were brought to Le Paréage by a bowman of the local *vice-sénéchaussée* (vice-seneschal's jurisdiction) named Jean Chaleppe. Chaleppe owned a small amount of property in the parishes, and also had the right to administer justice in one of the forest settlements, the hamlet of Breuilh. He arrived with his warrants in Sanilhac, at the mouth of the forest, a village which contained the shrine of Notre-Dame-des-Vertus, the most sacred place of pilgrimage in the whole of Périgord. An old woman of the village asked him what sort of warrants he was carrying. Chaleppe was foolish enough to indulge in a sick joke. He said with a snigger that he was bringing the warrants for the *gabelle*. He was promptly chased from the village, and his house there was burnt to the ground. A local gentleman called Antoine de Ribeyreix thereupon harangued the people of Le Paréage and urged them to rise in revolt. Church after church rang the tocsin, and a crowd of 4,000 to 5,000 people gathered from all around. This crowd immediately set off to lay siege to the nearest town – Périgueux. Périgueux enjoyed the privilege of being exempt from the regular *tailles*, and was at the same time, to add insult to injury, the home of the excisemen.

On 1 May the peasants appeared before the town 'in an armed mass'. They called on the citizens to open the gates to them, to provide them with cannons, and to hand the excisemen over to them for execution. The citizens however ignored this call and kept a close guard on their gates. The rebels consequently went off to devastate the neighbourhood. They ransacked the country houses of the burgesses and ravaged the estates of the most notorious excisemen. The next step was to hold their first assembly. This gathering took place in some large meadows known as Les Terriennes which stretched from the Taillefer gate at the western end of Périgueux to the town's small river-port on the banks of the Isle. The rebel communities used the assembly to announce the rules they had adopted to govern their activities and the name of the leader they had chosen. This leader was a gentleman of Périgueux called La Mothe-La-Forest. Finally the rebels appointed a number of envoys who were to fan out through the province and summon all the communities to a general meeting. The meeting was set to take place in a few days' time.

The mayor of Périgueux and the *lieutenant-général* of the local *sénéchaussée* were away in Bordeaux. On 4 May Bordeaux got word of the rebellion, and the two men both set off for their homes with all due speed. The mayor reached his destination: the *lieutenant-général* was not so lucky. Jean de Jay, seigneur of Ataux, had been one of the principal targets of the rioters who rose up in Périgueux in 1635. Now, two years later, the Croquants were equally anxious to catch him, since it was he who had been responsible for conducting the assessment for the rations tax. He tried to hide in the house of a friend, but was found and taken captive. Between 8,000 and 10,000 peasants were involved in the operation, and they led him under close guard to the forest of Vergt, which was only a short distance off.

On 7 or 8 May the rebels held their second assembly. This second gathering proved to be the largest and most decisive in the history of the revolt. It took place in the heart of the forest, between the hamlets of Bordas and Pont-Saint-Mamet. The site of the assembly was referred to as La Vernide, after a pool of stagnant water which lay somewhere in the vicinity, or alternatively as Plaistidiou, after a stretch of bare moorland which flanked the Périgueux–Bergerac road in this area for a distance of several leagues. No less than 30,000 men are said to have attended. Their leader, La Mothe-La-Forest, was presented to them. He picked out the likeliest soldiers from the various communities, and selected the best weapons from the motley arsenal in the hands of the peasant host. By this means he was able to form an organized peasant army of about 8,000 men. He appointed officers to lead them and arranged for their parish syndics to keep them on a war footing. The rejects he sent back home.

On 10 May a third assembly gathered in front of Bergerac, in the meadows beside the Dordogne. The army of the communes drew itself up in battle formation, sixty well-ordered companies with their banners flying in the breeze. At the end of the afternoon four rebel horsemen rode beneath the walls of Bergerac to the sound of a drum. They stopped before each of the town gates and called on the citizens to let their army in. Bergerac was unfortified and had no garrison to defend it.[3] The following day the Croquants made their entry into the town.

---

3 According to a description of the time, the town of Bergerac was 'situated at the heart of Guyenne in a fertile territory, rich in corn and wine. The river Dordogne flows past it, and there is a fine bridge which supports a large trade between the adjoining provinces; and the river is easily navigable. A large number of people consequently made their homes in this town in the time of the late King Henri IV, and as a result of its convenience for trade and the goodness of the local soil, the town became powerful and full of wealth in the pleasant peacetime conditions.' See Archives Nationales, E157b, fo. 283.

The town consisted of two parishes and 800 households. It levied minor duties on trade, which

The Croquants were now masters of a thriving town inhabited by a prosperous Protestant bourgeoisie. Bergerac was both a commercial centre and a seat of the royal justices. It also possessed the strategic asset of a stone bridge which crossed the Dordogne.

Well equipped, ably organized, the people of the communes were now in a position to march wherever they pleased. They could head for either Guyenne or Agenais as the fancy took them. There was, for the moment, no force powerful enough to resist them, and the whole of Périgord seemed to be swinging to their side. 'All the communities', a chronicler noted, 'were so well disposed to this faction that there was scarcely a town in the province they could not claim to control.' Another writer observed how 'several persons of rank and people from every walk of life were instigating this rising and supporting the rebels with the most brazen effrontery.' The victory of the Croquants, however, was only superficial. It lasted exactly twenty days.

Those twenty days were, none the less, an exceptional episode, unique in the long, monotonous, heart-rending record of abortive peasant revolts. Let us take advantage of this interlude to pause for a moment and examine the personalities of the men who led the communes, the aims which inspired them and the documents they drew up.

The leaders of the peasant army

According to the account of the rising written by Chevalier de Cablanc, the first leader to emerge was Antoine de Ribeyreix, nicknamed the Turk, or the Turk of Grignols. The Turk was in fact a knight. He was seigneur of Lartige, La Jarthe and La Cottebouille, and captain of the county of Grignols. The county of Grignols marched with the western border of Le Paréage, and Ribeyreix was consequently well known to the peasants who lived in the villages of that district. He had led them before, in crises when the communes armed to defend themselves against raids launched by the Protestant strongholds of southern Périgord, and also on more ordinary occasions when the woods were beaten for wolves. Chevalier de Cablanc tells us how he placed himself at their head. 'Ribeyreix the Turk persuaded the people of Le Paréage to rise in revolt, and drummed it into them that they should set this affair in motion.' The Turk played a crucial role in the first few days of the rebellion. He served as spokesman for the Croquants. He may have been the spokesman who called on Périgueux to surrender, and he certainly was the herald who bore the

---

brought in revenues of up to 1,720 *livres* a year. At the same time it enjoyed a signal privilege in the form of exemption from the state taxes (see Bibliothèque Nationale, ms.fr.24056, fo. 45).

Bergerac's walls had been slighted in 1631 as a punishment for its participation in the Protestant uprisings. The people were almost all Huguenots. In 1636 they had started building what they intended to be the finest Protestant church in the entire province, and on 10 April 1637 the roof had been formally installed in the presence of the Lady of Monbazillac. The church was put up in the centre of the town, and a clock was fixed to its pediment. Work on the building was completed in 1643, and from them on it served as a meeting-place for the Protestant convocation of Basse-Guyenne. See *Jurades de Bergerac*, vol. 7, pp. 7–10, 306–8.

challenge of the communes to the citizens of Bergerac, and subsequently to the citizens of Sainte-Foy.

The general chosen by the communes was, to give him his full name, Antoine Du Puy, Esquire, lord of La Mothe and La Forest. La Mothe-La-Forest was a gentleman of good family. He was the scion of a noble house dating back to the fourteenth century, and his ancestors had married well. He was the elder son of François Du Puy, lord of La Forest and Cenat, and Marguerite de Bayly, daughter of the seigneur of Razac. At the time of the rising he was about fifty-five, and had spent all his life in the army. The chroniclers give a uniformly favourable account of his qualities, describing him as a 'man of mature years and ripe intelligence . . . an elderly man, well versed in the use of arms'. In 1622 La Mothe had married Jeanne de La Douze. His bride's father, Gabriel d'Abzac, who was already dead at this date, had been Marquis de La Douze, seigneur of Vergt and a gentleman of the bedchamber; her mother was Jeanne, Baroness of Lastours. The wedding was witnessed by La Mothe's brother-in-law, Charles d'Abzac, the new Marquis de La Douze, and his uncle, Alain de Bayly, seigneur of Razac. The family had estates in the neighbourhood of Périgueux, at Cornille to the north of the city and Sanilhac in Le Paréage, but La Mothe lived as a rule in the city itself, in a mansion owned by his wife, the château of Barrière. A naturally well-intentioned and unassuming man, he seems to have accepted the command of the Croquant army in a spirit of pure dedication and a belief that steps would quickly be taken to come to terms with the rebels as soon as the king became aware of the level of desperation to which his subjects in Périgord had been reduced. La Mothe was approached by the Croquants at the end of April. He asked for a few days to consider their request to lead the rising, and spent them praying in the oratory of Notre-Dame-des-Vertus. He emerged to announce 'that the Virgin had made known to him in a revelation the justice of their cause, and that he embraced it with all his heart'. He was hailed as leader either during the assembly at Les Terriennes or during the subsequent meeting at La Vernide. He dressed simply in a suit of linen clothes with lace cuffs, which he turned into a sort of rustic uniform by decorating it with wisps of straw, and assumed the title of general of the rebel communes of Périgord.

Another major leader was Léon de Laval, Baron de Madaillan, who was appointed to the rank of *maréchal de camp* (commanding officer) in the army of the communes. Madaillan, like La Mothe, was the scion of a modest but genuine noble house, and could trace his lineage back to the thirteenth century. His father, Jean-Jacques d'Albert, seigneur of Laval and Lévignac and Baron de Madaillan, had been killed in 1619 while besieging Les Échelles in Savoy at the head of his regiment. In 1616 the younger Madaillan had married the daughter of a certain Charles de Montalembert, who was serving as captain of a regiment in Picardy. Madaillan himself had served with the Swedes, and boasted of having been the lieutenant-colonel of a cavalry regiment which took part in the battles at Leipzig and Breslau in 1631. He was captured by the Imperialists at Lauenburg, and subsequently freed in return for a ransom of 1,000 *écus*. Later, in 1636, he raised two companies of cavalry at his own expense and led them into Roussillon. Two of his sons had been killed in action, one of them before Salces and the other before Corbie.

In the spring of 1637, Madaillan was staying on his estates between two expeditions. His château and property were situated in the parishes of Isaac and Saint-Romain, in the valley of the Dropt. The parishes lay between Eymet and Miramont, on the borders of Périgord and Agenais. Madaillan's family was Protestant, and he was currently involved in an inheritance dispute which was being heard by the *Chambre de l'édit* (bipartisan court containing both Catholic and Protestant members).

His reputation was nothing less than notorious. One chronicler described him as 'the most infamous and abominable gentleman in the kingdom by reason of his vices and execrable crimes'. A more detached observer called him 'a wicked, seditious man, uniquely skilled at intrigue and mischief-making ... He was strong and courageous, charming and quick-witted, capable of both devising plans and carrying them out. His family background was good, but his career was chequered with scandal'. Madaillan proved to be the cleverest and most determined of the rebel leaders.

According to the chroniclers, it was La Mothe-La-Forest himself who chose the officers of his army. He did so by singling out among the Croquants at the assemblies those who had most experience of war. Some of them had fought in the royal regiments, while others had simply served in the militias raised during the religious wars of the previous decade. La Mothe recognized them as captains of their parishes, or jurisdictions, or even admitted them to his council of war. These men are known to us only from laconic references made by witnesses in their testimonies and victims in their indictments, and the list of persons excluded from the royal amnesty after the rebellion was put down. Such sources have, however, enabled me to identify a total of sixty-three names. In twenty-five cases the names are literally all we have, and no further description is appended. This would have meant that the men were ploughmen from neighbouring hamlets, and their names alone were sufficient identification in the eyes of the plaintiff. Among those who had a title, a qualification or a trade, we find fourteen professional persons, namely: six judges of townships, four candidate attorneys, two notaries, a clerk and a lawyer. A further six were gentry. They included Pierre Bouchard d'Esparbès, Marquis d'Aubeterre, whose arrival the rebels awaited eagerly, Bernard de Montesquiou, Baron de Fages, and Jean de Fettes, known as La Mothe-Grignols or La Mothe-Selleys. All of these three men passed themselves off as captains.[4] Little is known about the three other gentlemen. Their names

---

4 In a judgement delivered by the intendant Foullé on 7 January 1638, Bernard de Montesquiou was condemned to death *in absentia* along with the consuls of Saint-Cyprien. On 18 February the vice-seneschal had the consuls' houses razed to the ground, together with Montesquiou's château of Fages overlooking the Dordogne. The parish bell of Saint-Cyprien was dismantled, and a stake was erected in the town square. The stake bore a bronze plaque setting out the details of the sentence.

Jean de Fettes bore the summons of the rebel army to the gates of Sainte-Foy. He was beheaded under a sentence passed by the commissioners of the provincial *parlement*.

are given as Périllac, a *maréchal de camp*, Des Marais, and Constantin de Bessou, known as Old Constantin. All of them were minor country squires who sat on the council of the communes. Six of the Croquants identified were traders or village craftsmen. There were two barbers, a messenger, a weaver, a carpenter and a currier of leather. Five of the leaders are described as being the owners of some smallholding. The Croquant high command included four priests, and just three merchants.

Only two commoners are known to have played a leading part in the rising. Buffarot, a weaver at Capdrot, near Monpazier, was the captain of the communities of Sarladais. His band on the borders of Périgord and Quercy numbered some 4,000 to 8,000 men according to contemporary accounts. He was said to have been 'a man of high courage and no experience'.

Jean Magot, a doctor of Périgueux, had played a role in the riot which broke out at Périgueux in June 1635. He had 'stirred up a commotion with his seditious harangues'. Magot was a sworn enemy of Jay d'Ataux, the *lieutenant-général*, as the result of various lawsuits which he had either lost or was currently engaged in. He was followed by peasants from three parishes of Le Paréage, around Montagnac-la-Crempse, 'where he carried on his intrigues'.

This dissection of the social background of the leaders reveals, then, that the rebellion took place within the customary framework of peasant life. In the three main categories of leaders, country gentlemen, parish priests and village craftsmen, we find the three familiar estates of the realm, intact and functioning at the lowly level of the commune. Even bearing in mind that both the victims of a rebellion and the authorities who put it down had a tendency to lay the blame on prominent individuals, it is evident that the communes were organized as a hierarchy. They reproduced in microcosm the traditional and respected order which prevailed in society as a whole.

The manifestos of the rebel communes of Périgord

Most of the texts which were written by the Croquants of Périgord are known thanks to an anthology which appears to have been put together by a citizen of Brienne. Other documents come down to us through a different channel. They would seem to have been passed on by informants in Agen or Bordeaux to Parisian correspondents like Pierre Dupuy, the royal librarian. We can identify a total of fourteen texts of Croquant origin.

The first in date of these texts was the 'Declaration of the Assembled Communities'. It was drawn up before the first assembly was held at Les Terriennes, or in other words right at the end of April. It broke the news of the uprising, announced the election of La Mothe-La-Forest as general and prescribed the rigorous means through which the assemblies were to be organized. The document took the form of a circular to be distributed among the parishes. It is not so much a summons as a set of rules. Precautions are taken against any possible outbreaks of violence, the aims of the movement are specified, a hierarchy is designated and a system for policing the assemblies is laid down. All of these measures betoken a cautious approch to the rising, and suggest that the document should be attributed to the moderating influence of La Mothe.

The terms of the summons pronounced in front of Bergerac on 10 May have been preserved in the minutes of the *jurats*. We can also find scraps of the arguments which the rebels shouted to the citizens of Périgueux, and subsequently to the people of Sainte-Foy.

Following his entry into Bergerac La Mothe gathered the leading citizens into the town hall on two separate occasions and subjected them to a harangue. These two addresses were delivered on 14 and 17 May. The gist of them has been preserved in indirect speech in the minutes of the *jurats*.

A 'Petition made to the king by the rebel communes of Périgord' must also be dated to these first days of the rebels' stay in Bergerac. The petition is addressed to King Louis XIII. It opens with the words, 'Sire, the most glorious name of Just which Your Majesty has acquired . . .' The petitioners address the monarch in classic style. They implore his attention, and present a range of requests and wishes. The preamble to the document justifies the rising and introduces a catalogue of demands. It is quite clever and well constructed, and we can probably see in it the hand of the *lieutenant-général* Jay d'Ataux, who was at that time prisoner of the Croquants. Indeed, according to Chevalier de Cablanc, Jay d'Ataux 'wrote some petitions addressed to the king, which were forwarded from hand to hand, but never got as far as Paris'. These texts circulated at least as far as Auvergne, where they were shown to the governor, and some also found their way into Agenais and even Poitou. It is clear, at any rate, that copies of the petition were prepared, and that messengers carried them to every point of the compass.

Five different documents written from Bergerac are dated 15 May. They follow an identical formula. The general calls a new assembly, summons jurisdictions from Sarladais to Agenais to rally to the cause and appeals to one of the principal barons of the province to come to the Croquants' aid. La Mothe had evidently become conscious at this stage of the precarious and fleeting nature of his power. He was anxious to draw in more adherents and give the rising an irresistible impulse. He uses these documents to promise safe-conducts to any merchants and speaks in the style of a supreme commander.

On 24 May La Mothe issued a summons to the jurisdiction of Savignac in Sarladais. On 28 May he was prompted by the approach of royal troops to write a personal letter to the king in the hope of obtaining a settlement in the form of an honourable submission. A final batch of summonses were sent to some parishes in Quercy on 18 June. The author this time was Madaillan, who had taken over the leadership of the revolt.

We can say with fair certainty that these documents were written by dignitaries, whether the author was an elderly soldier of noble origins or an official of the *sénéchaussée*. It is also true that some of the apparent awkwardness in the texts may be the result of errors made by copyists outside the province. At the same time the documents do seem to bear the stamp of a genuine popular style. They are full of lamentations, highly coloured complaints and items of fabricated news that teem with thousands of 'poor' ploughmen and 'rapacious' villains ('thousands of robbers', 'thousands of new duties', 'thousands of ravenous predators'). The images and parallels they use are drawn from the land ('changing ploughshares into swords', 'changing stones into bread, ferns into money', 'better that the water should be lacking from the soil than to have to endure the gilded thefts [of the excisemen]', 'the schemes of the [unhappy] kings have been cemented with the blood and sweat of the people'). The rebels also sometimes assumed a legalistic tone in their written reports of events in an attempt to imitate the vocabulary of royal edicts and the style of notices issued by the jurisdictions. But the overall flavour of the documents is a popular one. Bearing this flavour in mind, we shall now proceed to examine the themes with which the documents are concerned.

The revolt is traced first and foremost to the increase in taxation. This increase is portrayed as both the reason and the justification of the rising. The increase is held to have taken place at two specific times – twenty years earlier, when power struggles were taking place during the king's minority and the Protestant wars were raging, and two years before, when France went to war with Spain. The new taxes are described as 'extraordinary' (the word recurs four times) and for good measure 'intolerable, illegal, excessive, unknown to our fathers', and beyond the province's ability to pay, even if it contributed its entire revenues.

Trade, we are told, has ceased. 'Livestock, wine, and chestnuts are no longer transported to other regions.' In time of peace, chestnuts were indeed loaded on to boats at Limeuil, Mouleydier and Bergerac and the other Dordogne river ports and exported to the various regions of northern France. But all this traffic has been obstructed by the war. In addition troops have been crossing the province and taking up billets there as a result of the military operations being conducted in Roussillon and the Basque country. The petition also contains an account of the sack of a village by the soldiers. Everyone at that time had either personally witnessed such brutalities or at least heard horrified witnesses describing them. The soldiers are said to be 'cruel and barbaric, rascals and harpies. They treat our land like conquered territory.'

The effect of these ordeals has been to leave the province 'exhausted' and the peasant 'poor' or 'ruined'. But the Croquants will never submit to 'oppression' (the word recurs four times). This oppression is reducing them to 'beggary, to misery. It is enraging them, drowning them in despair, putting swords in their hands.'

The oppression is blamed on 'Your Majesty's financial officials, thieves greedy to fill their own purses'. They are as rapacious as beasts of prey. 'They are *ravenous* . . . they are *eating* the poor ploughmen right down to the bone.'

These officials are robbing and lying 'behind the king's back'. The *lieutenants-généraux* are 'neglecting the people', or are 'overtaxing them'. The armies paid by means of the new taxes 'think they are the cat's whiskers', and all talk of service to the king is a 'specious pretext'. The Croquants refuse to accept this state of affairs.

What then is the notion which the rebels hold of themselves, and the image which they aspire to give to their movement in the face of this oppression? They declare themselves to be 'the most humble subjects and most obedient servants of the king'. In all his documents, La Mothe appends to his title of general a longish qualification protesting his loyalty to the king . He calls himself 'the most faithful, most humble and most obedient servant and subject of the king'. The rebels refer to their duty of serving the king each time they touch on the reasons for their revolt; but this incessantly reiterated concept of service is always accompanied by a rider which subtly alters its meaning. It is mixed up with or 'coincides' with 'public freedom', 'the general good' or 'the relief of the populace'. The 'good servant of the king' is also a 'lover of the public', and the struggle against the oppression of the taxman is, consequently, identified with the service due to the king. It follows that the rebels never think of their movement as a revolt. It is an 'uprising' , an 'insurrection'. Above all it is a 'justified . . . all too justified . . . recourse to arms'.

Contemporaries invariably referred to the rebels as Croquants, but the rebels themselves never used the name. The terms they most frequently use in the titles of their documents are 'communes' or 'rebel communities of Périgord'. These two terms usually occur in the plural, but we sometimes find them in the singular, i.e. 'the Commune' or 'the Community of Périgord'. The rebels are encouraged by their numbers to declare that they have 'risen up', 'assembled' or 'united'. They associate themselves not only with Périgord, but also, more ambitiously, with Guyenne. The summons delivered to Bergerac was issued in the name of the 'general of the rebel bands of Guyenne'. In his letter to the king, La Mothe wrote that 'your communes of Guyenne have risen up'. In his summons of 24 May he styled himself 'general of the communes of Périgord, Agenais and the other communities of Guyenne'. At this point the royal forces had not yet regrouped in the valley of the Garonne, and the rebellion had reached the peak of its territorial expansion. The rebels had consequently developed larger ambitions, as reflected in this novel title. In the same spirit Madaillan signs his communiqué of 18 June, 'general of the political communes'.

The Croquants were headed, then, by an 'elected' general, La Mothe-La-Forest. In the various Croquant documents La Mothe repeatedly characterizes his power as 'absolute'. His 'commandments', his 'authority' and his 'power' are always 'absolute'. He speaks in the tones of an undisputed leader, and presents himself as one vested with a kind of sovereignty. He refers to '*our* troops, *our* ordinances, *our* camp, *our* army'. He gives commands 'in his Council' and he 'makes them known to all'. He affects in his correspondence a formal and stately style of diplomatic address, and his documents are stamped in red wax with his family seal. Anyone who violates his orders is threatened with martial law. 'Any failure to co-operate', he declares to his addressees, 'will be treated as insubordination.' They must carry out his orders 'on pain of being found guilty of disobedience and disloyalty, on pain of infringing our ordinances, and on pain of death'.

The declared aim of the communes is to *re-establish justice and freedom*. The insurgents reserve the right to administer justice themselves in the body they call the 'Council of the ruined poor' or the 'Council of the rebel communes'. They demand in the declaration that 'anyone in sympathy with the *gabelle*' should be handed over to the heads of the parishes. The parish captains are summoned to pass judgement upon the prisoners, and anyone who hangs back is threatened with being treated as 'a true enemy of public order'. The rebels call on the communes to 'go into action against the excisemen'.

The king, however, continues to be viewed as the ultimate source of justice. Up till now he has been deceived. 'It is certain', say the rebels, 'that all these things have been taking place behind the king's back and against His Majesty's wishes.' The communes' manifestos will open his eyes to their grievances. They will 'convey the true character of our oppressions and give an accurate picture of our needs'. The communes would like to have a syndic appointed 'to submit their grievances to His Majesty'. The sole purpose of their uprising, they insist, is 'to ask for justice'. As soon as their request is heard the king will undoubtedly lose faith in his bad advisers, and will take steps to ensure that his subjects benefit from the 'effects of his clemency . . . and his justice and mercy'. At five places in the documents the king is described as 'most just'. He is also referred to as being 'most virtuous, generous, fatherly and merciful'.

The peasants have been denied justice for too long. They have been exposed, for example, to the lawless violence of passing soldiery. The petition describes an episode of plundering, setting out the whole range of scandalous and humiliating treatment to which the victims were subjected. 'The menfolk were pinioned and put to the torture, and their wives and daughters were raped before their eyes.' The rebels demand that the authorities should respect their dignity as Christians and subjects of the king. They express their determination in words like 'rage' and 'despair', and announce that they are prepared 'to die in this travail . . . to die like men'.

The principle most often alluded to besides justice is that of freedom. The declaration twice refers to the need for freedom to be preserved. The excisemen are described as being 'enemies of public freedom', and the merchants are given their safe-conducts in order that 'they may carry out their accustomed business in free and open conditions'. In the address he delivered to the peasants of Le Paréage, Ribeyreix invited them to become 'the founders of public freedom'. La Mothe was hailed as the 'liberator of public freedom' in the speeches made to welcome him when he arrived in Bergerac.

In spite of all this rhetoric, there is little evidence to suggest that the rebels had worked out any specific programme. Only the declaration sketches a handful of policies. The authors of this document call, without further elaboration, for the 'new duties' to be abolished. They offer to pit the army of the communes against the Spaniards for a period of three months. Above all they are concerned that the authorities should rescind any measures that seem to point to the imposition of a *gabelle*. They are thinking, in particular, of the appointment of *élus*. 'Rid us of these financial officials and make this province a *pays d'état* [province taxed through the old representative Estates] . . . give the people a syndic.' The demand was a long-standing one. Périgord had been a *pays d'élection* (province taxed through the system of *élections*) since the reign of Henri II a century earlier, and the peasants had ever since been struggling to regain the freedom from taxes they had enjoyed before that time. Meetings of estates had continued to take place in Périgord right up to 1611, and the delegates to these various meetings had voiced similar demands to the ones which the Croquants were making now. They had called for the dismissal of the *élus*, the holding of regular assemblies by the estates, and the appointment of a permanent syndic to treat with the king on behalf of the province as a whole.

Once the king had granted the demands which were being made of him, the rebels anticipated that a golden age would dawn. The documents explain how the king will grow rich: 'Your money will go straight into your coffers.' His enemies will be demoralized. 'Astounded that a small province can support so many soldiers, they will humble their pride and lay down their arms.' The king's subjects will devote themselves to his service. 'We and our children', the Croquants say, 'will dedicate our lives to enhancing Your Majesty's greatness.' Finally, Heaven will grant the king a long and glorious reign, 'Heaven will hear our prayers and accord you many years of life.'

The peasants of the communes of Périgord portray their revolt in vague and idealistic terms. Their demands never get beyond the level of principles, of calls for justice and freedom. They are looking, in other words, for the punishment of the excisemen, the restoration of ancient customs and the coming of the golden age. Such things are no more than the stuff of popular legend.

Hunting down the excisemen

Rebellions always started, for practical purposes, with the hunting down of those persons whom the peasants felt to personify the oppressive taxation system. The communes set out to take their revenge upon the 'people who sympathized with the *gabelle*', or in other words the financial officials who had taken shelter in the towns. They vented their fury upon the country estates of these officials, and ravaged them right up to the city gates.

The immediate cause of the rising, as we have seen, was the ration tax. This tax had been allocated among the communities by Jay d'Ataux, the *lieutenant-général* of the *sénéchaussée*. The clerk of the *élection*, Alesme, had organized the dispatch of the tax warrants, and sergeants or bowmen had distributed them. Jay d'Ataux, as we saw, was taken captive by the Croquants, but was rescued from lynching by the successive intervention of clergy from the various communes and of La Mothe-La-Forest himself. La Mothe actually summoned his captains on 17 May for the precise purpose of ensuring that the *lieutenant-général* was given a proper trial. Jay d'Ataux got away with his life. According to Chevalier de Cablanc his reprieve can be put down either to the substantial ransom he offered or to the skills which he made available to the rebels by composing their petition and advising La Mothe on the negotiations they had to conduct with the royal troops. His house, however, was ransacked and his woods were all cut down. He remained in the hands of the rebels for five weeks.

The clerk of the *élection*, André Alesme, had faced retribution as early as July 1635, when rioters threatened to throw him into the well of Couderc. His town house was looted. The damage came, by his reckoning, to 10,000 *livres*, plus 2,000 *livres* spent on lawsuits arising from the incident. From June to October he and his family had to remain in hiding. In 1636 the mob killed two or three of his sergeants and bailiff's escorts. In 1637 the rebels ransacked and burnt a house he had recently bought on the edge of the suburb of Périgueux known as Chapeau Rouge. They ravaged the garden, tore up seven vines, cut the trees down and filled in the well. Alesme calculated his loss this time as 80,000 *livres*. The house had contained his jewellery and tapestries, an assortment of valuable furniture and all his papers.

The two tax collectors for the *élection*, Jean Vincenot and Jean Salleton, were both hard hit by the rioting of 1635. In May 1637 both men had to flee as fast as their legs would carry them and take refuge with the Council. Vincenot estimated the damage inflicted by the rebels on his house and garden at 20,000 *livres*. Salleton lost a house, a barn and some vines. Some of his trees were chopped down, and some of his corn was cut before it had ripened. In 1640 he succeeded in getting the government to promise him an indemnity of 3,000 *livres*.

Two officials were unlucky enough to live in Le Paréage. Louis de Bessot was the auditor of the *élection*, and Jean Chaleppe, as we saw earlier, was the bowman sent to distribute warrants there. The rebels burnt their houses and farms with the livestock inside. The communes of Chanterac and Saint-Vincent-de-Connezac in the neighbourhood of Double plundered the house of a certain Simon de Guivry, Esquire, who served as warrant officer of a company of bodyguards. They blamed Guivry for having slapped a surcharge of 8,000 *livres* on top of the regular taxes to finance the time he spent razing the citadel of Sainte-Foy between April and September 1635.

Popular fury seems, then, to have been directed at tax gathering to the exclusion of everything else. Alesme and the five other victims just mentioned all brought actions for damages before the Council. Thanks to these actions we know a certain amount about both the men and the losses they suffered. All of them were notorious for their involvement in tax collection.

The communes in power

Provincial officials like governors, magistrates, financial administrators and the consuls and *jurats* who ran the affairs of the walled towns all liked to depict the revolt as a surge of unbridled disorder. If we examine the actual conduct of the communes during the twenty-odd days when they held sway in Bergerac, we find that it does not altogther conform to that standard image.

The peasant army was rigorously organized. Its leaders gave thought to the quality of both the soldiers they recruited and the officers they appointed over them. The 8,000 men in the force were 'mostly veteran soldiers from the most warlike provinces in the realm', and the captains were 'old soldiers selected from all over Périgord, the best who could be found'. The Agenais chroniclers tell us that La Mothe chose the twenty sturdiest men from each parish that answered his summons. He required the parish to pay for their upkeep on a basis of five *sous* per head per day, making a contribution of roughly five *livres* a day from each village. The figures are plausible ones. Given that 400 parishes took part in the rising we find, on this calculation, that the parish *syndics* must have provided a total of something like 20,000 *livres* over the twenty-day period. Such was the cost of the rising in Périgord. The rules laid down by the leadership were effectively implemented. 'They pay for the corn they eat and the wine they drink . . . These people have orders to keep out of debt. No one has ever seen such a display of restraint and courtesy in a rebellion of this size.'

The citizens of Bergerac suffered little from the Croquant occupation. All the Croquants did was to forbid the export of sacks of corn and casks of wine, so that they would have adequate provisions if the town were besieged. The burgesses were allowed to go in and out of the town as they pleased. These burgesses did not respond in a similar spirit. Some of them had had their furniture moved to the safety of the Augustinian monastery,[5] before fleeing to the territory of the Marquis de La Force on the right bank of the Dordogne. On 14 and 17 May La Mothe was obliged to resort to threats. He demanded that the citizens should 'rally to his cause, fortify the town, rebuild the bastions and agree to provide a loan towards the maintenance and provisioning of his army'. On 15 May he had a proclamation issued in the streets to the sound of the drum. The citizens were ordered 'to go and work on the fortifications'. The Croquants had the town fenced round with a bristling ring of barricades. The bridge over the Dordogne was blocked, and twenty companies of armed men were assigned to stand guard.

The assembled communes were faithful in every particular to the established military procedure of the day. They used the same hierarchy of ranks as the regular armies. Their orders were phrased in the same style, and their rules of daily conduct were equally conventional. They set bodyguards at the town gates and on the crossroads. Their soldiers camped in the suburbs and the meadows beside the river, and their general established his headquarters in the town hall. La Mothe made his appearances surrounded by his captains. All of them had hats on their heads and swords at their sides, and musketeers marched beside them with fuses ready-lit. The ceremony they followed when they summoned a town to surrender was also a traditional one. The herald would ride to the ramparts ringed by a troop of cavalry. His proclamation would start and end with the roll of a drum, and he would repeat it using an identical form of words at each of the town gates. Even the threats the Croquants used to terrorize their opponents were in accordance with the established customs of war. Towns were informed that unless they surrendered they would be 'reduced to rubble, razed to the ground and burnt to ashes', and their inhabitants would be 'put to the sword'. Standard reprisals were

---

5 'When the Croquants were in the town in May 1637, the Augustinian Fathers allowed the citizens to deposit all their property in the monastery, and promised to give them personal sanctuary if they needed it. This has placed them under a great obligation, as they have admitted on several occasions.' See Bibliothèque Nationale, ms. Périgord 48, fo. 373, *Histoire des récollets*. The full meaning of this text becomes apparent when we recall that the population was entirely Protestant. The six Augustinian Fathers had settled in Bergerac precisely in order to refute the preaching of the Protestant clergy. They had spoken out against Protestant teaching in the public squares and even ventured into the Huguenot synods.

used to chastise anyone who continued to hold out. The country house of the mayor of Bergerac, who had fled to the provincial governor, and the outlying estates of the citizens of Sainte-Foy, who had refused to open their gates to the rebels, were systematically wrecked. The Croquants burnt their farms, smashed their casks, slaughtered their livestock and ravaged their cornfields and vineyards. The devastation was both organized and precise. Soldiers called it 'wreaking havoc'.

Such acts of violence were both deliberate, and limited in scope. At all other times La Mothe made sure that his army behaved in an orderly way. He entrusted the task of keeping order to a number of clergymen who had followed their flocks into revolt. Chevalier de Cablanc observes that 'a number of priests were at the head of this rabble'. Gaufreteau records that 'a priest cut a striking figure in the violent insurrection of the commune of Périgord because of his valour and strength'. Four priests are mentioned in the surviving lists of rebels. The first was a curate of Pissot in the forest of Vergt, the third the parish priest of Puyguilhem and the fourth the archdeacon of Bergerac. The Declaration states that the function of these priests was 'to outlaw vice . . . to call the people to prayer and to forbid people to utter blasphemies and to perpetrate scandalous acts against the honour and glory of God'.

The fact is that a large number of the Croquants, and La Mothe in particular, felt that their cause was profoundly just. They were sure they had Heaven's approval. The declaration says at one point, 'May God be pleased to sustain and bless our sacred resolve.' La Mothe, we remember, sought the protection of Notre-Dame-des-Vertus when he first became involved. 'He was anxious', an observer reported, 'to make his damnable venture appear respectable, and to give the impression that he was responding to some kind of special call. Consequently he spent some days shut up in a shrine near Périgueux . . . He carries an image of Our Lady and pretends to hold discussions with it.' Further evidence for a cult of the Virgin may be detected in the emblems which were chosen by La Mothe's army. On 11 May sixty companies of the rebel communes hoisted their new blue and white banners in the meadows of Bergerac. We must surely recognize in these flags the symbolic colours of Mariolatry and conclude that the Croquants had placed themselves under the protection of Our Lady.

By gathering in arms, raising taxes and seizing fortified strongholds the Croquants were guilty, on three counts, of treason and lese-majesty. But the peasants of Périgord who had enlisted to fight for their communes would probably not have been conscious of any dereliction of duty. It would not have occurred to them that they were taking part in a scandalous revolt against their natural masters. After all, they had genuine commanders leading them, and priests were urging them on. They believed that God was behind them and that they were fighting in the service of the king. They were sure they were going to bring their province justice and liberty.

La Mothe's plan was to march down the Dordogne towards Bordeaux, rallying any towns he passed through on the way. He knew that he needed artillery. Without it his troops could do nothing against the smallest fortified town, still less against a regiment of royalist forces in the open countryside.

The Croquants had originally hoped to get cannon from Périgueux when they appeared there on 1 May. On 15 May they set out in the hope of obtaining guns from Sainte-Foy. Forty rebel companies pitched camp beneath the town walls. Sainte-Foy was a large stronghold that dominated the river. It was the gateway to the Bordeaux region. Its citadel had been dismantled in 1635 after only seven years' service, but the walls with their accompanying moats, towers and bastions were strong and well maintained, and the burgesses were inured to war by the recent religious struggles.[6] The capture of this town would have represented a decisive victory for the communes. On 13 May, however, three or four guards dispatched by the Duke of Épernon had hurried in to bolster the town's resistance. Ribeyreix went to make the ritual proclamation to the town along with three other captains, some sergeants and a drummer. While the party were delivering their summons, however, the inhabitants staged a sortie. Two of the Croquants were killed and the others were thrust into the town. 'The drawbridge was raised and the citizens jeered at them.' La Mothe had no option but to beat a retreat, burning local barns as he did so.

After the army had got back to Bergerac, the local people remembered the existence of some old iron castings which had been buried there ever since the Wars of Religion. Nobody knew for certain whether they were hidden in a corner of the cemetery or under the flagstones of the church, but a hasty search was conducted. On 16 and 21 May the excavators even broke open some tombs. But the search was in vain, and the Croquants were still without artillery.

La Mothe none the less redoubled his appeals to the countryside. Summonses were issued to the communes of Beynac, La Roque-Gageac and Saint-Cyprien, near the confluence of the Dordogne and the Vézère, and to the jurisdiction of Puyguilhem on the south bank of the Dordogne, on the borders between Guyenne and Agenais. All of these proclamations are still extant. Contingents came flocking from every part of the province of Périgord, but certain local groupings were conspicuous. By examining the list of Croquants whose names are mentioned in the records, we can distinguish four principal breeding-grounds of revolt. The first of these breeding-grounds stretched from the Dordogne to the Isle, the forest of Vergt and the neighbourhood of Périgueux, reaching its limit approximately at the point where the Isle meets the Auvézère. A second group of rebels rose up in the area between the Vézère and the Dordogne, or in other words in the patch of countryside that separated Limeuil and Saint-Cyprien. To the west of the province, on the

---

6 The town had been a secure Protestant stronghold. All the inhabitants 'with the exception of one or two, professed the reformed religion'. Protestantism was so strong that no Catholic residents could be found to sit on the council of *jurats*, even though joint membership of this body had been compulsory since 1629, and in March 1636 clergy had to be called in from outside to fill the vacant Catholic seats. From 1632 up to August 1634, the *chambre de l'Édit* of the *parlement* at Bordeaux held its sessions in the town. The burgesses were ready for the approach of the Croquant army. When the first wave of disturbances broke out in July 1635, they had mounted a guard against 'the rebels and dissidents who might seek to make their way in there'. See Archives Départementales, Gironde, E.suppl.4989. The record book containing the debates which were held by the *jurats* between April 1636 and January 1638 is significantly missing.

border with Angoumois, trouble broke out in the communes of Bourzac, Aubeterre and Chanterac. The fourth and final breeding-ground was situated in the south-west of the province, on the south bank of the Dordogne near the border with Agenais. All the communities of this district from Puyguilhem to Eymet rallied to the rebel cause. Forest parishes played, on the whole, as important a part in the movement as the villages in the river valleys. But no town, large or small, adhered to the Croquant insurrection. The rising was truly a rising of country people, and the army which fought for the Croquant cause was composed of peasants alone.

On 17 May the communes held a fourth gathering in the meadows of a place called L'Artigue. They were one league upstream of Sainte-Foy and in sight of its ramparts. This meeting was marked by the presence of communes from the north bank of the Dordogne. They came from the direction of Double and Angoumois, and specifically from the district which extended between La Mothe-Montravel and Montpon. La Mothe put the communes to work making ladders for scaling the walls of Sainte-Foy.

The fifth and last meeting took place on 24 May. The peasants assembled at Lamonzie, close by Bergerac, in another of the low-lying meadows which stretched beside the Dordogne. This meeting was attended by the communes from the region between the south bank of the Dordogne and the north bank of the Lot. On the same day La Mothe appealed for the help of the communes on the borders of Sarladais and Brivadois. These communes occupied the lands between the Dordogne and Vézère more than thirty leagues away.

The council of the communes debated a number of possible options. One possibility was to attempt an assault on Sainte-Foy with a view to advancing on Bordeaux. A second was to stay put and wait for reinforcements. The army could occupy itself with ravaging the estates of local notables who had shrunk back from joining the rising as a warning to any other waverers. A third alternative was to turn and march south. This third alternative was proposed by Madaillan. He undertook to win over the communes in his canton and to take either Agen or better still Cahors, which the army could easily blockade by seizing the spurs that overlooked the Lot a little way downstream. In the end it was Madaillan's idea which prevailed. The Croquants left a garrison in Bergerac and advanced into Agenais. Madaillan commanded the vanguard, and La Mothe was in charge of the main body of the army. The various market towns gave in with little or no resistance. Eymet fell to the rebel troops on 28 May, and La Sauvetat, Miramont and Lauzun capitulated soon after.

The government's turn

The officials whose duty it was to keep order in the province were slow to react to the rising. They were distracted by the danger on the frontiers, and unprepared for the startling speed at which the rising spread. On 4 May Pontac, the *procureur général* (provincial solicitor-general), denounced the revolt before the *Grand-Chambre* (principal chamber) of the *parlement* at Bordeaux. The *parlement* issued a decree directing the officers of the courts to launch an investigation and commanding the seneschals to move against the rebels.

'They were to proceed on the basis of this enactment alone, and no other warrant was needed.' Otherwise the response was feeble. The *cour des aides*, a detested body, took refuge in Libourne. The provincial governor, the Duke of Épernon, was eighty-two years old and bedridden in his château at Cadillac. He had at his disposal only his personal bodyguard, a force of thirty-odd horsemen led by the Count of Maillé. It is true that there were three regiments currently quartered in Guyenne. They were there to raise recruits for a season, before setting off once again for their base in Picardy. But these regiments were under strength, and scattered in different places. They evacuated their billets in Bas-Périgord as soon as the communes approached. On 12 May Épernon wrote to Richelieu admitting that he had no idea what to do. An observer in Agen noted that 'everyone is astonished, and especially the men of property. Most of them are wondering what on earth will become of them.'

On 23 May the king sent a letter commanding Épernon to crush the revolt with all the troops he could muster and by every means in his power. Épernon appealed for the help of his son, the Duke of La Valette, who was currently commanding the army at Labourd. La Valette promptly left the Marquis de Poyanne to deal with the Spaniards and hurried towards the Garonne. On 27 May he organized a regiment of 3,000 infantry at Marmande and a troop of 400 cavalry at Monségur. Some of these men were troops withdrawn from the frontier army, and others were soldiers whom La Valette had picked up haphazardly in his march across the province. At the same time the duke asked the *parlement* to send him commissioners to try the rebels when he had caught them. He was sure of an easy victory.

The fall of La Sauvetat, 1 June 1637

The Croquants had organized an outpost at Eymet. As the royal troops drew near, the 200 to 300 men who made up the rebel garrison decided to retreat. They withdrew under cover of darkness, marching 'in single file, through the cornfields'. Madaillan deployed a force of 2,000 to 3,000 men to defend La Sauvetat. They were, says a chronicler, 'the best troops the communes had . . . the worst of their ruffians'. La Sauvetat was a large market town with a Protestant population. It was a difficult place to defend, being incompletely fortified and situated in the low-lying meadows beside the River Dropt. La Valette had no more artillery than the Croquants did, and his troops were no more numerous than theirs; but he reckoned that his hardened veterans would easily get the better of a band of peasants. On Whit Sunday, 1 June, he issued a formal call for the communes to surrender.

At the third summons the Croquants shouted to La Valette's trumpeter, 'If you come back with any more fanfares we will haul you up and hang you so high that your master will see you from miles away.' The duke immediately gave orders for the assault. His soldiers set to with their halberds and overturned the Croquant barricades in the face of heavy musket-fire. They then set fire to the houses where the Croquants were holding out. After two hours of hand-to-hand fighting the Croquants were forced to retreat, leaving a heap of corpses behind them. Scipion Dupleix observes that the battle was 'a massacre of the bloodiest kind. The rebels refused the army's offer of quarter, and defended themselves with the stubbornness of madmen from street to street and hovel to hovel. They fought in the church, and in the citizens' houses too.' All our sources agree that the royal troops suffered heavy casualties. La Valette reported that 200 of his men had been killed, including twenty officers, and a large number more had been wounded. The Malebaysses record in their journal that 600 men were killed on the government side, and the anonymous correspondent in Agen puts the figure as high as 800. Between 1,000 and 1,500 Croquants were reckoned to have been killed. Twenty-five houses had been burned to the ground along with their occupants, women and children included. But in spite of all their exertions, the royal forces had managed to take only forty prisoners.

The resistance put up by the communes had turned the battle into a Pyrrhic victory for the Duke of La Valette. Contemporaries were astounded and saddened by the desperation with which the peasants had fought. The Duke of Épernon remarked that the officers present 'would regret to their dying day that the exploits performed on both sides had not been directed against the enemies of the crown'. All the letters written at this time allude to the number of casualties. It is clear from the insolence with which they answered the trumpeter's summons, the desperate tenacity with which they conducted their defence and the tiny number of prisoners they left in the hands of the victors that the Croquants were passionately committed to their rising and determined to conquer or die. We may deduce, consequently, that these peasants had been inspired with a heady confidence by the successes they had won. Their rising had lasted longer and spread farther than they had ever thought possible. They were certain that their principles would triumph, and the golden age would return.

Madaillan knew the country perfectly. He escaped from the royal forces with a handful of faithful followers, and took refuge in a nearby château in the parish of Puisserampion which belonged to a lawyer attached to the provincial *parlement*. La Mothe had set out too late to help Madaillan. But he gathered together the 1,000 to 2,000 Croquants who had survived the battle at La Sauvetat, and was consequently able to continue holding out in Bergerac. His army now totalled 6,000 men, and the barricades were strong. In addition he was expecting reinforcements. The Marquis d'Aubeterre was believed to be approaching at the head of the communes of Double, and the weaver Buffarot was thought to be on his way with the communes of Sarladais. All through the region from parish to parish the tocsin rang. Peasants who had up till now stayed aloof from the rebellion began to hold meetings. The people of Puyguilhem, for example, gathered in the woods on the heights of Théobon. Another band of rustics met in the lofty château of Montcuq, which commanded the approaches to Bergerac. On 3 June the consuls and magistrates of Bergerac who had taken shelter in the lands of the Marquis de La Force left the marquisate and crossed the Dordogne to link up with the royal army. They were anxious to restore their town's reputation by lining up behind La Valette. But they soon had to turn back. The roads were full of musketeers in the service of the communes and peasants trying to carry whole cartloads of old clothes and furniture out of reach of the soldiers in the marquisate. The wharves of the Dordogne river ports were jammed at the same time with carriages heading in the opposite direction from towns up and down the south bank.

The Marquis de Duras negotiates

La Valette had sent to Bergerac a local gentleman called the lord of La Grave. La Grave was attached to the retinue of the Marquis de Duras. Son-in-law of the Duke of Bouillon and colonel in the army of Labourd, Duras was one of the great Protestant seigneurs. His estates lay only one or two leagues from Bergerac, and he is likely to have had a number of friends or tenants among the rebels. Ever since the revolt began he had been attempting to interest La Mothe in a 'possible compromise'. Now La Grave was dispatched to the rebel camp with instructions to 'ascertain the reason for their rising and find what it was they were asking for'. The leaders of the communes replied 'that they sought of the king two things only. In the first place they wished him to accord them an exemption from all special taxes, and secondly they wished him to grant them an amnesty.' But the communes also demanded a rapid reply. They insisted that they should be given an answer within a fortnight, and had the audacity to maintain that they would gather in even greater numbers after that deadline than they had done up till now. Half of their following, they declared, had still to arrive on the scene. La Valette for his part was anxious to avoid any further bloody confrontation. But he was unable to grant any kind of legal recognition to the rebel communes or to make them any promises, since he had not received any warrant or any formal instructions to take such a step. The Marquis de Duras duly set off to parley with the rebels on this basis. The negotiations lasted several days. They were held on a high road two hundred yards from the gates of Bergerac. La Mothe was the spokesman for the rebels, and four other leaders of the communes were also present.

La Mothe's hand was forced by the news that cannons had been delivered to the royal army. Word had also reached him that frightful reprisals were in store for his men. The enemy were threatening to hang any rebels they captured and to raze their leaders' houses to the ground. On 6 June he agreed to disband his troops in return for an assurance that they would not be hunted down and that La Valette would make a personal plea to the king to pardon them.

The last-ditch stand of Jean Magot, 6 June 1637

It took a soldier's eye to detect how weak the communal forces were. La Mothe saw the hopelessness of the rebel cause, and resigned himself to surrender. His attitude contrasted with the resolve of the peasant host and their confident expectation of reinforcements. At Bergerac La Mothe was denounced by a fellow-leader. This diehard condemned him as a 'perjured traitor who sought to hand them over to the enemies of their freedom and was the cause of all their ruin and wretchedness'. The diehard was Jean Magot, a physician from Périgueux. Magot was a dubious character. Madaillan had suspected him of playing a double game, and had ordered some of his soldiers to keep him under guard. The rout at La Sauvetat, however, gave Magot the chance to break free. He succeeded in winning over some twenty parish syndics and about a thousand of the peasants, persuading them that the pact with Duras was a dead letter, that Ataux had been killed and that the Marquis d'Aubeterre was on his way to take over the command of the rebel army. The first two of these three assertions were plausible enough, and the third was a simple statement of fact. Magot's adherents responded by throwing up barricades in the citadel. It was now four o'clock in the afternoon.

La Mothe promptly intervened with a force of a hundred followers, most of them citizens of Bergerac. Magot was struck down, and his corpse was left lying on the cobbles.[7] By the end of the evening the communes had evacuated the town.

La Valette took his time, however. It was only on the following morning, 7 June, that he made his entry into Bergerac. The corpse of Magot was hoisted on to a wheel. The officials of Bergerac returned to their homes, and the peasants went back to their parishes. La Valette made no attempt to pursue the rebel forces, either because he felt bound by his promise to La Mothe, or because, as he wrote to Richelieu, he was physically unable to advance. The communes had taken care to destroy the bridge as they retreated, and the river was impossible to ford.

It seems puzzling that the Croquants should have been so quick to disperse. Their behaviour contrasts sharply with the diehard resistance of Magot and the stubborn defence put up by the men who fought at La Sauvetat. The chroniclers were sufficiently struck by this contrast to judge that La Mothe and his lieutenants were 'negligent'. They were 'rashly committed' to a policy of surrender, 'lulled by promises' or even 'weary of the fighting'. We know that La Mothe did his best to exculpate himself personally in the course of his talks with Duras. He dissociated himself from the other rebels, insisting that he had been 'put at their head in spite of the fact that he had no stomach for the venture'. He claimed that the rebels had forced him to march with

---

7 B. Porshnev has sought to ascribe a special significance to the role played both by Magot and by Greletty later on. See Boris Fedorovich Porshnev, *Les soulèvements populaires en France de 1623 à 1648*, translated from the Russian by Mme Ranieta and Robert Mandrou, École Pratique des Hautes Études, VIe section, Oeuvres Étrangères, 4, Paris, 1963). In political terms he has seen these men as representing a more radical point of view than the rest of the rebel leaders, and he has even claimed to detect a social antagonism between a rural petty bourgeoisie and a nobility associated with the 'aristocratic-feudal' State. There is in fact nothing in the sources to give grounds for such a conjecture – not an anecdote or even a reference. Porshnev's idea is based solely on the theoretical framework into which he would like to fit French society at this period, and not on the actual events. So far as we can judge from the documents, the clash between the rebel leaders reflected nothing more than personal rivalries. The mutiny staged by Magot was not caused by La Mothe's surrender. He had already been detained as a potential troublemaker several days before the surrender took place. His captor, Madaillan, later emerged as one of the leaders who favoured persevering with the revolt. Nor was Magot antagonistic to the nobility. He justified his stand by pointing to the imminent arrival of the Marquis d'Aubeterre and urging the rebels to flock to the Marquis's side.

them by threatening to burn down his house and murder his family. He drew attention to the set of rules he had prescribed in the Declaration of the communes, and boasted of his skill in preventing excesses and keeping the movement within bounds. Finally he swore that he had always been ready to lay down his arms the moment the king gave him orders to do so. La Mothe's posture seems equivocal. But the role he played was in fact quite typical of the attitude which most of the provincial nobility adopted in the face of the popular rising.

The provincial nobility and the rising of the communes

Right from the outset the rising of the communes of Périgord was a peasant upheaval. It followed immediately after the assemblies held in Charente, and reflected the rage which was felt in every country parish at the growing burden of taxes. The documents of the movement were singularly lacking in any invective against the traditional social order which prevailed in the countryside, and every act of violence the rebels perpetrated was directed against the taxman and the taxman alone. The sheer prestige of the Marquis de La Force, for example, was enough to ensure that any fugitive could take refuge on his lands, even though his lands were unprotected by either soldiers or battlements. The property of the Marquis de Beynac, the Marquis de Duras and the Count of Gurson lay right in the heart of the rebel cantons; but the onslaught of the peasantry passed all of these nobles by. And just as the communes made no attempt to rise against the châteaux, the gentry for their part showed little anxiety to rush to the defence of the forces of law and order. The appeals of the Duke of Épernon were greeted with little more than kindly promises. The nobles contented themselves with declaring their loyalty or lamenting their inability to come to Épernon's aid – 'They complained that none of their subjects and tenants were willing to follow them.' The upshot was that the nobility of Guyenne offered no practical help to the provincial governor, either because they feared that the communal forces might retaliate if they did so or because they had actually taken the rebel side. Attitudes began to change only as the tide of rebellion ebbed. 'Before the lord of La Valette captured La Sauvetat, he had fewer than half a dozen of the Périgord gentry behind him; after the rebels there were beaten, however, he had over 200 of them flocking to join his forces in less than three days.'

At the same time the nobility showed little inclination to come out openly in support of the rebel cause. La Mothe made a point of summoning the seigneurs of the rebel parishes. He proclaimed himself well aware that 'the nobility were the right arm of war'. Among the gentry summoned was Claude de Beynac, seigneur of Tayac and La Roque-Meyrols in the country between the Dordogne and the Vézère. Beynac's was one of the leading baronial families of Périgord. In 1605 his father had risked his neck by joining the Bouillon conspiracy, and the peasants on his estates were all in the process of rising up. But Beynac was careful not to compromise himself in any way whatever. There is, furthermore, every reason for suspecting that La Mothe and a number of the men who surrounded him were more concerned to restrain the revolt than to see it triumph. They appear to have hoped that the rising might be brought to a peaceful end through the mediation of either Duras or alternatively the seneschal of Périgord, the elderly Marquis de Bourdeille. At the end of May Bourdeille had made his own bid for a settlement by dispatching his vice-seneschal, La Brousse, on a mission to the court. La Brousse's task was to try to induce the Council to grant the rebels a tax exemption and a political amnesty: the hope was that this would have the effect of pacifying the whole of the countryside. The attitude of the nobles is best understood if we remember that one of their principal duties was to ensure the security of the realm. They were collectively responsible for keeping order in the provinces. In their eyes to serve the king was a matter of honour: it was their duty and calling to uphold his interests. No decent gentleman could take part in any kind of revolt without the utmost unease and reluctance, however much he might share in the resentments and dreams of the rebels.

Such at least was the view of the overwhelming majority of the gentry. But there were a number of mavericks who shook off the conventional inhibitions and embarked on the risky course of conspiracy or revolt. Ribeyreix and Madaillan were cases in point. It is even possible that these two may have been in league with the Count of Soissons or the Duke of Lorraine on the other side of the kingdom. The manifestos issued by the insurgents at Sedan were couched in language identical to that used by the communes of south-west France. The ringleaders at Sedan complained how the Cardinal Minister had built up his fortune out of 'the blood and sweat of the poor.' They spoke of 'the new extortions, these wicked and frightful taxes', of how 'the poor have been fleeced and eaten out of house and home … to the point where they have nothing left but the skin on their backs and a mouth to voice their grievances'. These phrases can be found in a pamphlet entitled 'The people speak to the king' which circulated at Sedan in this same year of 1637. Dupleix maintains that the Croquant leaders actually drew the events in the east to their followers' attention. 'To encourage and reassure them, they gave them to understand that their rising had met with the approval of the Count of Soissons and the greatest nobles in France, and that these dignitaries even shared their loathing of the present government. The government was hateful to every order of society (or so they said).' A Walloon gentleman named Mérode was said to have spent six months with the Croquant forces, and another gentleman suspected of working for Soissons was arrested by Épernon in July. Duke Charles IV of Lorraine actually did send an agent called Rochevalon to make contact with the Croquants, but this agent arrived on the scene only after the communes had already been routed. Chavigny was able to write to one of his envoys in Spain, 'The enemies of this state pinned great hopes on the revolt of a handful of peasants; but the revolt has come to grief.'

It is clear, then, that the mass of the nobility were profoundly sympathetic to the demands which the communes voiced. But the number of nobles who gave active support to the rising by plunging recklessly into open rebellion was inevitably very small. With the scattering of their army the grand design of the Croquants was brought to a premature end. We must now consider the impact which this amazing peasant rebellion made upon the surrounding provinces. The Croquant manifestos had circulated throughout the whole of south-west France. Everywhere word had spread of the victories which had been won by the peasant army. People learnt with astonishment and a sudden surge of hope how the communes had controlled the entire countryside of a province for the period of a month, and how they had even made their entry into some of the larger towns. The consequence was that the troubles began to spread. From May to July the peasants rose up in a number of other provinces, and swept through the parishes in pursuit of the excisemen. The first and most violent of these sequels to the Périgord revolt took place in the province of Quercy.

The troubles in Quercy, June–August 1637

The people of Quercy were quiet right up to the beginning of June. The first disorders in the province only broke out on 7 June, when the revolt in Périgord was over and the peasants of that region had returned to their homes. The disorders were caused by the arrival in the town of Cahors of a party of officers from the Biscarrat regiment. The officers were in transit, but a rumour spread that they had come to arrange the quartering of their regiment in the town, and the populace started to riot. The consuls dispersed the mob without any apparent difficulty, but early on the morning of 9 June the disorders started again. This time the mob were no longer content with shouting, as they had been two days earlier. The action they took was violent and carefully prepared. A large band of craftsmen's wives, accompanied by a handful of journeymen and vine growers, carried off the cathedral pew where the *élus* sat in a body during religious ceremonies and burnt it in the town square. They devastated the courtroom where the *élus* sat in judgement, snatched up the furniture and added that to the flames. They were just beginning to plunder the houses of three or four officials of the local *élection* when the town militia bore down on them. The burgesses were commanded by the consuls and the seneschal of the province, the Count of Cabrerets. The rioters streamed back into the suburbs pursued by the mounted burgesses and bombarded with volleys of musket fire. Several of their number lay dead on the streets, and the remainder took to the hills. The consuls remained in control of the town, but their victory was a distinctly Pyrrhic one. The *élection* office was wrecked, the *élus* had fled to Montauban and no further tax collection took place for several months.

Four days later the news spread that Cahors had been blockaded. Some bands of insurgents had unexpectedly captured the château of Mercuès, three leagues further down the Lot. This château had at one time been a feudal stronghold, but was currently used as a country house by the bishops of Cahors. Perched on a hillock that overlooked the river from a height of 100 metres, it commanded the route into the Lot valley. It was occupied only by a steward and a handful of domestic servants who were entirely unprepared for such a startling turn of events. The raid was masterminded by none other than the Croquant leader Madaillan. After fleeing first from La Sauvetat and then from Puisserampion, Madaillan had slipped through the royalist lines.

He had made his way through the whole of Haut-Agenais and had now finally reappeared 100 kilometres further east. In spite of the setbacks he had suffered he was still pursuing the plan he had worked out at Bergerac.

Madaillan had gathered around him the peasants of Sarladais. These peasants were led by Buffarot, who was in control of the territory between Monpazier and Montflanquin. Madaillan's band consequently numbered almost 800 men. On 16 June he sent Buffarot with a contingent of 200 to seize the château of Albas, which also overlooked the Lot a little further downstream. He himself remained at Mercuès. On 17 June he called on the citizens of Luzech to open their gates to him. Styling himself the 'general of the political communities', he issued orders from Albas on 18 June to the villages on the left bank of the Lot. These villages consisted of a dozen parishes from Trespoux in the neighbourhood of Cahors to Bouloc on the borders of Agenais. His aim was to take Montcuq, the largest town in the canton. Little by litle he hoped to rebuild a peasant army which would ultimately have the strength to capture Cahors and Agen.

Cabrerets appealed to La Valette to come to his rescue. La Valette responded by sending out a troop of horse from Bergerac. This cavalry force was under the command of the Count of Maillé. The horsemen besieged Mercuès, which surrendered after three days. Madaillan and his men got away. It is not clear whether they managed to escape under the cover of darkness or whether the besiegers deliberately allowed them to leave. Whatever the truth, Madaillan proceeded to throw himself on the mercy of a member of the Quercy gentry, the lord of Lacoste-Grezels. Lacoste-Grezels gave him shelter. In the meantime the royalist forces had been reinforced by the regiments of Navaille and Roquelaure, and they moved on to besiege Albas. The garrison at Albas surrendered on the same terms as the defenders of Mercuès: resistance would cease on condition that they were granted their lives and their freedom. These two rebel strongholds both fell in the first week of July. The weather had been dry for several months, and it was already time for the harvest. People said the peasants had only disbanded to attend to their seasonal labours. 'The lowest orders in the countryside seem full of ill will . . . they are only waiting till they have got the harvest in, and then they will make trouble again as vigorously as ever.'

Round about 20 July word spread that Buffarot had entered Figeacois in Haut-Quercy, where he was issuing orders to the parishes of the limestone country. Communal assemblies took place at Assier and Fons, two walled towns in the neighbourhood of Figeac, and both of these towns opened their gates to the Croquants. On 26 or 27 July a further assembly was held at Gramat. The Baron de Gramat was the brother of the provincial seneschal. Finding himself isolated in this small town he judged it prudent to take to his heels before the rebels arrived. The latter may at this point have numbered some 300 to 400. On arriving in the town they murdered two of the local attorneys and sacked their houses. They also ravaged the property owned by the burgesses of Figeac in different parts of the limestone belt. Most of these burgesses were officials attached to the *élection* of Haut-Quercy.

At the beginning of August the communes of Haut-Quercy appeared before

Figeac itself. Their army was now approximately 6,000 strong, and was under the command of a blacksmith known as Captain Basque. Their object was 'to force the people of the town to join their party'. After that they apparently intended to capture Villeneuve, and then to march on Villefranche-de-Rouergue. But Figeac resisted. The burgesses rallied behind the leadership of the Baron de Lacapelle-Marival and the lord of Camboulit. They sallied forth from their battlements in a vigorous sortie. Eighty of the Croquants were killed, and the remainder ran for their lives. The Figeacois gave chase to the retreating communes and besieged their stronghold of Fons. The defenders surrendered on the usual conditions that their lives should be spared and their freedom guaranteed.

This reverse more or less put an end to the rising in Quercy. Only Buffarot and a handful of diehards attached to him were still at large in the countryside. They tried to take shelter in the border country adjoining Agenais and Sarladais. This border country, unfortunately, was controlled by the Count of Espenan, who maintained strong detachments of troops there to protect the sergeants assigned to collect the taxes. He bribed Buffarot's companions and got them to turn him in.

The communes of Quercy: their numbers and aims

The rising in Bas-Quercy never spread beyond the valley of the Lot. It was confined to the immediate vicinity of Cahors and the parishes which lay within the jurisdiction of Montcuq on the south bank of the river. The rebel strength in this area never totalled more than a thousand. In Haut-Quercy, on the other hand, the upheaval was appreciably more serious. All of the parishes which lay in the limestone country round Gramat took part in the Croquant assemblies. These parishes included a total of some thirty villages in the territory between the Dordogne and the Lot. To judge from the list of guilty parishes which was drawn up subsequently by the *élus* of Figeac, the trouble extended all the way from Padirac in the north to Livernon in the south (a distance of some forty kilometres), and from Rocamadour in the west to Lacapelle-Marival in the east (twenty kilometres in all). Several thousand armed peasants are recorded as having taken part in the rising, or in other words nothing less than the entire population of this bleak, rocky countryside.

The rising was headed by the two Croquant leaders from Périgord, Madaillan and Buffarot, and also by a third figure we have just encountered, Captain Basque. The citizens of Figeac regarded Captain Basque as the 'general' of the communes of Haut-Quercy. Like their counterparts in Périgord, the communes of Quercy had a fully structured army with a hierarchy of military ranks. They went round the parishes issuing formal summonses to the villagers, and held a series of assemblies designed to rally each jurisdiction in turn. In addition they followed the tactics laid down by Madaillan. They began by capturing any points of strategic importance in the neighbourhood, and rallied the local villages to their cause. After that they blockaded the towns and endeavoured to take them by storm. They maintained their troops by requisitioning victuals from every parish they crossed. In a word, their military arrangements were almost identical to those of the communes of Périgord.

The communes of Quercy typically began their campaigns by sacking the property of the 'excisemen'. They burnt down the excisemen's country houses and smallholdings complete with the mills and even the dovecotes. They ravaged the cornfields and haystacks and devastated the orchards and the vines. An outraged contemporary chronicler, the notary Besse, observed that the peasants were cutting armfuls of unripe corn to feed their horses. As you might expect, he remarked (*Quod est notandum*). All of these depredations were mentioned in the indictments brought in the aftermath of the rising. The persons who had committed them were peasants from the limestone country. The documents actually record the names or nicknames of eleven of the offending villagers. Most of them were tried *in absentia*.

A year after the rising collapsed the provincial intendant embarked upon an attempt to reckon up the damage it had caused. He was obliged to give ear to the clamour of no less then twenty-seven plaintiffs who maintained they had suffered substantially from the revolt. The losses they reported ranged from the order of 100 to 7,000 or 8,000 *livres*. The plaintiffs included the widows of two burgesses of Gramat who had been murdered by the communes, Master Gaspard Perra and his son-in-law Master Antoine Decas. Both of these men had been doctors of law and attorneys attached to the *parlement* at Toulouse. Gaspard Perra's son, Bertrand, a merchant of Gramat, had also been to a lesser degree a victim of the rising. His house had been looted by the rebels. The total loss undergone by the family was eventually calculated as being 12,330 *livres*. The Baron de Gramat similarly felt himself entitled to initiate a lawsuit against the populace of his town. Yet another prominent plaintiff was Antoine de Laporte, the *lieutenant-général* of the *sénéchaussée* of Figeac. A particularly numerous group of victims were the officials employed by the various *élections*. Eleven officials attached to the *élection* of Quercy had their property damaged by the rebels, and similar damage was reported by eight officials in the *élection* of Figeac and three in the *élection* of Cahors. The list of victims concludes with an assortment of citizens of Gramat including three of the consuls, two merchants, a notary, an apothecary and three individuals who are named but not futher identified. Some of the victims such as the *élus*, for example, were evidently singled out for vengeance by the rebels as known and notorious excisemen. Others were held to be culpable of something more in the nature of guilt by association. They were punished because they were relatives, in-laws or friends of the excisemen, or because they had voiced disapproval of the revolt.

Only a few of the slogans used by the peasant rebels in Quercy have been preserved. The slogans are similar to those recorded in Périgord, and suggest that the rebels of Quercy had very much the same aims as the insurgent Périgourdins. Guyon de Malleville declares that the Croquants of Quercy rose up 'claiming that their object was to prevent the introduction of the *gabelle* and to drive the *élus* out of the province'. The Villefranche chronicler states that they 'claimed to be anxious to safeguard the common weal'. When Madaillan issued his summons to the jurisdiction of Montcuq, the order he gave was 'Down with the excisemen!' Buffarot posted up a number of proclamations in the parishes of Haut-Quercy. He urged the parishioners to 'put an end to the *élus* and *gabelles*'.

This last phrase encapsulates the essence of the rebellion. The peasants in Quercy were aiming at precisely the same objective as their cousins in Angoumois and Périgord. The scapegoats marked down for particular vengeance, 'the real excisemen', were the officials of the *élections*.

Up until 1621 the collection of taxes in Quercy had been based on the system employed in all the regions of Guyenne which were subject to the *tailles réelles* (poll tax levied on non-noble land). Assemblies of the local estates had met each year to accord their consent to the annual levy and to spread the burden of payment among the taxpaying population: the allotment of dues this entailed was traditional and unchanging. In 1581 and 1603 the authorities had issued edicts designed to set up *élections* in the regions to the south of the Garonne; but delegates from those regions had protested strenuously, and the edicts had been revoked. In September 1621 a further edict was issued. The people of Quercy believed that they could get this edict cancelled as easily as they had the earlier ones. The syndics of Quercy and Agenais offered a total of 200,000 *livres* to buy out the tax farmer, Jean Saubat. But the syndics had failed to take account of the more significant profit which the Council hoped to make from the new system. Séguier, who was at that time serving as *maître des requêtes* (chancellor's deputy), was given a special warrant to go ahead with the setting up of *élections*. The price of this policy was a peasant revolt.

This rising was Quercy's first expression of violent hostility to the new-fangled *élections*. It broke out in May 1624. A band of 5,000 to 10,000 peasants smashed up the property of three local entrepreneurs who had taken advantage of the new system to purchase offices. The area affected by the rising was precisely the same as in 1637. The marauding peasants all hailed from the parishes of the limestone country between Gramat and Figeac. The names of the three victims were Pierre Reynal, Gabriel Dufour and Jean Dupuy. All three were *élus*, and all three owned property in the rebel cantons of Haut-Quercy.[8] Pierre Reynal was singled out for vengeance a second time during the rising of 1637; he consequently had the distinction of being the victim of two peasant rebellions in thirteen years. The lot of a man who bought offices was scarcely an enviable one. He offered himself as a target for public execration, and was liable to be hunted down any time a disturbance broke

---

8 Jean Dupuy and Pierre Reynal were citizens respectively of Loubressac and Gramat. They were in fact the very first men to buy offices in the region. The down payments they made for their posts were registered at the *cour des aides* of Languedoc as early as 25 August 1622. Dupuy bought the post of counsellor and Reynal the post of controller: these offices each cost 6,200 *livres*. The petition which was subsequently addressed to the Council on their behalf related how 'a number of persons and communities, 10,000 men in all, had risen in arms to murder the present plaintiffs. They looted their property and devastated their houses with a view to deterring anyone else from obtaining these offices ... this violence was inflicted on the plaintiffs purely out of hatred for their posts.' The total cost of the losses suffered by Dupuy and Reynal was reckoned to be 31,228 *livres*. See *Archives Nationales*, E79b, Fo. 358, 17 August 1624; *Archives Départmentales*, Hérault, B32, fos. 479v and 484v.

out. The rising of 1624, however, was a short-lived episode. The seneschal of the province, the elderly Marshal de Thémines, sent in his troops immediately and scattered the peasant band.

These two uprisings in Quercy had a good deal in common. They broke out for the same reasons, and in the same geographical area. They were aimed at the same victims and lasted for about the same period of time. And both of them expressed the intense hostility people felt for the new institutions which the state had established to tax them.

The revolts in Périgord and Quercy differed in one respect alone – the behaviour of the provincial nobility. None of the gentry of Quercy were to be found in the ranks of the rebels. On the contrary, the seneschal and the greatest barons of the province rode out together against the peasant bands. The Croquants of Quercy had made their move too late in the day. Political circumstances no longer favoured the rising, and the fortunes of war had changed. The nobles of this province had no reason for hesitation. Even the most deluded member of the local gentry could no longer see anything to be gained whatever from joining the rebel side.

The impact of the rebellion on the towns of the Garonne

The rest of Guyenne was virtually untouched by the disorders. The Duke of Épernon had taken steps to forestall any rising as early as 11 May. He sent messages to all the towns under his administration enjoining them to 'keep the closest possible guard . . . and stand firm in the service of the king'. The towns responded. The authorities in Libourne, La Réole, Aiguillon and Agen proclaimed a state of alert which remained in force from the middle of May right up till early July. The citizen militias stood guard at the gates, on the bell-towers and in the town halls. A rumour had circulated that the communes were marching on Coutras with the object of seizing the château and recruiting the prisoners held there. The authorities at Coutras promptly reinforced the château with a squad of thirty soldiers and fifty pounds of gunpowder. Consuls in every town in the region gave similar proof of their zeal for the government cause. They made a point of sending envoys to Épernon to assure him of their loyalty to the crown.

On 11 May the *jurats* of Bordeaux received an anonymous warning 'of a revolt which was being hatched in the town on the model of that of the people of Périgord'. The *jurats* were alarmed. They posted guards in the districts of Sainte-Croix and Saint-Michel, on the Hâ and in the town hall, and distributed hundreds of muskets to the houses of reliable burgesses. Those measures were apparently felt to be adequate. By 20 May the *jurats* were able to write to Épernon that 'the populace were behaving'. After the fall of La Sauvetat they sent the Baron de Mornac, a nobleman who was also a member of their council, to present their congratulations to the Duke of La Valette.

South of the Garonne there is nothing in the consular records to suggest that any special precautions were taken against the rebellion. None of the records even gives news of it.

Some notice of the uprising was taken, however, at the other end of south-west France. The aldermen of Toulouse took the trouble to mount a guard in their city. The president of the *parlement* wrote a letter to the chancellor boasting of the vigilance which he and his colleagues had shown. He hoped that this might be the chance to win the city an exemption from some new taxes which had recently been announced. In spite of the city's exertions no disturbance in fact took place in either Rouergue or Gascony – let alone in Languedoc.

The disturbances in western France, April–July 1637

At the beginning of 1637 the Council had been seriously concerned by the possibility of an upheaval in western France. The threat to Poitou undoubtedly seemed graver than that to Guyenne. Some of the Protestant gentry there might well encourage the Huguenot dissident Soubise to abandon his temporary refuge in England and attempt a landing on the coast. Saintonge and Angoumois were also potential trouble-spots. The peasants in both those regions had been refusing to pay their taxes ever since the assemblies organized by their communes the previous spring. From January onwards, then, the governor, Des Roches-Baritaut, was busy keeping order in Bas-Poitou. His task was to hold the local nobility to their duties and to secure the coastal strongholds of La Chaume and Beauvoir, which a Protestant landing party might use as a beach-head.

In April the government decided that the taxes of western France would have to be gathered by force. In Bas-Poitou, for example, the bailiffs assigned to collect them were no longer prepared to risk the trip to the villages. Fifty of the parishes in the *élection* of Sables had failed to draw up assessments for two whole years. Tax agents had been murdered, and the tax farmers' offices stood empty in the towns of Charente, Sèvre and Rivière de Marans. Des Roches-Baritaut was given command of a body of troops, whom he directed to muster at the town of Montaigu. He now had at his disposal a force of 6,000 infantry and 800 horsemen consisting of his personal force of elite troops, the mounted provincial constabulary and the regiments of La Meilleraie and Roquelaure. His staff was composed of officers whom he had specially selected as being 'energetic and law-abiding persons who are well suited to dealing with the masses'. His orders were to disarm any rebels he encountered, to set upon any peasant bands and cut them to pieces, to besiege any towns that resisted him and bombard them into submission. The provincial intendant, Villemontée, was assigned to bring up the rear. His function was 'to reduce the rebels to obedience . . . and make them pay their dues'.

From May to June Des Roches-Baritaut paraded his troops through the 'rebel marshlands'. The regiment of La Meilleraie was stationed in the towns of Luçon, Fontenay, Niort, Saint-Maixent and Lusignan. The garrisons had to stay for a year, but Poitou was pacified.

No rebel meetings were organized in Angoumois until the middle of June. It is possible the peasants there were still hoping for the exemptions they had been promised in 1636, or alternatively they may have been waiting to see what happened to the insurgents in neighbouring Périgord. By about 20 June, however, quite formidable assemblies were being held in the *châtellenies*. The Count of Brassac, who was serving as governor of the province, was obliged to ask for reinforcements. La Valette responded by sending the regiments of Montagnac and Vigan under the command of the Count of Espenan. Help also came from Des Roches-Baritaut, who advanced rapidly through Saintonge. In early July he succeeded in breaking up a number of peasant bands in the district of Cognaçais. Three hundred prisoners were taken, including Gendron and Estancheau, who had led the assemblies of 1636. In August the authorities posted letters patent throughout the province ordering the rebels to hand in their arms at the offices of the various local courts.

The muddled revolts in western France broke out independently, and there is no sign of any collusion with the rebels in Périgord. It would seem that a handful of peasants from the southern *châtellenies* of Saintonge and Angoumois made their way through the forest of La Double to join La Mothe's army. But these peasants were probably acting in response to the huge prestige which the dissident Marquis d'Aubeterre enjoyed in these southern cantons; and otherwise there is no evidence of contact between the revolts. When harvest time came the governor of Saintonge put out a conciliatory announcement. He invited the rebels to return to their homes, and promised that they would not be hunted down.

The disorders in central France, May–July 1637

Riots broke out in Limousin as in every other province in the first months of 1637. Once again the trouble was caused by the appearance of bowmen employed by the local *maréchaussée* bearing writs from the tax collectors. By May the disorders were serious. The Council requested the provincial governor, the Duke of Ventadour, to return to his post as fast as possible. In July Ventadour reported that 'the country people were little inclined to pay their taxes ... they could only think of rising up or winning their liberty'. He asked the authorities to send an intendant to back him up. The government responded swiftly, and on 27 July a royal warrant was duly dispatched to the intendant Le Tonnelier de Conti. The text of this document was to be published in Limousin, and much thought went into the wording. On Ventadour's own advice the Council judiciously refrained from implying at any point that the intendant was being sent in to quell the resistance to the taxmen. His official function was simply to ensure that the passage of troops through the province took place in good order and oversee the administration of the government's 'borrowings'. The intendant's real task was set out in a confidential instruction which was sent to him through the agency of the *maître des requêtes*. The Council required him to put an end to the risings and speed up the tax gathering.

Yet another peasant revolt took place still farther afield, in the region of Apchon in Haute-Auvergne. This rising coincided with the upheaval in Périgord. Apchon was a green and varied stretch of countryside, where the northern slopes of the Cantal mountains were broken up by streams. The peasants of the region had foregathered from several parishes to resist the intruding bailiffs, and the regiment of Effiat, which was currently quartered nearby, was ordered out to confront the peasant host. The *vice-bailli* (deputy law enforcement officer) of Haute-Auvergne, who served as guide to this force, has left an account of the expedition. He relates how the soldiers arrived on 26 April to find the entire contingent of 1,500 peasants drawn up on the Moussages hill. At the sight of the troops the peasants scattered and vanished among the rocks of the neighbouring valleys.[9] The regiment of Effiat resumed its journey towards Champagne, and Mesgrigny, the local intendant, was left to restore order with the help of a few companies of cavalry.

The tide of revolt had been stemmed, but the authorities were unable to collect any further taxes that summer. The peasants all went into hiding the moment the bowmen drew near. Mesgrigny reckoned that there were over 6,000 taking refuge in the woods. Even in this remote district people had heard of the rising in Périgord, and the Croquant manifesto had circulated there.

One final trouble-spot was to be found in the mountains of Marche. The tax collector employed by the *élection* of Guéret had as little success as his colleagues at raising revenues in 1637. In August the tax sergeants had to face a whole series of isolated revolts. Places afflicted included Guéret, Felletin and Aubusson, and above all the villages on the wooded plateau of Millevaches, La Mazière-aux-Bons-Hommes 'and other parishes of the Croquant League'. The disturbances had grown so acute that 'neither sergeants nor bowmen were willing to venture into the mountains any more'.

The peripheral risings as a whole

Little is actually known about the upheavals which took place on the periphery of south-west France. These revolts were both short-lived and scattered, both disorganized and lacking in any specified goal. They were entirely peasant affairs, confined to the rural cantons, and met with almost no positive response in the towns at all. They posed little threat to public order, and the authorities had only to send a few detachments of cavalry to break them up. It is, consequently, no surprise that so few traces of these risings survive in our sources.

The revolts in Périgord and Quercy were another matter altogether. The authorities in those provinces had to contend with real peasant armies. The armies were large, and were welded together by at least a crude code of discipline and system of ranks. The other revolts involved little more than disorganized mobs. Generally these mobs consisted of several hundred peasants, and now and again, in Angoumois and Haute-Auvergne, for example, some thousands might take the field. But none of these peasants were able to stand up to professional soldiers: they panicked the moment they found

---

9 See *Procès-verbaux des chevauchées des Lacarrière, vice-baillis de Haute-Auvergne (1587–1664)*, published by Ulysse Jouvet in *L'Auvergne historique . . .*, Riom-ès-Montagnes, 1900, p. 139. The northern slopes of the Cantal range between Mauriac and Riom-ès-Montagnes were a forbidding and almost uninhabited area.

themselves within range of the soldiers' guns. The last and most critical weakness of the peripheral revolts was their lack of co-ordination. Each of them sprang up on its own, raged for a few days over a few leagues of countryside and fizzled out in the same isolation in which it had started. It is true that some of the risings gathered head at about the same time. The troubles in Poitou and Haute-Auvergne, for example, both flared up, like the great revolt in Périgord, at the end of April. But this timing reflects nothing more than the regular order of the tax year. Spring was the season when the tax warrants were sent to the countryside. Every disturbance that took place, every outbreak of peasant resentment was strictly localized. The rebels campaigned exclusively within their immediate neighbourhood, and made no attempt to link up with insurgents in other provinces. Their revolts come across as nothing more than abortive provincial rebellions which disintegrated for want of leaders and troops.

Yet these minor outbreaks offer us a useful yardstick for comparison. They enable us to see more clearly just how important the rising in Périgord was. They also give us the chance to assess exactly how far away the impact of the Périgord rising was felt. It is clear that only those regions which lay on the borders of Périgord felt the full impact of the rising. The response was dramatic, for instance, in the *châtellenies* of Angoumois on the northern border and in the Lot valley and the limestone country to the south. In the more far-flung areas the occupation of Bergerac and the exploits of La Mothe and his army were never regarded as models. They were nothing more than sensational pieces of news which aroused the interest of the gossips at the fairs. It is true that this news succeeded in making its way to regions as distant as Auvergne and Haut-Poitou. The Croquant manifestos also percolated startlingly far. The aldermen of Poitiers judged it advisable to have a refutation published, and deep in the heart of Auvergne the provincial intendant Mesgrigny denounced the Croquant literature. All the same, there was never any question of a general, concerted rebellion. The idea was inconceivable. These scattered manifestations of an inchoate uprising took place of their own accord in different parts of the country, and no single model or incident was needed to spark them off.

The localized nature of the trouble is instructive from still another point of view. Old centres of insurrection came to prominence once again as the hotbeds of the most alarming disturbances. One major hotbed, for instance, was the district surrounding the town of Crocq on the edge of the plateau of Millevaches. It may well have been from this town that the Croquants derived their name. Much agitation also took place in the forest of Vergt and the meadows of the Dordogne, where the first Croquant bands had assembled in 1595. Peasants rampaged around the limestone district of Gramat, as they had when they rose up to resist the introduction of *élections* in Quercy in 1624. Turbulence was endemic in the patchwork fields of Bas-Poitou and the *châtellenies* of Angoumois. Some of the parishes in these two regions had failed to perform the invidious task of preparing the tax assessments for several years. When the sergeants or tax farmers' agents arrived in the spring, the peasants just drove them away. A peasant revolt was not simply a venture launched at a given time for specific reasons and with particular objects in mind. The country people were never disposed to submit to the grip of the taxman, and rebellion from their point of view was a custom and way of life.

The crushing of the revolt

A rebellion unfolded in several phases, and the scattering of the rebel band by government troops was seldom the end of the episode. In the first place the government usually took steps to punish the rebels. When punishment had been meted out an amnesty would be granted. Finally the revolt would sputter on in isolated areas, and memories of it would linger in the minds of the local people. These last three phases of a rising often had a decisive effect on the way it was treated by later historians. The image which subsequent generations would have of the rising, the value-judgement they would make about it and the haze of nostalgia through which they would view it all took shape at this time.

The punitive phase

In the letters he wrote in May and June La Valette incessantly dwelt on the need to punish the rebels. He appeared before the *parlement* at Bordeaux to request that commissioners be dispatched to try the ringleaders, and explained that he was quite certain such judges would have a deterrent effect. 'He said that they would do much to pacify the masses.' When it became apparent that unrest was still continuing even after the settlement which had been reached at Bergerac, he became even more convinced that punitive measures were required. 'As a result of their failure', he wrote, 'the masses have been obliged to lay down their arms. But their hatred and malice are as virulent as ever, and they continue to indulge in brazen and seditious talk.' He ascribed the outbreak of the rising precisely to the fact that 'the masses in Saintonge got away scot-free'.

To be fully effective these punitive measures would have to be directed at 'those persons of high condition in every walk of life who are openly instigating and supporting the disturbances'. La Valette observed that such leaders 'have something to lose', and he insisted that an example be made of them. He proposed that their houses should be razed to the ground, and their property confiscated and distributed among those captains who had served him best in the course of the campaign. 'It is vital that we should cow them and intimidate anyone who has fallen by the wayside ... these punishments may perhaps provide us with a means to hold them in check.' The commissioners sent by the *parlement* argued in very much the same terms. They wrote how 'the best results will be achieved by punishing those persons of rank and importance who have acted as ringleaders'. 'Even the most stubborn of the rebels' would be 'terrified' by 'the victorious arms of the king' and by 'sentences designed to set an example'.

The rebels had already been subjected to those 'victorious arms' even before the machinery of justice was set in motion. La Sauvetat was sacked with a brutality typical of the most ruthless practices of seventeenth-century warfare. The soldiery were given free rein, and a number of different sources bear witness to their excesses.[10] After the fighting was over, government troops were left behind to garrison the province, and the towns which had welcomed the Croquants were obliged additionally to receive and support this army of occupation. Wherever they went the conquering troops carried out reprisals in the heat of battle and helped themselves to whatever loot came their way by the fortune of war. They had an unwritten right to do so. The custom was a savage one, but nobody questioned it.

The real punishment of the rebels, however, took a rather different form. It was a systematic operation which the government conducted for strictly political ends. Their objective was not so much to mete out justice to the insurgents as to make their authority felt. They wished to make the populace fear them and to drive home the message that their cause had prevailed and any further rebellion was futile. On 27 May the *parlement* at Bordeaux dispatched one of their oldest counsellors, Jean de Moneins, to inaugurate the proceedings. Moneins was given full powers to try the rebels who had been captured at Sainte-Foy and La Sauvetat. He summoned the magistrates of the local *sénéchaussées* to sit in judgement at his side and was accompanied, for good measure, by a deputy public prosecutor on the staff of the *procureur-général*. The Duke of La Valette lent this tribunal the authority of his presence, and made his troops available to ensure that the sentences which the tribunal passed were duly carried out. From the middle of June right through to the middle of July the commissioners pursued their investigations and questioned suspects in Bergerac, Sainte-Foy and Périgueux. They issued warrants for the arrest of rebels who had gone into hiding, and passed sentences *in absentia*. At least four of the several dozen prisoners who had been taken were put to death. One man was condemned to the galleys, and the others were either deported or left to languish in the *parlement*'s prison until such time as the commissioners had completed their inquiries.

Equally rigorous punishments were inflicted in western France by the intendant Villemontée. Villemontée was assisted in his investigations by the *lieutenant criminel* (magistrate attached to the *bailliage* court) of Saint-Jean-d'Angely. He passed the death sentence on anyone who was convicted of murdering an agent of the tax farmers, and a number of such persons were hanged at Charroux in July. The 300 prisoners whom Des Roches-Baritaut had rounded up in the neighbourhood of Cognac were interned in various strongholds in different parts of the province. Villemontée tried their cases

---

10 See Scipion Dupleix, *Histoire de Louis le Juste, XIII du nom, roy de France et de Navarre,* Paris, 1633, p. 43; Bibliothèque Nationale, ms. Périgord 182, fo. 245; Dupuy 473, fo. 255. Madaillan reported that the government forces 'attacked, burnt and pillaged La Sauvetat, and looted and burnt the churches there. Not content with raping the wives and daughters of the citizens, they paraded them stark naked through the army for a period of three days. All the people of La Sauvetat can testify to these outrages.' See statement submitted by Madaillan to Machaut, the provincial *intendant*, in May 1639, *Revue de l'Agenais, 1896,* p. 377.

during the autumn, and a number of them were executed in November at Angoulême.

We may note that the people of Périgord were by no means reduced to apathy or cowed into submission by this judicial terrorism. The authorities were obliged to deploy large numbers of soldiers to make sure that the executions took place. La Valette reported that he 'was obliged to help the commissioners of the *parlement*, who were afraid to carry out their sentences without my assistance'. At Périgueux the soldiers who were stationed around the scaffold broke ranks in panic themselves. Their fright was caused by the din of falling masonry when the crowd of onlookers on the roof of a nearby porch brought the edifice crashing down in the middle of the proceedings. The townspeople of Poitou went so far as to kidnap the hangman whom the provincial intendant had brought from Fontenay to dispatch a number of rebels. The executions were held up, and the intendant had to call in the regiment of La Meilleraie to ensure that justice took its course.

These punishments were designed first and foremost as public spectacles. Executions were deliberately held at times and in places where they could be seen by as many people as possible, and were staged in such a way as to make the maximum impact upon the crowd. Ribeyreix, for example, was executed in mid-afternoon in the town square of Périgueux, to the sound of drums. The authorities in Poitou decreed that the rebels of that province should be dispatched in La Mothe-Fouquereaux 'at one of their official fairs. The news will spread a long way, as livestock merchants from all the surrounding provinces will be there'. Buffarot's execution was actually postponed for two days to ensure that it coincided with a fair which was to be held in the market-place of his home town of Monpazier. The executioners dismembered his body and exposed the severed limbs at the gates of Monpazier and Belvès. Other pieces were hung on a cherry tree which stood at a neighbouring crossroads.

The total number of executions was fairly small. Barely a dozen rebels were put to death, not counting the men who had been killed in the fighting at La Sauvetat. The victims included three of the rebel leaders who were taken captive at Sainte-Foy – Léonard Bonami, Jean de Fettes, commonly known as La Mothe-Grignols, and Antoine de Ribeyreix. Bonami, a notary, was hanged at Sainte-Foy: the other two men, however, were members of the gentry, and were consequently granted the privilege of death by decapitation. Ribeyreix was sentenced at the *présidial* of Périgueux. He had antagonized the burgesses of that town by inciting the rebels to besiege them and lay waste their property, and the burgesses duly took their revenge by including in the sentence a provision stripping both him and his descendants of their status as noblemen. The authorities in Périgueux prided themselves on the sentence, and cited it in later years as a demonstration of their unwavering loyalty to the crown. Another prominent victim was Jean Bonmartin, the lord of Lescansou. A lawyer and a burgess of Eymet, Bonmartin was convicted of bringing the communes into his town, and was sent to the gallows. Charles Lallegrand, another of the prisoners taken at Sainte-Foy, was condemned to the galleys but subsequently released 'with the help of his friends'. Captain Basque, his

standard-bearer and two other members of his band were sentenced to death
by the vice-seneschal of Quercy and executed at Figeac in accordance with
his decree. Buffarot was convicted in the provost's court by the vice-seneschal
of Agenais and was broken alive on the wheel. Similar treatment was meted
out to Estancheau, the leader of the assemblies of Angoumois, who was broken
alive on the wheel at Angoulême. The commissioners of the *parlement* issued
a warrant for the arrest of La Mothe-La Forest. But La Mothe was never
caught. The likelihood is that his numerous friends and relations gave him
shelter, or alternatively took steps to ensure that the authorities made no great
effort to look for him.[11] Madaillan was afforded similar protection by the
gentry of Quercy who took him in. We may cut a long story short by saying
that none of the ringleaders excluded from the subsequent amnesty was ever
rounded up. All of the leaders of the communes apart from Ribeyreix, Basque
and Buffarot got away unpunished. We may further note that the clause by
which Ribeyreix's judges had stripped him of his noble rank was never
implemented. Twenty years later his son was able to take his place among the
king's squires. It is clear that so far as the bulk of the nobility were concerned
no disgrace or dishonour attached to the act of leading a peasant revolt.

The amnesty of June 1637

The authorities had justified their punitive measures on the grounds that the
rebels were persistently refusing to pay their taxes, were 'abusing their excisemen' and indulging in 'brazen insolence'. Before very long they were citing
exactly the same phenomena to argue that the time was ripe for an amnesty.
Punishment and amnesty, in fact, were two complementary ways of dealing
with a rising – two successive stages in the government's response to an
outbreak of unrest. In embarking on this two-stage operation, the authorities
were merely acting in accordance with well-tried political maxims. Messengers
from the Dukes of Épernon and La Valette and the Count of Espenan were
hastening to Paris to propose the terms of a possible amnesty even while the
magistrates were still conducting their hearings in Périgord. On 23 June the
court resolved that the amnesty should be granted. The proposals made by
the dukes were followed down to the smallest detail. Only a handful of
ringleaders whose names had been reported to Paris were excluded from the
terms of the amnesty. Their lands were to be confiscated and distributed
among the captains who had distinguished themselves on the government side
at the battle of La Sauvetat. The Marquis de Duras was accorded the honour
of conveying to Périgord the letters patent from the court, and the king
additionally promoted him to the rank of *maréchal de camp* on the recommen-
dation of La Valette. The final text of the amnesty was drawn up by no less
a personage than the king's secretary, Cartier, who also served as the Duke

---

11 I have been unable to find any document which refers to La Mothe after his departure
from Bergerac on 6 June 1637. We know only that he must have been dead by 1648, when his
wife Jeanne d'Abzac remarried.

of Épernon's business agent in Paris. Richelieu had instructed both Bullion and Sublet de Noyers to give the two dukes their full co-operation.

The preamble to the letters patent ascribed the outbreak of the rebellion to the schemes of foreigners and enemies of the crown. These elements, it said, had 'aided and abetted the uprising of our people'. The king was prepared to forgive and forget the various crimes of the rebels such as 'holding unlawful assemblies, raising men and money for purposes of warfare, using soldiers to administer justice and carry out policing functions, storing up armaments and capturing and fortifying towns'. We may note that this list of the rebels' principal crimes conspicuously failed to allude to the actual cause of the uprising – the peasants' refusal to pay taxes they considered to be unjust. The authorities contented themselves with citing the different forms which the insurrection had taken. The letters patent went on to list the persons excluded from the amnesty. The list contained the names of the twenty-five men who were generally viewed as the ringleaders. In return for the amnesty the government merely required that the peasants should pay the taxes due from them. The Croquants had proposed that 4,000 of their number should be dispatched to spend three months serving against the Spaniards. The letters patent took note of this suggestion, but the government also attached an accompanying note to the dukes which left it to them to judge when the time was ripe for such an arrangement. In the event they took no steps whatever to implement the Croquant proposal. The amnesty did not extend to protect the rebels from claims made by persons who had suffered at their hands under ordinary civil law. Some protection in exceptional circumstances was offered by the clause 'saving our right in other matters and that of other people in all' – but the interpretation of this ambiguous clause gave rise to considerable wrangling. The letters patent concluded by revoking the warrants which had empowered the sergeants to raise the ration tax for the army, and withdrawing the army's right to requisition supplies of corn. Cartier had been thoroughly briefed by the dukes, and was perfectly well aware why it was the revolt had started. He had insisted that this stipulation should be written into the terms of the amnesty. 'It is a small thing to grant', he observed, 'but will none the less be a great comfort to the mass of the people in the communes.'

The government were in no hurry to publish the amnesty. It was only on 23 July that they finalized it by issuing a binding decree designed to conform with the myth which prevailed among the rebels that 'the king had been robbed'. The purpose of the revolt had been 'to persuade the masses that a large part of the taxes which were being levied upon them was finding its way into the pockets of the tax-farmers who were assigned to collect the funds'. The king was accordingly 'anxious to make known the sincerity of his intentions'. He was directing that the moneys raised should be 'conveyed directly to the Treasury, and that the tax-farmers should have no chance to hold back any part of them'. The authorities arranged for the decree to be posted up and read in the provinces where revolts had broken out.

On 30 July the dukes convened a kind of provincial assembly at Périgueux. The assembly was attended by the local justices and the parish *procureurs d'office* (official solicitors). The object was to discuss the implementation of the amnesty 'which the king has been pleased to grant the communes'. On 4 August the *parlement* at Bordeaux made a formal record of the amnesty and had it printed. Espenan introduced the amnesty to the people of Quercy in much the same way. On 18 August he gathered together the consuls of all the townships in the *sénéchaussée* together with a crowd of the local people in the town hall of Cahors. He 'harangued the crowd, assuring them that there was no question whatever of imposing a *gabelle*'. It is evident that the authorities went to particular pains to publicize this act of royal clemency. The amnesty, like the punitive campaign which preceded it, was a political manoeuvre, and the administration of the provinces would be significantly affected by the way it was received. The response to the amnesty would reinforce or alter both the public image of the king and the degree of resentment which was felt towards his taxes. Those factors in turn would decide the overall loyalty of the subject population and the resources which would be available to the government in their quest for a victory over Spain.

Richelieu hoped that the amnesty would free his hands and enable him to bring all his armies into action on the frontiers. The Council were irritated by the continued need to keep regiments in Guyenne and western France. On 1 September the king dispatched a letter expressing amazement that the *parlement* had released a number of rebel peasants who had been arrested in July. 'Your failure to punish these rebels', he observed, 'has emboldened their fellows to resume the uprising.' He insisted that the *parlement* should continue to act with severity, and reminded them 'how essential such an example is to the tranquillity of our state'. Under the terms of the amnesty the authorities were barred from launching any prosecution related to the events which took place in the spring of 1637. But the Council found opportunities to display their resolution and behave severely in dealing with the numerous outbreaks of tax resistance which took place in the autumn of 1637 and the spring of the following year.

La Valette's campaign had ended in victory; but the revolt was not over. It had gone too far and aroused too many hopes to collapse without trace. The aftermath was protracted. As might have been expected, the rising had an immediate and serious effect on the country's revenues, and on top of that there were repercussions in the world of high politics. Finally the troubles in Périgord persisted to such an extent that rebellion appeared to be becoming endemic there.

The revolt and the revenues

The officials of the *élections* had taken to their heels as soon as they got word of the insurrection. It was only at the beginning of July that they were finally induced by the orders of the provincial governor to draw up the tax demands for the current year. The government advanced the *bureau des finances* (fiscal supervisory body established within the *généralité*) the funds necessary to cover the cost of transporting the demands; and the task of distributing the demands in the parishes was assigned to the vice-seneschals and their bowmen rather than to the sergeants of the *élections* who had previously tried to perform it.

In spite of this precaution the demands proved difficult to serve. We need only consider the evidence supplied by Jean Fournier, who was *procureur d'office* in the duchy of Fronsac. Fronsac was an attractive domain which overlooked the Dordogne a league downstream of Libourne. The domain belonged to Cardinal Richelieu, and Fournier had to report to Michel Le Masle, the steward-in-chief of the Cardinal's property. It was his responsibility to set an example for the rest of the province by ensuring the Council's orders were carried out faithfully in the territory he controlled. In mid-July, unfortunately, the bowmen of the *vice-sénéchaussée* found themselves unable to enter his duchy. The villages all rang the tocsin when they drew near, and the peasants chased them away. Fournier was anxious to avoid having punitive garrisons stationed on Richelieu's lands. Accordingly he formed, at his own expense, a body of troops made up of his personal friends along with the servants of the Cardinal-Duke. On 27 and 28 July he marched round the duchy taking dozens of prisoners in each of the parishes which had refused to admit the vice-seneschal's men. At the beginning of September the time came for gathering the first two quarters of the annual *taille*. Fournier duly repeated his military demonstration. He was assisted on this occasion by two of the Cardinal's guards who had been sent from Paris specifically to give him support.[12]

The situation in Fronsadais was paralleled in every province of western France. Everywhere columns of soldiers marched through the villages trying to speed up the tax collection. The regiment of La Meilleraie, for instance, had been scouring the countryside ever since 1636. Following these operations it stayed in the region a further year, and made its departure only in July 1638, when four companies of infantry arrived to relieve it. The regiment was supported by a company of carabineers. Combisan, the vice-seneschal of Saintonge, had been given the assignment of raising this force in May 1636. The company was now organized, and was playing a conspicuous part in the tax-gathering operations. By September 1637 the taxes were beginning to flow into the government coffers once more. The provincial intendants now had at their disposal an armed force sufficiently powerful to enable them to implement their ordinances – by fair means or foul. They responded to the appeals that came in from the chief tax collectors by systematically billeting troops upon recalcitrant communities to force them to pay up.[13]

From this time on the authorities habitually resorted to terrorist methods

---

12 At daybreak on 27 July 1637 Fournier appeared before the town of Cadillac-en-Fronsadais at the head of a force of 150 infantry and 50 horsemen. He surrounded the town and barony and took all the inhabitants prisoner. Some of these peasants were released in August – a step which drew down upon the *parlement* the letter of reprimand referred to above. At the end of the year the *parlement* and the *cour des aides* sentenced a number of the offenders to banishment or the galleys. See L. Brièle, *Document pour servir à l'histoire de l'Hôtel-Dieu de Paris*, in *Collection de documents pour servir à l'histoire des hôpitaux de Paris*, Paris, 1887, vol. 4, p. 295. See also sentence passed on Guilhem Neyrac, barber of Cadillac, in Archives Départementales, Gironde, 2 B 88, 7 November 1637.

13 The cost of maintaining the regiment of La Meilleraie and Combisan's carabineers amounted to 64,000 *livres* a year. Two-thirds of this sum were charged to the *généralité* of Poitiers, and the remainder to the *élections* of Angoulême, Cognac and Saintes. See Archives Nationales E1386, fo. 317; E141c, fo. 25; E145c, fo. 326.

in their attempts to gather the taxes. Such methods often proved to be their only effective way of overcoming the stubborn resistance of the taxpayers.

Several months passed before the regular fiscal machinery was working again. In the meantime demands for tax were made known to the public through the ordinances issued by the provincial intendants. The intendants appointed agents to administer the taxes, and supplied warrants to the troops who had been assigned to conduct the tax-raising operations. Their intervention was badly needed. In the course of May and June the regular financial officials had fled from the headquarters of every *élection* in Guyenne. The officials in Cahors had won the Council's permission to move to Montauban, and the officials in Figeac had obtained a similar imprimatur for their transfer to Capdenac. At Agen and Bordeaux certain steps were taken to stem the tide. On 23 July the government issued a binding decree that directed the officials of those cities to return to their posts within eight days. If they failed to comply with the decree the Council threatened to dismiss them; if they did as they were told they were promised the protection of the crown. The *élus* of Quercy, however, made their way back to Cahors and Figeac only in March 1638, when the provincial intendant officiated at a formal ceremony restoring them to their posts. Périgord took still longer to get back to normal. In March 1638 the tax collectors were still afraid to venture into the countryside, and the officers who collected tithes and fines for the *présidial* were equally unwilling to risk their necks. The rebellion, in other words, had caused a breakdown in the established fiscal institutions. But by doing so it also gave the authorities the chance to try out an emergency system of tax gathering which proved to be both faster and more efficient than the traditional mechanism.

The size of the shortfall incurred by the royal treasury in consequence of the rising is difficult to assess. The tax rebates granted by the government in 1637 were undoubtedly less generous than they had been the previous year. The superintendents of finance were obliged to abandon the levy which had touched off the explosion – the rations tax designed to support the army of Bayonne. They also had to desist from imposing the system of borrowings on the towns of Agenais and Condomois in place of the *tailles* which were levied upon those *élections*. Instead the *élus* were simply required to allot the year's taxes in conformity with the assessment which had been drawn up the year before. Still greater losses had to be endured in the two *élections* of Périgueux and Sarlat in Périgord, where the government were compelled to waive in its entirety the last of the five instalments of the regular annual *taille*.

The tax known as *droits aliénés* had been introduced in 1635–6. It was suspended in 1636, but the suspension was only momentary, and the tax was introduced once again the following year. In spite of this hardly any of the sum demanded was ever paid. The authorities were unable to find anyone in Guyenne who was willing to take on the task of collecting it. The arrears owed by the three *généralités* of Guyenne, Limousin and Auvergne were reckoned to amount to more than 10,500,000 *livres*. It is also instructive to examine some fragmentary calculations which have been preserved in the records of the *chambre des comptes* (sovereign court responsible for fiscal cases). These calculations are concerned with the total quantity of revenue that flowed in from the *élection* of Fontenay in the course of the 1630s. The figures reveal a dramatic increase in the amount of bad debts. In 1636 only 6,309 *livres* of arrears were recorded – a relatively modest sum which amounted to less than 10 percent of the government's tax demand. By 1638 the arrears had shot up to 194, 184 *livres*, or over half the total tax levied. The fact was that tax-gathering operations had fallen well behind schedule in every part of south-west France. In Saintonge, for example, the parishes only began to pay their taxes for 1636 at the end of 1637, and the tax assessments for 1637 were not drawn up till well into 1638. 'In most of the parishes', the tax collector reported, 'they paid only half of the levy imposed on them; and in some they paid nothing whatever in the hope they would get a remission as they had done the year before.' The chief collector of the *droits aliénés* complained how 'the taxpayers are claiming that the sums they owe have been waived by His Majesty – a rumour which has been spread by certain persons ill-disposed to His Majesty's service. Under this pretext the taxpayers are gathering together and rioting against the agents and bailiffs.' The damage inflicted on the tax system was, consequently, twofold. In the first place the rise in the number of bad debts and the late arrival of such taxes as were collected seriously undermined the credit of the Treasury and made it more dependent than ever on the whims of the moneylenders. Secondly the persistent myth that taxation was being abolished was given a new lease of life. The peasants were encouraged in their delusion by both the initial success of the rising and the concessions that followed it – the formal proclamation of an amnesty and a tax rebate.

Political repercussions

The rebellion, then, had a wide-ranging impact on the tax system. But the political repercussions were arguably even greater.

The court in Paris had viewed the Croquant rising as nothing more than a minor irritation. Any steps taken to scatter the Croquants were regarded, by the same token, as nothing more than the prelude to greater and more glorious victories over Spain. But by winning the battle of La Sauvetat, La Valette did at least succeed in regaining the confidence of Cardinal Richelieu, which he had forfeited as a result of his well-known connections with the Duke of Orléans and the Count of Soissons. This turn of events is reported in numerous letters of the time. The Count of Chavigny, for instance, notified Cardinal de La Valette that his brother had been restored to Richelieu's favour. 'If he will only make some slight effort Monseigneur the Cardinal will be completely reconciled to him. For God's sake tell him to behave.' Richelieu himself confirmed the rehabilitation. He wrote to La Valette expressing his hope that the duke 'may be as successful against the Spaniards as you have been against these wretches'.

Unfortunately La Valette proceeded to forfeit the Cardinal's confidence all over again. He left his troops in their camp near Bayonne right through the summer, and made no attempt to engage in any operations against the Spanish forces. Gramont wrote to Richelieu from Labourd denouncing La Valette as an incompetent. He observed that the pass of Le Passage could have been taken in June, and that the Spanish trenches should have been stormed in August under cover of artillery fire. The Spaniards were poorly provisioned and decimated by fever, and would have made an easy target for an assault in the hot season.[14] What actually happened was that on 21 October the Spaniards abandoned their positions under cover of darkness and withdrew to Socoa, where they took to their ships. And on 30 October the Prince de Condé was appointed *lieutenant-général* of the armies of Guyenne.

The appointment was a humiliation for both La Valette and his father. The reasons for it were spelt out in a letter issued by the king. 'We have witnessed the course of events this summer with the greatest pleasure', he proclaimed. 'By God's grace our armies have prevailed on every front. The sole exception to this has been the army of Guyenne, which has taken no action whatever against our enemies, at great cost to the province.' In November the Council recalled François de Verthamont, a friend of the Épernons, from the post of provincial intendant which he had occupied ever since 1630. He was replaced by Étienne Foullé. In April 1638 Condé made his formal entry into Bordeaux. Épernon withdrew to his château of Plassac in Saintonge, and La Valette was from now on obliged to submit to Condé's orders. To avoid the indignity of having to dance attendance on his rival, he set off on a trip to court.

The dukes had fallen from favour in spectacular style. Their fall gave the many enemies they had made the chance to put in the knife. Already in 1635 Épernon had been accused of stirring up the revolt of the tavern-keepers. It was claimed that he had been using the rage of the populace as a weapon against his personal adversaries. Now, two years later, the charges laid were almost identical. The dukes were accused of having fomented the Croquant rebellion. Their accusers maintained they had been seeking to strengthen the dissident Sedan faction, or at any rate hoping to enhance their reputation by winning an easy victory over the disorganized peasant bands. The accusations rained down on the dukes from a number of different quarters. Most of the delegates who attended the *parlement*, for example, raised their voices in condemnation of Épernon's oppressive rule. 'His rations taxes', they told the king, 'have ruined the countryside and driven your people to unlawful acts ... the leading men of this body have been singled out as targets for the explosion of popular rage ... his troops have not been defeating your enemies, but instead have been winning their victories over your long-suffering people'. When Condé arrived in Guyenne he acquainted himself with these grievances and took it upon himself to draw them to the attention of the court and the government. The aged governor and his son were also reviled by the common people in an outburst of hostility that may have been orchestrated by the delegates to the *parlement* at Bordeaux. Ordinary citizens jeered at the rations

---

14 See Archives Nationales, KK 1216, fos. 189, 201, 226 and 234. Gramont was one of Richelieu's regular sources of intelligence. On 1 March 1636 he wrote to the Cardinal how he hoped 'you will please advise the king how honest and loyal I am, seeing that I am your *protégé* and am bound to the service of your house' (KK 1216, fo. 423).

tax as a levy which was being gathered for 'the wedding of Mme de la Valette'. Further indignation was aroused by some cartloads of corn which were sighted heading down the road to Bayonne. People complained that the dukes were reselling the corn to the Spaniards to enrich themselves still further while they left Guyenne to starve.

The Dukes of Épernon and La Valette had been expected simultaneously to contain the provincial insurgents and to launch an invasion of Spain. This double assignment proved to be beyond their capacities, and their failure brought them down. In this sense their fall was the most clear-cut example of the impact which the Croquant revolt had made upon the world of high politics. The changes which now took place in Guyenne as an unmistakable consequence of the local disorders amounted to very much more than a simple substitution of personnel: they affected the very nature of the administrative machinery through which the province was governed. So long as the aged Épernon was the dominant figure there, Guyenne had enjoyed a degree of autonomy: from now on, however, it was closely controlled by the central authorities in Paris. The role of the provincial governor diminished in importance, while that of the intendant increased. Condé, the newly appointed *lieutenant-général*, was a newcomer to south-west France. He had no estates or dependants in that part of the country, was a king's man rather than a semi-sovereign governor, and never possessed the kind of local power base that the indefatigable Épernon had succeeded in building up. Real power in the province was wielded by Foullé, the intendant, and all the decisions taken there were taken by him.

Verthamont, the previous intendant, had kept a low profile. He had exercised his authority in an inconspicuous fashion, and had often shown himself willing to champion the interests of local people. Foullé was an administrator of an altogether different stamp. His arrogance was colossal, and his power was unrestrained. The Council had sent him to promote the all-important war effort, and he was single-minded to the point of ferocity in ensuring that their wishes were carried out. Verthamont had been issued with a number of warrants by the Council in the course of his tenure of office. These warrants, however, were both highly specific and limited in scope, and Verthamont was usually content to leave the conduct of local affairs to the governor and sometimes even the seneschals and *lieutenants-généraux*. He had little choice, insofar as he had not been granted a military command of his own and was consequently in no position to enforce his decrees. Foullé's position was far stronger. The Council had made him 'intendant of justice and finance in the province' – an office which carried with it enormous if ill-defined powers. The governor's duties, by contrast, were confined to the military sphere. His task was to set his seal at the foot of Foullé's ordinances, thereby empowering the intendant to borrow the troops he needed to ensure that his decrees were obeyed. Foullé even had a company of carabineers at his permanent disposal in the same way the governor did. This company served as an escort and stood ready to come to his aid in any emergency. The chronicler Scipion Dupleix had the chance to see Foullé in action. He observed how the intendant was free to do whatever he wanted with the troops that were stationed in the province and the provincial *maréchaussées*. He remarked that Foullé had 'made himself so feared that he was able to exercise absolute power. He kept a lavish table and surrounded himself with a magnificent retinue. As a result he invested his office with far greater dignity than other provincial intendants had been accustomed to do.'

In sending Foullé to Guyenne, the Council abandoned all attempt to pursue a moderate policy. They no longer had any interest in granting tax rebates to offset the burdens which they had inflicted on the communes by requiring them to contribute towards the upkeep of passing troops. Instead they were opting to prosecute the war with Spain whatever the cost might be. They were going to raise taxes by force, and to resort systematically to terrorist methods whenever such methods seemed necessary to keep their coffers full.

The Council were plainly encouraged to adopt a hardline policy by the course of recent events. The taxpayers in the provinces drew rather different conclusions. So far as they were concerned the news of the Croquant revolt afforded an excellent reason for persisting in their refusal to pay their tax. Difficult though it is to establish with any certainty what ordinary people thought, few of them seem to have been inclined to regard the developments which took place at La Sauvetat and Bergerac as dazzling victories. Few of them seem to have taken the view that the royal forces had beaten a deluded mob. We may gauge their opinion from a letter which the intendant of Auvergne sent to the chancellor Séguier. The intendant was writing to relay the news which had been spreading into his province from Guyenne. The picture he gave was scarcely one of undiluted success. 'Every day', he wrote,

we get fresh rumours of the vast number of Croquants at large in Guyenne . . The Marquis d'Aubeterre is said to have joined them recently, and we hear that M. the Duke of La Valette was allowed to regain control of Bergerac and Sainte-Foy only *on condition* that he agreed to secure the government's approval for the petition these rebels had drawn up.

Still more revealing evidence of the outlook of ordinary people may be found in the language of the official minute-book which was kept by the *jurats* of Laplume. The *jurats* reported that the Marquis de Puységur, the noble who acted as the protector of their community and the whole Lomagne region, had set off to join La Valette in Périgord. 'As soon as the agreement was made at Bergerac', however, 'he went on leave with a view to taking the waters in his estate at Encausse.' These provincials, then, were not disposed to believe that the Croquant forces had been broken up by victorious government troops. So far as they were concerned the Croquants had scattered voluntarily because their appeals had at last been heard.

In the eyes of the Council a part of the subject population had risen against their rightful lords and masters, and the rebellion had ended as it had to end, in their defeat and disgrace. The people thought otherwise. In their view the excisemen had been repudiated, and justice done to the poor. No wonder, then, that 'the war of the Croquants in Périgord', as the spring revolt of 1637 came to be called, had a lengthy aftermath. Resistance to the taxman continued for over twenty years. In several places the trouble became endemic. Tranquillity did not return to a number of parishes in Sarladais till well after 1660, and the turmoil was equally protracted in the Isle and Dronne valleys, the Libournais country and the *châtellenies* of Saintonge and Angoumois. The original revolt sputtered on for months and even years, and some of the Croquants turned to banditry.

During its long afterlife (or protracted phase of decomposition), the Croquant revolt was distinguished by a number of colourful episodes. Later generations turned these episodes into epics of heroism, and legend took over where factual records left off. We shall now examine the episodes with a view to disentangling fact from myth and tracing what really happened.

Sequels to the Croquant rising

The history of these sequels is poorly documented, but we can at least make out the identity of some of the leaders involved. Some of them were diehards who had fought in the shattered army of the communes and refused to accept defeat. Others were peasants whose livelihoods had been ruined by the marching of government forces across their land. And a conspicuous number were men who had played a leading part in the original rebellion and had been specifically excluded for that reason from the government amnesty. Forced into hiding, they now re-emerged to head the continued Croquant resistance. The most noteworthy of these captains were the Marquis d'Aubeterre, Pineau le Jeune and Pierre Greletty. Let us glance briefly at them in chronological order of the risings they led.

The Marquis d'Aubeterre

The marquis arrived on the scene just a little too late. Word of his advent spread through the countryside at the very time that the bulk of the original Croquant rebels were returning to their homes. If he had appeared in time he would have brought to the Croquants' aid not simply the cachet of a famous name but also the artillery which the rebel army had tried and failed to obtain in the course of their descents upon Périgueux, Sainte-Foy and Bergerac. The marquis proposed to lead the communes 'with a view to besieging the château of the afore-mentioned Aubeterre. He promised the rabble that he would strengthen their faction by giving them the cannons which were to be found in this château.' In September and October 1637 the marquis took the field in the company of Madaillan and Constantin de Bessou. Dodging the attentions of government troops these commanders rode all the way from the Aubeterre estates on the borders of Angoumois to the forest of Vergt. They rallied to their cause 'all the local malcontents . . . and as many friends as they could'. Épernon responded by sending a company of guards to Périgueux. This move was enough to stop the trouble developing into a second major rebellion. By December it was all over. 'Old Constantin' was rumoured to be skulking amidst a troupe of wandering tumblers. Madaillan was reduced to buying his pardon with a promise to betray his former comrades. The marquis found himself sentenced to death *in absentia* by the *présidial* of Bordeaux. He took to his heels.

The background of this leader is of some considerable interest on account of his family. The Aubeterre family was a grand one, and its name was by far the most prestigious of those associated with the peasant revolts of the seventeenth century. The marquis's full name was Pierre Bouchard d'Esparbès de Lussan. He was born in 1605, and died around 1650. He was the elder son of François d'Esparbès, a marshal of France and state councillor who served as the seneschal of Agenais and Condomois. By the time that old d'Esparbès died in 1628, the young marquis was already terrorizing the neighbourhood. At the age of nineteen he had set himself up as the leader of a small private army. This band marched into the villages on market days, drums beating and armed to the teeth, and raised taxes from the parishes of the local *châtellenie* for the marquis's personal benefit. On 17 February 1629 the marquis was disinherited by his widowed mother, and on 19 February 1630 the provost of Angoulême condemned him to death. The marquis took refuge in Piedmont, where he was befriended by the Count of Soissons. In August 1634 he returned to his native province and set about organizing a number of gatherings of gentry who had sided with Monsieur. The court issued orders to keep him under surveillance. This task was assigned to his brother-in-law, the Count of Jonzac, who was currently serving as *lieutenant-général* in Saintonge. In January 1637 the marquis was informed that he had been wholly dispossessed by his younger brother, François, Viscount of Aubeterre. The viscount had not merely succeeded to their father's estates, but had now in addition inherited the post of seneschal of Agenais and Condomois. By plunging into the revolt, then, the marquis was in effect embarking on a kind of personal crusade to recapture his lands. The remainder of his life was just as adventurous and violent as the earlier part had been. The Marquis d'Aubeterre was a full-time conspirator, and proud of it. And he was, by the same token, a typical representative of the French provincial nobility, who maintained their independence against all comers and in due course fought for the Fronde.

Pineau le Jeune

After Aubeterre's disappearance the parishes of Le Paréage found a new leader in the person of Jean Pineau, otherwise known as Pineau le Jeune. Pineau was the son of a Protestant clergyman from Bergerac. He served in the army of the communes as captain of Maurens, a parish which lay to the south of the forest of Vergt. Foullé, the intendant, issued an order for Pineau's arrest, and Jean de La Brousse, vice-seneschal of Périgord, duly succeeded in capturing him in January 1638. La Brousse set off towards Périgueux with his prisoner and an accompanying guard of bowmen, but the party were ambushed on their way through a stretch of woodland and Pineau managed to escape. La Brousse himself was killed in the skirmish, and several of the bowmen also fell. Pineau had been wounded, and his freedom did not last long. He was recaptured shortly afterwards and beheaded at Périgueux.

Pierre Greletty

Pierre Greletty achieved the distinction of keeping the *maréchaussée* at bay for three whole years. Trouncing his pursuers in the depths of the woods, he became a popular hero, and the local chroniclers gave more space to his minor victories than they did to any number of other events which took place in their province at the time. Greletty was a native of Peyrafon, a village situated on the estates of the Marquis de La Douze not far from the township of Vergt. His father, brother and cousins were all ploughmen on the La Douze estates, but Greletty preferred to describe himself as a soldier. He spoke Low Gascon, and knew only a few words of French. An anonymous member of the peasant host in 1637, he emerged as the head of a rising of his own in December the following year. He was close on forty years of age.

Greletty's revolt is said to have been provoked by the violent conduct of a company of soldiers who were billeted in his village. The captain of this force was a certain Chevalier de Chavigny, who was also related by marriage to the seneschal, Bourdeille. Chavigny's arrival was greeted with a clamour of 'Down with the excisemen!' and the likelihood is that the government had issued a warrant instructing him to use his troops to escort the local tax sergeants. At all events he was forced to flee, and the peasants plundered his baggage. In addition to being implicated in this disturbance Greletty was also accused of having murdered a Périgueux attorney with whom he was engaged in a legal dispute. The accusation may or may not have been justified; but Greletty was from that time onward obliged to go into hiding.

It is clear that Greletty had several hundred associates right from the start. On 7 January 1639 Bourdeille issued an ordinance requesting the villagers of Le Paréage to return to their homes. On 30 January the seneschal gathered a force of 2,000 men at the château of Atur, in the northern part of the forest of Vergt. He proposed to attack the peasant contingents and to raze their leaders' houses to the ground. The soldiers were accordingly dispatched to the depths of the forest. This first attempt at repression proved entirely ineffectual, since the rebels simply scattered the moment the seneschal appeared, and a second expedition had to be mounted the following April. On this occasion the government troops were accompanied by Amelot de Beaulieu, a *maître des requêtes*. The Council had issued Amelot with a warrant directing him to restore order in the district. He rounded up a few dozen prisoners and assumed that with this small step the object of pacification had been achieved. A garrison commanded by the Count of Grignols was left on the edge of the forest for the remainder of 1639. Greletty's father was captured and taken to Bordeaux. On 8 December he was broken on the wheel.

But the pacification was not after all the success it had been supposed. By January 1640 we find that the citizens of Périgueux were sick of the constant raids being launched by Croquants from the forest. They armed at their own expense a force of 120 men. This garrison patrolled the forest paths for some time under the leadership of a young burgess named Pierre Grand du Pouzet. The following March the Count of Grignols advanced into the forest at the head of his royalist force in a third attempt to put down the rising. This time the rebels resisted. The soldiers were bloodily beaten, and in the next three months, March to June 1640, Greletty's insurrection reached the climax of its success.

Every day new recruits arrived to swell the peasant contingents. Faced with this challenge the provincial intendant, Foullé, got the Council to adopt a resolution directing that the forest should be cut down. The Marquis of Sourdis, currently *lieutenant-général* of Guyenne, hurried across to the district from the other end of Gascony to take personal command of a fourth campaign. Arriving in June 1640, he set two regiments to work felling trees and burning thickets. Peasants from three leagues around were drafted in to help with this operation, which continued for nine whole days. Before setting off once again Sourdis made a point of organizing a temporary encampment of the army of Guyenne. A supply base was set up at Bergerac to provide this new garrison with victuals and arms. In the course of September, however, the regiments were obliged to return to Languedoc by the pressures of the Spanish war, and the Croquant bands resumed their raids with a vengeance.

In the autumn of 1641 the veteran rebel Madaillan reappeared in the public eye. The Sedan plot had just collapsed. Madaillan had probably been involved in the conspiracy, and his object now was to turn its failure to his advantage. He consequently accused the Dukes of Épernon and La Valette of having sought to get Richelieu assassinated through the agency of Greletty. Madaillan's plot was abetted by the Duchess of Aiguillon, the Cardinal's niece, who was one of the Agenais landowners, and the Baron de La Rivière, who was Richelieu's vassal in the latter's capacity as Duke of Fronsac. The duchess arranged for Madaillan to be given a safe-conduct, and the baron acted as his witness. The unmasking of this supposed plot had gratifying results. Greletty was granted an amnesty, and Madaillan won golden opinions as the provincial peacemaker. Both the Marquis de La Douze and the Duke of La Force spoke up on behalf of Greletty, and in November 1641 the letters containing his pardon were issued by the king. On 19 December Greletty and his men appeared in the village of Lembras to make their formal submission to the *lieutenant-général* of Bergerac. Greletty obtained a captain's commission in the royal armies, and persuaded a hundred of his associates to enlist at his side. On 25 January 1642 the band left the province for good.

The peasant bands of Le Paréage: background and organization

Various different places are mentioned in the sources as the homes of Greletty's associates. On closer inspection we find that these places were all located in the same dozen parishes stretching from the heart of the forest of Le Paréage into the surrounding countryside as far as the gates of Périgueux. Greletty's bands never numbered more than a few hundred men. They reached their greatest strength after the Count of Grignols was put to flight in the spring of 1640. At that time they may have totalled some 700 to 800 men. By the time they finally submitted, however, in December 1641, their ranks had thinned considerably, and they numbered no more than a hundred men in all.

They were scattered through the forest in isolated groups of twenty or so, and it took their leader several days to gather them all together.

The rebels none the less succeeded in scoring a number of major successes. The attempt which the burgesses of Périgueux made in January 1640 to station a garrison in the forest proved ineffectual. The garrison ran short of provisions and forage, and consequently found it impossible to hold out for any length of time. It was this débâcle which tempted the Count of Grignols to take a hand. Bourdeille, the provincial seneschal, was old and visibly failing, and Grignols had an eye on his post. He persuaded the Marquis de Sourdis to issue a warrant authorizing him to use prime-quality troops against Greletty. Armed with that warrant he levied some regiments from Tonneins and Ventadour along with a troop of horse from the company based at Marsin. In March 1640, as we saw above, he led this small army into the forest – and disaster. The Croquants ambushed the soldiers and routed them. The action which took place was nothing short of a bloodbath. Over 200 members of the royalist force were killed, including fourteen of its officers. Grignols himself was wounded, and the regiment from Ventadour had to be completely reorganized.

Even the major expedition which Sourdis led in June was cheated of victory. The army met with no resistance, since the rebels had simply resorted to a well-tried tactic and scattered in all directions before the government soldiers arrived. By the end of 1640 the peasant bands had re-formed and were once again in control of the territory. They stormed a couple of fortified posts which Sourdis had left behind him in the townships of Vergt and Saint-Mayme. They set upon a detachment of the regiment from Tonneins, drove the troops into the forest and slaughtered them in the château of Rossignol. They raided the local tax collectors and confiscated their takings. Finally they turned their attention to the worst of all their enemies, the *lieutenant criminel*, Martial d'Alesme. Alesme owned estates in Meycourbi, a village which lay on the edge of the forest not far from Périgueux. The Croquants descended on his country house and burnt it to the ground.

Quite a lot of blood, then, was spilt in the course of these various skirmishes. But the trouble was only sporadic, and barely affected anyone living outside the forest. Greletty's men were bandits rather than rebels in the fullest sense. Sometimes, indeed, their excesses actually drove the peasants to take up arms against them. The bowman Chaleppe, for example, was able to rally a local following against Greletty. (Chaleppe, as we noted earlier, was himself a native of the forest – a fact which presumably helped.) The seigneur of Razac could count on the support of his loyal peasants to keep the Croquant contingents away from his lands. Bourdeille, finally, was able to call on hundreds of tenant farmers from his estates in Nontronnais to comb the forest for rebels. We should note, all the same, that these armed expeditions which the communes dispatched to the forest to assist the authorities scarcely ever succeeded in coming face to face with the rebel bands. Greletty's men survived in their woods, and they did so for two reasons. They were experts at guerrilla warfare. And the local communities gave them enough support to ensure that they could continue holding out.

The villagers of Le Paréage gave Greletty's bands food and shelter and supplied them with information. They collaborated out of a mixture of motives. The rebels were genuinely popular, but they were, at the same time, feared. In the view of the Marquis de Sourdis the peasants supported the rebels 'partly from the ill will they bore us, and partly because they were afraid that the Croquants might burn their homes down as they had threatened they would do'. Chevalier de Cablanc indicates that the rebels succeeded in forging certain kinds of 'alliance between one parish and the next'. Greletty used a whole range of people to act as his envoys in this forest diplomacy. Parish priests, village lawyers and even simple ploughmen were sent round the neighbourhood on behalf of the rebel bands. One typical envoy was Jean Daniel, a one-time soldier who had since settled down as a burgess in Bergerac. Cablanc informs us that Daniel often used to go to the forest to visit Greletty,

whom he greeted as an old friend. He would beg Greletty to support him against anyone in the area who was giving him trouble; and if Greletty's associates happened to be threatening any of his friends, he would go to the rebel leader and beg him to make sure that the threats were not carried out. Greletty was always happy to grant these favours, since he enjoyed complete authority over all the associates who were with him in the forest, numerous and powerful as they were.

The rebels, in other words, had ensnared the local communities in a web of intelligence-gathering and intimidation. 'They threatened that they would kill anyone who denied them the help they needed, or burn down his home. These threats terrorized the whole neighbourhood to such an extent that no one dared to betray them to the authorities or refuse what they asked.' The rebel band itself was held together by mutual terror. Greletty assured his followers that 'it was as much as their lives were worth to desert his company', while 'his soldiers threatened that they would kill him if he ever went off and left them unprovided for'.

The forest people knew everything there was to know about ambushes, raids, sudden scatterings and the hidden cache of arms. The Duke of La Force reported that 'they have learnt how to fight with skill and how to advance or retreat when necessary in these regions which no one except themselves is able to penetrate'. Scipion Dupleix recorded how 'they shut themselves up in the shelter of various strongholds and entrenchments which they had built in the most terrifying depths of the forest'. Greletty never embarked on any large-scale operation. He never tried to rally the parishes outside the forest district or to march on a local town. He was content to harry his enemies and frustrate their attempts to destroy him.

The bandits and their doctrine

Contemporaries referred to the rebel bands in the forest as 'Grelettys' or Croquants for short. They also called them robbers, the 'robbers of Le Paréage' or 'robbers of the forest of Vergt'. These rebels never produced any sort of written manifesto or indeed made any utterance suggesting that they had an agenda in mind. They justified their rebellion in bleakly simple terms. They cited the wretchedness of the taxpaying population and the enormity of the crime they had committed in rising up. Such a crime could not be atoned for. It placed them outside the law. If caught they would be consigned without fail to the harsh and summary justice of the provost's court. Further indications of the rebel outlook are given by Dupleix. 'This rabble', he wrote, 'were engaging in every kind of banditry. They justified themselves by claiming that the people were ground down by taxes and special levies, and that their rising was an attempt to resist this oppression.' Greletty and his followers used similar language to the envoys whom the Duke of La Force sent to treat with them in 1641. They maintained that they had been 'driven to this extremity by their wretchedness and despair ... They insisted none the less that they would abandon this life altogether if the king in his mercy were pleased to grant them an amnesty for their crimes.'

The 'Grelettys' directed their animosity first and foremost at the burgesses of Périgueux and the officials of the provincial jurisdictions. They launched their raids on the property of these dignitaries, burning their smallholdings, plundering their livestock and forcing them to send their merchandise on long circuitous routes to avoid the dangerous road through the forest. The Croquants referred to their targets explicitly on the occasion when they burnt down the country house of Martial d'Alesme. Some of them boasted that they 'had singed the tails of the rats in Meycourbi, and before long they would be burning some other rats' nests too'. Punitive expeditions into the woods proved fatal for a number of burgesses. Two of the more prominent casualties were Pierre Grand du Pouzet, the captain of the guard at Vergt, and Géraud Chancel, whose father was serving as councillor on the local *présidial*. Both of them fell in the course of an assault on the outlaw entrenchments. To the vast indignation of the Périgueux burgesses, the Croquants appeared to be getting away with their crimes. A number, indeed, were captured. They were duly condemned by the *présidial*, and the burgesses had them broken on the wheel. Much of the time, however, the bandits succeeded in evading every attempt to catch them. They stayed free because they had the local gentry on their side.

Time and again great cavalcades of nobles rode through the woods in the train of their seneschal. Ostensibly they were riding to crush the rebels, but their efforts were suspiciously ineffective. These nobles appear to have been in remarkably little hurry to capture the Croquants, in spite of the fact that the Council had issued them with the most particular orders to do so. A glance at their backgrounds is revealing. Two of them, for example, were relatives of La Mothe-La-Forest. The seigneur of Razac was his first cousin, and the Marquis de La Douze was his brother-in-law. Razac and La Douze were two of the five principal seigneurs of these forest cantons: the others were the seigneur of Fonlongue, the Baron d'Auberoche and the Count of Grignols. All of them except Grignols came out openly and unambiguously in favour of the Croquants. Dupleix confirms that 'certain members of the nobility supported their lawlessness, or covered it up'. How this collusion worked is indicated in the records of a trial which took place at Périgueux at the beginning of 1641. Two Croquants were being cross-examined before the magistrates' court. They explained to the court that the gentry had been giving the rebels prior warning of the dates on which the seneschal planned to launch his expeditions and the routes he proposed to take. (Chevalier de Cablanc lays the blame at the door of the seneschal himself: he explicitly states that Bourdeille took care to advise the rebels every time he marched through the forest.) A valet of the lord of Fonlongue was assigned the task of alerting the bandits to the approach of the seneschal's cavalry. The rebels accordingly fled, and were given shelter by the gentry on a number of their country estates in Faure, Bourboux and Fonlongue. The court was informed that some traders from the township of Vergt joined forces with some of the servants of the Marquis de La Douze to keep the Croquants supplied with powder and weapons. They also bought up the livestock which the Croquants had plundered during the raids they launched on the smallholdings of the Périgueux burgesses.

The accused rebels shook the court with the still more serious revelation that four of the stewards employed on the lands of the Marquis de La Douze had personally organized or led a number of Croquant raids. La Douze's men had been responsible, among other things, for instigating the burning of the country house at Meycourbi which had belonged to Martial d'Alesme. A lawyer named Gabriel Desmaisons who had been appointed to the post of magistrate for Vergt had apparently come to seek out the 'Grelettys' and had advised them 'that they should go and burn down this house at Meycourbi. He told them that this was the way to bring the authorities to terms, and that it would be pleasing to M. the marquis.' The names of the two Croquants who were examined by the court were Milor and Bonnet. They recalled one occasion on which they pilfered guinea-fowl from a farmyard, and were arrested and held in detention by La Douze's stewards. 'Why the hell', asked the stewards reproachfully, 'didn't you eat the fowls in Périgueux? If you'd only picked on those we'd never have come and arrested you.'

These episodes reflect the profound antagonism that existed between the burgesses of Périgueux and the people of the surrounding countryside. This rural population included both the gentry and peasants of Le Paréage. Nobles and peasants alike were girding themselves to resist the invasion of the countryside by an alien bourgeoisie. They rebelled against the extensive and in their view excessive power which the bourgeoisie had acquired as a result of the sale of offices and the shift to a new tax system. The nobles inevitably sympathized when the bandits in the forest of Vergt swept out of their strongholds and surged up to the very gates of Périgueux. By the same token it was the military commanders in the province, and not the judicial authorities, who stepped in to negotiate an amnesty for Greletty. The magistrates in Périgueux, indeed, did everything in their power to discourage the government from granting it. When the letters patent arrived from the crown announcing the amnesty the event was duly entered in the records of the *présidial*. But none of the urban magistrates who sat on the *présidial* made the formal request for an entry. The request came, significantly, from a seigniorial judge whose calling was pursued on the lands of the Baron d'Auberoche.

Greletty was probably the most celebrated of the various peasant leaders who took part in the chaotic and little-known struggle between the cities and countryside of sixteenth- and seventeenth-century France. He presented himself to the public as a soldier and 'man of honour'. The hatred with which he was viewed by a handful of families in Périgueux was vastly outweighed by the admiration of villagers throughout his forest canton; and the barons of Périgord protected him from his foes. In certain respects his rebellion was little more than a shadow of what had gone before. Only two years had passed since the great uprising of the communes, but already the changes were startling. The communes had put their case in a series of written manifestos. Greletty's band left no record apart from the scraps of a few reported speeches whose principal characteristics were ferocity and despair. The communes had gone round the countryside in broad daylight summoning the fortified towns of the province to rally to their cause. Greletty's band preferred to move about under cover of darkness, and contented themselves with the pillage of isolated farms. These rebels were shorn of doctrine compared with their predecessors, and the demands they made of the government were sadly and visibly trimmed. In fact, they were no longer rebels in the strictest sense at all: they had turned into bandits. Yet Greletty's adventure none the less provides us with a glimpse of the same social panorama that formed the background to the upheaval of 1637. Once again we can see the traditional society of the countryside rising up in protest against the new-fangled apparatus of state control and against the intendants and tax-farmers, the fiscal officials and agents, the bowmen and bailiff's ushers and all the other provincial functionaries who served as the cogs in that infernal machine.

In the years between 1637 and 1648, outbreaks of peasant resistance to the new tax system recurred again and again. The rulers of France had no choice but to try to live with these outbreaks and view them as a kind of occupational hazard. Trouble was provoked by a series of major political events. In 1641 the government invested the provincial intendants with full tax-gathering powers. Little more than a year later Cardinal Richelieu and Louis XIII died in quick succession, and in 1643 the boy-king Louis XIV acceded to the throne. The peasants reacted to each of these events with a surge of anger or optimism, and used them as pretexts for refusing to pay the government's latest taxes. They considered the taxes to be both unwarranted in principle and unacceptable in the specific form in which they had been imposed. Most of the trouble at this time was concentrated in Rouergue, where a revolt broke out in 1643, and Gascony, where the peasants of Astarac and Pardiac withheld their taxes continuously from 1642 to 1645.

The Council of the new king was not unaware of these persisting domestic threats. Cardinal Mazarin, however, was bent on pursuing Richelieu's policy of making war on the Habsburgs in Vienna and Madrid. The tax revenues which the government were able to raise in the countryside (always assuming that it was possible to raise them at all) were evidently not going to be substantial enough to meet the needs of the royal armies; and a change of policy was consequently tried. From 1646 to 1648 Particelli d'Hemery, the Superintendent of Finance, issued a series of edicts shifting the burden of war contributions on to the towns. Most of the towns of France had up till now been exempt from the obligation to pay the tailles, *and Paris in particular had basked in its tax-free status. Particelli's efforts proved fruitless. The populace in the towns were already suffering from war-weariness brought on by the unending European conflict, and the government's measures were cordially loathed. The government was ill-placed to confront this degree of unpopularity at a time when the king was a minor and the chief executive who had pushed through the measures in his name was a figure like Mazarin. The new Cardinal was viewed as a foreign interloper, and a liar into the bargain. He was little feared, and widely despised.*

The members of the sovereign courts of Paris who formed the political elite of the capital made up their minds to reject the Cardinal's measures. Their act triggered off a crisis which gripped the country for five whole years. The Fronde, as this crisis was called, posed a serious threat to the very survival of the state. One after another the major interest groups in the kingdom made their bids for immediate power – the members of the parlements, *the officials of the provincial administrations, the great princes and their regional followings. These groups even went so far as to demand control of the central government and to seek changes in the basic principles on which that government was run. Historians generally assume that the views of ordinary people can hardly have constituted a significant force at this early date. They take it for granted that the political duels of the Fronde years were altogether beyond the grasp of the poor. Seen in this light the thesis which I am advancing in this study may well seem both heterodox and a trifle provocative. I have tried to show that the peasants too made demands in the course of the Fronde, and have argued that peasant unrest may indeed have exerted an influence on the overall course of events. The peasantry were involved in the Fronde in several different ways. Sometimes the villagers simply followed their local seigneur. They rose up and fought on whatever side the seigneur happened to be. But the peasants also rose up spontaneously on a number of occasions when they had been goaded beyond endurance by the depredations of passing troops. Their views emerge still more clearly from the slogans which the chroniclers record them as yelling when riots broke out, and most clearly of all from the handful of petitions which various meetings of provincial estates submitted to the government in 1649 and 1651. The fact remains none the less that the opinions of the masses made a significant impact only now and again. The aims of the Fronde as a movement were essentially unconnected with the troubles in the countryside, and popular grievances had little bearing either on the way the movement developed or on the ups and downs of the civil war. I have consequently felt obliged to omit this particular portion of the study from the present abridged edition. Interested readers will find a more substantial discussion on pp. 463–523 of the complete text published in 1974.*

Isolated popular risings continued to break out incessantly right up to the end of Mazarin's ministry. In 1660–1 the political scene was transformed by another succession of major events. Louis XIV married, and peace was at last concluded with Spain. The Cardinal-Minister died, the king claimed the right to rule by himself, and Fouquet, the Superintendent of Finance, was placed under arrest. People responded to the news of these various developments with one final surge of hope. They believed that the government might now at last accord them a tax remission, and that the country stood on the threshold of a new and better era in which the monarchy would be shorn of all the fearsome characteristics it had acquired in recent years. The new tax system would be dismantled, and the trend to an ever more centralized and authoritarian regime would be steadily reversed. The hopes were sadly misplaced. From the 1670s onwards a utopia of this kind was no longer even conceivable. Peasant revolts were now being systematically and harshly suppressed. One typical case was that of the peasants of Vivarais, who had risen up to resist the introduction into their province of the government's tax reforms. In July 1670 these peasants were scattered by government forces. Their leaders were hunted down tirelessly: once caught, they were handed over to the magistrates and subjected to the utmost rigour of the law. A fresh wave of troubles broke out when the government introduced stamp duty in 1675. Much of the agitation took place in Bordelais, the traditional hotbed of popular risings. But there were also disorders in Brittany, where bands of peasants rose up in the viscounty of Cornouaille. As well as opposing the new tax these peasants were also motivated by resentment of their seigneurs. Outbreaks of violence against the seigneur were unusual at this early period. At all events these various disturbances had been quelled without difficulty by the end of September that year.

By this time the Council in Paris had developed swift and effective methods for gathering intelligence and suppressing unrest. The peasants of this generation were in any case less disposed than their parents had been to resort to the weapons of riot or insurrection as the obvious means of pressing their political demands. Better educated than their forefathers, they were also more docile. Their heads were not turned to such a degree by the heady excitements of violence. And they were more accustomed than their forebears to the state's fiscal apparatus and its annual appearance in their midst. No one by this stage seriously questioned the government's essential right to levy the regular yearly tax.

The eighteenth century opened with the revolt of the Camisards, which lasted for just over two years, from July 1702 to August 1704. This episode, however, was quite clearly linked to the state's persecution of Protestants and the very specific circumstances which prevailed in the Cévennes region and had driven the villagers there to despair. The Council were afraid that the revolt might lead to a general bout of resistance to the taxman all over the south of France. But nothing of the kind took place. On the contrary, for many decades peasant protests were small-scale, and none of them took on the character of a province-wide uprising. The quiet remained unbroken until the start of the great rebellion which convulsed western France in March 1793. But before that quiet set in there was one final outbreak of traditional peasant insurrection. This outbreak took place in Quercy in 1707. The peasants on this occasion expressed themselves and behaved in ways reminiscent of risings dating right back to 1548.

The rebels of Quercy began by reviving the old name of Tard Avisés. The object of their revolt was to protest against some edicts the government had issued which would have the effect of increasing the tax on legal fees. The government had farmed out the work of inspecting the legal documents to a number of local agents. The peasants marched to the offices of these agents and set them on fire. The next target was the town of Cahors, where the intendant of Haute-Guyenne had taken shelter. Between 10,000 and 15,000 of the rebels converged on the town and subjected it to an unsuccessful siege. Other peasant columns advanced in the meantime to threaten Sarlat and Gourdon. The townspeople subjected them to a volley of gunfire, and a few companies of dragoons were enough to complete the rout. The entire revolt had lasted for no more than two months. It began in May 1707 and was over by the end of June. The rout of these latter-day Tard Avisés was the last event of its kind. No further peasant armies are referred to in the records of current political events. For the whole of the eighteenth century the kingdom of France was singularly free of rural disturbances. No agitation seems to have lasted for more than a few days or affected more than the merest handful of cantons. (An account of the uprising of 1707 may be found on pp. 524–533 of the 1974 edition.)

4

Types of Riots in the Seventeenth Century

This study accepts the sociological concept of perennial violence. I assume, that is, that riots are not merely unique and irreplaceable components of a historical episode, but to a certain extent resemble each other, conform to patterns, and exhibit conventional and often repeated features. These similarities allow us to group them into families of events, which I have defined on the basis of their immediate causes, their institutional circumstances, and the bugbears which stirred them up. To assign the ultimate causes to these events we should doubtless need to invoke the different systems of interpreting history. Such a step would exceed the scope of this typology. I prefer to remain at the level of describing and analysing the basic structures of the historical phenomena, as I have done in the remainder of this work.

I have distinguished four separate causes of riots. They broke out in protest against the price of bread, the billeting of troops, the collection of taxes and, finally, the practice of farming taxes out. The *cause* of a riot seems, indeed, the element by which a particular episode can be most easily classified, as well as being the element most likely to alter the other components of the affair. It would be possible to imagine other such elements. We could classify riots according to the view taken by the rioters: 'They are trying to starve us', 'They are coming to live off us' or 'They want to rob us'. Alternatively we could classify them according to the forms the violence took: the riot of rejection, in which tax agents were driven out and the gates of the city closed; the riot of attack in which grain was plundered, and the tax collector's office or the guard of fusiliers assailed; the riot of popular justice, in which ritual murders took place, excisemen were imprisoned and the public's grievances avenged in kangaroo courts. We could classify them according to the people who took part: women's riots, smugglers' riots and general riots. We could classify them according to their outcome, as riots of jubilation or riots of despair. Finally, we could classify them according to their various purposes: the search for a scapegoat for the public misfortunes, the urge to defend a long-established order of things, the desire to strengthen local solidarity. We shall look at these various different elements under the heading of the four principal types of revolts we have defined, considering in turn their causes (i.e. the institutional cause of a riot and the popularly transmitted idea of that cause), the forms the violence took (i.e. the words and deeds of the rioters), the roles played by the people involved (i.e. the victims who provoked the trouble, the rebels who turned to persecution and the notables who acted as mediators), the effects of the disturbance and finally the purpose it was intended to serve. This account will inevitably contain repetitions – repetitions which only serve to show how difficult it is to categorize events which are themselves so complicated, and how many-sided and hard to reduce to any particular category each individual episode proves to be.

Riots at the price of bread

These riots were naturally the result of a subsistence economy in which each group of peasants cultivated its separate plot of soil in isolation and autarky. Provoked at the same time as they were by the most basic daily necessity, they remain readily understandable to the reader of another period. Their simple motive readily attracted the attention of historians. Another reason we know more about them than the other types of riot is that troubles connected with the grain supply broke out with particular regularity and seriousness at the end of the *ancien régime* (e.g. in 1766, 1772, 1775, 1789, etc.), at a period for which the sources are more numerous and fuller – a period which has also proved particularly attractive to historians insofar as it covers the eve of the French Revolution.

Our argument here will be based on a relatively limited number of episodes. The reason for this lies purely in the defects of the sources. The scattered incidents which took place in times of dearth did not always give scope for legal proceedings. The offenders who might have been prosecuted were often, as we shall see, anonymous and diverse, and repression often seemed an inappropriate course to take. Above all, the episodes which did stimulate inquiries were handled only at the lowest level of jurisdiction, in communal or seigniorial courts or the common crown courts. The archives maintained by all these places have either disappeared or are hard to come by. Riots of this kind should certainly be regarded as frequent and commonplace. At the same time they were confined to the years of dearth, or in other words to a mere ten or fifteen years of the century under consideration.

Immediate causes of bread riots

As might be expected, these outbreaks followed the annual fluctuations in the grain price. They took place when prices went up. Most often they took place in the interval between harvests, a period whose length depended on the degree of shortfall experienced in the harvest just over and any delay which might affect the reaping of the crop to come. Most of the recorded riots, nineteen in all, took place between March and early August, and the greater part of these, ten of the nineteen, were concentrated in the months of May and June. A particularly bad harvest could engender a fear of dearth as early as the previous autumn or winter: the winter of 1708–9 is the best known case of this.

Two types of incident were liable to provoke a riot. In fifteen cases the cause was the removal of grain from the village, town or province, and in ten cases it consisted of real or imagined embezzlement by the police of the grain being stored within the community. In the first of these circumstances merchants from outside the province had contracted to export corn from it in spite of the increase in the local grain price, and the provincial governor or town council had seen fit to grant them passes to facilitate their journey. Boatmen were seen handling sacks of grain on the watefront, or some of the wealthier ploughmen were heard making arrangements with a merchant in the village. They were seen loading carts up in the barns.

To the humble people who lived in a river-port or the next-door neighbours in a village, shipments of corn of this kind represented an intolerable threat. When supplies were running short, and the price of grain and bread was rising at every market, people would be made cruelly aware in the weeks that followed of the quantities the merchants had taken away. If the merchants were selling their corn at a distance from the village, it was because they were getting a scandalously high price there which no one could afford to pay them locally. In other words they were jeopardizing the lives of their fellow-villagers for the sake of making a profit. The officials who had given them passes had an interest in the trade, since the merchants had had to pay them to get their travel permits. This assault on the community's welfare consequently took on the appearance of a conspiracy, a deliberate attempt to exploit the famine and the public misery.

In the second circumstance the craftsmen's wives, who lacked the means to bake bread at home as women in the more prosperous houses could do, found that the only bread which remained in the bakers' shops was lighter or dearer than usual. The bakers maintained that the ordinances which the town hall issued governing the weight and price of bread were no longer valid, since the price of grain was rising and the millers were milling less flour with every passing day. If the town council insisted on freezing the price of bread in spite of these protestations, the bakers insisted they could no longer get in their stock for the payment of such an inadequate price and they began baking less and less bread. Their entire batch of loaves was already sold in the early morning, carried off by the wealthier families in town who were also running short of grain supplies in this period of dearth and consequently also resorted to the baker's shop. Consequently there was no bread left for the craftsmen's families, and crowds of the poorer women formed in front of the bakers' stalls vainly demanding their daily bread.

Whether the scarcity of grain was real or exaggerated, the bands of women nursed a traditional picture of fraud. They accused the bakers of hiding away their supplies until they could force the town council to authorize them to raise their prices. By emptying their shops they had created an artificial scarcity. They were waiting till the people were starving in order to sell their stocks off at the price of famine years, in which the price of corn would rise by 100 per cent in some months, and sometimes more.

Riots took place on the route the corn had to take. They began on the highways leading from the barns to the mill and from the mill to the town gates. In the town they broke out on the square where the corn-market was organized, in the market, in the streets of the merchants where the bakers' shops were grouped, and at the river-bank where the moored boats were waiting for the grain to be transferred from the carts. In Bordeaux, for example, crowds gathered in a number of different places. In August 1643 they assembled in front of the bakers' shops on the Rue du Hâ. In March 1643 they flocked to the wharf of Pont Saint-Jean where merchants were selling some grain which had just been unloaded from the boats. Above all they mustered at the Chapeau Rouge gate, where rioting started in both March and August 1643, and again in August 1648. This gate was the liveliest part of the entire waterfront. People standing there could watch the boats going by. The foot of the ramparts was lined with well-stocked street stalls including the 'pantry', a large counter where the *jurats* used to organize distributions of free or price-regulated grain to the city poor in time of dearth. Of the seventeen outbreaks of grain-related rioting which can be pinned down to a specific location, the largest group (seven) involved plundering on the highways. Five of the others took place in the wharves, and five in the markets.

Acts and slogans of the bread rioters

The form the collective reaction took depended on the circumstances which had provoked it. Particular events which aroused public indignation gave rise to appropriate outbreaks of violence. Peasants gathered in ambush to halt the convoys of carts carrying grain outside the neighbourhood, and townspeople attacked any boats or carts they found to be loaded with grain. Bakers who put up the price of their bread or refused to bake it found disturbances breaking out in front of their shops, and sometimes the tradesmen themselves were assaulted in return for their double-dealing.

Rioters lay in wait for the carts as they passed along the roads. The peasants carried their customary weapons, their double-ended sticks, pitchforks and halberds, and some of them had muskets. Their women had gathered stones. Merchants were thrown from their horses, and they and their drovers had only just enough time to flee. If the merchants had anticipated the danger and brought along an armed escort, the tocsin would be sounded for some hours before they were due to pass by, and some hundreds of men would gather from several villages round about and would lie in wait for them in the cornfields or behind the hedges.[1] In river-ports the merchants' boats would be pulled on to the bank, unloaded and set on fire. The scene of plunder which followed was the same both in the town and the countryside. The strings of the grain-sacks would be cut. The men would load them on to their

---

1 Only about thirty people took part in the peasant ambushes which were staged in Angoumois in 1643. They took place at night, since the merchants had tried to cover up their movements by waiting till nightfall before setting out, drinking in a tavern on the fairground. When the tocsin sounded the entire small village community sprang to arms. In June 1699 300 men and women held up a merchant from Châtellerault in the village of Saint-Romain-sur-Vienne. In June 1693 and May 1694 several hundreds of Angevin peasants attacked some convoys of corn which were headed for Angers. The aldermen of Angers had combined with a body of armed burgesses and the bowmen of the *maréchaussée* into an effective escort which put the peasants to flight. This episode was known as the 'war of Craon'.

shoulders, and the women would gather up as much grain as they could in the folds of their skirts. The sacks which could not be carried off would be ripped open and the good quality grain would be poured out on the ground.[2]

The looters were people of few words. On the wharf at Bordeaux on 3 March 1643, they 'shouted incoherently that grain was being carried out of the town without Messieurs the *jurats* knowing'. On 26 August 1648 the market women paid their respects to the Duke of Épernon, then told him frankly 'that they would not allow grain to be taken from the city'. When the peasants of Angoumois attacked the merchants of Périgord who were taking corn to their homes, in a clash which took place at Nanteuil-en-Vallée on 30 May 1643, their battle-cry was 'Kill, kill *the robbers*'. In June 1643 the peasants of Aignes said that 'they would take by force all the grain they encountered and could find, and would kill everyone who tried to stop them'. In November 1643 a skirmish took place at La Jaufrenie, near Villebois-Lavalette. Some peasants of the *châtellenie* of La Valette threatened a miller from Mareuil in Périgord that 'if he attempted to carry off any corn in future, they would kill him'.

The first reaction of rioters against the bakers or merchants in the towns was to break down their doors, to ransack their booths, and to threaten to set fire to their houses. The bakers had no option but to flee, climbing over the rooftops or escaping under the protection of the watch. The crowd called out that 'the bakers are trying to starve us'. They promised that they would 'toast them and bake them in their own oven if they went short of bread'. Failing to catch the miscreants during a riot in 1709, the women of Saint-Jean-d'Angély went and took down a dried-up skeleton from the local gibbet, and stuck it in front of a merchant's door. At Limoges in 1714, the grain merchants had satirical songs made up about them and were derided in the streets. They were painted in effigy like criminals who had been sentenced to death *in absentia*, and a baying mob took the dummies through the town and burnt them in a public square.

On one occasion a sedan-chair bearer in Bordeaux had himself carried round in state in his sedan-chair, sword at his side, from one shop to another. He demanded bread at the fixed price of two *liards* (farthings), and paid up punctually. The procession was intended to make fun of the bakers. It did not constitute a grave affront to the authorities, since the chair-bearer was asking no more than his due; but the *jurats* none the less condemned him to the gallows.[3] His demonstration expressed, in fact, the demand for a kind of popular control, a right to help police the grain trade which the poorer citizens claimed they should have. In calling their victims robbers, in calling the members of the town council or the governor to come to their aid, in demand-

---

2 The town mobs shared out the grain roughly in the place where they had seized it. The organizers of the peasant ambushes carried the sacks into the woods to distribute the grain at leisure. The denunciations which were made at the local *présidial* were the work of those people who had not had their fair share.

3 On 11 June 1675 the *parlement* commuted the sentence passed by the *jurats* to six years in the galleys.

ing that respect be paid to the municipal regulations and in claiming they were entitled to stop grain circulating anywhere outside their community, the bands of looters were conscious of being within their rights and of exercising, by means of their riot, a legitimate power against the enemies of the public welfare.

Merchants, millers and bakers

Merchants, millers and bakers were the chosen victims of the disturbances. They owned their own mills or ovens, or trafficked in the *banalités* (minor obligations of peasants to use the seigniorial mills, barns etc.) that were farmed out by the seigneurs, and were consequently considerable figures in the village economy. They were generally held to be dishonest. The miller was said to keep back flour on his millstones, to moisten it and mix in oats with the wheat, and to add in bran, sand or plaster. In the period between harvests the bakers were accustomed to buy up all the corn available and to put only a very small quantity of it out for sale. The grain merchants were readily hated insofar as they made their profits in the months of dearth and earned their money without doing anything. 'They had nothing in their shops except hay rolled in some paper.' In addition it often happened that a single person traded as merchant, miller and baker, all at the same time.

Merchants were generally rich enough to be able to avoid exposing themselves to the mercy of the riots. The peasant bands could only get at a handful of boatmen, drovers and petty tradesmen who owned no more than four or five donkeys, or alternatively that member of the fraternity of aldermen, *jurats* or consuls who was responsible for policing the market and who was consequently inundated with insults and abuse.

Humble people and poor women

The make-up of the crowds involved in grain riots was rarely specified in the records. In Poitiers, in May 1630, they are described as 'vagrants and good-for-nothings', in Thouars in December 1698 and in Limoges in August 1699 they are called the 'poor', and in Bordeaux in August 1648 and Limoges in 1714 they are referred to as the 'humble people'. In actual fact those involved were not wholly destitute, but belonged to the mass of craftsmen who formed the body of citizens known as the lesser people of the towns – people who 'lived from hand to mouth' and were cast into the ranks of the true poor by the first dearth that struck.

The most constant element in these riots was the presence of women. At night on the high roads there were women armed with stones who even took part in the peasant ambushes. Aldermen noticed the presence of women carrying swords and halberds in the crowd which ran riot in Poitiers. Some of the crowds in our survey, six out of thirty-one, were even made up exclusively of women. They yelled, threw stones, broke into shops and plundered the grain. This flocking of women to the riots at the price of bread is a reminder of the almost biological nature of this kind of episode. Bread riots were the most spontaneous and essential of all the types of rebellion – but also the most short-lived and the easiest to disperse. The women were there because they were in charge of the home and the day-to-day purchases;: they were involved in ensuring the immediate survival of the family, and institutional interventions were alien to them. They plunged into the riots over the bread price without having any other programme than anguish at what the future might hold and the basic rights of the starving.

The town council and the policing of the grain trade

The first step resorted to by the rioters was to go and seek out the aldermen, *jurats* or consuls and to demand that they stock up the shops, fix the price of bread and visit the granaries of the merchants. Each time the town council lived up to their expectations. In 1624 the council at Niort had an ordinance published prohibiting grain to be taken out of the town, in 1631 the council at Bordeaux gave orders that the boatmen should be imprisoned, and in March 1643 the same council got the bowmen of the watch to confiscate any corn found in the carts that were leaving the city. In 1628 the council at Cognac acceded to the demands of the assembled crowd of craftsmen in limiting the amount of grain to be sold to any single purchaser to a few bushels only, in order to prevent the merchants from buying up the whole stock in massive quantities. In May 1630 the council at Poitiers and in May 1675 the council at Bordeaux fixed the price of bread at an affordable level and ordered the bakers to keep their shops fully stocked. In August 1643, finally, the council at Bordeaux warned the bakers to 'make bread, and brown bread especially, without any slackening, on pain of death'. All these measures were adopted in the aftermath of riots. They show that the town councils followed the lead of the population.

Not only the town councils but also the officers of the law and the king's representatives in the crown courts issued public condemnations of speculators. The provincial intendant at Limoges faithfully transmitted the opinions voiced by the spokesmen of the craftsmen who had massed beneath his windows. Riots at the price of bread were understood and listened to; and they aroused the attention and pity of the leading members of the community. By lending the aid of the bowmen against the merchants and encouraging the condemnation of speculators, the authorities accorded a kind of official imprimatur to the grain-related disturbances, a recognition that the rioters had a right to protest as they did.

Tolerance and pity in society as a whole

The mere rumour of an imminent scarcity of grain was enough to make it disappear from the market. Some people laid in supplies in anticipation of the dearth, and others stocked up to await the inevitable rise in prices. It was in the context of such dearth-related panics that riots broke out at the price of bread. The universal loathing of speculators induced officials to adopt provocative attitudes which in turn gave rise to the panic. The *lieutenant de police* (magistrate in charge of the police force) at Limoges authorized the printing of satirical songs against the merchants, saying in justification 'that these merchants who had wanted to make their fellow-citizens starve thoroughly deserved to be mortified'. The *procureur du roi* (solicitor-general) at Tulle ordered searches to be made in the granaries, and openly called for the punishment 'of the ravening wolves who have no feeling of either pity or religion, who *delight in the public misery* ... the misers and usurers of this town.' The *parlement* at Bordeaux waxed indignant at 'the avarice of certain individuals, *enemies of the common weal* ... [who] in hopes of a sordid profit ... are filling cellars, granaries and warehouses, and awaiting the opportunity to convey them secretly to other regions or simply to keep them until the months of May, June and July to make the price go up'. This decree gave legitimacy to the hunting down of monopolists. It was published and posted up throughout the jurisdiction of the court, and especially in the port of Bordeaux. The choice of terms and the particular publicity given to the document confirmed the poorer people in their obsession with the agents of starvation and constituted a virtual invitation to riot.

Some of the most illustrious dignitaries of the day have preserved in their writings a number of scathing attacks on speculators, which were probably composed in their original form by one of those village doctors who usually acted as spokesmen for the rebels. The Count of Jonzac wrote how 'a number of greedy individuals have built granaries in order to profit from the ruin of the people at large'. The presiding magistrate Suduiraut observed that 'the tradesmen are making every kind of grain expensive and scarce. They are storing up the grain in their warehouses, and the people have to buy it from them at whatever price they choose to ask.' A decree issued by the Council declared that 'a number of merchants are buying grain dirt-cheap and loading it up in the ports of France to convey it to foreign parts .. or to sell it at the end of the season at an exorbitant price. This could give rise to an acute dearth and famine.' Everyone plainly shared in the general dislike which was felt for the usual victims of the bread riots.

The upsurge of popular violence against the trafficking of the merchants is easy to account for, and, for that matter, easy to justify. It was known that grain riots generally took place in the larger towns: outbreaks of peasant plundering were not, as a rule, very serious. One author wondered whether the weavers were likely to prove more rebellious than the vine growers. 'They are not', he wrote,

more rebellious, but they are hungrier. In a year of bad harvests the peasant farmer in the country is not the most outspoken in his complaints ... The real sufferer is the day labourer: he finds himself caught, as the saying goes, between the devil and the deep blue sea, and doesn't know which way to turn. The price of bread has gone up, but he cannot hope for a corresponding increase in wages. He despairs, and despair breeds riot.

'Nothing is more *natural*', a lawyer reflected, 'than to fight to save one's life. As bread is the most basic foodstuff, people strive all the harder to have it. The poor can never be sure of having it, and consequently fear they will never have enough; and the anxiety they feel leads them to read a famine into every rise in price." After the corn-boats were ransacked in the port of Niort in 1624, a Capuchin friar called Father Calixtus went to preach in the town market. He endorsed the reason for the riot and declared 'openly that these women had committed no sin in carrying off a certain amount of corn last Friday'.

Results of the bread riots

The general consensus to the effect that bread riots were justified was reflected still further in the relative impunity on which the culprits were able to count. In May 1675 at Bordeaux two of the culprits had indeed been sent to the galleys; but the idea on that occasion was to set an example. The authorities had dismissed from their minds the role played by the bread price in causing that particular riot, and had chosen instead to view it in the context of the continual outbreaks of seditious violence which had been shattering the city's peace. In the same way the prisoners taken after the disturbances in Saintonge in April 1709 were sentenced in the provosts' courts. The authorities were bent on curbing the bands of wandering peasants who were holding out in the woods. We should also bear in mind that these two examples of harshness are taken from the end of our period – from the intolerant reign of Louis XIV. In fact the most usual sentences passed by the city judges on rioters caught red-handed entailed no more than the lightest forms of corporal punishment such as the pillory and the birch, if the prisoners were not actually acquitted 'in view of the wretchedness and need of the time'. In most cases, however, the culprits were either unknown or impossible to catch. If the victims had managed to identify some of their assailants, a judge would certainly not refuse to give orders for their arrest. When the sergeants went to the culprits' houses, however, to carry out those orders, they would find that the birds had flown; and the matter would go no further. This was what happened in Angoumois, for example, in 1643.

The immediate effect of the riot might well be to frighten the bakers and merchants so much, in the first few days, that they would be even more reluctant to put their grain on the market. This negative consequence would be counteracted, however, by ordinances issued by the town councils or the royal jurisdictions. Riots would force the authorities to pay attention to the public grievance, and a disturbance would soon be followed by prohibitions on the export of grain, the freezing of the bread price and the regulation of sales. If the dearth had merely arisen from the ill will of the merchants, these measures would be enough to put a stop to it. If on the other hand there had really been a shortfall in the harvests, the riots would not bring the populace a single extra grain. In the final analysis the riots emphasized the isolation not merely of provinces but of each small neighbourhood. They were rich in illusions alone.

Object and purpose of the bread riots

Speculators cut themselves off from the rest of the community. The fortunes they made affronted society's sense of morality and order. They battened precisely on the disasters suffered by the community at large. People of no account, they made their sudden pile and established themselves in the space of a single season without regard for the traditional hierarchy of the estates. They had deliberately sought to infringe the norms of a society which believed in the duty of almsgiving and the permanence of social rank. Riots were consequently launched to punish outrageous behaviour and to quell an unwarranted leap up the social scale. The women of Châtellerault cried that they wanted 'to crumble the bread to powder, without paying for it, to shock the shady profiteers'. At Limoges rumour had it that the king had frozen the price of corn at a single low level which was meant to operate throughout the kingdom, but that this well-meaning decree had never filtered through to the population. 'It is thought that it fell into the hands of some usurer who is hiding it.'[4] We see here the myth of the king deceived combined with the myth of a planned starvation. The bread riots assumed the character of an assertion of morality, a defence of the established order against social climbers.

The hunt for the agents of starvation had also a reassuring function. Natural disasters that came from out of the blue were too appalling to contemplate. People preferred human culprits, to smoke out the troublemakers who had brought the calamities upon them. The riots fulfilled, in this sense, the need people felt to find human explanations for abstract misfortunes.

The attacks launched by peasants on carts of grain had a special significance. They formed part of the war between the countryside and the cities, and were part of the rural reaction against the dominance of the towns. In Craonnais and Châtelleraudais armed burgesses setting out to buy corn in the villages and channel the produce of the countryside within the walls of their towns ran up against the risings of entire communities. In 1709 peasants seized the gates of Libourne to stop grain getting into the town. The gentry of Haute-Auvergne denounced the rule of town magistrates who forcibly gathered up corn from the countryside and stockpiled it in their towns, thereby driving the country people to abandon their villages and resort to a life of vagrancy and begging.[5]

Bread riots were related, finally, to the urge of communities to defend their local privileges. The free circulation of grain against which these peasants and craftsmen were rebelling could only be guaranteed with the aid of a central government. By contrast the maintenance of local autarky which resulted from the disturbances was associated with the safeguarding of provincial freedoms and tax exemptions.[6]

---

4 Letter written on 29 August 1709 by M. Lapoumelie of Limoges to Desmarets, the controller general. See Archives Nationales, G.7, 340.
5 Article 21 of a petition submitted by the nobility of Haute-Auvergne in 1614. See *Revue de la Haute-Auvergne*, 1948, p.121.
6 The revolt which took place at the same period in the small city of Fermo in the Papal States

The riot which took place in Bordeaux in August 1643 was broken up by the simple expedient of distributing bread 'to the most vociferous women'. Bread riots seemed to contemporaries the least fearsome form of civil disorders. Fonteneil quotes them as saying that such riots were the 'commonplace disturbances of a population, which are over almost as soon as they have begun'. Even the troubles of 1643 or 1709, the most widespread of their kind to take place at this period, each amounted to no more than a rash of simultaneous incidents. They never constituted a revolt.

If the fear of dearth did not have the quality of stimulating revolt, it was none the less a factor in most of the disturbances which took place at this period. In 1643 and 1675 the citizens of Bordeaux were rising up nominally against the '*gabelle*'; but the bread price was an additional cause for their agitation, and a conspicuous one.[7]

The fear of dearth was liable to well up at any moment in the course of the seventeenth century. It was an inevitable feature of a subsistence economy. Bread riots were equally an intrinsic part of such an economy. The advent of rapid communications meant the end of a subsistence economy in France, and the bread riots vanished with it.

Riots against soldiers

Riots against passing soldiers are an ancient defensive reaction of any community – as ancient, indeed, as the passage of soldiers itself. They go hand in hand with a particular military institution, the practice of quartering troops on the country and billeting them in the houses of its inhabitants. They are the direct result of that institution, the specific response and sinister corollary to it. In the period we are considering all the rules by which armies claimed to curb the soldierly customs of violence and pillage had been proved illusory by the involvement of the kingdom in the Thirty Years War. All kinds of fraudulent practices had taken root at that time: raids conducted in the neighbourhood of places where the armies halted, deals struck with the local people and ransoms extorted from them, the customs of arranging special

---

offers an outstanding example of the connection between a riot against the free circulation of grain and the defence of provincial autonomy. At a time of dearth in 1648 the local governor had tried to enforce a large-scale removal of corn from the city in order to supply the population of Rome. Rioters promptly lynched the governor and hoisted the banner of the city on the roof of the city hall.

7 In investigating the types of riot which may provide us with some kind of pattern I run the risk of neglecting the multifaceted quality that riots possessed. Persons in authority such as the Count of Jonzac were well aware how easily one cause of discontent could fuse with another. 'If we allowed corn to be transported', wrote Jonzac, 'all the lower orders would set upon the merchants. Once they developed a taste for taking their corn without paying, they would unquestionably band together, and the next step would be that they would deny the freedom of the high roads to all those officials who go about collecting the king's revenues, and would make the gathering of His Majesty's taxes a risky business. The moment the masses have armed and risen up, they use their arms against anyone who asks for their money' (letter of Jonzac to Séguier, 12 December 1643).

protection or buying exemptions from billeting, and above all the *routes brûlées*, the 'burning of roads' which took place when soldiers were induced to change their route by the personal recommendations or antagonisms of their commanders or the possibilities they had scented of amassing loot. Each billeting of soldiers, then, seemed suspicious to local people, tainted with illegalities or abuses of one kind or another.

Ordinances dictated that a company of soldiers should not arrive in a new locality without giving prior warning. The way would be prepared some days or hours beforehand by a quartermaster, a deputation of captains or a cavalry sergeant. Even if an orderly billeting was not prescribed in the soldiers' rulebooks, they still could not hope to take a village by surprise. They would not know the way, and would consequently have to send out scouts, thereby giving notice of their advance along that particular road. Peasants would have risen from their fields and householders raced from the nearby hamlets to spread the news of their approach.

The soldiers would also be preceded by their reputation. Regiments that came into winter quarters usually had local connections: they belonged to the provincial gentry. The soldiers in the regiment would have been enrolled in the province the previous year, and the regiment now returned to the province to rest up and make new recruits. If one regiment had conducted itself in a disciplined manner, another would be notorious for the havoc it had wrought. The community on which the troops were to be billeted would accordingly have the time to make appropriate preparations. It would either get ready to welcome the troops or alternatively, if it viewed the billeting as an assault, an unjust persecution, it would take up arms and get organized to resist the soldiery.

The dates on which this kind of riot took place are not unimportant. Of the thirty-seven disturbances whose dates have been recorded, nine are concentrated in the winter months, November to January, and a still larger number, sixteen, broke out between April and June. These were the two chief times of the year at which troops were in transit through the kingdom, making for their winter quarters and setting out again for the frontiers the following spring.

The site of the riots varied. In twenty cases they broke out at the gates of the town, when the soldiers made their appearance and the inhabitants resisted their entry. In fourteen cases they started on the high roads where the people lay in ambush, waiting for the soldiers to pass. In eight cases, finally, they began in the city streets, when the riot was provoked by a brawl between soldiers and citizens.

Closing the gates or an ambush

The site of an outbreak of rioting reflected merely the environment in which it took place. Riots which began at the town gates were, naturally, urban in type. They took place in cities and market towns which were either enclosed by a wall or had a topography suitable for the raising of barricades. In eleven recorded cases the closing of the gates, the appearance of the citizens in arms on the ramparts and a few volleys of musket-fire were enough to drive the troops off. In May 1638 two companies of infantry were repelled in this fashion when they bore down on Grenade-sur-Garonne. 'In the course of their advance they had stopped to catch some chickens they had noticed in a smallholding which gave on to the road. Some women who were weeding the nearby cornfields caught sight of this act of looting. They raced to the town gates and closed them as soon as they got there.' In January 1639 the cavalry force employed by the Baron de Linard, a gentleman of the Marche region, took up its winter quarters in the town of Dorat. The townspeople rioted. When the horsemen came back to the town the following August they found the gates shut against them and burgesses armed with arquebuses peppering them with gunshot from the ramparts. For two weeks they had to take up their quarters in the adjoining hamlets. They ransacked the hamlets, then dug themselves in there in order to repel the successive sorties launched by the citizens of Dorat. It was only natural that the people of Dorat should mount such attacks. The lands which surrounded the city, the gardens, fields and vineyards which were visible from the walls did, after all, belong to the burgesses. The people who lived in the neighbourhood were their sharecroppers and servants; and any plundering which took place in the adjoining countryside affected equally the families in the town. If the town, furthermore, enjoyed some privilege that exempted it from the billeting of soldiers, the surrounding villages which fell within its jurisdiction were entitled to share in that exemption. On these grounds the town militia sallied forth on six recorded occasions to drive soldiers out of their suburbs. In August 1636 the mayor and consuls of Périgueux learnt that a company of mounted troops had billeted themselves in a town which lay within their city's jurisdiction. They sallied forth from the city at the head of 500 armed men and marched as far as Atur, 6 kilometres away. The horsemen got word of their approach and cleared out 'in great haste'. In June 1636, similarly, 400 citizens of the town of Montmorillon issued forth to attack the regiment of Périgord, and in November 1651, 300 inhabitants of the town of Mur-de-Barrez marched out against the regiment of the Count of Chavagnac.

Ordinary villages could ward off approaching soldiers by barricading their streets with barrels and carts. As soon as word came that soldiers had arrived in the district, the tocsin would be sounded in a number of parishes. Throughout the neighbourhood the peasants would abandon their work, the markets would break up and the taverns empty. Livestock would be herded into the farm of one of the gentry or into the courtyard of the local château. Sentinels would be stationed at the crossroads, guards would be set on the approach roads, and musketeers would be posted behind the barricade. On nine recorded occasions troops of horsemen descended on villages to find the people well prepared to resist them.

Peasants seldom attempted to barricade themselves in their fragile houses, but instead took shelter in the village church. The church with its stout stone walls became a refuge for the rural community in every period of danger. As time went on the peasants fortified it with certain extra features, watchtowers flanking the walls, bartizans girdling the bell-towers, turrets overlooking the gates, a parapet walk above the apse. These 'look-out stations' or 'galleries' transformed country churches into small fortresses. The entire population of the village could find shelter in the nave, while musketeers hidden in the embrasures could direct a brisk fire upon the attackers. Peasants held out against contingents of horsemen by these methods at Abjat in May 1640, at Gradignan in May 1649 and at Chéronnac in August 1649. In the autumn of 1649 the villagers of Camblanes held out for an entire day, only to perish in the night when the attackers set fire to their church. In November 1653 the people of Rocamadour took refuge within the walls of their church and beat off the regiment of Aubeterre. In 1661 the peasants of Benauge rose up against the horsemen who had been assigned the task of collecting their taxes. According to the intendant Hotman the fortified state of their churches gave them 'an opportunity for insolence and rebellion'.[8]

Finally, peasants resorted to ambushes in landscapes dotted merely with scattered settlements, where they had no protection other than the slopes of a ravine, the rows of vines in a vineyard, fields of growing corn or the hedges overlooking sunken roads. Eight cases of such ambushes are mentioned in the records. The peasants of Camblanes slaughtered some fifty horsemen of the regiment of Créqui in their local vineyards and woods. The highlanders of Lavedan were in theory exempt from the requirement to lodge soldiers, and they set upon any troops who tried to violate that exemption. In June 1654 they brought a cavalry force commanded by Marshal d'Hocquincourt to a halt in the gorges of Geu, and in March 1665 they ambushed the troops of the Marquis de Saint-Luc in the same place.

The country people could win still easier victories over companies of raw recruits, who were both untrained and poorly armed. They would wait for these bands of greenhorns in the middle of the woods, charge at them suddenly with their flails and iron-shod sticks, and send them scattering. Often the captains had to rally their companies back into line two or three times in a single encounter. The hatred the peasants felt for the soldiers was reflected in the relentlessness with which they dragged in the dust and stripped and mutilated the corpses of any they killed. Any soldiers who managed to flee left their horses and baggage behind them. The funds the captain carried coupled with the pay the recruits received and their arms and harnesses represented a considerable booty for the peasant rioters, one that could sometimes come to as much as several thousand *livres*. On one occasion the people of Lavedan captured a captain from the regiment of Roquelaure. They kept him in their villages and would release him only in return for the payment of a ransom. We may recognize in this strategy of peasant self-defence, in these obscure battles fought out in the woods and on the high roads, the theme of 'the peasants' revenge' which the great engraver Jacques Callot

8 A detailed study of this rising has been made by Loirette. As part of this study he prepared a map of the county of Benauge, or in other words the right bank of the Garonne near Cadillac (see *Annales du Midi*, 1966, p. 530). This map shows a total of fifty-six parishes. Twenty-three of the parish churches, such as the churches of Cantois, Coirac, Bellefond, Targon, etc., were endowed with defensive features which still survive.

(1592–1635) illustrated in his set of etchings 'Miseries of War' (*Malheurs de la guerre*).

The justification of the rioters

At Abjat in 1640 and Cognac in 1653, the citizens called out when the soldiers drew near, 'We must kill all these robbers and not allow them to be quartered here.' They saw themselves as defending their property against those who wished to steal it from them. At Montmorillon in 1636, and again at Abjat in 1640, the citizens denounced the soldiers as excisemen as well as robbers. 'Down with the excisemen! Here are our excisemen, kill them, kill them!' They expressed in this word 'excisemen' all the resentment the people felt against different kinds of intruders who came to demand from them financial contributions they viewed as unwarranted and detestable.

It may indeed be said that in a great many cases the billeting which provoked the riot was thought to be unjustified in one way or another. Orders might deliberately have been given, for instance, to billet soldiers on places which were in theory exempt from such billeting. The step was taken for political reasons and as an emergency measure; but the locals refused to surrender their privileges and rose up in riot instead. Such, at least, was the cause of the minor peasant war which broke out in the suburbs of Bordeaux in 1649, of the sorties staged by the people who lived in the suburbs of Périgueux in 1636 and 1640, and of the rebellions which took place in the seven valleys of Lavedan in 1654 and 1665.

In other places the parishes were given no notice that soldiers were to be billeted on them. The soldiers in effect roamed off their intended route and sought to install themselvs in a village by force, without any official authorization. At Saint-Geniez in Rouergue, for instance, a company in the employment of the Marquis de Cadillac presented the inhabitants with out-of-date billeting warrants. Soldiers who arrived in Thiviers had no valid documentation to show to the consuls there.

In other places again the troops arrived in part of a province where they had already made themselves universally loathed by conducting a series of plundering raids. The regiment of Périgord, for example, set out on one occasion to gather recruits in Saintonge and Poitou. The soldiers devastated the parishes they passed through to such an extent that they actually provoked the local authorities to lodge a complaint with the Council in Paris. Their march through the region led to several disturbances, which reached a climax when the citizens of Montmorillon surged forth to attack them. The provincial intendant instituted legal proceedings against the rioters; at the same time, however, the crown decided to deprive the regiment of the precedence it had formerly enjoyed in the marching order of the royal armies as a form of punishment. The regiment of Aubeterre spent an entire season ravaging the parishes of Quercy in similar fashion. The soldiers arrived at Rocamadour to find themselves shut out.

The people who held out in these towns were grimly determined. They knew that if they lowered their guard their town would be sacked without pity,

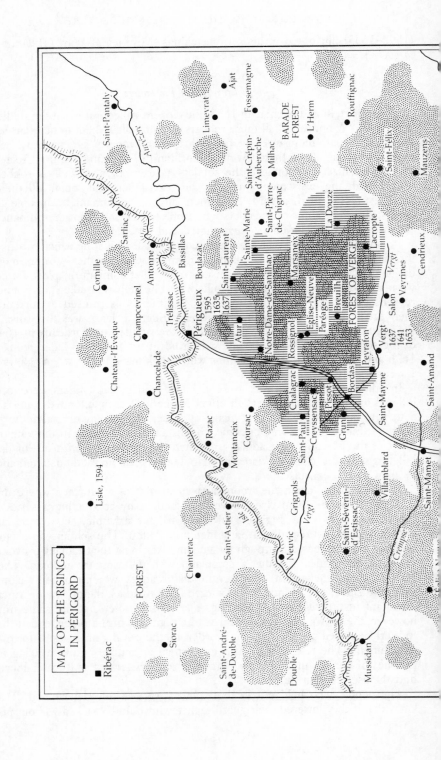

MAP OF THE RISINGS
IN PÉRIGORD

■ Ribérac

● Lisle, 1594

FOREST

Saint-André-
de-Double

Double

● Siorac

● Chanterac

Saint-Astier

Neuvic

Grignols

Saint-Severin-
d'Estissac

Mussidan

Vern

Crempse

Vilamblard

Saint-Mamet

Saint-Amand

Montanceix

Razac

Coursac

Chancelade

Trélissac

Bassillac

Antonne

Champcevinel

Chateau-l'Évèque

Cornille

Sarliac

Saint-Pantaly

Auvezère

Limeyrat

Ajat

Fossemagne

Saint-Crépin-
d'Auberoche

Saint-Pierre-
de-Chignac

Milhac

BARADE
FOREST

L'Herm

Routfignac

Saint-Félix

Mauzens

Sainte-Marie

Saint-Laurent

Boulazac

Périgueux
1595
1635
1637

Atur

Notre-Dame-de-Sanilhac

Rossignol

Marsaneix

Église-Neuve

Pareage

Breuilh

La Douze

FOREST OF VERGT

Lacropte

Cendrieux

Veyrines

Salon

Vergt

Peyraton

Vergt
1637
1641
1653

Chalagrac

Saint-Paul

Creyssensac

Dussot

Grun

Bordas

Saint-Mayme

Isle

Vergt

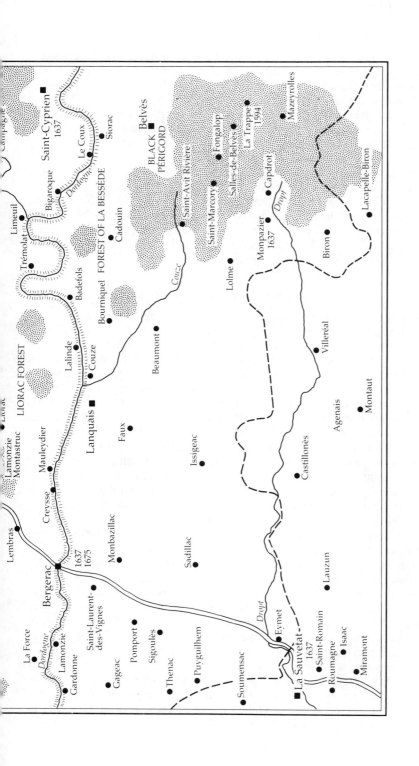

since in confrontations of this kind the officers of a besieging force usually promised to give their soldiers 'licence to plunder' if they broke through the town gates. One chronicler described the attitude of the citizens who defended Rocamadour in 1653. 'The inhabitants saw that they were in a hopeless predicament. They were quite unable to feed such a large contingent of soldiers, and in view of this they decided not to let them in at all.' At Vic-en-Bigorre in 1638 a similar mood prevailed. 'The citizens are resolved to die rather than let the soldiers enter their town.'

Citizens engaged in this form of collective violence with an entirely clear conscience. They did not doubt for an instant that God was on their side. The parish priest of Rocamadour articulated this certainty. 'Since the soldiers', he declared, 'were ill-intentioned and were bent on nothing but plunder and other vile purposes, the Lord withdrew His blessing from them. He granted that the first of them to be sent against us should perish, and that the rest should see they had no hope of gaining entry to our town.'

The communal nature of the riots

Uprisings against marauding soldiers expressed the united will of the community to a greater extent than any other form of collective violence. The residents of a given locality found themselves abruptly confronted with the imminent danger of being subjected to an orgy of brute force. The troops who were bearing down on them could not be expected to spare a single one of their number: even the humbler people, sharecroppers and domestic servants, who were exempt from the obligation of providing billets for soldiers, would have no hope of escaping maltreatment at their hands. Everyone in the city or village under attack was, consequently, ready to take up arms.

On 3 May 1640 a company of horsemen from Thiviers descended on Abjat in search of lodgings. The community was immediately given warning of their approach. Drums rolled to summon the citizens, and the tocsin sounded in the bell-towers. The town was barricaded, and the judge and the parish priest went out and tried to dissuade the twenty-five horsemen from entering it. The company fell back on the neighbouring hamlets. In the course of their withdrawal the horsemen were surprised by an ambush of 300 to 400 peasants, and their captain was killed. This captain was a man called François de Vaucocour, the son of one of the noble families of the province, and the family in question instituted legal proceedings against their offspring's killers. The records of these proceedings have, as it happens, survived intact. The indictment lists 100 of the local residents by name, and also embraces, more sweepingly, 'all other residents and householders of the town and parish of Abjat'. The list of names reveals the entire social structure of the village. There is the parish priest; twelve village officials including the judge and deputy judge, the solicitor, the notaries and the clerks of the court; four sergeants; four merchants; fourteen persons in trade such as tailors, locksmiths and millers; and seventy-five other individuals including ploughmen, sharecroppers and domestic servants. Only a dozen of these defendants could in fact be brought to justice, and only two of them were convicted by the courts.

One of the two, a sergeant in the royal armies, was broken on the wheel, and the other, a miller, was sent to the galleys. All the defendants lived either in the village of Abjat itself or in one of the twenty-one other hamlets which lay within the same jurisdiction. Everyone hailed from a single area. The list also tells us something about the social milieu the defendants belonged to. It shows the various ties of kinship that existed between them. Seventeen surnames appear more than once, and five more than 4 times; and fifteen individuals are described as being the son or son-in-law of someone else. We can see from this evidence how far a rural community extended in the eyes of the people who felt they were part of it. Rebellions radiated well beyond the confines of a market town or a parish. They attracted adherents throughout the surrounding jurisdiction, and sometimes even farther afield than that.

The initial impulse for a rising was often both popular and spontaneous. The call to arms might be given by the first people to observe the approach of the soldiers. At Grenade in 1638 the initiative was taken by a group of women in the fields, and at Thiviers in the same year, by some 'rascals', as the chronicler put it, who happened to be passing through the town gates. At Granges in 1640 some peasants on the high road led the way. But the rest of the community were seldom slow to follow. Dignitaries such as the members of the town council, the local justices and the neighbouring gentry rallied to the call to resist the advancing soldiers and in so doing implicated themselves, as well, in the violence that entailed. A number of episodes are known in enough detail to enable us to distinguish the roles played by different groups of people in a particular course of events. The dignitaries in general played a different role while the upheaval was in progress from the one they assumed when the disturbance was over and the community had crossed the brink into lawlessness. During the upheaval they were concerned to mediate between the populace and the soldiers, or alternatively to put themselves at the head of the rioters. Afterwards all they could do was to protect the people and their property from repression by the authorities, or to launch a prosecution against the soldiers to counter the one that was being mounted against them. Aldermen, consuls and *jurats* appear in the records nine times as ringleaders or mediators in a disturbance that had newly broken out. Local officials played this role on seven recorded occasions, and local gentry twice. The breakdown of activity in the aftermath of the rising is a rather different one. Members of the town council and town officials are recorded as acting as protectors of the community only on three or four occasions, but the local gentry, on the other hand, took upon themselves the role of protectors of the community at least eleven times.

The reasons for this differing breakdown are not far to seek. The members of the town council were the walking embodiments of the community as a whole. It was their responsibility to carry out policing duties like opening or closing the town gates and calling the people to arms; and by virtue of those functions their place was necessarily at the heart of the communal insurrection. Once implicated in the rising, however, they were no longer in a position to act as mediators between their community and the royal authorities. The consuls of Couthures-sur-Garonne, for example, were implicated up to their necks. They threatened the soldiers of the Estrée regiment that they would stir the inhabitants up and have them cut in pieces if they did not withdraw at once'. A consul at Auch plunged into a street battle in full livery – and was killed by a group of soldiers. An observer sympathised: 'It was a miracle that the other consuls were so restrained and prudent that they forbore to allow their people to cut these ruffians to shreds.'

Local officials and justices were invested with a political authority in their capacity as officers of the crown. They believed that this authority entitled them to repel by force any attempt to billet soldiers on their community which did not appear to them to be legally warranted. Sometimes they paid the price of their conviction. The judge of Mur-de-Barrez, for example, was taken prisoner by a contingent of soldiers, and the judge of Razès was killed. Some officials of the *présidial* at Limoges emerged more happily from a similar confrontation. When the intruding regiment of La Rochette had resumed its journey after devastating their town, they closed the town gates and took prisoner a couple of officers and a number of common soldiers who had stayed back to shoe their horses.

Country gentlemen sometimes led their peasants out to scatter bands of marauders who had intruded into their lands. For the most part, however, it was after the confrontation that the gentry played their main role in the communal resistance to the unwanted quartering of troops. They gave shelter in their mansions to peasants on the run from the authorities, hid their livestock and threatened any sergeants who came to look for them. Soldiers themselves, the gentry were in a strong position to negotiate with regimental officers or the provincial governor. Some of them enjoyed a rank and reputation sufficient to enable them to draw a case to the attention of the king himself. In this way they managed to arrive at a satisfactory settlement. They induced the troops to depart, and persuaded the authorities to pardon the community. Finally they secured official recognition that the community had been justified in rising up.

Local gentry intervened effectively on a number of different occasions. In 1602, for instance, Le Dorat was threatened with punishment for closing its gates on a company of horsemen. Schomberg and La Rocheposay dissuaded Henri IV from razing the town to the ground.[9] The Viscount of Pompadour[10] pleaded in similar vein on behalf of some parishes which had risen against the soldiers in Bas-Limousin, and Gramont made representations in defence of the parishes of Labourd. At Niort a brawl which took place in October

9 The king was proposing to employ what looks at first glance like an abnormal degree of terrorism. The reason is that the disturbance broke out at a delicate time when the towns of Poitou and Limousin were already in revolt at the tax of 'a *sou* for every pound' imposed on the circulation and consumption of goods. The king was marching troops through these towns with the object of stemming the trouble.

10 In 1625, seven or eight parishes in the barony of La Roche rose up against the regiment of Verdun. Pompadour succeeded in arranging for the regiment to be withdrawn. In 1639 the same parishes rebelled a second time. The mediators on this occasion were the Jesuit fathers of Tulle, who owned the revenues that were collected from the town of Saint-Pardoux. They arranged for the authorities to return to the villagers the arms they had confiscated from them.

1668 between the citizens and a company of soldiers drew down punishment of some ferocity upon the townspeople. Royal policy by this time was to wipe out resistance in the provinces and make examples of any community which continued to offer it. The local chroniclers, however, did not touch on these developments as a possible explanation of the new severity. They attributed the fate of Niort, significantly, to a complex of relationships which existed between people on different rungs of the social ladder. The calamity which befell the town resulted, in their view, from the fact that the Niortais had failed to offer a gift to the provincial governor at the appropriate time. In addition the *lieutenant-général* in charge of the troops had been on bad terms with the governor of the town, and the governor had been at odds with the provincial intendant, who happened to be the uncle of the minister in charge of the affair. In the opinion of the chroniclers, it was only the intercession of the Count of Harcourt which in the end saved the town from utter destruction.

We can detect these networks of collusion between the dignitaries at every stage in the Abjat episode. Most of the land at Abjat belonged to the burgesses of Nontron, and any single one of those burgesses owned more livestock at Abjat than all the local inhabitants put together. As a result the Vaucocour family openly accused the burgesses of Nontron 'of advising the people to revolt'. The officials of Nontron did in fact refuse to initiate legal action against the people of Abjat, and would not even serve them with a summons. They sheltered the principal culprits and concealed their property. The principal local nobles, the Baron de La Valade and the seigneur of Maraval, persuaded the sergeants to leave the village alone; and the nearest country squire, Thibaut de Camaing, lord of Verdoyer, openly supported the villagers when the Vaucocours' prosecution was finally brought. He accompanied them to Périgueux and supplied them with solicitors and lawyers. He arranged for the sergeants to be intimidated, and helped the culprits to escape from detention or hide. The vice-seneschal was suspected of having made a deal with the villagers, and Bourdeille, the governor of Périgord, was no more to be trusted to take a stand against them than any of the others. In the end the provincial intendant was obliged to take personal charge of the case, and to hear it at the judicious distance of Nérac. He was confronted by a province-wide conspiracy to protect the agitators, a general determination to defend the rights of the local people against the assaults of marauding troops.

Resistance to marauders in the eyes of society

During periods of disturbances, the sufferings of peasants who had fallen victim to marauding soldiers were reported in a whole literature of indignant and sympathetic works. Everyone knew that peasants in the hands of the soldiers would be treated brutally, and their fate was the subject of constant well-meaning laments. 'It was all too common for these soldiers to escape unpunished, and this emboldened them to engage in every kind of violence. The people were already gravely oppressed with taxes and levies and the exactions made by passing troops, and this additional maltreatment drove them to despair.' Some warlords arranged for loot to be returned to its owners as a way of courting popularity. In 1650, similarly, the Princess of Condé had her followers return some livestock they had taken in the course of some raids in Médoc; and in 1652 Colonel Balthazar took over the goods which were carried in the baggage-train of the Marquis de Sauveboeuf, and had them distributed among the people of Périgord. 'He had this booty carried', says the chronicler,

into the public square in Périgueux and got his men to summon the citizens at the sound of the trumpet. He told the citizens that he was well aware that this booty was made up of property taken from the poor ... and that he had gathered them, consequently, in order that everyone might identify what belonged to him and take back freely what he had found to be his own.

As the war with Spain continued and military maraudings grew worse, the authorities even issued ordinances permitting 'the communes to assemble in arms and set upon' any troops that did not respect the king's regulations. The ordinance from which this quotation is taken was issued by the intendant of Auvergne in 1639.

On 5 March 1642 the Duke of Bouillon ordered his subjects who had gathered at the meeting of the estates of the viscountcy of Turenne that 'if any passing company ... should wish to take up billets in any parish in the viscountcy without having the king's express instructions to do so, the parish concerned should ring the tocsin to warn all the surrounding parishes, and these parishes should be bound to render it immediate aid'. During the Fronde the *parlement* at Bordeaux, which had sided with the rebels, had decrees printed ordering the communities within its jurisdiction to keep their territory clear of marauding troops. Mazarin for his part arranged for a similar decree to be published at Bourg-sur-Gironde on behalf of the king. In it the king committed the royal justices who represented him in each area 'to gather the local inhabitants by sounding a peal on the bells and turn them upon the marauders'.[11] In all these documents the act of rioting was given legitimacy in the form of an official authorization. We may presume that the peasantry did not always register the borderline between an officially authorized rebellion and a wholly spontaneous one.

The method adopted to repress an outbreak of criminal activity gives one of the clearest indications of the attitude taken towards that activity by society as a whole. In this case the authorities recognized that the violence taking place was communal in nature, and they held the community collectively responsible for it. This meant in practice that they adopted one of various types of collective punishment. They imposed symbolic penalties intended to humiliate the community as a whole, indicted the consuls as the community's representatives or slapped huge collective fines 'on the mass of the population'. At Thiviers in February 1638 a symbolic punishment was inflicted: the community had its walls and gates razed to the ground. The demolition work was

11 This decree was issued on 29 August 1650 with a view to enabling the people of Entre-Deux-Mers to gather the grape harvest in safety.

supervised by the vice-seneschal of Agenais on the instructions of the provincial intendant. At Abjat, similarly, in 1641, the town bells were dismantled. The market was destroyed and a memorial pyramid set up in its place as a warning to posterity. The vice-seneschal of Périgord was in charge of operations. The consuls were made the scapegoats on several occasions. At Massac-Séran in 1640 and Saint-Geniez in 1646, the whole body of consuls were sentenced to death. At Thiviers in 1638 the consuls were stripped of their rank, and their counterparts in Grenade were threatened with similar treatment in the same year. At Couthures and Saint-Lizier in 1637 the consuls were condemned to pay a collective fine. Large amounts of money, finally, were exacted in many cases from the community as a whole in the form of fines, indemnities and legal expenses. The citizens of Abjat were fined to the tune of 28,000 *livres*. Thirteen thousand *livres* were demanded of the people of Thiviers though only 8,000 were ever actually paid. Fines of 4,350 *livres* were imposed on Grenade, 2,500 *livres* on a village in Bas-Limousin, and so forth.

At first glance these measures look harsh; but they were not uniformly adopted. Much depended on the political needs of the moment. The government resorted to repression only when the authority of the crown appeared to be at stake and circumstances required them to make an example of an offending community. The *ancien régime* in France, like similar societies elsewhere, had a taste for concealing its ultimate weakness by an occasional dramatic display of punitive justice; and anyone wishing to escape such justice had only to survive the odd burst of severity. The people of Thiviers, for example were sentenced by the provincial intendant at a council of war which took place on 20 April 1638. One year later, however, they won permission from the Council to rebuild the demolished walls of their town, and two years later their consuls were formally restored to the rank from which they had been demoted. On 8 May 1641 ten citizens of Abjat were sentenced *in absentia* to be broken on the wheel, and a further eight were condemned to the gallows. But they too won through to better times. For three years they evaded the clutches of the bowmen by resisting their incursions or going into hiding, and in August 1644 they procured a pardon from the king. In October 1668 four citizens of Niort were condemned to death only to receive an absolute discharge the following year. The rebels who had prevented the garrison from Socoa from entering their town of Labourd actually managed to secure the removal of that garrison two years afterwards. The rebels of Lavedan provide the most striking example of all. Just two months after they had barred the way to a company of soldiers they received official confirmation that they would in future be exempt from any requirement to quarter troops. In all of the forty-odd episodes I have investigated in this connection I have been able to identify only three death sentences that were actually carried out.

Much depended, too, on the specific agents who were chosen to implement the repression. Under the terms of the ordinances this duty devolved upon the provosts who were employed by the provincial marshals. Many of these officials, however, lacked an adequate constabulary to enforce the sentences, and some were hand in glove with the local people. All local justices were suspect, and the officers in charge of troops who had been refused a billet had consequently to appeal to the superior authority of the Privy Council. The Council would refer the matter to the provincial intendant, and when the latter had delivered his sentence the offending communities, in their turn, would have recourse to the Privy Council to lodge an appeal. Thirteen of the disturbances discussed here were for this reason the subject of files in the Privy Council archives. Nine of the files consist of petitions lodged with the Council by military officers, and four of appeals from communities. No systematic law existed, in other words, to deal with acts of violence committed by communities against roaming bands of soldiers. The treatment meted out to these communities depended entirely on local circumstances and the political climate of the time.

The formation of rebel areas

In studying these various cases we find that no less than ten towns, villages or groups of villages were the scene of incessant rioting against contingents of troops. Sometimes the dates of these outbreaks are extremely close together, and this indicates that the communities concerned were reacting in self-defence to the depredations they suffered in a phase of protracted insecurity when soldiers were continually traversing their lands. In times like that the people would be on a constant war footing and would spring to arms the moment they heard the call. A typical exhibition of self-defence was given at Granges-sur-Lot when four light cavalrymen arrived there at nightfall to ask the way. The horsemen were promptly greeted with musket-fire, and peasants came flocking from all sides as the tocsin sounded the alarm. This incident took place in July 1640, when troops were incessantly passing through the region on their way to the Basque country or Catalonia. The peasants were on the watch, and the progress of the soldiers was punctuated by riots. The uprising at Abjat broke out in the same year. According to the chronicler, the people of this town had the reputation of being 'in the habit of rising up against the king's forces and of robbing and murdering the soldiers who were billeted on them.' As early as February 1640 they put to flight a newly recruited troop of infantrymen, killing some of the soldiers and plundering their baggage. In May they launched their onslaught against Vaucocour's cavalry; and they succeeded in driving off the sergeants who descended on the town right up till February 1641. They were still resisting incursions in January 1645. One night that month a sergeant crept up to the town and tried to throw an ordinance of the provincial intendant into its streets. The sergeant was greeted with a volley of arquebus fire and forced to take to his heels. For at least five years this town of Abjat had remained under arms against intruders, stationing sentinels and maintaining barricades.

Sometimes, on the other hand, we find outbreaks of violence against soldiers taking place in the same locality at two quite different dates. In cases like this we must assume that some sort of tradition of rebellion persisted in the area. Le Dorat, for instance, closed its gates to the troops sent to garrison it in 1602 and again in 1639. Montmorillon did the same in 1636 and again in 1649, Grenade in 1638 and again in 1661. The citizens of Périgueux drove soldiers away from the territory which fell within their town's jurisdiction in both 1636 and 1640. Describing these episodes half a century later, Chevalier de Cablanc drew the attention of his fellow-citizens to an important conclusion which could be deduced from them. 'We may notice from this', he wrote, 'that there is no need for us to endure the quartering of soldiers in our suburbs if the consuls are only prepared to do their duty and stop it.' A similar tradition of revolt can be traced in the town of Saint-Geniez. In January 1638 the Marquis de Canillac designated this town as the assembly-point for forty recruits who had been raised for his company of light cavalry, even though he had not received proper orders to do so. The townspeople promptly rose up under the leadership of the vice-seneschal of Rodez. They put these unwanted horsemen to flight and plundered their baggage. The rights and wrongs of the incident were so debatable, and the authorities appointed by the Council to investigate it so much in conflict with each other that no punitive action was ever carried out. Eight years later, in May 1646, another company of light cavalry marked time in front of the closed gates of Saint-Geniez for a period of four days. This company belonged to the Queen's Regiment, and their orders for billeting were properly made out; but it made no difference. On the fourth day the citizens sallied forth from their walls, routed the company, killed their horses and plundered their baggage-train. Four village risings against passing troops took place within an area of only a few leagues on the borders of Haute-Auvergne and Bas-Limousin. In 1625 the trouble centred on the barony of La Roche-Canillac, in 1632 on Saint-Chamant and Saint-Martin-Valmeroux, in 1639 on Saint-Pardoux-la-Croizille, and in 1659 on Jaleyrac. We can see, then, that there were a number of quintessentially rebel areas where people sprang to arms almost from force of habit. People in areas like this persuaded themselves for various reasons that they could not endure to have any soldiers billeted on them and that they could enforce by their own efforts the *de facto* exemption from billeting they had enjoyed. Sometimes they took this view because the place they occupied was easy to fortify, and the neighbourhood hard of access. Sometimes it was because they were following the example of the turbulent seigneurs who lived round about, or counting on them for protection. And sometimes it was simply because they were used to resisting passing troops and getting off scot-free. Their attitude was the product of a range of special factors: the chances of geography as they affected historical events, and their own experience of profitable rebellion. The effect of their attitude was, over time, to breed pockets of resistance in certain particular areas – zones of disaffection whose contours could never be found on the maps.

The villager's ethic – and the soldier's

It is easy enough to see what function this form of collective violence played in a community's social life. The arrival of soldiers constituted an aggressive incursion from outside, a brutal intrusion by strangers into the hermetic world of the village. The community's feeling was expressed in the answer given in 1651 by the people of Saint-Florentin to a quartermaster who had come to announce the impending arrival of horsemen to take up winter quarters in their village. The villagers yelled that 'if the community had any further garrison, it would have trouble getting through the winter; that they were in no mood to take strangers into their towns, or to allow themselves to be eaten out of house and home'. By closing its gates to the soldiers and leaving them out in the cold, the community gave a display of unity at the expense of the aggressor. The aggressor became a scapegoat. The effect of the disturbance was to strengthen the cohesion of the nuclear commune. It rejected the alien body that had tried to penetrate it, and turned in upon itself.

This outbreak of violence involved at the same time a confrontation between two different value-systems. On the one side was the ethic of the soldier, warlike, nomadic, essentially idle, and living from day to day. On the other side was the ethic of the villagers, peaceful, sedentary people whose lives were based on the need to work and husband resources to carry them through the years. Young, landless peasants might, of course, cross this gulf by going off to enlist. It was their only path to adventure, the only way in which they could remotely hope to share in the values of the nobles. But once they had turned their backs on their native community and become part of a warrior band, they reacted to their exclusion from the community by displaying a constant aggressiveness towards the villagers who had stayed behind. They were driven by an urge to scorn and abuse their old environment, to insult the village worthies and disrupt the local festivals. Let us consider a few examples of the conflicts which broke out between these two competing group ethics.

The consuls of Agen had forbidden the soldiers stationed there to walk the streets in bands after curfew. A garrison commander reacted to this prohibition by sending out a drummer to make the rounds of the garrison and forbid the troops 'to go about the town in parties of less than twenty, on pain of being hanged in his back yard. He gave them permission to kill anyone, even a consul, who tried to bar their way, and granted them, in advance, a free pardon for any crimes they might commit.' On another occasion some young people in a village were dancing to the sound of oboes. A group of dragoons beat drums to drown them out. Once a party of festive villagers set out to plant a maypole. They marched along in procession beating a drum. Their celebration offended a company of soldiers stationed in the district; the soldiers poured out of the tavern where they were drinking to beat up the merrymakers and break their tabor. In one town a financial official tried to stop some houses being ransacked by visiting troops. A party of drunken gentry got their batmen to give him a drubbing with their sticks.

Villagers who rebelled against the excesses of the soldiery excited in them not pity, but contempt. Condé, for instance, talked of 'the war of cobblestones and chamber pots'. Chavagnac remarked how the burgesses of Mur-de-Barrez had turned themselves into a 'savage infantry', and Vaucocour complained of the 'vile men of Abjat'.

Stiffened by their military ethic, soldiers refused to respect the regulations issued by the *bureaux de guerre*. They regarded such regulations as outrageous and demeaning. On one occasion the *jurats* of Bergerac posted a set of regulations at each of the various crossroads in their town. These notices laid down the rules for military halts, and specified the exact rate which the soldiers currently in the town were expected to pay for the goods they bought. The soldiers tore down the notices. They had every intention of living as they pleased. They set off through the streets to ransack the houses of the two burgesses who had been assigned the task of distributing the rations specially prepared for their consumption, calling out as they went, 'Long live the king, and no rules for halts!' Any attempt to punish crimes committed by the soldiers often led to mutiny in the ranks. On one occasion the authorities at Bordeaux tried to hang a soldier for looting. The garrison stationed in the city rose up and set upon the bowmen of the watch who had been posted around the scaffold, shouting 'Down with the redcoats!' The bowmen just had time to retreat to the town hall and place themselves under the protection of the provincial intendant. The chronicler Pontis gives an account of a similar mutiny. He reveals how even the officers at a top-level council of war insisted that the local community should release a soldier in their ranks who had been convicted of murder. They believed that 'it was a matter of honour on their part to support a soldier against a handful of burgesses who wanted him punished'.

Local people rose up with precisely the opposite end in view. Their onslaught was directed against the military ethic in every form it took. Crowds gathered to stop soldiers engaging in dissolute behaviour. At Auch, for example, the citizens set upon a soldier who was molesting a respectable girl. Crowds also tried to stop soldiers disrupting an entertainment. At Niort a group of towns-people who were watching a tumbler attacked a company of dragoons. Rioters hamstrung the horses of the military or cut out their tongues. Another time a group of villagers assailed some gipsies whom they had recognized in a newly recruited troop of light cavalry. The settled people of the commune had spurned these gipsies, but there was, significantly, room for them in the nomadic military life.[12]

The behaviour of the soldiers reflected, to a certain degree, the values of the nobility. To that extent we may detect faint traces of a resentment against the nobles in the revolts which so often broke out in the villages against the military bands. The burgesses of Nontron, for instance, showed signs of this resentment when they intervened in the lawsuit that resulted from the Abjat affair. They argued before the provincial intendant that a gentleman like Vaucocour was not doing anything especially meritorious in serving in the army, since he was doing no more than his duty and was drawing a good salary into the bargain. 'His Majesty does not intend soldiers to make their fortunes out of the ruin of the local people . . . or to make war on innocent

---

12 The villagers concerned were the people of Saint-Geniez, who were led by a band of youths known as the 'Kids' (*Marmots*). On 5 January 1638 they recognised in Canillac's light cavalry the gipsy captain La Jeunesse and four of his companions. See Archives Nationales V 6. 128, 13 April 1638, no. 26; V 6. 135, 7 January 1639, no. 3. For the protection which the gentry usually gave to gipsy bands against the legal proceedings instigated by local justices and villagers, see the chapter 'Les Bohémiens au château' in F. Vaux de Foletier, *Les Tsiganes dans l'ancienne France* (Société d'édition géographique et touristique, Paris, 1961).

folk.' Similar resentment may also be detected in some remarks made by Fonteneil, a lawyer of Bordeaux. Fonteneil was describing the death of some carabineers in the service of the Duke of Épernon. These carabineers had been killed by a group of rebels who had barricaded themselves in the Gradignan church. Fonteneil interjected the curious observation 'that a rifle in the hands of a skilful peasant can kill a gentleman no matter how valiant he may be'.

We have considered here about forty outbreaks of violence against intruding soldiery. A majority of these disturbances fall into one or the other of two distinct chronological clumps. Nineteen of them took place between 1638 and 1640, and a less conspicuous concentration of six broke out between 1649 and 1653. The first of these periods was precisely the darkest phase of the Thirty Years War, when the whole of France was convulsed by the military struggle. The second period is conterminous with the Fronde, when communities reverted to old techniques of local self-defence to protect themselves in the insecure conditions caused by the civil wars. From the time when Louis XIV began to rule in his own right rioting against soldiers virtually ceased. This type of rioting seems, then, to have been dependent on circumstances. It was rendered obsolete in Louis XIV's reign by a series of new developments. Military discipline was beginning to be inculcated, and the authorities were beginning to enforce on the armies strict observance of the rules regarding the routes they were to follow and the lodgings they were to occupy at their halts. A still more decisive innovation was the establishment of barracks and permanent garrisons.[13]

Riots against intruding soldiers had highlighted the cohesive nature of the commune. As these riots passed into history so too, coincidentally, did the military role which the commune had played. The authorities began to consider it more dangerous than useful to have closed towns and fortified cities in the heart of the kingdom. They issued financial edicts that ordered the confiscation of the revenues amassed in the town halls. The ramparts slowly caved in, and the town halls no longer had either the authority or the money to rebuild them.

As the commune stopped rioting against the billeting of troops it also lost its autonomy. In the meantime France began to create an army for modern times.

---

13 At the end of the seventeenth century militias began to be raised, and in the course of the eighteenth century militiamen began to be drafted into the regular army. These developments led to a number of desertions on the part of individuals and collective displays of resistance on the part of communities. It was the start of a new type of revolt, unknown at our period. In the seventeenth century the state had confined itself to tax gathering: now it was also imposing a programme of conscription. It had, in other words, devised for itself a new coercive function. The new form of dissidence was a response to this trend.

Riots against the taxmen

The development of the fiscal system was, as we have seen, a basic factor in the building of the modern French state. The increase in tax-gathering methods was an inseparable part of the process by which the central government was tightening its control of the population. The riots which broke out against tax collectors must consequently be assigned a position of some importance in the political history of this period. Numerous and widespread, affecting the whole of the country and persisting for many decades, they were an appropriate accompaniment to this major advance in the development of French institutions. From the point of view of a seventeenth-century chronicler, however, they were little more than trivial news items, and a modern researcher has to peer intently to make them out in the general rush of events. I have collated for the purposes of the present study the accounts of some sixty upheavals of this type. My selection of sources was a random one, and I have not tried to focus on any particular group of places or years.

Rebellion of this kind was viewed, for practical purposes, as a criminal activity in the legal treatises which were produced at this period on the subject of taxation. It was described as being a crime of high treason in the second degree. This carried the death penalty, but the legal commentators added that the circumstances had to be serious before that penalty would actually be enforced. Such a rebellion was defined in the first instance as a protest involving the use of force and violence against a government official; but the concept also extended to cover such displays of passive resistance as a refusal to draw up the tax rolls or to appoint solvent citizens to gather the tax. There was a certain logic in this. The methods used by the government to extort taxes from the populace were so heavy-handed that they sooner or later drove people who had simply refused to co-operate to resort to violence after all. It is cases like these, when a group of individuals resisted the tax collectors and by doing so laid themselves open to the charge of violent rebellion, that we shall now proceed to consider.

Sometimes the resistance took the form of a dozen people slamming their doors in the face of a bailiff. At other times as many as a hundred peasants might gather to resist the fusiliers sent by the government to enforce the payment of tax. It will clearly be seen that both events had the same institutional roots. Other incidents, however, do not always have the same common standard, and to add them to my survey I have imposed the further unity of a single day and location. Incidents which I have circumscribed in this way may be found taking place in a very similar fashion over larger areas and longer periods of revolt. We shall consider the reason for these larger groupings further on. The division into the day-long episodes is, none the less, a valid one. The words performed and the actions taken on those days are of interest in themselves, regardless of their immediate context. The intendant Charreton described one of these episodes in a report he wrote to the chancellor in 1644 on the state of the tax collection in his province of Gascony. 'Wherever an attempt is made', he declared, 'to enforce the payment of taxes, an outbreak of rebellion takes place.' Each of these outbreaks, considered separately, offers us a microcosm of the general resistance which characterized the century as a whole.

Tax-gathering practices that led to revolt

It will be no surprise to discover that physical compulsion in the form of imprisonment for debt was the tax-raising technique most liable to engender violent resistance on the part of the subject population. Nineteen of the sixty disturbances surveyed here broke out in response to coercion of this kind. Eleven others were provoked by seizures of moveable assets such as bed linen, kitchen utensils, weapons and pewter plate, and ten by seizures of livestock in regions such as the Pyrenees and Limousin.

We may consider, to begin with, whether these disturbances occurred haphazardly over the course of the year. The answer is plainly no. I have identified a total of seventy-nine recorded outbreaks, giving us an average figure of 6.5 per month. At certain times of the year, however, the figure is well above the norm. Twenty-nine of the outbreaks took place between March and June, fifteen in August and seventeen in November and December. In the other months, however, the figure is below average. Only eight outbreaks occurred in January and February put together, three in July, and seven again, in September and October together. This pattern can be readily understood from a glance at the fiscal calendar. Spring was the time when the tax warrants were distributed in the parishes and the assessment books were drawn up. Turbulence slackened at the beginning of summer and in the autumn, when the corn and grape harvests were being gathered in. The tax collectors were usually advised by the intendants to withdraw their sergeants at these periods and leave the peasants free to fill their sacks and casks undisturbed. Trouble resumed, however, in November and December. This was the time when the troops were moving into their winter quarters, and the tax officials had the chance of using force to suppress the resistance they had been obliged to put up with during the earlier months of the year.

Taxpayers refused to co-operate with the authorities for two different reasons. Sometimes they took exception to the form in which a demand for tax was presented, and sometimes they rejected the basic assumption on which the demand was made. The various forms of compulsion were obviously aggressive in character, since the object was to collect a given amount of arrears by force. A bailiff's writ was always resented as an insult and an invasion of privacy, even when the officials concerned had taken all the precautions provided for in the government ordinances. These ordinances actually laid down careful rules regarding the way in which the bailiff was to conduct himself when he served his writ. In addressing the taxpayer he was to issue 'an express and emphatic command to pay at once and without delay, in the name of our lord the king'. Alternatively he was to instruct the taxpayer 'to liquidate his debt by handing over gold and silver coin for the king'. If the taxpayer refused, the bailiff was to order him 'to open his doors to them, in the name of the king, so that they may take his moveables and put them on sale. The proceeds are to be used to liquidate whatever debt may be owing to His Majesty, and to meet their own expenses.' The bailiff was careful to state his rank and the commission under which he was acting. He handed over a copy of the notice or summons being issued, and pronounced the formal sequestration of any goods that might have been seized. All these proceedings would be duly mentioned in the report he prepared, even if he had done no more than gallop through a village and throw a paper into the street, or yell his announcement of a sequestration in the hurly-burly of a riot. In getting the bailiff to serve his writ with all this care and formality, the government had a very definite aim in view. The idea was to forestall any attempt at pleading ignorance on the part of the taxpayer – to invest the bailiff's operation with the authority of the crown and thereby to stigmatize as rebellion any resistance that he might encounter. The report drawn up by a bailiff to denounce an act of rebellion tended consequently to conform to a basic stereotype. The rebel in question was portrayed as having openly derided the legal injunction under which the writ was being served. He was said to have flouted the authority of the crown, and denounced, for good measure, for having 'blasphemed against the holy name of God'.

A bailiff's task ranged from searching a peasant's cottage for goods to confiscate to stripping a room of its furniture against the wishes of the occupants and haling a refractory taxpayer off to prison. Work like this was bound to involve a fair degree of brutality; and the complaints lodged by private citizens against the excesses of the bailiffs are as stereotyped, in their way, as the reports the bailiffs drew up. If a bailiff was a Huguenot, for instance, or if an element of scandal attached to his private life, the petitioners never failed to point it out. Bailiffs were portrayed as offending against the most sacred values. A citizen would complain that a bailiff had intruded on his religious observances in the middle of a church, or molested his pregnant wife. Protests of this kind were voiced at Lusignan, where the tax collector was calling on the householders to liquidate their debts by surrendering their moveables, even though they claimed to be exempt from any such requirement. The citizens submitted a petition to the Council denouncing 'a large number of bailiffs and bowmen who had been sent to arrest some of the residents of this town. These officers had committed some outrageous acts of violence. They had beaten and upset a great many people including even pregnant women, several of whom went into labour in mid-term.'[14] The archives of the lawcourts are full of similar complaints. The sergeants are said to have knocked

---

14 Petition filed at Lusignan, May 1656. See Archives Nationales, E 292b, fo. 396. Criminal investigations often contained references to pregnant women whom the plaintiffs alleged to have been maltreated by the other side. It was a classic plaintiff's device. In an instruction manual designed for the guidance of tax agents and sergeants, the author warned his readers how crooked innkeepers had a habit of getting their wives to carry the keys to their cellar or their false compasses, 'especially when they are pregnant. A tax agent runs truly dreadful dangers in arresting such a woman, especially if she gets hurt in the course of the struggle. If that happens he can only clear out and flee.' See Pierre Asse (former collector of *aides*), *Traité des aydes pour tous les lieux où ils ont cours* . . ., republished Paris, 1964, p. 11.

out a woman as she clung to the cooking-pot they were trying to confiscate, and cut off the fingers of a man to stop him clutching the door from which they were trying to drag him away. They are accused of dragging taxpayers by their hair, of binding them hand and foot and throwing them into a cart. Violence of various kinds which broke out in the process of tax collection was the subject of 18.1 per cent of the lawsuits brought before the *présidial* of Angoulême in 1643 and 1644. This figure includes the outbreaks of violent protest which took place among the taxpayers. Such cases alone constituted 6.7 per cent of the total number of lawsuits.

The bailiffs' proceedings were not merely exhibitions of aggression: they could also seem fundamentally illegal in the eyes of the victims. The serving of the writ was viewed as being an act of private vengeance disguised with a show of judicial propriety. In many cases it was, after all, a personal enemy who denounced the offending taxpayer and got the bailiffs sent in to search and distrain upon his goods. It was the residents of a neighbouring community who acted as guides when the fusiliers were sent to a given canton to force the parishes to accept collective responsibility for a debt. Incidents like these were the cause of the minor wars which broke out between different *communes* in the reign of Louis XIII. A conflict would arise, typically, when the principal town in a *collecte* (tax district) or jurisdiction was obliged to provide billets for a company of soldiers or to pay an advance instalment of a tax on its own. The town would then turn on the other parishes in its jurisdiction which had not borne their share of the burden and which were known variously, in the different regions, as its 'helpers', 'goddaughters', 'fortresses' and 'cantons'. For several days the consuls of the town and a party of armed citizens would go round from village to village in the company of a force of soldiery, carrying off livestock from the smallholdings of those parishes which had not contributed their share to hold in pawn for the payment of the money. Raids like this were launched from the town of Casteljaloux in 1636, from Laplume, Layrac and Mauvezin in 1638, and from Verdun-sur-Garonne in 1644. Sometimes it happened that the villagers resisted these neighbours 'who presumed to deal out justice themselves ... This had forced them to arm and meet force with force.' Clashes took place on 5 November 1636 between the citizens of Casteljaloux and the villagers who lived in the rural parishes of Pindères and Les Lugues, and on 11 February 1638 between the citizens of Laplume and Montagnac.

Communities sometimes claimed exemptions from the taxes demanded of them. Small country regions that had enjoyed long-standing privileges in respect of taxation felt that those privileges should entitle them to a comparable exemption from any new levies. The larger towns equally could cite any number of rights and freedoms when confronted with the prospect of an unprecedented tax. The taxpayers in these places thought that the bailiffs were no longer the true representatives of the king. Rather, they were acting as agents for a tax-farmer engaged in raising an iniquitous levy. People were generally willing to pay taxes to the king, but refused to comply with demands for taxes on offices or for contributions towards the salaries and expenses of the bailiffs and the upkeep of the fusiliers. Under these circumstances communities could appeal to a rival jurisdiction and win a reprieve from the coercive measures with which they were threatened. Taxpayers often felt free to challenge the validity of the bailiff's warrant. In January 1643, for instance, the people of Champagne-Mouton declared that 'these robbers have no authority whatever for coming and distraining upon the goods of people in Poitou'. In August 1667 the people of Montesquieu-Volvestre told the bailiffs, 'Folk in this region are not used to seeing a rabble like you.'

Finally people objected to the latest measures which the authorities had devised to coerce them, such as the imposition of collective distraints and the stationing of fusiliers in their midst. They resisted such measures constantly and vigorously. The government's attempt to introduce new coercive machinery was the cause of most of the riots that took place at this period – and the most serious ones.

The neighbourhood to the rescue

Taxpayers rose up, in the first instance, because the conduct of the bailiffs had goaded them into doing so. We should remember that the upper classes of society were exempt from taxation, and that a delinquent payer of taxes or 'greencap' was an object of contempt. This meant that to be served with a writ by a bailiff was regarded in some sense as a shameful event. The victim resented the bailiff's arrival as a disgrace, a stain on his reputation. The shame which the bailiff's advent was felt to entail is reflected in the insults with which the taxpayers greeted him and consigned him to the depths of public scorn. 'Rascal', they called him, 'good-for-nothing bailiff, rogue of a sergeant, layabout, man of straw'. People of standing felt that their homes were entitled to a certain degree of immunity which the bailiff had violated. He had offended social propriety, and they gave him a drubbing for his pains. 'That will teach you to go into respectable houses . . . houses of decent people.' 'God's death, this ruffian has had no respect for me . . . Anyone who stays in my house will get a taste of the stick . . . This is no way to treat a man of my rank.'

Crowds gathered to thwart the bailiffs. They wanted to stop them carrying off the moveables they had seized, to reclaim the livestock they had started driving off down the high road and to snatch from their clutches those villagers whom they had arrested and were dragging off to prison in the local town. Local people felt an immediate sense of solidarity when confronted with the bailiff. A victim of the bailiff's attentions had only to call for help; and if he happened to be a reasonably prosperous master-craftsman or ploughman with a family, his wife, children and domestics could give the bailiff a fairly unpleasant time even before the neighbours arrived on the scene. A citizen of Maintré appealed to his household in 1706, 'Have I no servants to put an end to these persecutors?' A tailor of Civray cried likewise in 1698, 'Have I no friends to get me out of the hands of these bloody robbers?' Women would scream at their gates and set the whole neighbourhood in an uproar. Even in a lonely hamlet, several dozen people would come flocking in a matter of minutes. The crowds would be mostly composed of women, since the men would be working in the fields. People carried whatever weapons they were able to snatch up. Women bombarded the bailiffs with stones and spattered them with cinders and slops, while the men set about them with sticks, cattle-prods, pitchforks and hatchets. The neighbourhood always came to the rescue in no time at all. People in a community felt a duty to help one another, and none of them would have dreamt of questioning it. 'Close the gates', cried a woman at Saint-Maixent in 1645, 'The tax crooks are carrying off my husband.' 'Down with the robbers', called the people of Linars in 1643. 'Ring the town bell!' The citizens of La Réole declared in 1668, 'We must seize these people who have come to extort from us ... and not let them carry off a single craftsman.' 'We've just killed one of your taxmen', the crowd at Maintré yelled in 1706. 'We must throw these rascals in the river.' All the reports of the bailiffs emphasize how suddenly these disturbances flared up. 'Large numbers of people arrived all at once from both the village itself and the neighbouring parishes ... More and more people gathered with every passing minute.'

Sometimes it happened that the sergeant did not take to his heels fast enough, or was chased for several leagues and then caught. In this case the unfortunate bailiff would be showered with blows. The crowd would snatch off his hat and baldric and would tear his clothes to shreds. They would steal his horse and baggage and even his shoes. They would seize his official papers and rip up his warrant. They would shut him in a barn to beat him up and would cut off his beard and moustaches. Finally they would want to push him into a river or toss him into a well. Throwing the sergeant into the water was a kind of ritual. In Périgueux in 1635, and Carcassonne in 1664, the town well served as a place of execution. The lynching of the sergeant was felt to be an act of justice, like everything else the rioters did. The community had been exempt from paying taxes for all sorts of good reasons. By pressing for taxes the sergeant had committed an aggression against the community, and deserved to be punished for the upheaval he had caused. The peasant crowds had no doubt that they were in the right. All they were doing was refusing to pay an unwarranted tax, a *gabelle* or extortion. 'Down with the robbers', they cried. 'We must kill them. There is no need for us to pay, we are under no obligation to do so.' In outbreak after outbreak the bailiffs were abused as 'robbers and thieves'. It was the favourite insult. At Montesquieu-Volvestre in 1667 the bailiffs were also referred to as 'excisemen who plunder the people and eat up their livelihood'. A chronicler writing in Gascony in 1643 reported how 'the people believe they are obliged to pay only the old royal *taille*. They think that the special warrants and even the warrants of the intendants have been revoked.' The people of Limousin declared in 1645 that 'they would certainly pay the taxes if they could. But they would never take in these soldiers and they would cut to pieces anyone who turned up in the name of the king.' In 1636 a tailor of Agen was asked by a visiting bailiff to contribute to his expenses. The tailor replied 'that he knew very well what the man was really levying – the *gabelle*'. Another recalcitrant tailor was the one who appealed for help at Civray in 1698. He was not prepared to contribute his share of a tax which was being raised on jobs in the gift of the town hall. He called in his neighbours. 'We must kill these buggers', he said, 'and anyone else who comes to make us pay an illegal tax.'

Consuls or aldermen threw their moral weight behind these justice-loving riots by seizing an offending bailiff and throwing him in prison. Sometimes the bailiffs and their heavies put up a resistance. They fired on the crowd in an attempt to break free, and wounded or even killed one of their assailants. This made them murderers from that time on in the eyes of the community. At Migné near Poitiers, on 24 December 1643, the crowd threw nooses around the necks of the bailiff and his men and dragged them to the foot of a tree with a view to hanging them. In the end cooler counsels prevailed. The captives were taken under close guard to the courtroom of a local judge. The judge ignored their protests, declared them to be under arrest and consigned them to the mercies of the law.

Equally drastic upheavals took place when fusiliers were stationed in a province to enforce the payment of taxes. News of the route they were taking spread rapidly through the countryside, and the villages emptied as they drew near. The horsemen arrived to find the cottages abandoned. All the moveables had been carried off and placed under the protection of the seigneur or village priest. The men had all taken flight, and there was no one left in the villages but women and children. There was nothing for them to seize, and no one to take prisoner. In some places communities would prepare to defend themselves as though there was a war on. They would throw up barricades, and post sentinels and snipers. In 1641 the villagers of Saint-Cricq in Les Lannes 'swore to kill the first person who came to take their cattle'. People in neighbouring parishes would promise to help each other. If the fusiliers appeared on the borders of any one of them, the tocsin would be sounded. The peal would be taken up by one church after another, and within the space of a few hours all the people in the canton would abandon work, take up arms and rush to their barricades. A typical campaign of resistance was mounted by the inhabitants of the *châtellenie* of Montguyon in 1657–9. A chronicler reports how 'they had made up their minds not to pay any taxes, and not to let any agents or bailiffs come to collect them.' An account of the resistance which broke out in Pardiac in 1642 illustrates the extent of the collusion which could develop within a neighbourhood. 'They had plotted among themselves and had schemed with a number of neighbouring parishes, fifty or sixty in all, that as soon as the authorities tried to force any one parish to pay tax, the tocsin would be sounded, and all the other parishes would send in reinforcements, one armed man from every household, on pain of being fined.' The fusiliers usually contented themselves with delivering a single volley of musket-fire. After that they headed about and went back to the town they had come from to draw up their reports.

Once they had gathered together, the peasants would typically decide to go and rescue their consuls, syndics or fund-raisers – leading members of their community whom the authorities had thrown in gaol. The protracted revolt in Pardiac began in just this way. For a period of about ten days some tens of thousands of Croquants moved about the district from town to town with the object of freeing people who had been imprisoned for non-payment of taxes. Not content with resisting the companies who came to harass them, they actually went and attacked the fusiliers in their quarters. They stormed their tormentors' barracks and chased them across the countryside. Incidents of this kind took place in Astarac in July 1640, at the town of Puydarrieux. In Pardiac the revolt which raged between 1642 and 1644 affected the towns of Plaisance, Estampes and Bétous. Bas-Limousin experienced two separate bouts of resistance: one of them broke out at Viam in January 1645 and the other at Rilhac-Xaintrie in July 1648. In September 1659 there was trouble at Leynhac in Haute-Auvergne, and in December 1661 the fusiliers were assailed at Escoussans in Benauge.

Some of the fusiliers taken prisoner by the Croquants were held for ransom. Others were simply lynched. At Sauze-Vaussais in Bas-Poitou in 1624 and at Estampes in 1643 the peasants buried the fusiliers they had slaughtered and tried to forget they had ever passed that way.[15] In 1656–9 the peasants who lived in the regions of Coutras and Montguyon embarked on a course of open rebellion. They abandoned their villages and went into hiding in the forests and outlying hamlets. The only objective of people waging these hopeless little wars was to win an amnesty for their past offences. The people of Coutras, for instance, submitted a petition in the hope of obtaining a pardon for their crimes. They had wiped out a brigade of soldiers and had harassed visiting bailiffs over a period of several years. Significantly, the rebels defended their conduct by repeating the familiar arguments that they were in the right and that even their revolt had been undertaken in a blind search for justice.

They said they had been driven to take up arms because the soldiers who came to their place had raped their wives and daughters, plundered their houses and maltreated them in various other ways. That was the only reason for their rebellion. And they had only committed the other excesses they were accused of in order to keep alive and ward off starvation during the time they were banded together, and at the same time to preserve their goods from being plundered by those horsemen, so that they would have the means to pay the *tailles* you required.

In a sense this was special pleading. The rebels suddenly found themselves in the role of suppliants, and they needed to present their revolt in a favourable light. At the same time their petition faithfully represented the overall programme of the Croquants and the overall aim of the riots which they staged against the taxmen. They wished to see a return to the old, established taxes, and they were not prepared to accept the new-fangled terrorist methods of

15 According to reports drawn up by Charreton, the provincial intendant, in October 1643, eighteen fusiliers on a tax mission who had been captured by the people of Estampes were led into a field at night and clubbed to death. Their bodies were thrown into pits. The peasants quickly ploughed over the graves and sowed flax there. See Archives Nationales, KK 1217, fos. 38 and 69, and *Affaires Etrangères Mémoires Docmentaires*, France, 1743, fo. 75. Contemporaries were fascinated by both this crime and the punishments which were subsequently inflicted upon the culprits, and the oral tradition through which the story was preserved was embroidered with extraordinary details. 'The women braked flax so that no one would hear the noise of the execution. The impudent rascals kept their own counsel, and the authorities questioned them in vain. The corpses were found by a dog.' Notes made by Larcher, a specialist in feudal law, and referred to in the *Revue de Gascogne*, 1897, p. 76.

tax collection which the fiscal authorities of their time were bent on trying out.

The dramatis personae of the revolt

The victims of the rioters all belonged to a particular type of institution. They were the regular or special agents used by the government in its tax-collecting operations. They ranged from the bailiffs, sergeants and bowmen employed by the *maréchaussées* to the fusiliers assigned to tax raising, the guards of the provincial governors and the companies that were detached from local regiments to help conduct the levies. In many cases an angry crowd succeeded in catching only a handful of unfortunate bailiffs' men. These men were typically village craftsmen, doctors, soldiers and journeymen recruited in the taverns. The bailiffs had hired them for the price of a few *sous*. They were expected, if the need arose, to come to the bailiffs' assistance in a scuffle and to bear witness in court. When the bailiffs found themselves faced with resistance on the part of the taxpayers, their task was to assess the danger that threatened them. If their own force was strong enough, it was their duty to charge the crowd 'to preserve the authority of the crown and the laws'. If, on the other hand, the odds seemed to be against them, they would retreat 'in order to avoid any undesirable consequences . . . to ensure their personal safety . . . and to prevent matters taking a still more scandalous turn'.

The forces of order had to contend with entire communities. Whole streets and townships, hamlets and cantons rose up against the taxman. Collective prosecutions were brought against whole parishes in the aftermath of forty-four of the sixty-odd outbreaks of violence I have studied. In March 1643, for instance, we learn from the legal records that all the villagers of Maillezais in Poitou had risen up. They were armed with guns and sticks. In April 1644 'all the people of a place called Bétous' rose up in Gascony. They were helped by a number of soldiers newly recruited into the regiment of Roquelaure. A wide range of craftsmen played their part in the various revolts. The villagers who rioted at Migné in December 1643 were led by a miller, the townspeople who ran amok at La Réole in September 1668 were led by a hatter and his son, and the people who rose up at Laugnac in November 1719 had a shoemaker at their head. The riot which broke out at Civray in April 1698 was started by the arrest of a master-tailor. All the other residents in his street came pouring out of their houses to deliver him from the clutches of the sergeants. In the end there were almost a hundred people involved in this riot. Women and girls for the most part, they set upon the sergeants with sticks and stones. They were led by a tavern-keeper who brandished an axe. The women from the master-tailor's home were prominent in the riot, and so too were his apprentices, a butcher and his wife, the son and mother of a locksmith, the son of a baker, the son of a cobbler and all the local children.

A spontaneous outbreak of rioting could evolve into organized resistance only if it had the support of the traditional community leaders such as the consuls, justices and local gentry. As often as not it did. At Fleurance in November 1637, Siros in January 1660, Sauveterre-en-Nébouzan in June

1660 and Montesquieu-Volvestre in August 1667, consuls had the tocsin sounded, or marched at the head of the rioters. At Le Dorat in June 1638, Champagnac in July 1653, Carcassonne in August 1664 and Saint-Maixent in July 1665, local justices gave orders for the tax sergeants to be arrested and thrown into prison. Gentlemen of the district often led the peasants in the small-scale wars they waged against the bands of fusiliers. One such blue-blooded leader was Anguittard, the seigneur of Saint-Germain. From May to November 1642 he raised the parishes around Jonzac in revolt against some bowmen who had come to serve writs on the taxpayers there. A similar kind of leadership was provided by Étienne d'Asta, the seigneur of Estampes. In September 1643 he gave the signal to the people of that village which incited them to embark on their notorious massacre of an entire brigade of fusiliers. In August 1659 the seigneurs of Jarnac and Roissac between them captured another complete brigade which had been sent by the provincial intendant to enforce the payment of taxes in the *élection* of Cognac; and the following month the barons of Fargues and Saignes along with three other members of the local gentry led a force of 300 peasants against the barracks occupied by a troop of cavalry. These risings attracted participants from every level of rural society. When the third in a series of rebellions broke out in Gascony in 1642, six of the ringleaders were condemned to death. Their names offer us a fair sample of that old country hierarchy. Top of the list was Hercule de Monlezun, Baron de Saint-Lary. He was convicted of 'instigating and leading the uprisings which have taken place in the district of Pardiac'. After him came Jean Dargaignan, a notary at Villecomtal, and Simon Dargaignan, who served as clerk of the court at Betplan. Both of these brothers were executed on 30 March 1643. A third Dargaignan brother, the parish priest of Malbat, and two ploughmen, Jean Gardeilles, known as 'Ropey' (*Cordelle*), and Pierre Davesies, known as 'Matey' (*Petit Amic*), completed the list. All these last three were executed on 18 April 1643.[16]

The whole community, then, was involved in resisting the tax collectors, just as it was in resisting the quartering of troops. In theory the community was held to be jointly responsible for paying tax, and the aggressive intrusion of the bailiffs into a single house was consequently perceived as an assault upon the entire population. The unanimous impulse to riot was intensified by the outrageous character of the bailiffs' distraint proceedings and the duty which people felt, no matter where they lived, of coming to their neighbours' assistance in time of need.

Recriminatory lawsuits

If the community leaders themselves took part in the riot, they gave it, in effect, their moral endorsement. They bestowed the approval of the law on

---

16 Hercule de Monlezun was executed in effigy at Marciac on 5 May 1643. He had been sentenced *in absentia*, and escaped with his life. In March 1644 he submitted a petition to the queen to win himself a pardon. See *Affaires Etrangères, Mémoires Documentaires*, France, 1743, fos. 77–80; *Journal de Sentex, Revue de Gascogne*, 1903, p. 73.

the backlash of popular rage. Sometimes the local officials intervened to prevent the riot going to extremes and to save the bailiffs from lynching. But they did so on condition that the bailiffs desisted from the attempt to serve their writs. Sometimes the officials sheltered the bailiffs by putting them in the municipal gaols, beyond the reach of the mob. But the fact remained that they were throwing them in prison like criminals, and the purpose was also to subject them to a criminal investigation. The revolt had taken a complicated turn. To outward appearances it looked as though an ordinary legal dispute was in progress. But taxman and taxpayer had changed places, and the plaintiff had become the accused. The fund-raisers whom the sergeants had held captive as surety for the payment of their community's debts had their freedom restored to them, and the tax agents whom the rioters had managed to seize were imprisoned in their place. The sergeants were forbidden to continue performing their official functions. The bailiffs' men were found to have criminal records. They had deserted from the army or committed murder or theft. Sometimes they also turned out to have beaten up one of the local people while effecting his arrest. The man would lodge a complaint against them, and the bailiffs' heavies would consequently find themselves at the receiving end of a lawsuit, on trial for an offence in which they had been caught red-handed. The effect was to hold up the writs which had been made out by the tax collectors and the decrees which had been issued by the provincial intendant, and to delay their implementation for some considerable time.

Sometimes, however, the sergeants were able to get away and lodge complaints with the intendant or the local *élection*. In this case the rebels would initiate rival proceedings before a local justice, or even before a *cour des aides* or a *parlement*. These authorities were jealous of any attempts which the government's representatives might make to encroach on their jurisdiction. They made a practice of taking cases of this sort. Such lawsuits were known as *récriminations* or *diversions*. They were usually initiated in the name of a figurehead. Sometimes this figurehead might be the widow of a rioter who had been killed in the commotion, and sometimes it might be a distinguished protector of some kind. The deputy-seneschal of Auch, for example, joined forces with the syndic of Quatre-Vallées to champion the people of Siros. Cardinal d'Este, who was also abbot of Bonnecombe, took up the cause of the citizens of the little town of Naucelle, and the Duke of La Trémoille went to court on behalf of the peasants who lived in his parish of Berrie.

A session of the court of *Grands-Jours* was held at Poitiers in 1634. The session was entrusted with the task of dealing with outbreaks of local resistance of this type. The advocates who spoke there drew attention to a number of revolts and murders of sergeants which had gone unpunished for a dozen years. Provincial intendants had latterly been appointed right and left, and their powers had been extended: they were, consequently, in a good position to look into cases of this kind. But as communities continued to initiate actions before local sovereign courts, the intendants found that they had to make frequent appeals to the Council to get their ordinances confirmed. This resistance through the lawcourts actually intensified as the drive to increase taxation reached its peak in about 1640. In 1642, for example, the *élus* of Saintes heard a whole series of actions which had been brought against the bowmen and fusiliers in the pay of the intendant Villemontée. The *parlement* of Bordeaux decreed that they should be arrested and thrown in the city gaol if they happened to come that way. The agent in charge of collecting the taxes in Saintonge expressed his dismay. 'If an appeal is not lodged quickly', he wrote, 'we shall not be able to find a single bailiff or sergeant who is willing to serve writs for extracting the taxes and provisions for the army.'

After the Fronde the government sent the fusiliers back to the provinces. The communes responded with a new wave of recriminatory lawsuits. The *cour des aides* in Guyenne ordered the arrest of the captain of a company of fusiliers which had been active in Bordelais, and forbade anyone to give him shelter. 'The writs which this man has been carrying', it proclaimed, 'could not merely bring to a halt the raising of His Majesty's moneys but could even provoke a general rising among the people who live in the places where his company has been proposing to pass.' A party of gentry brought a band of fusiliers from the *élection* of Cognac to the prisons of Angoulême, and the *lieutenant criminel* stationed in that town promptly instituted legal proceedings against the prisoners.[17] Rebels in Cozes and Aubeterre appealed to the *cour des aides* in Paris. The *cour* forbade the tax collectors to declare collective distraints without its consent, and prohibited the use of fusiliers in any place which fell within its jurisdiction. Some fusiliers who were captured by the people of Montesquieu-Volvestre were sentenced to the galleys by the *présidial* of Toulouse. The agent assigned to collect the taxes in the area voiced similar consternation to his counterpart in Saintonge. 'This verdict', he wrote, 'is the produce of pure rancour. They hate these soldiers because they are used to collect His Majesty's funds. They also hate them because they even descend on the farms of officials to force them to pay their tax.' In the end, naturally, the Council issued decrees declaring these judgements null and void and giving the intendants permission to override them. But the conflicts of jurisdiction which had taken place encouraged the defaulting taxpayers to believe in the justice of their cause, to hope for better times and to persevere in their resistance.

Typical bouts of rebellion

The outcome of these disturbances depended on the political events and troop movements that were taking place in the neighbourhood, and also on the personal disposition of the local intendant. The treatment meted out to the

17 In an ordinance issued on 5 March 1659, Hotman, the provincial intendant, posted a special detachment of twenty-four fusiliers to the *élection* of Cognac. The communities immediately resisted. They were led, as we saw above, by two members of the local gentry, the *seigneurs* of Roissac and Jarnac. The *lieutenant criminel* of Angoulême, who was also judge of the town of Jarnac, agreed to issue a warrant for the arrest of the fusiliers. One day the following August the entire brigade was surrounded by a host of peasants. The fusiliers were captured along with their horses and weaponry, and taken off under guard to Angoulême. See Archives Nationales, E 329b, fo. 383, 18 September 1659.

rebels varied according to whether the intendant was more or less inclined to take repressive measures. In some places a community which had risen against the bailiffs got bloodily chastised. In other places the result was that the community grew hardened in its refusal to pay taxes and won various kinds of *de facto* exemption.

During the first drive to extend state control in the years before the Fronde, the intendants were determined to punish rebellion by terror as a warning to future malcontents. They were anxious to stem the tide of revolt and to check the spread of subversion before it deprived the king's ministers of the resources they needed to implement the grand design they had drawn up for enhancing the glory of France on the European stage. Judicial terror was employed on a number of occasions, at Galan in August 1640, Estampes in October 1643 and Saint-Bonnet-Elvert in March 1650. The risings which had taken place in these villages were suppressed with a ferocity that inflamed provincial opinion. These were, however, isolated cases. The authorities did not take long to recognize, in fact, that they had nothing to gain from their policy of imposing crushing burdens of collective responsibility upon a population and distraining upon whole cantons in order to force them to pay huge fines. All they were achieving was to prolong the rebellion. They were driving entire communities to desperation, regardless of the fact that their members might not all have been implicated to the same degree in the original offence. Sometimes the penalties they imposed went altogether too far. In 1643, for example, they tried to exact the huge sum of 48,913 *livres* from the communities of Pardiac as a punishment for their revolt in the previous year. In 1656, similarly, they slapped a fine of 20,000 *livres* on the people of Coutras, and in 1661 they endeavoured to collect 17,500 *livres* from the parishes of Benauge. In each case they were eventually forced to admit that the money could not be raised because of the 'extreme wretchedness and poverty of the population'. The authorities found themselves confronted with the prospect of interminable revolts. Intendants and tax collectors had to adapt to this awkward reality by accepting that such recalcitrant localities were not going to yield much tax and putting the blame on the wretched conditions which prevailed there or the seditious mood of the people.

We have seen that revolts often tended to break out repeatedly in the same place. By examining these cases of repeated upheaval we have identified a number of special theatres of insurrection – regions where outbreaks of collective violence had become virtually a local tradition. The history of such cantons was punctuated by intermittent rebellions – risings which did not necesarily burn themselves out in a few days of mob fury, but could carry on sometimes for months or even years. During such risings the people lived on a constant war footing, ready to snatch up their weapons at the first intimation that bailiffs, fusiliers or other government agents were drawing near. Revolts of this kind broke out so persistently that they had, in effect, become endemic to the district. I propose to call such protracted episodes bouts of rebellion.

Let us consider the case of the county of Pardiac in the period 1638–45. Pardiac was a small region in Gascony situated between the Rivers Adour and Baîse. It consisted of about fifty parishes, and Marciac was the county town.

For tax purposes the region belonged to the *élection* of Auch. It lay in the hilly country of Armagnac, where a handful of dirt tracks ran to isolated farmsteads in the middle of the woods. The region suffered terribly from hailstorms. A few herds of livestock were raised there, but the wine was of poor quality, and the people lived on chestnuts and rancid bacon. In December 1638 the parishes of Pardiac gathered together to free their consuls and fund-raisers, who had been thrown into prison because the local communities had failed to pay their tax. On 26 December 1638 it appears that a band of 6,000 to 7,000 men succeeded in breaking open the prisons at Marciac. On 4 January 1639 they forced the prisons at Mirande, and on 7 January they devastated the country around Mirande when the burgesses of that town refused to let them use their bridge to cross the Baîse and march on Auch. In May 1642 fresh trouble broke out. Peasant bands from the parishes of Pardiac attacked and routed some companies which had been detached from the regiment of Roquelaure to gather the taxes there. These bands numbered 2,000 to 3,000. On the night of 22 June they marched up to the town of Plaisance. The general tax agent for Montauban was staying there in the company of the deputy vice-seneschal of Armagnac and his bowmen. The rebels took them by surprise. The officials were captured, but a member of the local gentry, the seigneur of Pouydraguin, intervened and persuaded the peasants to spare their lives. The officials were then led off under guard to Villecomtal, a hillside village 30 kilometres away, and released five days later in return for a ransom of 3,000 *livres*. The tax agent also lost the money he had collected, which amounted to some 12,500 *livres*. Risings against the fusiliers continued to break out in Pardiac the following year. News was just then spreading through France of the death of Louis XIII. People believed that the hated provincial intendants might now be recalled; and the whole of Rouergue was convulsed by rebellion. In July 1643 the citizens of the little town of Aignan drove off a brigade of sixteen horsemen who had been sent to collect their tax. Two months later a second brigade was captured by the people who lived in the small market town of Estampes. The brigade consisted of an official bearing writs for distraint from the local tax collector, a sergeant and sixteen horsemen. The peasants held them prisoner for three days, then massacred them.

The massacre had been instigated by the local seigneur. In February 1644 the seigneur of Estampes returned surreptitiously to his estates. A number of peasants had been executed for the crime, and the seigneur had them decently buried. He also drove off some labourers who had been employed in setting up a pyramid commemorating the government's vengeance. On 21 April yet another brigade of fusiliers encountered resistance in the region. They were chased away from the village of Bétous, and four men were killed in the skirmish. In June, and again in November, the provincial intendants denounced the local nobility for continuing to hold seditious assemblies; and reports from this time make it clear that the sergeants were still unwilling to risk their necks serving writs on the parishes of Pardiac. For over six years, then, the county of Pardiac had been in open revolt. This little area which stretched for no more than 50 kilometres in each direction had refused to pay its taxes, and backed up its refusal with arms.

This bout of rebellion unfolded according to a pattern which is hard to understand at first glance. Risings against the taxman were taking place to a greater or lesser extent in every part of the country. But why did they carry on for so long in Pardiac in particular? A study of the events suggests that the decisive factors were the exhilaration the peasants felt as the result of their early success, the failure of the authorities to punish them effectively, their faith in the justice of their cause and their hopes for a better future. All they had had to do initially was to gather together. The prisoners held by the government for non-payment of taxes had been freed without a shot being fired, and the fusiliers had turned tail at the first encounter. The authorities had made no attempt to put down the first wave of disturbances in 1639. Collective fines had been imposed on the region in 1643, but the officers sent to collect them had been frustrated by widespread passive resistance. In the meantime the government had granted a series of tax rebates to the parishes stricken by hailstorms in the period between 1637 and 1644. This had convinced the peasants that they could force the Council to make concessions. Everywhere they detected hopeful signs. On 8 June 1643 the *parlement* at Toulouse had an ordinance printed and published revoking the agents' special warrants, and on 10 June 1644 it forbade the staff of the local intendant to exercise any kind of judicial authority. Bands of Croquants were led by masked representatives of the gentry. Marshal de Saint-Luc gave the nobles permission to hold assemblies. They issued proclamations opposing the government's current tax policy, and went into the townships to tell the fusiliers to clear off. All these spectacular developments excited the people of Pardiac. In view of the changes they were witnessing they saw no reason to lay down their arms. Rather, they felt encouraged to persist in their dissidence.

We shall now look briefly at three other bouts of rebellion. The first of these bouts affected the southern *châtellenies* of Saintonge and Angoumois, and lasted from the summer of 1635 till the spring of 1643. The second raged in a dozen villages on the plateau of Millevaches. It broke out in about 1637 and continued till 1645. The third bout swept through the moorlands of Coutras and Montguyon between 1656 and 1660. In each case the revolt was sustained by much the same dynamics as the one in Pardiac. The peasants were encouraged to persevere in their resistance by the success of their first uprisings, the failure of the authorities to punish them, and the example of defiance which had been set by the local gentry. The rebels who rose up in 1635 and 1636 had ended by securing tax rebates from the government, and the government's concession had been seen as a victory throughout the countryside of western France. Everywhere the peasants seemed to be prevailing with ease. Prisoners were freed at Saint-Bonnet on 21 May 1642 and at Nieul-le-Virouil in September the same year. Excisemen were lynched at Saint-Estèphe on 31 August 1642 and at Coutras on 7 April 1656. Fusiliers were put to flight at Perols, Saint-Setiers and Le Bugeat between 27 and 31 August 1644, at Viam on 11 January 1645 and at Coutras on 12 August 1660. Gentlemen like the seigneur Anguittard in Saintonge and the Count of Bonneval in Limousin were setting an example of resistance to the bailiffs, or appeared to be doing so. Many regions escaped the attentions of the authorities.

The lands which belonged to the Lady of Pompadour in Limousin or the Duke of Épernon in Guyenne were regarded as being safe from the aggressive intrusion of the taxman, and had for a long time been exempt from any punitive action the government might take. In the same way the parishes of Saintonge which drove away the bailiffs in the spring of 1642 had paid no tax whatever, or almost none, for the previous four or five years. The intendant of Limousin described the communities that lived on the plateau of Millevaches as having been 'in a state of revolt for five or six years past'. And the moorland parishes of Montguyon are said to have 'resolved not to pay any taxes to His Majesty, and stood their ground by violent means for three or four years'. In the course of such bouts of rebellion, insurrection became for these districts a habitual method of getting their way. Eleven revolts are reported, for instance, from the *châtellenie* of Jonzac in the six months that elapsed between May and November 1642. Seven are reported from the Coutras-Montguyon area between May 1659 and October 1660.

Bouts of rebellion came to an end in various ways. Sometimes a change of intendant was enough to pacify an area. The recall of Charreton from Gascony and Villemontée from western France in 1644 brought calm to both regions. But a period of insurrection could also be ended more brutally, when the king's armies routed the peasants and in so doing extinguished any hopes they might have nurtured that the tax burden might be lifted and better times return. The government succeeded in inflicting defeats of this kind at Montendre on 28 March 1643, in Limousin in March 1645, in the *châtellenie* of Montguyon in the autumn of 1660 and in the county of Benauge the following winter. Such events halted the impetus which had kept the rising going, at least in the canton affected and at least for a few years.

The advantages of a rising

Contemporaries tacitly conceded that outbreaks of violence had a certain kind of *de facto* validity. If it was not for that recognition it is hard to see how theatres of insurrection could have flourished or bouts of rebellion lasted as they did. The fact was that revolt was often profitable. The villagers of Payzac, for instance, had a long record of putting up resistance to the bailiffs. By virtue of that resistance they managed, in 1644, to divert the bailiffs into surrounding villages where the people were less well prepared to defend themselves against insistent demands for money and consequently got their neighbours to pay the regular taxes on their behalf. The people of the Pyrenean valleys had similarly found a way to dodge the taxman. They had won themselves privileges and exemptions for the simple reason that their valleys were impossible to take by storm. In the words of the chronicler they 'held the law in contempt, placing their trust in the geographical location of their district and in the unfair privileges they had enjoyed for so long'. The act of rebellion, in other words, was often enough to discourage a creditor and get a debt annulled. A debt was worth no more than the power, determination and persistence of the person who tried to collect it. Equally, it was not always worth diverting soldiers from their assigned routes and sending them into rebel villages merely to extort a handful of *livres* from armed and unwilling peasants. A doctor from Blésois wrote a letter on these lines to the controller-general, possibly remembering a beating that he himself had received:

Rebellions often take place against the sergeants and bailiffs, and they sometimes get gravely maltreated, beaten and abused by the peasants when they go to distrain upon them. Matters usually rest there, however, since it would be too expensive to initiate an inquiry. The crime consequently remains unpunished, just as the original judgements and writs put out by the courts remain unimplemented.

The instruction manuals from which sergeants and tax agents learnt their profession made a point of reminding them that the law could be enforced, in practical terms, only to a limited extent. If rebellion did break out, the usual advice to officials was to flee for the time being. After that the manuals counselled them to seek a compromise with the offenders, and always, whatever happened, to opt for a civil action against them rather than embark on the burdensome and unpredictable venture of a criminal case. 'There is limitless scope for appeals, and even when sentences are confirmed it is impossible to get back even part of the legal expenses. Most of the time a case bankrupts plaintiff and defendant alike.'

For the authorities to identify a crime, then, did not necessarily mean that the crime was going to be punished. But there was room none the less for a range of customary proceedings on the fringe of the official law. Just as communities knew how to make good use of a rebellion, so certain bailiffs also knew how to turn a rising to account. 'What is a bailiff?' a contemporary pamphlet enquired. 'He is a man who rejoices in another person's trouble, and who can make his fortune out of a bout of fisticuffs.' Bailiffs were pastmasters in the art of drawing up reports and initiating legal actions which were solely intended to frighten their opponent into coming to terms. On one occasion some merchants of Béarn were threatened with prosecution for having assaulted a sergeant. They agreed to pay their victim 300 *livres* to get the action halted. The local intendant agreed to hush the matter up, noting that 'this settlement is more generous than an ordinary compensation'. In the eighteenth century it became standard practice for agents in the pay of the tax-farmers to settle their disputes with the help of this kind of amicable compromise.

The community kept up a tradition of revolt to win itself a *de facto* exemption from taxes. The bailiff used the reports he prepared on a rebellion to increase his personal profit. We may discern in the behaviour of each of these two parties a hidden meaning which underlay this type of disturbance. The object of all concerned was to secure a *fait accompli*, so important in a society based on custom. A person might feel he had every chance of winning a legal action; but violence offered more certain and more immediate rewards. In forcing the legal system to hold back while it protected rights secured on a *de facto* basis, society was, of course, acting in a thoroughly contradictory manner, and contemporaries knew it.

Exemption from tax was a sign that you belonged to the upper classes. In defying the bailiffs, the taxpayer and the relatives and servants who sprang to his aid were asserting their claim to social status and resisting attempts to prise them off the rung of the social ladder they believed to be rightfully theirs. When a rising spread to the neighbourhood or the whole inhabited area, the usual reason was that the community had up till now enjoyed a tax exemption, *de jure* or *de facto* as the case might be, and the residents wished to uphold it. People resisted the bailiffs, then, to defend their own privileges or the privileges of the place where they lived, to ward off an assault on their personal standing or their community's ancient rights. Their rebellion also had a larger, political meaning. People were signalling their refusal to accept the coming of state control and the new, terroristic methods of tax raising through which the government aimed to impose it.

Riots against tax-farming

Aides (sales taxes), *traites* (customs dues) and other kinds of indirect taxes that hampered the circulation of goods were levied in growing numbers and at ever-increasing rates in the course of the seventeenth century. The raising of this kind of levy formed an important part of the government's overall campaign to increase taxation. Between the reigns of Henri IV and Louis XIV indirect dues rose as sharply as the *tailles*, and were farmed out in lots that extended to cover almost the whole of France. The government's growing tendency to impose direct taxation on places that had traditionally been exempt from it affected only a number of specific towns and regions. The disruption it caused was limited. The extension of tax-farming, however, struck at the commerce of entire provinces; and it provoked a violent reaction at every level of society. The reaction was all the more serious for a number of reasons. In the first place these indirect dues were tainted by the simple fact of being so obviously new. Secondly, the person who made out the warrant for the levy in a given area was an outsider, isolated and disliked in the very district he wanted to coerce. Thirdly, this person was nothing more than the agent of a tax-farmer. He did not come to gather the king's tax, but seemed in the eyes of the people to represent merely the interests of one greedy man. I have managed to identify a fairly considerable number of disturbances which broke out in response to this particular kind of state provocation. Much of this source material is rich in detail. The unusual wealth of evidence may perhaps be attributed to the fact that the agents involved enjoyed a privileged status and were able, consequently, to appeal to the Council every time they found themselves confronted by a revolt.

We are talking of roughly a hundred different episodes. Studying these episodes, we find that *aides* and *traites* were approximately equal in importance in terms of the opposition they aroused. Fifty-eight outbreaks of violence were directed against *aides*, and sixty-one against *traites* and other duties. If we look at the geographical distribution of the outbreaks, we can see without difficulty that the centres of agitation corresponded to the various different departments into which the provinces were carved by the tax-farming system. We can identify in this way five regions of south-west France, unequal in area, which served as the fields of operation for the principal tax-farms. Thirty-nine risings, for instance, broke out in Poitou. The resistance was aimed at the *traites* which had been introduced in Marans and in the duchy of Thouars, at the imposition of *aides* and at the salt tax being levied in Anjou and Touraine. Fifteen revolts took place in Limousin and Marche. Antagonism here was directed, once again, at the *aides*, and resentment was also aroused by the fraudulent practices of the excisemen who had been operating in Berry. A total of sixteen disturbances were reported from Guyenne, Gascony and the Basque country. The rebels in this area had taken exception to the range of taxes which were farmed out in Bordeaux under the collective name of 'Convoy et Comptablie'. This name was derived from two medieval duties on merchant shipping, and the taxes were imposed on all merchant vessels entering or leaving the Gironde estuary and the river Garonne. Finally there were five upheavals in Quercy and Rouergue. The main sources of trouble here were the salt tax levied in Languedoc and the *traites* which had just been imposed on the town of Arzac.

These outbreaks seem to have been distributed fairly evenly throughout the year. They did, however, reach a peak between June and August, when 37 per cent of them took place. This pattern is probably best explained by the convenience of travel in the summer months. Merchants took to the high roads, and the agents and officers in charge of collecting the duties set off on their trail. The salt trade was not confined to any particular season. The salt was extracted from the marshes between June and October and was then put in casks and covered with straw. After that it was safe from the weather and could be transported at any time. Loads of salt were carried in the same boats which brought wine and spirits to Bordeaux and Brouage in the spring. Convoys of salt substitute could arrive at any time of the year in the moorlands of Gascony, on the borders of Rouergue, in the moorlands of Berry or the marshy country around the Loire. On the other hand the specific disturbances which were caused by the collection of *aides* did have a noticeable peak between November and January. Nineteen of the 58 recorded incidents took place in these months. The reason for this phenomenon is not far to seek. November to January was the time when the new wine was on sale in the taverns; and the agents collecting the *aides* sought to make this traffic liable to duty.

Trouble provoked by the agents

To discover the reason for a riot we have to study the exact moment at which the disturbance broke out and to examine the institutions which were prevalent in the area immediately before the trouble began. The synthetic account of a rising which we read in the chronicles is, consequently, no more than the sum of the moments that triggered it off, when the tax-farmers were stopped in their tracks and halted in village after village by the violent resistance of the subject population.

The first step in raising a new tax was to send an agent to distribute warrants to the prospective taxpayers, or to open an office from which the levying of the impost could be administered. Word quickly spread through a town when strangers arrived at the inn. The news would get round the community with particular speed if the strangers had done something to arouse their suspicion or if they were actually expecting officials to descend on them with warrants or distraints. A chronicler writing in Bordeaux in 1637 reported the arrival at an inn there of 'a man from Paris who had come to raise new taxes'. 'A horseman arrived here', recorded a citizen of La Rochelle in 1619. 'He had been sent to publish an edict.' A correspondent writing from Guéret in 1705 announced that 'we have here two tax-farmers and a party of bailiffs who have come to impose some duties'.

The next step was for the agent to apprise both the local justices and the consuls or aldermen of the imposition of the duty. Sometimes he had to register the lease of his tax-farm with the clerk employed by the court of the local jurisdiction. He formally requested the magistrates he found there to go ahead with the registration, and also demanded the help of the consuls or aldermen. This meant that the corporation or community would find itself collectively responsible if any trouble broke out. On leaving the court the agent went off to post up a notice proclaiming the powers which had been conferred upon him and the rates of tax he intended to impose. Usually he fixed this notice to the town gates, the church door or one of the posts in the market. His final step was to nail a plaque embossed with a fleur-de-lis on the outside of the house or cabin which he was using as his office or booth. In a community liable to rebel at any moment this ostentatious procedure looked very much like a deliberate attempt to enrage. The mobs soon gathered.

Sometimes it happened that a revolt was actually expected. The authorities were already aware that trouble was brewing, and certain that a disturbance would break out. The inauguration of the new tax would then be entrusted to an armed force to forestall any possible resistance. Generally the agent would be escorted by a company of guardsmen whom the tax-farmer had been authorized to maintain in his theatre of operations by one of the clauses in his lease. If the lease had not granted him this special prerogative, the farmer could still use bowmen recruited from *maréchaussées* outside the province where he was to operate. These bowmen were entitled to exercise their functions in any part of the kingdom, and the farmer consequently hired them out on a temporary basis. Sometimes, as in Poitou in 1633, the farmer was able to obtain the support of officers from the *prévôté de l'Île* the elite corps of bowmen assigned to keep order in Paris and the Île de France. If he was even luckier he might get help from the *prévôté de l'Hôtel* the police force directly attached to the royal household. The bowmen of this *prévôté* had their jackets embroidered with the royal arms, and their intervention was an explicit sign that the farmer had the crown's authority behind him. On other occasions the farmer's aim was to levy a tax on maritime trade. In this case he arranged for a warship to enter the port concerned and moor there with the objective of blocking the passage to the open sea. Operations of this kind were conducted in May 1641 at Bayonne, and in March 1643 at Bordeaux.

Even the day-to-day routine of administering the levy was a sensitive business. It entailed a good deal of violence on the part of the agent and could easily lead to a riot. To collect the *aides*, for example, the agent would force the innkeepers to open up to him and if necessary break down their doors. He would go to the cellars to count the casks, measure their capacity and mark them with his compasses. He would search the entire building, look inside any disused doors and probe the walls to see if any other casks were hidden behind a panel. These operations earned the agent the name of *cellar rat*. On festival days he would appear at the fairground as soon as the vintners arrived in the morning. When evening came and the gathering was about to disperse he would plunge his measuring rod in their casks to find out how much wine they had sold. The agent had no hesitation in disrupting the festival. He carried out his inspection on the very carts of the vintners, with the customers thronging around him and the hubbub of the fair on every side.

An agent responsible for administering the *traites* had a different set of duties. His task was to station himself at the entrance of the town. When merchants arrived in their carriages he went up to them and took the horses by the bridle. He then inspected the carriages. If a merchant was liable for duty the agent would collect the money from him. Sometimes however the merchant might be carrying a *transire* issued by one of the agent's colleagues in a tax-farming office elsewhere. In this case the agent would simply check that the document was valid. The river trade was monitored in a similar fashion. Tax-farmers kept up a fleet of customs vessels armed with cannon or fishing smacks with musketeers on board. The function of these vessels was to force the river craft to dock at the point on the bank where the agent had set up his customs house. On fair days the agent went up and down the streets of the town inspecting each of the traders' carts as it went by, and asking the traders where they intended to take their bundles of goods. Finally the agent was expected to keep an eye out for smugglers. If somebody tipped him off that a smuggling racket was in progress, it was his job to follow the information up. To this end the agent would organize night-time patrols or ambushes on outlying roads, at the docks or at breaches in the ramparts. Anyone caught was inevitably subjected to a brutal interrogation which only served to fuel the community's rage.

Such, then, were the circumstances in which a revolt broke out. The trouble was caused by a stranger intruding upon the community. People identified the agents of the tax-farmer as representatives of a single greedy merchant whom they imagined to be launching a deliberate assault upon the community's well-being. It was a challenge to communal loyalties. Neighbourhoods, craft guilds and whole communities felt an impulse of duty to come to the rescue of the unfortunates upon whom the tax-farmers had chosen to prey.

Besieging the inn

The first and most classic stage of a revolt against the tax-farmers was the siege of the inn where their agents had come to stay. Episodes of this kind figure in almost forty of the surviving reports, to the point where we can imagine the precise form that a typical siege would take. A report submitted in Poitiers in November 1624 gives a fairly standard picture:

At about midnight last Sunday, 25 November, a large crowd of people surrounded the house of Hersan, the crown notary, where the office for collecting the *aides* had been set up. They tried to break down the door, but were unsuccessful and instead smashed the windows of the hall and the bedrooms with showers of sticks and stones and volleys of pistol fire. As they did so they swore and blasphemed against the holy name of God. They said they were going to kill those robbers who were raising illegal taxes and throw them in the river. They were going to do the same to Hersan, too, for giving the swindlers shelter ... Not content with that they went off to the front of the Windmill Inn, where a number of other agents were staying, and made the same sort of scene there ... They said they were going to look for a match so that they could start a fire and burn the place down. The inmates were cooped up under siege, and none of them had the courage to show their faces until it was already broad daylight.

The mobs always knew where to find the excisemen. They put up invariably either at a well-known local inn, or alternatively at the house of a burgess who had some degree of financial interest in the raising of the tax – a notary, for example, or an attorney. If the agents had opted to stay at an inn, the mobs would go and threaten the innkeeper. In the rising that took place at Poitiers between 10 and 26 June 1663, the rioters informed the landlord that they intended to burn his inn to the ground. The frightened landlord asked the agents who had taken lodgings with him to clear off his premises. The agents found themselves having to move from one inn to another. Each time they settled in a new place the mob came and threatened the landlord, and they had to leave again. Elsewhere the innkeeper was harassed by parties of rioters who passed underneath his windows during the night. They threw stones at the windows, and threatened to put him to death.

One day the mob would gather in strength outside the offending building. The rioters would demand that the agents be handed over to them. The narrow street in front of the house would be packed with several hundred people. At Montaigu, for example, in the autumn of 1653, a company of guardsmen who had been sent to enforce the payment of *traites* in Anjou were confronted by a crowd of 600, and at La Rochelle in July 1661 a single tax-farmer had to face no less than 1,200 rebels. It was now that the violence started. The crowd would smash the windows of the house to smithereens with a hail of stones. They would hack at the doors with axes or heap up straw with a view to setting the entire building on fire. Sometimes it happened that the crowds were not quite enraged enough to light the straw or give the signal to take the building by storm; and sometimes the agents and bowmen inside the building were numerous and determined enough to put up a stiff resistance. In cases like this the siege might last all day. Sooner or later, however, the rebels would make their way in. They would break down the doors, or set fire to the building by lighting a handful of straw and throwing it through an open window. At Soulac in 1642 and Lalbenque in 1695 the crowd climbed on to the roof, tore out the tiles, broke the roof-tree and descended on the agents from above. The moment an entrance had been forced the mob would rush into the building. They would ransack the agent's office, tear his official papers to pieces and plunder his baggage together with any funds he had so far raised. Usually the agents would succeed in making a getaway. They would slip out of the building in disguise, or under cover of darkness. Sometimes the innkeeper would think of a trick by which to smuggle them off his premises, or the local worthy in whose home they wre staying would find a way of protecting them. Bleeding, half-naked and without either horses or kit they would beat a retreat across gardens, over rooftops, walls and ditches, till they finally reached the safety of the open countryside.

Now and again, however, an agent would be unlucky enough to fall into the hands of the mob. The triumphant rebels would then embark on a ritual designed to purge their community of the intrusion, by haling the excisemen through the streets of the town. This ceremony usually ended more or less grotesquely: every so often the outcome was tragic as well.

Haling the exciseman

We know of some thirty occasions on which an exciseman caught by the mob was made to undergo this degrading ritual. In view of the fact that the ritual was staged so frequently, we may conclude that it was traditional, and hallowed by custom. A riot, in the last analysis, was a performance in which the actors played their parts on every occasion in the same unchanging and time-honoured ways; and in this performance the haling of the exciseman was an indispensable scene. Criminals condemned to the gallows were regularly led through the streets, squares and crossroads of their town before their execution. The object of this proceeding was to enable them to make due apology for their offences, and at the same time edify the watching crowds with the spectacle of their humiliation and remorse. The haling of the exciseman followed a similar pattern. Stripped to his shirt and bound with cords, the unfortunate agent was dragged ignominiously through the town while the citizens rained jeers and blows upon him. By taking part in the ritual the citizens showed their determination to resist and made it clear what their attitude to the agents was likely to be on any future occasion. In 1656, for example, an exciseman was haled through the streets of La Rochelle. The citizens threatened that 'they would treat all the other excisemen and monopol-ists in just the same way'. Anyone who came to the community to extort illegal taxes as the victim had planned to do could expect to be punished, as he had been, with the haling ceremony.

In haling the exciseman the citizens were administering a form of popular justice. Often their rituals were a transparent imitation of the sentences imposed by the regular courts. At Saint-Jean-d'Angély, for instance, in 1629, the rioters had the idea of fastening their captured exciseman to a hurdle as though to drag him to execution. The rebels who rose up in La Rochelle in 1656 tried to take their victim to a gallows. At Saint-Benoist-sur-Mer in 1633, and Le Gua and Marennes in 1656, where the exciseman was actually killed, the rioters chopped up the body and exposed the remains to public view.

At Chauvigny in 1633 and Marennes in 1644, the rioters ended their procession by throwing the agent in the river. At Châtellerault in 1642, La Valette in 1654 and Montmorillon in 1661 they beat him up. Once this last ritual was over the humiliated victim was generally allowed to make his escape.

At Bouresse in 1635, however, and at Soulac in 1642, the whole point of the parade was to escort him with all due ceremony to the town gaol. In other places the procession ended with the agent being lynched. This was what happened in 1629 at Saintes and Saint-Jean-d'Angély. The great cycle of urban riots which broke out in the summer of 1635 in Bordeaux, Périgueux, Agen, Port-Sainte-Marie and Aubeterre all ended with the murder of the excisemen. Agents were slaughtered at Le Gua in 1656, and at Fresselines ten years later.

The attitudes of the local justices gave convincing evidence of the unanimous local backing the riots enjoyed. These justices sometimes went so far as to uphold the killing of the exciseman by wrapping it round in a veil of legality. If rioters delivered the captured agents into their custody, they sentenced the agents to death. Often they managed to get the agents executed in the presence of a vast crowd of people before the tax-farmers had had time to halt the proceedings by lodging an appeal with the Council or the intendant of the province.

Antoine La Butte, the agent for the tax-farm of Convoy et Comptablie in the city of Bordeaux, was a victim of this kind of quasi-legal proceedings. In February 1631 he was dragged on a hurdle to the Bordeaux scaffold and hanged. Another victim was Simon Brettier, an agent who had been hired to collect the salt tax in Anjou. He was hanged at Poitiers in October 1655. In such episodes the ritual of a popular rebellion was given the blessing of the legal system. We shall now pause to consider two revealing accounts which show this phenomenon at work. Both accounts date from the aftermath of the Fronde, when the myths which that great insurrection had generated were still circulating freely throughout the kingdom.

In October 1655 the agents responsible for raising the salt tax in every part of France had been active in Châtellerault for a whole year. They were trying to reinstall in the town the brigade of bowmen which had been used before 1648 to prevent the smuggling of substitute salt from Poitou into Anjou and Touraine, provinces where the tax on ordinary salt was high and the black market for substitute produce correspondingly extensive. In addition the agent had initiated legal actions against the local manufacturers of substitute salt. The citizens of Châtellerault struck back. They took 'a decision to put to death anyone whom the government tried to establish in their town in the capacity of agents and bowmen', and also decided to kill anyone who had acted as a witness in the legal proceedings launched by the excisemen. Rumours raced round the town, and the finger was pointed at a man called Simon Brettier. He was promptly seized by the rioters. His house was ransacked and his moveables were burnt on the open street. A party of citizens took Brettier to Poitiers, 'where', the chronicler tells us,

they succeeded in persuading the judges and all the people that he was an exciseman. All the attorneys and counsels were thereupon forbidden either to defend him or offer any resistance on his behalf. The prohibition was so effective that Brettier was promptly sentenced to death and executed in this town of Poitiers, even though he had committed no crime and been convicted by no court. He was executed for the sole reason that he was believed to be an exciseman and that it seemed generally expedient to put him to death. He himself cried out openly to the people from the scaffold that he died an innocent man.

In July 1659 a brigade of a dozen guardsmen responsible for policing the collection of the salt tax in Languedoc descended on the village of La Bastide, on the borders of Quercy and Rouergue, and made the rounds of the house in search of substitute salt from Poitou. The local seigneur responded by having the tocsin rung. He attacked the guards at the head of his peasants, captured them and locked them up in the dungeons of his château. On 28 July a commissioner arrived from the *parlement* at Toulouse. He was Antoine de Commère, a counsel at the High Court, and he had come to take delivery of the prisoners. The chronicle informs us that he brought them back to Toulouse 'in conditions of the utmost disgrace and ignominy in order to stir the people up against the men who worked for the tax-farmer'. He had them seated

on a cart, with their hands and feet tied behind their backs. Their escort consisted of 100 gentlemen and 200 musketeers, who had been commandeered for the purpose by Master Delong, a lawyer from the *Grand-Chambre*. Delong had placed himself unofficially at their head in order to make the impact of the procession all the more shocking. Everywhere they went he announced that they were going to hang all the excisemen, and that no tax agents would be allowed to enter the province any more.

The spectacle described in these two accounts is reminiscent of an ancient Roman triumph. The captive excisemen were led in procession to their punishment, and their downfall heightened the glory of the men who had conquered them, the rioters, magistrates and gentry who had risen up to champion the traditional freedoms of the province.

The siege of the inn and the haling of the exciseman were standard episodes characteristic of every riot. In addition to the main types of riot each had a number of special features of their own. Revolts against the levying of *aides*, for example, were often accompanied by a traditional orgy of drinking and merrymaking. Smugglers often triggered off the risings against the *traites* by calling upon the neighbours to come to their rescue.

The riot of jubilation

Jubilant riots broke out as a form of retaliation against the spoilsport officials who tried to stop the wine going round. They were a sign that gaiety had returned to the community, that drinkers and merrymakers could do as they pleased. Jubilant riots began with the beating of a drum. At Limoges in May 1705, a small boy went through the streets beating a tabor and calling out, 'Anyone want to come and stop the salt tax?' At Guéret the following month the town crier went round proclaiming that the excisemen were going to be driven out. He danced with the local children, who followed him wherever he went, and had a drink in every house he passed. Just for a laugh he also stuck a woman's coif on his head. This gave him an excuse for kissing the maidservants he met in the street. At Lalbenque in 1695 the riot was led by a couple of innkeepers. Both of them had dressed up in women's coifs and gowns, but they also brandished halberds. They danced together in the town square surrounded by a ring of rioters. Many of the rioters involved in these episodes wore comic masks or masks to hide their faces. Agents making their calls in Confolens in 1654 were accompanied by an unwanted escort of protesters in masks and false beards, and inspectors from the tax-farms making their nightly rounds of the Bordeaux merchants in 1692 got similar treatment. At Bordeaux in 1656 the maskers patrolled the streets. They said they were looking for excisemen.

People did not gather spontaneously to drive out the tax-farmers as they did to protest against a rise in the price of bread. Their risings were planned and deliberate. They spent several days working out how to mock the excisemen. Men did not generally play a prominent part in the proceedings: at most there were a few young sparks dressed up in disguise. The lead on these occasions came from the distaff side. At Angoulême in 1629 we are told that 'the people decided to put the women in command. The women gave orders like captains, surrounded by armed bodyguards.' In May 1705 the houses sheltering a number of excisemen were set on fire in Limoges. The arsonists turned out to have been 'a large number of women, girls and children sprung from the dregs of the common people. Their husbands and fathers played no part in the riot at all.' In February 1707 some tax agents were assigned the unpopular task of searching for wine in the taverns of Montmorillon. They were warned that 'the people had dressed up as women and armed themselves with knives. They would cut their throats if they tried to enter their cellars.' In spite of these threats the agents sallied forth into the street. They found the inn doors closed against them and heard the coded warning passing from house to house, 'Watch out, little sheep – the wolves are coming.'

All the people needed to do to obstruct the collection of the *aides* was to close the taverns. Inn signs consisted of a bush made up of a clump of straw. The landlord hung up his bush above the door of his tavern to indicate to the passers-by that he had barrels open there. This was because a straw bush was the object he used to stop up the bung-holes of his barrels. In 1659, then, when the innkeepers of Bressuire wished to signal their refusal to pay the *aides*, they simply removed the bushes from the tavern doors. They said they were 'taking the bush down'. The taverns were then shut up and even barricaded. At Rochechouart in February 1635 the innkeepers gathered together and marched in procession beneath the vaults of the covered market. They made a bonfire of their bushes, and took a solemn oath that the first man to start trading again without the agreement of the others would be fined 100 *livres*. If he repeated the offence his house would be burnt to the ground. When trouble broke out in Poitiers in August 1639, the rioters went through the town destroying the signs of the taverns and inns. Wine would of course still be sold while the innkeepers were on strike in the backs of shops, and also in private households. Citizens would publicly offer to sell their neighbours a jug of wine and a meal and scant regard was paid to either the royal edicts forbidding this or the indignant reports which were filed by the agents.

Sometimes the local judges or aldermen gave a degree of official sanction to the tavern-keepers' strike. They issued ordinances prescribing the closing of the taverns on the pretext that this was necessary in the interests of morality or law and order. The justice of Melle, for instance, had an ordinance posted prohibiting the sale of wine in the local fairground. His object was not to prevent the peasants from going to have a drink and a gossip in the fairground taverns, but simply to find an excuse for keeping the tax agents away from the festival. When his clerk of the court saw the agents disrupting another fair in the court's jurisdiction, he actually threatened to have them put in the pillory and boasted 'that he knew still better means of preventing the collection of *aides* in this town'. In Saint-Jean-d'Angély, similarly, the *lieutenant-général* threatened to fine anyone who went into a tavern. The aldermen acknowledged laughingly 'that the only reason for the ban was to teach the extortioners to take a holiday'.

Riots of this sort reeked of wine. The casks would be broached and the rioters would drink themselves silly. When the agents entered the tavern to make their official call, the customers would drink their health with grotesque mock toasts and throw the jugs at their heads. In every incident they came out with the same heartfelt cry of resentment: 'Bloody extortioners, the price of this wine is all your fault.'

As we have seen, the agent was a professional spoilsport. So far as we can judge from the sources at least fifteen of these riots broke out on a holiday. Agents were instructed to maintain a heightened degree of vigilance on such occasions. An agent reporting from Saint-Jean-d'Angély in July 1667 observed that 'smuggling takes place on days of public rejoicing, like the day when they lit bonfires to celebrate the fall of Tournai'. For similar reasons the companies of guards employed by the tax-farm of Convoy et Comptablie sent detachments to keep an eye on the crowds at parish festivals. The crowds got angry. At Barcelonne-du-Gers on 10 August 1657, and at La Souterraine on 25 November 1689, fairgoers were confronted with a dramatic spectacle. The agents and guardsmen were chased from the fairground with jeers, and hurried off to the village inn to look for their horses. At Liguué on 2 August 1639, a noisy, drunken crowd of rioters came rolling into the fair, firing salvoes of musket-fire into the air and shouting, 'Liberty!' On 16 August 1694, a similar outbreak of violence took place at a festival which was being held in the town of Eyrans-en-Blayais. When night came the fairgoers scattered to the country taverns and described the day's happenings. The talk went on for months.

Outbreaks of jubilant rioting were a festival in themselves. They were a chance for the taxpayers to take their revenge by playing jokes, and people flocked to them. An intendant wrote how 'the masses take pleasure in rioting'. Festivals and drinking sessions were jolly events, and it was only right to defend them in a jolly manner.

Rescuing the smugglers

There were a considerable number of ways of cheating the collectors of *aides*. A tavern-keeper could falsify the measures of his wine. He could mark his casks with forged compasses, make false declarations to the agent, take his wine away down a tunnel and store it in a different cellar, use casks with false bottoms or secret taps, and so forth. The methods of dodging the *traites* were equally varied. Traders are said to have forced their way through the town gates and transhipped their cargoes at night. Above all they are said to have relied on the use of well-armed and organized convoys which travelled at night on remote and unfrequented roads. Sometimes, however, the traders found the agents waiting for them. At Le Gua in 1660, the smugglers were taken by surprise and thrown into confusion. Their reaction was to call for help. 'Here, quick', they shouted, 'it's the excisemen!'

When a call for help was given the entire convoy of friends, servants, employees and accomplices would rush to the smugglers' aid. A shoot-out ensued, and the agents were often forced to retreat. If the agents had managed to confiscate the smugglers' livestock and carts, the smugglers would have no hesitation in coming back in strength. They would attack the guards and recapture the confiscated transport. On 21 April 1656, for instance, several hundred people assembled from the parishes of the *bailliage* of Marennes to recapture some bundles which the guards appointed by the tax-farmer had seized from a party of smugglers. The ensuing skirmish ended in the slaughter of three of the guards and their captain. A similar episode is recorded in 1705. Some merchants in Limousin were anxious to recapture a convoy of about fifteen carts which had been confiscated by guards two days earlier. To this end they organized a force consisting of 600 peasants or seasonal reapers, with several of the local gentry at their head. On 10 May this little army surrounded the villages of Rochechouart and Vayres, where the guards were staying, and blockaded them in their lodgings throughout the night. The makers of substitute salt who lived in the Grandes Landes of Gascony were a particularly resourceful group. From 1627 to 1663 they organized smuggling convoys of about a hundred men several times a year. The route they followed was well known, but they were far from being the only smugglers to use it. At Clermont-Ferrand in 1692 there were ironmasters getting iron ore out of the County of Foix. At Poitiers in 1706 there were butchers trying to dodge an assortment of duties whch were levied on round-hoofed and cloven-hoofed animals. Merchants in the towns and villages of the Haut-Pays were anxious to find their way past the offices of the Convoy tax-farm in Bordeaux. All of these traders knew how to put the agents on the defensive by using armed escorts, forcing their way through town gates, and smuggling openly.

Smugglers could also count on the help of ordinary passers-by. People felt an automatic duty to rescue their neighbours, just as they did in the incidents we looked at earlier, when the bailiffs arrived with their writs of distraint. Bystanders turned into rebels. Citizens going past the town gates or the docks in the course of their daily business spontaneously snatched up arms to resist the agents. All kinds of riots began with this spontaneous seizure of weapons: in this case, however, we may note that it was specifically the craftsmen and merchants who reached for their arms. Boatmen brandished oars, poles and cutlasses. Merchants had swords, and dockside carpenters had axes. Butchers, always prominent in this kind of brawl, were especially well armed. They carried skewers and kitchen knives, coshes and eelskins stuffed with lead. Fishmongers and market gardeners threw stones, eggs and vegetables, or took off their clogs and beat the guards with them. Finally the peasants flocked from their fields with their crowbars and *volants* (long sticks used to lime birds), pitchforks and scythes and iron-shod sticks to take part in the confrontation between smugglers and guards. The aroused population presented an alarming spectacle. The inspectors who examined goods at the gates of Bordeaux, for example, often had to take shelter behind their bodyguards when the current wave of rioters surged up around them threatening to set fire to their office, drown them in the river or hang them on the gallows. In December 1663 a boatman in Pontonx-sur-l'Adour called for help against the agents of a tax-farmer who had been sent to levy duty on whale oil. The agents fled to Dax, where a merchant similarly raised a hue and cry against them and had them driven out. In April 1693 a brigade of guards were besieged in an inn in the village of Oradour-sur-Glane by some peasants who were trying to stop them seizing a load of contraband. In September 1701 the people of Ussel rang the tocsin in their town and drove out a party of agents to free a tobacco smuggler whom the agents had detained. The people of Villefranche-de-Rouergue took similar action in July 1711 to punish a company of guards who had beaten up a manufacturer of substitute salt.

A smuggler released at Riberou in April 1644 escaped, in the view of the chronicler, 'as the result of the violent conduct of a large number of townspeople who went to his aid'. The agents expelled from Ussel in 1701 had no other option but to flee. 'They were obliged to yield to superior force and cry for mercy. Otherwise they would all have had their throats cut.' The agents who were driven from La Souterraine in 1689 described their predicament in similar terms. 'When we saw how many people were descending upon us, and realized how determined they were, we were forced to let go of those merchants and their goods and take thought for our personal safety.' If the tax-farmers took them to court, the smugglers were never short of witnesses to defend them. 'All the people were convinced that it was permissible to give false evidence against the agents.' In all these episodes the bystanders behaved in exactly the opposite way to that prescribed for them in the royal ordinances. The government sought to bind the communes to give the agents and guards whatever help they needed. But this string of incidents in which the populace rescued the smugglers gives us an altogether different picture. Smugglers were able to rely on a highly organized network of collaboration. The people hated the tax-farmers with a hatred that was both intense and quickly awakened. Bystanders saw it as their duty to help the smugglers against the agents, and revolts against indirect taxation broke out at the drop of a hat.

Abusing the excisemen

Rioters abused the tax-farmers in a variety of ways. The insults they used reflect the usual grievances of tax rebels. The most common yells in a riot were 'Down with the excisemen!' 'Down with the extortioners!' Each of these two words was used within a clearly defined area. North of the Garonne estuary, in *langue d'oïl* (northern French), people said 'extortioner' (*maltôtier*); south of the estuary, in *langue d'oc* (southern French), they said 'exciseman' (*gabeleur*). If used outside its region, each word was usually accompanied by its native equivalent. A chronicler would write, for example, 'the communes have risen up . . . against the excisemen and extortioners.'

Gabelle and *maltôte* were synonyms. Both words referred to an indirect tax which had just been introduced, and was felt to be unlawful for that reason. People rioted equally against 'the introduction of a *gabelle*' and the imposition of a 'programme of *maltôtes*'. *Gabelle* with a definite article had a special meaning, however. '*La*' *gabelle* referred first and foremost to the tax imposed on salt. In south-west France, where the salt tax was not in force, the word *gabelle* had another meaning again – a meaning that was both more specific and more laden with emotional overtones. In 1548 the provinces of south-west France, from Poitou to Gascony, had risen up in a bid to prevent the introduction of the salt tax in that region. The revolt had been successful, and Henri II had very rapidly been forced to grant those provinces a permanent reprieve from the tax. From that time on the people of the south-west appear to have looked on this exemption from the salt tax as an inalienable and essential part of their heritage, paid for as it had been by a bloody rebellion and ratified as it had been by the king himself. In the south-west, consequently, *gabelle* did not just mean any new tax, and nor did it just mean the salt tax. It implied an infringement of provincial privileges, a violation of rights which had been sanctified by tradition and by the promises of kings.

When rioters gathered to resist the imposition of any sort of indirect tax, their driving concern was to thwart the government's imagined purpose of introducing the *gabelle*. The mythical introduction of the *gabelle* was looked on as being the final, disastrous stage in the process by which the people were gradually being reduced to slavery. It is clear from the slogans which were bawled out on days of riots that the population repeatedly thought the *gabelle* was on its way. Rioters shouted their fear of this prospect in 1635, when the government imposed an annual duty on the city innkeepers. They voiced it again in 1641–3, when the authorities tried to introduce a tax on the basis of a *sou* for every pound. Finally they vented their panic in 1666, when the government installed a line of customs offices five leagues inside the borders of those south-western provinces which were exempt from the salt tax, in a bid to prevent the smuggling of substitute salt into other provinces where the yield on the salt tax was high. The chroniclers despaired. 'It is difficult to make them listen to reason', one lamented, 'because there is no one individual for us to address. We are dealing with a whole population run riot. They always defend themselves by saying that they want to stop the *gabelle* and burn the houses of the excisemen and the folk who give them shelter.'

We can easily form a picture, in this connection, of the kind of person the exciseman was thought to be. The word 'exciseman' was bracketed with a whole vocabulary of insults. The exciseman was variously called a robber, a bugger, a rascal, a rogue, a scum, a scoundrel, a beggar, a chaffinch and a crop-eared criminal. He and his colleagues were referred to as 'worthless fellows', 'jumped-up lackeys' who had probably just escaped from the galleys or the gallows and in any case deserved to be sent there. Merchants were unable to look on the exciseman as anything more than a sordid criminal. Both business people and craftsmen were exasperated by the sometimes haphazard way in which the tax-farmer's agents and guards were recruited, by the insolence of their conduct and their public display of idleness. From this point of view the choice of insults was entirely apt.

Excisemen were believed to act together in a kind of conspiracy. At Pamproux in 1662 the citizens said to a local official or resident they suspected of having a financial interest in the tax-farming, 'You are associated with them, you are one of their gang.' At Loudun in 1668 they added that the suspect was 'one of the gang of the excisemen, in favour of the *maltôte*'. This fantasy worked two ways. Any official noted for issuing ordinances that tended to obstruct the farming of the taxes would earn a high reputation as 'a strong defender of the public good'. The excisemen were viewed, in other words, as public enemies. Citizens complained how 'the excisemen and extortioners levied new taxes on the people'. In 1694 the people of Riom called a party of visiting agents 'filthy scum, disturbers of public order'.

People threatened the excisemen with punishments of a most appalling kind. 'Kill the excisemen, kill them', the mob yelled, 'let's beat them all to death.' In a riot at Saint-Jean-d'Angély in 1643, the citizens vowed to the agents that they were going to 'flay them alive'. At Pamproux in 1662 the people threatened to 'open them up and eat their hearts'. In reality the usual fate of the exciseman was to have his lodgings burnt down and his body thrown in the river. This punishment was carried out or threatened so incessantly that it became tantamount to a ritual. 'Drag them in the river . . . teach them to swim . . . drown these dogs of extortioners.'

As we have seen, a new tax was held to be unwarranted precisely because it was new. The town or region affected would claim to be exempt from such an innovation by virtue of a long-standing privilege. 'An agent is trying to bring in a new kind of tax', cried the people of Thouars in 1643. 'We'll have to beat him up.' The people of Châtellerault declared in 1655 that they 'would rather die than have this inspection started'. At Riom in 1694 a rioter appealed for support on similar grounds. 'This way, gatekeepers, citizens, help me catch these rascals . . . Riom's a free town and there's no reason why we should put up with these filthy scum.' 'God's Death and Head', cried the rebels of La Souterraine in 1689, 'who's going to help find these rascals who've got into the town? We've got to get on to them.' The rioters at La Rochelle a hundred years earlier gave a concise summary of the issues at stake. The question, in their view, was whether the citizens of their town were going to preserve or lose 'the privileges exempting them from all taxes and levies which their predecessors had managed to obtain'.

Rebels believed that they were inaugurating a better world. From now on the king would respect his people's ancient exemptions and freedoms and would refrain from imposing any more taxes on them. Even the shortest slogans expressed this hope. On 1 June 1705 the people of Guéret shouted, 'Long live the king and no more *maltôtes*!' 'Long live the king and no more *gabelle*!' cried the people of Montauban on 26 April 1641 as they burnt the intendant's coach in the market square. 'Freedom!' and 'Down with the extortioners', yelled the rioters who rampaged in the Old Market of Poitiers and the nearby fairground of Ligugé on 2 August 1639. They declared that 'they had to kill all persons who came to levy duties. They had come there with this intention, and to make the people free.' These rebels stuck up seditious posters in the different cantons of Poitiers, on the doors of a number of local dignitaries who had made themselves scarce. These posters were entitled '*In the name of the king and the people*'. The linkage was significant. A rift between king and subjects was never envisaged in the rebel scheme of things. The same kind of mental outlook may be detected at Limoges on 20 April 1602, when the populace rose up to resist the introduction of a new set of taxes. The leader of the rising had belonged to the 'royalist' party which was formed in the city in the course of the civil wars. Referring to his achievement in getting a crowd to expel the excisemen, he boasted that 'he had found 500 men *to serve the king*'.

Dramatis personae: the victims

The victims of this kind of riot were, naturally, the agents and guards employed to carry out the instructions of the tax-farmer. They were lowly individuals whose misfortune it was to be made scapegoats of the explosion of popular rage. It was only on rare occasions that a riot affected anyone occupying a more important post in the tax-farming system, and I have been able to identify only three risings in which some more senior men got caught. On 22 April 1633 an assistant farmer of *aides* in western France named Pierre de Gallières was besieged in the château of Niort. The rebels also directed their wrath at his relative, Antoine de Gallières, who had a financial interest in the same farming operation. Antoine was the target of a revolt whch broke out at Civray in May 1635. On 26 July 1661 the citizens of La Rochelle drove out a man named Jean Pinet who was the farmer assigned to levy *aides* there; Pinet had already had a number of lucrative warrants leased out to him by the Treasury. In 1683, finally, a man named François Hocart was attacked by the merchants of Aigre, where he had been sent by the controller general to inspect the tax bureaux. Hocart had a financial interest in five large farming schemes.

After it had driven off the agent who came from outside, the community quite frequently turned in on itself, as the citizens switched their attention to hunting down the excisemen whom they fancied to be lurking within their walls. Local residents, passers-by and unknown members of the public were all liable to excite suspicion if they had just returned from a journey, or had uttered an indiscreet word, or if news of a legal action had just spread through the town. In 1629, for example, two royal sergeants from Loudun were in Saint-Maixent on business when a crowd unexpectedly set upon them and chased them all the way to the open country. Ten years later in Poitiers the rioters seized control of a prison run by the aldermen and used it to shut up a person whom they claimed to be an extortioner. A Treasury agent who happened to be staying in the town was similarly detained, and the papers he was carrying were read out in public by an attorney who had sided with the rebels. On 6 June 1641 an almost identical episode took place in Bayonne. A crowd of insurgents took over the town gaol and used it to incarcerate a tailor whom they accused of having had secret dealings with the excisemen. 'They tortured him to make him confess his complicity and tell them the names of the excisemen in Bayonne.' In Bordeaux a counsel at the *cour des aides* was made out by the mob to be an 'administrator of the *gabelle*', and in Châtellerault a number of citizens were persecuted for their supposed collaboration with the excisemen. The search for scapegoats was particularly vigorous in the neighbourhood of Limoges after rioting broke out in that town in May 1709. The local peasants 'are said to have mustered in little bands and taken up their station on the high roads. They are detaining any travellers bound for Limoges and are asking them if they are excisemen and whether they are on their way to introduce the *gabelle*. If they answer in the affirmative, the peasants are threatening them with physical violence.' Communities, then, were obsessed with the dreaded prospect of the *gabelle* to the point of paranoia. They imagined themselves surrounded by persecutors and traitors who were socially no better than they were and could, consequently, be caught and delivered up to their vengeance. Any mysterious stranger was suspect in their eyes, and so was any local resident who had recently made his fortune and was too often out of town. Any such person was liable to be cast in the role of exciseman, and victimized.

Dramatis personae: the rioters

I have included in this survey a total of 169 individuals who can be identified as having taken part in a riot against the levying of *aides* or *traites*. All of these people are mentioned by name in the official investigations which the government habitually launched in the wake of such riots. Their degree of involvement varied, but all of them had a share of responsibility for the outbreak of rioting in their town and the subsequent course it took. Seventeen of the culprits, or 10 per cent, turn out to have been officials. The involvement of these officials – nine judges, five *élus* and three provosts – took a number of different forms. Some of them had vociferously refused to register an agent's lease. Others had headed the crowd which ejected the agents from their town or had set an example of resistance by refusing to pay their taxes or let the agents into their cellars. One of the reports drawn up by a fleeing tax official protests indignantly how 'the agents were hounded through the countryside, beaten, robbed and molested by those very persons who were supposed, on their own admission, to uphold the authority of the king'. There is plenty of evidence for this kind of collusion between officials and rioters. On 23 December 1642, for instance, the *élus* of Fontenay stuck up an ordinance on a post in the covered market forbidding the agents to levy *aides* in their town. On 13 January 1643 the *élus* of Thouars urged their fellow-citizens to resist some agents who had arrived to collect a *subvention*. They delivered harangues to this effect in two separate places, first in their audience chamber and then in the market. On 26 January 1655 a chief justice in the *élection* of Saintes went further still. He not only informed the agents who approached him 'that he had no intention of getting involved in their operation', but even allowed the people to molest them when they left his house.

Sixteen of the offenders referred to in the investigations, or 9.4 per cent of the total number, were members of the gentry. Some of them lived in Gascony, and others in Bas-Poitou, where no less than five were vassals of the Duke of Thouars. These men were personally involved in cheating the collectors of *aides* or producing substitute salt. If a clash took place between their retainers and the guards employed by the tax-farmers, they had no hesitation in plunging into the fray.

Of the total number of identified rebels, then, 19.4 per cent were men of some distinction. The remainder were drawn from the mass of the populace. Only the common people were involved in actual rioting. The largest category of commoners were the keepers of inns and taverns. Forty-four of the culprits, or 26 per cent of the total, were men of this calling. A further thirty-eight, 22.4 per cent of the total, were craftsmen. They included five blacksmiths and three shoemakers, five carpenters, all from Bordeaux, and three pin-makers, all from Limoges. Eighteen offenders, or 10.6 per cent of the total, were merchants and retailers, sixteen, or 9.4 per cent, were men connected with the judicature such as lawyers, attorneys and sergeants, and thirteen, or 7.6 per cent, were day labourers, dockers and boatmen. One final group of offenders were the surgeons. There were seven of them, representing 4.1 per cent of the total catalogue of rebels. If we compare this breakdown with the numerical strength of the various categories in society as a whole, we notice certain anomalies. Day labourers, for example, account for a surprisingly small proportion of our offenders. The likely explanation is that the named individuals who are listed in our sources were persons of some means from whom the authorities could hope to exact compensation for their misdeeds. No compensation was likely to be forthcoming from day labourers, and the government was accordingly content to leave most of them nameless in the crowds from which they had sprung. The number of tavern-keepers, on the other hand, is astonishingly high. This is presumably because so many of the disorders revolved about the levying of duty on wine. In addition we should perhaps remember the very special role which the tavern-keeper played in society. As a source of news and a master of ceremonies at every major event in the life of the community, he occupied a pivotal place in the popular culture of the time. To understand how important a tavern-keeper could be in a rising, we need only consider the activities of Jean Gaillouste, otherwise known as Nanet. Gaillouste was a man of fifty who kept a tavern in the town of Lalbenque. He was also the ringleader of the rebellion which broke out there on 20 April 1695. It was he who had the idea of organizing a demonstration of women to put the sergeants to flight. He strutted about in the crowd with a halberd which he described as being 'a weapon to end all weapons'. He dressed up as a woman and sang and danced in front of the house where the exciseman was staying as the rioters burnt it to the ground. The authorities acknowledged the central role he had played by sending him to the galleys.

Often the agents cast their net rather wider. They used their reports to pin the blame on entire social groups. In 1656 an agent expelled from La Rochelle denounced the coopers of that community. Salt merchants were blamed for the trouble that broke out on various occasions at Soulac, Marennes and Le Gua. At Bordeaux the watermen attracted particular condemnation, and at Poitiers the butchers were usually seen as the source of major unrest. Broadly speaking, it is clear that the revolts against the tax-farmers were started by the people who lived in the cities and market towns, and the craftsmen especially. It was they who suffered directly from the duties the government imposed on the production or circulation of goods.

The mayor versus the agents

In the eyes of both agents and rioters, the mayor represented the town. Some agents who appeared in Montmorillon in 1707 went to call on the mayor there as soon as they arrived. They wanted him to help them carry out their assignment 'insofar as he was the person best able to control the mood of the people'. The rioters who rose up at La Rochelle in 1589 approached their mayor with the opposite aim in mind. They asked him 'to deal with these imposers of taxes in his capacity as father and protector of the people, and not to let anyone levy taxes at the expense of their traditional exemptions and liberties'. The mayor was supposed to defend at one and the same time the mutually exclusive concepts of traditional order and royal authority. The citizens appealed to him to protect them from the *gabelle*, and the excisemen appealed to him to protect them from the wrath of the citizens. Most of the time the mayor ended up heading the resistance to the advance of taxation. This was because taxation affected the community as a whole. Given the nature of his office and the place he occupied in society, the mayor was not surprisingly disposed to take the side of the other people in his town.

Only the mob and its ringleaders seem to have engaged in acts of open violence. The mayor was seldom seen at the head of an actual riot. Sometimes, however, he did go so far as to cause the town drums to be beaten and to set the militia marching against the agents. Incidents of this sort are recorded at La Rochelle on 4 October 1624, at Fontenay between June 1632 and October 1635, at Châtellerault in May 1655 and at Montluçon on 28 December 1656. On 8 November 1629 the mayor of Poitiers, who also sat on the local *présidial*, was audacious enough to inform a party of agents who had been sent to levy the *aides* 'that so long as he was in office, he would not allow this duty to be raised in the town in any form whatever. If the agents pressed him any further, he would have them dealt with, and they would not be in any hurry to come back again.'

Ordinarily the mayor resisted the agents in a more passive way. He appealed to the intendant, had the agents sued for damages in the provincial courts or sent emissaries to plead before the Council. If a riot broke out he pretended to be unaware of it, minimized its importance and refused to receive the formal petitions of complaint which the agents lodged with him. Sometimes he also tried the opposite tactics. He used the riot to threaten the agents. He depicted the mob as a blind and uncontrollable force, and emphasized that he could not guarantee the agents' safety. Tactics of this kind were used in August

1619 to frighten an agent away from the town of La Rochelle. 'M. the mayor promptly went to see him and told him that he would have to get back on his horse and leave the town without delay. He explained to the agent that he would not be able to save him, if the people knew the reason for which he had come to this town.'

'Whether through connivance or laxity', as the king wrote to the aldermen of Poitiers, the officials of a community, mayors, aldermen, *jurats* or consuls, were always more or less inclined to side with the rioters against the agents who came to organize the farming of new kinds of tax. They were, after all, local citizens, and any misfortune which struck their town affected them as well. At Cognac the agents complained how 'the mayor and the aldermen along with the leading citizens are giving their blessing to these revolts. They want to be able to carry on distributing their wine to the retailers without paying any duty.'

The local judges versus the agents

A mayor, in short, took the part of the rioters in his town out of a sense of local solidarity, a feeling that his interests coincided with those of the city where he lived. The same applied to the officials of the local judiciary. They expressed their allegiance to the community by bringing actions for damages. Legal investigations would be set in motion against the agents of the tax-farmers just as they were, on other occasions, against the sergeants who came to collect the regular tax. The inquiries might be launched in the name of a merchant the agents and guards had beaten up or the widow of a rioter they had killed. Sometimes a lawsuit might even be brought on the initiative of the *procureur du roi*, when the latter had taken the view that the activities of the agents were disrupting the public order prescribed in the royal edicts. Actions for damages were so frequent that we may reasonably regard them as an ordinary sequel to a riot. Of the 120 riots of this type I have surveyed for the present study, no less than twenty-eight – 23.3 per cent of the total – are recorded as having been followed by such an action. We may conclude, in other words, that in almost one in four cases the local officials tried to use a diversionary lawsuit to distract attention from the original outbreak of violence.

Officials behaved in this way for two reasons. In the first place they wanted to safeguard their own material interests. Secondly they were anxious to ward off any collective punishment that might fall upon the community as a whole. The *lieutenant criminel* at Saint-Jean-d'Angély, for example, had an obvious personal motive for forcing the agents sent to collect some *aides* to leave his town. He is said to have been 'delighted to find an opportunity to get his revenge on the agents, since they had been badgering him to pay duty on the wine he had been retailing in his house throughout the previous year'. The local judge at Soulac sought to protect his fellow-citizens. Following a violent clash between the salt merchants of the town and the agents of the Convoy tax-farm, he conferred with the persons who had been the ringleaders in the rising in order to work out a means of shielding them from the responsibility for this outrage. He hit on the idea of launching a legal inquiry in which the sole witnesses would be those very individuals who had had a hand in the crime. In pursuit of this inquiry he had the guards consigned to the prisons in the town of Lesparre, half-dead though they were.

Similar brawls between the tax-farmers' guards and the citizens took place at Guéret in September 1635, at Saintes in May 1644, at Montluçon in December 1656 and at Niort in February 1664; and each time it was the guards that the local judges threw into gaol. The *lieutenant criminel* of Montmorillon gave a classic display of partiality. On 7 May 1661 he allowed the mob to hale a couple of agents through the streets for their efforts to gather *aides* without making any attempt to launch an inquiry. The agents fled, but returned to the town on 24 July, fortified by a wage increase they had got from the tax-farmer. The *lieutenant criminel* had them arrested the moment they stepped inside the town gates. Two years later another couple of agents were man-handled by the mob. They were found three days afterwards lurking in the bushes, injured and half-naked. The *lieutenant criminel* clapped them in irons.

Sometimes the tax-farmers got their case referred to the provincial intendant, and consequently thought they would get a fair hearing. But both plaintiffs and defendants still had to win the ear of the subordinate judges to whom the intendant had delegated the case. On one occasion we are told that the rioters succeeded in 'distracting attention from the evidence and winning the favour of the provincial officials who were called upon to testify'. On another occasion 'the offenders had sufficient influence to ensure that the judges from the royal or intermediate courts whom the tax-farmer had summoned to preside at the trial were conveniently away.'

The lawsuits brought by the local officials achieved their intended aim. The agents found themselves caught between the riot on the one hand and the prospect of prison on the other. They were forced to abandon their offices and their tax-raising operations and leave the town. Sometimes they had to clear right out of the province. To protect themselves from catastrophe they swallowed their pride and signed reports stating that they had not been maltreated in any way. They agreed to acknowledge the competence of the local justices, to pay the appropriate damages and legal costs, to make due apology for the harm they were found to have caused, and to leave their horses, weapons and baggage in the hands of the local authorities. Episodes of this kind are recorded at Layrac in 1609, Châtellerault in 1642, Sarlat in 1643, Saintes in 1658 and Dax in 1663. As soon as they were safely out of reach, however, and had made their way back to Paris, the agents changed their tune. They drew up new reports and secured the agreement of the tax-farmer to back them in any action they might bring. Finally they got the Council to quash the verdict of the local court. The prison sentence imposed on them was struck off the records as having been 'an atrocity and an insult'. Orders were given to end the confiscation of their baggage. The Council took over their case and either referred it to the provincial intendant or even included it in the petitions submitted to the royal household; and the local judges were forbidden to take any further cognizance of it.

If we study the entire history of struggles between provincial communities and tax-farmers, we notice that a number of jurisdictions showed particular enthusiasm for bringing these actions for damages. Such actions were brought so often that we must surely recognize in them a form of political protest. The *présidial* at Poitiers, for instance, intervened no less than six times in the weightiest possible manner against agents sent to gather *aides* and tax-farming in general. The *parlement* at Bordeaux delivered repeated hostile judgements in an attempt to block the collection of the Convoy et Comptablie dues. And the *parlement* at Toulouse and the *cour des aides* in Haute-Guyenne adopted an attitude of marked and consistent antagonism to the levying of customs duty on the borders of Languedoc.

Retribution and patronage

Sometimes the risings were serious. Major disturbances broke out, for example, at Limoges in 1602, La Rochelle in 1661, and Limoges again in 1702 and 1705. Even in cases like these, however, the courts were usually satisfied with hanging one or two of the rioters. The government's retribution was short-lived. The authorities were more concerned to ensure that their duties could still be levied. At the same time they hoped to persuade the offending towns to come to an adequate compromise by repurchasing, as it were, the tax imposed upon them, and thereby enabling the government to buy the farmers out. An amnesty would be granted a few months later, if the disturbances had been sufficiently extensive to warrant such a formality. Amnesties were accorded at Niort in July 1633, at Bayonne in July 1641 and at Châtellerault in October 1658.

Retribution in any case could often be stopped in its tracks by the deployment of patronage. The Count of Gramont, for instance, spoke out on behalf of his province of Labourd. The tax-farmers were clamouring that the province should be punished, but Gramont's intervention persuaded the authorities to stay their hand. La Trémoille in the same way came to the rescue of Poitou. The holder of the benefice of La Porte wrote to the chancellor, Séguier, in defence of an exemption that had been enjoyed by the city of Niort. He claimed somewhat conceitedly that he was 'obliged to uphold the privileges of this town by virtue of the citizenship I have purchased there. It is a town I regard as my particular client.'

Of a hundred or so disturbances, only one appears to have been put down by terroristic means. Following the protracted revolt which took place at Audijos, Colbert authorised the intendant, Pellot, to take a bloody revenge for the thirty to forty murders committed by the 'Invisibles'. The captured offenders were either broken on the wheel, or hanged, or sent to the galleys 'in batches'. Pellot arrived in Lannes in August 1664. By September 1665 he was able to write to Colbert, 'So that makes fifteen or sixteen of them hanged, broken on the wheel, or caught and killed on the spot. I shall try to find some more.' He succeeded. By 1667 almost twenty further executions had taken place.

In 1641 the people of Bayonne rose up in an open and successful revolt against the imposition of the tax of 'a *sou* for every pound'. Twenty-five years later, in 1665, they put up no more than a minor disturbance when the tax bureaux were installed in Lannes. The resigned way in which they behaved on this second occasion affords a striking contrast. Only a generation separated these two events, and one man, David d'Etcheverry, was a member of both the missions which the town sent to Paris on each occasion to plead its case before the Council. Both missions got an identical reception from the government of the day. 'You've got yourselves in a fine pickle', said Bullion in 1641. 'You're backing a losing horse.' 'M. d'Etcheverry', echoed Colbert in 1665, "you people in Bayonne are gluttons for punishment.'

But there the resemblance ends. In 1641 a whole chorus of protest rose up on behalf of Bayonne. Three delegates from the town council went to the court to complain, and so did a number of the local country squires. The bishop of Bayonne, François Fouquet, went all the way to Abbeville to seek an audience with the king and Cardinal Richelieu, and the Count of Gramont made a personal intervention in the hope of persuading the king to agree to have the tax-farmers driven from the town. Six days after the delegates arrived at court, the chancellor, Séguier, sent for them. 'Gentlemen', he announced, 'the king and Council have duly been informed of your loyalty and made aware of the difficulty in which your town has been placed by the new taxes. His Majesty is consequetly pleased to forget what has happened and to exempt you from the taxes.' Louis XIII invited Bishop Fouquet to join him in his coach. 'Shaking his head', he acknowledged 'that the tax-farmers had been the cause of this disturbance'. The intended tax bureau was never set up. Instead the government instituted an annual duty of 50,000 *livres* to be paid simultaneously with the regular state taxes. This duty was divided among the three *élections* of Comminges, Lannes and Armagnac, and was levied on the salt which they imported from Poitou by way of the River Adour.

In 1665 the government took another line altogether. Pellot, the provincial intendant, wrote in scathing terms to the court before the delegates from Bayonne had even arrived there. 'Desperate diseases', he wrote, 'require desperate remedies ... Bayonne is the only place left in France where the king's commands are not heeded. His authority is supreme in all other parts of the kingdom, and I believe that the time is ripe for us to implant it as firmly in this town as we have done everywhere else.' Both Etcheverry and Borda, the *lieutenant-général* at Dax, pleaded eloquently for Bayonne, but to no avail. On 8 August 1665 government troops entered the town. On 13 August a couple of craftsmen were hanged, and in September a tax bureau was established at Dax to inhibit the shipment of merchandise down the Adour.

The contrast between these two episodes provides a dramatic illustration of a well-known change. By 1665 the Thirty Years War was over. France had defeated Spain, and its victorious government was firmly in the hands of Louis XIV and Colbert. From this point onwards the state began to tighten its grip. The government issued the great ordinances through which it streamlined the farming of taxes, and accelerated the creation of bureaux designed to levy *aides*, *traites* and *gabelles*. The process was soon irreversible. It had become the state's settled policy to humble the pride of the communes, and to curb their ancient freedoms through a programme of cautious but steady attrition. The change had taken no more than a single generation to come about.

Rebellion in triumph and defeat

Let us picture the aftermath of a victorious riot. The excisemen have fled, leaving behind them only the ruins of their office, which the rioters have ransacked or burned to the ground. Tax gathering has come to a halt, and the town council has sent a delegation to the court. One day, a little later, an edict arrives from the king announcing that the installation of the tax bureau has been postponed or even cancelled. 'Thank God, gentlemen, no *gabelle*!', write the members of the delegation.[18] The king has acknowledged that the complaints of his subjects are warranted and that the excisemen have behaved with insolence. The excisemen are on their way back to Paris, and will never reappear in the province. The local collaborators have repented, and their remorse has assumed a symbolic significance in the eyes of the population. Take the case of James Hondarast. Born in Bayonne, he worked as a pilot helping to steer boats through the narrows of the Adour. He agreed to act as a guide for the boat in which the tax-farmers descended on the town. When he arrived in Bayonne, however, he was surrounded by a threatening mob who shouted that 'he came off the excisemen's boat'. He was manhandled, and would have been lynched if some friends had not come to his rescue. He went back on board one last time to report on his venture into town, gathered up his baggage 'and left the vessel that very minute, saying that he would not be back again'. Or take the case of Armand Fenix, a corn merchant of Layrac. Fenix had agreed to act as the customs supervisor for his town in exchange for a regular salary. 'He soon realized, however, that these duties were unjust and that the people were crying out against them from all sides. Consequently he decided to leave his post.' Yet another repentant sinner was a merchant of La Rochelle named Jean Dupin. Dupin had a financial interest in some new duties which were being levied on the maritime trade of his town. When rioting erupted in June 1589 he took to his heels

and was only too glad to be out of it. He had already been on the point of taking the plunge and resolving to impose no more taxes or other levies either on his own town or anywhere else. When he left the town he declared that he would never again get involved in any such dealings.

Such scenes were not unusual. Sometimes rebels did triumph and did succeed in forcing the government to abolish the latest *gabelle*. In November

---

18 These words were actually used by Daccarrette, Etcheverry and Ségure, the delegates from Bayone, in a letter they wrote to their aldermen from Paris on 19 June 1641. See *Archives Historiques, Gascogne*, vol. 24, p. 22.

1602, for instance, the sales tax or duty of 'a *sou* for every pound' which the crown had imposed on Limoges was repealed after only five months. In July 1609 the agents in charge of collecting the customs duty for Languedoc were driven from the town of Layrac. By November the Council had disowned them. A delegation arrived from Guyenne with a petition objecting to the duties, and the Council satisfied its demands in every particular. When the annual duty which the government had imposed on the innkeepers ended by provoking the great cycle of urban riots in the summer of 1635, the government promptly revoked it. In November 1640 the authorities made a second attempt to levy a *subvention*, or tax of 'a *sou* for every pound'. By February 1643, however, the edict had been suppressed, and the levy had been converted into a tax of 1,500,000 *livres* which the government would raise from the towns. The decree suppressing the original document declared that 'the expenses involved in raising this duty and the exactions made by the collectors amount to more than three or four times the sum which accrues to His Majesty';. Such edicts of revocation were solemnly printed, published and posted up in every part of the kingdom. Their importance is amply attested in a large number of sources. They did much to foster the general spirit of rebellion which prevailed at this time.

In certain places local revolts against the tax-farmers became persistent and even habitual. We have seen how this happened in the case of the other revolts against soldiers and bailiffs. A town or region would be confronted by an attempt on the part of the tax-farmers to encroach on its traditional freedoms such as its right to retail wine or salt as it pleased, and would defend those freedoms stubbornly over several dozen years. The people of Châtellerault, for instance, were in revolt throughout the period 1643–57. They were asserting the right to sell salt to anyone they chose without having any agent to supervise them. The people of the Lannes and Chalosse regions were in constant rebellion for forty years. From 1627 to 1667 they fought to protect the traditional salt trade on the rivers Adour and Midouze. Let us try to identify some common features in these risings – in the length of time they lasted, the results they attained and the destruction which eventually overtook them. Their essential impetus was derived from the persisting faith of the rebels that their region would triumph over the outsider and the excisemen would vanish from the scene. This confidence in turn was based on the solid local feeling of sympathy for the rebel cause. Everyone inclined to the rebels, up to and including the social groups on whom public order depended, such as the gentry, the justices, the officials of the *maréchaussée* and even the officers in charge of the troops the government sent to put the rising down. Revolts made most progress in periods when the central power was weak: the tax-farmers, conversely, flourished at times when the royal armies were victorious and military force could be exerted on their behalf. They gained ground as the social consensus behind the rebellion began to fracture, revealing potential agents like attorneys, sub-contractors and informers within the very bosom of the community. After the rising was suppressed, however, the tax-farmers still had to contend for some time with the activity of professional smugglers and criminals who had been excluded from the government amnesty. People like these kept the spirit of popular vengeance alive, and maintained a resistance on the fringe of society. We can, then, identify six characteristic features of a rising. There was the confidence of the rebels that their cause would be victorious; the local consensus behind them; the accommodating attitude of the officials whose task it was to put the rebellion down; the connection between the progress of the rebellion and the fortunes of the king's armies in the field; the betrayal of the revolt by local collaborators of the excisemen; and the desperate resistance which sputtered on after the main revolt had been crushed. Let us now take a closer look at each of these features in turn.

The rebels believed that it lay within their power to wipe out the excisemen. They cried death to their oppressors, and vowed to exterminate them. Language of this kind was used by the surgeon Bourdeau, who acted as standard-bearer of the companies of burgesses in the town of Châtellerault, and by Bernard d'Audijos, a gentleman-adventurer who led the 'Invisibles' of Chalosse. On 4 June 1641 the 'rebels of Bayonne' addressed their tormentors in still more explicit terms. 'Robbers and excisemen', they cried, 'we are going to take your lives and wipe out the whole race of you, so that not so much as a memory of you will remain.' The rebels had no doubt that their cause would prevail. 'They believed that by murdering the guards employed by the Convoy tax-farm, they could get rid of the tax bureaux. They persuaded the masses that there would be no *gabelle* so long as Audijos lived.'

The rebels had no doubt, either, that their cause was a righteous one. The delegates sent to court by the rebel towns drew attention to letters patent issued by Charles VII and Henri II. They used the word freedom to describe not only the traditional exemption from taxes enjoyed by their community, but also the organized smuggling through which the community exported black market salt to neighbouring provinces where the price of salt was higher. We learn from the information provided by the tax agents that Châtellerault was the centre of this traffic in substitute salt. On market days the smugglers could be seen stocking up on this contraband openly for the run into Touraine and Orléanais. 'Every citizen', said the agents, 'has at least 500 to 600 *minots* of salt in his house . . . and every year at least 300,000 *livres* of salt are sold openly in this town.' The entire Haut-Pays got its salt from Poitou by way of Bayonne and the River Adour, thereby circumventing the offices which had been set up to collect the Convoy et Comptablie duties from the river traffic on the Garonne. Estimates given by the tax-farmers suggest that the Haut-Pays consumed a total of something like 12,000 hectolitres of salt each year. In 1639, a peak year for smuggling, 51,000 hectolitres of substitute salt came up the Adour. After the salt reached Dax it was forwarded along either of two alternative routes. One route led by way of Hagetmau and Castelnau-Rivière-Basse to Bigorre and Armagnac. The other route ran through Mont-de-Marsan to Lannes, Condomois, Bazadais and ultimately Quercy. In 1657–8 over 10,000 hectolitres of substitute salt were transported up the river Midouze, which flows past Mont-de-Marsan. Many of the people in the region, then, depended for their livelihood on local privileges of a highly remunerative kind. Sometimes the tax-farmers agreed to accept annual indemnities in compensation for the shortfall in their takings which had resulted from the activity of the smugglers. The Duke of Épernon, for instance, was charged an indemnity of 2,000 *livres* to compensate for the smuggling conducted from his estates, where the tax-farmers had set up the bureau of La Teste-de-Buch. Twelve thousand *livres*, similarly, were exacted from the town of Mont-de-Marsan, where the farmers had established their first bureau in the Lannes region. The effect of this arrangement was that the smuggling was accorded a degree of official recognition.

The unanimous local feeling in favour of the rebels can be accounted for precisely by the extent of this smuggling activity. At Poitiers in October 1655, Pouydraguin in August 1657, and Nogaro in November 1661, the judges sentenced the tax guards who were brought before them. Members of the nobility intervened in favour of the smugglers. The Duchess of Orléans, for example, was also Duchess of Châtellerault, and she came to the defence of the salt smugglers in that town. The Duke of Gramont spoke out on behalf of the people of Hagetmau, where he was seigneur. The Marquis de Poyanne pleaded for the citizens of Dax and Saint-Sever, where he served as governor, and the Viscount of Poudenx championed the smugglers in Chalosse. He held lands in that district, and was in addition the principal spokesman of the nobility of Béarn. Certain country squires like the seigneur of Pouydraguin and the barons of Arblade, Banos and Brocas went so far as to give the rebels material aid. Now and again officials of the local *maréchaussée* (marshal's jurisdiction) were themselves implicated in the smuggling. A man named Le Coq who served as lieutenant in the *maréchaussée* of Châtellerault had a hand in the local black market, and all of the bowmen in his company were implicated in a general sense. Another culprit was David de Saint-Paul, the vice-seneschal of Lannes. He was relieved of his office by Pellot, the provincial intendant. A noble named Christophe de Borrit, who served as crown judge of Chalosse and provost of Saint-Sever, was hanged for offences of this nature in May 1665. The officers of the troops that were sent to put down the rising showed no enthusiasm for serving the interests of the tax-farmers and made deals with the rebels. On one occasion, for instance, a judge of Rivière-Basse named Jean Duclos was found guilty of passing an unwarranted death sentence upon a guard employed by the Convoy tax-farm who had been captured at Pouydraguin. The judge was imprisoned – only to be released by the officers who had been sent to restore order from the citadel of Blaye. They got him set free without so much as a word to the tax-farmers, by showing the prison governor an ordinary letter with the great royal seal on it, and even let him have a horse with which to escape from their clutches. In a similar spirit the officers of the Podewilz regiment came to an understanding with Audijos, the leader of the 'Invisibles'. They would give him advance notice of their movements, on condition that the 'Invisibles' refrained from firing on the blue coats of their dragoons.

Rebels consistently secured their short-lived victories at periods when the king's wars were raging most fiercely, and the grip of the central government on the provinces was correspondingly weak. On three such occasions, in 1628, 1638 and 1641, the people of Lannes prevented the agents of the Convoy tax-farm from opening offices in their territory; and in 1648 the people of

Châtellerault succeeded in expelling the brigade of troops who had been installed in their town to obstruct the traffic in salt. In 1655, at the height of a riot against the agents, a burgess of Châtellerault named Grimaudet who had been sent to the Council to plead the town's case actually had the audacity to call out to his fellow-citizens in the open street 'that they need have no fear, since His Majesty was embroiled elsewhere and in no position to send any troops against them'. This period was also the heyday of the traffic in substitute salt which took place in the Landes region.

The tax-farmers, conversely, took their revenge at periods when the wars were over and troops were available for dispatch to the provinces. In August 1664, for example, the government was able to withdraw its dragoons from the provinces of eastern France and could consequently turn its attention to suppressing the resistance in Landes. This operation was completed by the time the royal forces were once again needed on the frontiers, when the War of Devolution broke out in 1667.

In every disturbance that took place the most detested scapegoats were the men who had betrayed their community. Certain of the tax-farmers' agents showed their true colours late in the day, when it was obvious that the Council were determined to crush the rising. We have already looked at the fate of Simon Brettier of Châtellerault. Both he and Jean Petit, an assessor of the *maréchaussée*, lost their lives or property for having collaborated with the excisemen or given evidence on their behalf. The assistant magistrate of Mont-de-Marsan was another collaborator. He accepted a commission to march against the rebels in Lannes. The local people retaliated by setting his property on fire. The citizens of Saint-Sever, Aire, Hagetmau and Bayonne vented their indignation upon 'certain individuals in the town of Mont-de-Marsan who have gone to the extreme of receiving the excisemen and permitting them to establish the office designed for collecting the *gabelle*'. The murders and arsons committed by the 'Invisibles' were undoubtedly directed at the guards employed by the Convoy tax-farm. But the guards were not the only or even the principal targets. The 'Invisibles' were also wreaking revenge on the villagers of Chalosse 'because the people there were in sympathy with the guards'.

Once troops were stationed in a town and the agents installed in strength, the rebels were reduced to staging sporadic attacks on the oppressors and smuggling their goods in secret convoys. 'They called themselves desperate men', the chronicle tells us. 'They said they were martyrs to the common weal, and were not afraid to die.' In the opinion of the consuls of Saint-Sever, the arrival of the excisemen and the punishment inflicted on the community in retribution for the rising which the excisemen had provoked led the way into 'a labyrinth of troubles'. Profits would no longer be made from the traffic in substitute salt, and the region was consequently bound to experience at least a temporary stagnation. The consuls were filled with foreboding. 'I fear they may seek to establish a bureau to raise the *gabelle*, which would be a great burden on the poor region of Chalosse. What misery afflicts us! I pray the good Lord that he may be pleased to bestow his holy blessing upon our land. Amen.' 'They say Hagetmau will never recover from this treatment . . . not even in sixty years.' In Châtelleraudais the mass of the people were forced to abandon their traffic in substitute salt. The authorities had set up a permanent office to halt the trade, and anyone who continued to engage in it found himself implicated in a criminal activity, with all the risks that entailed. Châtellerault was consequently hard hit by the dearth that broke out in the region in 1662. Tradesmen were driven to shut up shop, and craftsmen moved elsewhere. In 1665 the town council cited the ruin which had overtaken the leading citizens as a reason why the authorities should consider exempting them from the obligation to buy shares in the French East India Company. They blamed this disaster exclusively on the tax-farmers who had been sent to collect the *gabelles*. The farmers had initiated legal action against the citizens, and the citizens had been ruined by the ensuing costs and fines. It is not difficult to see why the suppression of the substitute salt trade was such a calamity. France was still a subsistence economy. Life was precarious in the outlying towns and regions, and smuggling represented a considerable source of extra income. If the central government was enfeebled and the tax-farmers withdrew, people might still hope to realize their traditional profits: if, on the other hand, the government grew stronger and the farmers reappeared, those profits would be wiped out. Here, yet again, is evidence of the impact which the advent of state control was liable to make on the fate of the provinces.

People took pleasure in looking back to a golden age of freedom. In their belief, the tax-farmers were destroying that legacy, and they rose up, in part, to defend it. In defending their old local commerce, however, they were also trying to protect a genuine way of life, and one on which many of them relied for their daily bread. Tax-farmers struck at this commerce, and were, consequently, always liable to be viewed as the heralds of dearth and famine. In this way the original grievance which lay at the root of a rising was often exacerbated by the obsessive fear that the price of bread might go up. On one occasion the aldermen at Bayonne gave the spread of this obsession among the craftsmen of their town as a reason for insisting that the tax-farmers should withdraw in the boat by which they had come.

Ever since this vessel had arrived at the town and moored in the river there, all river commerce had come to a halt, and many rumours had spread among the people. It was quite impossible for them to feed themselves and their families under these conditions, seeing that they depended on this traffic for their living – the poorer classes in particular.

An equally revealing episode took place at Bordeaux in March 1643. The tax-farmers had anchored a vessel off the citadel of Blaye, trained their guns on the Garonne and blocked the river trade. The crowd on the city wharves retaliated by setting upon a boatman whom they found loading grain to supply the citadel. They accused him of shipping the grain off 'to feed those persons who are trying to starve our population to death'. The citizens who rose up against the salt tax in Limoges in May 1705 were haunted by a similar fear of famine. 'The lower orders imagined that the duty was being imposed, in a general fashion, on every commodity they needed for their daily lives. They already had the utmost difficulty in surviving, and felt, consequently, that this duty sealed their doom.' Dearth was never far from the minds of the poor in the cities, and it is no surprise to find their obsession rearing up in this context. In these disturbances, however, the dread of starvation was no more than a subsidiary factor. The principal aim of the rebels was to drive out the extortioners and excisemen.

Most reviled of all were the excisemen who slapped duties on salt and wine. Any attempt to meddle with these two foodstuffs provoked a violent emotional reaction that may possibly be connected with the part they played in Christian symbolism. Both were ubiquitous commodities, essential to life and pleasure. Neither was scarce, but neither could be produced outside a range of very specific areas. They were traded along ancient and well-established routes, and the tax-farmers who blocked those routes were consequently disrupting a vulnerable and precious rhythm of social intercourse. In the eyes of many people the *gabelle* was a violation of a basic and essential human right. The exciseman who levied the *gabelle* was viewed as an enemy of mankind, a person without feelings, and the natural scapegoat for every grievance and hate.

Riots against the *gabelle* also had an orgiastic quality. They were an opportunity for drinking and merrymaking and the cruellest of practical jokes. This was the reason why the authorities came to frown on the Midsummer bonfires and the boisterous parish gatherings which so often served as a backdrop for rioting of a more subversive kind. Evidence for this may be found in the decree which the government issued condemning the rebels who had risen against the excisemen in Saint-Sever. The authorities made a point of forbidding the citizens of that town to hold any further gatherings on Midsummer's Day. The advance of the tax-farmers, in other words, formed part of a larger process. The state was imposing on society a new kind of culture in which the people would be expected to repress their wilder instincts and behave in a dignified manner. This culture was intended to take the place of the long-standing popular culture of the drinker in the tavern. Hortensius was getting his revenge for Francion's tricks.

Riots at the price of bread were the least dangerous type of disturbance, and the type which the authorities were quickest to forgive. But the obsessive dread of famine was always present, liable to manifest itself in outbreaks of violence at any time. Often a fear of starvation was voiced in the course of quite different risings, in which concern at the price of corn had initially played no part. Of all the various types of riot which raged in the seventeenth century, the bread riots were the slowest to die away.

Riots against the quartering of troops, on the other hand, came to an end as soon as the military authorities began to tighten their control of the troop movements. And the riots provoked by the tax collectors and tax-farmers also became less frequent as time went on, as the government increasingly used force to secure the consent of the populace to its taxes, and provincial loyalties ruptured, and the old exemptions were flouted and forgotten. Such riots were characteristic of a social order in which the subject was attached to his locality by a network of group and community ties, and the king was still revered for his love of justice rather than loathed for his greed for money. When that old social order disappeared, the riots went with it. They had expressed, in spectacular fashion, the values of a traditional and customary culture which prided itself on its just application of popular law. The excisemen who got punished were victims chosen to atone for the sins of their masters and to serve as the necessary scapegoats for the community's sufferings. Traces of these phenomena lingered on even after the reign of Louis XIV. Minor vendettas organized by the traders in substitute salt persisted with some intensity during the eighteenth century. But these were essentially criminal operations conducted on the fringe of society. They had little in common with the province-wide rebellions which had broken out at the time of the Thirty Years War. The fact remains that the old tradition of resistance had not been entirely buried. It survived, indeed, right down to the present day. Peasants still gathered together within living memory to bar the road to the bailiffs, and rang the tocsin to warn their neighbours that the inspectors of indirect taxes were coming by. We may detect in these activities a last dim memory of the assemblies of the seventeenth-century communes.

5

The Rebel Imagination. Traditions of Insurrection in South-West France

The condemnation of taxes

An entire body of doctrine based on the principle of resistance to taxation was current in seventeenth-century France. This body of doctrine was unique to the period. It gave expression to a general consensus which had arisen on the subject of taxes, and the issues on which it fed were drawn from every part of the social scene. Good Christians were filled, for example, with a sense of compassion and an impulse to charity when they contemplated the sufferings of the poor, and these emotions probably did much to turn them against the idea of taxation. Many people thought it scandalous that a peasantry ravaged by famine and disease should in addition be called upon to shoulder an ever-growing burden of levies. Pamphlets were written describing how the peasants had been reduced by the taxman to vagrancy, begging and despair. These descriptions bore a striking resemblance to the stories told by the beggars who actually roamed from parish to parish in Paris trying to induce the families of the burgesses to give them alms. One pamphlet related how 'whole bands of paupers were seen spending months beneath the hedgerows and under the bushes. They kept alive for a time by eating a few wild berries, but now they have no other recourse than death.' Similar doleful accounts of the conditions in the provinces were approved by the court of the archbishop of Paris and sold at the gates of every church in the city. 'The poor ploughmen are oppressed by the tax officials with an infinite number of legal actions, distraints and imprisonments ... Some die ruined in the prisons, which are full to the roof with them, and others perish in the towns and the open fields where ... poverty has driven them to beg their wretched living.' The foregoing is a fair example of the tone adopted by the authors of these pamphlets in their attempts to counter the new tax system which the state was seeking to impose.

The evil of taxes appears to have been a common topic in both conversation and literature. In a novel of Paul Scarron we find a merchant, an actor and an innkeeper seated at a table laden with jugs of wine. 'They talked of taxes, railed at the extortioners and sorted out the state.' The discussion was brought to an end only when the sodden participants were carried from their table and put to bed, fully clothed. At another point in the novel a lawyer at the *cour des aides* described the successful plea he had made on behalf of a doctor who wished to be exempted from the task of collecting taxes. The doctor had insisted that his function of tax collector would worsen the condition of any patient he might have to treat. 'In his overheated imagination the sick man will call to mind all the *tailles* and *taillon* he has been required to pay ... and his mind will be filled with visions of sergeants and joint distraints. These mere ideas are enough to give a poor man the shivers and make his fever twice as bad.'

Seventeenth-century historians and essayists were unable to touch on the subject of taxes without resorting to language of the most morbidly gloomy kind. In his *Mémoires d'État*, Michel de l'Hospital declared that a king could set his finances on a firm foundation only by swindling and fleecing his subjects. A certain Lazare Ducrot wrote a treatise on taxes in which he referred to financial officials as 'leeches who feed off the substance of the poor'. (The first edition of his treatise was dedicated to Marshal d'Effiat and the second to Cardinal Richelieu.) The chronicler François Mézeray accused the provincial intendants of 'battening on the sweat of the people and the blood of the soldiery'. According to one tradition Mézeray went still further than this in the final years of his life. Deprived of a pension by Colbert, he poured his resentment into a 'History of Extortion'. After his death the manuscript fell into the hands of his heirs. They were terrified, and burnt it at once.

Two kinds of treatise in particular bore the stamp of this crusade against taxation. The first kind were manifestos. They were drawn up by persons who were actively engaged in conspiracy and revolt. The second kind were warnings. They were composed by a variety of writers in the provinces, and sent off in large quantities to the ministers of the crown.

Taxes condemned in subversive manifestos

In June 1605 the gentry of Périgord were hatching the Bouillon plot. They gathered together, in their own words, 'to relieve the plight of the people, crushed and worn out with levies as they are'. In 1632 the exiled queen mother addressed a letter to the *parlement*. She pointed out how 'the people have been drained of all their wealth ... the countryside is depopulated, and the cities have been ransacked.' When the House of Habsburg went to war with France three years later, they issued a manifesto deploring the 'loud cries coming from the poor, who have been virtually ruined by the greed and folly of the Cardinal'. The princes who rose in the Fronde maintained that they had banded together 'to lighten the burden of the poor'. They declared in their manifesto that the peasants 'have been reduced to eating and sleeping like beasts. They have been dying of famine and plague. They have been forced to abandon their work in the fields and take up arms. Some of them have even been driven to beg their bread, or take refuge in foreign lands.' In 1672 the Chevalier de Rohan drew attention to 'the general wretchedness, and the pitiful condition to which the realm has been reduced by the cruelty and greed of the tax-farmers'. Twenty years later, in 1692, Marshal de Schomberg circulated a manifesto promising to 'deliver the people from the taxes which are eating them up'. This list of examples could be protracted *ad nauseam*.

When commanders led their troops into a foreign country they habitually proclaimed to the people there that they proposed to free them from taxes.

When the king of France, for example, entered Habsburg dominions, he assured the population that he meant to leave their country 'freer from taxes and levies than it has ever been before'. The king of Spain took a similar line when he crossed into Guyenne. He vowed to the people 'that they would pay no tax to the Catholic King'.

Some observers were unimpressed by these constant allusions to the tyranny of the taxman. In their view such references were simply a rather easy way for conspirators to justify their venture. A provincial intendant was moved to some ironical reflections by the declarations which were issued in 1643 by the nobles of western France. 'They suggested', he wrote,

a variety of methods for relieving the provinces. Among other things they proposed to get rid of the minister and the intendant and to bring about a reduction in the taxes and other levies. These gentlemen called for the people to be succoured on every ground imaginable, and assured them that the whole of France had an interest in their plight.

Jean Sirmond, a writer employed by Richelieu, refuted the manifestos of the various dissidents in similar terms. 'The mask they assume in public is so old and so well-worn it is amazing that they can still bring themselves to use it. Every rioter, troublemaker and rebel in history began that way.'

Taxes condemned in warnings

Ministers in charge of finance received admonitory letters from the provinces. These warnings also made it plain how hatred of taxes had degenerated into a cliché. Pontchartrain remarked that he had 'more than enough memoranda informing me how I am enriching the king and ruining the people'. Both the intendants and the secretaries in the controller general's office made irritated allusions to provincial 'writers' and 'visionaries'. Most of these compulsive correspondents were minor officials, tax agents or village priests.

Some of these writers can fairly be regarded as representing public opinion. One of the more convincing correspondents is Pierre Gaschet, an apothecary of Saujon, in Saintonge. Gaschet was a convert to Protestantism who had previously sat for twenty years as a delegate in the local Catholic synods. He had also been the captain of a company of militia. The memorandum he submitted was one of the more elaborate of its kind. He proposed that the administration of taxes should be placed in the hands of the parish priests, or alternatively entrusted to 'justices of the peace'. He wanted the authorities to designate a number of families of burgesses which would be exempt from taxation, but suggested at the same time that their consumption on clothing should be curbed. The tax sergeants should be abolished, and their functions taken over by officials specially appointed to serve notices of distraint. Gaschet's manifesto was not, in fact, an entirely novel one. His ideas for entrusting the administration of taxes to priests or local worthies and for abolishing the post of sergeant had been put forward only a short time previously in a programme submitted to Richelieu by Simon Estancheau. Estancheau was the judge of a village in Angoumois. In 1636 he had led the Croquants who took up arms in his canton.

Certain letters written by priests in the country parishes can be linked with a popular tradition. We find in them the strand of Christian charity which played such a prominent part in the anti-tax doctrine. The controller general was besieged with compassionate letters from an array of clergymen. A priest in Angoumois declared himself 'moved to pity by the sorrows and lamentations of the people'. A priest in Périgord was 'distressed by the ruin and hell into which his parishioners had fallen'. A priest in Bordeaux was 'unable to sit by in silence while extortioners make their demands on the people and get away scot-free'.

The correspondents all professed to know of infallible methods for filling the Treasury with record revenues. Money, they claimed, could be brought in without any difficulty. It would strengthen the king and ruin his enemies, without harming his subjects in the process. The two basic themes which ran through their letters were the need to promote the king's interests and ease his subjects' lot. They pointed to the instances of dishonesty and corruption on the part of the taxmen, and inveighed against them. They favoured increasing the duties which were imposed on local commerce, and also envisaged the establishment of new official posts. The duties previously performed by the tax agents would be institutionalized, and additional taxes would be imposed on those persons who had previously served in the tax administration. These writers of warnings had little to say that was new. An unimaginative breed, they contented themselves with conventional denunciations of evils like profiteering and the sale of offices. They discoursed at length, for instance, about the 'great taxes which His Majesty is raising from his subjects, to the ruin of the population' and the 'large-scale wastage of public money'. 'People are lawless', they noted, 'because they are too poor to deposit the money which is needed to bring a suit.' These abstract comments indicate the trivial nature of much of the opposition to taxes, or what a Limousin intendant described as 'the spirit of resistance to levies'.

The mythology of tax resistance

Certain strands in this doctrine of hostility to taxes seem to have been particularly prevalent among the common people. A glance through the sources reveals a number of popular themes. The king, for example, is held to have been deceived by his wicked ministers, or robbed by his financial officials. Rumour has it that the king has remitted his people's taxes; that the *gabelle* has been introduced; that a poll tax has been brought in; that the excisemen have been punished. These various fantasies combined to make up a kind of mythology of tax resistance. The mythology shows us how the subject population reacted to the steady increase in taxes, and how they attempted to explain that increase to themselves. The myths served a double purpose. They reassured people, and goaded them as well. They were reassuring when they depicted the king as being the victim of deceit and robbery, and thereby affirmed the guiltlessness of the monarchy on which the state was based. They were reassuring, too, when they promised a remission of taxes and the return of the golden age. This prospect diverted people's thoughts from the crime they had committed in rebelling by reminding them that their cause was just and certain to prevail. But by justifying the rebel cause the mythology also served as a spur to action. News of imaginary levies like the poll tax and the *gabelle* in south-west France shocked people violently and goaded them to rise up. Accounts of the popular risings of the period give us a clear impression of the role that was played by these myths. Written specimens of the legends are harder to find. For them we need to direct our attention to the literature that burgeoned during the period of the Fronde. This literature presents certain problems. It is often difficult to determine where a particular document originated or how it came to be transmitted to other parts of the country. The corpus of Fronde texts is, all the same, a uniquely valuable source. The sudden outpouring of writings that took place at the time of the Fronde reveals all the passions and tensions of the seventeenth century. The Fronde helped to give those feelings articulate expression. By the same token it also gave us the chance to analyse them.

Myths about the king

The king deceived

Rebels engaged in panic-stricken witch-hunts for the persons who had brought disaster upon the population. But they let the king alone. A contemporary text observes that 'the love of princes towards their peoples and the instinct which subjects feel to respect and obey their sovereigns are like sacred bonds uniting ruler and ruled together, and preserving that happy understanding which exists between them and by means of which empires are supported and made strong'. The king was regarded as the epitome of all that was just and good. Louis XII, for instance, was known as the Father of the People (*Père du peuple*), and writers often alluded to this monarch and his prosperous reign. It was said that he wept every time he had to impose a tax on his people. In the same way the reign of Henri IV was remembered as a golden age, and the masses waited expectantly for that golden age to return. Many traditions survive about the good King Henri IV: we may take as a typical example the character sketch provided in the folk-tales of Gascony: 'Once upon a time there lived at Nérac a king called Henri IV. This king was as rich as the sea, as charitable as a priest, as brave as a lion, and as good as gold.' Louis XIII's entourage gave him the nickname 'the Just' and did their best to popularize it. 'Knowing well', they declared, 'that justice is undoubtedly the virtue of kings, he prefers the title "Just" to all others. He wishes his successors to understand that zeal for the good of the people is the passion by which their conduct should be governed; and such zeal is never found when a Council of wicked ministers exercises tyrannical power over the land.'

So rebels never put the blame on the king. They never even mentioned his name except in very unusual circumstances. Now and again, however, at

Bressuire in 1659 and Agen in 1695, rioters did go so far as to say that not even the king could persuade them to pay their taxes. Towards the end of the reign of Louis XIV some traders in Bourbonnais who dealt in substitute salt wrote up graffiti insulting the king's person; and a smuggler in Poitou yelled out to the agents sent to collect the *aides* who were trying to imprison him in the name of the king, 'The king is a bugger and a thief, he's not allowed to steal from his people.'[1] But these were exceptional incidents. The mass of French people concurred with the sentiment expressed by the burgess of Landes who went to Tartas to see the Court pass by on its return from Saint-Jean-de-Luz. 'I had', he exulted, 'the honour of seeing the king and the queen his wife with my own eyes ... I desire nothing more, except to see the King of Kings in Heaven.' To have seen the king with one's own eyes even once in a lifetime was an outstanding privilege. It was a privilege that was certainly not accorded to every peasant in south-west France.

Sometimes the king's subjects might be driven to despair by excessive taxation. But people felt this was precisely because the king knew nothing about it. The king had been deceived. His subjects were in agony, but that agony was being concealed from him. In 1629, and again in 1637, rebels in Périgord declared that the oppression they were suffering was taking place 'behind the king's back'. Parish syndics from Quercy who came before the Council in 1662 to complain at the rate of their taxes deluded themselves that 'all these abuses and irregularities are taking place against His Majesty's wishes'. In 1705 a dissident in Agenais wrote an anonymous letter threatening a local tax collector. He insisted that 'the king will not have his people persecuted'.

This concept of evil ministers who concealed their exactions from the king enjoyed a particular vogue at the time of the Fronde. One writer spelt it out at considerable length. 'If you wish to know the reason why so many empires have been left desolate and so many ages have been plunged into ruin, you will learn from this treatise that ministers, and ministers alone, are to blame.' History was full of examples. Alexander the Great had been poisoned by Antipater, and Mithridates of Pontus was hounded to death by subordinates who sought to usurp his throne. Charlemagne divided his empire 'because his favourites begged him to', and the finest of cities had been destroyed 'by their wicked consuls'. The writer accordingly castigated, and marked out for revenge, 'those enterprises which the ministers and favourites set in motion under cover of the name and authority of their kings'. 'Access to the king is blocked by his evil ministers ... Their sole idea is to make the king's authority hateful through the proclamations ... which they publish in the name of His Majesty. They strew them around the country like so many snares.' The time had come to 'deliver His Majesty from oppression and endow him with a law-abiding Council once again ...France must be rid of the vermin who are eating away at the fleur-de-lis.'

---

1 In the episode at Agen in 1695, the rioters said that 'even if the king was there, he would have no better success than you'. In October 1707 rioters at Thouars declared that 'the king is a robber'.

The king robbed

The king was not merely being misled by the wicked ministers and their creatures. They were actually robbing him. This idea seems to have caught on with particular effectiveness insofar as it became a cliché alluded to by some of the most distinguished men in the land. Michel de l'Hospital, for example, described the duties of a good prince to the young François II in the following terms: 'He will not allow stupid courtesans to get their impious claws into his money ... Too many officials get their chance to handle the wealth of our state. This is the real reason why such a scanty revenue accrues to the king.' On one occasion Henri IV won a sum of money at tennis. He pretended to put the coins in his hat, observing as he did so, 'I shall keep this money safe, and no one shall filch it from me, since it will not pass through the hands of my treasurers.' Plentiful rumours attached to the ministers. Richelieu was supposed to have hidden away 'the richest pickings in France' in his native town of Richelieu, as well as in Brouage and Le Havre. People said correspondingly of Mazarin that 'none of the money raised from the subject population was spent on prosecuting the war. He diverted it for his own private use.'

The idea that the king was being robbed had a similar effect to the notion that the king was being deceived. Both theories served, to some extent, to hold society together. They depicted the interests of the king and people as being identical, and threatened by a common enemy.

Glutted with the blood of the people a number of individuals and other persons motivated by financial gain ... are continuing to scheme and collaborate with the foes of this monarchy to the ruin of the king and his poor subjects ... If the people are not contented, royal authority cannot be maintained . . . The king has been robbed and the people have been seriously maltreated by the petty functionaries who have assumed authority over them.

A pamphlet which circulated in Bordeaux at the time of the famine in 1631 sought to enlist the king on the rebel side. 'Your Louvre is as liable to plunder as any of our villages. Your palace is being looted just like our huts, and the looters are getting rich at the expense of all of us. Your interests, Sire, are intertwined with ours.'

The notion was a directly subversive one. Carried to its logical conclusion it meant that the people were entitled to refuse any tax not destined for the royal treasury. Evidence of this is provided by an incident in which a team of local commissioners were sent to distrain upon a tax-farmer. The commissioners are said to have called out to the passers-by that the man had taken to his heels and 'carried off the king's funds ... and uttered a variety of other insolent remarks calculated to stir up sedition against the farmer and get the mob to ransack his house'. On another occasion a citizen of Verdun-sur-Garonne was incensed by a new tax. He cried out in the market square 'that this money was being gathered purely and simply for those persons who were devouring the wealth of the town. Not so much as a coin would go to the

king, or find its way to his coffers.' In April 1648 a correspondent wrote from
Guyenne, 'There is reason to fear that the people may shake off the yoke of
their long-standing fiscal burdens, claiming that the taxes are no longer going
to the king but are being diverted by the tax-farmers. I assure you, this kind
of thinking is gaining ground among the peasants in the countryside.'

The Council for its part tried its best in the documents it issued to persuade
the subject masses that the taxes imposed upon them were genuinely sought
on the king's behalf. 'The most effective relief we can bring to the people',
wrote Colbert, 'is to see to it that they pay nothing other than what they owe
to the king.' After the Croquant revolt of 1637, the government circulated a
conciliatory decree. They announced that the money raised in taxes would be
transported straight from the collector's office to the Treasury, so that the
taxpayers could see quite clearly that the tax-farmer was getting no profit from
the sums they paid in. A royal directive issued in the years of the popular
risings emphasized the point still further. 'In allocating and levying these taxes',
the king commanded, 'the strictest possible order must be observed. I wish to
be sure that the money raised has been spent properly and according to my
original intentions. The people must perceive this as well.'

The myth of no more taxes

The grand remission

Rumour persistently had it that the king had at last discovered the wretchedness
of his subjects, and had granted them, in his goodness, an exemption from
their taxes or even a wholesale remission of their debts. It was the most
tenacious and enduring of the myths which spread in reaction to the fiscal
demands of the time.

The myth gained plausibility from the fact that exemptions actually had
been accorded on many occasions to parishes ravaged by hail and to provinces
made desolate by war. Sometimes remissions too were made, though these
amounted to no more than an acknowledgement by the authorities that they
were not, in practice, ever going to recover certain arrears. When a disaster
struck the king would grant a reduction in taxes. The concession was extended
collectively to the whole region, *généralité* or *élection* as the case might be, and
the intendant, or the elected representatives, had the task of distributing the
royal bounty among the places most affected by the catastrophe. In the disaster
area the rebate was merely accepted as a sign of royal awareness that tax
gathering was out of the question there: in the neighbourhood, however, the
spread of the great news was apt to give rise to wild hopes. An exemption
accorded to a single parish would conjure up visions in the minds of the
people of an entire *élection*. The king, they surmised, had awoken to the
suffering in the countryside. The remorseless demand for taxes had been
curtailed. The oppressors were leaving for good.

The impact of the myth was reinforced by the solemnity with which some
tax remissions were announced. In November 1625, for example, the authorities made known to the public letters which the king had issued lifting and

abolishing a range of taxes that had been imposed without his blessing by officials in Bas-Poitou. The news was spread by means of proclamations made in the towns to the sound of drums and trumpets and placards erected at the crossroads. In March 1627 a 'Declaration made by the king to restore to their rightful place all the classes in his kingdom and to relieve the sufferings of his people' was circulated throughout the whole of France. In it the king promised to 'lessen by every possible means the burdens which weigh upon our poor subjects'. 'It is', said the king, 'our express wish to declare more especially by these presents . . . and to take upon ourselves, on our word and honour as king, the obligation to relieve [our people] and reduce their burdens'. On 18 January 1634 Louis XIII returned once again to this dangerous theme. 'Wishing to add the name of Father of our people to our august title of Elder Son of the Church . . . and to give by our actions notable proof of our desire to relieve the people's hardships . . . we have resolved that several taxes which presently oppress them shall be abolished from this time on.'

There was always a considerable gulf between the concession actually granted and the exaggerated meaning which the taxpayers read into it. After the peasant revolts of 1636 and 1637, for instance, the king agreed to allow his subjects a delay in the payment of their dues. This extension was widely viewed by the public as a wholesale remission of tax. 'The said reprieves were granted only for a certain period . . . His Majesty had no intention of exempting the taxpayers from their duty to contribute the monies owed by them.' The authorities had acted to gain time, but their move was interpreted everywhere as giving grounds for subversive hope. One intendant reported, 'I see no sign that the measure has done anything to open their purses . . . on the contrary, everyone sees it as paving the way for a fuller exemption.' 'Consuls and debtors alike', declared a decree, 'pretend that His Majesty has remitted the funds the people owe him and that they are among the exempted. Under this pretext they are rebelling and refusing to pay.'

A declaration made by the king on 17 July 1648 had similar results. According to the declaration, the king desired to 'reciprocate the love which all of our subjects show us . . . by devoting ourselves continually to all which may bring them relief'. Here, noted the *Parlement* in Paris (principal sovereign court), was 'a truly royal deed, to deliver the masses from oppression, to hear the cry of the people and to lighten the burdens which weigh them down'. The taxpayers maintained that the exemption applied to arrears of all kinds, to those incurred that year as much as to those of the year before. 'The remissions accorded to them have given them the impression that by withholding payment they can expect the same rebate in the future.' Enthusiasts soon sprang up to champion this myth of an extended rebate. Letters received from the provinces and decrees issued at the request of the fiscal authorities were full of vague but continual condemnations of 'rumours sown and bills posted by persons ill-disposed to the service of His Majesty to the effect that all outstanding debts had been remitted and that none of them need be paid'. 'There are a number of persons in the provinces who, imbued with the spirit of revolt, have not merely perpetrated acts of rebellion and violence against the authority of the crown but are continuing to circulate rumours and pamphlets in the parishes and are filling men's minds with notions of a complete remission of tax.' Charges of this kind had reached the Council from every part of the kingdom.

The myth of the grand remission spread with especial vigour in periods like 1636–8 or 1648–50, when a crisis of confidence gripped the land. But from time to time it also appeared in a random fashion in a particular province or year. The cause might be variously a tax increase which the public felt to be unwarranted, a build-up of debts in a given canton or an exemption accorded to a handful of parishes which had been stricken by disaster. No more than that was needed to start the glad news circulating, to set seditious tongues wagging and seditious pamphlets passing from hand to hand. Faith in a remission was promptly greeted by an intensified endeavour on the part of the authorities to force the debtors to pay. 'The hope they have invested in the supposed remission has caused them to suffer heavy losses as a result of being subjected to incessant proceedings of distraint.' The Council issued statements denying the remission reports. Parish priests were expected to read them out as part of their sermons, and consuls had to post them publicly in their communities. Intendants were empowered to seek out the authors of this lying gossip, to inform against them and try them without right of appeal. They were to make war on unknown criminals, fatherless rumours, fleeting conversations and unsigned pamphlets.

Who were these mysterious dissidents? From what plots did their rumours derive? Now and again we have access to records of the inquiries conducted into exceptional cases in which an offender was caught red-handed. These give us the opportunity to follow the progress of a rumour, and even to trace it to its source. Sometimes, for instance, it happened that a pedlar was caught at a fair selling booklets for a few farthings and calling out news of the tax remission to pull in customers. The supposed royal document he was selling turned out to be a reprint of one or several ordinances or decrees which were either out of date or had been abridged in such a way as to deprive them of their original meaning. The pedlar led the way to the printer. Both were small-time operators who made their living out of public gullibility and had no objective more grandiose than selling their little book. At other times the rumour was stirred up by a letter received from town, or an overheard conversation. In the Forez region, for example, the clerk in one of the villages showed the peasants coming to market a letter he had received from one of his sons in Montbrison. The letter reported that the *tailles* had been abandoned and that distraint was to be forbidden from that time on (15 December 1649). At Clermont-Ferrand, on 25 February 1692, the tax-farmers were threatened by crowds that had gathered outside their office. Poor folk and children were calling out news of the end of the *maltôte*. Shrillest among them were a sedan-chair bearer and a trumpeter. 'The *gabelle* and the *maltôte*', they said, 'have been done away with. I've got it on good authority, I heard a letter read at Mme Labournat's, and the letter says the king's abolished them.'

The chain of rumours started with an ambiguous ordinance, a badly phrased decree, or, even more trivially, with a legal dispute over debt collection or a piece of idle talk. One case of this was a rumour which developed during the summer of 1653 to the effect that the costs incurred by the communes for billeting troops were to be deducted from their taxes. The rumour originated in Saintonge and spread to Angoumois, Guyenne and Gascony, where the people who had heard it stubbornly refused to pay the balance of their dues. The cause of the rumour was a judgement passed on 2 July 1653 by the *élus* of Saintes in favour of two local communes which had been impoverished by fulfilling their obligation to accommodate a brigade of light cavalry. The *élus* had ordered a stay in the execution of some distraint proceedings to which these communes had previously been condemned. In the same way, and in the same area, the country round Charente and Bordeaux, word spread in the summer of 1656 that the king had given up collecting the arrears attributable to the year gone by and had banned the use of fusiliers in tax-collecting operations. The entire rumour sprang from an ordinance issued by one of the royal treasurers, in the course of a tour of inspection, on 3 June 1656. The treasurer had initiated an inquiry into the excesses committed by a band of fusiliers in one particular parish. In Anjou, in 1664, the lease awarded to a tax-farmer was suddenly revoked. For several days afterwards the district concerned was the scene of a rivalry between the agents brought in by the new tax-farmer and those of his predecessor. The new agents drove out the old ones calling out to the villagers 'that the king had remitted the balance of the taxes and that the said bailiffs were thieves' (3 April 1664). The story got around, and debt recovery became impossible to effect in any part of the *élection*.

One final example relates to an agent who had been appointed to gather the taxes in the region round Bordeaux. The agent himself had failed to pay a particular tax, and was wanted by the courts, and the bailiffs were hot on his heels. Eventually they caught up with him in a village of the Médoc district. The bailiffs shouted out to anyone who would listen

that they had orders from the king to arrest the said agent because he was collecting taxes which His Majesty had commanded that his subjects should be spared. Although this was mere conjecture fabricated by them with a view to making the people well-disposed towards them, and thereby to making the arrest of the said prisoner easier to effect, this lying rumour none the less made such an impression on the minds of the people, and spread so widely in the province of Guyenne, that the tax collectors gathered almost nothing.

A study of these various episodes makes it obvious that the rumours of a grand remission of taxes did not, after all, spread as the result of a conspiracy. The remission was a myth which took shape spontaneously under the stimulus of a trivial incident or a scuffle in a village street. It was a piece of news which the public always expected, and instantly believed, for it answered, only too well, to the visions and hopes they nursed in their collective consciousness.

The myth of the grand remission flourished with especial vigour at two particular times – on the death of a king, and the conclusion of a peace treaty.

Remission on the king's death

Even before the official announcement had been made in royal dispatches, news of the king's death would be spread throughout the kingdom by messengers sent from Paris on the instructions of merchants who had come up from towns in the provinces to do business in the capital. The news would then percolate to the countryside from the main provincial towns, or from the château of a nobleman who had been alerted by one of his retainers.

Hope that the fiscal reign of terror might at last be nearing its close was given an initial stimulus by news of the death of Richelieu on 4 December 1642. 'Rejoicing was extreme' in the country mansions, and bonfires were lighted in many villages. Louis XIII fell ill the following March. Rumour had it he had disclosed to his confessor that he meant, if God spared him, to make peace soon and call his armies home. On 25 February 1643 the Council had revoked the highly unpopular levy of a *subvention* or tax of 'a *sou* for every pound'. The dues outstanding from 1635 to 1638 had already been remitted in a proclamation issued on 4 July 1641, and a decree of 2 May 1643 extended the moratorium on debt recovery proceedings to include the arrears which were owed from 1639–41. By January 1643 the taxpayers of Rouergue were withholding their contributions. By March rumour was active in Touraine and Gascony. On 14 May 1643 the king died – and the myth of a grand remission spread like lightning.

Rumour maintained that all special taxes were to be suspended, now that the king was dead. All the mandates conferred on the intendants of provinces or the tax-gathering companies of fusiliers had been automatically cancelled. The new king would mark his accession by awarding a generous remission of arrears and an exemption from the taxes newly impending. Town councils and associations of local functionaries were no longer required to comply with the orders of the intendants or even to accord them official recognition. Taxpayers were no longer obliged to endure the harassment of the fusiliers and could even drive them away.

As early as 20 May the authorities were forced to react. The Council issued a decree enjoining local officials to be on their guard against false rumours of tax remission. On 30 May a further decree was promulgated denying a piece of news which had spread to the effect that the government had revoked the tax imposed on alienated church property. In the meantime the magistrate of Villefranche-de-Rouergue, who had been sent to Paris as a delegate representing the regional estates, went back home to advise the local communes 'that they should in no wise enforce their taxes or pay them either; that there seemed to be disorder in the country at large, and they would win an exemption from their dues, if they tried hard enough'.

On 8 June the *parlement* of Toulouse issued an order forbidding the local authorities to implement any edicts and decrees which had not been endorsed at court. The order even went so far as to annul the special tax-gathering mandates which had been formally entered in the records in the late king's reign. The preamble to this document dwelt on the whole range of familiar themes, the deceiving and robbing of the king by his subordinate officials and the grand remission of taxes. The government's financial edicts, for example, were condemned as being ruinous for king and people alike. They were the work 'of petty men who were taking advantage of the dire condition of the state to play on the generosity of the king and his Council and to squeeze out these concessions by means of abhorred and damnable lies'. For every *écu* that found its way to the coffers of the king, the agents took fifty. The *parlement* went on to recall how after the death of Henri IV the queen regent had abrogated fifty-four edicts or special mandates at a single stroke of the pen. This document, in other words, presented all the main arguments of the anti-tax mythology; yet it was, at the same time, printed and published under the auspices of the court. The response was instantaneous. Violent, seditious gatherings of nobles took place in Gascony, and tax collectors were driven out of Toulouse and Lavaur. 'The people believe that this decree excuses them from payment of all but the old royal *taille*, that the special mandates and even the mandates of the intendants have all been rescinded.' The *parlement* of Bordeaux, for its part, passed an order on 3 July forbidding the intendant Lauson to engage in any of his regular duties. 'These gentlemen', Lauson wrote to the chancellor, 'appear to believe that everything died with the king.'

In the summer of 1643 resistance to taxation led to violence in Poitou, Guyenne and Gascony. Rumours of royal remissions continued to circulate intermittently right up to the end of 1644.

In September 1715 news of the death of Louis XIV gave the myth a fresh lease of life. Rumours of a rebate promptly filtered through Bordeaux and the whole of Guyenne.

The enduring nature of the state was an intellectual concept unknown to the general public. Ordinary people associated the machinery of government with the person of the monarch and expected it, consequently, to perish when he did. The accession of a young king meant for them a renewal or, more exactly, a resumption of ancient customs – customs which prescribed, in their view, generosity on the part of the monarch and emancipation as the rightful due of his subjects.

Remission after a peace

Proponents of this particular myth maintained that taxes were no more than an emergency measure to which kings were obliged to resort at times of danger to the throne. 'Taxes were originally ordained for no other purpose than to meet the expenses of war. Our kings even declared that they would be abolished when all cause for raising them had ceased.' The winning of a 'just peace' was held to entail automatically the relief of the subject population, and the king was felt to be duty-bound to proclaim a remission of taxes so soon as peace was restored.

Between 1596 and 1600 Henri IV made an effort to satisfy the expectations of the public by initiating a series of tax cuts. The Marquis de La Force even made the somewhat exaggerated claim that 'as soon as peace was made, the king repealed half the taxes to relieve the hardships of his people'.

In January 1659, peace negotiations began between France and Spain. By the following May the tax gatherers were meeting violent resistance, which the resisters sought to justify by maintaining, among other arguments, that a tax remission was warranted by the peace. A decree issued by the Council on 17 May observed that 'as a result of the peace the people have been exempted from paying the balance of their dues ... False rumours of this kind are driving the taxpayers to rebel against the bailiffs.' At Gaillan, in Médoc, the parish priest had the tocsin rung on the arrival of the tax fusiliers, and shouted to them 'that the inhabitants were under no obligation to pay tax, since it had been remitted as a result of the peace' (12 July 1659).

On 2 February 1660 a royal letter was dispatched throughout the whole of France to announce the conclusion of peace and the marriage of the king. Once already in the summer of 1659, and again in the spring of 1660, the people of Aquitaine saw and hailed their youthful sovereign. These events were celebrated universally and in every manner of ways – by bonfires, solemn masses, drinking sessions, tournaments and dances. Accounts of these festivities were printed and circulated. Magistrates made pompous speeches in which they predicted the imminent end of the evils afflicting the kingdom and the return of the Golden Age. A prophetic tract printed at Toulouse declared that 'the Golden Age is certain to return during the glorious reign of Louis the God-Given ... His entrails will resemble a pile of corn surrounded by lilies.' A speech printed at La Rochelle was more explicit. It looked forward to 'a succession of golden centuries ... the abolition of subsidies and taxes which were only instituted in response to the exigencies of war'.

The Council took advantage of the peace to initiate an overall adjustment of fiscal policy which gave at least the appearance of fulfilling the hopes of the populace. In two resolutions, issued on 23 August 1660 and 5 January 1662, the Council wrote off the arrears which were owing from the period 1647–55, and gave orders that a directive should be sent to the local intendants instructing them to re-examine the arrears recorded as owing from 1657–9. A decree dated 2 April 1661 even provided for a small reduction in the tax rate which had been set for the following year. All of these various documents insisted on the king's desire to 'enable his subjects to enjoy the fruits of peace by relieving them entirely of the extra burdens they have borne throughout the war ... to spread abundance in his lands and to ensure that his subjects appreciate the true fruits of a well-founded peace'.

Each time, however, the measures adopted by the crown fell short of the hopes which had been aroused in the general public. In 1659–62, as in previous years, the government had to use troops to collect arrears from the taxpayers. Their operations provoked a series of disturbances, in Périgord, Angoumois, Poitou, Limousin and Auvergne. The rebels justified their risings 'on the grounds that their taxes have been remitted because of the peace ... by advancing their fanciful notion that their taxes will be remitted after His Majesty is married'. Local officials refused to pay the taxes imposed on them, claiming that the decrees which related to those taxes were out of date. The people of the Pyrenees, whose contribution had been revised upwards during the war, wanted it brought down again to the minimum rate to which they had been entitled previously as a special privilege. 'They claim that now the kingdom is at peace they are under no obligation to pay any of the levies which have been imposed on their lands.' The inhabitants of Montmorillon took up arms and declared that 'they had only paid what they wanted while the war was going on, and they were certainly not paying anything in peacetime'.

Hope of an end to taxes was given fresh stimulus by the death of Mazarin and the arrest of Fouquet. 'Certain disaffected subjects have taken advantage of the reform which His Majesty has effected in his financial administration and are circulating false rumours to intimidate those officers who are entrusted with the collection of His Majesty's revenues.' 'Conclusions may readily be drawn from the unfortunate consequences which remissions have had in the past. The masses become convinced that such concessions will always be accorded them from time to time. They harden their hearts and refuse to pay the taxes currently owing.' The authorities found it necessary to publish and display mandatory decrees intended to rid the taxpayers of their illusions. The myth that remissions followed a peace was refuted in a particularly striking manner by a demand made on the towns to contribute taxes 'in the form of a free gift to help meet the exceptional expenses which His Majesty has incurred in the course of his journey, and to show appreciation for the general peace he has bestowed upon his people, and for his marriage'. This tax was imposed by a decree of 21 August 1659. It led to a number of scattered uprisings, in the Île de Ré (4 July 1661), at Guéret (10 November 1661), and above all at Limoges (11 September 1660).

Directives issued to the intendants after the treaty of Nijmegen in 1679 were couched by the authorities in familiar terms. Once more the king was depicted as being concerned to relieve the hardships of his subjects at the end of a war, and anxious to 'enable them to enjoy the fruits of peace'. Six weeks after the treaty of Ryswick, on 27 December 1697, the poll tax was officially abolished. The Duke of Burgundy's marriage had been celebrated three weeks previously, on 7 December. There once again were tokens of the future, first signs of a new era, of the ever-awaited end of taxation. Some years later, in 1706, peasants in Poitou were mobilized during the summer to guard the coasts against enemy fleets. A rumour spread through the region that the king was remitting their taxes in recognition of the damage which had been inflicted on their livelihood.

Colbert was well aware of the power of tax remissions to stimulate revolt, and invariably did his best to avoid giving the impression of granting any such relief. 'I do not protest', he declared, 'against the excesses of the tax-farmers, because financial matters are sensitive and it is extremely dangerous to make it evident to the masses that one disapproves of those persons who are appointed to collect His Majesty's dues.' The controller general was approached on a number of occasions by intendants seeking an exemption for certain parishes. His response was a definite no. 'The moment such hopes are raised among the masses we can abandon all hope of collecting not only their past but even their future debts. They will harden their hearts and believe that the favour we have done them in remitting these arrears will be a sure precedent for another, more considerable favour to come.' 'Take care', he wrote on another occasion, 'that the masses never claim the right to an exemption. They must not even be conscious of such a possibility.' This rough-and-ready grasp of the taxpayer's psychology may well have played a part in fostering the undoubted growth of public submission to taxes during Colbert's ministry.

Imaginary taxes

Most of the myths which surrounded taxation were optimistic ones. People dreamt that better times were just round the corner. But there was also a constant fear of imaginary taxes which were thought to be on the way.

The legend of the gabelle in south-west France

In 1549, as we saw in the last chapter, the provinces of south-west France had bought themselves a permanent exemption from the salt tax. 'This agreement', observed a chronicler, 'is one of the greatest assets of these provinces . . . and successive kings have kept to it faithfully.' 'All rights to levy the *gabelle* and other duties on salt were abolished in those regions, and they are free and exempt from such taxes in perpetuity.' The south-western provinces took the opportunity to remind the authorities each time they submitted a petition of the sacred and permanent privilege which they had won through a formal agreement with the king himself. People in these provinces were keenly aware of their privileged status. They were jealous of their privilege – and doubtful that it would last. They detected in each new tax an attack on their treasured exemption; and the word *gabelle* had consequently come to denote any levy they perceived as unjust. On one occasion, for instance, a *mande* or constable in the town of Laplume was aggrieved that the consuls there had deducted the cost of his livery from his wages. 'He went through the market-place shouting that to make him pay for his uniform was nothing less than a *gabelle*.'

Any unusual event like the appearance of an unknown traveller or the unexpected arrival of a royal commissioner was immediately suspect. People assumed that a *gabelle* was about to be imposed. One year, for example, some Treasury agents took lodgings at an inn in the town of Tulle. The agents had been sent to inspect the accounts of the tax collectors; but their coming caused a commotion. A crowd gathered outside the inn calling out, 'The excisemen (*gabeleurs*) are here!' The rioters chose a spokesman in the shape of an apothecary, who went into the agents' inn 'to find out if they were *gabeleurs*'. The terminology varied. When the Marquis de Villeroy entered Poitou to raise an army in the spring of 1644, he was accused of coming 'to set up "a" *gabelle*'. When the Prince de Condé, on the other hand, was appointed governor of Guyenne in October 1638, he was accused of being about to introduce '*gabelles*'. And when the Count of Estrades was made mayor of Bordeaux the public presumed that he was on the point of establishing 'the' *gabelle*. Printed leaflets were passed round the city warning 'that if Arras gets to work they will impose the *gabelle* in Guyenne, and implement twenty-four new edicts.

We must pray God He will ensure that bread is sufficient and that the lot of the poor is relieved.'

The *gabelle* (or *gabelles*) was regarded, then, as an ever-present menace. Right through the century the people of the south-west were on the alert, always ready to take up arms against a possible assault on their privileges. A burgess of Périgueux diagnosed their obsession in his family's record book. The *gabelle*, he observed, was nothing more than 'a bogey, a figment of the popular imagination'. Sometimes the haunting fear of the *gabelle* even extended to a morbid play on words. 'In July this year a rumour spread far and wide among the people that the *cour des aides* had authorized a fraudulent (*cabaliste*) tax assessment. Actually it was the merchants and innkeepers who were defrauding (*cabalèrent*) the masses. They went round announcing that the *gabelle* was being levied, and the masses were so stupid as to believe them.' Another contemporary observer trembled at the prospect of 'gentlemen excise-men (*cabaliers gabeleurs*)'. 'I gather', he wrote, 'that these troopers dislike being called excisemen (*gabeleurs*). They refer to themselves as the king's gentlemen (*cabaliers*).'

We saw in our survey of the great waves of rebellion how the hunt for excisemen acquired an almost pathological character. The rioters were possessed by a kind of persecution mania which was exacerbated by the most harmless incidents. On days of rioting the mania blazed out in full fury. But even on ordinary days it is clear from dozens of anecdotes that the neurosis was always there, dormant perhaps but liable on the smallest provocation to stir into angry life. One typical episode took place in a Pyrenean valley in September 1667. A commissioner in charge of the reorganization of the forests, a man named Froidour, was riding through the valley with some guards employed by the *prévôté de l'Hôtel*. The guards all wore bandoliers embroidered with the fleur-de-lis. Some women from the mountain villages caught sight of these liveries and imagined that the company was preparing to institute the *gabelle*. When the news reached their menfolk several hundred peasants sprang to their arms. 'Fortunately', Froidour reported, 'I had with me a party of gentlemen who were free from any suspicion of being in league with the excisemen. These gentlemen sent some of their number to ride out among the peasantry and explain who I was ... If we had really been excisemen neither I nor any of the people with me would have come out alive.' In 1670 the priest of a little church in Lannes climbed into his pulpit to read out a pastoral letter which had been issued by the bishop of Aire. 'Most of the folk who were there for mass were convinced that he was about to announce the introduction of the *gabelle*, no less, and that this would be their ruin. All the congregation began to cry out against the priest, the women and girls especially.' Similar incidents were reported from the parishes of Saint-Aubin, Chalosse, Saubrigues and Maremme. The parishioners were so suspicious that the priests had to take to their heels. Hostile gatherings and even full-blooded revolts were provoked by such innovations as an edict relating to coats of arms, a revision of title deeds, a tax to be levied on carters and a duty to be imposed on the sale of oil. The outbreaks were not directed at the measures themselves, but at the mythical introduction of the *gabelle* which they were assumed to be heralding. The intendant of Limousin, for one, was fully aware of this. 'In my view', he wrote after an eposide of this kind,

the people were affected by the news that the cost of transporting salt was to be made subject to a surcharge levied at the rate of a *sou* for every pound. The salt trade has always been free in this province, and they got it into their heads that the introduction of this duty meant that a *gabelle* was to be imposed.

Many of these displays of obsession serve to remind us of the formidable prestige which printed matter commanded in an unlettered society. Any printed poster attracted a crowd of passers-by. People wondered what the words meant, and looked for someone literate enough to decipher them. Even if someone could be found to decipher a document, it was likely to be written in an abstruse style, and the crowd would speculate whether the *gabelle* was not the real subject of the notice, if you read between the lines. At Limoges in 1705 'the peasants saw some old poster stuck to the walls of the town gatehouse, and the rebels cried out yet again that this was the *gabelle*'. When the *lieutenant-général* arrived on the scene he was obliged to have the poster torn up in front of the crowd. All it took to create a disturbance was a notice put up by the bishop of Agen to advertise the liturgical calendar, or a pastoral letter circulated by the bishop of Bayonne to call for public prayers, or an English nautical chart pasted on to a wall in Saint-Jean-de-Luz. Noisy crowds of women would gather at the first sight of these documents, certain that the mysterious letters spelt out the advent of the dreaded *gabelle*.

Taxes on life

The *gabelle* was not the only tax dreamt up by the crowds of anxious commoners. In 1635, for example, a rumour ran round Guyenne that the tax-farmers were going to institute communal ovens, and had plans to designate a number of special inns which would have the exclusive right to sell wine. In 1643 it was reported in Poitou that a royal tithe was to be imposed on all the property of both nobles and common people. In 1670 the peasants of Vivarais whispered that taxes were to be slapped on a range of items that included new suits of clothes, hats, shirts, pairs of shoes and even their daily bread. Finally in 1709 the market women of Bayonne were convinced that the government was preparing to levy taxes on 'everything that could be eaten or burned'. They expected to have to pay duty on goods ranging from their herbs, eggs and butter to their weekly laundry.

The most common bugbear, however, was a tax which the authorities were thought to be planning to levy on individual births. 'From now on women will have to contribute a certain sum of money for every child they bring into the world.' Sometimes the rebels even claimed to know the intended rates. At Pau in 1657 the rate was said to be thirty *livres* for every newborn child, while at Aubenas in 1670 it was ten *livres* for a boy, and five for a girl. This crazy idea can be traced to the duty which was imposed on persons wishing to withdraw their birth certificates from the parish records and use them as evidence in court. The duty was known as document control. First introduced in 1568, it was reaffirmed by the government in 1654. In 1690 the post of parish clerk was created, and in October 1706 the documents were placed in the hands of official controllers. The duty was raised each time.

People regarded the notion that human birth might be taxed as loathsome and sacrilegious. The claim that such a tax was in prospect sparked off a considerable number of seventeenth-century risings. It was one of the major causes of the insurrection which broke out at Villefranche-de-Rouergue in 1627, of the riots which swept through the towns of Guyenne in 1635, and of the revolt which took place at Montpellier in 1645. In 1649 a *Catechism of Tax-Farmers* (*Le Catéchisme des partisans*) was published. The author denounced those businessmen who 'were formerly so presumptuous that they even suggested the Council should impose taxes on the holy baptism of children'. The myth continued to surface in a series of later disturbances. It was a theme of the rising which broke out at Carcassonne in 1655, at Pau in 1657, at Aubenas in 1670, and at Bayonne in 1706 and 1709. Finally it was one of the reasons behind the last of the Croquant rebellions, the great revolt which convulsed Quercy in 1707.

The government were also thought to be contemplating a tax on marriage. Rioters talked of the marriage tax in the same breath as the dreaded duty on births. In May 1697 the women of Bayonne even thought that the authorities were proposing to slap a duty on sexual relations. They complained of 'shameful levies . . . on things which we cannot decently refer to . . . on the freedoms of marriage'.

Finally people feared that there might be death duties. Their fears are set out in some detail in the pamphlets circulated by the Fronde. The authors suggested that the day might come when the extortioners would have the idea of plundering the dead 'to make a profit out of their shrouds and winding sheets, their funeral regalia, their coffins, biers and caskets, their tombs and epitaphs . . . They would even raise taxes and levies on the road to Paradise, if they only had the nerve and power to do so.' This myth generated an incident in the town of Montauban in September 1691. 'A number of wretched women and children armed themselves with sticks and stones and banded together to tear down the notices concerning the administration of burial rights which the authorities had posted up at the corners of the streets.' In fact the authorities were merely seeking to impose a duty in support of a post they were creating for a funeral director. Such an official was employed as a rule only by Parisians. Few people in the provinces could afford to pay for such a service, apart from a tiny number of bourgeois families. But in trying to remedy this deficiency the authorities had only succeeded in conjuring up the popular fantasy of the loathsome extortioner 'feeding on sighs and battening on tears'.

The government were sometimes suspected of plotting to impose a tax on the water from rivers and springs. 'It was said they would tax every jug of water the women took at the fountain.' Rumours of this kind circulated at Villefranche in 1627, at Pau in 1682 and at Bayonne in 1709.

Most of the risings against these non-existent taxes on life were the work of women. We may notice here once again the visceral, biological character of women's revolts. We considered in the last chapter the strikingly important role which women played in the most spontaneous and unorganized of all the eruptions of the period – the riots at the price of bread. Women were generally confined by society to the traditional sex-determined roles of wife and mother; but society by the same token allowed them a degree of exemption from the responsibility and the threat of punishment which hung over their menfolk. In addition we may note that certain groups of women like the lacemakers of Saint-Maixent or the fishwives of Labourd broke away altogether from the conventional stereotype and began to create a niche for themselves outside the home. Such women were especially prone to indulge in riotous behaviour. Their riots excited nothing more than pity and scorn in the local officials, who referred to them as displays of 'imagination, fantasy and excess'. These women of the people were illiterate and knew nothing of civic affairs, and the risings they staged were marked by a certain lack of consistency. At one level they were ridiculous, little explosions which died down almost as soon as they had started. At another level they undoubtedly reflected a genuine despair. A chronicler recounting a disturbance which broke out in Saint-Maixent on 2 September 1641 records that the women there 'had despaired. They had nothing with which to feed themselves and their families.' On 21 July 1709 the women of Saint-Maixent revolted once more. An observer reported that 'they would rather be hanged than endure this tax'. But the troubles were easily quelled. On every occasion the women were persuaded to return to their homes by some soothing words from the magistrates, or a small posse of soldiers arrived and chased them off the streets.

All of the people who took part in these various upheavals were convinced that they were defending a natural and fundamental right. They were fighting for the freedom to eat and drink, to be born, to get married, and to be given a Christian burial without being subjected to the attentions of the taxman. The idea that a tax might be imposed on the rites of the Church was sacrilege in their eyes; and the idea that the populace might be obliged to purchase their right to live seemed frankly perverted. These rebels were rising up in defence of their basic human dignity. Every instinct within them cried out against the excisemen and tax-farmers, and they looked on such persons as the enemies of mankind.

Myths about the exciseman

We may reasonably suspect that the rebellions were characterized more by hatred than by zeal for any positive goal. The rioting mobs were impelled first and foremost by a common detestation of the excisemen (*gabeleurs*) or extortioners (*maltôtiers*). These two words, as we have seen, were identical in meaning, and the appearance of one or the other in a particular text reflects nothing more than the division between the land of the *langue d'oc* and the land of the *langue d'oïl*. Who, then, were the excisemen? Our sources describe them as 'those gentlemen who serve as agents or tax farmers. They are commonly known by the hateful names of excisemen and monopolists.' The crimes of the excisemen afflicted society at every level. An agent writing in

1649 acknowledged the widespread loathing his calling had aroused. 'We have made enemies of the entire population of France. We have forced the farmer to abandon his plough, the merchant to give up his business, the noble to pawn his sword, the official to relinquish his post and the churchman to bid farewell to his living . . . We have mauled the fleurs-de-lis.' Laborde-Péboué included the excisemen in the list of public disasters he made for his family record book. 'I would now like to inform you', he says, 'of the wolves which have been causing great havoc in this region ever since September . . . I would like to tell you of the excisemen who have caused great havoc in this region. They descended on us in about May . . . I would now like to speak to you of the Huguenots, etc.' The excisemen, in other words, were classified midway between wild beasts and heretics. They were regarded as one of the constant and inevitable evils of life. An ordinary decent villager, like the author of this record, could do nothing whatever about them. All he could do was learn to endure them, and put his trust in prayer.

The exciseman as cannibal

People expressed their loathing of taxation by referring to the taxman as a cannibal or a vampire. It was a handy and well-worn cliché. Money raised in taxes was equated with the flesh or blood of the taxpayer. The individual citizen on whom the taxmen descended was compared to a quivering, terrified animal. The taxmen were shearing the animal's fleece so hard they threatened to flay it, or milking it so vigorously they threatened to drain it dry. Sometimes our sources even describe them as eating the animal alive. The official who raised the tax was referred to by a number of abusive names. Usually he was called a leech, but sometimes he was also alluded to as a man-eater, or a ravening wolf. The literature of the Fronde is predictably full of such gruesome imagery. All the Fronde writers were doing, however, was to echo a series of commonplaces which make their appearance unfailingly in every work on the subject of taxation. In 1648, for example, the chief justice, Molé, described the excisemen as gorging themselves on the blood of the people, and in 1680 the abbé of Saint-Réal wrote how the taxmen were drunk with the people's blood. A pamphlet of 1637 entitled the *People's Word to the King* (*Voix du peuple au Roy*) referred to Richelieu as bathing in the blood of the taxpayers. Another typical diatribe denounces the various acts of pillage in which the taxmen have indulged. 'Their houses are mortared together with the blood of the people, and their furnishings are made of widows' tears. They have raided the substance of the orphaned and the destitute for their pomp and their purple trappings, and wear them unblushing to the foot of the altar-table of Jesus Christ.' Yet another writer envisages Mazarin giving directions to his butler. The Cardinal requests twenty-eight dishes made up of the loot he has raised in levies, with side orders to match, and gets the butler to bring to his table 'a stewed peasant, garnished with taxes'.

The theme of the predatory taxman is still not entirely exhausted even today. By the eighteenth century, however, the crazily realistic language in which people had once spoken of fiscal cannibals had disappeared. Jules Michelet

(1798–1874) revived this language in his *Histoire de France*, in line with the early texts from which he drew his material. In recounting the origins of the royal exchequer during the reign of Philippe the Fair, Michelet described it as 'a monstrosity, a cyclops, an ogre, a ravening gargoyle ... The terrible hunger of this prodigy could never be assuaged. It would eat flesh and drink blood if it needed to.' In using such phrases Michelet was rediscovering the style of those Croquant manifestos which had complained how the poor ploughmen were being 'eaten down to the bones'. Such language was the product of the same visceral terror we encountered just now in considering the legend of taxes on life. The peasants were giving voice to their nightmare fear that the taxmen were coming to devour them. They saw themselves being herded to their deaths like cattle by the exactions of sergeants and tax farmers.

Excisemen were associated in the popular mind with two main characteristics – the insolence with which they flaunted their fortunes in the face of the public misery, and the staggering speed with which they had risen from rags to riches in the first place.

Insolence of the excisemen

It is clear from a number of documents that people believed they could trace a direct connection between the rise to wealth of the taxmen and the deteriorating conditions of the poor. 'These vultures', one writer comments, 'never soar higher than when the people have fallen low.' 'We are not a fat breed', admits the frank agent of 1649. 'We are bloated from drinking the blood of private citizens.' One peasant petition to the king complains that the excisemen 'make their profits out of the public wretchedness. They make hay out of disasters, batten on your ravaged provinces and found their fortunes upon the ruin of your people.'

Not content with acquiring their fortunes by criminal means, the excisemen were said to be unveiling those fortunes in the most spectacular possible way. The extent of their gains, rumour had it, was reflected in the size and pomp of the palatial residences which they were getting built for their personal use. 'Built as they are from the blood, sweat and substance of the people, their mansions sometimes surpass even the palaces of kings in the symmetry of their architecture and the comforts and adornments they contain.'

Fortunes of this kind entailed serious consequences in the religious sphere. In accumulating riches by wicked means, the excisemen, it was felt, had gone openly and without compunction beyond the accepted bounds of Christian morality. They were living 'unconstrained by faith, religion or the law'. They were people 'who have plundered mankind, misanthropes and werewolves. It is no use expecting them to show either fear of the Lord or loyalty to the fatherland.'

'We nurse in our hearts only godlessness, and nothing but blasphemy escapes our mouths.' The agent's admission is apt. The insolence of the excisemen was expressed in the sickest of jokes. They made fun of the general wretchedness in offhand remarks that goaded the peasants into revolt. One of the victims of the great city riot that broke out in Agen in 1635, for example, was an official who had announced with a snigger that he was deducting the *gabelle* from the wages of the labourers in his pay. In 1637, as we saw in chapter 3, a bowman from Périgueux who was distributing tax warrants in the surrounding parishes tried to play a practical joke on the villagers by pretending that he had come to introduce the *gabelle*. His house was burnt to the ground. Pleasantries of this sort were current at a higher level as well. Bullion was said to have remarked 'that the people were happy as long as they had bread', and Mazarin was supposed to have commented that at any rate the townsfolk weren't yet reduced to wearing clogs. A tax-farmer named Monnerot was said to have declared that he never went to bed

unless he had a million gems under his pillow. He even had the impudence to add that he was amazed any sensible man could go to bed without having that . . . Marshal de Gramont went to see him one day, and could not resist giving him a warning. He told him he seemed to be unaware that by acting so arrogantly he was putting a rope round his own neck, and that one of these days he would find himself hanged from one of his own fine rafters.

Tales like these ran round the provinces. The persons who spread them always claimed them to be authentic, and the dates and place names attached to them were varied in different regions to make them seem more plausible – and more provocative. A typical example is a story of 1690 about a sergeant who was supposed to be rolling in money. On this occasion the story was set in Saintonge.

About six months ago I heard from an informant of absolute honour and integrity of an astonishing act of embezzlement which had been committed by a sergeant in this district. This man had gone the rounds of the entire island of Alvert . . . and had exacted a large amount of silver there. He went back to the tavern [where he was staying], fed some oats to his horse, and then made off with the sieve, which he filled with silver. After that he sieved some gold through it too, and declared with the utmost insolence . . . 'I would want my horse shod in silver if I lived in Alvert.'

'The excisemen get rich quick'

So far as the public were concerned, the excisemen had made their money all too fast. The speed with which they had got rich was a token of their dishonesty. It was also a source of scandal insofar as it brought about a degree of social upheaval in traditional communities that were unaccustomed to change. The social hierarchy was thought to be eternal and preordained. By transcending that hierarchy an exciseman marked himself out in the collective judgement of the people as a social climber and a villain. Upward mobility was not merely a token of crime, but a crime in itself.

The distinguishing feature of the exciseman consisted precisely in this contrast between his humble origins and his dazzling success. 'God knows where they have come from and how they have made their money. But they have got themselves splendid mansions and are splashing out on them.' The archetypal exciseman, of course, was Mazarin himself. Leaders of the anti-tax movement spread stories to the effect that the cardinal was the grandson of a bankrupt Sicilian hatter and his father had been a stable-hand. All his relations were thieves. 'That was what his ancestors did, and his parents and grandparents, and it's his main calling today.' Mazarin, so the stories went, had started off as a footman and risen to the rank of butler. He had made all his money from backhanders. 'He was born poor, but has since become one of the richest men in the world.'

The correspondence which flowed into the office of the controller general included a large number of anonymous letters denouncing persons who had made their fortune with scandalous speed. The authors of these letters were probably village merchants or parish priests. The characteristics which they ascribed to the businessmen they detested conformed in every detail to the stereotype of the wicked exciseman. They portray him in the familiar way as a person of humble origins who has grown obscenely rich. One of the classic sketches of an exciseman, for example, was given in a letter attacking the tax collector employed in the *élection* of Périgueux.

M. Delpy is the son of a poor carter from the estates of the Viscounts of Turenne. In 1670 he came to Périgord to take up a post as sergeant there. His wife was the daughter of a poor tailor of Bordeaux, and they were so poor at that time they had less than fifty *écus* to their name. Now, however, they live like lords off a fortune estimated at more than a hundred thousand *écus*.

Stock condemnations of this kind were accompanied by an incessant demand for sumptuary laws. People were not supposed to rise above the rank in society to which they were born, and were expected to wear the dress appropriate to that rank on every occasion. The exciseman was betrayed by both his rise from humble origins and the borrowed finery in which he was clothed; and his neighbours denounced him accordingly.

The exciseman figures in our sources as a cultural archetype. It is harder to say if he represents a definite social category. If we study the lists of persons who fell victim to the disturbances we may sometimes fancy we can identify a particular social group, like the burgesses who bought their way into civic posts. Such schematizing is dangerous, however, and all too often the schema proves to be riddled with contradictions. When people of this period spoke of excisemen they referred first and foremost to members of a particular institution rather than a particular social class. The insult was not aimed at any burgess or peasant who had happened to strike it rich: the anger of the public was directed specifically at those townsmen or villagers who had received a commission to raise taxes or a job in one of the tax-farming operations. But even if you had identified the offending institution you could not necessarily pinpoint the exciseman. It is evident from a number of official inquiries that bailiffs and *élus* were sometimes to be found at the head of a riot. Agents employed by the tax-farmers enthusiastically accused each other of being excisemen, and no one was prepared to admit that he belonged to that hated calling. People with an interest in the tax-farms never turned out to be excisemen, nor did financial officials, or burgesses in the towns, or people from Paris. Excisemen were people who had a larger interest in the farms than you did, or had a hand in more offices than you, or had bought more property than you had in the surrounding countryside, or went to Paris more often than you had ever done. The exciseman was always someone else. He was the man who outstripped his neighbour in taking advantage of the opportunities for profit which were offered by government institutions in a system based on the sale of offices and the farming out of the money-raising activities of the crown. The exciseman was left in no doubt of the fate that awaited him. He faced death at the hands of the rebels and damnation in the other world. He was the scapegoat for public misfortune. Everyone else off-loaded their guilt on to his shoulders and vented their resentment upon him. Naturally the man in the street had no hesitation in making money in just the same way if the chance arose. But he stoutly denied it and condemned anyone who visibly attained the desired objective in the name of public morality. People like to assert their sense of collective identity by harping on the foul and revolting nature of whatever they may perceive as representing the antithesis to themselves. For the seventeenth-century public this antithesis was, precisely, the exciseman.

The punishment of the exciseman

The punishment of the exciseman was, as we have seen, a ritual enacted in every popular rising. One of the principal myths of the tax resistance movement consisted of reports that the taxman had met his just deserts. It was a development which people awaited impatiently.

Everyone agreed that to burden the population with taxes was a sin. The most upright of the French kings were traditionally supposed to have been troubled on their deathbeds by remorse for the dues they had forced their subjects to pay. The earliest such tradition attached to St Louis (Louis IX). This monarch had been obliged to raise a tax in order to provide himself with the means to go on crusade. 'On his deathbed', we are told, 'he expressly commanded the heir to his kingdom, his son Philippe the Fair [error for Philippe the Bold] to remit this tax and to make no further financial imposition upon the people ... He made it plain that his soul was filled with remorse.' Three centuries later Charles IX was said to have repented on his deathbed in a similar fashion.

The myth of the conscience-stricken exciseman was always believed. We may consider, for example, the case of Bullion. Despised and detested in his lifetime, he was supposed to have confided on his deathbed to Louis XIII that Cardinal Richelieu was making war for his own exclusive profit and was devoting all the money in the kingdom to that unworthy cause. Mazarin too was rumoured to have been overcome by guilt in his final agony. He reproached himself, it was said, 'for having plundered the people too much'. Colbert and Louvois were reputed to have left testaments vociferously deploring the various forms of corruption that were practised by government officials. These testaments were, naturally, apocryphal.

But people were not entirely satisfied to think in terms of the exciseman repenting. They preferred to imagine him in torment. The document of 1637 entitled *La Voix du peuple au Roy* demanded nothing less than the most condign punishment for Bullion and Cornuel. The popular hunger for retribution is reflected in an edifying story which spread through the kingdom during Mazarin's ministry. This story was set down by the priest of Saint-Amable, a scholarly man from Limousin of conservative inclinations who was grieved by the death of Richelieu and disposed to blame it on a conspiracy organized by the dissidents of the day. The story went that a relative of Pope Innocent X made use of his connection to get a new tax established in the Papal States. This tax was to be farmed by him personally. After attaining this objective the newly licensed tax-farmer set off for his home. Before he got there, however, his coach was waylaid by a swarthy man with horns. This monstrous assailant strangled him – and vanished.

News of his tragic end ran through Italy like wildfire, and Pope Innocent X revoked the tax. We may learn from this the fate which awaits excisemen, tax-farmers and devisers of new levies. People like these are leeches who feed off the blood of the poor. They are displeasing in the sight of God, and the Lord will consign them for torment to the talons of the King of Hell.

In the period of the Fronde, rebel pamphlets were constantly calling for the punishment of the excisemen. It was one of the commonest demands. 'Sire,' a petition insisted, 'all of your land of France is astounded by their insolence. The people are crying out to you ... and are asking you to render justice upon those persons who have so cruelly sucked their blood and wolfed their entrails through cunning larcenies.' 'What are the Last Things which will befall the man called Mazarin? They are four in number – judgement, torment, death and hell.' 'With a *pistole's* worth of rope (or even less, in my opinion), we could fill the king's coffers to the tune of 20 million *livres*.' The pamphleteers took delight in surveying the history of the kingdom and pointing out instances of the nemesis which had overtaken former 'devisers of new levies'. They cited the names of Enguerrand de Marigny, Pierre Rémy, Jean de Montaigu, Pierre des Essarts and a host of lesser officials who had helped to administer the country's finances – and paid for their corruption with their lives.

By the seventeenth century, however, an offending financial official was seldom sent to the scaffold. Kings no longer cared to indulge their subjects with such edifying spectacles. From this time onwards an official whose activities had given rise to controversy was usually dealt with through some form of out-of-court settlement, and the authorities rarely initiated criminal proceedings against him. In surveying the records of south-west France for this period, we can identify no more than a bare handful of cases in which legal action was brought. One such exceptional case was that of a secretary of the Council named Jean Biou. Biou was sent to Poitou in November 1637 to organize the collection of the army rations tax for that province. The following April he was found to have spent his assignment taking gigantic bribes from the local communities by the carrot-and-stick technique of promising them exemptions while threatening to billet troops in their homes. He was recalled from the province, and the government launched a judicial inquiry into his conduct: matters do not, however, seem to have been carried much farther than that. Action was also taken against an official called Joachim Dubourg who served as tax collector for Saintes. Dubourg was convicted of having tampered with the seals of the tax warrants he received from the *bureau des finances* in order to alter and exaggerate the demands which were made in them. On 31 August 1638 the *cour des aides* in Paris pronounced him unfit to hold a public office, and in September 1643 he was forced to resign his post. A third case was that of Nicolas Tabouret. Tabouret was the official responsible for gathering taxes in Limousin. He discharged his duties with the aid of methods so brutal that the people rose in revolt. On 15 June 1650 Marshal de La Meilleraye met Tabouret at Confolens and put him under arrest. 'He had Tabouret's pony tied by the bridle to the back of his baggage-cart.' Finally there was Jean Pinet. Pinet was an agent employed to gather *aides* and crown duties in Aunis and Saintonge. On 26 July 1661 his activities provoked a disturbance in the city of La Rochelle. He was obliged to take to his heels, but subsequently managed to extract large sums from the city in damages and interest payments. From 1662 to 1668 he served as chief tax collector for Poitou; and this time retribution overtook him. He was found guilty of having embezzled a total of 200,000 *livres* in the course of his posting, and was hanged at Poitiers on 16 May 1670. Insofar as Biou and Pinet had been the objects of rioting before they were brought to justice, the crown was in their two cases setting its seal upon a verdict already arrived at by the general population.

These cases notwithstanding, the practice of offering scapegoats to a vengeful populace would seem, then, to have been abandoned by the seventeenth century. In theory the responsibility for punishing financial officials devolved upon certain specially appointed courts. Special courts of this kind were convened on seven occasions in the reigns of Henri III and Henri IV. In the whole reign of Louis XIII, however, a court sat only once, from 31 October 1624 to 2 June 1625. In the edict they issued in May 1625 to announce the court's dissolution, the government declared that future sessions would be held on a basis of once in ten years. But just when the next court was due to meet, in April 1635, the government cancelled the session. Instead it brought in a new duty to be levied on tax collectors and business people 'by way of exempting them from the setting up of the special court and the inquiries this would entail'. In 1643 the government pre-empted the holding of the next session too, with a view to obtaining an out-of-court settlement from the various financial officials. In the summer of 1648 the country was shaken by a major outbreak of resistance to the taxman. The crown was sufficiently impressed to promise the convening of a new special inquiry into such crimes as might have been committed by the tax collectors. In December 1652, the board that had been entrusted with this investigation was dissolved. Matters changed somewhat after Louis XIV began to rule in his own right. By an edict issued in November 1661 the young king set up a special court and endowed it with an unaccustomed power. The court embarked on a series of proceedings that were not terminated officially until August 1669. Some of the cases it brought to light were distinctly sensational, and a number of sharks were, for practical purposes, ruined. The fines which were handed out by the court to discipline these offenders reached a total of no less than 110 million *livres*. There was scope for the culprits to haggle with the officers sent to fine them, and the amount of money recovered was undoubtedly a good deal smaller than this figure might suggest. This court was, even so, the most effective of all the ones that were convened in the course of the seventeenth century. It sent subcommittees out to the provinces, kept up its activities for five whole years, and was buttressed by the support of a monarch secure in his new-found power.

From May to August 1676 a court was convened to investigate the black market traffic that flourished on the highways and at the wayside halts. This court, however, was quickly superseded by the introduction of a tax to be raised from the chief tax collectors and toll-keepers. Yet another court was summoned at the outset of the regency which held power during the minority of Louis XV. The court sat for just over a year, from 13 March 1716 to 22 March 1717, and imposed no less than 4,410 new taxes on the financial bureaucracy. The sum to be raised amounted to a total of 220 million *livres*. But again the court's decision was implemented only very imperfectly. By 1726 the recovery operations were still unfinished, and only seventy million *livres* had been brought in.[2]

Set up, as they usually were, at the end of a war or the opening of a new reign, special courts of this kind fulfilled an important psychological role. They provided a means by which a government might hope to induce the people to forget the years of privation its campaigns had inflicted upon them, and a king could show himself to be virtuous and concerned for his subjects' well-being. Often the authorities were deliberately seeking to respond to popular aspirations: the courts of 1563, 1577, 1597, 1648, 1661 and 1716 were all convened with this aim in view. Most of the time, however, the only extortioners who were dramatically punished in consequence of the hearings were the small fry. A bailiff, for instance, or a tax-farmer's clerk, might be sentenced to the gallows. After a few months of this severity the courts would stop short and would wind up their proceedings by preparing a roll of taxes to be imposed on the financial officials who had committed the major crimes. Hearings tended, as we have seen, to be held on a regular basis irrespective of whether or not there were any particular incidents that called for investigation. The courts passed what amounted to criminal sentences, only to commute those sentences in a systematic manner into taxes whose rate was agreed on with the defendants by a process of vague and arbitrary compromise. The net result was to dignify the incessant acts of embezzlement with a sort of official recognition.

The people, then, were no longer given the satisfaction of seeing the exciseman punished, and the prospect they awaited had become no more than

2 See Daniel Dessert, *Argent, pouvoir et société au grand siècle*, thesis published by Fayard, Paris, 1984.

a nostalgic dream. The judicial machinery of the state was no longer designed for exacting vengeance, but was instead devoted to the pursuit of what the authorities conceived as the public interest. The punishment of the exciseman was no longer, consequently, an option available under the law, and the people could gratify their appetite for such punishment only at times when riots broke out. 'We see every day', notes one writer, 'the effects of the hate which the people bear for the tax-farmers. There is scarcely a province or town in France where a farmer has not been lynched in the last thirty years.' It is clear from the history of popular uprisings of this period that the danger of such lynchings was very real. The punishment of the exciseman had been dropped from the cognizance of the official legal system and relegated to the domain of customary law. By the seventeenth century it figured only in that body of informal traditions from which the common people selected their penalties. But the implementation of popular law, when it took the form of rebellion, was a fearsome development. We shall now consider the ways in which rebellion was viewed by those who engaged in it.

Myths of rebellion

An act of justice and cleansing

We can arguably look upon the traditions of the people and the standards of conduct enshrined in them as a kind of customary law. In the context of customary law an uprising may be seen as the ultimate penalty. To use the word 'law' in connection with such a rising is, of course, to talk with the wisdom of hindsight. None of the rebels were conscious of asserting any legal rights, and it becomes apparent that they believed their cause to be righteous only when we examine the various ritual acts in which they engaged in the course of the disturbance. Such rituals, as we saw earlier, recur incessantly in contemporary accounts of the revolts. Rioters subjected their victims to the ordeal of mockery in the *charivari* and the ceremonial haling of the exciseman. They set up improvised tribunals and imitated the forms of the regular courts. In May–June 1635 short-lived tribunals of this kind were organized by the insurgents at Bordeaux, Périgueux and Lectoure with a view to deriding or terrorizing the persons brought before them. In 1548 and 1636 the local communes set forth in arms to lay siege to Angoulême. Their intention was to sustain the siege until such time as the citizens should hand over the excisemen and enable the peasants 'to mete out justice to them'. Similar events took place at Cahors in 1624 and 1637. The rebels subjected their victims to the normal judicial practices of the day. The authorities were given, for instance, to executing in effigy offenders whom they had condemned to death *in absentia*; and in just the same way the rebels made symbolic dummies representing the excisemen and hung them on the town gibbets. In 1659 the gibbet which stood in the market square at Libournais was laden with the effigies of rebels sentenced to death by the *cour des aides*. On the night of 12 June, however, a band of insurgents carried the gibbet off and set it up on a new site in front of the tax collector's office. Similar warnings of punishment were given at Saint-Jean-d'Angély and Limoges to merchants who had been speculating in grain. On 8 December 1656 a tax agent who lived at Tonnay-Charente and handled the Convoy tax-farm had his hat knocked off in a brawl. The following day he found it fixed to the local pillory. Beside it was a poster daubed with a series of caricatures. Underneath each sketch was the name of one of the officers employed on the tax-farm. In July 1658 some salt merchants of Marennes were helping to levy the salt tax at their community's expense. One day they all found notices posted up outside their houses. They assumed that these notices referred to themselves. The notices contained a decree purporting to emanate from the Council, 'to the effect that the Council had sentenced these merchants to be hanged'. The rebels concluded their show of legality by dispatching their victims in certain specially designated execution grounds. They drowned them in a particular well, for example, or hanged them from a gibbet in the public square, or flung them into the river which flowed past the town. After the execution they disposed of their victims' remains in the prescribed manner. They quartered their bodies and exposed them, and razed their houses to the ground.

Sometimes the rioters drove the exciseman from their community, and sometimes they put him to death and destroyed his home. In either event they were performing something more than a simple act of justice. The punishment of the exciseman was also a ceremony of purification. The excisemen, as we have seen, were scapegoats for the community as a whole. A pamphlet circulated by the Fronde made the point explicitly. The taxmen, it declared, were 'more laden with sorrows and curses than the scapegoat of the desert'. In addition the exciseman took with him the stain he had inflicted on the community which cast him out. The community was, in effect, conceived of as a virgin whose honour remained inviolate only so long as the world respected the privileges of the town or province concerned. To see this symbolism in operation we need look no further than the mottoes which surrounded the coats of arms of the different towns. Most of these mottoes were composed between the fifteenth and seventeenth centuries, at the dawn of the modern period, when towns still enjoyed their freedoms and the language of heraldry was still fully understood. They reflected the feminine essence of a town which was felt by the citizens to be, at the same time, maternal and vulnerable. The town was thought of as being eternal, protective and sacred like the Virgin who guarded her. Sometimes the mottoes made specific reference to the town's imagined maidenhood. Uzerche, for example, was descrbed as '*Non polluta*', and Bayonne as '*Nunquam polluta*'. Epithets of this kind were of special importance to the citizens. The people of Bayonne made a number of unmistakable allusions to their motto in the course of the protracted struggle they waged against the Convoy tax-farm. In 1625 the town council wrote to Richelieu denouncing the tax-farmers in the following terms: 'The persons embarking on this course are ravishing by devious means that maiden whom our kings have honoured with the title of "unpolluted". They are using these flimsy pretexts to seduce the virgin who was given to David in perpetual maidenhood. And by David I am referring, Your Eminence, to our kings.' Forty years later, in 1665, the town council's delegate Etcheverry used very similar language to plead the cause of Bayonne at court. Assuring Colbert of 'the love and loyalty with which the citizens of Bayonne regard the person and interests of the king', he observed that 'the town has had many suitors, but no one has ever induced her to waver or forced her by open assault. In consequence she has won an irrefutable right to the motto of *Nunquam polluta* which surrounds her coat of arms.' In making such a comparison between town and inviolate maiden the people of this period were using the symbolic languge of heraldry as a way of expressing their world view. It followed that they perceived the punishment of the excisemen who had broken into their town as a process of cleansing. They saw themselves as restoring the integrity of the town's ancient privileges after the intrusion of change. They were seeking refuge in an era when time stood still, and their object was to recreate the vanished world of their ancestors and bury themselves inside it.

The return of the golden age

The delusions harboured by seventeenth-century rebels were powerful ones, and the machinery available to put down their uprisings was sometimes inadequate. Disturbances were consequently apt to take on an optimistic, carefree quality. The riots which broke out at Agen on 28 May 1635, at Bourg-sur-Gironde in July the same year, at Bourges in January 1636, at Bordeaux in 1651, at Lalbenque-en-Quercy on 20 April 1695 and at Guéret on 2 June 1705 were all accompanied by singing and dancing. We may note that the riot at Bordeaux broke out in the carnival season. It is clear from the regularity with which the authorities moved to ban carnival festivities and Midsummer bonfire nights in periods of unrest that a masquerade could turn into a riot on the slightest provocation. Police reports drawn up in the aftermath of a riot sometimes note that the offenders had worn masks or other disguises. They put their hats on inside out, or fastened false beards over their mouths or black velvet masks around their eyes. The most common disguise was for a man to slip into a woman's bonnet and skirt. Masks were worn either to conceal a person's identity or to frighten or amuse the passers-by. Usually the masker was animated by the simple desire to avoid the prying eyes of spectators who might give evidence against him while he proceeded to paralyse his victims with the fear of the unknown. Such, at least, was the evident intention of the masked rioters who ran amok at Loudun in May 1637, Castillonnès in May 1641, Plaisance on 22 June 1642, Tulle in May 1644 and Fontenay on 28 June 1659; of the 'Invisibles' who troubled the Chalosse region in 1663–5; and of the rebels who rampaged in disguise through Clermont-Ferrand in August 1692 and Montmorillon in February 1707. But the comic side of masking may also have played a part on some of these occasions. The maskers would select an appropriate target for ridicule. The infuriated victim would not know whom to lash out at, and would consequently turn into the carnival sourpuss whom everyone loved to deride.

Riots, like festivals, created a break in the monotony of daily life. The rioters swept away the nightmare of the impending *gabelle* which had brooded over their town. They drove off the parasites who had revelled in the public misery, and drew their community together once more in the shadow of the bell tower.

Wine flowed like water, and the people danced for joy. The outbreak of rioting had given them a fleeting taste of Utopia. Within hours, or days at most, they would be jolted back to reality; but so long as the interlude lasted they felt that the golden age had returned.

Prophetic writings had circulated foretelling this epoch-making upheaval, this unlooked-for restoration of lost content. One of the leaders of the Croquant rising which broke out in Quercy in 1624 had actually been a caster of horoscopes.[3] No less than two prophetic documents emanated from the revolt of the *Nu-Pieds* in Normandy. The first was a poem entitled *À La Normandie* and the second a work called the *Dialogue de Jean Nu-Pieds*. This dialogue contained the lines,

> I shall restore, in a word, the freedom we used to see
> To Holy Mother Church, to nobles and peasantry.
> I shall bring back, I say, the conditions we used to know
> In the golden age of Louis the Twelfth a hundred years ago.

A quatrain purporting to derive from the *Centuries* of Nostradamus and apparently predicting a Croquant victory gained wide currency during the rebellion which raged in Rouergue in 1643. The quatrain ran,

> In Guyenne in sixteen forty-three
> The great by the small shall vanquished be.
> Gold straw and jabbing fork shall each
> Drain out the blood from the biting leech.[4]

At the time when the Fronde held Bordeaux a priest with 'mathematical' pretensions claimed to have seen in the stars that Bordeaux was going to become a 'mighty republic'. This claim was succeeded by a prophecy of Poitevin origin. The prophet foretold how the minority of a boy king would be troubled by a series of dreadful calamities. At the height of these trials, however, 'the lion will drive off the wolf ... You will be comforted, poor people, but more than that, it will be a pleasant time. Your king will be upright in all his works and will toil full hard to set up good laws again.'[5] The prospect of peace with Spain encouraged the soothsayers to combine two separate pieces of fantasy: the myth of no more taxes and the myth of a new golden age. The peace treaty of 1660 and the young king's Habsburg marriage were

---

3 This Croquant leader of 1624 was a man named Douat. He is said to have been 'a keen practitioner of physiognomy and palm-reading, who dabbled in horoscopes'. See *Mercure françois*, 1624, p. 473.

4 The *Centuries* of Nostradamus were frequently adapted to fit such contemporary events as the Huguenot wars and the wars of the Fronde. See Geneviève Bollème, *Les Almanachs populaires aux 17e et 18e siècles: essai d'histoire sociale*, École Pratique des Hautes Études, Livre et Sociétés 3, Paris, 1969, pp. 17–21.

5 *Prophétie curieuse et remarquable d'un certain Rouallon ...*, 1652. The publisher who disseminated this prophecy maintained that it was composed in 1480. The prophet anticipated that various misdeeds would be committed by a 'great rake'. The publisher explained this as Richelieu, 'who raked in everything'. The prophet also foretold the advent of two boy kings who would stray far and wide through their kingdom. The publisher noted that this should be taken as referring to the minorities of Louis XIII and Louis XIV.

seen as tokens of returning prosperity. A writer of anagrams based on the sovereign's name predicted, '*Le vieus royaume de France qu'on admire sera tout d'or*', ('The ancient and admired realm of France will be solid gold').

People waited nostalgically for the return of a mythical past. They located this past in the reign of a king with a legendary reputation for justice. The specific choice of reign varied from one generation to another. The myth was originally associated, as one might expect, with the reign of the good St Louis (Louis IX). In his time, it was believed, there had been no taxes whatever. '*Tailles*, fortunately, were unknown, and no one had the least idea what was meant by taxes, excise or extortions.' People in the sixteenth century looked back to the time of Louis XII. Taxpayers demanded that the government should reduce their assessments 'to what they were paying in the time of the late King Louis'. In the seventeenth century paradise was felt to have been lost at the moment when Henri IV was assassinated in 1610. The Croquants who rose in rebellion in Périgord and Rouergue, the *Nu-Pieds* of Normandy and the delegates from the estates who drew up petitions to the crown in 1649–51 all shared this assumption. They wanted to see a general return to the conditions which had prevailed under Henri IV – in the sums to be raised in taxes, the numbers of officials assigned to collect them, and the ordinances on which the tax system was based. These people were not simply waiting for a miraculous restoration of past prosperity. They were also filled with a latent hatred of anything new. The *jurats* of Bordeaux were well aware of this attitude. 'The masses here', they acknowledged, 'are naturally intolerant of any kind of change.' All the popular risings of the period showed this tendency to resist the new-fangled operations of the state. Ordinary people were distressed at the way in which the symbols and values of traditional society were getting disparaged and phased out. They wanted to resume their ties with an older order of things.

Popular violence and the self-image of the people

Even when a rising was bolstered by the assistance of local dignitaries, it remained essentially a popular act. The rebels derived their strength from sheer weight of numbers. The upheaval was accompanied by violence of the crudest kind, and it brought to the fore individuals whom society ordinarily held in the deepest contempt. We may detect from time to time in the accounts of these violent interludes the outlines of a genuine popular power centre with methods and traditions of its own.

Risings which broke out in cities threw up a number of ringleaders. Previously unknown leaders rose to prominence in the course of the secret discussions which took place in shops and taverns and the seditious meetings which were held in broad daylight in the open space afforded by a churchyard or a public square. Innkeepers or master craftsmen were elected to captain the rebel bands. They set up barricades and placed themselves at the head of companies formed by the town's artisans or the local householders. When the rising seemed about to collapse in the face of general apathy and fear of government reprisals, a core of diehards would also emerge from the ranks of the population to make an unexpected last-ditch stand. These diehards no longer had any hope of help from the leading citizens. Instead desperation drove them to the suicidal tactics of setting the town on fire and lynching the magistrates. Such extremism was typical of the people. They clung to the legends which circulated in the world of tax resistance, and preferred to die rather than to lose a traditional freedom or submit to a *gabelle*. Educated observers described these attitudes as 'delusions of the rabble'.

Revolts in the countryside invariably began with parish assemblies. Following these meetings the dissidents sent out circular letters with a view to convening assemblies on an altogether larger scale. Their envoys went round the district from village to village seeking to persuade the local communities to side with the rebel cause. The rebels maintained that their proceedings were wholly lawful. They invoked the memory of the provincial estates which had met at earlier periods, and cited the permission which a governor or supreme court was supposed to have given them, or actually had given them in a fit of absence of mind. The legality of their assemblies was further proved, as they saw it, by their appointment of syndics or delegates whose function would be to undeceive the king and to open his eyes to their plight. They had risen up purely, they claimed, in response to exceptional circumstances: their sole objective had been to attract the king's attention and to ensure that justice was meted out to the excisemen who had fled to the shelter of the towns. These risings also threw up leaders in the form of parish captains. If the local seigneur or parish priest was unwilling to play that role, the peasants would elect someone who was reasonably well travelled, like a lawyer who had pleaded cases in a nearby town, an innkeeper with the gift of the gab, or a veteran who was used to giving orders.

Police reports often allude to the weapons the rebels carried. A glance at these references is enough to show how precarious the rebel prospects were. The weapons insurgents carried scarcely varied from province to province or even from one century to another. They were typical weapons of the people, and an obvious reminder of the essentially popular nature of the risings in which they were used. The weapons used by the people fell into three broad types. They had small quantities of firearms, iron implements, and sticks. On days when disturbances erupted the rioters generally produced a variety of weapons which had been left over from the wars of the previous generation such as arquebuses, halberds and partisans. In addition they had a certain amount of more up-to-date equipment which the verterans among them had hidden in their village when they returned from the king's campaigns. Quite a large number of ploughmen had muskets, and some were even the owners of pistols and guns. They used these to guard their houses and to engage in either poaching or any hunting the local seigneur might deign to tolerate. Town-dwellers also had firearms. They carried them proudly in the guild processions and the parades of the city militia. When rebellion broke out, consequently, the popular forces were never short of musketeers. They posted them on their barricades or stationed them at the head of their companies.

Rioters in the cities were most likely to brandish the tools of their trade.

Butchers snatched up their cleavers, watermen their boat-hooks and shoe-makers their fleshing knives. Tanners and curriers, coopers and carpenters all had recourse to their assorted 'ironmongery'. Peasants wielded two-pronged pitchforks and also *hachereaux* – hatchets with small blades fixed to handles four or five feet long. The great majority of the Croquants, however, had only sticks. Every peasant carried an iron-shod club or cudgel or staff. The weapon was made by hardening a stick in the fire and fastening an iron cap to each end. This 'double-ended stick' became something of a symbol of peasant life. It was constantly mentioned by observers. Montaigne, for example, reported in his *Journal de voyage* how he had seen the peasants in one of the villages he visited vying with each other in contests that tested their skill in wielding the dagger, the falchion, the two-handed sword – and the double-ended stick. Ability to handle the stick was the peasant equivalent of swordsmanship. A chronicler of Libourne tells a typical story. In the winter of 1660, he records, the Dordogne was frozen over, and the people of Libourne organzed a skating competition. In the course of this competition a burgess who was serving as captain of one of the districts in the town gave a display of prowess with the double-ended stick. The feature of this episode which impressed the chronicler was the fact that a burgess should have been so skilled in using a peasant weapon. The double-ended stick was a real hallmark of rural insurrection.

For offensive purposes the peasants relied on 'long stakes' and 'burnt poles'. They also wielded *gallebots*, staves which were normally drawn between the legs of cows to hobble them, and *volants*, or long sticks which were used in liming birds. The peasant weapon most commonly referred to by observers apart from the double-ended stick was the back-hafted scythe, or in other words a sickle whose blade was fixed in the handle in such a way that its cutting edge faced outwards. We find the process referred to in our sources as *manglar* (hafting) the *oun gaje* (iron). The name for the weapon varied in differnt regions. In Marche it was known as a *gouyard*, in Angoumois as a *cerceau* or *gibot*, in Périgord as a *gibot* and in Guyenne and Gascony as a *daille*.

Rebels also had their own songs. We learn from our sources that seditious songs were sung in the course of the popular risings which took place in 1643 in the town of Espalion and in 1665 at Bayonne. We know nothing more about these songs except that the one in vogue at Bayonne was known as 'the song of Audijos'. It was sung in the streets and taverns, and the authorities were eventually goaded into banning it.[6] The Croquants are traditionally supposed to have launched their revolts to the sound of mournful ballads. Collections of these ballads were compiled in Périgord in the early nineteenth century. The antiquarians who published them referred to a number of specific peasant sources such as a group of young people in Lalinde and a sharecropper in Brantôme. The material contributed by these particular informants consisted of a lament composed in the low Gascon dialect on the death of Marshal de Biron. The ballad related how on the eve of Biron's execution his master, Henri IV, was overcome with remorse and went to visit his former comrade-

6 Ordinance issued by the aldermen of Bayonne on 15 May 1665.

in-arms in the Bastille. The marshal reminded the king how he had once used his body to shield him when they were on campaign together in Piedmont. A summarizing couplet observed that kings forgot the blood which was spilt for them, but many counts and barons, gentlemen and ladies grieved for the death of Biron. The song concluded by calling on the entire province of Gascony to rise in revolt in his memory:

> In Biron's chapel, brothers,
> Let all of us arise.
> Let's pray for both father and son, and spread
> Their glory far and wide.[7]

There is no real way of checking either the authenticity of this ballad or the accuracy with which the text has been handed down; but the language is so obscure and ambiguous that a forgery seems unlikely.

We may gain some additional insights into the nature of these popular risings through considering the names by which the rebels described themselves. We can start by clearing up the obscurity surrounding the word 'croquant' which was so often used to refer to rebellious peasants. This epithet was never claimed by the peasants themselves. It was a name which contemporaries used to insult and ridicule them.

A 'croquant' meant a rebel peasant. Specifically, it meant a rebel peasant in south-west France. The word was first used in this sense at the time of the rebellion which broke out in Périgord in 1594. Subsequently it was applied to the peasants who rose up in Quercy in 1624, in Angoumois in 1636, in Périgord and in Quercy again in 1637, in Gascony in 1639–43, in Rouergue in 1643, in Limousin in 1650, and in Agenais, finally, in 1652. That, however, is as far as the catalogue goes. After the Agenais rising the usage disappears. 'Croquant' was never used, for example, as a term for the peasants who revolted in Quercy in 1707, even though this rising was characterized by much the same features as the peasant movements of earlier decades.

The term 'croquant' broadened over time to include not merely a rebel peasant but every kind of riff-raff. 'Croquants of Bordeaux,' demanded an orator in 1649, 'are you afraid of battle?' The expression also came to mean a rustic pure and simple. We meet it already in this sense in a pamphlet written in 1615 to denounce the rebellion of the Prince de Condé. The writer quotes the sententious opinions of a typical peasant he refers to as 'the croquant of Poitou'. We also meet this usage in the *Fables* of La Fontaine. The *Fables* became so famous that they gave the word a new lease of life.

There is no doubt the word was used pejoratively right from the start. A chronicler in Villefranche wrote of the rebels of 1594, 'They styled themselves the *Tard Avisés*, but more law-abiding people called them Croquants.' The amnesty granted after the rising of 1637 declared how 'this multitude had taken up arms and gathered together under the infamous name of Croquants

---

7 Lament for Biron. Collected at Lalinde in 1835, this song was published in 1837 in *La Mosaïque du Midi*. In 1876 it was reprinted in the *Bulletin de la société historique et archéologique du Périgord*, p. 167: the name given in this version, however, is Bourbon rather than Biron.

– a name well suited to the vile and shameful rebellion which they had mounted with such pernicious and criminal aims'. The peasants who rose up in Angoumois in 1636 murdered a craftsman from one of the towns there who was rash enough to call them Croquants.

The word 'croquant' lent itself readily to fanciful derivatives. A glance at these derivatives suggests that they too were coined in a spirit of contemptuous satire. In a letter of 1637, for instance, Jean Fournier, the functionary who served as official solicitor for Cardinal Richelieu in his duchy of Fronsac, referred to a gathering of Croquants as a *crocquandaille*. The intendant Charreton used the word *croquandage* to describe the crime of rebellion or involvement in sedition. Hosten, a city clerk of Bordeaux, coined the term *croquantisme* in one of his letters as a nickname for the rebels' aspirations and general outlook. An account of the rising in Quercy in 1624 called the rebel outlook *croquanterie*.

The sudden vogue for the term 'croquant' in 1594 aroused widespread curiosity. Many writers puzzled over the origins of the word. Chilhaud, the author of memoirs from Périgord, and Mézeray, the historian, followed the chroniclers de Thou and Palma Cayet in maintaining that the word 'croquant' derived from an accusation which the peasants used to hurl at the warrior gentry. The peasants complained that the gentry liked 'to crunch (*croquer*) the poor country people between their teeth and gobble them up'. When they drove out marauding soldiery the peasants accordingly shouted, 'Down with the crunchers (croquants)!' Subsequently their enemies appropriated the nickname for use against them. It could even have been that the peasant assemblies had created such havoc in their turn that this synonym for plunderers seemed the obvious name to call them. De Thou remarks that 'the word "Croquants" is used in vulgar parlance to describe people who gobble up all that lies in their path' ('obvia cuncta devorantes in vulgari dicterio *Crocans* vocarentur.') Chilhaud records that the peasants 'engaged in looting and violence everywhere they went. They were known as Croquants because they swallowed up all the plunder they could lay their hands on.'

Other proposed etymologies were even more bizarre. The philologist Ménage believed that the peasant rebels were known as Croquants 'because they were poor country people who were unable to sign their names when asked to do so. All they could do was to scrawl a tick (*crochet*) or a cross (*croix*) with their heavy fists.' The scholar Moreri claimed that the word had its origins in the fame of a certain Crocas, 'king of the Alemanni. He marched into Gaul in AD 260, and plundered and ravaged Auvergne, Gévaudan and other regions.'

One popular explanation was advanced by the historian d'Aubigné, as well as by Tarde, who recorded the details of the Périgord rising of 1594, and the Villefranche chronicler. These writers all derived the word from the simple fact that the first assembly of rebel peasants met in a place called Crocq. D'Aubigné claimed that Crocq was a village in Limousin near Saint-Yrieix-la-Perche; the Villefranche chronicler, however, located it in the viscountcy of Turenne. 'The rebels first rose up', he informs us, 'in the town called Crocq which is situated in the viscountcy of Turenne . . . Later on the other peasants followed the example which had been set by their fellows in Crocq, and this was why they were known as Croquants.'

The town clerk of Périgueux insists similarly in his *Gros livre noir* that all the earliest outbreaks of peasant resistance at this period took place on the lands of the Viscount of Turenne. He even maintains that the viscount instigated the risings himself. A writer of memoirs in Limousin who is known as the Anonymous Chronicler of Saint-Léonard makes the same point in his *Chronique*. This connection between the Croquants and the small town of Crocq is a surprising one, on the face of it; but it is one which nevertheless deserves serious consideration in view of the general support it receives from contemporary narrative sources. The town of Crocq is not, in fact, associated with a specific outbreak of violence in any surviving description of the 1594 revolt. It was at least 50 kilometres away from the epicentre of the upheaval in Limousin, and communications were poor. On the other hand it is true that the people of Crocq were known as Croquants. It is also true that the Viscounts of Turenne had been the seigneurs of the town since 1460, and had actually borne the title of Baron de Crocq for about half a century by the time the *Tard Avisés* rebelled. We may note that Crocq was, in one respect, strategically situated, lying as it did on the borders of the three provinces of Auvergne, Limousin and Marche. It was close to the communes of Marche; and we know that these communes, at least, played an active part in the rising of 1594. Finally there is some evidence that a tradition of rebellion persisted in Crocq in the following century. Tax collection came to a complete halt in the area during the troubles of 1637. The tax collector for the *élection* of Guéret lodged a complaint with the Council, reporting that 'neither sergeants nor bowmen are prepared to venture into the mountains any more . . . They are particularly reluctant to go to La Mazière and the other parishes *in the Croquant league.*' The reference is plainly to Crocq. La Mazière, or La Mazière-aux-Bons-Hommes, to give it its full name, was one of a cluster of ten or twelve villages which dotted the little valley of the Tardes; and Crocq was the heart of the cluster.[8]

To satisfy ourselves that this etymology might have some substance, we must first of all pause to consider the history of Crocq, and the circumstances which prevailed there at the time when the 1594 rising began. We may start by noting that Crocq was a mountain town. The climate was cold, and the nearest roads were a long way off. The surrounding landscape varied from wooded plateaux and moorlands where the peasants pastured their sheep to forest pools and low-lying meadows where the cattle grazed in the summer. Most people in the region lived cheek by jowl in sizeable villages, and great stretches of forest and tableland were entirely uninhabited. Winters were long and bitter. Even at this early date the peasants were tending to emigrate in search of work on a temporary or seasonal basis. The population conversed

---

8 La Mazière-aux-Bons-Hommes was located at what is now Creuse in the canton of Crocq. The 'Bons Hommes' were some monks from Grandmont who lived in seclusion in a nearby château.

in the Auvergnat dialect of *langue d'oc*, and spent their leisure hours dancing the traditional *bourrée* and *montagnarde* to the sound of the bagpipes and the hurdy-gurdy.

The town of Crocq was built upon an easily defended site 768 metres above sea-level. This site had been fortified as early as the twelfth century by the *dauphin* of Auvergne. The town had consuls of its own, and annual fairs had been held there for quite a long time. A château with two round towers rose up alongside, and the town was enclosed by a rampart with four gates. Within the walls was a square separating the town church from the château. Four or five streets climbed the slope of the hill on which the town stood, and each street was provided with deep wells to enable the population to draw water from under the slope. In 1594 the affairs of the town were dominated by Henri de La Tour d'Auvergne, Viscount of Turenne and Baron de Crocq. For the past nineteen years Turenne had been the leader of the Protestant faction in Limousin. He maintained in the château at his own expense a garrison and a captain to command it. From time to time troops of the Catholic League in the service of the Duke of Nemours had camped on the outskirts of the town; but rival forces rubbed shoulders in this way in every part of the kingdom. Crocq, in other words, was no more than one of a thousand fortified townships to be found at this period in the provinces of central and south-west France.

This seemingly ordinary place, however, had one conspicuous feature. Contemporary administrators included Crocq in a portion of the map they referred to as the *Pays de franc-alleu*. This *Pays* encompassed, in addition to Crocq, some twenty other parishes in the Combraille region such as La Mazière, Bellegarde and Mainsat. The term *Pays de franc-alleu* was never used in the fiscal documents of the late sixteenth century to denote an administrative district. It was nothing more than a long-established place name for a very specific part of the countryside. We find the name mentioned for the first time in a tax assessment dating from as early as 1435. *Franc-alleu* was generally a word used in feudal law to describe a territory whose inhabitants were free of any obligation to pay homage to a seigneur. In this context, however, it meant simply that this particular group of parishes had tax-free status. *Pays de franc-alleu* was, in fact, a misnomer. The term had no basis in law, but was merely an invention of the local people. Even the tax-free status to which they were laying claim was *de facto* rather than *de jure*. It was the consequence of a series of tax exemptions which the authorities had repeatedly accorded to the district over a period of more than seventy years. The concessions had been prompted by the fact that the district lay, at that period, in a vulnerable frontier zone.

In 1357 the district of Crocq was ravaged by Anglo-Gascon soldiers in the first of a series of devastating raids. The French kings responded to these raids with incessant grants of tax relief, 'seeing', as they put it, 'that the town of Crocq is located close to the borders of Guyenne, and that this region of Guyenne has always been exposed to the aggression of our enemies in England'. The people of the district grew accustomed to paying no taxes, and as time went on they began to assume that this tax-free status was theirs by right. By 1438 they were voicing this assumption explicitly in a complaint to the government. 'They protested shrilly', says the chronicler,

about the injuries they had suffered lately at the hands of a number of mercenaries who had stayed a long while in their district. At the same time they pointed out that they were entitled to certain privileges which had been accorded to their forefathers by the late kings of France. By virtue of these privileges they were paying no taxes, *aides* or levies, and were under no obligation to do so either.

The town and district of Crocq, then, were endowed at a very early date with privileges in the form of consuls and fairs. They were granted tax exemptions consistently enough to enable them to evolve, over time, into a tax-free entity, and to coin for themselves a place name which expressed that freedom. Finally they were protected over the centuries by a series of extremely powerful families such as the Counts of Auvergne, the seigneurs of Peschier, the Viscounts of Turenne and (subsequent to the 1594 revolt) the Marquis d'Effiat. The people of Crocq felt that they had inherited from their ancestors and held in trust for their children a very special right. They conceived of their district as a unique area where freedom prevailed and taxation was not to be tolerated. We can appreciate in the light of such a distinctive historical and psychological background how the revolt of 1594 might have started in this canton, and how the contingents of rebel peasants in other provinces might have derived the name which was used to label them from this isolated town.

We may note in passing that this theory identifying Crocq as the region of the Croquants ties up, to a certain extent, with the far-fetched etymology which Moreri proposed. The town of Crocq was traditionally supposed to have been named after a Vandal king called Crocus or Crocas, who pitched camp in the area in 408 while he was ravaging the surrounding provinces. Another baleful figure with a closely similar name appears in the pages of Froissart. Froissart relates in his *Chroniques* how a number of strongholds were seized in the course of 1348 by bandit chieftains who proceeded to use them as bases for terrorizing the neighbourhood. 'And these chieftains included', he tells us, 'a man called Crokart who had risen from humble origins.' Crokart's companions chose him to lead their band. He fought with the English in Brittany, made a fortune in ransom money and stormed any number of towns and châteaux only to meet an undignified end by falling from his horse. 'I do not know what became of either his riches or his soul, but I know for a certainty that this was the end of Crockers [Crokart].' We should not need to dwell on this story if an unexpected allusion had not been made to it two centuries later. In 1594 the deputy seneschal of Cahors, Antoine de Peyrusse, made a speech before the assembled estates of Quercy. In the course of his speech he addressed himself rhetorically to the rebel multitude. 'I urge you', he cried, 'to hold in loathing this vile name of Croquant which the world is giving you. It reminds me of a page-boy called Crokart who set himself up as chief of a band of English brigands. Large numbers of those brigands appeared in our region.' There are, of course, no serious grounds for supposing that the word 'croquant' had any connection with either Crocas or Crokart. At the same time the readiness with which people at the time of the peasant risings alluded to these men cannot be wholly disregarded. It was no accident that they remembered these two pillagers of bygone times, each of whom had grown fearsome for a season before disappearing into wretched obscurity. The impression the Croquants made on observers was a pitiful one, and their name evoked only pathetic associations.

We have still not exhausted the possible etymologies of 'croquant'. There was a kind of cudgel known as a *croc*, from the Latin *crocus*. The same word is also found in the variant forms *croquet* and *croquebois*. The scholar du Cange quotes some fourteenth-century texts in which the *croc* is alluded to as the regular peasant staff. Peasants are depicted as using the *croc* to fight each other or gather their flocks. 'The grape pickers set down their baskets and exchanged several blows with the *croques* which they used to support the baskets and various other sticks.' 'The shepherd caught up a *croquet* and rounded up his sheep.' The verb *croquer* meant to hit something with a *croc* – to lop off branches, for example. In Guyenne the people employed to remove the bodies of plague victims were known as *crocs* or *croque-morts* after the iron-shod staff which they used to drag the corpses along. We can see, in this context, that a 'croquant' could well have meant a peasant armed with a stick, even though this usage is not attested in any dictionary. Possibly the 'Crokart' of Froissart was not a name at all, but a nickname referring either to the bandit's rustic appearance or his skill at wielding a staff. By the same token it might be conjectured that the word 'croquant' was neither more nor less than a joke designed to make fun of the peasant bands that were raised by the Viscount of Turenne. The term would have alluded both to the viscount's title of Baron de Crocq and the rustic appearance of his troops. I will conclude this lengthy digression by proposing that the word 'croquant' conceals two different layers of meaning. On the one hand a croquant was a peasant wielding a *croc*. On the other hand it referred to the people of the town of Crocq, who had either risen in rebellion or were generally held to have done so. These two meanings merged unobtrusively in contemporary minds, and the result was a word which conveyed, *par excellence*, the idea of a rebel peasant.

The rebels described themselves by names of a rather different kind. They spoke of themelves as the Third Estate, as the countryside and above all as the assembled or rebel communes. Their leaders referred to themselves in a variety of ways. The men who led the rising against the salt tax in 1548 were described as captains of the communes and colonels of the provinces. The great Périgord rebellion of 1637 was directed by self-styled generals of the ruined poor. In Normandy two years later the rebels were headed by generals of the army of suffering, and in Vivarais in 1670 generals of the oppressed population were in command. The rebels of 1548 were also known as *pitauds*. *Pitaud*, like 'croquant', was a word with pejorative overtones. A *pitaud* was a peasant, an oaf, a ridiculous figure with rustic manners who spoke in a thick country dialect. Ronsard declares at one point in 'Les Amours de Cassandre',

I would I were a mere village *pitaud*
Dull, without reason or intelligence.

By the seventeenth century, at all events, this term was obsolete. The rebels of south-west France called themselves by only one name with any consistency. That name was *Tard Avisés*. First mentioned by our sources in 1594, it was used by assemblies of rebel peasants in every part of the region, from Marche to Périgord. Forty years later it was revived in a rebel 'ordinance' which circulated in Angoumois in 1636 and Périgord in 1637. One of the rebel leaders responsible for organising the massacre of the guards of the Duke of Saint-Simon at Coutras in 1656 was known as the *Tard Avisat* captain. The name *Tard Avisés* was used above all by the peasants of Quercy who rose up in 1707 in the final episode of this cycle of insurrections. In choosing this name ('Out-of-dates') the peasants drew attention to their long-suffering endurance of hardship while acknowledging that they were ill-informed people, out of touch with the news. They declared their own shortcoming, and by so doing asserted their collective identity all the more strongly.

We may catch a further glimpse of the popular character by examining the conventional nicknames which were bestowed on some of the ringleaders. An innkeeper in Poitiers got called 'Jack Flour' (Jean Farine), and a ploughman from the Île de France was nicknamed 'Cornstore' (Sauvegrain). The leader of the communes of Angoumois, Estancheau, was known as 'Captain Clog' (le capitaine La Galoche). A Poitiers currier was referred to as 'Captain Barelegs' (le capitaine Va-Nu-Jambes). He was an exact contemporary of the celebrated 'Captain Jack Barefoot' (Jean Nu-Pieds) from Lower Normandy. A leader of the riot which broke out at Tours in November 1643 was called 'Captain Woodsoles' (le capitaine Sabot). The rising which flared up in Rouergue in May 1643 brought to prominence a saddler from Villefranche who was commonly known as 'Fork' (Lafourche), and a country mason and tavern-keeper called 'Straw' (Lapaille). Finally, the peasants who rose in revolt in Benauge in December 1661 took their orders from a villager who went by the name of 'Captain Straw' (le capitaine Lapaille).

These nicknames bear a striking resemblance to the *noms de guerre* which are known to have been given to soldiers by the recruiting sergeants or non-commissioned officers who enrolled them in the regular armies. The choice of such sobriquets was traditionally limited to names of plants such as 'Rose' and 'Flower' (Larose and Lafleur), items of equipment like 'Forge' and 'Needle' (Laforge and Laiguille), personal characteristics such as 'First Strike', 'No Quarter', 'Liberty', 'Justice' and 'No Regrets' (Frappe d'abord, Sans Quartier, La Franchise, La Justice, Sans Regret), and a few other categories. A contemporary monologue which was written on this subject in Médoc mentions two *noms de guerre* very close to 'Straw' and 'Fork'. The monologue depicts a sergeant presenting recruits to his captain. The sergeant suggests a name for each of the men. The names include 'First Strike', 'Branches' (Larameye), 'Greenery' (Laverdure), 'Straw Pallet' (La Paillasse) and 'Pitchfork' (Lafourcade). Rebel nicknames seem, consequently, to have been invented in much the same way as *noms de guerre*. The handful of nicknames which are recorded for rebel leaders, however, are not to be found in the long lists of *noms de guerre* which have been preserved in the recruitment registers. This tends to confirm that the rebel nicknames were original ones.

We may carry our analysis a step further by observing that these superficially peculiar nicknames like 'Barefoot', 'Barelegs', 'Clog' and 'Woodsoles' are, in fact, very obvious allusions to the distinctive features of a peasant's appearance. The average labourer in the fields wore neither boots nor shoes. Such articles were expensive, and to possess them was a first sign that a man had made his fortune and had risen above the mass of the rural poor. In the picturesque language of the sixteenth century, a peasant was known not only as a *pitaud*, but also as a 'dusty-foot' (*pied-gris*). This usage reflects the extent to which rustics were traditionally thought of as going barefoot; and we may accordingly deduce that the rebel leaders were given nicknames symbolic of the peasant condition.

It is also worth pausing a moment to consider the nickname 'Straw'. People in the seventeetnh century wore wisps of straw as tokens by which they could be identified. In 1637, for instance, the general of the communes of Périgord, La Mothe-La-Forest, wore a piece of straw in his hat. In 1652 during the second phase of the Fronde, the partisans of the princes sported small button-holes of straw in both Paris and Bordeaux. There was even a brotherhood of 'Knights of the Straw'.

Straw was a symbol of the daily life of the people. As such it figured in the imagery of the countryside in many parts of Europe, including England, Germany, Flanders, Picardy and south-west France. Its connotations were obvious and universally known. A twist of straw could take many different forms, and the words which referred to it were legion. People spoke, for example, of armfuls of straw, of rags and bushes and brands, of squares and banners and scarecrows. In England they talked of *wisps*. In Poitou people alluded to a straw *chapeau* or *chapel*, in Picardy to an *escouve* or *escoive*, and in Gascony to an *empaillou*. In some places a twist of straw was used for the same purpose as a *may*. On these occasions it was put up to indicate either the boundary of a jurisdiction, the inn or common which served as the seat of the jurisdiction where the local judge held his assizes, or the gallows where justice was meted out. It was used to mark a city's limits and to designate, by the same token, the borders within which the seigneur could enforce his authority, strangers could seek asylum and merchants could take advantage of the freedoms and privileges the town enjoyed. Elsewhere a twist of straw was liable to be used for the bush which served as a tavern sign. The original purpose of the bush was to bung up the hole in a barrel. By hanging it above his door the landlord indicated that the barrel was open and passers-by were invited to drink and dine. The twist of straw might also be set alight as a firebrand on Brand Sunday, the first Sunday in Lent, when the weeds were swept together and burnt on a bonfire. People believed that anyone who drew near this bonfire might be cured of whatever ailments were afflicting him. Finally the twist of straw could serve as the torch or staff of justice which was used to 'brand' a confiscated estate. The first step in this process was to confiscate the harvest as it was gathered. After that a sergeant set twists of straw up at either end of the field to 'put a ban on the estate'. Generally speaking, a twist of straw was tied to a hedge or a tree-trunk to mark a boundary. It was used to delimit the common territories agreed on in the conventions which were negotiated between the people of two adjacent seigniories. It also served to identify communal mills and bakehouses, and to indicate the area of common land where people were at liberty to let their livestock roam. At harvest-time it informed villagers that the crops on the lord's land were not yet gathered and the left-overs, consequently, could not yet be gleaned. Sometimes the peasants were forced to perform certain kinds of labour service as soon as the harvest was in, and in this event the question of access to the gleanings was a matter of life or death.

In every region the twist of straw acquired this complex of uses. We can only presume that it had become something more than a mere sign. It was also a symbol. It stood for the right of the populace to enjoy a certain *freedom*, either by asserting the existence of that freedom or by marking out its limits. It formed part of a rustic language that was instantly understandable, and constituted a typical piece of peasant imagery. The step from symbol to myth is only a short one. It was natural that straw should become a recognised Croquant emblem.

Walking in clogs or barefoot and pitching the straw were quintessential features of life in the countryside; and the peasant bands consequently used them as the insignia of their revolts.

We can, then, identify a way of life and mode of conduct peculiar to the peasant rebels. It was reflected in the proceedings of their assemblies, in their choice of weapons and songs, in the imagery of their manifestos and the myths which they wove in their hatred of the taxman. Finally it was reflected in the names they gave each other when the rising broke out. The people of the communes made a conscious decision to adopt and abide by this characteristic style. They were fully aware that they stood for a distinctive culture and an independent social force. We may say that our study of the rebellions reveals the existence of a kind of 'People's Power'.

The mass of the rural population play little or no part in a state's political history. As a result historians seldom trouble to take an interest in the peasantry as such. They are content to examine nothing more than the way in which their societies have evolved. In exploring this subject they are aided by the wisdom of hindsight. Few of them can contain the sense of superiority which they derive from the simple fact of knowing what happened in later years. They are also puffed up by their faith in whatever ideologies and schools of thought may be prevalent in their time.

Common people in the seventeenth century knew little of the world outside their basic social unit, the hamlet and parish in the countryside, the street and district in the town. It was only rarely they played a part in a larger organization by joining, say, a political party or religious sect. Even when they did their concern was rather to express their knee-jerk hostility to an increase in taxes or an extension of state control than to engage in the building of any kind of new political order. We must take their environment as we find it. Any attempt to bring some sense of predestined historical progress to bear on their society can only lead us to interpret it in a simplistic or disparaging way. Free of such preconceptions we may perceive that the world of these commoners had none the less an unmistakable freshness and flavour of its own. They were fired by what I have just described as a sense of People's Power.

Hotbeds of insurrection

People lived by the sound of their own church bells. The only reason they rebelled was to protect their own communities. But they did sometimes show an awareness of belonging to a community which extended beyond their village, irrespective of whether that community was an administrative division marked out by the state or a geographical unit determined by the landscape. This larger community might correspond to the local *sénéchaussée* or even the province. We know of a number of crises in which a rebellion spread beyond the neighbourhood where it started, and took on the character of a region-wide epidemic. The risings of 1548, 1594, 1635 and 1675 were all examples of this. Both fairs and taverns played, as we have seen, a crucial part in circulating news and ideas. The spread of rebellion was also apt to be furthered by a number of specific social groups. Subversive notions were propagated, for instance, by seasonal labourers like the peasants from Charente who went to Guyenne in 1637 to help with the corn and grape harvests. In 1635 and 1675 the watermen played a similar role in stimulating unrest. Accounts of the risings against the *aides* which took place in Charente in 1629 were carried directly by eye-witnesses as far as Périgueux and even Angers; and the manifestos of the Croquants of Périgord were disseminated all the way to Auvergne. In August 1637 malcontents at Brive drew attention to the example set by the rebels at Bordeaux four months earlier, and the rioters who rampaged at Sarlat in September 1643 took their cue from the troubles in Rouergue. Taverns in every river-port upstream of Bordeaux buzzed with the news of the riots which broke out in that city in 1675. Not all rebellions can be pin-pointed, in other words. Certain revolts were infectious, and spread from place to place. But if we endeavour to trace these infections back down the rivers or roads by which they were transmitted, we invariably arrive at the same heartlands or hotbeds of dissidence. From emergency to emergency these hotbeds never change.

We have now taken a reasonably broad cross-section of the popular risings which took place in the seventeenth century. Our survey leaves little room for doubt that the location of these risings was no coincidence. Groups of places and districts are referred to by the chroniclers in connection with rebellions too often to be ignored. Contemporary observers noticed that revolts had a tendency to recur in particular areas. They ascribed this to the innate disposition with which the inhabitants of certain regions were held to be endowed. People in Guyenne, for example, were thought of as being hot-blooded and mercurial. Guyenne was supposed to be 'the nurse of factions ... and the mother of Mars'. The Poitevin was believed to be peaceful and given to moralizing, while the Gascon was absurd and quarrelsome. Society was not content to type-cast the provinces. Even towns and cantons were held to have a distinctive character. The people of certain cities like Bordeaux, Agen and Bayonne were generally agreed to be bloody-minded, fierce and seditious. It is clear, at all events, that there were a number of places which won notoriety as centres of tax resistance and breeding-grounds for revolt. In these reservoirs of dissidence obstructing the taxman seems to have become a way of life, and the violent hostility displayed by the people to any financial official ended by gaining them a sort of *de facto* tax-free status. Let us try to draw up a catalogue of the major trouble-spots.

The marshlands of Riez

The first area we shall examine consists of the marshland parishes of Riez, Monts, Challans, Machecoul and the 'island' of Bouin. These parishes were situated in the far north of Poitou, between the river Vie and the Retz district of Brittany. The area was dominated by the châteaux of La Garnache and de Beauvoir, which belonged at this period to the Rohan family. The villages huddled together on the 'islands' which protruded from the marshes, and visitors from outside could reach them only in the summer months. Only the marsh-dwellers knew how to make their way to the villages through the maze of assorted creeks and channels, causeways and fords. The parishes of the marshlands were attached to the *élection* of Les Sables, but from 1636 to about 1660 they were almost unscathed by taxation. The contribution demanded of them rose to almost 100,000 *livres*, but all that accumulated in response was a mountain of bad debts. In June 1637, May 1643, August 1643, spring 1644 and at various other times the provincial intendants led punitive expeditions into the 'rebel marshes' and stationed garrisons in the towns on the edge of the marshes and the local châteaux. In 1658 the intendant Colbert du Terron recorded that the marshland parishes had persistently withheld their taxes over a period of twenty years.

This reservoir of dissidence seems to have come into being partly for geographical and partly for historical reasons. The marsh-dwellers knew they were protected from any intrusion by their waterlogged meadows. As a chronicler put it they were 'emboldened by their inaccessibility'. At the same time they were influenced by living on the borders of Brittany. Brittany had, after all, been an independent dukedom in the relatively recent past, and it continued to set an example of freedom and resistance to central authority. One of our sources observes that the area was 'quite difficult to handle because of its closeness to Brittany'.

The hotbed of tax resistance which centred on the Riez swamplands stretched eastwards along the marches of Brittany and Poitou, where the frontier had been tangled for centuries. The chronicles make it clear that revolt was endemic in the neighbourhood of Palluau, Rocheservière, l'Herbergement and Montaigu. In 1633, 1636, 1642, 1648, 1653, 1658 and so forth, the people of these villages rose up in protest at *aides, traites* and *tailles*. A certain number of these parishes on the borders of Brittany enjoyed a complete exemption from taxes, and their tax-free status was confirmed by each succeeding monarch. Now and again, in 1661 and 1680, for instance, the king tried to make them pay for these confirmations with some free gift, or to send the tax-farmers in to erode their privileges. The parishes responded with rebellions that eventually forced the king to a compromise.

This reservoir of unrest on the northern border of Poitou made its presence felt in each of the major revolts that broke out in 1637, 1643 and 1648. It was the first part of the province to rise in rebellion, and the last to be pacified.

The southern châtellenies of Saintonge and Angoumois

The border between the regions of Bordeaux and Charente was defined by the landscape. A belt of sandy soil extended south-east from the Gironde estuary and the marshes of Blaye all the way to the impoverished region of Double between the Dronne and the Isle. This area was shaped like a rectangle some 60 kilometres long by 30 kilometres wide. It consisted solely of stretches of woodland and moorland. The country between Cozes and Jonzac was covered by the forest of La Lande, and the country between Mirambeau and Guîtres by the moors of Tout-l'y-faut and Bussac. Similar woods and moors filled the landscape from Barbezieux to Saint-Aigulin. This belt of empty, wooded country continued into Périgord with the woods and pools of Double. To the north of this border zone lay the *châtellenies* of Cozes, Pons, Jonzac, Barbezieux and Montguyon in Saintonge, and beyond them the *châtellenies* of Baignes, Blanzac, Brossac, Chalais, Montmoreau and Aubeterre in Angoumois. The soil there consisted of good sedimentary deposits. The *châtellenies* fanned out along the edge of the Cognac wine region, with its patchwork fields and extensive woodlands. Although the region was covered by considerable tracts of forest there were large villages in the clearings. The peasants who lived in these villages raised poultry and grew corn. When the corn was ripe they transported it to Bordeaux and Guyenne, where they earned some additional money by helping with the grape harvest. These *châtellenies* occupied a transit area. They stretched along the Paris–Bordeaux road on the threshold of Poitou. They were also a frontier zone. From time out of mind the line they traced had more or less corresponded with the limits of dioceses and jurisdictions, the linguistic border between the *langue d'oïl* and *langue d'oc* dialects and the boundary between the area in which disputes were settled by written law and that in which customary law continued to prevail. The precise borderline actually ran a little further to the south, so that the country round Blaye, Libourne and Double, for example, still formed part of the *langue d'oïl* region. Even today a traveller crossing this area notes a marked change of accent within the space of a few kilometres. Pons, Jonzac, Montendre, Montguyon, Barbezieux, Blanzac, Aubeterre and the other townships in the area were all defended by large châteaux.

It was in this area that the great revolt of the *Pitauds* gathered head between May and August 1548. The revolt began in the villages of Châteauneuf and Archiac. Boismenier, the 'colonel of Angoumois, Périgord and Saintonge', arrived from Blanzac to lead it, and another rebel leader, Puymoreau, came down from Barbezieux. Puymoreau was a gentleman. Rumour had it that he was the bastard son of a noble of the Aubeterre family. By August the movement had spread to Guîtres in the part of the frontier region closest to Bordeaux, where a third leader, Tallemagne, was employed as a blacksmith.

The rising of the Croquants of Périgord in June 1594 found a sympathetic response in this area. The area's greatest prominence came, however, forty years later, when it suddenly emerged as the hotbed of the rising of 1636. The first of the peasant assemblies which were held on this occasion took place in the villages of Blanzac and Barbezieux. The only leader of this revolt whose name is preserved in the chronicles was a village judge from the *châtellenie* of Brossac named Estancheau. The revolt of the communes of Périgord which broke out the following summer spread to the area as a result of the activities of the Marquis d'Aubeterre. In July 1637 the royal forces staged a punitive raid on the area in the neighbourhood of Cognac, and in March 1638 they repeated the operation in the neighbourhood of Pons.

Many of the parishes in this area resisted the taxman constantly. In the spring of 1642 they resorted to arms yet again. This outbreak lasted a year. On 28 March 1643 it was stopped in its tracks when government forces routed a host of peasants who had risen up at Montendre; but the *châtellenie* of Aubeterre was still withholding its taxes as late as 1644 and 1645. During the Fronde wars this frontier zone acquired a strategic importance in the crown's campaign to regain control of Bordeaux. It was organized as a special command, and placed in the hands of a *maréchal de camp*, the lord of Folleville.

In April 1656 a fresh rebellion flared up in the area, and was not quelled till 1661. According to our sources the most serious violence took place in Cozes, Coutras, Saint-Aigulin and Aubeterre, where the tax fusiliers suffered heavy casualties. As late as 1673 the provincial intendant was still denouncing this area as a hotbed of tax resistance. He complained that the assessment lists were never drawn up, and that bad debts accumulated instead of taxes.

We may trace the seditious tendencies of the area in part to the influence of nearby Bordeaux. Bordeaux was a town with a history of exemptions and revolts if ever there was one. The area may also have been affected by the experience of the privileged district of Marennes, where the peasants extracted salt from the marshes of Brovage and La Seudre and were consequently allowed to enjoy an almost total immunity from taxation. The two most important characteristics of the area, however, were rather different. The first of these characteristics was that the area was covered with moorland and woodland which made it difficult for outsiders to penetrate. The second was that it lay in a frontier zone, which made it easy for the people to dodge the attempts of the courts to force them to pay their debts. The fate of this region also was decided, in other words, by a combination of geographical and administrative factors.

Le Paréage

The landscape in this case consisted of an expanse of thick forest. The forest of Vergt was located close to the outskirts of Périgueux, in between the rivers Isle and Dordogne. Administratively it consisted of a group of some twenty parishes which were jointly owned on a *paréage* or revenue-sharing basis by the Counts of Périgord and the canons of the cathedral of Saint-Front. When the rising of 1594 began the forest was the scene of a number of parish assemblies. It was the people of Le Paréage who struck the first blow in the great rebellion which started in May 1637, by laying siege to Périgueux and demanding that the citizens handed the excisemen over to them. From 1638 to 1641 Greletty held out in the forest and resisted the series of punitive expeditions which were sent against him from Périgueux. In September 1649 the peasants of Le Paréage aligned themselves with the Fronde, and they served in its armies continually up till July 1653. This history of rebellion was still not forgotten in 1675. When riots against stamp-duty broke out that year in Bergerac, the rebels threatened 'to go and find the people in Le Paréage and join forces with them'.

Contemporary observers noticed how the people of Le Paréage, or the 'Paréages', as they called them, had a hand in all the disorders of the time. They appreciated that a tradition of revolt had developed in the forest. It was a reservoir of dissidence and a refuge for malcontents. Local seigneurs like Ribeyreix, La Douze and Auberoche encouraged the rebels to rise up and protected them when they did so. The most striking feature of these risings was the hatred which the forest-dwellers displayed at every opportunity for the burgesses of Périgueux. The troubles which raged in Le Paréage in 1594 and 1637 provide us with two of the most dramatic examples of the perpetual conflict between the countryside and the towns.

The fiefs of the house of Turenne

Simply known as 'the viscountcy', the Turenne domain constituted the largest of all the fiefdoms in south-west France. The viscountcy straddled the borders of Haut-Quercy, Bas-Limousin and Haute-Auvergne. Fifty-seven of its parishes lay within Limousin, and thirty-nine within Quercy. The area was equally divided from a geographical point of view, insofar as the landscape varied from the beautiful plains of the Dordogne to the moors of the *causse* (limestone plateau) region and the plateaux and valleys of Brivadois. The viscountcy was said to contain approximately 100,000 people. The Viscounts of Turenne, who were also the Dukes of Bouillon, were not prepared to accept that their territory was merely a fief which the crown had bestowed on them and could transfer at will. They claimed that it was a free and independent dominion which had no obligation towards the king apart from the duty to pay him homage and respect the verdicts of his courts. The people of the fiefdom paid annual dues to the viscount: the sum to be paid was decided by vote at a meeting of the local estates. In troubled periods such as the Wars of Religion and the Fronde the people of the viscountcy also supplied their lord with contingents of troops. The viscountcy was exempt from any kind of imposition on the part of the state. It was not even required to furnish billets for the royal armies. It made no difference whether a man was a soldier crossing the country or a tax official touring the neighbourhood to serve warrants for distraint. When he came to the borders of the viscountcy he had to turn back. 'Taxpayers' and 'crown lands' began only when you left the viscount's domains. The people of the viscountcy were conscious that their status was unique and precious. 'The viscountcy', one of them noted, 'enjoys privileges quite different from those which are enjoyed by the various other estates in the kingdom. Its rights are sovereign rights, and their origin is so old it is lost in the mists of antiquity.' A rebel who hailed from the territory made the point more simply: 'Turenne is a land of freedom.'[9] The poet Maynard, who was born there, spoke of the 'golden age which Turenne enjoyed while the state was undergoing its bitterest blows'.[10] The inhabitants themselves agreed, then, that the viscountcy was an island of bliss and a bastion of prosperity.

It is clear from the chronicles that the people of this territory played a significant role in stimulating the outbreak of the first Croquant rising in 1593–4. The revolts which took place in Quercy in 1624 and 1637 both began on the edge of the viscountcy. In all the conspiracies and revolts which were hatched in south-west France, the viscountcy acted either as a meeting-place or a beacon of liberty.

When revolt swept across the country in 1675, the viscountcy sprang to arms. From 25 to 27 May the drums were beaten and the tocsin sounded in every part of Turenne. Messengers were dispatched from the principal town of the viscountcy to tour the surrounding parishes and muster the peasants 'in the name of their freedoms and ancient rights'. On Sunday 28 May two battalions each numbering 300 to 400 men were formed from the people of Turenne and some peasants from other regions who had flocked to their banner. The battalions marched in procession, with liveried consuls at their head. A doctor called Courèse posted up a notice which proclaimed, 'Long live the king and Monsieur de Bouillon, and down with the *gabelle*! We must drive out the excisemen, and death to anyone who tries to stop us!' The stamp-paper was burnt in the market, and the tax-farmer who had caused the disturbance fled from the town with all convenient speed.

From January to March 1696 a fresh wave of messengers made the rounds of the parishes of Turenne. They brought along powers of attorney for the villagers to sign, and asked them to choose some syndics to represent them. The issue on this occasion was the poll tax. The people had made up their minds to resist the tax, even if it was levied by the viscount's own officials. Once again the people prevailed. The poll tax was never enforced in Turenne, and a subsequent attempt to impose a special tax known as the *dixième* was equally unsuccessful.

People in the viscountcy, then, were keenly aware of their privileges and

9 See Archives Nationales, R2.501, Turenne, 28 May 1675.
10 See Maynard, *Oeuvres* (1653 edition), letters CXLIV, p. 403, and CLXI, p. 466.

determined to defend them. Early in the eighteenth century they manifested this determination yet again. The object this time was to maintain the exemption the viscountcy enjoyed from the farming out of the tax on tobacco growing. Tobacco was first cultivated in the valley of the Dordogne in about 1675. Before long the crown had imposed duties on the packaging and sale of this new product. In July 1681 the king issued an ordinance relinquishing his right to levy these duties to the Viscount of Turenne. In 1693, however, the viscount in turn waived his right to tax this commodity, and from then until 1726 tobacco production in the fiefdom expanded at a staggering rate. In 1700 the viscountcy produced 2,000 quintals of tobacco for a profit of 80,000 *livres*. By 1715 the output had risen to 15,000 quintals for a profit of a million *livres*. By 1725 the output was 80,000 quintals and the viscountcy's fortune was made. Then came a thunderbolt. On 22 March 1723 the Compagnie des Indes had been granted a monopoly on the sale of tobacco. In a decree issued on 16 February 1724 the Council gave the Compagnie the further right to buy up the entire output of the viscountcy and to uproot any plantations whose produce had not been sold to them. On 28 August some guards who had been sent to Turenne to enforce this arrangement were confronted for the first time by a community in arms. The confrontation took place in the town of Gagnac. One of the consuls of Gagnac marched up at the head of the citizens and ordered the guards 'to leave the viscountcy and keep a good league away from its borders'. Further outbreaks of resistance took place at Martel on 24 June 1726 and at Montvalent the following October. This time, however, the people of the viscountcy had to give in. The government was threatening to abrogate their privileges altogether. Regiments of grenadiers had been sent to quell the unrest, and were well on their way to Souillac and Terrasson. The planters of Turenne were obliged to limit themselves to selling their tobacco leaf to the Compagnie's agents at a fraction of the market price. Squads of government troops made the rounds of the viscountcy checking that no additional tobacco was being grown on the sly in the middle of the maizefields or in between the rows of vines. The farmers none the less continued to nurse stubborn hopes that free cultivation would once again be permitted. Such hopes were particularly widespread in 1734 and 1737, and large-scale smuggling set in. The Compagnie des Indes made representations to the government, and in 1738 the Duke of Bouillon finally agreed to sell the viscountcy to the crown.

The viscountcy of Turenne affords us perhaps the best example of the way in which the institutions prevalent in a particular district were apt to shape the mentality of the people who lived there. After being one of the major hotbeds of revolt in the seventeenth century, the old viscountcy of Turenne had become extinct; but its tradition of tax resistance lingered on in the area for many generations. Right up to the 1930s the Tobacco Board recorded a particularly high incidence of smuggling in the Lot region and the departments adjacent to it. Much of this smuggling took place in the Souillac and Sarlat areas. In the summer of 1954 the region became conspicuous as the birthplace of Poujadisme, a movement which sprang up to resist new types of oppressive taxation and protect the interests of declining rural areas. The Poujadiste movement rose to prominence in Saint-Céré, a town which lay in the heart of the long-forgotten viscountcy.

The viscountcy was not the only fief of the house of Turenne. It also owned a number of other territories in different parts of south-west France. These territories never enjoyed any freedoms as extensive as those of the viscountcy, but they too seem to have been infected by the contagion of tax resistance. One troubled area was Xaintrie. The district of Xaintrie occupied a granite plateau which stretched along the south bank of the Dordogne upstream of the viscountcy, on the borders of Haute-Auvergne and the forest of Mauriac. The landscape consisted of birchwoods and moorland, and the climate was cold. The people grew rye and raised livestock. Xaintrie was organized into seventeen parishes. Together these parishes made up the *châtellenie* of Servières – and the *châtellenie* was a fiefdom of the house of Turenne. Xaintrie was mentioned by chroniclers in the same breath as the viscountcy as a hotbed of the troubles which broke out in 1594. The district paid no taxes whatever in the seven years which elapsed between 1591 and 1598. Half a century later it was prominent once again as the first district from which the royal fusiliers were driven on the outbreak of the Fronde. On 11 July 1648, 400 peasants gathered at the sound of the tocsin from five or six of the parishes on the Xaintrie plateau. The fusiliers had taken shelter in a strongly fortified mansion, and the peasants accordingly marched off and laid siege to them. Yet another rising appears to have broken out in these parishes ten years later. Details of the rising are given in a series of five police reports that were filed between December 1658 and April 1659. On this occasion the authorities used the rising as a pretext for sending fusiliers to enforce the payment of taxes in every part of Bas-Limousin.

Another unquiet fiefdom was the plateau of Millevaches. Millevaches lay further north than Xaintrie, but the countryside was much the same. This district too was influenced by the proximity of a number of powerful families. They included not merely the Turennes, but also the houses of Noailles, Bonneval, Sauveboeuf and Pompadour. And in this district, like the others, resistance to taxation was stubborn and not to be rooted out. On several occasions the plateau was the scene of rebellions, when a few dozen parishes joined forces to drive out the bailiffs. In 1594 and 1637 the unrest centred on Crocq and La Mazière. From 1640 to 1645, however, the major upheavals were taking place at Bugeat and Saint-Setiers, and in 1648 Treignac was the focus of the revolt.

Xaintrie and the Millevaches country, then, were both typical examples of this very distinctive kind of trouble-spot. Both of these districts were characterized by an unusual landscape which attracted outsiders seeking a hideaway. And both of them were governed by archaic institutions, and subject to the persisting influence of the seigniorial past.

La Châtaigneraie

La Châtaigneraie is a further case of a lonely moorland plateau in a frontier zone. The people lived in groups of hamlets which dotted the occasional dells.

The plateau extended along the borders of Haut-Quercy and Rouergue, from Maurs to Montsalvy. Administratively it was a canton of the province of Haute-Auvergne, and its tax affairs were conducted by the *élection* of Aurillac. In the autumn of 1643 the revolt which had broken out in Rouergue spilled over into the canton. The government's regiments were harried by bands of several hundred Croquants over a period of two months. Major disturbances took place at Maurs on 24 September, and at Saint-Constant on 4 October. In March 1647 the household servants of the lord of Senezergues set upon the local bowmen with a view to rescuing some persons whom they had taken prisoner for non-payment of tax. From 1649 to 1653 the twenty-odd parishes on the plateau refused to pay any taxes of any kind, and it was only after troops were dispatched to the area in the autumn of 1653 that the tax collectors were able to resume their work. On 4 September 1659 a force of some forty tax fusiliers was put to flight at Leynhac by a mob of 300 peasants armed with guns and staves. Unrest was still seething in the district in November 1678, when a cavalry regiment had to be sent to put down a rebellion there. In 1705 the provincial intendant filed reports denouncing the area as a haven for bandits and traffickers in substitute salt.

The valleys of the Pyrenees

Our next major breeding-ground of insurrection is situated right at the other end of south-west France. Tax fugitives could find in the valleys of the Pyrenees the same combination of a mountainous landscape and a privileged fiscal status that attracted their fellows to the more easterly districts we have just been considering. The Pyrenean valleys can be divided into a number of different areas. Westernmost of these areas was the viscountcy of Soule, which consisted of sixty-nine small parishes in the valley created by the Mauléon mountain torrent. Next to the east were the valleys of Aspe, which extended from Somport to Oloron, and Ossau, which stretched from Pourtalet to Laruns. Both of these valleys formed part of the province of Béarn. Next after them came the viscountcy of Lavedan, which consisted of the valley created by the Pau mountain torrent and the seven smaller valleys which opened into it. These seven valleys extended from Gavarnie to Lourdes, which was the principal town of the area. Yet another viscountcy occupied the Quatre-Vallées district, which lay close beside the plateau of Lannemezan. The first of these 'four valleys' was the valley of the Magnoac, which lay outside the Pyrenees proper. The Magnoac region also included thirty-eight other parishes which stretched across the plateau and alongside the banks of the River Gers. The second of the valleys was that of the Neste. This valley included seven parishes which flanked the River Grande-Neste in the region surrounding the town of La Barthe. The third valley was in reality simply the upper valley of the Neste. This neighbourhood consisted of the Aure region, and Arreau was the principal town. The fourth and last of the 'four valleys' was the valley of the Ourse. It contained eighteen parishes, which together made up the Barousse region. The next major area to the east was the Val d'Aran, to use the name commonly given to the upper valley of the Garonne. This area only came under French rule belatedly in the course of the years 1640–59. Furthest to the east was the area known as Couserans. Couserans was another name for the upper valley of the Salat. The area centred on the towns of Saint-Lizier and Massat, and was walled off from neighbouring regions by a barrier of mountain gorges and defiles.

All of these areas were exempt from the obligation to pay either the regular *tailles* or any form of *aides* or duties on salt. They sent the king nothing except an assortment of gifts in recognition of his ultimate suzerainty. Matters changed slightly in the mid-seventeenth century. From 1638 the valleys were expected to contribute to the rations tax, and in 1641 the tax in support of military halts was also introduced. Both of these taxes, however, were assessed at very modest rates. They were payable in instalments, and the authorities had to obtain 'the express consent' of the syndics and delegates of the local estates before they could be raised. The valleys were entitled to import supplies of salt from within a clearly defined zone of the region of Aragon in Spain. The boundaries of the zone were laid down in very ancient agreements known as *lies* and *passeries*. Béarn and Basse-Navarre enjoyed the additional right of supplying themselves from a number of salt-water springs. The most celebrated of these springs was the fountain of Salies. Traders bringing goods to the valleys from other provinces were obliged to pay a special duty on their entry into the district. This duty was administered as part of a tax farm which went under the name of the *traites foraines* (border customs dues) of Arzacq.

In 1622 the province of Béarn rose up in defence of its religion and privileges. From 1638 to 1640 the Comminges region was convulsed in similar fashion by rebellions against the bowmen who had been sent to enforce the payment of tax. Disbanded Croquants from Astarac and Pardiac came to the mountains in search of shelter. The Val d'Aran took the French side in the Franco-Spanish war, only to revolt in 1642 on receiving the news that the king of France 'was going to introduce his taxes there'. In 1644 the valleys all combined to drive off officials who had been sent to serve writs of distraint for the rations tax; and in May 1654 the people of Lavedan rebelled in an attempt to frustrate the quartering of troops in their midst. From 1659 onwards there was a growing proliferation of riots directed against the tax fusiliers and the agents who were sent to collect the *traites*. Trouble broke out in May 1659 at Castelnau-Magnoac, and in June 1660 this upheaval was followed by two further disturbances at Sauveterre-en-Nébouzan and Siros in Béarn. In 1662 Soule rose up at the summons of Matalas, the parish priest of Montcayolle. Order was not restored until the authorities had routed the peasants, hanged two of their ringleaders and sent two others captive to the galleys. In November 1663 the communities of Couserans revolted in their turn. Pellot, the provincial intendant, arrived at Saint-Girons to blockade the rebel valleys. The consuls of the rebel parishes had their houses razed to the ground, and seven or eight peasants were sent to the galleys. In February–March 1665 the valleys of Lavedan rose up once again. The turbulence was provoked on this occasion by the approach of troops who had been dispatched to hunt down the rebel leader Audijos. The peasants responded by blocking the roads upstream of Lourdes for a period of several days. Disturbances continued to break out from time to time in subsequent decades as the populace reacted against an assortment of provocations. In the Ossau valley in 1680 and the Aspe valley in 1683 the trouble was caused by the activities of land surveyors. Other outbreaks were provoked by the government's efforts to reorganize forest administration and the appearance in the valleys of officials in the service of the intendants. Crowds of peasants would band together, and rumours would circulate 'that the king meant to introduce the *gabelle* in this region'.

We can form a clearer picture of the way in which these episodes unfolded by considering the history of one of the last in the series of risings – an abortive insurrection which took place at Lavedan in 1695. The people of the seven valleys there had been lodging complaints with the intendant's envoys and the commander of the château of Lourdes. The complaints focused on a number of grievances such as the steps which had been taken to raise militias the previous year. At the beginning of March a circular letter was dispatched to the consuls of the various communities of Lavedan. The letter bore the real or pretended signature of the syndic of the estates of Bigorre, and was stamped with a wax seal. 'The king', it ran, 'has received petitions at court informing him of the excesses which have been committed in this neighbourhood, and he is filled with pity for his people ... The time has come to complain to M. the intendant about the ill-treatment which we have been suffering in this region.' The circular was carried from village to village either by peasants or by the children who acted as messengers in the valleys. Most of the consuls who received the circular were illiterate, and were consequently obliged to get the local parish priests to read their letters to them. A number of parish assemblies were organized shortly afterwards, and on 14 March the estates of the valleys held two meetings at Salles and Arca. Each community was required to appoint one man per household to represent it at these meetings so that the peasants could pool their grievances. Word soon arrived from the government that the circular was a forgery and the assemblies were against the law. The authorities picked out scapegoats in the form of two parish priests, a notary and a gentleman, all of whom had manifested conspicuous zeal in the course of the assemblies. Orders were issued under the king's private seal banishing these ringleaders from the valleys. One of them, Caussade, the priest of Agos, was denounced by his bishop as being 'a natural demagogue'. Caussade had been acting as secretary and adviser to the consuls of several communities. The rogue gentleman was a certain François de Barèges, Esquire, seigneur of La Hitte in Bigorre. Barèges did considerable business in the valleys, and was known to everyone there. He took part in village discussions, and lent his stallions round the villages to cover the mares. Sourdis, the *lieutenant-général*, observed that Barèges 'is regarded as the defender of public freedom and avenger of any attempt to infringe it. He's a dangerous man.'

These rebel assemblies seem to have been remarkably easy to convoke. People in the valleys were keenly aware of their ancient privileges. They resented every intrusion on the part of the government as an assault on their basic rights, and were always ready to believe reports that the crown was confirming their freedoms, no matter how flimsy the evidence might be. The sheer isolation in which they lived knit these highlanders together in a strong solidarity, and their tradition of helping each other brought them to meetings with great swiftness in time of need. The Pyrenean region was defended as well as defined by its forbidding geography.

Contemporaries had no difficulty in accounting for the frequency and violence of revolts in the Pyrenees. The most obvious explanation for these phenomena, in their view, lay in the character of the people themselves. Attention was drawn to the 'evil disposition' of the mountain-dwellers, to their 'insubordination' and 'treacherousness'. They were, an observer noted, 'prone to revolt . . . and extremely difficult to govern . . . since they have no more sense than bears'. Contemporaries also pointed to the faith of the highlanders that they were entitled to certain legal privileges, no matter how ill-founded those privileges actually were. Sourdis remarked in 1695 how 'the mountain people are extremely jealous of their real or imagined privileges . . . After all, they live next to the Spaniards, whose privileges have made them thoroughly stubborn.' An intendant wrote that he had 'been able to find no other justification' for the exemptions the region enjoyed 'than the ferocity of the people who live there'. The explanation most commonly cited for the troubles, however, was the remoteness of the region. Walled off from easy physical access by its mountains and gorges, it was at the same time a dangerous area to venture into from the political point of view. It lay on a frontier, and the people might well switch loyalties. 'The inhabitants laugh at our writs', an official lamented, 'and trust to their rugged surroundings to protect them.' The Council made similar comments in a decree it issued to the commanders of the châteaux which guarded the mountain passes. The decree observed that the refractory conduct of the highlanders could be put down 'to the fact of their being situated in the Pyrenean mountains which command the passes into Spain. Numerous murders and uprisings take place there and go unpunished. The result has been that the local authorities have not dared to claim any taxes from the people of these valleys for several years.' The intendant Faucon de Ris declared similarly in 1682 how

these people live on the frontier with Spain and control a number of mountain passes. They can easily desert us and go over to the Spaniards, since no taxes are enforced on the Spanish side of the border. It is all the more important, then, that we make sure of their loyalty, since we have no stronghold from which to hold them in check in time of war.

We have now considered a series of different hotbeds of insurrection. Let us review the essential characteristics they shared. All of them enjoyed a *de facto* immunity from government interference as the result of their geographical position. Sometimes they were hard of physical access. Sometimes they lay close to a foreign country, and interference consequently entailed a political risk from the government's point of view. Sometimes they bristled with rebels who had made their way there from another province or kingdom in search of asylum. These trouble-spots also enjoyed, or professed to enjoy, a *de jure* immunity from taxation thanks to long-standing local exemptions or the protection which had been accorded to them by important local seigneurs. The people who lived in such districts believed that this supposed immunity entitled them to take up arms in revolt if the need arose. The distinction made here between a *de jure* and *de facto* immunity is purely one of convenience. In actual fact geographical considerations are likely to have played a major part in determining the original shape of such administrative units as viscountcies and *châtellenies*. Certain groups of communities were naturally linked by the landscape. A plateau or valley, for instance, was an obvious entity.

People were buoyed up by this sense of immunity, and rebellions snowballed. In certain respects they became self-perpetuating. The morale of the peasant rebels was invariably boosted by the initial successes they scored against the taxmen. People became convinced 'that this was the way to get rid of them'. Later, when the authorities struck back, the uprisings were prone to drag on as fear spread among the rebels that the government were sending troops to crush their revolt, seize their goods and throw them into prison. People felt they had no alternative but to reinforce their defences and maintain themselves on a permanent war footing. In the meantime their tax arrears mounted up. The debt was made worse as fines were imposed and legal expenses incurred, and the point was eventually reached where the authorities had to abandon any hope of recovering it. The intendant Villemontée made some pertinent observations when he toured the insurgent area of Bas-Poitou in June 1637. 'I have come to realize', he declared, 'that the towns which have paid no taxes at all for five or six years are poorer than the ones which have paid their dues. This is partly because they have not dared to pursue their regular business, and partly because they have squandered the money they would previously have spent in taxes on extravagant and dissolute livng.' The intendant Argenson found a similar situation when he travelled through the same region seven years later.

The parishes which have paid least tax and are most in arrears are as poor as or poorer than the ones which have made the largest contributions . . . Fear of the law has led them to abandon their property and businesses. The result is that the rebellion has ruined them at least as much as their fellows – and they still have their debts to pay.

The immunities which these areas enjoyed derived their validity from long-standing privileges. Ordinary people liked to depict these privileges in an outer coating of legend. In the first place they maintained that the privileges were sacred ones. They were guaranteed by kings, and the word of kings was not to be questioned. But the privileges also had contractual force. They were not simply concessions which had been handed down by the monarch: they had been offered by him to the people as the price of their loyalty, and the people had accepted the bargain. By the same token the king's evil counsellors were all thought to be devoting their energies to getting the privileges revoked. 'They are using all their borrowed authority to abolish the privileges enjoyed by the provinces, and to reduce our provincial institutions to a state of wretchedness. This has been the object of their efforts for many years.' People had such complete faith in the validity of these notions that they were even brought up in letters to the Council. Bertrand de Borda, the *lieutenant-général* at the *présidial* of Dax, wrote to Colbert on one occasion that 'privileges are, as it were, the sacred creations of our monarchs, and [the ministers of the crown] have never sought to violate them'. The bishop of Lescar went still further. 'This province', he noted,

is a region where ancient privileges and customs prevail, and its people have always shown the utmost anxiety to make sure that they are observed. All of our kings have acknowledged the legitimacy of their aspiration, and have taken a special oath to maintain the province's privileges. This oath has given the people a shield with which to defend themselves against any kind of innovation or unscheduled tax.

A third writer expanded on this point. 'Privileges and exemptions', he wrote, 'have enabled our towns to increase their wealth, heighten their reputation and maintain their dignity. Taxes and levies, conversely, turn our towns into deserts, our houses into hovels and our country estates into stretches of waste ground.'

The English legacy

People in the south-western provinces, then, were keenly conscious of their freedoms. They recalled, for example, the exemption from the salt tax which their forefathers had been granted in 1549. And their feeling of being privileged was strengthened still further by the distant memory of English rule. People looked back on the period of English domination in different ways, depending on circumstances. When an uprising started the rebels were apt to refer to it as a golden age. At other times, however, it became expedient for the subject populace to stress their loyalty to the crown, and in that event they changed their tune and reviled the English occupation as an age of darkness.

In 1514 the people of Agen rose up in revolt against a duty which the government had imposed on wine. They vowed that 'they would rather submit to English rule than accept this new levy'. When Bordeaux rebelled against the salt tax in 1548, the English banner with its red cross on a white ground was hoisted above the walls. A century later Bordeaux was held by the Fronde. The rebels sent delegates to London, leading Milton to imagine 'all the *Gascoins* that are the rightful *Dowry* of our ancient Kings, come with cap, and knee, desiring the shadow of the *English* scepter to defend them from the hot persecutions and taxes of the *French*'. As late as 1675 'the most insolent talk relating to the old days of English rule' was still to be heard in Bordeaux.

This nostalgia bred a mythology of its own. People began to imagine that Guyenne had not, after all, been conquered by France but had submitted of its own free will. The Gascons had either risen up in revolt against the exactions to which they had been subjected by the English, or had won a promise from the French kings to exempt them from taxes in perpetuity. The people who lived in the viscountcy of Turenne, for example, connected the freedoms they enjoyed with a past exhibition of loyalty on the part of their seigneurs. They thought that these freedoms had been conferred upon the viscountcy in reward for the services which their seigneurs had rendered to

France 'ever since the earliest times, and especially during the period when the English held Guyenne'. The citizens of Bordeaux, Dax and Bayonne were all convinced that their towns had become attached to the crown of France as the consequence of a non-existent revolt against the English. 'When these populations succeeded in ridding themselves of English rule and submitted to the crown of France, Charles VII granted them special terms and privileges which have remained intact from that day to this.' According to a tradition recorded by the *jurats* of Bordeaux, the Gascons originally balked at an attempt to levy upon them an English tax known as a *maltôte*. They rose in revolt, and the result of the outbreak was that they passed 'under the more benevolent and auspicious sway of the kings of France'.

English influence had extended well beyond the relatively narrow bounds of the historic duchy of Gascony. The Plantagenets made their presence felt in every part of south-west France. Regions like Armagnac and Fezensac, Bigorre and Béarn were all expected to pay due homage to the English king; and the Plantagenets asserted their right to accept the allegiance of vassals and handle the local revenues as far south as Quercy and as far north as Limousin. The territorial struggle in which the English and French kings were engaged in these south-western provinces was unquestionably a factor of major significance. On the one hand it encouraged warrior noblemen to spring up in especial profusion in this part of the country, and build their châteaux there. On the other hand it enabled towns and districts to elicit large numbers of privileges from the rival monarchs. In this sense the Anglo-French conflict served to mark out south-west France as a highly distinctive area, where people were keenly aware of their privileges and the spirit of independence was stubborn and strong. The communities in this area were deeply attached to their freedoms, and intolerant of any attempt to subject them to state control. We need only recall the example of the town of Crocq and the *Pays de franc-alleu*. During the trials of the Hundred Years War the strongholds which dotted this neighbourhood had lain in the front line of the conflict, at the mercy of English raids. The kings of France had favoured these strongholds with preferential treatment, and the Crocq district had consequently evolved into a tax-free area where any kind of fiscal intervention was bitterly resisted. We may adduce two further arguments in support of our contention that the Anglo-French rivalry had a major impact on the social evolution of the region. Both of these arguments are easy to verify. The first relates to the density of châteaux in the south-western provinces, the second to the proliferation of freedoms the towns there enjoyed.

The struggle between the houses of Capet and Plantagenet for power in south-west France was reflected in the abnormal number of fortified strongholds which sprang up in every corner of the south-western countryside. Scholars in the nineteenth century thought that the Plantagenets had made a systematic effort to put up a barrier of fortresses which would make it easier for them to resist the incursions of French troops into their duchy of Gascony. We now know that the reason for the springing up of these strongholds was rather different. The fact was that neither of the two rival courts had more than a feeble grip on this outer edge of their spheres of influence. The way was consequently left clear for those minor seigneurs of the frontier provinces who fancied themselves as independent warlords. The results are startling. The relatively limited area of Agenais, for instance, was dotted as early as the thirteenth century by a total of no less than 130 châteaux, while the larger province of Bourbonnais contained only forty-five. The same phenomenon may be noted in Armagnac, Fezensac and Périgord, though in these regions the proliferation of fortified manor houses dates back no earlier than the fourteenth century and the outbreak of the Hundred Years War. None of these strongholds were ever strategic fortesses, and indeed the majority played no part in the Anglo-French struggle. They amounted to nothing more than small seigniorial mansions or ramparts put up with a veiw to defending hilltop towns. Defensive sites of this sort do not suggest a trip-wire put up by the Plantagenets to protect their outpost of Gascony. Rather, they point to the freedom enjoyed by the vassals of both the two rival crowns, who were blithely erecting walls and towers throughout the region, secure in the knowledge that their distant suzerains were in no position to bring the full force of their authority to bear on them. The unusual density of strongholds in these provinces may be seen, then, as an indication that a zone of freedom existed in south-west France, in an area corresponding to the lands of the duchy of Gascony.

We can find some additional support for this thesis by taking a glance at the history of civic institutions in the region. It is well known that towns grew up at a remarkable rate in thirteenth-century Aquitaine. This growth took two principal forms. Vast numbers of towns were granted rights and freedoms, and numerous new towns were founded under the names of *sauvetés, castelnaux* and *bastides*. The two rival monarchs vied with each other in granting charters to the various south-western communities: in the period 1256–1331, for example, over 500 charters were granted to towns in the territory which stretched between the Pyrenees and the Dordogne. The granting of charters was too widespread a phenomenon to be regarded as uniquely characteristic of the province of Gascony. The trend towards new towns, on the other hand, was unique and conspicuous in every part of the region, from Gascony to Périgord. It was particularly marked in the second half of the thirteenth century. On one calculation a total of more than 300 *bastides* complete with their formidable ramparts were built at this period by the seneschals of either the French or the English king.

The privileges which the towns won in the course of the thirteenth century survived intact through the conflicts of the following hundred years. They were unaffected by either the ravages of the Anglo-French war or the recession that war ushered in. No matter which of the two sides had the upper hand in the fighting, the towns were always the winners in the sense that their institutions continued to benefit. The king of France, for example, would grant privileges to the towns which had taken his side and resisted his English enemies. These privileges might take several different forms. The king might bestow special honours on the magistrates who had been elected by the people of a given town. He might give the town permission to hold fairs and markets or to put up defensive ramparts. He might exempt the town from the duty to furnish billets for troops or pay taxes, or alternatively he might accord it the right to levy communal taxes of its own. Favours of these various types were bestowed in 1372 on the towns of Capdenac, Cognac, Domme, Eymet, Excideuil, Issoudun, La Rochelle and Saint-Jean-d'Angély, in 1374 on Angoulême, and in 1427 on Lusignan and the Île de Ré. Certain towns, on the other hand, resisted the French and had to be taken by storm. In this event the king would try to win the towns to his cause by confirming all the privileges which the English kings had showered upon them so generously in the previous centuries. Tactics of this kind were used at Saint-Junien in 1224, at Lectoure and Limoges in 1371, at Bergerac and Brive in 1374, at Bayonne in 1451 and Bordeaux in 1453.

The question arises whether or not civil privileges were bestowed in similar fashion in every part of the kingdom. We can explore this question by considering the specific example of *noblesses de cloche*. *Noblesses de cloche* were collective peerages which the French king conferred on certain towns by bestowing them on the municipal corporation. Such peerages were awarded only to cities which had given outstanding proof of their loyalty to the crown in the course of conflicts like the Hundred Years War and the Wars of Religion. These aldermen's peerages were abolished, for practical purposes, when the government threw municipal offices open to public auction in their edict of 1692. The peerages do not seem, however, to have become an object of general controversy till 1667. Only a tiny number of cities were actually privileged to receive this unusual honour during the centuries in which it remained in the gift of the crown. To be precise, only sixteen cases of such an award are recorded from any part of France. And of the sixteen towns so honoured, no less than thirteen were recorded in western France, on the fringes of the territory which the English controlled in medieval times.[11] Puffed up by royal favours, these privileged towns ended up by addressing the world in a style uniquely their own. The aldermen of Issoudun still showed vestigial traces of this style as late as 1663. In a petition they submitted that year requesting the government to exempt them from taxes, they wrote how

their ancestors had always rendered services of the utmost importance to this state in resisting the encroachments of the English ... At the time when the civil wars of the rival religious factions were raging throughout the land, they were the only people in Berry to persist in the obedience due to their sovereigns; and this at a time when all the other towns in the province were against them. Their devotion and loyalty were rewarded with many noble privileges, and all our kings have confirmed them.[12]

---

11 See François Bluche and Pierre Durye, 'L'Anoblissement par charges avant 1789', article published in the journal *Les Cahiers nobles*, 1962. Bluche and Durye list thirteen towns that were dignified with the *noblesse de cloche* in this region, namely Angers, Angoulême, Bourges, Cognac, Issoudun, La Rochelle, Le Mans, Nantes, Niort, Poitiers, Saint-Jean-d'Angély, Toulouse and Tours.

12 Issoudun had been exempt from the obligation to pay taxes or billet soldiers since the time of the Hundred Years War. Its aldermen were raised to the peerage only at a very late date, however, as a reward for the loyalty it showed to the crown in the period of the Fronde. In

For people who lived in privileged towns like Issoudun resistance to taxes did not constitute a revolt. Such people felt they were rising up in defence of their heritage. They had earned their exemptions by virtue of their past displays of loyalty; the crown had bestowed them freely; and in fighting to protect them they were merely upholding a noble custom which had stood the test of time. Over the years a number of powerful traditions had taken root in the south-west part of France. People had grown used to enjoying a *de facto* autonomy. From time out of mind they had been free from any attempt at extending state control. They felt that they had a natural bent for freedom. Their ancestors, they believed, had won this freedom by their own merits, and had handed it down to subsequent generations as a privilege which could not be taken away. Naturally the word 'freedom' has to be understood in its traditional sense. It meant nothing more than the independence of communities which had never been exposed to the pressures exerted by an absolute monarchy. But the word cannot be underlined too strongly in the context of our period. It was constantly being used. Rebels used it in their manifestos, and provincial syndics used it in the petitions which they submitted to the crown. The privileged towns we have just considered were the hotbeds of 'freedom', and as such they afforded both an example and an encouragement to malcontents hatching revolts. We may conclude our survey of the trouble-spots in south-west France by suggesting that these hotbeds lay precisely in the lands which were once fought over by the houses of Capet and Plantagenet.

Attitudes to the risings

We shall round off our study by considering what impressions these risings made on the contemporaries who witnessed them. We shall also examine how the risings were portrayed by historians in later centuries.

Public opinion viewed as ignorant or pathetic

Popular risings broke out all the time. In spite of their frequency, however, they were never regarded with hatred or fear by society at large. Society's attitude was one of pity or indifference. The events which occurred in the course of these risings were seldom judged worthy of mention in a news sheet or history. Now and again a rebellion was reported in the press. The *Mercure français* gave an account of the rising which broke out in Quercy in 1624, and the *Gazette de France* alluded to the bloody confrontations which took place at La Sauvetat in June 1637, Galan in August 1640 and Estampes in October 1643. On the other hand the great wave of riots which swept through the cities of south-west France in 1635 attracted no press attention whatever. Scipion Dupleix was the only historian to give a significant place to popular risings in his account of the period. A native of Gascony, he had personally

---

October 1651 the town fell victim to arsonists. Subsequently 1200 of its families moved to other parts, and from that time on the government no longer respected the town's traditional exemptions. See Archives Nationales, E 363b, fo. 378, 23 June 1663.

witnessed a number of the revolts. We may contrast the work of Vittorio Siri. Siri as a general rule never fails to mention a single battle. He describes how the Spaniards invaded Labourd in 1636 and were driven out by La Valette the following year. But he never allots so much as a line of narrative to the clash between government and rebels at La Sauvetat. Upheavals of this nature were regarded with sheer contempt. The most staggering example of this contempt may be found in the history compiled by a certain Jean Danes, a lawyer at the *parlement*. Writing in 1644 Danes records,

A handful of nonentities rose up in Périgord under the leadership of a weaver called 'Jack Barefoot' (Jean-va-Pieds-Nuds). They ravaged the province, only to be defeated on two separate occasions. In May they were routed by Cardinal de La Valette. He took control of the town of Bergerac, which the rebel forces had seized. The following August the rebels were put to flight by the Duke of Longueville. Longueville captured their leader and broke him alive on the wheel. The capture and execution of the rebel leader brought this squalid war to an end.

In one short passage this author has succeeded in confusing the Croquant rebellion in Guyenne in 1637 with the *Nu-Pieds* rising in Normandy in 1639, and the Cardinal of La Valette with his brother, the Duke.

The vagueness and inattention to detail with which these events were handled need not surprise us. They are fully in keeping with the attitude which society adopted in that century to manifestations of popular unrest. Observers viewed the people who gathered together in a crowd, a town or a canton as a kind of corporate entity. A disturbance implied that this entity had been taken ill. Contemporaries who witnessed the risings referred on countless occasions to the brainsick populace, carried away by frenzy and racked with fever. Once infected, the population became blind, irresponsible and ignorant, easy prey for the blandishments of that handful of seditious persons who were enemies of the state. But these risings were never felt to constitute a serious danger. They were a nuisance liable to hinder the activity of the taxman, but nothing worse than that. The moment the town militias took the trouble to engage them or a party of troops were dispatched to restore order, it became apparent immediately 'that courage mattered more than numbers, and military skill and discipline were certain to triumph over the savagery of the mob'. The rebels were generally agreed to count for nothing either in political or military terms. We find this assumption clearly expressed in a set of instructions which the government issued on one occasion to the Marquis d'Aumont. The central authorities found themselves confronted by two simultaneous upheavals in western France. Dissident nobles were holding assemblies, and the marshland parishes of Bas-Poitou had risen in arms. But the authorities detected only one challenge of any importance. Sublet de Noyers wrote to the marquis that it was 'far more urgent and necessary to break up a faction of gentry than to spend time punishing rebel parishes and forcing them to pay their tax arrears'.

Eminent people looked on the rebellions largely in a spirit of heartfelt pity tinged with contempt. The most famous expression of this attitude was undoubtedly the remark which Pierre de L'Estoile and Agrippa d'Aubigné ascribe to Henri IV. In June 1594, they tell us, word reached the court for the first time of the rising in Périgord. 'Swearing by his holy drunken gluttony and jesting in his usual manner', the king is said to have declared 'that if he were not what he was and had a little more spare time, he would gladly become a Croquant'. Another typical illustration of the attitude which the nobility adopted towards the rebels is provided by the policies of the old Duke of Épernon. Épernon was basically opposed to increased taxation. He was disturbed by the hardship which was afflicting his province, and full of abuse for the profiteers who were taking advantage of it. He was also personally acquainted with many of the rebels, and acknowledged the grateful tributes they paid to his mild administration. His biographer Girard tells us that he gave orders to his guards 'to avoid shedding the blood of this rabble as far as they could. He was rather grieved by their blindness than annoyed by their audacity.' Girard further comments on the massacre of rebels at Saint-Seurin, 'It was incredible what distress the duke felt at the loss of these wretches.' Most of the scholars in Épernon's province expressed themselves in similar terms. When government troops succeeded in scattering the Croquants of Angoumois in 1636, Guez de Balzac voiced his satisfaction. 'God grant', he wrote, 'that our other wounds may be healed as easily, and that the Croats will give us as little trouble as the Croquants have done.' Maynard delivered himself of some disdainful comments regarding the troubles which broke out in Quercy in 1637. 'In all probability', he observed to a correspondent, 'the news of our uprising will have reached you by this time and you will have had as good a laugh about it as I have done. The rebels have succeeded in harming only the people they claimed to want to help, and they have weakened themselves so much by now you can only pity them.' This note of pity is sounded with particular clearness in the writings of the two provincial chroniclers, Scipion Dupleix and the *abbé* de Foulhiac. Both men deplored the 'disastrous' nature of the risings. But they wound up their comments by voicing considerable sympathy for the reasons which had induced the rebels to take up arms. They talked of the 'violent conduct and greed of the tax-farmers' and the 'destruction of the main privileges these communities have enjoyed'. They referred to the 'oppression endured by the masses in south-west France' and lamented 'the burden of wretchedness which weighs them down'.

Religion and rebellion

France at this period was still a wholly Christian society. In studying the impact these risings made on contemporary opinion, we can scarcely afford to ignore the views of the churchmen of the day. At the same time we may usefully investigate the possible role which particular religious groups played in the various insurrections. The Protestants are an obvious case in point. Large numbers of them were concentrated in Guyenne, for example, where they took part in the religious wars of the early seventeenth century and later engaged in a vain attempt to revolt in response to the persecutions they suffered during the reign of Louis XIV. In certain important strongholds like La Rochelle and Montauban they had succeeded in coverting the entire population. Where this was the case it very often happened that the members of the community who took part in religious riots were also the ones who became involved in riots against the taxmen. Both kinds of disturbance were started by the same humble citizens who lived in the craftsmen's quarters. Both kinds of trouble broke out, for example, at La Rochelle in 1617 and at Montauban in 1638, 1656 and 1659; the object of the riots might vary, but the rioters never did. Freedom of religion, like freedom from taxes, was thought of as being part of a town's long-standing privileges; and the common people sprang to defend whatever privileges they felt they had. In defending their privileges these perpetual agitators believed they were simply acting as the champions of ancient custom and the established order of things. They considered themselves to be perfectly justified in resisting any attempt by the central authorities to do away with their privileges and introduce change. It was only natural, then, that the manifestos issued by the persecuted and dissident Huguenots should have taken up the old nostalgic themes of the tax rebels. We find this familiar nostalgia in both the manifesto issued under the name of the Marquis de Miremont in 1689 and the Duke of Schomberg's manifesto of 1692. In 1709 a number of Protestant envoys toured the Foix region and Rouergue on a mission intended to spread propaganda for their cause. These envoys were careful to play down any reference to religion. They were setting out to appeal to Catholic peasants as well as Huguenot ones. Their message was simply 'that there was going to be a general uprising, and that anyone who was tired of paying taxes should arm himself thoroughly and get ready to take his place in the front line'. Huguenots aimed to restore the freedoms of the churches, and tax rebels sought to re-establish the exemptions which their communities had enjoyed in earlier years. Both were agreed that the advance of state control was obnoxious and had to be resisted.

But the interests of Protestant and tax rebel did not always coincide. Generally speaking, the burgesses who lived in the towns along the Garonne were converts to Protestantism, while the peasants in the surrounding country-side had clung to their Catholic faith. The *chambres de l'Édit* were incessantly bombarded by requests that the agents of the tax-farmers should be brought to justice, and it is clear from these petitions that the agents in question were often Huguenots. When the great waves of insurrection swept through the countryside, the Protestant cities prudently shut their gates and avoided experiencing the terrible outbreaks of violence which took place in the Catholic towns. In 1635, 1637, 1643 and again in the Fronde years the Protestant towns of the Middle Garonne remained staunchly royalist. The town councils sent out envoys to convey their expressions of loyalty to the provincial governor and the Council in Paris. The Protestant towns, in other words, consistently followed a course of maximum prudence in political affairs; and they had no share in the resentments which seethed in the countryside. The consequence was that the tide of insurrection passed them by.

Leaders of the Catholic Church contemplated popular risings with much the same revulsion as the secular authorities. Catholic doctrine taught that it was a sin for the lower orders to rise up against the prince to whose care the Lord had entrusted them. It was equally sinful for them to refuse their prince the taxes he was raising in order to guard their country's borders and defend them against their foes. The Church made its position unequivocally plain on 12 June 1602 when riots broke out in Limoges after a notice announcing a new tax was posted there. Two of the rioters subsequently confessed to having stolen a number of sacred objects from a church. Before they were broken on the wheel they revealed that they had taken the host from the pyxes they had stolen, wrapped it respectfully in a linen cloth and hidden it in a cranny in the church wall. The local bishop promptly set off at the head of a procession of 7,000 to 8,000 people to retrieve the missing host from its hiding-place. A Jesuit preacher took the opportunity to draw the people's attention to the fact 'that these two wretches had been led on from sedition to far worse crimes'. The same point was made by another Jesuit in the aftermath of the Fronde. On 12 April 1654 this Jesuit father delivered a sermon to an immense crowd which had just completed a pilgrimage to the shrine of Notre-Dame-des-Vertus on the edge of Le Paréage. He informed the crowd 'that the only way for communities and individuals to live in comfort and security is to persist in steadfast service and obedience to the king. The town [of Périgueux] should give thanks to God for its happy deliverance from the hardships into which it has been plunged by the intrigues of a handful of ill-intentioned and muddle-headed people.' In the Jesuit's view the extreme distress which Périgueux had experienced resulted purely and simply from the exceptional wickedness of the people there. They should see it as a cue for repentance, not as a reason for continuing with their impious revolt.

Our *tailles* have tripled in the course of this unhappy period. In addition we have had to pay a further tax in the form of the army provisions. Hardest of all we have had to feed the same gangs of insolent soldiers who have wrecked all our property ... All the ills we are suffering have been caused by our wickedness, and the Lord has resolved to punish us for our sins.

The Church's efforts were directed, then, to reducing social tension and bringing together the various different elements in the body politic. But the clergy were also driven to adopt a rather different standpoint by the emphasis they placed on achieving reconciliation between the kingdoms of the Catholic world. Bichi and Scotti, the papal nuncios, and Caussin, the Jesuit who served as Louis XIII's confessor, were well aware of Richelieu's unpopularity in the provinces and barely troubled to conceal their distaste for his schemes. The Cardinal is known to have been opposed by a peace party whose members included some of the most prominent ecclesiastics in the Catholic Church. One obvious representative of this Catholic dissidence was Châteauneuf, Guardian of the Seals, who was imprisoned in the château at Angoulême from 1633 to 1643. On one occasion Châteauneuf voiced his indignation at the readiness Séguier had shown to compromise the dignity of his office by putting down risings in Rouen and Lyon.

Lower-ranking clergy were deeply rooted in their parish communities and infused, to a great extent, with the popular notions of the time. It followed that some of them were heavily involved in the risings. Village priests marched at the head of their armed parishioners in both of the two revolts which broke out in Angoumois in 1548 and 1636. Other priests came to prominence during the great rebellion of the communes of Périgord. A chronicler in Bordeaux records how 'one clergyman cut a striking figure in the course of the great uprising of the communes of Périgord on account of both his courage and physical strength'. This Croquant priest justified his involvement 'on the grounds that there was no rule forbidding clergy to go to war, and he was defending the common weal'. Large numbers of monks were involved in the Fronde conspiracies, and took part in the clashes on the streets. Bordeaux was filled with Jesuits and Franciscans preaching sedition.

On 12 June 1659 the parish priest of Gaillan in Médoc sounded the tocsin and urged his flock to rise in rebellion against the tax fusiliers. The soldiers beat the priest up and arrested him. The archbishop of Bordeaux appointed a special commissioner to investigate the incident. Summoned to give evidence, the villagers of Gaillan launched into a heavily symbolic account of the hardships their priest had undergone. They explained how the unfortunate clergyman had been set upon by the soldiers just as he was getting ready to celebrate the Eucharist. They beat him on the head with their musket-butts and dragged him by his feet all the way from the church porch to the churchyard. 'They tied his hands behind his back as though he had been a thief, stripped off his hat, shoes and cassock, and sat him on a horse in the most demeaning possible way. The horse had no pack or saddle, and they bound his feet together beneath its stomach.' As if to add insult to injury one of the soldiers decked himself out in the priest's black hat, and rammed 'a peasant's cap' down on the head of the priest. 'The blood which flowed from his wound', the villagers reported, 'caused this cap to turn red in several places.' It is clear that the villagers were seeking to depict the seditious priest of Gaillan as a Christ figure suffering humiliation for the sake of his parish flock.

Sometimes the rebels received unexpected help from miracles. At Bourg, for example, a rebel leader named Galtery who had been hanged for his part in an uprising was said to have come down alive from the gallows. At Montpellier the legends accumulated around the rebel Antoine du Roure. Roure too had been executed, and his body had been exposed on a public highway. But decay did not set in, and the flesh remained uncorrupted for days on end. In an age of intense devotion like the seventeenth century, no one would have been especially surprised at the interweaving of secular and religious motifs, however accidentally, in stories of this kind.

The clergy exercised a particularly striking influence on the communities of Bas-Poitou and the Pyrenees. Country priests in Poitou went round preaching against *tailles* and *traites*. They hid their parishioners' chattels and spurred them on to resist the taxmen. One of the provincial intendants wrote to Chamillart deploring this state of affairs. 'You cannot imagine the trouble the parish priests have been causing in this *département*.'[13] Priests in the Pyrenees

---

13 Letter written by Marillac, the intendant of Poitou, on 28 January 1680. See Archives Nationales, G7.449. See also the letters written by Marillac's successor, Doujat, on 26 October and 19 November 1707, Archives Nationales, G7.454.

played a leading part in the risings which took place in the Val d'Aran in the winter of 1643, in the valley of the Soule in November 1661 and in the valley of Lavedan in February 1665 and March 1695. These priests as a rule were the only educated people in their valleys. As the only literate members of their community, they were responsible for preserving the documents in which the community's ancient privileges were set down. In past years they had stirred up their parishioners to repel the incursions of Protestants from the plains, and now they led the communities to battle and served as the spokesmen for their cause. It was their advice which carried the most weight at gatherings of the provincial estates.

Religion played at most a subsidiary part in these episodes. Senior prelates discharged their duty of keeping order in the kingdom, and country priests shared in the subversive hopes of their rustic flock. In either case the attitude the clergy adopted towards a rising was dictated not by the mission laid down for them in the Scriptures but by their position in society.

In general there is no doubt that the religion which prevailed in this classical age of French civilization was a logical, uncompromising and authoritarian creed. Its champions frowned on the unruly character of traditional law. We may speculate that in doing so these clergy were moving ever further away from the outlook and way of life of their predecessors, who had turned a blind eye on the various traditional expressions of popular unrest. In the time of their predecessors, however, the institutions connected with the commune still had plenty of life in them, and local allegiances had not yet been eroded by the state.

Reasons of state

The most serious outbreaks of violence were brought to an end by the issue of an amnesty from the crown. All of these amnesties emphasized that the king was mild and merciful, and filled with kindness and gentleness. When the king sent troops to put down a rising in Poitou he was said to have commented, 'We are truly grieved to have to use force.' Amnesties granted at Bayonne in August 1641, at Bordeaux in April 1675 and a number of other places pointed out that the king had chosen to exercise leniency rather than subject his people to the rigours of the law 'in conformity with his kind and gentle nature'. A petition of 1653 spoke in similar terms.

Our tragic discords are always resolved by magnanimity. It is through pardons, reprieves and amnesties that our rulers subdue the masses, confound troublemakers and scatter conspirators; through proclamations and letters patent that they calm the cities and constrain the provinces to lay down their arms. The kings of France use sealing-wax, not fire and sword, to impress on their subjects the need for fear and obedience. They strangle rebels with silken cords and laces of love.'[14]

Under Louis XIV, however, the government increasingly lost faith in this

14 See *La Voix du peuple à Mgr le prince de Conty*, 1653.

system of reciprocal moderation. From this time onwards reasons of state dictated that 'the king's laws should run their course'. Louis XIV and Colbert made their intentions perfectly clear. They issued binding decrees and directives to their intendants to make sure that every disturbance met with a suitable punishment. From now on no rioters should ever be seen to have got away scot-free, as had so often happened before the 1660s. The classic manifestation of this new policy was the threatening letter dispatched by Colbert to Bidé de La Grandville, the intendant of Limoges. La Grandville had retreated in face of some peasant bands that had gathered to resist the collection of *aides* in Angoumois. Colbert informed him that

it is the bounden duty of those officials who uphold His Majesty's authority in the provinces never to show any fear at any time. In a crisis they must even be prepared to run certain risks in order to make their presence felt and recall the masses to their duty ... You may rest assured that the king maintains a permanent army of twenty thousand men within twenty leagues of Paris. This army is ready to march into any province where a rebellion may break out to subject the rebels to the most spectacular punishment and to remind the entire population of the obedience which they owe to His Majesty. You should make this known in your province.

Châteauneuf harshly critized the leniency which the *parlement* of Bordeaux exhibited in the aftermath of the rising of 1675. 'We could have wished', he observed, 'that the picklock and the sedan-bearer had been sentenced to a more exacting penalty than the galleys. There is no other way to keep the masses dutiful and obedient.'

We should note at the same time that the amount of severity which was used to put down a particular rising depended as a rule on the character of the intendant or governor involved. Certain officials such as Verthamont and Lauson in Guyenne, Argenson in Poitou and Chaulnes in Limousin adopted a moderate attitude, and even managed to win a degree of popularity in the course of their postings. Other officials made their names through acts of ferocious repression. Foullé and Villemontée, Charreton, Pellot and Foucault were all of them typical exponents of the new *raison d'État*. The methods they used could fairly be described as terrorist.

Étienne Foullé served as intendant of Guyenne from the winter of 1637 till the spring of 1641. Subsequently he was transferred to Limousin, where he served as intendant from the summer of 1649 to the summer of 1650. Foullé was originally sent to Guyenne to conduct a mopping-up operation in the wake of the Croquant rising. Within a few days of arriving in the province he gave ample proof of his ruthlessness. A description of him is given by Scipion Dupleix, who rode with him as he travelled round the province to round up forgers. 'He made himself so feared that he was able to conduct himself with an absolute authority. His progress and banquets were marked by splendour and magnificence, and the consequence was that he made a greater show of his office than provincial intendants were accustomed to do.' Foullé's name was associated with two atrocities in particular. The first of these took place at Galan in Astarac in August 1640, and the second at Saint-Bonnet-Elvert in Limousin in March 1650. Foullé took both towns by storm. He deliberately consigned them to the mercies of his plundering soldiers, and then proceeded to subject them to sentences designed to snuff out the very spark of community life. During the Fronde Foullé served as *maître des requêtes* to the Council. In this capacity he was obliged to appear before the *Parlement* of Paris when the provincial *parlements* voiced the unwillingness of the countryside to submit to intendants again. Letters dispatched by the *parlements* of Bordeaux and Toulouse on 18 June and 27 July 1650 respectively had been placed in evidence before the Court, and these letters indicted Foullé in the most damning terms. 'M. Foullé', they declared,

used his provincial office to hand out sentences which entailed the destruction of whole parishes by fire. He condemned whole populations to exile, the galleys or the gibbet without distinction of age or sex, and all because they had been unable to pay all the money the greedy excisemen had sought to extort from them. He treated their lack of means as a criminal offence, and punished it with violent and inhuman acts behind an outward show of justice.

The court granted Foullé a hearing on 19 July. A legal battle began to unfold in the course of August, but the incipient lawsuit seems to have been terminated abruptly after the Peace of Bordeaux.

Villemontée was a rather different case. This intendant deluded himself that his mild policies had pacified the rebels in Charente, and had even had a medal struck to perpetuate his memory. His over-confident nature is confirmed by Guez de Balzac. Villemontée served as intendant in Poitou for eleven whole years, from 1633 to 1644. In the course of this long posting he made a number of enemies, notably the commander of the royal army, Des Roches-Baritaut. In December 1642 Des Roches-Baritaut lodged a complaint at court against a number of extortions in which Villemontée had become implicated as a result of the activities of his company of fusiliers, 'Les Combisans'. On 12 March 1644 an anonymous pamplet entitled 'The Complaints of the Province of Poitou' denounced the intendant a second time, and Villemontée was recalled. A 'Letter from the People of the Province of Poitou' dated 16 June 1649 took up the charges yet again. These documents describe how 'the intendant was often seen making a triumphant entry into the town of Poitiers, where he returned after giving battle to the local taxpayers. He arrived with his troops at the head of a host of captive peasants, and filled the prisons with them.'

Charreton, lord of La Terrière, served as intendant of Haute-Guyenne. His assignment was to suppress the disturbances which had broken out in Rouergue and Gascony. He proposed to the Council that the hundreds of rebels he had taken prisoner in those regions should be consigned to the galleys in chains. 'Only through acts of especial severity may we ever hope to quieten the turbulence of these marauding scum.' Charreton used the massacre of fusiliers at Estampes as the pretext for an act of collective retribution. A report sent to Séguier described this punishment as 'exceptional and unprecedented'. The intendant had prescribed that the five offenders condemned to be broken on the wheel should be left to die in their torments, and the usual last-minute deliverance should be withheld from them.

Pellot directed the suppression of rebellion in Chalosse from 1663 to 1667. In the course of his posting he inflicted collective punishments on the communities of Hagetmau and Saint-Sever. His correspondence reflects a zeal for punitive measures and an exasperation with the attempts of local governors and gentry to intercede on behalf of the rebels – attitudes which received Colbert's support. Each year Pellot had two batches of convicts escorted in chains from his province to the galleys. An annual total of sixty to seventy rebels were chastised in this way. In 1667 the intendant excelled himself by deporting no less than 136.

Foullé, Charreton and Pellot, in other words, made it their trademark to mete out collective punishments to entire communities. To judge from the number of times such punishments were inflicted when the government sought to put an end to revolts against heavy taxation, we can scarcely doubt that the law was being deliberately applied in a terroristic manner. The penalties designed by the state to chastise rebel communities fell into seven different groups. As a first step a community's privileges would be rescinded. The government would abolish all its assorted exemptions and freedoms, festivals, markets and fairs. The second step was to demote the community's magistrates. Anyone implicated in their official capacity would be subject to individual punishments incuding, in some cases, death. The citizens would be forbidden to wear scarlet livery in future, and debarred from electing any further magistrates to represent them. The government's third measure was to confiscate or burn the town records. The effect of this punishment was to deprive the commune of its personality. As a fourth step the authorities burnt the gates of the town from their frames. The fifth move was to raze the walls, towers and buildings to the ground. Special attention would be paid to the gate-towers and clock-towers, the town hall and the houses of the consuls and the principal rebels. As a sixth step the town bells would be taken down and smashed. The seventh and final punishment was to set up memorial pyramids. The pyramids bore a brass plaque on which the community's sentence had been engraved. Measures of this kind were used to chastise the community of Bordeaux in 1548, 1651 and 1675. They were used at La Rochelle in 1628, at Saint-Cyprien in February 1638, at Galan in August 1640, at Abjat on 8 May 1641, at Estampes in October 1643, at Bugeat in March 1645, at Saint-Bonnet in March 1650, at Montpellier on 15 June 1655, at Carcassonne in April 1657, at Cantois in November 1660 and at Saint-Sever in October 1663. Large-scale punishments were more often threatened than carried out. By applying them every so often, however, the government demonstrated that punishments of this nature were valid under the law, and that they were quite prepared to use them when necessary in order to set an example to future offenders. It was the apotheosis of *raison d'État*.

The new policy of harshness began to take effect only in Colbert's ministry, when government troops were poured into every province in France. We have noticed the change that took place at this time as the authorities set about stamping out the old baroque local customs, as they rounded up vagrants and wanderers and revoked the traditional freedoms of the communes. A similar change may be detected in the methods which were employed to put down popular risings. The authorities had equipped themselves with the weapons of absolute power. Previously the intendants had needed special warrants to prosecute rebels. A special warrant did not necessarily confer on an intendant the right to pass sentence without appeal: the warrant might equally order him to forward the results of his inquiry to the Council and leave the final verdict to them. The Council was bombarded by petitions from the victims of civil disorders, and its records were filled with the decrees it issued authorizing the intendant of the province concerned to investigate their complaints. Even before the death of Séguier, however, as early as the very first years of Colbert's ministry, these decrees are no longer to be found. From now on a plaintiff had only to appeal to the intendant, and the intendant, in his turn, was free to issue ordinances without needing any warrant beyond the authority he had been granted when he first arrived in the province. The Council archives make no further reference to rebellions, apart from an occasional mention in the file devoted to decrees with binding force. Such decrees became necessary when the activity of the rebels had given rise to a dispute between two different local jurisdictions, or when a disturbance had grown so serious that the crown was forced to assert its authority publicly. Another basic reason for the new approach to quelling unrest was that the king now maintained a standing army large enough to enable him to fan out his troops through every province in the land. The government was consequently in a position to break up any rebel gathering by force of arms as soon as it took shape. A report dispatched from Bayonne in 1699 affirmed that 'the offenders will be dealt with on the field of battle by military means and without any further ceremony'.

The ending of the revolts

The reign of Louis XV was untroubled by civil unrest. It is clear from the Council's decrees that only a few dozen disturbances broke out in the kingdom each year. Often these disturbances amounted to little more than expressions of indignation at the serving of writs for distraint, gatherings of Protestants or assaults committed by gangs of cornered smugglers. Most of the trouble was connected with the substitute salt trade, with tobacco smuggling or alternatively with the raising of the local militias, which frequently led to brawls. The series of communal risings which had marked the seventeenth century came to an end with the revolt of the *Tard Avisés* of Quercy in 1707. Eighty years elapsed before major violence broke out once again with the French Revolution and the wars of the Vendée. During that period there were no further peasant wars in the sense of confrontations pitting government troops against the armed strength of dozens of rural parishes.

South-western France was affected like other parts of the country by the peasant uprisings which broke out in the course of the Great Fear between 20 July and 6 August 1789. The principal hotbed of violence was the Forest of Chizé on the borders of Poitou and Saintonge. The National Assembly agreed to abolish seigniorial rights on a long-term basis, and the seigneurs were granted no scope for repurchasing their rights at some future date; but this measure only gave rise to the same misunderstandings as the tax rebates which the crown had conceded in earlier years. Peasants in every part of the countryside were certain that the government had accorded them a complete and unconditional remission of all their dues. They looted and burnt down the châteaux and murdered the officials whose task it had been to raise the seigniorial taxes. These incidents have been analysed in a number of different studies. To take a few random examples, they included disturbances in the neighbourhood of Tulle in January 1790, at Madaillan and Laugnac in Agenais from 8 to 11 February 1790, and at Saint-Thomas-de-Cosnac in Saintonge. The curate of this last village, Jacques Roux, was soon to become famous. The anger of the peasantry blazed up once more at Whitsun 1791. This time the trouble centred on the southern *châtellenies* of Angoumois, where such places as Chalais, Aubeterre and Condéon came to occupy a conspicuous niche in the history of the risings. These peasant movements of 1790 and 1791 were nothing new. We need only examine their causes and the ways in which they started and spread to see that they have a direct affinity with the communal riots which raged in response to the myth of no more taxes.

It would be easy enough to identify a number of other traces of the seventeenth-century gatherings of rebel communities in the risings which broke out against the taxmen in 1830 and, above all, in 1848. Traces can even be detected still later than that.

The Croquants and the historians

Contemporary historians viewed the Croquant rebellions as contemptible or pathetic, and in any case trivial. They were quick to vanish from popular consciousness. A few isolated details which had excited curiosity or horror were, however, preserved by some of the local chroniclers. Chevalier de Cablanc, for example, was attracted by the adventures of the Croquant captain Greletty. He included Greletty's exploits in the long history of Périgueux which he composed at the end of the seventeenth century. Greletty conformed extremely well to the popular image of the heroic outlaw who goes about righting wrongs. Because of this he has continued even in our own time to serve as an inspiration for local poets. A poet whose work was published in the newspaper *Sud-Ouest* on 30 January 1967 even ascribed to Greletty a number of passionate love affairs. It was justifiable poetic licence.

A scholarly Benedictine named Dom Brugèles alluded to Foullé's sack of the town of Galan in a local history he composed in 1746. Dom Brugèles dated this episode erroneously to the end of the sixteenth century. He also gave credence to a legend relating to Foullé's motives for sacking the town. According to this legend the intendant was bent on avenging the death of his son, who had worked as an agent for the tax-farmers and been killed by the rebels for that reason. Larcher, a specialist in feudal law, supplied an appropriately colourful account of the massacre at Estampes. The destruction by government troops of the rebel village of Abjat is said to have provided material for a dirge. The author of this lost lament apparently claimed that Captain de

Vaucocour was lynched by the peasants only because of the outrage he had committed in seducing a village girl.

Romantic fictions do not, on the whole, have as lasting an effect as the distortions of historians. Those writers who happened to allude to the Croquant risings in the eighteenth and early nineteenth centuries got all their dates muddled up. The only events with which they were acquainted were the revolts of 1594, 1637 and 1643, and they even succeeded in getting those revolts confused with each other. Above all they tended to exaggerate the social conflicts of the time. They ascribed all manner of disorders to the rebellions and depicted them in apocalyptic terms. As often as not they referred to the rebel peasants as bandits. Typical language may be found in a chronicle dating from 1770 called *Les Annales de Toulouse*. This chronicle describes in its entry for 1637 the approach of '10,000 brigands known as Croquants. These Croquants gathered in the neighbourhood of Agen, Cahors and Ville-franche. They were armed, and committed numerous acts of appalling banditry. They were led by several of the gentry.' Fortunately, the narrator went on, the Croquants were routed by 'the worthy militia . . . composed of prosperous citizens whose morals were above suspicion'. A similar picture of the events which took place between 1637 and 1642 was given by the abbé Salvat, a historian of Quercy. 'Those malcontents', he wrote, 'had the effrontery to launch a political schism with the object of confounding all the laws and estates of the realm'.

Another typical author was the Baron de Verneilh-Puiraseau. Verneilh-Puiraseau represented the Dordogne in the Chamber of Deputies. In 1827 he dedicated to Charles X a work he had written entitled the *Histoire politique et statistique de l'Aquitaine*. He had drawn on such sources as the *Histoire* of de Thou and the *Annales du Rouergue*, and was heavily dependent on them. In consequence he covered only the rising of 1594 in any detail. To Verneilh-Puiraseau like the other writers of his time, the Croquants were bandits. 'They became a menace to the nobility. They seized mountain passes and wrought fearful havoc wherever they went. Their banditry continued for two whole years.' Yet another distinguished historian was the Marquis de La Grange, who served as the deputy for Gironde under Louis-Philippe, and sat at the same time on the Historical Committee of the Ministry for Public Instruction. La Grange referred to the Croquants in an edition of the *Mémoires* of the Duke of La Force which he published in 1843. He described them as 'hordes of savages who hurled themselves on the châteaux and devastated the lands of the nobles'.

This concept of the Croquants as foes of the nobles came naturally, as we might expect, to the more conservative authors. But it was taken up with even greater enthusiasm by historians of a liberal cast of mind. In 1880, for instance, a Walloon magistrate by the name of Hermann Pergameni brought out in Brussels a study of the *Guerres des paysans* ('Peasant Wars'). Pergameni's book has nothing to say on the subject of the Croquants, but his general attitude to the social problems of the period is perfectly clear. He talks of how 'Richelieu alone made an effort to protect the poor with his iron-fisted rule'. Above all he draws attention to 'the pitiful story of the peasantry and its struggle with the landowners, right down the centuries from the time of the Bagaudae to that of the Ruthenians in Galicia'. He asserts unmistakably, in other words, a view of peasant revolts as part of a constant and timeless struggle against the landowners. This theory of history has countless exponents, and there is no need for us to go into any further examples here. The theory may fairly be said to have a measure of truth to it, if we understand it to refer to the instinctive hostility between peasants and city-dwellers. It is not, however, sufficient to explain the majority of the events which took place in the seventeenth century.

The most famous account of the Croquants making 'war on the châteaux' was that provided by Eugène Le Roy in his novel *Jacquou le Croquant*. Le Roy was of Breton extraction. He ws born in 1836 in the château of Hautefort, where his parents were employed by the Count of Damas. His parents intended him to take holy orders, and with this aim in mind the count had him enrolled in the monastic school in Périgueux. At the age of fifteen, however, as the result of some conversations with a long-standing family friend, Le Roy became a convinced republican and anticlerical. In 1860, after a five-year spell in the army, Le Roy passed the examination for the state revenue service. From that time onwards he served as a tax inspector in different parts of the Dordogne. He married a woman in the postal service: the two of them were united in a civil ceremony. In 1877 Le Roy was dismissed from his post on account of his opinions, but the authorities reinstated him the following year. In 1880 he joined the Democratic Union for Anticlerical Propaganda. His first novel, *Le Moulin du Frau*, appeared in 1891, and *Jacquou le Croquant* followed in 1899. Le Roy was offered the *Légion d'Honneur*, but turned it down. When he died in 1907, he was given a civil funeral, and the only decoration was a tricolour flag. He was, then, a lifelong militant, passionately devoted to republican doctrine and the view of history it entailed. His hero Jacquou is portrayed as having risen up, like his creator, against the old order of things. He nurses an inherited hatred for the count of Nansac, and eventually has the count's château burned to the ground. The fires of his hatred are stoked by the memory of the sufferings which his ancestors have endured at the hands of the Nansacs and the other squirearchical families who own the local estates.

Le Roy sets his story in the château of Lerm. The château was already in ruins by 1750, eighty years before the events which Le Roy describes. Other châteaux, however, did get attacked in south-west France in August 1830. Insurgents in the Dordogne attacked the château of Pazayac near Terrasson and the château of M. de Moissac near Sarlat; and an assault was made on the château of M. de Saint-Georges at Chamberet in Corrèze.Le Roy might well have heard about these events in the course of his childhood. We may note that he revived the old word 'croquant' to describe both the social upheavals of the nineteenth century and the political passions which fired him personally. The word had a strong peasant flavour; and it was, at the same time, a long way removed by now from its pejorative origins. We can see, then, that the image of the seventeenth-century risings ran the gauntlet, as it were, of a whole series of different periods and outlooks. The school of thought that seeks to identify a social war or class struggle in the risings of the communes has found in the fictional portrayal of peasant risings by Eugène Le Roy a source of distinct satisfaction. It is, perhaps, unlikely that the adherents of this school of thought will find the present work convincing, since there is nothing as difficult to grasp as the fact that one's theories are out of date.

The socialists of nineteenth-century Périgord were convinced that they were the political heirs of the Croquants. Their conviction is, in itself, a matter of historical interest insofar as it reflects the outlook of people born into the same ideology-ridden world as the one in which we have to live. Other nineteenth-century activists looked at the past through a similar lens. A recent study has shown how the republicans of Cévennes convinced themselves in just the same way that the War of the *Camisards* was a prelude to the French Revolution.[15] Their delusion gained ground and turned into a widely accepted truth. But this attempt of a group of nineteenth-century republicans to identify themselves with the Protestants of an earlier time can certainly not be regarded as a contribution to history. It was a story, pure and simple.

15 See paper by Philippe Joutard, '*Les Camisards, "prophètes de la Grande Révolution" ou "derniers combattants des guerres de Religion"?*' in *L'Esprit républicain: actes du colloque d'études politiques tenu à l'Université d'Orléans (1970)*, Paris, 1972.

Conclusion

Certain popular uprisings have succeeded, albeit unobtrusively, in emerging from the obscurity of trivial, diverse events and in making their mark on what is conventionally called mainstream history, by which people mean political history. This has happened because of the scope, duration and repercussions of those disturbances. As far afield as Paris, they would be known about and discussed. The king and his ministers would be so alarmed that they would debate ways of calming the unrest, and even temporarily abandon government plans in order to bring it to an end. These revolts which have been deemed historic must be defined, however, and thereby distinguished from other, similar events. I would suggest that a popular revolt was characterized by the formation of an armed popular troop which was made up of men from several distinct communities or neighbourhoods and which remained on the march for more than a day. This definition can be supported with examples. Strict application of the term 'popular' would exclude the civil strife of the Wars of Religion or the Fronde where the masses became involved only as followers of other social groups. The term 'armed troop' permits a distinction between popular revolts and outbursts of ordinary street violence which merely serve to demonstrate how volatile the moods of crowds are. The passage of time and place implies that a revolt had a degree of organization which was absent from the less serious, spontaneous, local riot. According to these criteria, the great popular revolts which did not happen in south-west France can almost be counted on the fingers of one hand: the *Nu-Pieds* of Normandy (July to November 1639), the *Sabotiers* of Sologne (April to August 1658), the war of Lustucru around Boulogne (May to July 1662), the revolt of Vivarais (April to July 1670), that of the *Bonnets Rouges* of Brittany (April to September 1675) and the war of the *Camisards* in Cévennes (July 1702 to August 1704).

In south-west France, the first great popular uprising of modern times was undeniably staged by the communes of Guyenne when they rebelled against the salt tax in 1548. It became the model for all subsequent revolts and was the earliest to figure in the tales of seventeenth-century story-tellers. And when, in the seventeenth century, observers or delegates sought to show a chancellor or minister why an uprising occurred or to explain the status of their province and the opinions of its inhabitants, it was to the rebellion of 1548 that they referred.

The rebellion encompassed several provinces, Angoumois, Saintonge and Guyenne, and lasted from May to September 1548. Men from distant communes joined together and formed large troops; towns such as Barbezieux, Pons, Libourne, Bourg and Bordeaux opened their gates to them. The able-bodied of a village would be summoned by the ringing of the tocsin and set off in good rank and file behind their parish captain. Gentlemen adventurers and priests with their flock of faithful lined up beside them. Meeting points were designated where all these troops would converge to constitute a provincial army. The soldiers elected colonels and drew up catalogues of grievances which they sent to the king. They put to death those genuine or supposed tax collectors who had the misfortune to fall into their hands. And they claimed they were delivering the province from new levies. The uprising had tens of thousands of peasants on the move. Despite the bloody reprisals carried out against them by the Constable of Montmorency, the demands of the rebels were met a year later when the king finally exempted the whole of south-west France from the salt tax.

The revolts which occurred over the following century all had the same characteristics and pattern as this one. I would argue that more than ten uprisings in south-west France adopted the model for insurrection suggested by the *Pitauds* in 1548. At the end of the Wars of Religion (1593–5), the *Tard Avisés* rose up in Limousin and Périgord. They were the first to be labelled with the insulting nickname of Croquants. In spring 1624, Quercy was disturbed when Croquants took up arms a second time. The year 1635 was punctuated by a succession of urban riots in Guyenne. The peasant communes of Angoumois and Saintonge gathered together to rebel in 1636 and the following year those of Périgord and Quercy revolted in their turn. The latter was the most serious uprising of all on account of its unusually military character. The years 1638 and 1642 saw uprisings in Gascony (county of Pardiac) while 1643 found the peasants of Rouergue in revolt. The years of the Fronde were accompanied by a number of armed popular rebellions, short and ill-organized though these were. The followers of Audijos rose up against the imposition of the salt tax, and earned punishment for the Chalosse area between 1663 and 1665 as a result. From April to June 1675, a second wave of urban unrest engulfed the towns of Guyenne; the disturbances resembled those of 1635, although they were more confined and less violent than before. The last uprising led by a popular army was that of the *Tard Avisés* of Quercy in 1707.

All these disturbances broke out in springtime. Most of them ceased or slowed down in July and August, when the peasant army had to disband so that its men could return to the fields and bring in the harvest. They all lost their impetus quickly, within the space of five months; the nearer royal troops were, and the less responsibility for guarding the frontier those soldiers had, the quicker rebellion would be stamped out. Equally, the uprisings of the Croquants between 1593 and 1595 and the popular turbulence which accompanied the Fronde lasted only a few weeks at a time. Peasants would take up arms for a short while, simply attacking a place or confronting an aggressor before laying them down again and returning to the countryside a few months later. The longer periods of insurrection appear to have consisted of several shorter armed rebellions which varied little and which drew inspiration from the impunity enjoyed by preceding disturbances.

Four or five provinces, essentially the region between the Loire and the Pyrenees, were involved in the two revolts of 1548 and 1594. It was always difficult for an uprising to spread from one province to another as was shown when the *Pitauds* of Saintonge reached the Bordeaux area in August 1548, when the Croquants of Limousin and Périgord met up in the forest of Rochechouart in June 1594, when the Croquants of Périgord entered Quercy (July 1637) and when the *Tard Avisés* of Quercy tried to seize control of the areas around Sarlat and Agen in May 1707. On most occasions, a revolt was contained within the borders of a province. When it appeared to spread further, what actually happened was that several distinct groups of rebels rose up simultaneously. Although they all took up arms at the same time and were inspired by similar grievances, they did not merge their different armies.

Rebels involved in four revolts have left a total of thirty-five texts in the form of manifestos or codes of conduct. Little such evidence remains from the other movements except for what was recorded indirectly by witnesses in 1624 and 1707 and the slogans yelled or bills posted in 1635 and 1675. These texts are largely consistent with one another, revealing popular provincialism and a basic hostility to taxes which was common to the whole of society. Drawn up by village advocates, they did not attempt to sweeten the rebels' demands, yet they were not particularly radical either. Reflecting the actions of those in revolt, they were a frank statement of the peasants' intentions. This faithfulness of expression is, in my opinion, proven by the consistency of these texts throughout the region and the period.

Each of these provincial uprisings reflected some kind of local unanimity. The numbers of those coming to participate in assemblies or to take up arms would climb steadily as tens of thousands came from hundreds of parishes from miles around. The size of the largest insurrectional gatherings were considerable. On 7 May 1637, in the forest of Vergt, 30,000 peasants assembled. The *Pitauds* numbered about 15,000 three times in 1548: at Saintes on 12 August, at Ruffec on 16 August and before the gates of Angoulême several days later. On 31 May 1594 some 10,000 Croquants from Périgord assembled at La Boule. It was the same when the Croquants of the Angoulême area gathered for the assembly at La Couronne on 24 June 1636, in front of Villefranche-du-Rouergue in September 1643 and in front of Cahors on 15 March 1707. At the time, these assemblies appeared quite exceptional. On other occasions, when an uprising was more localized, only two or three thousand peasants would be involved. This was the case in Quercy on 6 June 1624 and at Plaisance in Gascony on 22 June 1642. Even fewer people were implicated in urban unrest: the most violent and populous riots of the summer of 1635, at Bordeaux, Agen, Périgueux, Port-Sainte-Marie and Clermont-Dessus, were certainly staged by fewer then 5,000. Yet even this number was sufficiently unusual and disturbing to warrant discussion and calculation by those who witnessed it. Thus the tens of thousands of peasants who assembled for the biggest revolts exceeded in number even those participating in the greatest fairs or the best-known pilgrimages; and they presented a spectacle quite beyond the previous experience of all those who saw them.

The sparks which fired these insurrections should be noted for their part in the history of the French tax system: they were events in the operation of this institution which appeared to the oppressed as unjustified aggression and intolerable provocation.

In 1541, it had been decided to extend to south-west France the system of government salt storage as part of the tax-farm there. It was the officials who put this into practice who provoked the great revolt of 1548 by their missions through the region. The peasant uprisings of 1593–5 were fundamentally a self-defensive reaction against the abrogation of tax agreements, the doubling of *tailles* and pillaging by passing soldiers. The establishment of an annual duty on innkeepers, the imposition of the so-called *droits aliénés* and the raising of the rations tax for the armies were responsible in their turn for the popular indignation which resulted in the unrest of 1635–7. During the Fronde, the dismissal of the agents of fiscal oppression, intendants, agents and fusiliers in the service of the tax-farmers gave rise to tremendous anti-authoritarian hopes which served as a motive for uprisings. Then, just as had happened in 1594 at the end of the Wars of Religion, peasants defended themselves in response to the ravages of the civil wars. The most unpopular levies of Louis XIV's reign were the extension of the salt tax to the Gascon and Pyrenean areas after 1663, the imposition of levies on the hallmarking of tin and the authentication of legal documents in 1675 and, finally, the duty on the issuing of writs in 1707. These taxes were particularly indicative of the burden which the standardization of revenue collecting placed on local privileges. The extension of existing taxes to provinces thitherto exempt made the inhabitants of those areas feel as if they had been attacked or invaded. Likewise, they especially resented the *aides* which restricted their wine-drinking, the salt tax which encroached on their freedom to season their soup, and the duties on the authentication of papers and issuing of writs which made it harder to take people to court or prove customary rights. Wine and salt were imbued with great symbolism while, to the seventeenth-century mind, paper carried unreliable but formidable authority. The story of the great popular revolts bore the marks of the military history of France: the Italian wars, the civil wars and the interminable Thirty Years War all required an effort which was met by the greatest achievements in tax-raising. The modern state of France was built by vigorous fiscal policies which were implemented according to the demands made by European wars. New ways of enforcing the government's plans and of tightening its grip on the provinces were necessary to defray military expenditure.

There is much to be learnt from the way in which the great revolts of south-western France conformed to repetitive patterns. It is possible to discover a basic formula for rebellion and to assign it its place in history. It was in the inns on the edge of fairgrounds that a new determination was born in the hearts of the peasantry. They would pass around messages to each other announcing rendezvous to be held on Sundays or festival days. Meetings would be held further and further afield and get bigger each time the tocsin was rung, drawing people from more and more parishes and across ever greater distances. Finally the point would be reached where those who had gathered elected captains and colonels. Then their army would set out for the nearest town. Before its closed gates, the self-styled communes, in arms, would command the magistrates to open up or send out the excisemen to receive their just deserts. Unable to force their enemy to come to terms, the communes then ravaged the rural possessions of the town. While waiting for the next assembly to be held, they compiled lists of grievances and they sent representatives to take these to the king or to the governor of the province. Then they would lay down their arms for one reason or another: the harvest would call them back to their fields; the promise of a royal commissioner would calm their anger or the swift rout of a few peasants by a handful of cavalry would frighten them into submission.

Urban uprisings lasted for a shorter time, but were better organized. Like their rural counterparts, they were hatched by plotters in inns or in the little shops in the streets where the craftsmen lived. The arrival of the tax gatherers would unleash the fury of the townsfolk. Driving out the excisemen began instantly; the bells called everyone to arms to protect the enemies of the commune. Some kind of judicial ceremony would be followed by the murder of the taxman. The rebels trooped through the city behind a leader whom they forced to put on a brave face and march at their head. In Bordeaux in 1548 and in Périgueux and Agen in 1635, it was a consul in his red livery or a magistrate who served as this kind of emblem of communal revolt.

Only when the militia of burgesses intervened, sometimes reinforced by troops of soldiers, was the unrest quietened. Then the barricades which had protected the artisans' part of the town would be torn down. If the burgesses were slow to react, it could be because they had been taken unawares, or because they were terrified by the outbreak of communal violence. Equally, however, their slowness could result from the unspoken sympathy of the whole town towards the intentions of the riot. Since it seemed better to trust to the designs of the rebels than to arms, the leaders of uprisings were sometimes left in charge of towns and cities for several days. In this way, the citizens of Saintes, Ruffec, Cognac, Libourne and even Bordeaux seized control in their cities in 1548; the Croquants of 1594–5 took charge of nine smaller places, including Chalûs, Excideuil and Penne; and Limoges, Périgueux and Agen received summonses. For several hours or several days in 1635, Bordeaux, Périgueux, Agen and twenty smaller cities were overwhelmed by strife. The Croquants of 1637 lost their nerve at Périgueux, Sainte-Foy and Figeac but succeeded in capturing Bergerac, Eymet and Gramat. The peasants of Pardiac took Marciac in December 1638 and Plaisance on 22 June 1642. Najac was stormed by the Croquants of Rouergue in September 1643 but Villefranche escaped. In 1707, the *Tard Avisés* besieged Cahors in vain. Each of these ephemeral victories allows the historian an unusual opportunity to analyse popular ideology. Two contradictory, yet often juxtaposed moods are discovered, of jubilation and despair.

Let us imagine a town in rebel hands. The rebels reinforce strategic points, set up a command system and enforce military discipline. By means of clumsily written proclamations, they summon all the other parishes in the province and they threaten the excisemen with death. They have leisure to draw up manifestos in which they reflect on their idea of Utopia, a king without ministers and a kingdom without taxes. The Provinces and autonomous cities would there rediscover the liberties of a golden past, much as had been enjoyed by a past generation, in a time when each estate or class had its own place. The disorder had begun when institutions which had once seemed unchanging were disrupted by the advent of easy money and upward social mobility. But, the rebels declared, the community would be *saved*, and the *freedom of all* would be restored after those responsible for the *sorrows of the time*, the excisemen, had met their end. The momentary success of the revolt was not accompanied by complete upheaval: life went on. It never occurred to the rebels that they might be doing anything illegal: they believed they were reinstating good laws.

In the country and in the towns alike, barrels of wine were rolled into the squares and opened up once an uprising had been successful. The cellars of the excisemen were opened for this purpose; the rebels got drunk and spent the nights drinking to their victory. The expulsion of the excisemen seemed like a carnival. People laughed and paraded in the streets. The riot was a festival.

By contrast, deep despair sometimes overcame the rebels. The very success of collective violence was frightening to the victors. They were afraid lest their triumph should bring down terrible vengeance on their town or lest troops should descend to make full-scale war on them. The militia of burgesses confined the disturbances to the craftsmen's quarter of the town. Left to their own devices, the rebels lost all hope that the town leaders would mediate, and had recourse to suicidal tactics. When it became clear that their violence would not be overlooked and the edicts of the excisemen would not be revoked, they threatened to set fire to the whole town, as at Bordeaux in 1635 and 1675. They showed in so doing a streak of extreme mob violence which reflected every bit as much as their carnival celebrations the authentic feelings of the people. The defence of local liberties rested with the poor. Magistrates were unconcerned because their offices and incomes made them susceptible to, or at least lured by, the promises of the excisemen; they were content to let their legacy of privileges and exemptions, which protected the inhabitants against new taxes, fall into disuse.

When all was said and done, revolt had its uses. Several months after the event, the crimes which it had involved would be pardoned. The levies which were most resented would be repealed. In September 1549 south-west France was declared to be exempt from salt tax for ever. When the popular assemblies sent deputies to court in 1594, they were given assurances of rebates. These promises were made good in 1594, 1596 and 1600. The result of the spate of uprisings between 1635 and 1637 was that the annual duty imposed on innkeepers, the introduction of the *droits aliénés* in addition to the usual *tailles*, and the military rations tax were all repealed and that the taxes owed by each province were remitted. Throughout the south-west, the recovery of taxes owed more or less ceased for three years. The optimistic legends which fed the growth of tax resistance among the people were given encouragement which would have serious consequences in the future.

Similarly, after the Fronde, tax collection was disrupted for years because assessments were annulled and innumerable rebellions were responsible for much hesitation on the part of the Council. These uprisings were suppressed by the brutal policies of Colbert. After 1660, the largest revolts ended in a bloodbath: the provinces were forced to drink the bitter cup of defeat and reprisals. When the *Tard Avisés* rose in 1707, taxation ceased only for three months, and none of the levies which had originally caused the rebellion was remitted. The year 1660 was indeed a turning point in the history of all institutions and attitudes. Before the accession of Louis XIV, revolt was profitable and useful; when arms had been laid down again, there was no reason to suppose that the utopian hopes for which they had been taken up were empty ones. The king would annul unjust taxes and reprieve his subjects from them. From this point of view, revolt was part of the ordinary course of events. When nothing had been achieved through complaints by provincial assemblies, the intervention of magnates, offers of lump sums of money and delegations to court, the town or province still had a weapon of last resort: popular uprising.

This then is the balance-sheet of historic revolts in south-west France. Their success was short-lived, but the huge numbers involved are proof of the strong support behind them. They occurred at the different stages in France's progress towards a centralized tax system. They were inspired by anti-authoritarian dreams of a provincial Utopia, and they were incessant and useful. Popular revolt can be considered to be an institution in the sociological sense of the word, that is to say a model for behaviour which is characterized by its collective nature. Revolt was a popular strategy, organized in exceptional circumstances to protect the community against fiscal aggression.

Obscure and forgotten instances of collective violence can be discovered not only in monographs about historical revolts; many also appear in accounts of prosecutions in judicial archives, in discussions recounted in the records of town halls, in letters of the time about politics and, above all, in the collected decrees of the Council. At this point, it is necessary to estimate the number of those popular revolts encountered by chance in the sources, and to explain why I have attempted to do calculations which are indispensable to research today. Sometimes only brief and cryptic information survives about a serious incident involving hundreds of people. By contrast, records of certain minor incidents which resulted in lawsuits have been perfectly preserved to this day. The difficulties caused by this inadequacy of seventeenth-century sources, at least where attitudes are concerned, are compounded by the complexity of collective acts of violence. Such events drew together many people, each with a different role and background; and all too many variables have to be taken into account when seeking to understand them. An uprising resembled a knot, or a bundle of inextricable strands. If one seeks to establish too much in the absence of documentation which would meet the requirements of sociological examination, one risks comparing facts and figures which bear no relation to one another. When attempting to plot them on charts, one soon enters a realm of shadows which only indicate how commonplace these events were. The only conclusions which I would wish to draw from this enumeration are that revolts were, indeed, an everyday affair, and that in this work they are accurately represented.

I have encountered a total of 450–500 revolts which occurred in south-west France between 1590 and 1715. To explain this figure, it is necessary to set out the parameters on which the survey is based. An event entails the intersection of a place and a time. The topographical parameter used is a city and its suburb or a town or village and its jurisdiction: the community within which people lived and worked, that smallest area of jurisdiction which corresponded to attendance at a particular church and which was used for tax assessment. It was in this neighbourhood, among the extended family, servants, people from the same street or hamlet, relatives, friends and loyal supporters that the duty to come to the rescue and resist tax increases asserted itself. The chronological parameter is the day when the uprising broke out and its immediate aftermath. Obviously, events which are isolated through these calculations form part of greater units which I have referred to as hotbeds or periods of revolt. Nevertheless, these minor incidents are worth consideration in their own right. When they are analysed apart from their immediate context, their repetitive and everyday characteristics are thrown into relief. In order to reconcile the differences between the various incidents examined here, it is necessary to identify each of the separate uprisings which made up the great revolts of the history books. In the crisis of 1635 in south-west France, for example, there were forty-eight different outbursts of violence, or sixteen per month. Twenty-five uprisings, or five per month, constituted the rebellion of the *Nu-Pieds* in Normandy. It is relatively easy to arrive at this analysis because great rebellions were not generally coherent single movements but groups of smaller spontaneous uprisings.

Before we attempt to arrive at any conclusions regarding the chronology of the risings which broke out in the 125 years under study, we must first bear in mind that our sources are highly selective. Even when this is borne in mind, however, it is impossible to ignore the impact of the Thirty Years War on the incidence of revolts. There were 282 uprisings during the twenty-five years from 1635 to 1660. This accounts for more than 60 per cent of the uprisings during the period in question and represents a yearly average which was three times that of the century as a whole. The outbreak of hostilities had a decisive effect. The average number of rebellions in any one year from 1600 until war was declared on Spain rose from one to ten. At the same time, taxes increased four- or fivefold. The connection seems clear.[1]

During the last thirty years of the reign of Louis XIV, tax revenue tripled in size. In the meantime the harvest failed increasingly often in 1693–4, 1698–9, 1709–10 and 1712–13. But this second rise in taxes prompted only sporadic violence. The reaction it received was different from that of earlier increases because acceptance of levies was determined not by their absolute

1 These are the figures yielded by my calculations. I would repeat, however, that they have no absolute value and are merely cited to give an idea of the relation they bear to each other. Altogether 459 uprisings have been identified during the 125 years from 1590 to 1715, of which forty-seven occurred before 1635, 282 between 1635 and 1660, and 130 after 1660.

value but by the way in which they were perceived. This time round, people had forgotten about violent resistance; the communities and the local independence which encouraged revolt had been worn away. Poverty alone was not enough to drive people to arms.

What was the seasonal pattern of these outbursts? It corresponds to that illustrated in the more limited analysis of the great historical revolts. Of the minor uprisings which formed part of the major rebellions, 71 per cent occurred between April and July; if this period is extended from March to September, 90 per cent are accounted for. In less serious rebellions, these proportions are reduced to 42 and 69 per cent respectively. Why, in these cases, were there fewer outbursts in the summer months? It was because minor disturbances usually occurred in direct response to tax collection. Levies on salt were collected all year round; duty on wine was charged from January to March when the new vintage arrived; the protests they provoked would be staggered throughout the year in a similar fashion. Moreover, these outbursts were confined to the towns and were therefore not affected by the rhythm of rural life. And perhaps the slight but pronounced increase in risings in springtime may be explained by the fact that people are more easily excited at that time of year.

By studying a period more than a century long and by examining a region which constitutes a quarter of France, we have been able to analyse an unusually large number of uprisings and have established a pattern for these outbreaks of collective violence. I have, however, confined myself to constructing a survey based on the study of institutions of the time. I have deliberately chosen to stop at this level because I refuse to subscribe to the finality of some philosophy of history, even if I have been imbued with one unconsciously. If disturbances can be classified according to their immediate causes, the best denominators are the operations of institutions. I have postulated four types of riot: those against the price of bread, those against the billeting of soldiers, those against the collection of overdue taxes and those against tax-farms. Each of these has its own pattern, its own authors, victims and mediators, forms of action, aims and specific results.

Different kinds of uprising attracted different kinds of participation. Usually, however, the community involved, be it hamlet or town, lent its unanimous support. We have already seen how the daily life of communities was reflected in their municipal regulations, legal procedure and military and fiscal arrangements; these rules reflected the long-standing sense of solidarity which was felt by local people and at the same time strengthened them. This harmony was also found in each of the four forms of violence outlined above, with the result that the inhabitants of a place would be as united in insurrection as they were in other aspects of their lives. Although collective violence at this time was a means of defending the whole community in a place, one group of inhabitants might however emerge as the leaders of the protest because of their particular role within the community. When disturbances first broke out, women would be particularly involved for a variety of reasons. When prices were too high, they protested because feeding the family was their responsibility. When tax arrears were collected, the excisemen found them alone at home while the men were in the fields. The innkeepers were often the ringleaders of the rebels in their capacity as representatives of local solidarity, spokesmen for community feeling and, of course, as the targets of the fiscal oppression imposed by wine taxes. When urban disturbances broke out, those responsible would include boatmen, ferrymen, cask-makers, tanners, butchers and shoemakers: all craftsmen who were regarded as dangerous by virtue of their clannishness or the tools they used in their trades. Riots against the salt tax were frequently the work of organized rings of tax-dodgers, groups of peasants who were usually led or protected by the gentry. When these dodgers were attacked by the tax-farmers' guards, however, the local people immediately came to their rescue, confirming their unanimous support for turbulent protest against duties. Revolts against the billeting of troops or tax collections were sometimes led by the nobility; more often, however, they would cover up the guilt of their own community by starting recriminatory legal proceedings against those who had provoked the violence, the tax collectors. The protesters recognized that the nobility were powerful defenders of community rights when the exciseman threatened: otherwise, they would have curbed the magnates' roles in rebellions. The real force however, lay with the ordinary people and even with the smaller landowners. It was the town or regional magistrates, and sometimes the lesser landowners, who could raise legal objections to taxes, make recommendations or permit tax evasion. The idea that popular radicalism was opposed by the swift enforcement of aristocratic power is refuted and shown to be no more than a distortion. Both had their place in resistance to taxes.

Each kind of violence was enacted against its own backdrop. Protests against high prices started in the market, by the harbour or on the streets. Protests against billeting drew the inhabitants to the city gates and walls. The revenue office and the agent's lodgings were the targets of violence against tax collection. Two particular features of seventeenth-century towns provided a framework for revolt and were indispensable to what may be termed the ecology of insurrection in this period. One was the concentration of craftsmen in specific quarters of the great cities, areas which became fortresses of rebellion, and the other was the survival of walls around even the smallest market town.

Each kind of violence was perpetrated in its own way. The anger of those protesting against the high cost of bread was directed against waggons or shops containing grain; they pillaged corn or imposed 'popular taxation' levied at a rate the poor could afford. Rioters opposed to billeting or tax-farming would seize the arms of the commune's militia and close the town gates in the faces of the aggressors. People who rebelled against the collection of *tailles* or the rights claimed by the tax-farmers caught up weapons and marched to the head-quarters of the excisemen, be it in a neighbouring town, at a military post or an office erected on the roadside. The tax agents who had ventured into the heart of the turbulent community usually provoked a siege of the inn where they were staying. And when, finally, the victims of this violence fell into the hands of the rebels, the haling of the exciseman took place: it was a ceremony which could be comic or tragic, humiliating or bloody, as the enemy who had aroused the community's wrath was punished for his aggression. This violence was ritualized; those involved took pleasure in executing it according to a set pattern. The rebels used time-honoured methods of punishment borrowed from folktales or legal procedure which confirmed the existence of a kind of popular justice. The juridical nature of their activity was further enhanced by the official sanction it received when the local magistrates, conniving with the rebels, imprisoned, judged and punished the unhappy exciseman who was delivered to them after being haled.

Our next task is to assess the part which these different types of disturbance played in daily life as we find it recorded at this time. Such disturbances reflected the special place occupied by violence in a society dominated by custom. Their purpose was to achieve their goal immediately: immediate and brutal action was preferable to a long drawn out lawsuit whose verdict would be forever challenged in the courts. As a result, those who led revolts were often successful in achieving their aim.

Those who joined in protests against high prices and tax-farms drew confidence from the fact that the very act of protesting unmasked the perpetrators of public crimes and human agents of catastrophe. These disturbances reflected the solidarity which the community felt against the victim who had goaded them to rage. By closing the gates on the exciseman or haling him through the town, the citizens showed their rejection of the public enemy. This rejection contrasted sharply with the sense of unity they felt among themselves. Far from disrupting or overturning social order, revolts reinforced and preserved the strength of custom.

These forms of riots were dependent on particular social and institutional situations; consequently they were impermanent. As transport developed, protests against high bread prices disappeared; as the quartering of troops improved, there were fewer outbursts against billeting; and as communities became less cohesive and lost their privileges, so there was less violence against the *tailles* and the tax-farms.

Because the motives behind revolts were often complex, types of collective violence were often less clear-cut than those outlined here and they tended to overlap. For example, when the Croquants of Périgord gathered to protest against taxes and billeting in May 1595, they also attacked the waggons of grain entering Périgueux. When the people of Bayeux rebelled against the levying of the Convoy et Comptablie dues in June 1641, they accused the tax agents of wanting to starve them. Conversely, hostility to taxes affected the grain riots in the Auvergne in May 1662, where the rebels labelled their enemies 'corn excisemen'.

The principal value of this kind of classification is rather that it enables us to include in our survey the great majority of recorded revolts. The hundreds of violent incidents analysed here fall into the categories I have suggested, with just a few exceptions. The disturbances which cannot be included are protests about monetary matters which, though similar to riots against taxes, were confined to the immediate area affected; fighting between rival factions in towns, especially in Gascony; and strife between religious groups. The latter two kinds of violence were but pale reflections among ordinary townsfolk of the great political conflicts which went above their heads and in which they were involved only as unimportant followers. Overall, therefore, our classification of revolts appears to work well.

The new character in the drama was the modern state, bureaucratic and centralizing. People who occupied one area, living and dying under the jurisdiction of the same by-laws, shared a common feeling of solidarity. Their spontaneous hatred of innovation prompted them to reject each new institution which represented the expansion of state activity. And so, when the state, which had been arbiter of justice and then collector of taxes, began to conscript men for the army in the eighteenth century, this latest role provoked a different kind of popular violence: rioting by militia men, conscripts and deserters. To have any impact, the new institutions had to be aggressive and restrictive, adopting attitudes which provoked the response of revolt. Each state institution thus prompted a particular reaction on the part of the subject. During the sixteenth and seventeenth centuries, the French monarchy developed machinery for collecting taxes which, in order to obtain something from every subject, had to undermine the barrier of privileges and customs which protected the individual from the state.

This study has also led us to a tentative survey of the beliefs which were associated with tax resistance. The ideas which inspired French rebels doubtless had their place in other uprisings of early modern Europe. It is possible to reconstruct the lore of hostility to levies from the attitudes and reactions of those who remained in arrears as taxes were increased. It had four basic themes: myths about the king, myths about the end of taxation, maddening rumours about imaginary taxes, and hatred towards the exciseman.

It was widely believed that the king was deceived by his wicked advisers who did not tell him about the woes of his subjects; and that he was robbed by his finance ministers who pillaged the royal treasury just as they despoiled the dwellings of the people. These stories perserved the fiction of royal innocence and justified a revolt which would release the king from the clutches of his obnoxious entourage.

Rumours that taxation would be ended altogether were even better incentives to revolt. People thought that levies were an extraordinary, temporary expedient which was bound to cease one day; and that that day had now come. They told each other that the king would repay taxes to his subjects. Such reports spread especially fast when the monarch died or when peace was made. After this long-awaited abolition of duties, they believed, a golden era would begin or the good old days return, and there would be no more taxes.

Hostility to taxes engendered rumours of levies which did not actually exist. The possible introduction of the *gabelle* haunted people in south-western France for the whole of the seventeenth century, as a terrible menacing threat or a disaster whose unjust imposition seemed all too likely. Similarly, people in many provinces thought the day would come when they had to pay duty just for living. They assumed it would be levied on births, marriages and deaths, irrefutable proof of the impiety and wickedness of tax collectors, and they felt compelled to defend their basic dignity. These ideas were reinforced by myths embodying the hatred felt towards the exciseman. In south-west France, this was the name given to the public enemy, that upstart who was made the scapegoat for all the community's misfortunes. The exciseman was regarded as an insolent *nouveau riche*. He had made his money by ruining his neighbours and got fat by shedding the blood of the poor. He was regarded as a cannibal; monstrous and inhuman, he was sure to meet a terrible end.Enforcement of his final, just and dramatic punishment was the culminating scene of revolts in which these stories were made to come true.

One term occurring in this corpus of beliefs which deserves special attention is that of 'public freedom'. The *public*, that is the people, have the right to *freedom* and *repose*. These three words often occur together both in royal ordinances and in the shouts of rebels. 'Public freedom' and 'public repose' were phrases uttered by the *Pitauds* of 1548, the rioters of Bordeaux in 1635 and 1675 and the well-born Frondeurs of Limousin in 1649. Similarly, provosts' regulations referred to the 'defence of public freedom' and those who disobeyed them were designated 'disturbers of public repose'. These phrases represented the only alternative or concrete ideas that seventeenth-century rebels put forward about their ideal government, in all their opposition to the expansion of the state. 'May God protect our poor Poitou.' The purpose of uprisings was to defend, not to subvert. They were inspired not by hopes of a new future but by memories of a golden past. The supporters of change at this time were to be found in positions of power: they were envoys of the Council, provincial intendants and reforming bishops. The language they used bears a curious resemblance to that of the prefects appointed after the French Revolution; they all sought to stamp out the vestiges of a past which had been declared despicable. By contrast, the ideals of those in revolt were conservative: they wanted to re-establish a Utopia founded on custom and the kingdom's most ancient laws.

Although these beliefs were popular in their simplistic imagery and violent consequences, the same arguments were voiced at every level of society. All groups accepted the ideas associated with opposition to taxes, from the landowners ready to leap on their horses each spring to go to war or, failing that, join a revolt, to the officials capable of orchestrating collective popular violence in towns for their own ends.

Other conclusions drawn from this work would take us beyond the scope of our subject. Nevertheless, we would suggest that geographical patterns of behaviour during this period can be discerned, and that much can be learned about popular law.

When the history of revolts of this time is analysed, it is possible to recognize reservoirs, hotbeds and bases of insurrection: communities which, first, remained almost permanently in arms and which, second, set an example of rebellion to other places where collective violence erupted. I believe I have identified several such places: the Breton marshes, the moorlands of Saintonge, the area of Le Paréage or the forest of Vergt, the viscountcy of Turenne, the plains of Xaintrie, Millevaches and La Châtaigneraie, the valleys of the Pyrenees. This list is not exhaustive: contemporary records of people's attitudes suggest that towns such as Bordeaux and Agen or cantons such as Labourd and Haut-Quercy could be added too. They spoke of people 'free for all time who would not tolerate levies and taxes' or of 'the madness with which folk in the marches are imbued'.

The areas which were prone to revolt distinguished themselves from neighbouring places by the physical realities of geography and legal traditions enshrined in history. Physical reality lay in the landscape. Somewhere that could be reached only by difficult journeys across marshes, moors, mountain passes and hilltop paths gave the appearance of being impregnable. The same was true of border country, of the frontiers of provinces or kingdoms. Rebels of one territory could seek to escape its jurisdiction by taking refuge in that of another.

Legal traditions stemmed from ancient privileges and the real or fancied immunity asserted by an area and its inhabitants. These, they believed, legitimized their uprisings. Actually, physical reality and legal tradition were complementary: in the distant past, the location of a jurisdiction where refuge might be sought was determined by landscape. It would be a geographical unit such as an island or a mountain, for instance.

The formation of rebellious areas in south-west France in the seventeenth century appears to have been much affected by the English occupation of the Middle Ages. This may have been due to the memory of English sovereignty. A more likely explanation, however, is that the edges of the region still enjoyed the vestiges of those special freedoms and privileges which had been accorded by rival English and French monarchs. The influence of Anglo-French wars on the origins and development of centres of tax resistance does not apply only to south-west France, but also to the whole of western France, from the Pyrenees to Normandy where provinces shared the same histories. The best example comes from the ancient viscountcy of Turenne, where hostility to taxes is documented right up to the present day. It seems possible to trace a continuous tradition from the Hundred Years War to the Poujade movement.

Such a theory helps to explain certain indistinct but undeniable features such as 'popular spirit' or 'national character'. These ideas are normally refuted on the grounds that they are no more than subjective fable. In fact, they can be attributed to the lasting impression made by an institution on a region. This is not difficult to illustrate. Changes in the distribution of taxes resulted when a province was exempted and another taxed in its place, when the jurisdiction of a revenue office altered, when a town fair was subjected to its first duties and when a rebel city lost its privileges; all these could create unjust regulations. Merchants and inhabitants would rush to trade where it was most profitable, bringing business to the routes they took. Local differences in the duties levied created opportunities for smuggling which benefited the borders of a region.

For these reasons, the marches and moorlands of the Poitevin parishes which bordered Brittany and Anjou and enjoyed age-old privileges were home to a surprisingly large rural population. They were apt to be frequented or deserted according to whether their liberties were respected or ignored. Their inhabitants were unusually united in the defence of their rights – a habit they had long learned from resisting encroachment by the state and which they put to good use by rebelling against the collection of *traites* in the seventeenth century and, a hundred years later, in the revolt of Vendée.

For peasants who eked out a precarious existence as arable farmers, smuggling offered an important secondary income and even provided a living for whole parishes on the borders of tax boundaries. In 1661 the consuls of Rodez, whose fellow-citizens frustrated the tax-farm of Languedoc, had no qualms about defending the source of their town's profits. 'The salt depot of Languedoc infringed the liberties and privileges of the town, drove certain artisans to starvation and put the donkey drivers out of work. The result of this was to deprive the inhabitants of the opportunity to buy and sell food and profit from the passing of the donkey drivers.' We can see how the immediate economic effects of tax decrees may have led over time to longer-term repercussions resulting from those statutes which were issued locally laying down a code of conduct which the people were expected to follow. In due course, they gave rise to a collective attitude of passivity or a tendency to violence, acceptance or rejection of these innovations. Modern geographers who account for disparities in the territorial distribution of families who wielded great political power or the discrepancies between rural environments and urban society are convinced that they must take collective attitudes into consideration. Mentalities have effects which are different from those of demographic, economic or social forces; and they develop at another pace. Obviously, they are partly shaped by geographical factors, but they are extremely influential in their own right in restricting, distorting or inspiring the actions of groups of people. There is no simple relation between the economic and social climate of a neighbourhood or area and the political or cultural leanings of its inhabitants. The interaction between them is complex. It has to account for trends of stagnation or expansion in a particular place which can only be explained by recourse to narrative, chronicle, long-term observation or, in other words, the study of history.

The purpose of this work has been to emphasize the importance of mentalities. Attitudes to taxes, for example, varied not according to how much was really being charged, but according to how much people thought they should pay. We have tried to move away from the link between poverty and revolt postulated by traditional historians. Grain riots are merely one type of rebellion, and one which occurred infrequently at that. Historians studying these revolts have traditionally assumed that they were preceded and caused by bad winters. In fact, the occurrences of rebellion and dearth diverge more than they coincide. There is no clear-cut link between the state of the economy and revolt.

It is likely that the conjunction of certain important phenomena – the growing power of France in the seventeenth century, the fall in population growing power of France in the seventeenth century, the fall in population and the rise in yields on capital and land – were most keenly felt in virtually the same areas as the trouble-spots we have examined. Although they form a framework for events, however, they do little to explain variations and locations of revolts. A revolt is a cultural event before it is the possible product of economic coincidence. In these pages, I have tried to show the dynamic of such happenings in time and space.

Even away from those areas where there was a long history of revolt, people everywhere regarded it as an easy and legitimate weapon. It was embodied in traditions and ways of life as part of what is known as popular culture, and it was an accepted way of voicing protest at norms imposed by society at large. The term *popular* is not altogether adequate for these purposes, however. Even if the most extreme aspects of this kind of culture were decidely popular, its forms and beliefs, especially where hostility to taxes was concerned, were shared by other sections of society. When higher social ranks shared in it, its essence remained the same, although some of its stronger beliefs and assumptions were diluted and the behaviour it resulted in was accepted only as part of a tradition already being lost to oblivion and disuse. Popular culture, however, is no mere collection of old-fashioned, decadent or vulgar manifestations of the elitist culture of a wider world. It takes its character from original creativity pertaining to the lowest social orders. It follows therefore that those participating in popular revolts had their own way of thinking and acting, illustrated by the activities of peasant assemblies, the choice of arms and songs, the content of their manifestos and the nicknames of their leaders.

An analysis of popular culture reveals that a turning-point occurred in the seventeenth century: most of the aspects we have examined suggest that the year 1660 was decisive in its development. During the course of the century, a number of festivals or customs thought to be shocking and disruptive died out or were adulterated either because they were prohibited or, simply, because they were forgotten. These included the colourful boisterous processions which were led through towns to celebrate a special day in the town's history or the bull-fights stamped out in Lower Guyenne. The rituals of craftsmen's fraternities, the jollifications of the young and the leaders of *charivaris* all vanished from town streets at the same time as gipsies and vagrants disappeared from the highways.

This watershed is also perceptible in the social organization of the kingdom. Between the Wars of Religion and the Fronde, the aristocracy had been free to make war on each other, raiding and conspiring in the name of honour and loyalty, unafraid of bloodshed and death. After 1660, they were kept on a tight rein. When the civil war ended, their power vanished together with the old link between protection and land rent, preparing the way for the erosion of seigniorial dues in the next century.

Town officials ceased rebelling because the king no longer needed magistrates who had bought their positions to govern for him when he could send Council envoys to enforce his orders throughout the kingdom. The French monarchy transferred judicial administration to the executive. The structure of corporations and communities was dismantled. Military and taxation arrangements which, thitherto, had upheld local custom now destroyed it. The offices of popular magistracies were seized, town militias were, thenceforth, only allowed to gather for parades, town walls were allowed to fall into ruin, local privileges were abolished and room was made for direct contact between sovereign and subject.

Further indications of this turning-point in the seventeenth century are provided by features only recently studied by historians: the disappearance of the Occitan language and the end of the persecution of witchcraft.

For the previous hundred years, French had been not only the language of the state, but also that of common usage. Gascon languages lent no support to south-west particularism in the seventeenth century. Rebels' manifestos and even the shouts uttered in streets that supported revolt were in French. The only evidence to the contrary that I have discovered is the interrogation of Greletty in 1642, where it was stated that he spoke only *Bas-Gascon*. If ever popular dialects had been vehicles for regional revolt, they were not so now. Within south-west France, the *parlement* of Pau had abandoned Gascon in 1622, and only the assembly of communities of Labourd, the Bilçar, still deliberated in Basque. Rebellious inhabitants of Labourd gathered to the cry of '*Héria*' or 'the country', and legal records show that at trials in the area, a quarter of the witnesses could not speak French. But Basque was the only language to be linked to expressions of local autonomy in the south-west, as is proved by the fact that Occitan was not connected with particularism. Popular revolts were certainly provincialist, but they drew no extra strength from their association with the land of Oc.[2]

In the seventeenth century, persecution of witches was an expression of popular sentiment. It was demanded spontaneously by rural communities in Gascony and Béarn in 1643 and 1671, for example, not imposed by demon-hunting magistrates. Like most aspects of popular traditional custom, witch-hunting was forbidden under Louis XIV. The sorcerer and the exciseman together had been the enemies of the community, but now their execution by a frenzied mob was a thing of the past. The age of classical reason and royal centralization consigned these practices to the barbaric past.

A chronicler from Quercy, Guyon de Maleville, who was writing shortly before the estates of his province stopped meeting altogether, can give us a final example of this cultural turning-point of the seventeenth century and of how people then were aware of what was going on. Our author concluded his local annals with a sad and resigned reflection on the faded glory of his region. Significantly, he associated the growth of the state, which destroyed ancient local institutions, with the poor climate which, to the seventeenth-century mind, stood for an impersonal and unavoidable fate. 'We men of Quercy protect the use and liberties of such privileges as remain to us, and in particular we uphold the authority of our assemblies, although this is daily eroded by inclement weather and the expansion of the monarchy.'

Let us take up the thread of our methodological arguments again. Certain scapegoats found themselves the victims of a popular hue and cry which had repetitive, ritualized features. This was one of the methods of coercion enjoyed

2 Marshal de Schomberg calmed rioters at Montpellier in 1645 'by speaking to them only in our Languedoc tongue'. Likewise, Épernon and the Duke of Gramont made a show of speaking Basque to rebels from Labourd.

by popular culture. Georges Lefebvre has emphasized this normative functional aspect of collective violence in his work on episodes that took place during the French Revolution. He detected the idea of popular justice at work during the days of bloodshed of the September massacres; and he perceived a notion of 'social law' which motivated peasant communities when they defended their communal rights and when their rebels imposed their own taxation. In using the term 'social law', he referred to an idea formulated by Georges Gurvitch in 1932.

Gurvitch considered that each social group developed its own internal, spontaneous and autonomous methods of control. Thus, not only the state but every group created its own laws, albeit of a very primitive, incoherent kind. The function of social law is to integrate and harmonize the group. Gurvitch did not, in fact, supply any illustrations for his model from societies of the *ancien régime* but drew them all from the modern world of work.

René Maunier (1887–1946), professor of law at the École Coloniale, studied the laws and customs of North Africa and developed a theory of customary law or judicial folklore based on the cases he came across. He made a distinction between those of its traditions which were punitive and those which were not. He included among the punitive traditions the normative and coercive features of folklore ceremonies which his analysis had revealed. He believed that, on the fringes of state legislation, each society had one or more bodies of its own traditional law which combined the themes of oral tradition and customary popular culture.

Recently, Pierre Bourdieu has drawn attention to the excessively legalistic outlook adopted by those who reduce everything to the execution of set rules and their corresponding sanctions. Each social action, in his view, is one of many possible expedients. It is adopted almost unconsciously as a traditional solution to a problem but, in fact, it represents a popular principle which has been internalized. The approach to life and the material environment inherited by the individual allow him or her to draw on the received wisdom of these unspoken principles and to put into practice any number of tested solutions. Every group has such a range of expedients at its disposal in order to ensure that its age-old powers and privileges are passed on to the next generation.

From the historian's lowly, empirical point of view, the definition of any system of rules for behaviour is only of secondary importance, whether that system be a pale imitation of state law, or the rudiments of a social law full of potential or a tangled, contradictory mass of ideas derived from the traditional principles with which an individual is imbued. The historian will merely concede that every culture possesses the means of controlling those who embrace it. The preservation of normal behaviour is guaranteed by sanctions whose sum may be called either a bunch of expedients or the punitive dimension of juridical folklore. In such a system, revolt is the ultimate customary sanction that popular tradition offers. It at once achieves and exceeeds the effects of all the scorn and disapproval which the social group may display. Thus the protection and preservation of a particular section in society is assured together with the links between the group's rights and its members' duties. Like popular culture in general, this normative aspect of it is usually not expressed and becomes apparent only during the course of certain events. This notion appears to be a useful theory in the study of all human groups but it yields particularly interesting results when applied to a traditional or rural society. In this context, popular law governs social activity; and state law remains unable to circumscribe or dismantle it.

It still remains for us to demonstrate the unusual nature of these popular uprisings by comparing them with other convulsions in French history. To do this, we must draw the reader's attention once more to two fundamental characteristics of peasant revolts, namely the unanimity with which they were supported in the area where they occurred, a unanimity which contemporaries acknowledged with the tag 'excitability of the communes', and, secondly, the instinctive opposition of the rebels to increases in royal taxes.

When described like this, popular revolts of the seventeenth century can be seen to have nothing in common with the millenarian movements which had drawn huge medieval crowds. The apocalyptic fatalism of millenarians stemmed from their position on the fringes of society; excluded, woe-begone wanderers, they formed groups which stood opposed to the evil world which had rejected them and driven them to despair; and they sought to destroy it. Their organizations were fundamentally religious and spiritual: a characteristic largely absent from the revolts of the communes in south-west France. In these revolts priests intervened only in the last resort and then to join in the fates of their parishioners whose convictions and dreams they shared.

Those peasant revolts known as *jacqueries* which took place during the captivity of King Jean the Good in the fourteenth century were not so different from those we are studying. As in the seventeenth century, peasants then countered the ravages of war and the absence of royal authority by defending themselves and refusing to pay royal and seigniorial dues. The most interesting difference lies in the exact forms that the uprisings took. In the sixteenth and seventeenth centuries, peasant communities proved to be more united. The procedures by which taxes were collected had themselves created an opportunity for village assemblies to develop, and the least of country parishes had its communal discussions. Revolts were more organized and lasted longer. Instead of being directed against the local castle, they depended on it for support. The lord might call on the peasants to take arms or they might decide to make him their leader. Sympathies of landowners lay indisputably with the solidarity exhibited by the countryside or province. The enemy was the exciseman, and he lived in the town. So it was there that peasants went to beat him out of his hiding place behind the gates that the townsfolk had hastily closed. The towns seemed to be besieged by rural tocsins. The revolts of south-western communes were one episode in the long struggle between country and city; the city stood for the incursions of the state and the much-resented aggression of the modern world.

By 1789, the château had fallen into the hands of a landowner who had become a total stranger to country ways and offered his tenants no protection. He was a city-dweller who sent an agent to collect his seigniorial dues. To the peasants, he seemed no more than the distant beneficiary of a 'feudal' tax-farming system which was changing its form in keeping with the revisions of the *terriers* (documents recording obligations within a seigniory). Paradoxically, it was at this time that the principle of government taxation, long unavoidable, ceased to be disputed. This was the most important shift in the equilibrium of rural society in this period. But the other characteristics of uprisings remained the same. Peasant revolts of the years 1789–92 had much in common with their seventeenth-century counterparts: unanimity of the rural community, rejection of new taxation to which they were unaccustomed, defiance of enemy townsmen and a belief that there would be a general remission of taxes, particularly when the king decided to convene the estates general. In spite of all that is suggested by the political history of the period, the peasant disturbances at the beginning of the French Revolution did not depart from the typical communal revolt of the preceding century. On the contrary there was continuity; the ancient forms survived and there were no new kinds of violence. Moreover, the huge uprising in western France in 1793, which was directed against the Revolution, also marks the most radical expression of the reciprocal hostility between town and country. The same tension is evident in the many Italian counter-revolutionary revolts which came to an end in 1799.

The term 'primitive' as a description of the conduct of revolts is inadequate. No behaviour can be given a precise date; and if it is described in terms sufficiently abstract, aspects of it can be found in extremely different contexts. All the time that a community maintains its solidarity, it will furnish examples of unanimous uprisings against the incursions of the tax collector particularly at periods when government institutions are either new and not yet accepted, as in the case of an innovation which improves the machinery of the state, or are subjected to complete dismemberment when events overtake them. This was the case during the revolutionary crisis of 1848 when a political vacuum created by the provisional nature of the ruling assembly was combined with the imposition of the new tax of 45 *centimes*. It was also true whenever there were wars on French soil, as in 1814, 1870, 1940 and 1944. Insecurity, coupled with the absence of central political power, revived old local loyalties and responsibilities. The autonomy which towns or regions enjoyed for days or weeks at a time would prompt the inhabitants to organize themselves collectively, for example, by taking hostages and condemning their *ex officio* guardians for negligence.

The peasantry's ancient habits of self-defence would reassert themselves too: people would take refuge in the nearby church or the largest cellars and ambush enemy soldiers in the woods. Many of the dramatic scenes of those troubled years were reminiscent of past events going right back to the seventeenth century. It is therefore inaccurate to label nineteenth- and twentieth-century revolts by communes as primitive or anarchic. Instead, it should be observed, albeit at greater length, that the reactions expressed in such revolts are characteristic either of societies whose ideas about social order are simple and few, or of groups which are led by extreme circumstances to forget the ideological disagreements which divide them in ordinary times.

The term 'anarchism' which some authors have retained to define communal revolts appears particularly inappropriate. The Croquants did not reject the idea of authority or attack the social hierarchy; they merely limited their obedience to what they called their *patrie*, which might be their parish, or, at most, their province – the totality of their existence and destiny. Beyond that, they acknowledged only the king. To him belonged the duties of defending the kingdom and administering justice to his subjects. The ideal monarch had none of the new functions claimed by the modern state, which they saw, essentially, as the tyrannical innovations of tax and conscription.

In a work which has been rightly acclaimed, Carlo Levi gave an excellent account of how the educated city-dweller reacted when confronted by the astonishing, inconceivable world of the peasant. In this case, he was referring to the mountain villages of southern Italy. There, it was enshrined in collective memory that for centuries the oppressors of rural communities had come from the towns: first tax-farmers and collectors of old baronial dues, and then the supporters of Unification who had driven out the king of Naples and had filled the countryside with their inspectors and policemen. The peasants were united in their hatred of all these social, political and cultural developments which were sweeping their old southern kingdom aside along with all its traditional customs and practices.

The only wars with which the peasants sympathize are those waged against this civilization (of towns), against History and *states, theocracy and armies*: they fight their battles under black flags, with no attempt at rank and file, without skill or hope. These are miserable battles, always lost before they have been begun, fierce, desperate and incomprehensible to historians ... From time to time, the peasants of a village will rise up, hungry for blood, when they find no reaction from the state and no protection from the law. They burn the mayor's house or the police station, kill those there, and go off to prison resigned to their fate.

Not all of this agrees with our picture of seventeenth-century France. The Croquants, *Nu-Pieds* and *Bonnets Rouges* took great care to conduct their gatherings in military fashion. When they set out on their campaigns, they always believed that victory was within their grasp; they did not take up arms out of despair but because they wanted to drive out the enemy whom they thought responsible for the grievances of their province. These features, which are so different from desperate anarchism, also characterized the uprisings of the Italian 'brigands' of 1798 and 1813. Nevertheless, Carlo Levi has drawn attention to certain aspects of revolt which are similar to those of our study. In both cases, there is suspicion and hatred towards towns, legislators and property purchasers. There is the same resistance towards the distant state which appears on the scene only to demand taxes or conscript young people. Such are the unchanging characteristics of a particular rural way of life.[3] In all these campaigns, the memory of a golden past is evoked. The good kings Louis XII and Henri IV of the Croquant manifestos correspond to the rosy

3 See Paul Blois, *Paysans de l'Ouest: Les structures économiques et sociales aux options politiques depuis l'époque révolutionnaire*, thesis published by the École Pratique des Hautes Études, VIe Section, Paris, 1960, for important discussion of the hostility of 'countrymen towards the city-dwellers' and 'the revolution imposed by the city-dwellers'.

legend of Conrad of Swabia in Calabria and, in Mexico, to the memory of Zapata, who stored away underground the title deeds which proved that the land had once belonged to the peasants in the distant past. These stories of the good old days were much repeated because, in an agrarian society, tradition seemed reassuring while innovation was regarded as dangerous and even shocking.

The examples of peasant uprisings cited above allow us to conclude without difficulty that revolts of this kind were never subversive in their intentions but that they always constituted a response to aggressions perpetrated by towns. The popular culture that French revolts reveal was barely evident to its participants; it was revealed not by positive statements but by the scorn it received. When the age of revolts came to an end, it was denoted negatively by the disappearance of all kinds of folk festivals and ceremonies which future generations would deride. The history of the inhabitants of Saint-Sever is a good illustration of these parallel trends. These people had whole-heartedly opposed the establishment of an office of the Convoy tax-farm within their walls. Their privileges entitled them to do so, they believed. But as they had protested collectively, so they were all punished together. Their assembly was dissolved, two aldermen were hanged, their gates were torn down and their bells were smashed. The inhabitants were forced to pay the sums sought by the tax-farms from then on and they were forbidden to celebrate the Midsummer festival, lest it offer a pretext for further disruption. So they all held a meeting to discuss ways of finding means 'to appease God's anger . . . to escape this tangle of woes'. They thought they should abolish bullfighting, 'an old tradition which seems to have survived here from pagan times'. That decision meant that the end of their fiscal freedom and their traditional entertainments corresponded precisely. They imagined that this cultural sacrifice would at once satisfy the wishes of the reforming bishops, who had condemned these unruly spectacles for the best part of a century, and the orders of the representatives of the centralizing, absolute state, which was tightening its institutional grip in every conceivable sphere.

Those who benefited from this expansion of taxation, the 'excisemen', were also the embodiment of social and political changes which bore witness to the continuing development of the state. They represented public interest and patriotism. Whether we like it or not, classical culture is not unconnected with the *gabelle*, or taxation. Pascal's father, an *intendant de finances* (financial commissioner), was one of the envoys the Council dispatched to Normandy to assist in putting down the revolt of the *Nu-Pieds*. In his youth, Pascal himself dealt with the affairs of Poitou in his capacity as a tax officer. Bossuet, moreover, was the son of a notorious financier who had made himself rich by tax-farming. The Croquants were not imagining things when they believed that their traditional way of life was threatened by the tiniest piece of inscrutable print.

January 1972

Postscript

On rereading this history of revolts in south-west France after an interval of over twelve years, I could not avoid an author's remorse at repetitions and omissions that I had made. As often happens when one first tries one's hand at writing history, I sometimes failed to see the wood for the trees. I therefore think it necessary to emphasize once more what I believe was the fundamental characteristic of the events I described: the strength of the local community. The feeling of belonging to a village or a town, the spontaneous solidarity dictated by the neighbourhood, the inevitable mutual support offered by members of relatively isolated communities to one another have all been conspicuous features of daily life since time out of mind.

When trouble threatened, the community would unite, bracing itself against any sign of incursion from outside. In any rural society, tensions could arise from many quarters. There could be conflicts between journeymen and farmers, sharecroppers and landowners, peasants and merchants in the nearby towns. Imminent dangers brushed aside these disagreements, however. When the grip of state taxation tightened, each and every person made common cause in a volatile, violent unanimity. Old family rivalries, inheritance disputes, contested customs and social and economic competition were buried or seemed wholly insufficient to warrant coming to blows. The most durable manifestation of these little village homelands lay in the defiance they showed to foreign envoys and in their instinctive and many-sided rural hostility towards men of the city, whether that hostility was latent or active. But it was not only in the countryside that this local unanimity existed in pre-industrial society. People also knew how to uphold their autonomy and local solidarity in little walled towns and in the quarters of great cities which were so ready to throw up chains and barricades.

The history of the growth of the modern state with its concomitant political changes has often concealed the strength and durability of local communities.[1]

---

1 The importance of community structure in everyday village life, its rural economy, rudimentary political dealings, religious observations and spiritual life was documented in Albert Babeau's great work of 1879. Pierre de Vaissière built on this in his account of the provincial nobility in 1903. These two writers understood perfectly the behaviour, beliefs, deeds and aspirations of former rural society. Unfortunately, neither book has been republished. In addition, the object of their studies has been given an unflattering and narrow label: it is designated vaguely as the history of 'mentalities'. This is a term borrowed from outmoded sociologists who used it as a simple category for everyday life, custom, trivialities or tradition.

Riots demonstrating village unanimity can be found occurring well into the nineteenth century when community rights and traditions, such as gathering timber or vine stakes for firewood, were called into question and began to disappear. Fossilized traces of activity lingered on in the countryside long after the village lost its corporate spirit. Paths still led to stretches of waste ground and communal farmland, and summer pastures were still used after the nearest hamlet had been deserted or its inhabitants had moved on.[2]

The solidarity of the local community accounts for the origins, goals and forms of popular uprisings which persisted in the French provinces until modern times. Its importance in this respect was greater than that of all other historical forces, greater even than the hostility to new taxes or the unfolding of major political struggles.

There were more outbursts of violence in south-west France in the seventeenth century than in any other part of the kingdom. We should therefore ask ourselves how representative this area was of the country as a whole; and whether an examination of revolts in other provinces or of the evidence offered by other sources would produce the same conclusions. Discrepancies in privileges, freedoms and exemptions, in other words in the status enjoyed by different people and places, were a fundamental characteristic of the social order of the *ancien régime*. Where other types of political and fiscal status existed, it would doubtless be possible to discover other models of behaviour. Moreover historians have pursued different avenues of inquiry, and had different preconceptions; they have used a variety of methods and sources. All of these aspects of their work may lead them to produce dissimilar results. We must therefore put our study to the historiographical test and see where it stands in comparison with the work of others.

In 1975, René Pillorget published a well-researched and perceptive thesis on insurrectional movements in Provence. It is full of details of incidents with

---

So much significance has been attached to the economic data of the past that historians have tended to forget the influence of repetition of events, isolation and changelessness. The publication of many monographs about rural communities, from parishes to provinces, has, nevertheless, quietly increased what we know. Community life has been well charted in the important research of Jean Jacquart, *La Crise rurale en Île-de-France, 1550–1670*, Travaux du Centre de Recherches sur la Civilisation de l'Europe Moderne, Paris, 1974, Jean-Pierre Gutton, *La sociabilité villageoise dans l'ancienne France*, Hachette, Paris, 1978, and others. The present generation of students are too young to have known the countryside of the 1950s which was still well populated and worked by largely non-mechanical methods. They have never seen the once familiar sights of the whole village harvesting and threshing the corn and picking and treading the grapes. These ancient reminders of the past which some of us witnessed in our youth now have to be explained like a lesson in ethnography. Survivals which disappeared only recently, they have been illustrated by Hervé Luxardo, in his book of pictures, *Rase Campagne. La fin des, communautés paysannes, 1830–1914*, Paris, 1984. I myself have collected texts documenting the persistence of communal revolts into the nineteenth century in *Croquants et Nu-Pieds*, Paris, Gallimard ('Archives' series), 1974.

2 Marcel Gautier, *Chemins et véhicules de nos campagnes*, Saint-Brieuc, Presses universitaires de Bretagne, 1971; Nicole Lemaître, *Bruyères, communes et mas. Les communaux en Bas-Limousin depuis le XVIe siècle*, Ussel (distribution De Boccard), 1981.

which the uprisings in south-west France can be compared in our search for likenesses and differences.[3]

In Pillorget's study, we encounter riots against high prices, billeting, taxation on the sale or consumption of salt and wine just as in the south-west. They happen at different times, but this can be attributed to geographical variations, other strategic strengths and weaknesses and the different personalities of those who held power locally, such as provincial governors or the chief justices of the highest courts. The Provençaux had a much greater propensity for relentless struggles, however: they would fight long and hard for the fair distribution of municipal posts and the control of the consuls' offices and against municipal taxes. Factional struggles to manipulate consular appointments were not unknown in the south-west either but they were largely concentrated in Gascony and on the borders of Languedoc. In the south-east, these kinds of tensions provoked greater anger than did the royal taxes that drove the people of south-west France to arms. Indeed, the only money paid by the Provençaux to the royal coffers in the sixteenth and seventeenth centuries came in the form of a free gift granted by the estates. Communities administered taxes themselves and opposed the royal *taille* with their own levies. The result of this was that even if most people could not escape central taxation altogether, they were not, at least, exposed to the full weight of it. On the other hand, it was impossible to avoid town dues which consisted of duties on goods and *per capita* charges imposed regardless of income. When there was a crisis, therefore, the Provençaux directed their anger against local taxation rather than distantly decreed *tailles*. Thus it can be seen that there was a considerable contrast between revenue taxation in *pays d'élections* and *pays d'états*. Under Louis XIV, however, local autonomy was eroded in Provence as it was elsewhere; the relation between taxation and revolt was modified accordingly, and the reaction in the south-east came closer to that of the rest of the country. To sum up, the nature of institutions in any one place shaped the mental picture people formed of taxation and thereby affected the ease with which it was collected, the amount that was raised and the political behaviour of ordinary people.[4]

Another thesis published in 1984 shed new light on a whole section of French society under Louis XIV. Daniel Dessert undertook exhaustive research to compile a genealogical, social, economic and statistical picture of some five or six hundred financiers from 1653 to 1720. This painstaking reconstruction of the financial and fiscal machinery of the modern monarchy is, in some ways, a rigorous counterpart to the study of revolts against taxes. Fiscal institutions and rebellions are, in some ways, the obverse and reverse sides of the same coin, with the well-documented revolts constituting the

---

3 René Pillorget, *Les Mouvements insurrectionnels de Provence entre 1596 et 1715*, Paris, Pedone, 1975.

4 Even fewer social and institutional differences were to be found in wooded areas such as those in Normandy where *Nu-Pieds* staged their great uprising in 1639. Cf. M. Foisil, *La Révolte des Nu-Pieds*, Paris, PUF, 1970.

obverse, overt side, and the secretive factions and intrigues of the tax-farmers the seamy reverse.[5]

Daniel Dessert argues that the image of a financial official as a nobody who embezzled money to get on in the world is pure myth. It started as gossip; then the government turned the story to their advantage. In fact, the principal tax collectors undoubtedly had noble status *de jure* by virtue of the privileges which the offices they had purchased at huge cost conferred on them. Of these men, 46 per cent had been ennobled by the purchase of their positions. They were far from humble by birth: some came from families who had held financial posts and had handled royal taxation for several generations. Among them 12.9 per cent were of the third generation to enjoy noble status. The financial official was no upstart flunkey who defied the common poverty of the time by making his way up the social ladder at other people's expense, ignoring the widely held belief that a man should remain in the station to which he had been born. But the legend of the self-made man offered a scapegoat on which to vent not only popular anger but also every other social resentment. The people were like the dog of seventeenth-century imagery which furiously bit the stones thrown at it while ignoring the hand which threw them.

The financial official occupied a position which was well integrated into French society. Doubtless he worked for his own ends; but above all he promoted those of the plutocracy, who often represented the cream of the landed aristocracy. The work was not without risk: 18 per cent of officials in the period studied certainly went bankrupt. The financier was skilled at deriving hard currency from seigniorial rents, many of which he administered himself, and from royal direct taxation which he farmed. Thanks to the economic developments which occurred under Richelieu's ministry, the financier was able to invest capital in stock and put the finishing touches to the government's machinery for collecting revenue. He could tap the incomes of the burgesses of the robe, and even overseas trade and manufacturing businesses by buying the farms of occasional levies such as those on the transfer of bonds or the sale of offices. These indirect taxes had been introduced when Colbert restructured the royal budget. Under Louis XIV, financial officials were drawn from an aristocracy of several dozen families who monopolized the best positions available in the Council and government machinery. It was they who supplied funds for investment, and made profit out of years of crisis when an emergency necessitated exceptionally high interest rates. Moreover, they used their discreet powers of political patronage to exert their authority on the taxation system.

If the reality of fiscal machinery differed from the yarns that seventeenth-century people loved to spin about it, this does not mean to say that contemporaries were necessarily either miserable dupes or masters of hypocrisy. Certainly politicians who were as shrewd as Richelieu, Mazarin and Colbert set out to make a personal profit out of tax-farming. But equally, many of

5 Dessert, *Argent, pouvoir et société;* Françoise Bayard, *Finances et financiers en France dans la première moitié du XVIIIe siècle,* University of Lyon-II, 1983 (state thesis, not yet published).

those who were involved in farming the revenues of transferred lands or who were engaged to collect overdue *aides* or *traites* were not in it purely for gain. During the Thirty Years War and the years of the Fronde, superintendents paid out pensions and pledges for generals, governors and other people owed money by the state on the strength of receipts which they had then to recover and which might be invalid. Even where real gains were made, the coexistence of a profit motive and a social ideal which contradicted it does not imply that the nobility were in any way hypocritical. Simple observation will reveal that any period sanctifies the values it inherits and firmly believes in a truth which must be accepted by all, even though this idea is partly based on an illusion. As a result, Richelieu contrived to mistrust financial officials, while simultaneously using their services to administer the state finances as well as controlling western France, supervising the salt-pans of Aunis and Saintonge and farming certain salt taxes for his personal benefit. By the end of the seventeenth century the state was wholly, indisputably and increasingly dependent on its tax-farms; ministers by that time were all too aware that the government could do nothing to reverse its reliance on this type of exploitation.

If, by chance, rioters ended up injuring the unlucky sergeant of a tax farm, were they taking their revenge indiscriminately? The tax-farming system must have enjoyed a degree of local complicity insofar as the smallest unit of administration for the *taille* was the *élection* and, for the *aides*, the parish. The network stretched far beyond its centre at Paris and the neighbouring provinces where most financial officers came from. The hierarchy of tax-farmers had its lowest rank in the villages with the guards and the agents who were paid a salary from the farm's profits. At the next level up, it consisted of the farmer's lowliest sub-contractors and of the merchants, innkeepers and butchers who had identified, denounced and taxed their colleagues and involved themselves in collecting local revenues in a number of ways. On these men was based the villagers' typical idea of an exciseman, a picture of a racketeer who had escaped from his poverty. Thus the image of an upstart profit-maker was not wholly unfounded, at least in Louis XIII's reign when tax-farms were still confined to certain parts of the kingdom, when their renewal was not guaranteed and they were split up and sublet. At this time, the myth of ill-gotten gains and fraudulent social climbing and the ignominious status of the tax gatherers still had some foundation in fact.

This was no longer the case in the eighteenth century, by which time the financial official had an accepted position in government administration. The aristocracy had deliberately involved itself in tax-farming. Social and political representation was transformed; peasant wars were stamped out; and state taxation provoked only sporadic and local violence.

The Fronde was the final expression of a political ideal which embraced local liberty, government by magistrates, the renunciation of state taxation and happiness created by social immobility. Sudden action taken by the young Louis XIV in 1661 resulted in Fouquet's arrest and the establishment of a new court of justice before which tax collectors could be tried; these two royal initiatives lent credence to the myth of an unchanging, tax-free Utopia. The turning-point of 1661 gave the impression that the supporters of the Fronde had won their revenge. Richard Bonney, author of several important works which have added much to our knowledge of the politics of taxation in seventeenth-century France, has analysed the forces at work in the politics of that episode. The *tailles* were reduced, the proportion of revenues raised by indirect taxes increased, the interest rates lowered; financial officials were harassed, false titles of nobility were denounced, and reforms in justice and administration were solemnly proclaimed. So, for a short time, it was possible to believe that that imaginary time had returned when all was peaceful because property was unharmed and those who disturbed people's repose or were unduly ambitious were punished.[6]

Jean de Briand, an obscure Poitevin financial official who served as chief justice in the *élection* of Niort, was typical of those who shared this optimism. Like most of his colleagues, he had been involved twelve years earlier in the cliques of officials and rested his hopes on the success of the rebellion of the sovereign courts that formed part of the Fronde. This former militant did not think he had been disappointed; in February 1662, he saw fit to address a light-hearted remonstrance to the young king in which he voiced his wish to see taxes abolished. He had seen the joy of the populace in Nantes and the whole of the west when Fouquet's arrest was announced. He envisaged the king commanding all his financial officials to assemble on the plain of Charenton, dressed in the clothes their forebears had worn fifty years earlier, in order that they could assist the work of the *Chambre de justice* (special tribunal set up to investigate embezzlement). He imagined people with four carriages and fortunes amounting to ten million *livres* would then be seen dressed as valets, second-hand clothes dealers and palace clerks. 'Everyone would chuckle when they saw people dressed up like this; and provided no one was suffocated by the crowd or split their sides laughing, nothing so entertaining or comic could be dreamt of. And no doubt, Sire, it would give the gentlemen of the *chambre de justice* much useful knowledge.'[7]

This treatise was not really about political conflict or a cosy conspiracy among the powerful. It was putting forward a vision of the world based on an enduring, ever-relevant and immensely appealing view of life. The expansion of state power, with all the changes in social position it inevitably entailed, was briefly but seriously obstructed by this formidable psychological barrier.

In 1662, the commonplace that people's fortunes ought not to change still seemed eternally valid. Chroniclers and political essayists working at the end of the sixteenth century had expressed the same disapproval of the insolence of self-made men. When, after a long time had elapsed, the *Chambre de justice* met in 1716, during the Regency, such thoughts were voiced again, though

---

6 Richard Bonney, *Political Change in France under Richelieu and Mazarin, 1624–1661*, Oxford University Press, 1978; *idem, The King's Debts. Finance and Politics in France, 1589–1661*, Oxford, Clarendon Press, 1981.

7 Jean de Briand, *Très humble remontrance faite au Roy, d'un style respectueux, burlesque, sérieux et de Carnaval, concernant les concussions et malversations commises par les financiers, partisans et traitants*, Niort, 1662, 89 pp.

they now had a somewhat old-fashioned and nostalgic quality. Right through the seventeenth century, this age of peasant revolts, most people felt that a permanent state of social immobility was a necessary precondition for civil peace and the happiness of estates and people alike. They upheld their view through a series of outbursts of wild collective rage.[8]

8 In 1976, my thesis was awarded the Grand Prix Gobert for history by the Académie française. Since then, I have embarked on the following further studies of the problem of revolts:

Fête et Révolte, Paris, Hachette, 1976.
'La mobilité sociale, argument de révolte', *XVIIe siècle*, 1979, pp. 61–71.
'Les aspects clandestins des déviances', *Histoire et Clandestinité*, Privas, 1979, pp. 89–96.
'La fascination du monde renversé', *Le Monde renversé*, Paris, Vrin, 1979, pp. 9–15.
Révoltes et Révolutions dans l'Europe moderne, XVIe–XVIIIe s., Paris, PUF (coll. 'L'historien', no.40), 1980, 264pp.
'Les chouans des Marches. La tradition de révolte des confins de provinces', *Vendée-Chouannerie*, Nantes, 1981, pp. 109–18.
'Rural Unrest', *Our Forgotten Past*, ed. Jerome Blum, London, Thames and Hudson, 1982, pp. 134–56.
'Droit des paysans et droit de l'écrit. Le projet de Code rural de 1808', *Annales de Bretagne*, 1982, pp. 205–13.
'Offene Fragen der französischen Bauernrevolten vom 16 bis 18 Jahrhundert', *Aufstände, Revolten, Prozesse*, ed. W. Schulze, Stuttgart, 1985, pp. 60–75.

Index

d'Abzac, Gabriel, 116
agents, tax, 153, 212–18, 220–8,
 238–43, 246, 254, 265–73, 308, 323,
 329, 338
aides (sales tax), 16, 214–17, 221–3,
 228–30, 234, 236, 249, 288–9, 297,
 323, 346
Aiguillon, Duchess of, 160
d'Albret, Jean-Jacques, seigneur of
 Laval, 116
d'Albret, Marshal, 44–5
alderman: dignity of, 5, 304; election of,
 3–4; fiscal power of, 16, 216; judicial
 power of, 9; policing power of,
 174–5; political power of, 7–8, 174,
 228; and rioters, 202, 222–3, 232,
 241, 341
Alesme, 123, 161, 163–4
Alexander the Great, 249
Ambleville, Count de, 103
ambushes, 180–3
amnesty, 101, 134, 148–50, 164, 234,
 237, 311
Anabaptists, 99
anarchism, 339–40
ancien régime, 170, 191, 337, 343
Angoumois, 290–1; *see also* insurrection,
 hotbeds of
Anguittard, seigneur, 211
Antipater, 249
Arblade, Baron de, 239
Argenson, 300, 312
army of communes (Croquant army),
 114–16, 117–18, 124–5, 143, 340
assemblies: composition of, 75–80, 117;
 end of, 102–4; history of, 72–106,
 285–7; leaders of, 80–2; of local
 estates, 139; military structure of,
 78–80, 124–5, 137–8, 340; nobility

and, *see* nobility; and tax resistance,
 141; see also *châtellenie*
d'Asta, Étienne, 206
d'Aubeterre, Marquis de, 75, 117, 130,
 142, 156–8, 291
d'Aubigné (writer), 68, 79, 82, 87, 96,
 280, 306
d'Aujidos, Bernard, 238–9
d'Aumont, Marquis de, 306
Auvergne, Count of, 283
d'Auvergne, Henri de la Tour de, 282

bachelleries (bachelor festivals), 28
Badefol, Seguin de, 100
bailiff, 153, 197–201, 205–6, 209,
 212–14, 216, 243, 254, 267, 271
bailliage, 94, 224, 291
bakers, 171–3, 175, 177
Balthazar, Colonel, 190
Balzac, Guez de, 307
banalités, 174
Banos, Baron de, 239
de Barèges, François de, 298
Barrault, Count of, 32
Basque, Captain, 137, 147
Bayly, Alain de, 116
Bayly, Marguerite, 116
Beaulieu, Ameliot de, 159
bell (communal emblem), 6, 40, 70,
 314, 324, 341
Besse (chronicler), 138
Besson, Constantin de, 118, 157
Bessot, Louis de, 124
Beynac, Claude de (seigneur de Tayac),
 133
Baynac, Jean Guy de (Seigneur de
 Tayac) 98
Beynac, Marquis de, 133
Bichi (papal nuncio), 309